INFLATION AND GROWTH
IN LATIN AMERICA

PUBLICATIONS OF
THE ECONOMIC GROWTH CENTER
Lloyd G. Reynolds, *Director*

INFLATION AND GROWTH
IN
LATIN AMERICA

Edited by
WERNER BAER
and
ISAAC KERSTENETZKY

A Publication of
The Economic Growth Center
Yale University

New Haven and London, Yale University Press

FOREWORD

THIS VOLUME is one in a series of studies supported by the Economic Growth Center, an activity of the Yale Department of Economics since 1961. The Center is a research organization with worldwide activities and interests. Its research interests are defined in terms of both method of approach and subject matter. In terms of method, the Center sponsors studies which are designed to test significant general hypotheses concerning the problem of economic growth and which draw on quantitative information from national economic accounts and other sources. In terms of subject matter, the Center's research interests include theoretical analysis of economic structure and growth, quantitative analysis of a national economy as an integral whole, comparative cross-sectional studies using data from a number of countries, and efforts to improve the techniques of national economic measurement. The research program includes field investigation of recent economic growth in twenty-five developing countries of Asia, Africa, and Latin America.

The Center administers, jointly with the Department of Economics, the Yale training program in International and Foreign Economic Administration. It presents a regular series of seminar and workshop meetings and includes among its publications both book-length studies and journal reprints by staff members, the latter circulated as Center Papers.

GUSTAV RANIS, *Director*

PREFACE

THE Conference on Inflation and Economic Growth was held in Rio de Janeiro from January 3–11, 1963. It consisted of seven sessions in which formally prepared papers and comments were presented. These are fully reproduced in the first part of this volume, with some alterations by the respective authors and the editors.

The second part of the conference consisted of five panel sessions. There were usually four or five speakers, followed by general discussion from the floor. The panel sessions were recorded and edited by us from tape transcriptions. This presented a number of difficulties, since some of the transcriptions in English originated from simultaneous translations from the Spanish or Portuguese which left much to be desired in terms of accuracy and completeness. In many cases, fortunately, participants were kind enough to review and revise the record. In order to stay within our space limitations and present as tight a summary of the discussions as possible, we were forced to make substantial cuts in the panel presentations and to include only those comments from the floor which seemed directly relevant to the panel topic.

Although the theme of the conference was inflation and growth, many other aspects of development are related to this central theme, and the discussion occasionally wandered off into most interesting, but not necessarily closely related topics. This, on occasion, somewhat diluted the central theme, but added considerably to the intellectual content of the conference.

The first section contains the summary paper of Professor Ruggles and the final address by Professor W. Arthur Lewis. Professor Ruggles' paper, presented on the last day in an attempt to synthesize the ideas which had emerged, may be recommended as providing a comprehensive initial overview of the proceedings of the conference. Professor Lewis' paper represents a general assessment and critique of the ideas and controversies aired in the course of the sessions.

WERNER BAER
ISAAC KERSTENETZKY

vii

INTRODUCTION

MANY economists have viewed the phenomena of inflation and growth in Latin America as the result of unsound monetary policy, government deficits, and unrestrained wage demands. Other economists, however, maintain that the problem of inflation in Latin America differs in a number of important respects from the problem as it presents itself in North America and Western Europe, and that the traditional theory of inflation as it has been developed in these latter countries is not always strictly relevant. In particular, it is claimed that the traditional theory, which, broadly speaking, attributes inflation either to excess demand of one sort or another or to "cost-push"—generally wage-push—does not provide an adequate explanation of the differences which are observed among the countries of Latin America in the relation between inflation and growth. Nor, on the other hand, do the present theories of economic growth throw very much light on the differences which occur in this region. Many combinations appear: rapid growth and rapid inflation, in Brazil; slow growth and rapid inflation, in Chile; moderate growth and slow inflation, in Mexico; and so on.

The problem of inflation and growth in Latin America has thus given rise to considerable controversy, with different points of view being presented by the various governments of Latin America, the United States, and international organizations such as the International Monetary Fund and the United Nations Economic Commission for Latin America. Unfortunately, however, relatively few economists outside of Latin America, aside from those connected with governments or international agencies, have been directly concerned with the analysis of Latin American economic problems.

In July 1960, therefore, under the sponsorship of the National Planning Association, a group of economists from Europe, North America, and Latin America met in Bellagio, Italy, to consider the desirability and feasibility of a conference on inflation and growth in Latin America.[1] Both the Rockefeller Foundation and the Dear-

---

[1]Those attending the Bellagio Meeting were: Roberto Campos, Hollis Chenery, Gerhard Colm, Alain Debiez, B. Kragh, José Antonio Mayobre, P. Mendive, Julio Olivera, Felipe Pazos, Anibal Pinto, Raul Prebisch, Nancy D. Ruggles, Richard Ruggles, Charles Schwartz, Dudley Seers, Robert Triffin, Pierre Uri.

born Foundation made grants to the National Planning Association in support of this meeting. It was the recommendation of the Bellagio Meeting that a conference on inflation and growth in Latin America be sponsored by a group of private economic research institutions. It was further recommended that no organizations, international or private, should be permitted to send official representatives to this conference, but that individual economists should be invited to participate irrespective of and independent of their affiliations.

On the basis of these recommendations, five private research organizations joined together to organize the Conference along the lines suggested. These research institutions are the DiTella Institute in Argentina, the Institute of Economics of the University of Chile, the National Planning Association in the United States, the Vargas Foundation in Brazil, and the Economic Growth Center at Yale University. The Ford Foundation, the Rockefeller Foundation, and the Economic Growth Center at Yale provided support for the conference.

In November 1961 a program committee[2] composed of the research directors of the sponsoring institutions, together with the steering committee designated at the Bellagio Meeting, met in New Haven to draw up the program of the Conference and make the necessary arrangements with respect to time and place.

The Conference on Inflation and Growth was held in Rio de Janeiro, January 3-11, 1963. The first half of the Conference was devoted to invited papers. Background papers on the analysis of inflation and growth in a number of countries were provided to the authors of the invited papers in order to give them the necessary material on which to base their own analyses. The invited papers were mimeographed and distributed prior to the meeting so that they were not read at the meeting itself; formal discussants evaluated and criticized these papers.

The second half of the Conference consisted of panel sessions on specific problems of economic policy in the area of inflation and growth. There were five such panel sessions over a period of two and a half days. The chairmen of the panel groups provided the members of their panels with an agenda of questions to be discussed.

Finally, there was a summary session at which the conclusions to be drawn from the formal papers and panel sessions were synthe-

---

[2]The program committee of the Inflation and Growth Conference was composed of: Richard Ruggles (Chairman), Roberto Campos, Gerhard Colm, Joseph·Grunwald, Federico Herschel, Alexandre Kafka, Raul Prebisch, Lloyd G. Reynolds, Charles Schwartz, Dudley Seers, Nancy Ruggles (Secretary).

sized. The success of the Conference depended in large measure on the extent to which it drew additional members of the economics profession into the analysis of Latin-American economic problems and provided a critical reexamination of conflicting points of view.

RICHARD RUGGLES

LIST OF CONFERENCE PARTICIPANTS

1. Adler, John M., International Bank for Reconstruction and Development, Washington, D.C.
2. Baer, Werner, Yale University, New Haven, Connecticut
3. Bloch, Henry, Zinder International, New York
4. Brown, Robert T., Instituto de Economia, Chile
5. Bulhões, Octavio, Fundação Getulio Vargas, Rio de Janeiro, Brazil
6. Campos, Roberto de Oliveira, Brazilian Ambassador to USA
7. del Canto, Jorge, International Monetary Fund, Washington, D.C.
8. Chamberlain, Neil, Yale University, New Haven, Connecticut
9. Chamberlain, Mariam, Yale University, New Haven, Connecticut
10. Chenery, Hollis, State Department, USA
11. Davis, Tom E., Cornell University, Ithaca, New York
12. Dell, Sidney, United Nations, New York
13. Diaz, Carlos F., Yale University, New Haven, Connecticut
14. DiTella, Guido, Instituto DiTella, Argentina
15. Dorrance, Graeme S., International Monetary Fund, Washington, D.C.
16. Escobar, Luiz, Finance Minister, Chile
17. Felix, David, Wayne State University, Detroit, Michigan
18. Ferrer, Aldo, Inter-American Development Bank, Washington, D.C.
19. Franco, Jorge, Consultant, Colombia
20. Furtado, Celso, Minister of Planning, Brazil
21. Goldsmith, Raymond, Yale University, New Haven, Connecticut
22. Gomez, Eduardo S., Jr., Superintendency of Money and Credit, Rio de Janeiro, Brazil
23. Gonzalez, Norberto, Economic Commission for Latin America, Chile
24. Gorban, Samuel, Universidad del Litoral, Resario, Argentina
25. Gordon, Lincoln, USA Ambassador to Brazil
26. Grunwald, Joseph, Brookings Institution, Washington, D.C.

27. Gudin, Eugenio, Fundação Getulio Vargas, Rio de Janeiro, Brazil
28. Haberler, Gottfried, Harvard University, Cambridge, Massachusetts
29. Harberger, A. C., University of Chicago, Chicago, Illinois
30. Harrod, Sir Roy, Christ Church–Oxford, England
31. Herschel, F. J., University of Buenos Aires, Argentina
32. Hirschman, A. O., Columbia University, New York
33. Hopenhayn, Benjamín, Economic Commission for Latin America, Chile
34. Iglesias, E. V., University of Montevideo, Uruguay
35. Kafka, Alexandre, University of Virginia, Charlottesville, Va.
36. Kaldor, Nicholas, King's College, Cambridge, England
37. Kaser, Michael, United Nations, New York
38 Kerstenetzky, Isaac, Fundação Getulio Vargas, Rio de Janeiro, Brazil
39. Krieger Vasena, A., Academia Nacionel de Ciencias Economicas, Argentina
40. Lerdau, Enrique, Organization of American States, Washington, D.C.
41. Lewis, W. A., Princeton University, Princeton, New Jersey
42. Lutz, Friedrich, Universität, Zürich
43. Lutz, Vera, Universität, Zürich
44. Magalhães, J. P. Almeida, Confederação Nacional da Industria, Brazil
45. Marquez, Javier, Centro de Estudios Monetarios de Latino America, Mexico
46. Marshall, Jorge, Banco Central de Chile
47. Martner, Gonzalo, Economic Commission for Latin America, Chile
48. Massad, Carlos, Instituto de Economia, Chile
49. Mendez, Jorge, Economic Commission for Latin America, Chile
50. Messy, Roger, Economic Commission for Latin America, Chile
51. Mitchell, G. W., Federal Reserve Board, Washington, D.C.
52. Molina, Sergio, Director of Budget, Chile
53. Montias, John M., Yale University, New Haven Connecticut
54. Navarrete, Alfredo, Nacional Financiera, Mexico
55. Pazos, Felipe, Organization of American States, Washington, D.C.
56. Pechman, J. A., Brookings Institution, Washington, D.C.
57. Pedersen, Hans T., Economic Commission for Latin America, Chile

58. Perloff, Harvey S., Organization of American States, Committee of Nine
59. Pinto, Anibal, Economic Commission for Latin America, Brazil
60. Pollock, David N., Economic Commission for Latin America, Washington, D.C.
61. Ranis, Gustav, Yale University, New Haven, Connecticut
62. Reynolds, Lloyd G., Yale University, New Haven, Connecticut
63. Ruggles, Nancy, Yale University, New Haven, Connecticut
64. Ruggles, Richard, Yale University, New Haven, Connecticut
65. Sammons, Robert, Federal Reserve Board, Washington, D.C.
66. Schwartz, Charles, International Monetary Fund, Washington, D.C.
67. Seers, Dudley, Economic Commission for Africa, Ethiopia
68. Schlittler, Silva H., Banco Nacional do Desenvolvimento, Brazil
69. Silvert, K. H., Dartmouth College, Hanover, New Hampshire
70. Simonsen, Mario H., Fundação Getulio Vargas, Rio de Janeiro, Brazil
71. Smith, Gordon, Harvard University, Cambridge, Massachusetts
72. Sunkel, Osvaldo, Economic Commission for Latin America, Chile
73. Thin, Tun, International Monetary Fund, Washington, D.C.
74. Thomas, Woodlief, International Bank for Reconstruction and Development, Washington, D.C.
75. Uri, P., Atlantic Institute, France
76. Urquidi, Victor, Banco de Mexico, Mexico
77. Villanueva, Javier, DiTella Institute, Argentina
78. Moura Castro, C., University of Minas Gerais, Belo Horizonte, Brazil
79. Costa, Margaret Hanson, Fundação Getulio Vargas, Brazil
80. Mallon, R. D., Harvard University, Cambridge, Massachusetts

TABLE OF CONTENTS

PART I: SUMMARY PAPERS

PART II: PAPERS AND COMMENTS

xvii

PART III: PANEL SESSIONS

SUMMARY PAPERS

Part I

1. SUMMARY OF THE CONFERENCE ON INFLATION AND ECONOMIC GROWTH IN LATIN AMERICA

Richard Ruggles

The Conference on Inflation and Economic Growth brought together a group of economists concerned with analyzing the major economic problems of Latin America. There is no lack of explanations for the inflation and growth experiences of the different Latin-American countries; rather there are too many conflicting points of view, and it was the purpose of this conference to sort out and clarify these various explanations.

The two most prominent explanations have been based on the monetary and structural theories of the relation between inflation and growth.

THE MONETARY ANALYSIS OF INFLATION AND GROWTH

The monetary school stresses the control of inflation as one of the major objects of economic policy in the developing economies. The monetarists recognize that rapid economic development is likely to provoke inflationary pressures, and they argue that one of the problems calling for high priority attention on the part of the authorities in a rapidly developing economy, therefore, is the restraint of inflation. In essence, the monetarists believe that price stability is a necessary prerequisite for sustained economic growth.

In their view, a continued inflation diminishes the volume of resources available for domestic investment. Not only is community saving reduced, but a significant part of this saving is channeled to foreign rather than domestic investment, and simultaneously the flow of capital from abroad is discouraged. Furthermore, a substantial part of the reduced flow of resources for domestic investment is diverted to uses which are not of the highest social priority. The accumulation of large inventories is encouraged. There is a diversion of saving away from capital markets, where investment decisions would be subject to longer-term economic criteria, and toward luxury housing and other kinds of investment which are socially less useful but may be highly profitable because of the inflation. Balance of payments difficulties also result, and to reduce the foreign deficits

3

the authorities are forced to resort to controls which in most cases protect uneconomic production. Political pressures lead to further restrictions which create further distortions. Economic activity thus becomes steadily more distorted.

In cases where the economic system has been allowed to get out of hand, the authorities must decide to stabilize or not to stabilize. The monetarists agree that the process of stabilization is difficult, but they argue that, difficult or not, it is the necessary basis for more rapid economic growth.

According to the monetarists, the theory that there cannot be development with stability and that development brings about inflation is not valid. There is no necessary conflict between stability and development. As long-run policy the monetarists do not recognize inflation as a serious possibility. Stability is the only viable policy, and the real alternative is between stability with development and stability without development. The monetarists do not claim that development with stability can be achieved through the exercise of monetary policy alone. They maintain that monetary policy is essential, but that it is only one of the elements which will be required. They recognize that well-designed fiscal policy, and in some cases other more direct controls, may be required. They are fully cognizant of the need for basic reforms such as land reform, increased emphasis on education, and provision of social capital for the purpose of fostering economic development.

THE STRUCTURAL ANALYSIS OF INFLATION AND GROWTH

In contrast, the structural position is that in developing economies with rapid urbanization, structural maladjustments themselves may be responsible for imbalances which cause unavoidable price increases. The attempt to restrain such price increases may result in unemployment and stagnation, which in turn may lead to political instability that threatens the very existence of the economy.

The structuralist argues that the growth of real income and economic potential in a country increases demand in some sectors of the economy where bottlenecks prevent the expansion of the supply of goods. For example, it is argued that a rise in real income will increase the demand for food by industrial workers, who are receiving more income for their expanded role in the production process. Agricultural output increases slowly in most Latin American countries, as a result of technological and institutional rigidities.

The increase in consumer purchasing power, therefore, results in a rise in prices of food and other agricultural products. There is no compensatory fall in prices elsewhere in the economy to offset the increases in prices of food. This is due partly to the fact that wages are not readily flexible in a downward direction, so that producers are faced with relatively rigid costs. In these circumstances they will not and cannot reduce prices. Furthermore, since the increase in food prices is not due to a redistribution of income but rather to an increase in total real income, the demand for nonagricultural goods will also rise; thus there is no economic reason why prices in this sector should fall.

The increase in food prices sets off further price increases elsewhere in the economy via its impact on the cost of living. With the initial rise in the cost of living there will be immediate pressure to raise wages. Governments usually respond to such pressure by raising the minimum wage rate. Unless there is a fall in employment, an increase in wage rates will result in larger wage bills and thus in an increase in purchasing power, which in turn will cause an additional increase in food prices, and thus an upward price spiral is generated.

In some countries other sectors may create structural difficulties. One such sector is exports and imports. Exports earnings may not keep up with the growth of the rest of the economy, because of either a failure of the export industries to grow or a continual decline in world prices of the export goods. Under these conditions it is argued that the increase in real income in the economy will cause an increase in demand for imported goods, which in the face of the failure of export earnings to rise at a similar rate will result in balance of payments difficulties and a rise in the prices of goods in the import sector. To the extent that import goods are directly reflected in the cost of living index or are indirectly linked through the supply of capital goods or raw materials for production, the price increases in this sector may generate a price-wage spiral.

This, then, is the mechanism of the relation between economic growth and prices as envisaged by the structuralists. An upward pressure on prices is considered a necessary concomitant of economic growth—a side effect which cannot be eliminated except by reducing overall growth to the rate of growth taking place in the bottleneck sectors. Therefore, according to the structuralist position, the maintenance of complete price stability in an economy would condemn that economy to a slow rate of growth, and at best to the rate of growth of its export or agricultural sector.

Conclusion

The difference between the monetary and structural positions thus essentially comes down to a difference in their view of the nature of price increases in the economy. The monetarists consider that price stability is a prerequisite for rapid economic growth and that governments should give it high priority and take the necessary measures, despite the difficulty of such measures, to insure it. The structuralists consider that, in an economy with major bottlenecks and weak export markets, the attempt to achieve price stability through monetary or fiscal means will result in unemployment, underutilization of industrial capacity, and slow growth.

STATISTICAL AND ADMINISTRATIVE REQUIREMENTS FOR STABILITY AND GROWTH

Merely because wide differences exist in the basic theoretical models underlying the relation between inflation and growth does not mean, however, that the monetarists and structuralists disagree on all questions of economic development.

For example, considerable consensus has emerged in the discussion of the statistical requirements for controlling inflation and stimulating economic growth. Both monetarists and structuralists agree that statistics on the structure and operation of the economic system are required for the design and implementation of current economic policies and for development planning. There is an increasing realization that the estimation of a few macroeconomic aggregates is not sufficient. To formulate a consistent and workable development plan, a fairly detailed picture of the economic situation in the base year and of past development during a reasonably long historical period is needed. A quantitative assessment of general economic growth during recent and past years, and of the contribution of the various industries and factors of production to this growth, is required to reveal the basic weaknesses and strong points in the economic structure and to show to what extent a balanced development has so far been achieved. To obtain an idea about the investment effort it is necessary to have information on the share of total resources which in the recent past have been devoted to the building up and renewal of the capital stock. The more detailed such an analysis can be made the more significant it is, and to achieve a reasonably detailed analysis at least some information about investment by main sectors of the economy is needed.

National income and national accounts estimates furnish the raw material for the construction of balances of total demand and supply by main components, which are indispensable in revealing the existence and sources of inflationary pressures or pressures on the balance of payments. The existence of such balances makes it possible for the policy makers to take measures which may prevent future moneary disequilibrium or a balance of payments crisis during the implementation of a plan.

National budgets or one-year economic plans which present as complete a picture as possible of the likely development of the economy in the year to come, and are intended to form a consistent framework for short-term economic policy, have been found useful in many countries. The national budget is usually presented to the parliament together with the government budget or as a supplement to it.

No Latin-American country so far prepares a national budget of this sort, but the need for such a tool is evident. Several countries are in the process of changing their budgetary procedures by adopting program and performance budgeting, and more analytically meaningful economic-functional classifications of their government budgets which could be directly fitted into a national budget. No doubt the main reason why complete national budgets have not yet been formulated is the lack of statistics on which to base them. For national budgeting, up-to-date, reliable, and fairly detailed national accounts data are indispensable.

It should be emphasized, however, that more than national income accounts will be required. Other forms of economic accounting such as input-output, flow of funds, and sector balance sheets will eventually be required. It is important that all of these different kinds of economic data be fitted into a single comprehensive and integrated system of economic accounting which will insure consistency and complete coverage of the economy, so that those making economic policy can move easily from one kind of data to other kinds of data about the economy. There was a general consensus in the conference that the lack of adequate economic data was impairing economic policy formulation and implementation in Latin America, and that a very high priority should be given to the development of the necessary underlying statistical sources.

ORGANIZATIONAL REQUIREMENTS FOR STABILITY AND GROWTH

With respect to organizational requirements for stability and growth, the frame of reference taken by the conference was that of a "mixed economy" in which both the private and public sectors own means of production and are entrepreneurs; and in which a democratic political system prevails, with political parties, labor unions, and other organized "pressure groups" which influence economic and political decisions.

The necessity to accelerate economic development has also been taken for granted.

Accelerated economic development with stability was understood to mean a process of development at a rate faster than the historical one achieved until now, accompanied simultaneously by: (1) full employment, (2) monetary stability, (3) foreign trade stability, and (4) the avoidance of sectoral bottlenecks and shortages of capital or human factors, and prevention of any geographical region from lagging too far behind the rest of the country.

Any process of development not complying with these prerequisites has inherent in it germs of instability.

It may be asked whether the free operation of market forces will not by themselves lead to faster economic growth with stability. The evidence of the past cannot be brought to bear to answer this question, since it is probable that in no Latin-American economy has there been a case of a free market economy operating during a period long enough for its benefits to come to fruition—although economists have never decided just how much time a free market economy requires to demonstrate its merits.

It is not likely, furthermore, that the free market economy will have a chance to prove its merits in the future. The pressure toward higher consumption levels in underdeveloped countries is extremely strong, not only as a result of prevailing low standards of living, but also from the powerful impact of the demonstration effect, both domestic and international, upon the expectations of the majority of the population. In countries with one main product like many of the Latin-American countries, decisions taken by companies, or even just one firm or a labor union, at times one whose membership is very small, have repercussions throughout the national economy. In these circumstances it is impossible for the state to remain passive. Other systems of economic organization must be sought to accelerate growth and to guarantee its achievement with stability.

In considering this question, certain limitations must be borne in mind. Economists often assume that Latin-American governments are capable of making legally effective any policies they want. There are, however, impediments to a completely effective rule of law arising from the nature of the social organization. What some economists like to call parallel market and subsistence economies also describe cultural boundaries: tribal societies are even more effectively outside the national policy than the national economy. Legal power is limited even in the cities by the existence of important traditionalist groups who deny the notion of the supremacy of law. These limitations upon the effectiveness of political decisions must temper all predictions about economic development and stabilization programs.

Despite these limitations on the scope of economic development planning, however, it has become increasingly obvious in all Latin-American countries that it is necessary to embark seriously on long-range economic planning. In order to accomplish this it is necessary to set up a planning organization within the government. Such an organization should not only have the function of the development and coordination of the plan itself, but it should be in a position to check on the progress of the plan and bring to bear those instruments of policy which will enhance the cooperative participation of different sectors of the economy and the general effectiveness of the economic development program.

INFLATION AND GROWTH IN THE INDUSTRIAL COUNTRIES

In examining the inflation and growth experiences of industrial countries, it is a remarkable fact that 17 years after the end of the war the governments of these countries have still not succeeded in finding a satisfactory relationship between the goal of price stability and the various other possible targets of public policy.

In the period immediately following World War II many of the industrial countries felt inflationary pressures created by liquid funds accumulaed during the war and immediate postwar period combined with acute shortages in the supply of many products. As the industrial countries recovered from the war, the problem of rising prices became less acute. In the period from 1953 to 1961 the cost-of-living increase in 12 industrial countries ranged from a low of 10 percent for Switzerland to a high of 38 percent for France. In comparison with many Latin-American countries these rates of price increase seem quite low. Nevertheless, there has been very considerable concern about inflation in a number of these industrial countries. For example, in the United States, where consumer prices, on average, rose by only 1½ percent per year, there has been considerable controversy as to the cause of the price rise.

Initially it was held that excess demand was the cause of the price creep and that policies of credit restriction and budget surpluses should be invoked. In the late fifties when the price creep persisted despite excess capacity and unemployment, the arguments about the causes of the price increase shifted to wage-cost push and administered prices of large firms. The government's policy therefore shifted to urging restraint on the part of labor unions and businesses.

Incidentally, it is interesting to note that a structural argument could be advanced with respect to this upward creep of the price index in the United States economy. As real income rose in the United States, the demand for, and the remuneration in, the service industries rose. It was this component of the consumer price index and the GNP deflator which rose. By and large, commodity prices did not rise. Thus this relative price increase in serivces, plus the fact that prices in the service sector are measured by inputs and not outputs, accounted for almost all the rise in the over-all price indexes.

With respect to the relation of the rate of economic growth to the rate of price rise in industrial countries, no satisfactory conclusions emerge. There have been very considerable differences in rates of growth, but similar price increases can be found in countries with very different rates of growth. The view was expressed by a number of members of the conference that more sophisticated multivariate analysis might well be able to reveal more than the simple correlations which have been made to date.

INFLATION AND GROWTH IN ASIAN COUNTRIES

The experience of Asian countries is not very much more revealing than that of the industrial countries. There are only three countries in Asia, Indonesia, China (Taiwan), and Korea (South), which have experienced moderate to high inflation during the last decade. Heavy military expenditures have largely contributed to inflation in these countries, and this should be noted in making a comparative analysis of the experience of inflation and growth in different regions. These countries have had varied experiences in growth; while the growth rates of Indonesia and Korea have been low, the growth rate of China (Taiwan) has been quite high. This is largely due to the fact that, in spite of high military expenditures, China also put great emphasis on economic development. Also, the availability of technical skills in China (Taiwan) is relatively greater.

In the moderate-inflation-to-stable group, with the exception of Japan and Thailand, the Asian countries are newly independent nations; before independence they had a long experience of monetary stability, and their monetary systems have been closely tied to important western currencies. After independence, economic growth has been the main ambition of these countries. They have pursued this objective with different degrees of success.

The common factors in these countries are: relative political stability, low per capita income (below U.S. $200 with the exception of Malay), and financially conservative governments with long histories of monetary stability. Moreover, the absence of large government expenditures directly creating employment opportunities in these countries makes it easy for a government to cut down its expenditures whenever it desires.

INFLATION AND GROWTH IN CENTRALLY PLANNED ECONOMIES

In centrally planned economies, the varying degree of susceptibility to inflation in the last decade is explicable only in part in terms of the quality and experience of the financial planners. There is also considerable difference among the centrally planned economies in the ability to resist spontaneous wage demands, to revise work norms periodically, and to force the peasants to deliver their compulsory quotas of agricultural produce despite poor harvests or other hardships.

A high rate of growth in the centrally planned economies has not proven an insuperable obstacle to monetary equilibrium. What causes problems in these countries is the inability of the planners to predict with exactitude the changes in the level of inventories, in marketed food supplies, in labor productivity, and in foreign trade balance corresponding to the growth they have targeted.

COMPARATIVE ANALYSIS OF EXPERIENCE IN LATIN AMERICA

With respect to the comparative analysis of experience in Latin-American countries, it is also evident that just as stability does not insure rapid economic growth, inflation in itself is not a sign of economic dynamism. It is best to separate the forces of growth and inflation, although there are obvious interconnections. The countries which have shown the fastest economic growth in recent years, such as Brazil, have also had the greatest possibilities for import substitution. In some of these countries, such as Colombia, this process commenced comparatively recently. Most of them have started their rapid growth experience from very low per capita income levels and their labor movements are still weak.

Industrialization through import substitution in countries with a highly unequal distribution of income is principally geared to the middle income groups. In large countries like Brazil, the inequality of the income distribution matters less because the absolute size of the middle groups will be large and therefore the import substitution process can proceed vigorously for a longer period of time. Since the market in these economies does not depend very much on the purchasing power of labor, even a decline in real wages will not dampen the sales potential of enterprises, but, on the contrary, will increase profit margins and therefore provide incentives to private investment.

On the other hand, in the smaller of the industrially more advanced countries of Latin America, notably Chile, the income distribution matters much more. The process of import substitution of consumer goods has just about come to an end there. For almost a decade now, the Chilean economy has grown not much more than its population, while the basic imbalances have continued to produce one of the highest inflation rates in the region. It is very unlikely that, in the absence of a significant change in the income distribution and the size of its market, this economy could sustain an acceleration in its rate of growth for an extended period of time.

In Argentina, government policies have played a much more important role in that economy's semistagnation than in Chile.

Countries like Colombia, Peru, and Venezuela can still go a long way in carrying forward industrialization on the basis of consumer goods import substitution, which they have begun comparatively recently. Eventually, however, economic development in the "old" and "new" industrial countries of Latin America will depend upon a widening of markets. In a normal process of industrialization this should come naturally as a by-product of development, but in most of the Latin-American countries severe obstacles will have to be overcome before a basic improvement in the distribution of income can be achieved. This is part of the economic significance of such fundamental measures as land, tax, and educational reforms. This is also the rationale of the striving toward a common market in Latin America which would make capital goods import substitution an economic feasibility even in the smaller countries.

Thus, whether a country has grown or not depends primarily on factors other than the existence of inflation. Nevertheless, inflation can have important effects on economic development through its influence on savings and investment decisions.

COMPARATIVE ANALYSIS OF POLICY INSTRUMENTS

The discussion of policy instruments in relation to inflation and growth pointed up a consensus that monetary and fiscal policy alone were not sufficient to insure stability and economic growth. Countries with social orientation defined according to the preferences of the authorities cannot expect to have economic development at a rapid pace, along with stability, from spontaneous market forces alone. These forces are very useful, actually indispensable, within the system of free enterprise, but they are not enough. In order to attain all these objectives, controls of many different kinds are needed, taking into account that some countries will be prepared to accept certain types of controls while others may prefer different ones. Acceptance of controls presupposes the acceptance of certain losses of freedom, and there will be different attitudes, depending on the kind and degree of freedom which is lost.

Merely because fiscal and monetary policy cannot be considered sufficient instruments for rapid economic growth and stability does not of course mean that they are not essential elements in any development program. Only with proper credit controls, adequate tax systems, and responsible government expenditures can a development program succeed.

It is very important that development programs not be overambitious in planning an investment program which is beyond the real domestic and external resources of the economy. Both monetary and fiscal policy are important in helping to make a high investment level possible by preventing excessive internal competition for specific resources, or over-all excess demand. Selective credit controls which affect different sectors of the economy differently may be very useful. Similarly, differential tax treatment of different kinds of activity and careful planning of government expenditures can make fiscal policy more effective.

In addition to these controls, wage policy may be an important element. Much of the inflation taking place in Latin America has been accentuated by the price-wage spiral, and although the underlying political conditions may not permit stopping all interaction, it is possible that the interaction may be somewhat modified.

There is also need for policies in the foreign sector to help maintain the balance of payments and to insure that the external resources which are available are used as much as possible for development purposes.

Finally, there are a host of more specific economic policies aimed at specific sectors in the economy. Thus export industries may be directly or indirectly stimulated. Educational policy should be directed at providing the technical and administrative personnel required by economic development. Other policies designed to improve the mobility of resources and to reduce institutional frictions should also be considered. It is in this context, then, that policy instruments for growth and stability must be evaluated.

CHANGE IN ECONOMIC STRUCTURE

In the discussion of changes in the economic structure, the panel members were in agreement that there exist very serious structural imbalances which prevent rapid economic growth in Latin America. In almost all countries there are sectors of the economy which constitute bottlenecks in the expansion process.

There was some discussion of the degree to which the price signals in a free market economy would lead to the necessary expansions and contractions. Even under the most optimistic assumptions with respect to this question there was general agreement that some problem areas would require special consideration.

As has already been pointed out, the slow growth of agriculture has created serious difficulties in many countries. Special policies concerning land reform, improvement in the use of land, greater use of fertilizer, and even in some cases the introduction of farm machinery may help increase the total output of the farm sector in these countries. In addition, there is a great need to improve the system by which farm products are marketed and distributed to consumers.

Another sector recognized as a common bottleneck was the public utility sector. Electric power, water supply, and the transportation system (including local transport) provide the backbone for urbanization and industrial development. A lag in these facilities seriously impairs economic development programs. From a financial point of view these industries are often victims of the inflationary situation. Their costs rise with the inflation, but the prices they are permitted to charge lag far behind, creating deficits. It was argued that uneconomically low prices overencourage the use of these scarce resources and at the same time discourage investment in these areas because of the lack of profitability. Some defense was offered for the lag in prices in the case of local transport. Raising prices in this area would be very regressive and might embarrass governments politically to an extent over and above the gain achieved. In the case of other public utilities it was pointed out that a low price did encourage use of their services and the shortage of capacity in these areas was in itself a powerful stimulant to expansion.

The discussion from the floor pointed up the necessity for increased emphasis on education. If there is to be rapid economic development the requirements for educated, trained, and skilled manpower a decade hence will expand manyfold over their present levels. The present level in most Latin-American countries is far from adequate and in order to insure a sufficient future supply immediate action is required.

Finally, the problem of the foreign sector was also discussed. The question was raised whether a correctly valued rate of exchange would by itself bring about the desired amount of import substitution and export expansion. Considerable doubt was expressed by some who felt that frictions and lack of mobility of factors of production were such that adjustment would be too slow to accommodate a high rate of economic development. Furthermore, if long-term planning is undertaken a government would be required to initiate in one period measures which would insure the emergence of the industrial mix which would meet future requirements. It was suggested that if long-term planning is to be taken seriously and if a rapid rate of growth is anticipated, existing price signals may not be an adequate basis on which to build future industry. In this connection, it was urged that the question of economic integration of Latin-American markets be considered. The export markets of Latin America may change drastically in the next several decades, and it is not at all inconceivable that these countries would become major exporters of heavy industrial manufactures, with the more highly developed countries specializing in technologically more advanced products.

INVESTMENT POLICY

In the panel on investment policy the view was expressed that there was no real proof that rapid inflation would raise the percentage of resources devoted to capital formation. Some members of the panel felt that the distorting effects would cause increases in inventories and housing investment. Other panel members indicated that, in some countries, this type of distortion had not taken place despite considerable inflation.

Investment was recognized as a key variable in the economy—key in part because it provides the basis for economic growth and in part because it is subject to control by economic policy. The view was expressed that excessive use of monetary policy to achieve price stability could be very harmful to investment. In such instances the private sector is often squeezed in order to achieve stability for the economy as a whole.

It was pointed out that well-designed tax policy can play a significant role in stimulating desirable forms of investment and controlling the overall level so that the economy does not attempt to employ more resources than exist. Stabilization which is attempted without careful planning as to where the impact of the restrictions will fall may have very serious economic and political repercussions on the economy.

The nature of the investment effort will of course be different for different countries. Several panel members indicated, however, that more emphasis on agricultural investment was desirable. There was no agreement on whether major attention should be given to investment in export industries or import substitution industries. In any case it was pointed out that investment mistakes in fast-growing economies often were not as vital as in slow-growing economies.

Finally, the argument was made that inflation discouraged foreign investment, due to exchange risk and uncertainty. Foreign credit by suppliers may be a significant source for investment resources. In this case it is the foreign companies which produce the specific products and which are willing to extend credit to sell their products. In the discussion of this kind of financing the hope was expressed that this type of credit could be internationalized.

FOREIGN SECTOR POLICY

The panel on foreign sector policy considered the problem of common markets. It was pointed out that the European common market is quite different from the Latin American common market. The high degree of intra-European trade is in marked contrast to the lack of trade among the Latin-American countries. Also, there are wide differences in the degree of inflation among Latin-American countries and in the role of government in these countries. These elements make a Latin-American common market somewhat more difficult. Some panel members questioned the fact that LAFTA had no provision for across-the-board lowering of tariffs and expressed the opinion that there might be more trade deversion than trade creation. Another comment pointed out that the creation of the European common market in fact discriminated against the present and potential export of manufactured goods by the Latin-American countries.

International commodity agreements were discussed at length. Some panel members felt that these agreements are necessary to prevent further deterioration in the terms of trade against the primary producers, but that it is also necessary to accompany them with some system of production control in the supplying countries. There is also the very serious problem that many commodity agreements do not sufficiently favor low-cost producers, but rather continue to support high-cost producers.

The suggestion was also made that industrial countries give serious consideration to the levy of a tax on primary commodities imported from less developed countries and that the proceeds of this tax be utilized to finance development programs in these countries. Some discussants raised the question as to whether for some products the elasticity of demand might be such that the net benefit of this device might not be significant, and that therefore small incremental taxes should be utilized in order to ascertain the elasticity of demand.

Finally, concern was expressed that the establishment of fixed commodity prices might be a deterrent to long-run adjustment in the demand and supply of primary commodities. It was therefore suggested by some discussants that a sliding scale of prices be established on an average of the prices over a preceding period. This would permit a downward pressure on prices to be distributed over time.

Neither the panel nor the discussants could agree on the degree to which the terms of trade would continue to move adversely against primary material-producing countries. On the one hand, the view was expressed that there would not be another major depression in the industrial countries and that this was the major cause of the change in terms of trade which occurred during the 1930's. Along the same line, it was argued that current deterioration in the terms of trade was more apparent than real, since the quality of industrial goods and the introdcution of new goods was not adequately taken into account in the price indexes of industrial goods. On the other hand, the view was also expressed that within any developed economy the industrial sector benefits at the cost of the agricultural sector; and it is for this reason that governments usually have domestic programs to support farm income, so that the benefits of increased productivity in the economy as a whole can be extended to the farm sector. It was argued that the same mechanism applies to the relation between industrial countries and primary material-producing countries, and that therefore some mechanism was required to protect the terms of trade of these countries.

MONETARY AND FISCAL POLICY

In the panel on monetary and fiscal policy it was emphasized that monetary policy alone was not sufficient to stop inflation and that monetary policy could not be used to solve structural problems. The view was also expressed by some members of the panel that structural factors alone could not be considered to be responsible for extremely rapid inflation. Some of the limitations of monetary policy cited were the inability to predict the behavior of financial groups and the role of financial intermediaries in the economy.

The monetarist position that inflation increases structural imbalances was presented. According to this view, investment is distorted during rapid inflation, resources are misallocated, productivity is impaired, the balance of payments deteriorates, and forced saving reduces the standard of living of the lower income groups. The suggestion was made by a number of panel members and participants that in a rapid runaway inflation the sooner the inflation was brought to a halt the better, and that a shock was necessary to accomplish this. The argument for this was that since the expectation of rising prices had to be changed it was not feasible to halt an inflation by slow degrees, and that experiene showed that when inflations did stop they stopped suddenly.

A number of participants disagreed with the desirability of achieving stability by shock. The shock required for stability might well result in drastic unemployment, cutback of essential investment programs of the government, or restriction of credit to such a degree that financial panic and business failures would ensue. It was argued that from a political point of view such a shock could produce extreme instability and would not be practical in many countries.

There was general agreement that fiscal reform was required in Latin America. Despite the fact that it would not in itself stop inflation, fiscal reform is necessary to permit better resource allocation and to improve equity.

First of all, it was agreed, a more comprehensive income tax system is needed in Latin-American countries. This would provide more equitable tax treatment of individuals. Besides income taxes, it is possible to have indirect taxes. At present many Latin-American countries place taxes on imports of luxuries, but as import substitution comes about attention must be given to the desirability of taxing these commodities when they are domestically produced. Land taxes and taxes on capital were also emphasized as especially important aspects of any tax reform system.

One panel member reminded the group that tax systems were subject to constitutional and legislative considerations. There is also the fact that the difficulty of applying taxes varies considerably by kind of tax and by sector of the economy. Thus taxes on agriculture are more difficult to apply than those on corporations. Governments can improve their fiscal systems considerably by reducing fragmentation in the administration of expenditures and revenue. A comprehensive overview of expenditures and the tax system cannot insure success, but it can avoid unintentional waste. It was also emphasized that with respect to changes in the fiscal system the problem of communication is very important. There should be participation of taxpayers in the development of the tax system. For example, tax hearings should be held and the government should endeavor to enlist the talents of lawyers and accountants.

Finally, in this panel there was some discussion of exchange rate policy. The view was presented that except for currencies used as reserves (the dollar and the pound) the exchange rate should correctly reflect the true exchange rate. According to this view this would in the proper degree encourage export industries and restrict consumption of imported goods. The effect of devaluation on inflation, it was suggested, was less than was popularly believed. Others expressed the view, however, that foreign exchange controls were a proper instrument of policy to protect the balance of payments, restrain inflation, and stimulate economic development through the protection of import substitution industries.

THE DISTRIBUTION OF INCOME

The final panel on the distribution of income did not find that inflationary pressures had much effect on the relative shares in the income distribution. One unfavorable aspect is, however, that some people profiteer because of the inflation and others are discriminated against.

The determinants of the income distribution in an economy lie in inequality in the holdings of land and other assets in the system, and in inequality in educational opportunities. One of the major routes of attack on inequality of income is to attack the sources of inequality directly. Thus land reform in Latin America would do much to improve the income distribution. Over the longer run, increasing educational opportunities will improve the mobility of human resources, make the needed kind of manpower available for economic development, and improve income equality.

The point was made, however, that there is a sharp limit to the degree of redistribution of capital and income that can be achieved in the short run. There is a considerable danger of flight of capital and human resources if the redistribution is of a confiscatory nature.

Another method of systematic redistribution which was mentioned was a change in the prices of agricultural goods relative to those of industrial goods. Raising agricultural prices more than industrial prices will redistribute income between these two sectors. This kind of redistribution has taken place in Argentina; it is interesting to note, however, that it did not result in greater agricultural output.

The thesis was also advanced that the initial stages of economic development might, through the expansion of profits and increase in demand for skilled workers, actually increase the inequality of income. With further economic growth, however, it was suggested that it was quite probable that inequality in income would decline. Such a decline in the inequality of income has been observed in the more developed industrial economies. In these countries the increasing educational level of the population has done much to increase labor mobility and to provide the kinds of skills required by the economy. In this context the benefits of increasing productivity are diffused more equally throughout the economy.

Although it was recognized that income taxation alone could not achieve an ideal distribution of income, several panel members emphasized the need for a comprehensive income tax which would have wide coverage of income groups at relatively low tax rates. Such an income-tax system should cover capital gains as well as other kinds of income. Even if such a tax system were mildly progressive at the lower income levels, it would have a favorable anti-inflationary influence. As incomes and prices rise, the tax revenue which would be generated would increase faster than income, thus helping to put a brake on the inflation.

In conclusion, it is evident that although there have been many points of disagreement among the participants in this conference, there have also been wide areas of agreement, and it is on these specific areas of agreement that we should try to build policies for economic development in Latin America.

2. CLOSING REMARKS

W. Arthur Lewis

I.

It was originally decreed that Dr. Prebisch and I were to share this session with you. Having regard to your desire that the conference should in this final session receive a balanced summing up of its problems, I told my speechwriter, "Just find out what Dr. Prebisch is going to say, and say the exact opposite." Unfortunately both Dr. Prebisch and my speechwriter have defected, so I am left to do the best I can for all three of us.

Thinking back over the mass of papers and speeches with which we have been entertained during the past nine days, what stands out most clearly in my mind is the importance of distinguishing between factors which cause prices to start to rise, and spiral processes which keep prices rising on and on far beyond any level that you can justify in terms of the original cause. Our economics have become much more unstable since 1945 than they ever were before. I use the word unstable in the technical sense, to indicate that if for any reason prices move from what may in some sense be an equilibrium level, there are no forces to bring them back. On the contrary, powerful forces at once take over to send prices rising and rising and rising to levels for which there is no justification in the original cause which started them off.

The mechanism is familiar to us all, and is not confined to Latin America. Every country in the world, including the Soviet bloc, has either experienced it, or views it with apprehension. It has three contributing parts: wages, budgetary deficits, and devaluation, and it runs somewhat as follows. First comes the original cause, which starts the mechanism working. This may be a rise in the price of domestic foodstuffs, or a rise in import prices, or an increase in the quantity of money, or a rise in the price of exports, or anything you like, provided it is something which raises the cost of living. Then the mechanism starts. Wages rise, and this raises prices more, wages more, prices more, and so on. Secondly, in those countries where the marginal ratio of government receipts to national income is below the average ratio, the price rise opens up a budget deficit, because government costs rise faster than government revenues. This

21

gives an extra twist to the spiral. Then thirdly the rise in prices forces devaluation, and this raises import prices proportionately to the devaluation and domestic prices in somewhat smaller proportion, so a third twist is given to the spiral. So what with wage pressures, budget deficits, and devaluation, prices may rise continuously and at a high rate for reasons which have nothing to do with the original cause.

Failure to distinguish between the original cause and the spiral mechanism can only cause confusion. If one asks why prices rise by 25 percent per annum in Chile, it is confusing to be told that this is because agricultural output is growing less rapidly than the demand for agricultural products. Chile is only one of 50 countries where agricultural demand is growing more rapidly than supply. The difference between Chile, where prices increase by 25 percent per annum, and India, where prices increase by only 2 percent per annum, is not a difference in the elasticity of supply of agricultural output, which is equally low in both countries, nor a difference in the rate of growth, which is higher in India than in Chile. The difference is that Chile is in the grip of the spiral processes to a much greater degree than India.

The spiral is not confined to Latin America; all the world's continents are having to cope with it. Yet it seems to have gotten much more out of hand in some Latin-American countries than in the rest of the world. If during 1963 the cost of living were to rise by, say, 10 percent in, say, Nigeria or Ceylon, one could not confidently predict that this would set off spiral processes which would raise the general price level in Nigeria or Ceylon by 30 percent in three years. But it seems that one could safely predict such a result in some Latin-American countries. Some Latin-American economists assert that this is because their people have acquired expectations of continuously rising living standards which make them more aggressive than the peoples of Asia or Africa. I do not believe this to be so. I do not think that Latin-Americans are more anxious to have a rising standard of living than Nigerians or Ceylonese. The difference is in the expectations, not about the standard of living, but about how prices will behave. A Nigerian is used to seeing prices rise, and then fall again; in fact, if you ask a Nigerian farmer what is likely to happen to agricultural prices, he is even now more likely to predict that they will fall than to predict that they will rise. This is in sharp contrast to those Latin-American countries where today no person under 40 years of age can remember any time when prices fell continuously over a period of two years. A country's expectations depend on its history, and the intensity of the spiral depends on its expectations. Prices rise much faster in Chile or Brazil than they do in Nigeria or Ceylon mainly because Chileans and Brazilians expect prices to rise much faster.

I think we are all agreed that this is a terrible state to be in, because this kind of inflation is quite pointless. One can argue for an inflation which sets out to achieve a deliberate purpose, such as to acquire more resources for a government which is engaged in military operations, or to bring about a change in the distribution of income such that proportionately more resources will be devoted to productive investment. I shall examine such inflations later in this paper. But the spiral has neither these purposes nor these effects. Once the whole community has been subjected to a high rate of inflation over long periods, nobody is caught by inflation any more. There are no unprotected contractual incomes any more. Even pensioners and professors of economics learn to keep up. So the spiral has all the usual evil effects of inflation without achieving anything useful. I think we are all agreed that, whatever may be the original fundamental causes which start prices rising, the spiral itself adds nothing and should be eliminated if this is at all possible.

Now, in order to eliminate the spiral you have to get at its fundamental cause and stop wages chasing prices. But you must also deal with its secondary contributor, the budgetary deficit.

A budget deficit is not a necessary part of a spiral and does not, in fact, contribute to the spiral as it is experienced in the advanced industrial countries. In most of those countries a rise in the general price level leads, on the contrary, not to a budgetary deficit, but to a budgetary surplus. This is because the marginal ratio of government receipts to national income exceeds the average ratio. These governments take 25 to 35 percent of national income, but their marginal rates of direct taxation exceed 50 percent, and many of their indirect taxes are well over 50 per cent on the goods for which demand rises most rapidly. Hence, as national income increases, their revenues rise faster than their civilian expenditures, and, in the absence of increases in military expenditures, the Minister of Finance is every year in the happy position of having to announce tax cuts in order to avoid an ever-increasing budget surplus. Most underdeveloped countries are in the opposite situation. Their marginal tax rates are too low; too many taxes are fixed in money, instead of being on a proportionate basis; and prices of public utilities are slow to adjust. So a general increase in prices raises the government's cost faster than its revenues, and the resulting deficit makes the spiral worse than it would otherwise be. This seems to be of enormous importance in the bigger Latin American inflations. Without the budgetary deficit the wage spiral by itself might raise prices by 5 or even 10 percent per annum. Increases of 20 percent per annum and more over long periods must mainly be due to the secondary contribution of the budgetary deficit.

To explain how the spiral can produce a budgetary deficit is not to explain why these large budgetary deficits are tolerated year after year. This seems to be a specifically Latin-American phenomenon. Public opinion in India or Nigeria would be shocked by the idea of a large budget deficit every year, financed by creating new money, but public opinion in many Latin-American countries seems to accept the right of the government to print money as it likes. Here again these psychological differences must have largely historical explanations. Whenever I find myself tempted to generalize about Latin-American opinion, I draw back hastily. After all I was chosen to give this talk, I am informed, mainly because I know almost nothing about Latin America, and am therefore neutral. Moreover, my Latin-American friends seem to hold as widely differing opinions as my friends of any other nationality. Indeed, usually when I take any particular opinion as being typically Latin-American, or in some sense the expression of *the* Latin-American point of view, the typical Latin-American who has expressed this idea turns out to be Mr. Dudley Seers. But I cannot foist upon Mr. Seers any *laissez passer* attitude to budgetary deficits, since in one of his papers he goes out of his way to attack budgetary deficits and argues for budgetary surpluses. All one can safely say is that in a number of Latin-American countries the government gets away with printing money to an extent which is puzzling to visitors from any other continent, and one cannot help feeling that the people deserve better governments than they get.

If one eliminated the budgetary deficits, prices would not rise so fast, but the wage-price spiral could still be there, just as it exists in many of the advanced industrial countries which have no budget deficit. This problem cannot be solved without the consent of the trade unions. Monetary weapons are inappropriate. By reducing the quantity of money, one may stop prices from rising, at the expense of employment and growth, but this is not even certain since the wage spiral may be continued even in face of much unemployment.

The spiral may stop temporarily, but unless the consent of the trade unions has been gained, it is likely to start again as soon as the deflationary pressures are removed. A lasting solution requires trade union consent, which can be secured only on two conditions.

First, the cost of living must cease to rise, and stability of prices must be maintained for a period sufficiently long enough to convince the unions that the government means to control the cost of living and has the means of doing so. At the technical level this requires a combination of means: price controls, subsidies, use of foreign exchange reserves to bring in wage goods and dampen domestic prices, even perhaps an upward revaluation of the currency. But behind these technical means must lie the will to achieve price stabilization. The other condition for winning the confidence of the trade unions is political sympathy between the unions and the government, such that the unions are not striving all the time to embarrass the government by every means in their power. Such sympathy exists in Communist countries, but it is not confined to Communist countries. It is found also in many of the new nationalist states, even in those which are quite democratic, like India or Nigeria. The basis for this sympathy is a belief, on the part of the union leaders, that they and the government leaders have pretty well the same objectives, and that these objectives are dominated by the interests of the common man. As far as one can gather, conditions for this sympathy do not exist in most Latin-American countries. The reasons for this lie in political theory. Of all social classes the most reactionary is the class of great landowners. As Marx himself recognized, the industrial capitalists are a progressive liberalizing class. Moreover, face to face with powerful unions living in urban centers, industrial capitalists have relatively little power when compared with the control which great landowners are able to exercise over the lives and votes of those who live in the countryside. Nowadays the power of great landowners has been broken all over the world except in the Middle East and in Latin America, and so Latin America is the most politically reactionary of all the continents. It is, for this reason, the angriest continent and therefore about the last place where the trade unions are likely to agree to any kind of wage control. In this sense the wage spiral in Latin America is fundamentally political and cannot be eliminated without fundamental political change. Whether the cooperative efforts of the Alliance for Progress can succeed in bringing about such fundamental change is more than I would know. On the other hand, one reads that Latin-American trade unions are pretty weak. So a combination of firmness with progressive policies might possibly bring the spiral to a stop.

II

So far, I have really said nothing about the relationship between economic growth and inflation, since the spiral is not essentially a phenomenon of growth. This spiral is, in the last analysis, a political phenomenon, arising out of political tensions in society and aggravated by poor fiscal policies. You could expect to find it in any economy, whether growing or stagnant. I began with the spiral in order to get it out of the way, since it seems largely irrelevant. If prices are increasing by 25 percent or more every year over several decades, this is because the society is sick rather than because it is developing.

When we turn to examine the relationship between inflation and economic growth, the subject matter breaks into two parts: inflation as a by-product of growth and inflation as an instrument of growth. We cannot, of course, entirely escape the spiral, since any inflation can set the spiral off. But it is important to distinguish between what sets the spiral off and how the spiral itself works, especially since, with good management, one can have price increases associated with growth which nevertheless do not spiral because the spiral itself is under control.

Economic growth will cause the general price level to rise through the effects of the expansion of some sectors of the economy on other less responsive sectors. The classical case is where extra income derives from an increase of exports. Part of the proceeds of these exports is spent on other sectors, and insofar as the output of these other sectors is inelastic and not completely substitutable by imports, prices rise in these other sectors. Prices will rise if demand puts pressure on supplies, but prices may also rise sympathetically, without such pressure. In the classical case, the price of rubber or cocoa or some other primary product rises on world markets, and one follows through the effect on other prices in Malaya or Ghana as the extra income of the farmers works its way through the system. Let me take instead the case of Jamaica, where, in the newly opened bauxite industry, the trade union is extracting a wage of £8 per week for unskilled work for which the normal Jamaican wage is £3 a week. This sets up two different strains. First, as the workers spend their extra incomes, they put pressure on the prices of wage goods. But, secondly, even if they consumed only imports and bought no domestically produced wage goods, there is a sympathetic upward movement of all other wages. If your cousin is getting £8 per week working on a bauxite mine, or reaping £8 per week because the price of rubber or cocoa has risen, you are no longer willing to accept £3 per week for working on the roads. The £8 a week serves as a challenge to all other unions to try to get increases in all other wages. In this conference we have heard a good deal about the direct pressure of demand on the output of stagnating sectors, but I think that in practice the sympathetic upward movement of incomes is just as important a source of rising prices. We have heard a good deal also about food, but the pressure of demand may affect all domestic output, including manufactures, raw materials, and services, such as the price of haircuts. From the angle of the spiral, any price which enters into the cost of living matters, not excluding the price of haircuts.

Since *de minimis non curat les,* let us concentrate on food. If the supply of food does not keep pace with growing demand, food will put a brake on growth unless one imports more food, in which case one must either export more of something, or import less of something else. This is very familiar territory, so familiar that it is puzzling to learn that this proposition now forms the basis of a new school of structural economics. The British economy met this problem head on as the economy developed in the nineteenth century. Its solution was to increase its propensity to export. Germany followed suit, and so did Japan. Other economies, faced with the same problem, have reduced their propensity to import: the Soviet Union, India, and Egypt are spectacular examples of import substitution. All these countries take this particular structural change in their stride. Why do we hear such pessimistic cries from those Latin American countries which now face the same problem?

Adjustment can be made either by increasing the propensity to export or by reducing the propensity to import. Particularly puzzling are those cries which seem to be founded on the belief that it is particularly difficult to expand exports because the world is buying fewer and fewer exports. The opposite is true. World trade has never grown faster. Between 1950 and 1960 the quantum of world trade in primary products increased at an average rate of 5½ percent per annum, and the quantum of world trade in manufactures by 7 percent per annum. The terms of trade for primary products could not retain the heights to which they were raised by the speculative fever of the Korean War and the heavy American stockpiling in the early fifties; nevertheless, the average terms of trade for the decade of the 1950's were better than for any previous decade in all the preceding 100 years. I do not know whether it is in fact true that in the 1950's Latin America had difficulty in keeping her exports growing at the same rate as national income, but if this was so, it cannot possibly have been due to failure of world demand to grow adequately, since the quantum of world trade was growing by about 6 percent per annum throughout the 1950's. Taking the continent as a whole, rather than individual countries, failure on this score can only have been a failure of effort.

Undoubtedly success in achieving major sectoral change, whether a fall in the propensity to import, or an increase in the propensity to export, or agricultural reform, creates pressures which will show up in rising prices. This is a temporary growing pains phenomenon, which should cease as the economic structure adjusts itself in the required direction, as the economy learns greater flexibility, and as increasing productivity takes effect on prices. One may note, incidentally, that this phenomenon is not confined to individual countries but exists for the world economy as a whole. Looking back over the past 90 years for which we have figures, we can see that whenever world manufacturing production has accelerated, or risen faster than 4 percent per annum, both the money prices and the terms of trade of primary products entering into world trade have risen, and whenever world manufacturing production has decelerated, prices have fallen. The world economy as a whole has the same difficulty with the inelasticity of primary production as have individual countries. But the associated changes in prices are relatively moderate: big changes can occur only if the wage-price spiral is set in motion.

In practice, in an open economy which has its spiral under control, the cost of living is determined more by price movements in the international markets for primary commodities than by domestic pressures. Every country both imports and exports primary products, whose prices enter directly or indirectly into its cost of living, and most other prices seem to take their cue from these international prices. If wage costs get out of line with international price movements, there are repercussions on employment and on the balance of payments, so most open economies pursue policies which are set, in the last analysis, by the direction of international commodity prices. Since the early stages of growth involve some increase in domestic prices, it is easiest to keep an economy open if its period of growing pains coincides with a period of general upward movement in international commodity prices; and one will find historically that periods when international commodity prices are rising secularly, whether à la Kuznets or à la Kondratief, are also the periods when development is occurring most widely over the whole world economy. If by misfortune one's period of growing pains occurs during one of the periods when international commodity prices are moving downwards, one must look out for trouble in the balance of payments.

III

From price increases as a by-product of growth, I turn to consider inflation as a deliberate instrument of growth.

One may decide to open the monetary tap to promote growth in two situations: if the propensity to invest is too low, or alternatively and paradoxically, if the propensity to save is too low.

In speaking of the propensity to invest being too low, one has in mind sluggish economies where investment is low, not because of a shortage of saving potential, but because entrepreneurs are too easily satisfied. For example, it is said of British entrepreneurs that the proportion who will invest for the sake of innovation is too small, and the proportion who will invest only because demand presses on capacity is too large. By contrast, it is said that German or Japanese entrepreneurs are driven by a devil which makes them invest in any circumstances whatever. If people invest not primarily to innovate but primarily because demand presses upon capacity, then a policy of keeping demand and supply exactly equal results in low investment and slow growth. The remedy is to keep the tap slightly open—just 1 or 2 percent per annum. One does this not to increase profits, or to redistribute income, but simply to keep order books slightly overfull. I think there is some evidence that Britain and France and the United States now fall into this category of needing just a little monetary stimulus if they are to keep at full stretch.

The case where the propensity to save is too low is very different. Here the object of opening the monetary tap is to divert income from those who spend on consumption to those with a greater propensity to spend on long-term improvement. In the typical underdeveloped country 80 percent or more of gross national product is spent on personal consumption, and the remaining 20 percent on capital formation and on public services, some of which, such as education and health services, may do as much for economic growth as is done by capital formation. One wants to get the 80 percent spent on personal consumption down to 70 percent, and investment and public services together up to 30 percent of national income. When inflation is used for this purpose it is only temporary; the object is to effect a permanent structural change in the distribution of income in favor of government and of savers. When this change is achieved, the inflation stops, and prices are stable at a higher level of growth. This kind of inflation is therefore self-liquidating.

Self-liquidating inflation is quite different from spiral inflation. Spiral inflation goes on forever, but self-liquidating inflation comes to a stop when the share of personal consumption has been reduced permanently to the new equilibrium level.

Large changes in the distribution of income, whether as between one class and another, or as between the public and the government, are not possible without inflation if they are to be accomplished over a short period of time. This is the proposition which inflation theorists have invited the statisticians to test. Instead we are inundated with diagrams relating the rate of inflation to the rate of economic growth itself, instead of to the rate of increase of the rate of economic growth. Nobody argues that a high rate of growth must be associated with a high rate of inflation. On the one side, we know that spiral inflation does not cause growth; and on the other side, you can have any rate of growth without inflation if the propensities to save and to pay taxes are already adjusted to that rate of growth. The proposition in which we are interested is that acceleration in the rate of growth causes inflation because the proportionate fall in consumption which this requires is resisted by the public, which therefore maneuvers to get higher money incomes. Will statisticians please note, and stop boring us with irrelevant comparisons between rates of inflation and growth in different countries?

Since the distinction between spiral inflation and self-liquidating inflation is so crucial, it is important to recognize the conditions which are necessary if inflation is to succeed in being self-liquidating.

The first condition is that it should result in an increase in the output of wage goods. You can get consumption down from 80 to 70 percent of national output if at the same time it is rising in absolute terms from 80 to 100, but not if it is falling in absolute terms, because the public will always fight to keep its absolute standards up. The corollary of this is that the purpose of the inflation must be to secure resources for investment in productive enterprises which yield a quick increase in the output of wage goods. Consumers then get something, and if their standard of living is rising absolutely, they are not so concerned about the fact that it is not rising as fast as productivity. However a rapid increase in the output of wage goods itself requires certain favorable factors: there must be natural resources capable of quick development; there must be enough foreign exchange to spare for importing equipment, and enough skilled labor to get on with the job. Giving the government money to spend does not necessarily result in increased output.

The second condition for success is that the inflation should redistribute income to the right people. Insofar as the purpose is to increase the government's share, this is relatively easy. One sets the marginal rates of taxation well above the average rates, so that government revenues automatically increase faster than incomes. A shift toward industrial profits is not so easy, because in economies dominated by cost accountants, industrial prices tend to be fixed on a cost-plus basis, which keeps gross profit a constant proportion of industrial prices. If left to themselves, farm prices will rise as fast as other prices, so farmers can be milked only by special measures, such as price controls, or collectivization, or using some foreign exchange to subject farm prices to international competition. The most likely result of inflation is to shift income from the non-unionized classes to get-rich-quick types of capitalists in retail or wholesale trade, and it is by no means certain that these will use their profits for productive investment. Inflation equilibrates most satisfactorily when its purpose is to increase the share of the government in national income, or when it originates, Schumpeter style, with entrepreneurs (whether private or public) actually increasing the amount of resources used in productive investment and so forcing the economy to accept a shift toward profits used productively. (Incidentally, as a social democrat I prefer the increase to be in public saving rather than in private profits.)

The third and final condition for success is command over the loopholes, command over the foreign exchanges, over flight of capital, over luxury consumption, luxury building, and such. But all this goes without saying if we are talking about successful inflations.

The size of the inflation depends on how big a proportionate change one is trying to achieve, and how soon. If the annual rate of exchange is large, the annual rate of inflation will also be large, and prices must rise, say, threefold to fivefold in ten years. A big inflation cannot go on for long without turning into spiral inflation, because in a big inflation everybody soon gets the point, and learns to protect himself by demanding higher money income. In this sense, by having prolonged large spiral inflations, which have achieved nothing, Latin America has already wasted her inflationary potential, and barred herself from turning now to useful self-liquidating inflations. If one takes a longer period in which to achieve the proportionate fall in consumption, one can get the same result with much smaller increases in prices. If, for example, the share of consumption falls each year by only one half of 1 percent of national income, while in absolute terms per capita consumption continues to rise by 1 percent per annum, some sluggish classes of the community will never get around even to trying to protect their position, and this, with the unsuccessful attempts of some others, will keep the rise of money incomes low.

For examples of self-liquidating inflation we must look, not at what is happening in Latin America today, but to other parts of the world where the gap between output and consumption has actually been widened. I think the satisticians will find, once they stop chasing hares and come to the real point, that virtually all take-off periods, which by definition are short periods of rapid acceleration of the rate of growth, have been periods of self-liquidating inflation. The so-called Lewis model was constructed to show how the share of profits and savings in national income can rise over a long period without inflation, but in practice there is usually a period when change is fairly swift. The classical examples in our day are provided by the Communist countries. For example, starting in 1928, when personal consumption was taking 80 percent of national product, Stalin succeeded in reducing the proportion to about 60 percent in 1939, at the cost of a tenfold increase in prices. His task was specially difficult because there was no significant increase in the quantity of wage goods. With better agricultural policies he might have achieved his end with only, say, a fourfold increase in prices. Anyway, by 1939 equilibrium had been reached, and price stability could thereafter have been maintained, with consumption at only 60 percent of national product, but for the outbreak of the war.

Now since any rapid increase in prices, even fourfold in ten years, is a pretty horrible process, one must also ask whether the same results cannot be achieved less painfully. Rapid growth can, of course, be achieved without this process if it is financed by foreign capital, as for example, in Puerto Rico or in Northern Rhodesia, but this is beside the point, partly because there isn't all that foreign capital to go round, and partly because our question is whether a rapid increase can be financed domestically by widening the gap between output and consumption without getting involved in inflation. I think the answer must be negative. It is fashionable to say that the gap can be widened by sharp increases in taxation, and to put forward such increases as an alternative to inflation, but this is misleading if it is exaggerated. A large increase in taxation is bound to be inflationary, if its purpose is to reduce mass consumption, because people will always try to get their incomes raised if their purchasing power is reduced, whether by taxation or in any other way. Taxes which fall on savings will not have this effect, but they are irrelevant to our present purpose, which is to reduce the share of consumption in national income. Taxes which fall squarely on the consumption of the rich, such as the great landowners, may also be noninflationary, and there is much scope for such taxes in Latin America. A drastic reduction in consumption cannot, however, take place only at the expense of the rich, because there are not enough rich. So far as I know, all attempts in recent years to effect a drastic reduction in consumption by means of taxes have been followed by industrial strife, even to the point of riot and bloodshed. Whether one proceeds via taxation or via turning the monetary tap, attempts to reduce sharply the share of consumption in the national income will always be inflationary.

For my part I do not believe that any country is wise to try for a sharp and swift reduction in the proportionate share of consumption, whether by taxation or otherwise, because I believe that a big inflation is a horrible experience and is too heavy a price to pay for achieving in five to ten years changes which could be achieved in fifteen to twenty years with only a moderate increase in prices. I believe that there should be a steady fall in the share of consumption, but that this should be within the limits set by the need to increase real per capita consumption all the time and should therefore not much exceed a relative fall of one half of 1 percent of national income per year. So, after one has squeezed what one can out of the landowners, taxes and savings taken together should not rise in real terms faster than about 6 percent per annum, when national income is rising by 3 or 4 percent. This, however, is a very personal judgment, based on my belief that civilization is pretty fragile and that if it gets torn apart in violent social conflict, it is hard to put together again. I do not want to force on the man in the street economic progress at a rate faster than he is willing to bear, defining this rate not in terms of individual savings, as the laissez-faire economists do, but in terms of the rate of change which the man in the street finds politically tolerable.

Since I am ending on this personal note, I may as well add that my highest preference is for rapid growth financed not solely as a bootstrap operation but also by massive foreign aid. But this is clearly outside my present terms of reference.

PAPERS AND COMMENTS

Part II

3. THEORETICAL FRAMEWORK

a. THE EFFECT OF INFLATION ON ECONOMIC DEVELOPMENT

Graeme S. Dorrance

I. INTRODUCTION

The Problem

In many of the less highly developed countries, incomes are not rising as rapidly as the desires of the community. In these countries personal savings are low, so that only limited resources are released for the expansion of the community's capital. At the same time, the tax systems provide only enough revenue to meet part of the community's desires for government services, with very small surpluses available to finance development. Under these circumstances, inflation may appear to be an easy method of providing finance to expand investment and, hence, to be an easy way of obtaining capital for a more rapid expansion of output. If a government can persuade the central bank to create money to finance a development program, or if the banking system freely makes loans to private investors for the finance of physical investment, the problem of expanding the community's real assets may appear to be easily solvable. Consequently, it is sometimes argued that "a case could be made for making inflation an instrument of (development) policy, rather than the control of inflation an object of policy."[1]

There is no doubt that, on occasion, a monetary expansion somewhat greater than the current increase in real output will introduce an element of flexibility into an economy, and lead to some "forced saving" releasing resources for development. However, there are strict limits to the amount of development which may be fostered in this way. Admittedly, the available simple evidence on the relation between inflation and growth is difficult to interpret. The difficulty is common in analyses of the effects of pervasive influences, such as

---

[1] H. J. Bruton, *Inflation in a Growing Economy* (Annual Lectures by Visiting Professor of Monetary Economics, 1960–61, University of Bombay, Bombay), p. 57; parentheses added.

the degree of inflation, on phenomena which are also subject to other, complex, forces.

Table 1 presents summary data gathered from three sources. This evidence varies from the simple comparison of average rates of growth for the years 1954–60,[2] as derived from UN national account statistics, to the conclusions drawn from data on specific periods of price change, identified by U Tun Wai.[3] The rates of growth in the simpler comparisons are based on one observation per country;

TABLE 1

RELATIONSHIP OF RATES OF INFLATION TO ECONOMIC GROWTH IN RECENT YEARS*

| | Annual Rates of Growth Per Capita (*percent*) | | |
	Stable Countries	*Mild Inflation Countries*	*Strong Inflation Countries*
Sample based on UN data.............	2	2	2
ECLA sample.......................	3	..	2
U Tun Wai samples, based on			
Per capita national income			
Unadjusted.....................	6	2	3
Adjusted for terms of trade........	4	1	1
Per capita social product...........	4	3	..

*For description of stable, mild inflation, and strong inflation countries, and for statement of countries and periods covered, see Appendix.
*For sources of data, see Tables 11, 12, and 13.

hence each observation reflects, not only the effect of inflation, but also the effects of the available natural resources and their stage of exploitation, the general political atmosphere, and other influences, such as the general social attitudes, in each country. The separation of shorter periods for individual countries when different rates of price increase prevailed, based on Tun Wai's observations, tends to strengthen the influence of the rate of inflation, as distinct from other forces, in the last three comparisons in Table 1. These latter data suggest that in the postwar years the less highly developed countries have, on the average, enjoyed annual increases in per capita output of approximately 4 percent during those periods when they maintained monetary stability. During periods of mild

---

[2]To be more precise: 1954–60 in most cases, in some cases shorter periods within that time span.

[3]"The Relation Between Inflation and Economic Development: A Statistical Inductive Study," *Staff Papers,* Vol. VII (1959–60), pp. 302–17.

inflation the increase in output in these countries was only half as great. During periods of strong inflation, the increases in output tended to be even smaller.[4]

It is true that individual units of investment financed by bank credit are likely to be created even in inflationary conditions. It is not the immediate products of monetary expansion which are in question; rather it is the over-all effect on progress which deserves consideration. An expansion of the monetary system's assets involves an equal expansion of its liabilities. Unless members of the community are willing to increase the real value of their money balances by an amount equal to the increase in bank credit, and thereby indirectly to provide finance for the new investment—either prices will rise, or imports will be so encouraged and exports discouraged that there will be a fall in the community's capital held in the form of exchange reserves, that is, a disinvestment in reserves offsetting the newly financed domestic investment. If prices rise, the real value of any increase in money holdings will be eroded. This fall in the real value of money may be considered as a tax on moneyholders. Inflationary policies, or policies which lead a government to be weak in resisting inflationary pressures, may be assessed by criteria similar to those used in assessing alternative taxation proposals.

The efficiency of any tax is largely dependent on the degree to which it cannot be evaded. The degree to which a tax "cannot be evaded" is, in turn, largely a function of the degree to which there are no incentives for evasion. A mild inflation may well encourage little or no evasion of the "inflation tax." On the other hand, a strong inflation, and frequently a mild one also, will lead to community reactions which have effects similar to those of widespread tax evasion.

A development policy may have wider aims than the encouragement of a high level of investment. It may be directed toward encouragement of types of investment different from those made by individual economic units acting without positive inducements by the government. If an attempt be made to foster development

---

[4]It should be recognized that these conclusions are more positive than the conclusions in some other studies. The difference between the conclusions in Table 1 and those of other studies may be explained by the fact that the data in Table 1 cover a fairly large number of countries where the rate of inflation is high, whereas the data used by most other authors are dominated by relatively low rates of inflation. For example, of the more than 100 annual rates of price change analyzed by Bhatia ("Inflation, Deflation, and Economic Development," *Staff Papers*, Vol. VIII [1960–61], pp. 101–14), only 14 were larger than 5 percent, and only 3 of these were in excess of 10 percent.

through an "inflation tax," the types of economic incentive induced by inflation are also relevant to its effectiveness. A strong inflation creates distortions in the economy, which may be regarded as comparable to the undesirable incentives induced by unsatisfactory forms of taxation.

It must be recognized that rapid economic development, by evoking supply shortages in certain specific fields, frequently leads to increases in the prices of certain commodities. The number of these may be fairly large. Under these circumstances, some rise in the average level of prices may frequently be an unavoidable companion of economic progress. This observation does not, however, lead to the conclusion that inflation aids development, or that its control should not have a high priority among the targets for economic policy.

The Significance of Expected Price Increases

The monetary system operates on the assumption that money serves as a satisfactory medium of exchange, *numéraire,* standard for debt repayment, and store of value. If prices are stable or rising imperceptibly, money will be accepted by the community for all these purposes. If prices rise markedly, individuals and businesses will cease to hold money for the latter two of these four purposes. If prices are not expected to remain stable, the economic adjustments attempted by the community will be different from those which will be attempted when price stability is expected.[5] In some respects, the problem facing the analyst is the comparison of these different adjustments.

The Effect of Inflation on the Desire for Liquidity[6]

Inflation has two effects on the desire for liquidity, which are related to the two basic reasons why individuals and businesses wish to hold liquid assets—the speculative and precautionary motives. Inflation increases the value of effective liquidity, thereby raising the community's desire for it, but it makes the most generally accepted store of liquidity—money and financial assets denominated in money—unacceptable sources of protection. This strengthening

---

[5]It must be recognized that the degree of price change required to influence expectations is not only rather indeterminate in any particular case, but will depend to a considerable extent on the degree of price stability in earlier years; even so, it will differ from country to country, and between countries with similar monetary experiences.

[6]This section, and Part III below, are based largely on A. S. Shaalan, "The Impact of Inflation on the Composition of Private Domestic Investment," *Staff Papers,* Vol. IX (1962), pp. 243–63.

of the community's wish for liquidity and weakening of the usefulness of the traditional store of liquidity will exert their greatest influence on the types of investment undertaken during periods of inflation, but they will also work to reduce the total flow of resources available for investment.

If an inflation were expected to proceed at a uniform rate, it might have little effect on the community's desire for liquidity. In practice, the rate of any inflation is unpredictable, and the variations in this rate are likely to become more pronounced as the average rate of inflation increases. In a stable economy, price movements are reasonably predictable. In an inflationary economy, if the current rate of price rise is 20 percent a year, the rate next year may almost equally well be approximately 10 percent or over 40 percent.[7] This uncertainty regarding the future course of prices creates an incentive for liquidity. With the future uncertain, the probability of unpredictable investment opportunities arising, or business difficulties occurring, is increased. Hence the desire to hold liquid assets for speculative and precautionary purposes is strengthened.

However, during an inflation money and financial assets denominated in money cannot be depended on as stores of liquidity, since they decline in real value as prices rise.[8] They even fail to provide acceptable liquidity to bridge the gap between transactions, because the intervals between cash receipts and disbursements may be long enough for prices to rise appreciably. In these conditions, attempts will be made to acquire assets whose value is expected to rise in the interval before the investment opportunity or other occasion for disbursement arises. This flight into nonmonetary assets is the source of many of the distortions which accompany an inflation, and is a partial cause of the decrease in the flow of resources to investment.

Inflation Is Not the Only Problem of Development

The control of inflation is only one of the problems facing a government wishing to encourage rapid economic development. The

---

[7]See, for examples, the data in Table 23. For a discussion of the effect of uncertainty regarding the rate of inflation on the structure of interest rates, leading to higher rates for long-term deposits than for short-term ones, and higher rates for short than for long loans, see C. D. Campbell and C. S. Ahn, "Kyes and Mujins—Financial Intermediaries in South Korea," *Economic Development and Cultural Change* (Chicago), October, 1962, pp. 64–65.

[8]Presumably, this is what Keynes had in mind when he stated that "money itself loses the attribute of liquidity if its future supply is expected to undergo sharp changes." (*The General Theory of Employment, Interest and Money*, [New York, Harcourt, Brace & Co. 1956], p. 241, n. 1.)

fight against illiteracy, the reform of bureaucratic practices, the building of basic sanitary facilities for the eradication of endemic diseases, the substitution of competitive for monopolistic trade practices, the encouragement of a widespread spirit of entrepreneurship, and the creation of an adequate amount of social capital may be important prerequisites for rapid growth. However, attacks on these problems are likely to be more feasible in an atmosphere of financial stability; a rapid inflation will make the failure of such attacks much more likely.

II. THE FLOW OF RESOURCES FOR DEVELOPMENT

Acceleration of development, or the maintainance of a high rate of economic progress, calls for encouragement of the flow of resources to development uses and their utilization in the most productive directions. These resources can come only from that part of total domestic output which is not consumed, or from foreign borrowing. Hence, a development policy may be judged by its influence on output, the rate of saving, the decisions of foreign lenders, and the uses to which the total flow of investment funds are put. The future level of output will be, in large part, determined by current and foreign borrowing, and by the productivity of the investments financed from these sources.

Domestic Saving

Amount. General Observations. In all countries, a considerable part of the community's saving takes the form of the accumulation of financial assets. In most poor countries, money forms the major part of the community's financial assets. Even in wealthy countries, financial assets denominated in money (money itself, savings deposits, insurance policies, bonds, etc.) absorb a large part of the community's saving. The willingness of individuals and businesses to hold an expanded quantity of money, or financial claims denominated in money terms, is influenced by their expectations regarding the future price levels. If prices are expected to rise markedly, holders of money will try to limit any increase in the money value of their holdings, or may even attempt to dispose of them. Evidence of community reaction to inflation is provided in Table 2. Historically, the ratio of money to income in all but the wealthiest countries has tended to rise, but in recent years this ratio, on the whole, has declined in countries where inflation has prevailed. The simpler comparison of the value, in terms of constant prices, of the increases in money leads to similar conclusions. In countries which have gone through fairly extended periods of strong inflation, the volume of savings accumulated in the form of money and quasi-money has been quite small, whereas in the more stable countries these accumulations have been substantial. In Argentina and Bolivia the real value of money holdings has even declined. It should be remembered that this latter comparison is limited to changes in the value of these holdings. It does not take account of any changes in the real value of transactions which these holdings are required to finance.

TABLE 2

COMPARISON OF RATES OF INFLATION AND OF INCREASES IN MONEY AND QUASI-MONEY*

(*In Percent*)

Countries	Average Annual Rates of Change in Recent Years in Ratio of Money to Income	Average Increases from 1948 to 1961 in Real Value of Holdings of	
		Money	Money and Quasi-Money
Stable countries.............	..	79	103
Mild inflation countries......	—2	100	138
Strong inflation countries....	—3	19	11

*See Tables 16 and 17.

Saving in the form of money accumulation is only one part of saving through the acquisition of financial claims. A large part of money accumulation is involuntary. Other holdings of financial assets are voluntary. These latter holdings are likely to rise less (or fall more) than those of money if prices are expected to rise. The experience of Argentina and Brazil, outlined in Table 26, may be taken as typical. Between 1950 and 1961 the money holdings of Argentine residents rose almost tenfold. However, the increase in quasi-money was only sevenfold and holdings of government debt remained constant over the period. While Argentine residents increased their money holdings by more than 800 percent (which in fact represented a decline of 25 percent in the real value of these assets), the wider group of financial assets rose by only 685 percent, representing a decline of more than 40 percent in their real value.[9] In Brazil, where money holdings have, until recently, tended to in-

[9]An examination of some unpublished data on insurance in Argentina indicates that the increase in all financial assets was less than 650 percent.

crease slightly in real value, all financial assets, taken together, have, until the last few months, been remarkably stable in real value. The decline in the value of financial assets other than money has offset any saving forced by monetary action.

It is true that this argument says nothing more than that one element of saving will be reduced. Yet it is the element of saving most widely accessible to nonproperty owners in less highly developed countries. Individuals who forego money savings will undoubtedly divert some of their saving to other forms. However, consumption is also a rival for expenditure, if saving in the form of accumulation of assets denominated in terms of money is unattractive. Consequently, a communal shift away from holdings of financial assets is almost certain to be associated with a decline in total saving.

Personal Saving. In part, the decline in saving may be explained by the changes in income distribution which are likely to accompany a strong inflation. In the early stages of a mild inflation, the belief that prices will not rise markedly may well lead wage earners to accept nearly constant money payments, and pension plans which promise fixed money payments. Consequently, in the early stages of a mild inflation, there may be a shift in income distribution from the relatively low-income wage earning and pension groups, who have a low propensity to save, to the relatively wealthy profit recipients, who are likely to have a higher propensity to save.

Once wage earners realize that the real value of fixed money earnings is likely to decline, they will press for higher wages or for sliding scale adjustments which will insure, at least, the maintenance of the real value of their earnings. At the same time, employers, with rising money profits, will be willing to compete for workers by agreeing to higher wage payments. Similarly, prospective pensioners will not be satisfied with retirement programs which relate benefits to past money incomes. Pressures will be exerted for the adoption of plans with escalator clauses. Governments, acting on the basis of humanitarian motives, will accede to these pressures. As a result, pension programs will be developed which, in effect, relate pension payments to the cost of living, the level of minimum wages, or some similar escalating provision. This process will result in a shift in income distribution from the wealthy back to the less wealthy, with a consequent decline in saving.

Whether these forces will be sufficient to make the final distribution of income more or less favorable to the relatively poor is probably impossible to determine. Table 27 suggests that if reasonably long periods are taken, the degree of inflation has relatively little influence on real wage rates. Similarly, the data in Table 28 suggest that the shift in the distribution of income may be quite small, with perhaps a slight increase in the share going to wage earners in periods of inflation.

At the same time, inflation will be associated with a qualitative redistribution of profits. Every rapid inflation provides an opportunity for fortunate speculators, and their ostentatious consumption gives an impression of a radical shift in the community's income distribution. However, these groups are not likely to be large savers relative to their incomes. The *nouveaux riches* are likely to be more typical of this group than the frugal entrepreneurs who reinvest profits to build industrial empires.

Business Saving. The pressures which depress personal savings will have a similar influence on business saving. In addition, strong inflation will bring forth two specific pressures encouraging businesses to distribute, rather than to reinvest, current earnings.

The strengthening of the desire for liquidity which results from inflation will discourage long-term investment. As a result, shareholders will press company managers to distribute profits.

Moreover, as shown below, in their search for liquidity and profitable investment, residents of countries where there is inflation are likely to shift from domestic to foreign investment. Shareholders in companies, being among the wealthy and more sophisticated members of the community, are persons who have the knowledge of, and effective access to, foreign investment. For this reason also, they are likely to put pressure on company managers to pay dividends rather than to retain earnings, so that the proceeds of these payments may be transferred abroad.

Comparative statistics on company practices are very scanty, to say the least. One admittedly unsatisfactory comparison is given in Table 19. Statistics on the activities of corporations controlled by U.S. residents, but operating in other countries, identify the data by country for only a relatively few countries. In the years 1957–60, the records relating to those less industrialized countries where prices were stable indicate that companies operating in these areas tended to reinvest half their disposable earnings. Similar companies operating in countries where prices were rising tended to reinvest only half as much.[10]

---

[10]A similar conclusion is obtained if the data relating to Venezuela (where investment in crude oil production is of a technological form which is not amenable to expansion through reinvestment of earnings) and to Brazil and Indonesia (where restrictions on capital repatriation led to forced reinvestment of earnings by foreign companies) are excluded from the comparison.

Government Saving. If saving by the private sector is inhibited by inflation, it is possible that the shortfall might be made up by government saving. The data in Table 3 indicate the reverse. However, this relationship reflects primarily the attempts of some governments to finance investment by budget deficits. That is, in effect some countries have made inflation an instrument of development policy rather than making the control of inflation an object of policy.

TABLE 3

RELATIONSHIP OF RATES OF INFLATION TO BUDGET DEFICITS,
SELECTED YEARS*

Countries	Average Budget Deficits as Percentages of Gross National Product
Stable countries.....................	2
Mild inflation countries.............	2
Strong inflation countries...........	5

*See Table 18.

There is one important factor which will tend to increase government expenditure and lead to budget deficits. Even though a worker realizes that his wages are increased, he strongly resents a rise in his rent or in the prices of bread or beans, and particularly resents any increase in public utility prices. In an attempt to forestall some of the undesirable effects of inflation, the government may attempt to restrain the rise in prices of consumer goods. Farmers and other producers will expect, and will provide supplies only if they receive the benefits of, rising prices. If the price of one commodity is controlled while other prices are rising, the demand for the price-controlled commodity will increase. If the supply of a commodity is to be encouraged, its price must rise relative to other prices. Hence, government restraint of price increases will only be possible if the production of the price-controlled goods is subsidized. The cost of these subsidies may well absorb substantial amounts of government expenditure. For example, the persistent deficits of government-owned public utilities, resulting from rising costs and opposition to rate and fare increases, are a common characteristic of government accounts in countries experiencing a strong inflation.

This is exemplified by the fiscal problems of the government of Ceylon. In the past few years, factors which might lead to rapidly rising prices have been present in that country. The government has striven to restrain these pressures, largely by using subsidies to suppress the effects of inflation, and has met with considerable success. Because of the country's high propensity to import (even though subject to controls, imports are equal to approximately 40 percent of gross national product and imported goods account for over 40 percent of consumer expenditure), the domestic price level is determined predominantly by foreign prices. The evidence of inflation has appeared primarily in a 60 per cent reduction in the country's foreign exchange reserves in the five years ending in 1962. Government revenue rose (Table 4), partly as a result of increased tax rates

TABLE 4

CEYLON: PRICES AND GOVERNMENT FINANCE, 1955–60

	1955	1956	1957	1958	1959	1960
Pre-subsidy cost of living index...	100	103	104	106	109	107
Effect of subsidy*.............	1	4	3	3	5	5
Subsidized index..............	99	99	101	103	104	102
			(million rupees)			
Government revenue†..........	1,185	1,280	1,271	1,293	1,349	1,413
Government expenditure........	1,068	1,322	1,507	1,554	1,774	1,863
Other than capital investment and inflation transfers‡.....	*563*	*670*	*831*	*713*	*895*	*948*
Capital investment..........	*357*	*431*	*396*	*499*	*493*	*496*
Inflation transfers...........	*148*	*221*	*280*	*342*	*386*	*419*
Surplus or deficit (−)..........	117	−42	−236	−261	−425	−450
Excluding capital investment and inflation transfers......	*622*	*610*	*440*	*580*	*454*	*465*
Excluding inflation transfers...	*265*	*179*	*44*	*81*	*−39*	*−31*

Source: Central Bank of Ceylon, *Annual Report for the year 1961.*
*Food subsidies as percent of personal consumption.
†Revenue plus grants under Colombo Plan and from other sources.
‡Food subsidies and losses of railway and electricity departments.

and new taxes, but government expenditure increased more rapidly in the six years ending in 1960 (the latest period for which data are available). Consequently, the government's cash accounts changed from a position of near balance to a deficit equal to approximately 7 percent of gross national product. If the government had been able to avoid the expenditures made to restrain the inflation, its excess of current revenue over current expenditure would have provided surpluses to finance its investment expenditure in the fiscal years 1955–58, and the 1959 and 1960 deficits would have been small.

The decision to provide food subsidies and to cover the operating losses of the railways and electricity departments induced inflationary deficits in the years 1956 to 1960. Even with the investment program, there would have been inflation-repressing surpluses in the early years.

Purchase of Foreign Assets. In an inflationary economy foreign financial assets serve to protect liquidity. Insofar as they are claims denominated in money terms, they provide the same quality of protection that domestic financial assets provide in a stable environment. Insofar as the expectation of price increases has, as a concomitant, an expectation of exchange depreciation, domestic claims will be expected to decline in real value, whereas foreign claims will not. Consequently, it may be expected that inflation will lead to an increase in the community's desires to hold foreign assets, and that savings will be diverted from the purchase of domestic assets to the purchase of foreign assets. Any expectation that the exchange rate will depreciate to a greater degree than domestic prices rise will strengthen the desire for foreign assets.[11]

Comprehensive statistics on the acquisition of foreign assets by residents of countries experiencing inflation are not available. A number of estimates of the total amounts involved have been made, but they can be no more than guesses. The few available statistics are depressing. In the five years ending in 1961, private residents of Latin America, other than banks, increased their investments in the United States by approximately one billion dollars.[12] The summary in Table 5 of data on the acquisition of short-term foreign assets by residents of Mexico provides an example of the relation between these capital movements and the rate of inflation. Indeed, "a particularly unfortunate feature of the international financial scene in the last decade has been the large flow of private capital from those less developed countries which have tolerated inflation to countries, frequently wealthy, which have maintained monetary stability."[13]

Purchase of Financial Assets. Even if inflation did no more than lead to a shift in the flow of saving from the accumulation of financial assets to the purchase of other types of assets, this would involve a decline in the "quality" of saving. It may be argued that if all domestic capital markets were perfectly linked, if the different availabilities of capital in each market were reflected solely in the differ-

---

[11]See Part IV for a discussion of this point.
[12]Derived from *Survey of Current Business* and *International Financial Statistics.*
[13]International Monetary Fund, *Annual Report, 1962*, p. 44.

ent rates of interest prevailing, and if these rates reflected only the liquidity and risk elements in the capital transactions, financial transactions might be considered to reflect purely economic forces. If these conditions prevailed, each economic unit desiring to invest would have to compete with all the others desiring to invest, and this competition would be based on the relative returns to be earned in different activities and the relative costs of borrowing from different sources. Under these conditions, investment should be channeled to the most productive uses. It must be admitted that these perfect conditions do not prevail in any market, and that the capital

TABLE 5

MEXICO: AVERAGE NET PURCHASES OF SHORT-TERM
FOREIGN ASSETS BY RESIDENTS, 1951–60*

(*In Millions of U.S. Dollars*)

Years of	Average Net Purchases
Monetary stability..............	..
Mild inflation..................	8
Strong inflation................	12

*Based on data in Table 20.

markets of all the less highly developed countries tend to be more inflexible than the markets of the more highly developed countries. Yet anything which encourages the flow of savings to the financial markets may be expected to increase the economic desirability of the resulting investment which the community's saving makes possible. Anything which limits the flow of savings to financial markets, or reduces the opportunity for self-investors to acquire financial assets, may be expected to limit the influence of economic criteria on investment decisions.

Foreign Capital

Amount. In addition to the release of domestic resources through saving, just discussed, resources for development may be obtained by borrowing abroad. But just as an outward flow of capital is encouraged by an inflation, so an inflow in the form of portfolio investment is discouraged by inflation.

A major part of private international capital transfers arises from equity investment by nonresidents. This flow is largely in the form of direct investment by experienced entrepreneurs interested in establishing types of production not previously undertaken in the developing economies. This is frequently one of the major sources of capital for the productive diversification of staple-exporting economies. The volume of this investment is largely a function of its expected return. Inflation may be expected to raise the money return on investment. If the exchange rate could be expected to depreciate at the same rate that prices increased, inflation would tend to have a neutral effect on prospective nonresident purchasers of domestic equity investments. However, as will be indicated below, the exchange depreciation is likely to be more severe than the increase in prices induced by inflation. Hence, the net return to nonresident equity investors in inflating economies may be expected to deteriorate. Therefore, the flow of equity capital to inflating economies will probably be lessened.

There is one very positive impediment to nonresident investment induced by inflation. It will be indicated that one of the effects of inflation is a deterioration of the foreign balance and that this induces the government to take protective action. One of these acts may be the restriction of payments to nonresidents. Payments on capital account to nonresidents are prime candidates for such restrictions. At the first sign of inflation in a country, nonresidents will fear that restrictions of this kind will be imposed and will refrain from investing there. They may even attempt to repatriate previous investments in anticipation of such restrictions. This type of reaction probably accounts for the disparate movements of international capital indicated in Table 6. This shows that net private direct in-

TABLE 6

AVERAGE INCREASES IN VALUE OF U.S. PRIVATE DIRECT
INVESTMENT IN LESS HIGHLY DEVELOPED COUNTRIES,
1950–61*

(*In Percent*)

Countries	Average Increases
Stable countries......................	214
Mild inflation countries..............	177
Strong inflation countries............	55

*See Table 21.

vestment in less highly developed countries by residents of the country with the largest capital exports increased at a rate 20 percent faster than the comparable increase in investment in a group of mild inflation countries during the 11 years ending in 1961. The comparable increase in a group of countries where prices were rising rapidly was equivalent to only a little more than the reinvestment of earnings at a rate equivalent to 4 percent of the capital invested.

Protection of Foreign Investors. It was suggested earlier that development policies are designed to make the flow of resources for investment greater than they would be in the absence of such policies. Since in the absence of government intervention, inflation is likely to have a depressing effect on the flow of foreign capital to a developing economy, it is likely to make a government more willing to protect foreign lenders. If this protection is to be effective, it is almost inevitable that it must err, if it errs at all, on the side of being excessive. That is, inflation may lead to the adoption of policies which give better terms to foreign lenders than they could command under stable conditions.[14]

The degree of uncertainty created by inflation may be greater in the opinion of foreign than of domestic investors. Not only is the uncertainty regarding the real domestic value of future earnings increased by inflation, but uncertainty regarding the future course of exchange rates is created and there is also the fear of exchange restrictions. To allay these fears, the government of an inflation-ridden economy may be pushed to borrow directly from abroad or to guarantee the repatriation of private loans raised abroad. However, development must, almost inevitably, include risky investment. No matter how astute investors may be, some investments will be unprofitable. If such investments have been financed through private channels, the process of bankruptcy will lead to a sharing of the cost of any unsuccessful investment between borrowers and lenders. If they have been financed by government borrowing or with a government guarantee, the full cost of investment, which in retrospect will be seen to have been unwise, will be borne by residents of the borrowing country.[15]

---

[14]This statement is not contradicted by the policies of certain governments restricting foreign investment in certain fields (for example, exploration for petroleum). These policies may be adopted for specific national purposes, and the inflationary or noninflationary climate is irrelevant. Within the constraints set by such policies, inflation is likely to increase the pressures on these same governments to take positive steps to increase the inflow of nonresident capital.

[15]These comments should not be taken as a generalized condemnation of government borrowing, or of intergovernment capital transactions. Under many circumstances, they serve highly useful purposes. Many forms of investment which are appropriate for foreign financing (for example, a part of social investment in roads, water, and sanitation works) can only be handled by the govern-

(Continued on next page)

Changes in Relative Prices

The distortion of the price structure created by inflation is likely indirectly to discourage saving and encourage consumption. In most nonindustrial countries, investment has a high import component. The excessive exchange depreciation induced by inflation, and the protective import substitution policies likely to be adopted by the authorities, frequently lead to relatively large increases in the prices of investment goods. The experience in nine Latin-American coun-

TABLE 7

RELATIVE PRICES OF INVESTMENT GOODS, SELECTED LATIN-
AMERICAN COUNTRIES, 1960*

(Average for All Countries = 100)

Countries	At Free Market Exchange Rates	At Parity Rates
Stable country......................	86	82
Mild inflation countries...............	100	95
Strong inflation countries.............	120	114

*See Table 22.

tries, summarized in Table 7, suggests that one unit of consumption expenditure foregone in a stable country would permit the use of 15 percent more investment, in real terms, than in the mild inflation countries, and almost 40 percent more than the average for the strong inflation countries. This rise in the relative price of investment goods decreases the money rate of return on investment, and consequently on saving, with a resultant discouragement of investment and encouragement of consumption.[16]

Conclusion

This analysis, which appears to be supported by the available statistics, suggests that inflation is likely to evoke forces which both diminish the resources available for development and reduce the true effectiveness of those funds which continue to flow to invest-

---

ment or its agencies. Many of the sources of capital in the modern world are governments or intergovernment agencies (International Bank for Reconstruction and Development, Inter-American Development Bank, etc.) which may be expected to make only loans with government guarantees.

[16]For a more complete discussion of this point as related to one country, see R. Hayn, "Inflación, formación de capital y balanza de pagos de la Argentina, 1940–1958," *Revista de Economia Y Estadistica*, Cordoba, Segundo Trimestre, 1962, Ano VI, Nro. 2, pp. 21–48.

ment. Saving is likely to be lower than under stable monetary conditions, and to take forms which lead to a lessening of the adaptability of the economy and to a lessening of the force of economic criteria in the choice of final investment. The inflow of foreign capital is likely to be reduced, and the terms on which it comes to the country are likely to become more stringent with regard to its eventual repayment.

III. THE DIRECTION OF INVESTMENT

Inventory Investment

If money, and financial assets denominated in money, cease to provide satisfactorily protected liquidity, other sources of this protection will be sought. The accumulation of salable inventories is one means of obtaining realizable assets whose real value is likely to be maintained in the face of rising prices. Consequently, inflation may be expected to encourage investors to forego the purchase of financial assets which could have financed long-term physical investment, and to accumulate inventories directly. As a result, the available resources will be devoted to inventory stockpiling rather than to long-term investment.

Moreover, in addition to the disadvantages of illiquidity attached to long-term fixed investment, there is an element of uncertainty. In an environment of unstable prices and rising costs, the long gestation period involved in fixed investment means that its eventual cost is indeterminate, and hence the possibility of financing the total outlay may be questionable. As a result, it may prove impossible to complete projects.

There are strict limits to the changes which may be made in the structure of a given stock of physical assets. Most of these changes must result from the channeling of currently accruing resources into the most desired form of asset. As the changes desired may well be large in relation to total annual investment, it may be expected that a large part of this total may be devoted to inventory investment, until the structure of the community's stock of physical assets is changed. Subsequently, the flow of investment resources will be divided between inventory accumulation and fixed asset formation, in the ratio which the community wishes to maintain between these components of its stock of physical assets. Hence, in a brief period of inflation, or in the early stages of a longer inflation, a marked diversion of investment resources toward the accumulation of inventories may be expected. In the later stages of a prolonged inflation, the ratio of inventory investment to fixed investment may be expected to be somewhat higher than it was prior to the inflation, but it should be less than in the early stages of inflation.

Table 8 indicates that in two relatively stable countries the inventory component of gross domestic investment has been relatively stable. There is some indication that in one of these, Ecuador, the ratio of inventory accumulation to total investment has been slightly correlated with the rate of inflation. In two mild inflation countries where the rate of inflation has varied (Colombia and Mexico),

TABLE 8

RELATIONSHIP OF INFLATION TO VARIABILITY OF INVENTORY INVESTMENT, SELECTED COUNTRIES, SELECTED YEARS*

Countries	Rate of Inflation		Inventory Investment as Percentage of Gross Domestic Investment	
	Annual Average (percent)	Standard Deviation	Annual Average Value	Standard Deviation
Stable countries				
Philippines...............	1	4	15	6
Ecuador..................	2	4	16	3
Mild inflation countries				
Colombia................	7	6	9	12
Mexico..................	7	9	14	9
Peru....................	8	3	11	3
Strong inflation countries				
Brazil...................	19	8	10	9
Chile....................	38	24	3	13

*See Table 23.

there is clear evidence of correlation between the rate of inflation and shifts in the stocking of inventories. In two strong inflation countries (Brazil and Chile), the rate of inventory investment has varied markedly. In Brazil, when the rate of inflation rose, inventories were increased sharply. Thereafter, even though inflation might be rapid, the rate of inventory investment reverted to a more normal level; when the rate of inflation was reduced, there was a temporary decline in the rate of inventory investment. In Chile, similar effects appear to have followed after a lag.[17]

[17]See Table 23, as well as Table 8, for the basis for these observations.

Housing

The implication of the above analysis is that inflation encourages excessive investment in inventories, which is a form of short-term investment, and at least temporarily discourages long-term investment in fixed assets. Nevertheless, it is frequently suggested that an inflationary economy is characterized by excessive investment in luxury housing—a form of long-term investment. However, this paradox is apparent rather than real. Encouraged to acquire physical rather than fixed-money assets, savers must find some asset which satisfies their demand. One of the physical assets most easily acquired by individuals is residential property. Hence, inflation may be expected to encourage the demand for houses, either for occupation or for rent. In many of the inflation-ridden economies, governments are prone to control money rents. Hence, the return on rental housing is prevented from rising in step with the increase in the level of prices. The outcome is that savers are encouraged to buy houses for self-occupancy and discouraged from investing in rental property.

Data on the distribution of expenditures between housing and other forms of investment are scarce, and data on investment in houses for owner occupancy are practically nonexistent. The indirect indication of the effect of inflation on the demand for building materials presented in Table 29 is consistent with an argument that inflation leads to a rise in the relative demand for buildings, as distinct from other forms of investment. While these data are consistent with the arguments presented here, they should be used with caution because the demand for building materials is more subject to the distorting effects of inflation than is the demand for most other products. The prices of all investment goods tend to rise more during inflation than the general level of prices. Stocks of building materials (other than cement) are prime targets for inventory investment, as they tend to be durable (bricks, pipe, tile, etc.), their cost of storage (on the sites of incomplete buildings) is relatively low, and they may be financed from a variety of sources (for example, both by bank loans for working capital and by construction mortgages).

Business Fixed Assets

The pressures exerted by inflation on the allocation of investment funds to the purchase of different types of fixed assets may be separated into those which may be termed "fundamental forces," and those which reflect the adjustment of individual economic units to the "inflation restraining" actions of the government. Requirements for investment in fixed assets differ markedly between industries. Some activities (such as railroad transport) require long-lived equipment, whereas others (such as highway transport) require much shorter-lived equipment. It may be taken that the most appropriate combination of investment in different activities will result from the interplay of competing demands by investors looking for the most profitable investments (adjusted to take advantage of subsidies and taxes where these are considered desirable for social reasons). However, some of these investments involve long-term commitments and hence will be influenced by the community's expectations. If investors believe that the prospective economic parameters will be similar to those presently existing, or if they can reasonably expect that changes in these parameters will be orderly, they can have a firm basis for their decisions. Technological factors will then be the primary determinants for the distribution of investment. If investors expect rapid change in basic economic relations, they will be hesitant to commit themselves for long periods. If capital investments may be amortized quickly, an investor has more frequent opportunities to review his decisions. The expectation of rising prices will therefore be likely to bias investment decisions toward the purchase of fixed assets with relatively short lives. For these reasons, an inflationary economy may be expected to evolve along lines where long-term industrial and social investment is discouraged, and where resources flow more readily to those fields in which returns may be achieved most quickly. In such an economy railway transport may be expected to deteriorate, while trucks have their useful lives curtailed bouncing roughly on potholed roads.

As suggested earlier, inflation brings forth two reactions by governments:

1. The impetus to imports calls for protection of reserves, which may involve active encouragement of import-substituting activity and exchange restrictions.
2. The reactions of the community to increases in the cost of living are likely to force the government to institute price controls over "the basic necessities of life."

An active policy of encouraging import substitution may involve protection of domestic production from foreign competition. This protection may be given by administrative restrictions, tariffs, or excessive currency depreciation. It is possible that the rapid development of import-substituting production may entail nothing more than an acceleration of part of the overall development process. It is also possible that it will lead to the encouragement of activity which, in the absence of protection, would remain unproductive almost permanently in the face of foreign competition.

Some indication of the extent of desirable diversification which has been achieved in recent years may be obtained by comparing the export data for individual countries. If a country is able to diversify its export sales, there are grounds for believing that it has been able to expand the production of goods other than its staple exports, and that this expansion has been in the fields where it enjoys some degree of comparative advantage. If it does not achieve diversification of export sales, there are grounds for believing that it has lost some of its comparative advantages, and that any diversification of production which has been achieved has involved the expansion of output in those fields where its costs are high by international standards. Table 9 summarizes the changes in the volume of exports between 1953-54 and 1958-59 in two groups of

TABLE 9

Percentage Increases, 1953–54 to 1958–59, in Volume of
Major and Minor Exports, Selected Countries*

Countries	Major Exports	Minor Exports
Stable countries............	18	39
Strong inflation countries....	10	—

*See Table 24.

countries. In both groups, the volume of staple exports (major exports) expanded. However, in the stable countries the volume of other exports (minor exports) expanded more rapidly than exports generally, providing some evidence that these countries achieved some economically desirable diversification of production. In the strong inflation countries the volume of minor exports was unchanged during these years. Whereas the minor exports accounted for approximately one tenth more of the total in the stable countries, this proportion fell by approximately one sixth in the strong inflation countries.

To protect exchange reserves from the erosion induced by inflation, many countries have resorted to exchange restrictions. Many restrictive systems have been based on multiple exchange rates, which have the adverse qualities to which attention has frequently been drawn.[18] They frequently provide minimum exchange depreciation for certain basic export products. This preferential treatment adds to the structural distortions of the economy discussed earlier. The favorable rates provided for the import of essential commodities serve to discourage domestic production and encourage activities (usually the production of nonessential goods) which are given the greatest degree of protection. Often these are not the most appropriate uses for the country's resources. For example, the exchange rate system of Indonesia at the end of 1961[19] could be described as a government production plan designed to penalize the production of rice and to divert domestic resources from investment to personal consumption, particularly of luxury items.

Investment decisions made by private entrepreneurs are primarily influenced by the expected profitability of investment. The relative profitability of investment in any activity is a function of the prices of final output rendered possible by the investment, compared with the prices of final outputs which could be achieved by alternative investment. Governments frequently attempt to restrain inflation by imposing controls on the prices of the basic necessities of life, or of community services. Under these circumstances, the general rise in other prices is equivalent to a relative fall in the prices of the basic necessities or services. If price controls are not accompanied by subsidies to the producers of the price-controlled goods and services, investment in the production of basic necessities and community services will become relatively unprofitable and will be discouraged. Consequently, if the consumer is protected, as he frequently is, from the evils of inflation, the result may well be to divert investment, so that he is deprived of access to potential supplies of basic necessities and community services.

This aspect of inflation is seen most frequently in the public utility field. Many public utilities are natural monopolies. Hence, their prices are frequently subject to control by regulatory bodies. This control, with the almost inevitable legalism involved in its administration, is likely to create a lag in the rise of public utility prices behind other prices. Moreover, the regulatory process makes this field a prime candidate for price control to restrain increases in cost of living indices. Hence, inflation will almost inevitably

---

[18]International Monetary Fund, "Decision on Multiple Currency Practices," *Annual Report, 1957*, pp. 161–62.

[19]See International Monetary Fund, *Thirteenth Annual Report on Exchange Restrictions, 1962*, pp. 174–75.

lead to a diversion of investment from public utilities. As a result, the recurrent power shortages, which are one of the aspects of life in an inflationary economy, are easily comprehensible.

Conclusion

These arguments, which are supported by observation, suggest that inflation is likely to evoke forces which divert the resources available for domestic investment to an excessive accumulation of inventories and the building of houses for occupancy by the relatively wealthy, rather than to the construction of productive facilities or the provision of housing for the major part of the community. Of the productive facilities actually built, a bias develops toward investment in relatively short-lived projects, and the attraction of truly low-cost production tends to be weakened, while resources are diverted from the production of basic necessities and investment goods to the production of consumption goods, particularly luxury commodities.

IV. THE BALANCE OF PAYMENTS

The frequency with which inflating countries have had to resort to the International Monetary Fund for assistance, together with the relatively small volume of continuing drawings by noninflating countries, provides clear evidence of the relation between strong inflation and balance of payments difficulties. These difficulties arise because strong inflations encourage capital flight, strengthen import demands, and reduce export supplies. They make large exchange rate depreciations necessary. The attempts to limit exchange pressures often lead to the imposition of restrictions which have distorting effects on the structure of investment and production.

Imports

When there is a generalized excess demand for goods it will quickly become evident as a demand for purchases from the most readily available elastic source, that is, from foreigners. Hence, one of the first effects of inflation will be a rise in imports. In the early stages, the effect of expanding demand on the price level may be dampened by the ability of the community to import. With a small rise in domestic prices, foreign supplies become relatively cheaper and the pressing demand from the domestic economy will be diverted to the larger world economy. This diversion will limit the demands impinging directly on the domestic economy and will restrict the immediate effects of inflationary pressures on domestic prices.[20]

In many countries, the impact of inflation on imports is repressed by trade controls, so that the level of imports is determined, not by relative prices, but by administrative decision. However, the trade controls and the exchange depreciation in inflating countries provide clear evidence of the payments difficulties of these countries.

Exports[21]

Just as inflation may be expected to encourage imports, it may be expected to discourage exports. Rising domestic demand will impinge on those export goods which are suitable for domestic consumption, and will divert them from export to domestic sales or stockpiles.[22] Of course, in many cases this diversion will be limited. An economy with only a few basic export products is not likely to increase its consumption of these products sufficiently to affect markedly the supply available for sale to foreigners. Even a doubling of domestic consumption of Brazilian coffee or Malayan rubber would lead to relatively small percentage declines in the supplies of these goods on world markets. However, it is easy to overstate this argument. All export production involves the use of some generalized resources. In any economy, excessive demand will impinge on these generalized resources, and bid them away from the production of export goods. This may be a somewhat longer-run effect, and is likely to be an influence leading to a structural distortion of the economy rather than to immediate short-term balance of payments difficulties. However, it is not merely coincidental that the volume of exports made available by Argentina, Bolivia, Brazil, Chile, and Haiti declined during the half century between 1913 and 1958, and that these countries have experienced almost continuous inflationary pressures since World War I.

In the period 1953 to 1959, the export experience of the three groups of raw material exporting countries differed markedly, as indicated in Table 10. These differences do not reflect varying market conditions, as the grouping bears no relation to the export products of these countries. Exporters of coffee, cotton, nonferrous

---

[20]See, for example, the discussion of Ceylon above.

[21]This section is based largely on Gertrud Lovasy, "Inflation and Exports in Primary Producing Countries," *Staff Papers*, Vol. IX (1962), pp. 37–69.

[22]One aspect of this problem is exemplified by the following quotation from a report on the decline in the marketable supply of sisal: "Brazilian growers are simply retaining their stocks as a hedge against inflation" (*The Statist*, November 2, 1962, p. 328).

metals, and rubber are in all three groups; of cereals, meat, and wool in the stable and strong inflation groups, and of fish and sugar in the stable and mild inflation groups. Consequently, it is not surprising that the average change in the world market prices (export price indices in terms of U.S. dollars) has moved in the same direction and by approximately the same amount for each group of countries. While the volume of exports of the stable countries rose by one quarter, and of the mild inflation countries by one fifth, the increase for the strong inflation countries was less than one sixteenth. The pressures of inflation led to a domestic absorption of resources in those countries where domestic prices were rising, preventing them from participating in the expansion of world demand for their products.[23]

TABLE 10

AVERAGE CHANGES, 1953 TO 1959, IN DOMESTIC PRICES, EXPORT PRICES AND
VOLUME, AND EXCHANGE RATES, SELECTED COUNTRIES*

(*In Percent*)

Countries	Cost of Living	Export Prices	Export Volume	Exchange Rates
Stable countries................	9	−5	24	..
Mild inflation countries.........	43	−10	19	64
Strong inflation countries.......	400	−16	6	700

*See Table 25.

The Exchange Rate

The incentives to capital exports and the discouragement of capital imports, caused by inflation, have been discussed above. These influences augment the balance of payments difficulties on current accounts so that, unless action is taken, an inflating economy's international reserves are soon dissipated. The action which is needed may take the form of restrictions on imports or on capital payments, or it may include exchange depreciation. If inflation is continued, it is practically inevitable that the exchange rate must depreciate.

Moreover, if imports are not restricted, the eventual exchange depreciation is likely to be greater than the rise in domestic prices. The excess demand caused by inflation will meet supply inelasticities. The spillover of demand into the foreign market and the reduc-

---

[23]Given the decline in average export prices, there was a rise in the volume of demand, but not necessarily a rise in the demand schedules for the products of these countries.

CHART 1

(As Percentages of 1951 Averages)

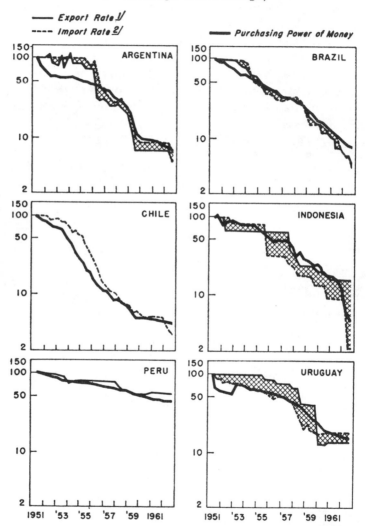

[1] For Argentina and Indonesia, implicit export rate; Brazil, implicit export rate excluding coffee; Peru, principal exchange rate, which does not differ markedly from the implicit export rate and the implicit import rate; Uruguay, principal export rate.

[2] For Argentina, Brazil, and Chile, implicit import rate; Indonesia, "other" import rate; Uruguay, free rate.

tion of exports consequent on inflation can only be offset by a greater rise in the domestic equivalent of foreign prices than of purely domestic prices. As shown by the comparison in Table 10, the depreciation of the exchange rate in mild inflation countries exceeded the rise in domestic prices in the period 1953–59 by almost 15 percent on the average. In the strong inflation countries this excess averaged 75 percent.[24]

While there is ample evidence to support the view that the exchange rate will depreciate by more than the increase in domestic prices, it does not follow that this is a smooth process. Most governments attempt, either consciously or unconsciously, to maintain confidence in the value of money. One of the quickest ways to destroy this confidence is to allow the exchange rate to depreciate. Therefore, it may be expected that the government will attempt to maintain the rate, for a period at least. Six examples of the pegging of exchange rates, at one time or another, are provided in Chart 1. Periods when the rate was pegged despite pressures toward depreciation are indicated by stability of the exchange rate (light) lines coinciding with decline in the price (heavy) lines. Such pegging action has two repercussions. First, as the domestic currency prices of exports and imports are maintained, the pressures of inflation are given full play; if the rate were allowed to depreciate, the depreciation would mitigate or even offset the balance of payments effects of inflation. Second, with exchange depreciation clearly forecast by the rise in prices, the inducements to capital flight, discussed above, are strengthened.

V. STABILIZATION PROBLEMS
The Difficulty of Stabilization

It is often alleged that, even though inflation may be undesirable, a cure by means of a stabilization program may be worse than the disease of inflation. Those who favor monetary reform are accused of placing a higher value on price stability than on economic growth. If the analysis presented in this paper is valid, an economy experiencing inflation must be one where development is proceeding less rapidly than it would if the economy were stable, all other conditions being similar. It does not follow, however, that a change in the climate will immediately ease an inflating economy's diffi-

---

[24]If allowance is made for the fact that world prices rose by approximately 10 percent during this period, and that hence a 10 percent rise in domestic prices would have been consistent with exchange stability, these percentages become 25 and 80, respectively.

culties. In particular, it does not follow that a stabilization program will bring an immediate increase in output.

The desirable reshuffling of the economy resulting from stabilization may lead directly to a temporary decline in the demand for physical investment. There is an inevitable lag between the decision to create physical capital and the actual consumption of resources in capital production. On the other hand, investment already in progress may be abandoned rather quickly. One of the effects of inflation is the encouragement of industries which would be uneconomic in a noninflationary world. Stabilization may bring a quick cutoff in the development of these industries, leading to a decline in the demand for investment resources. While a stable environment will make alternative industries appear to be profitable fields for investment, it takes some time for entrepreneurs to convert their investment desires into consumption of resources. Hence, the period immediately after the start of a stabilization program may well be marked by a lag in the consumption of investment resources, with a consequent decline in the production of capital goods.

It might be thought that, as inflation is a situation of generalized excess demand for goods and services, a reduction in demand might do no more than eliminate the excess. But the situation which develops in an inflation is that the supply of goods and services, which necessarily cannot be less than effective expenditure, includes types of commodities and services for which demand will exist only so long as inflation continues. The reduction of this demand caused by the cessation of inflation, and its replacement by expenditure appropriate to stable conditions, involves a corresponding readjustment of supply. It would be utopian to expect that all phases of this readjustment process would be closely synchronized. There are particular difficulties in the smooth adjustment of investment expenditures, which follow from the effects of inflation discussed above. In the first place, inflation induces an accumulation of inventories in excess of those which would have been built up in stable conditions. Necessarily, therefore, the cessation of inflation will lead to disinvestment in inventories, reversing this part of the flow of demand. Secondly, investment in industries during the inflation is likely to have been directed to those enjoying a high degree of protection. Insofar as the exchange rate is unified or changed to a more realistic one, or insofar as stabilization by strengthening the balance of payments (for example, by reducing purchases of imports for addition to inventories), enables exchange restrictions to be eased, the protection afforded these industries will be diminished, and their attractiveness for investment will decline. Thirdly, the increasing attractiveness of physical assets during an inflation may be expected to lead also to a rise in the demand for owner-occupied housing. Once stabilization is under way, the existing supply of this type of housing, together with the rising demand for financial assets, can be expected to lead to a reduction of investment of this kind. And even if stabilization and the easing of rent control make rental housing a desirable form of investment, it takes time to convert desires to invest. into orders for bricks and mortar.

Thus the flow of resources evoked by an inflation will be not only in excess of, but also partially inappropriate to, the flow of demand in stabilized conditions. The severity of the consequential adjustment problems, and the time required to solve them, will depend, in part at least, on the degree to which the economic system has been distorted. This degree of distortion will in turn depend largely on the duration and rate of the inflation which is being brought to an end. When the inflation has not been too severe, and in its current bout has lasted no more than about two years, as in Peru at the time of the adoption of its 1959 stabilization program, the problem is not too serious. When inflation has been rampant for decades, as in Argentina by 1958, the problem will have become very serious.

It should be emphasized that the depressive influences discussed above are temporary, rather than fundamental. After a relatively short period, they should evaporate. If the stabilization program is effective, the period of uncertainty must pass, and a new set of expectations should enable investors to make plans for future capital creation, with a consequent rise in their demands for resources. The decline in investment arising from the lag between the end of development of protected industries and the expansion of more economic (from a long-range view) alternative investment is by definition a temporary cutback in investment. Likewise, by definition, disinvestment in inventories must also be temporary. The general adjustment which should accompany stabilization (including the elimination of controls, such as ceilings on rents) may be expected to revive the demand for investment in rental housing to replace the decline in the demand for owner-occupied residences. The general flight from real assets to financial assets, which is one of the healthy signs of stabilization even though it may exert depressing effects on investment, should also be temporary. After a short period of adjustment, individual economic units may be expected to desire additions to their stocks of both physical and financial assets. At the same time, the capital flight resulting from inflation should stop. The switch in the flow of saving from foreign to domestic investment, and the repatriation of earlier accumulations of foreign assets, will lead to an increase in the demand for domestic resources.[25]

A government which decides to eliminate the distortions created by inflation will be faced with a host of problems while the economy is readjusting to a condition of monetary equilibrium. There is no doubt that the difficulties facing the community will be dependent on the imagination exercised by the government. A stabilization program which relies on monetary instruments alone will involve more stresses in the economy than one which includes fiscal and broader economic improvement measures as well. If a stabilization program can be quickly associated with measures for the development of previously neglected facilities (such as the rehabilitation of obsolescent railway systems and the development of public utilities), the stresses will be eased. Foreign assistance (drawings on the International Monetary Fund, to make more rapid elimination of exchange restrictions possible, and loans from the International Bank for Reconstruction and Development, to facilitate the redeployment of resources for development) will make the elimination of distortions in production easier. However, no cleaning-up process is pleasant. Stabilizing an inflating economy is one of the least pleasant of the operations facing a responsible government.

The Case for Firm Action

If an abrupt ending of an inflation is likely to bring a temporary decline in output, is not some alternative possible? Might not a tapering-off policy be adopted? Might not the rate of inflation be brought to an end slowly? The answer to these questions is that a gradual approach is fraught with more danger than sudden stabilization.

Among the real damages done by inflation is the distortion created in the economy. There is need to reorient the system. Drastic changes must be made in the community's expectations. These changes are not likely to occur if the community believes that the government may be lukewarm in its attack on inflation. If individuals see little change in the economic climate, they will be under

---

[25]For a discussion of one example of the change in direction of international capital movements, see the reference to this aspect of the changes in Spain following the adoption of a stabilization program in 1959, in International Monetary Fund, *Annual Report, 1962*, p. 49.

very few effective pressures to change their views. The fundamental changes which are required will not take place.[26]

The persistence of expectations as to the movements of prices is a particular problem to be faced in introducing a stabilization program. In the early stages of an inflation, individuals may continue ·to believe that prices will soon stop increasing. But once inflation is established, they will expect prices to go on rising; and even if they believe that the inflation has been halted, and that prices will be stabilized, they will not expect stabilization to take place immediately. Moreover, they will always be conscious of the possibility that the program may fail. Therefore, even when money and financial assets begin once more to appear attractive, the acquisition of such assets may be deterred by a lingering fear that they may again decline in real value. By contrast, the continued holding of inventories offers protection, even if the program succeeds, against any loss except that of the potential income from financial investments; and the holder of foreign financial assets risks the loss only of the possibly excessive returns on domestic financial assets over the return on foreign ones. If the program fails, such holders stand to gain much more. Thus, to enable a stabilization program to succeed, it is above all necessary for the government to convince the community that the value of money will henceforth be maintained.

In short, an attempt to slow down an inflation will take a long time to be effective and its final result will be uncertain. The restrictions on credit necessary to bring some stabilization will deter borrowers from investing, but the inflation-induced distortions of the economy are likely to persist. The continued rise in prices (even though it be slower than before) will deter the accumulation of financial assets and continue to act as a brake on the flow of re-

---

[26]The following is an assessment of the effect of these fundamental changes in one case:

"Now that the initial steps to stabilize the Spanish economy have been so successful the key to further progress seems to lie in the lowering of the import tariff and the abolition of the remaining import quotas. Spanish industry may be said to have grown up in the past 25 years in a hot-house atmosphere of complete freedom from foreign competition, and until imports began to be freed three years ago there had been no incentive or necessity to produce better goods at lower prices.

"But the limited measure of foreign competition to which it has already been subjected, together with free access to raw materials, has worked wonders. (In all fairness it should be said that during all that period Spanish manufacturers had to make do with substitute or makeshift materials in erratic supply, often smuggled in and sold at exorbitant prices.) Competition among manufacturers has made its appearance and quality has improved out of recognition." *Times* (London), November 23, 1962, p. 19.

sources to investment. Unless the authorities are firm in their attack, the atmosphere of financial stability necessary to induce a revival of output—to levels higher than those which would have prevailed under inflation—will not emerge.

VI. CONCLUSION

This review of the relation between inflation and economic development leads to the conclusion that the control of inflation should be one of the major objects of economic policy in a developing economy. It is true that, per se, rapid economic development is likely to provoke inflationary pressures. Therefore, one of the problems calling for high priority on the part of the authorities in a rapidly developing economy is the restraint of inflation.

Inflation diminishes the volume of resources available for domestic investment. Community saving is reduced, and a considerable part of this saving is channeled to foreign rather than domestic investment, while the flow of capital from abroad is discouraged. A substantial part of the reduced flow of resources for domestic investment is diverted to uses which are not of the highest social priority. The accumulation of large inventories is encouraged. The diversion of savings from the capital markets, where investment decisions are subject to longer-term economic criteria, is exemplified by the diversion of investment from productive uses for the entire community to the building of owner-occupied housing for the relatively wealthy. The apparent profitability of certain short-lived investments leads to distortions in the productive structure which make the economy less adaptable. Balance of payments difficulties are symptoms of the underlying stresses. To reduce the foreign deficits, the authorities are almost forced to resort to controls, which in most cases protect uneconomic production. Political pressures lead to further restrictions which, in the last analysis, create further distortions. Economic activity becomes steadily more distorted.

However, if the economic system has been allowed to get out of hand, the authorities must decide to stabilize or not to stabilize. There is no doubt that the process of stabilization is difficult, but, difficult or not, it is a prerequisite to rapid economic growth.

APPENDIX

Selected Countries

The term "Selected Countries" in the tables presented in this Appendix refers to all the less highly developed countries for which the relevant data are available in the sources. South Africa is not included, however, because its dual social structure makes statistical averages difficult to interpret; nor are the countries of the Eastern bloc. In several tables Finland and Greece are included. The tables do not include other countries in western Europe nor, of course, the United States and Canada.

Selected Years

In the tables compiled for this study, an attempt has been made to use series extending from 1948 to 1961. Many of the data, however, are not available for the full period. In these cases all the available data have been used, and the tables are stated to refer to "selected years." In many of the tables where annual averages are used, the time periods are not the same for all countries. Where tables are derived from other sources, no attempt has been made to alter the time periods covered by the original authors.

Classification of Countries

Countries are classified as stable, if the percentage increase in the cost of living index is less than 5 percent a year for the period covered. If the rate of increase is 10 percent or more, they are classified as being subject to strong inflation. The intermediate countries are considered to be subject to mild inflation. These boundary criteria should not be considered as separating clearly definable situations. Rather, they are arbitrary limits intended to identify different situations. They may be considered to be on the high side; in part they have been adopted because some price increases have been almost universal in the postwar period.

Ordering of Countries

Within each group, countries are arranged by the degree of inflation experienced, with the country experiencing the lowest rate of inflation placed at the top of the table, and the country with the highest rate at the bottom.

Weighting of Averages

Where averages are given for groups of countries they are unweighted averages, unless it is stated otherwise (for example, when the value of exports is relevant to a comparison of changes in exports).

TABLE 11

INFLATION AND ECONOMIC DEVELOPMENT, SELECTED
COUNTRIES, SELECTED YEARS[1]

(*In Percent*)

Countries	Rate of Inflation[2]	Rate of Growth Per Capita[3]
Stable countries	**2**	**2**
Philippines.....................	..	3
Ceylon.......................	1	..
Pakistan......................	1	..
Guatemala....................	1	2
Syria........................	1	−2
Burma........................	2	4
Malaya.......................	2	..
India.........................	2	1
Ecuador......................	2	2
Venezuela....................	2	5
Honduras....................	3	..
El Salvador..................	4	2
Mild inflation countries	**7**	**2**
Thailand.....................	5	1
Iceland......................	7	2
Colombia....................	8	2
Peru........................	9	1
Strong inflation countries	**35**	**2**
Brazil.......................	20	2
Indonesia....................	22	3
Paraguay....................	32	3
Chile........................	33	..
Korea.......................	66	1

Sources: Based on data in United Nations, *Yearbook of National Accounts Statistics, 1961,* and International Monetary Fund, *International Financial Statistics,* hereafter referred to as *IFS.*

[1]Generally 1954–60.
[2]Average annual increase in cost of living index.
[3]Average annual increase in real gross domestic product per capita.

TABLE 12

INFLATION AND ECONOMIC DEVELOPMENT, SELECTED LATIN-
AMERICAN COUNTRIES, 1955–59

(*In Percent*)

Countries	Rate of Inflation[1]	Change in Per Capita Product[2]
Stable countries...............	1	11
Guatemala...................	..	16
Ecuador.....................	..	4
El Salvador.................	1	4
Venezuela...................	2	21
Mild inflation countries..........	8	2
Mexico.....................	8	88
Colombia...................	8	1
Peru.......................	8	−3
Strong inflation countries........	35	8
Brazil......................	23	21
Argentina...................	39	−6
Chile......................	43	3

Sources: Based on data in Economic Commission for Latin America,
Economic Survey of Latin America, 1959 (E/CN.12/541), p. 57, and *IFS*.

[1]Average annual increase in cost of living index.
[2]Change from 1955 to 1959 in index of gross domestic product per capita.

TABLE 13

Inflation and Economic Development[1]
(*In Percent Per Annum, Compounded*)

Countries	Period	Rate of Inflation[2]	Rate of Growth Per Capita[3]
Selected Periods of Relative Stability			
Puerto Rico	1947–50	−4	10
Lebanon	1948–54	−2	4
Philippines	1947–54	−1	4
Panama	1948–52	−1	2
Cuba	1947–54	..	..
Egypt	1950–53	..	−5
Ceylon	1951–54	..	..
Dominican Republic	1950–54	1	4
Venezuela	1949–53	1	4
India	1948–53	1	1
Ceylon	1947–51	2	9
Turkey	1948–54	3	6
Brazil	1947–50	4	7
Guatemala	1946–54	4	2
Ecuador	1950–54	4	2
Argentina	1952–54	4	6
Northern Rhodesia	1946–53	5[4]	23
Colombia	1951–54	5[4]	6
Average[5]		2	6
(Average, excluding Northern Rhodesia)		(1)	(4)
Selected Periods of Mild Inflation			
Pakistan	1950–53	5	−3
Japan	1951–54	6	3
Honduras	1946–52	6	2
Puerto Rico	1950–53	6	2
Kenya	1947–54	6	4
Southern Rhodesia	1947–53	7	5
British Guiana	1948–51	7	1
Mexico	1947–54	8	2
Average[5]		6	2
Selected Periods of Strong Inflation			
Peru	1948–53	10	6
Thailand	1950–53	13	−1
Brazil	1950–53	17	−1
Chile	1946–52	22	1
Israel	1950–54	29	5
Paraguay	1950–54	84	5
Average[5]		29	3

Source: U Tun Wai, "The Relation Between Inflation and Economic Development," *Staff Papers*, Vol. VII (1959–60), Table 1, pp. 303 4.

[1]This covers all the cases in Tun Wai's table for the years after the end of World War II hostilities, except for those affected by rebellions, or immediate postwar reconstruction.

[2]Average annual increase in cost of living index.

[3]Average annual increase in per capita national income deflated by cost of living index.

[4]Between 4.5 and 5.0.

[5]Weighted by number of observations for each country.

TABLE 14

INFLATION AND ECONOMIC DEVELOPMENT

(*In Percent Per Annum, Compounded*)

Countries	Period	Rate of Inflation[1]	Rate of Growth Per Capita[2]
Selected Periods of Relative Stability			
Philippines	1947–54	−1	4
Panama	1948–52	−1	2
Dominican Republic	1950–54	1	6
India	1948–53	1	1
Venezuela	1949–53	1	3
Turkey	1948–54	3	6
Brazil	1947–50	4	5
Colombia	1951–54	5	4
Average		1	4
Selected Periods of Mild Inflation			
Pakistan	1950–53	5	−3
Japan	1951–54	6	2
Southern Rhodesia	1947–53	7	4
Mexico	1950–54	7	..
Average		6	1
Selected Periods of Strong Inflation			
Colombia	1948–51	14	..
Brazil	1950–53	17	−1
Israel	1950–54	29	5
Average		20	1

Source: U Tun Wai, *op. cit.*, p. 305.

[1]Average annual increase in cost of living index.
[2]Average annual increase in per capita national income, deflated by cost of living index and adjusted for changes in the terms of trade.

TABLE 15

INFLATION AND ECONOMIC DEVELOPMENT

(*In Percent Per Annum, Compounded*)

Countries	Period	Rate of Inflation[1]	Rate of Growth Per Capita[2]
Selected Periods of Price Stability			
Ceylon	1951–54	−1	1
India	1948–53	1	1
Japan	1951–54	3	6
Honduras	1946–52	4	3
Turkey	1948–54	4	4
Brazil	1947–50	5[3]	7
Average		**3**	**4**
Selected Periods of Mild Inflation			
Mexico	1947–50	5	3
Guatemala	1946–54	5	2
Argentina	1952–54	7	2
Ceylon	1947–51	7	5
Average		**6**	**3**
Selected Periods of Strong Inflation			
Brazil	1950–53	12	2
Chile	1946–52	22	1
Argentina	1948–52	27	−4
Average		**21**	..

Source: U Tun Wai, *op. cit.*, p. 306.

[1]Average annual increase in weighted averages of sector prices.
[2]Average annual increase in social product, deflated by the sector price index and adjusted for changes in the terms of trade.
[3]Figure in source is 4.9.

TABLE 16

AVERAGE ANNUAL RATES OF CHANGE IN RATIO OF MONEY TO INCOME,
SELECTED COUNTRIES, SELECTED YEARS[1]

(*In Percent*)

Countries	Change	Countries	Change
STABLE COUNTRIES..........	..	MILD INFLATION COUNTRIES...	**−2**
Very wealthy countries.......	−3	*Wealthy countries*...........	−4
United States.............	−3	New Zealand............	−3
Canada..................	−3	Australia................	−4
Switzerland..............	−1		
		Average countries...........	−1
Wealthy countries.............	−2	France.................	3
Sweden..................	−2	Norway................	−4
Belgium.................	−2	Finland................	−3
United Kingdom..........	−2		
Denmark................	−4	*Poor country*	
		Colombia...............	2
Average countries............	−3		
Venezuela...............	..	*Very poor countries*..........	−1
Netherlands..............	−5	Mexico.................	−1
		Peru...................	−2
Poor countries...............	2		
Austria..................	..		
Cuba...................	1	STRONG INFLATION COUNTRIES.	**−3**
Italy...................	3	*Poor countries*..............	−5
Lebanon................	6	Israel..................	−8
		Argentina...............	−3
Very poor countries..........	2	Chile..................	−3
Greece..................	6		
Portugal................	1	*Very poor countries*	
Japan..................	1	Brazil..................	..
Dominican Republic.......	3	Paraguay...............	−1
Guatemala..............	1		
Ecuador................	..		
Honduras...............	−2		
United Arab Republic.....	−2		
Ceylon.................	2		
Thailand................	1		
Pakistan................	4		
India..................	−1		
Burma.................	6		

Sources: Based on data in *IFS* and United Nations, *Monthly Bulletin of Statistics.*

[1]See page 69 for description of "Selected Years."
Because the ratio of money to income tends to be declining in the very wealthy and wealthy countries, and rising in the poor and very poor countries, this table incorporates a dual classification, by wealth and by rates of inflation. The classification by wealth is based on United Nations, *Per Capita National Income in Fifty-Five Countries, 1952–1954.* Countries estimated to have had, at that time, average per capita incomes equivalent to more than US$1,000 are classified as very wealthy countries; those with per capita incomes in the $750–$1,000 range, as wealthy; in the $500–$750 range, as average; in the $250–$500 range, as poor; and below $250, as very poor. Countries within each group are arranged by descending order of per capita income.

TABLE 17

RELATION BETWEEN CHANGES IN REAL VALUE OF MONEY HOLDINGS AND
CHANGES IN COST OF LIVING, SELECTED COUNTRIES, 1948–61

(*In Percent*)

Countries	Average Annual Increase in Cost of Living	Change in Real Value of Holdings of[1]	
		Money	Money and Quasi-Money
Stable countries....................	2	79	103
Dominican Republic...............	..	216	165
Philippines.......................	0.5	77	139
Ceylon...........................	1	84	109
Burma............................	1	162	178
Ecuador..........................	2	124	156
Guatemala........................	2	50	85
Venezuela........................	2	108	176
Portugal..........................	2	65	83
India.............................	2	13	47
Pakistan..........................	2	81	99
Honduras.........................	2	25	49
Costa Rica........................	3	72	101
Ireland...........................	3	14	9
El Salvador.......................	3	41	89
New Zealand......................	4	16	16
Thailand..........................	4	125	158
Nicaragua........................	4	73	88
Mild inflation countries.............	7	100	138
Iran.............................	5	61	..
Mexico...........................	7	97	102
Turkey...........................	7	131	187
Colombia.........................	8	141	158
Peru.............................	8	69	104
Strong inflation countries	27	19	11
Brazil............................	19	114	72
Argentina........................	29	−31	−40
Chile............................	33	8	41
Bolivia	56	−17	−26

Source: Based on data in *IFS*.

[1]Given by $M/L - 100$, where M is the 1961 index (base, 1948 = 100) of money (or money plus quasi-money) and L is the 1961 index (base, 1948 = 100) of cost of living.

TABLE 18

CENTRAL GOVERNMENT AVERAGE ANNUAL SURPLUSES OR
DEFICITS (−) AS PERCENTAGES OF GROSS NATIONAL
PRODUCT, SELECTED COUNTRIES, SELECTED YEARS[1]

Countries	*Percentages*
Stable countries	−2
Burma	−4
Panama	−1
Ceylon	−3
Ecuador	−1
Pakistan	−4
Venezuela	1
Honduras	..
Israel	−5
Australia	1
New Zealand	−3
Mild inflation countries	−2
India	−5
Peru	−1
Mexico	..
Colombia	..
Strong inflation countries	−5
Korea	−8
Chile	−2

Source: Based on data in *IFS*.

[1]See page 69 for description of "Selected Years."

TABLE 19

FOREIGN COMPANIES CONTROLLED BY U.S. RESIDENTS:
PERCENT OF EARNINGS RETAINED, SELECTED
COUNTRIES, 1957–60

Countries	Percentages
Stable countries	**49**[1]
Dominican Republic	19
Panama	72
Guatemala	−48
Honduras	47
Australia	60
Philippines	46
Japan	54
New Zealand	23
India	64
Mild inflation countries	**18**[1]
Venezuela	12
Mexico	22
Colombia	58
Strong inflation countries	**33**[1]
Peru	16
Chile	14
Brazil	52
Indonesia	47
Argentina	46

Source: Based on data in *Survey of Current Business.*

[1]Weighted by value of direct investments at end of 1957.

TABLE 20

Mexico: Price Changes and Net Purchases of
Short-Term Foreign Assets, 1951–60

Year	Change in Cost of Living Index[1] (percent)	Net Purchases of Short-Term Foreign Assets by Mexican Residents (Million U.S. Dollars)
1951	19	9
1952	..	21
1953	10	2
1954	13	44
1955	17	−23
1956	−2	−13
1957	13	17
1958	9	27
1959	..	−9
1960	8	−4

Sources: Based on data in *IFS* and International Monetary Fund, *Balance of Payments Yearbooks*.

[1]Year-end comparisons.

TABLE 21

CHANGES IN VALUE OF U.S. PRIVATE DIRECT INVESTMENT IN
SELECTED COUNTRIES, 1950–61

(*In Percent*)

Countries	Changes in Value
Stable countries[1]	**214**[2]
Panama	700
Dominican Republic	−1
Philippines	195
Guatemala	19
India	397
Venezuela	204
Honduras	53
New Zealand	52
Australia	373
Mild inflation countries[1]	**177**[3]
Colombia	120
Mexico	98
Peru	201
Strong inflation countries[1]	**55**[4]
Uruguay	−11
Argentina	78
Brazil	55
Indonesia	153
Chile	34

Source: Based on data in *Survey of Current Business*, August, 1962, p. 22.

[1] Averages for groups are changes in total value of investments in the countries in the group.
[2] Excluding Panama: 197. Excluding Panama and Venezuela: 188.
[3] Excluding Peru: 110.
[4] Excluding Indonesia: 54.

TABLE 22

COMPARISON OF PRICE RELATIVES OF INVESTMENT AND CONSUMPTION
GOODS, SELECTED LATIN-AMERICAN COUNTRIES, 1960[1]

Countries	At Free Market Exchange Rates	At Parity Rates[2]
Stable country		
Ecuador.	86	82
Mild inflation countries.	100	95
Colombia.	92	87
Mexico.	95	91
Peru.	114	107
Strong inflation countries.	120	114
Uruguay.	117	110
Brazil.	116	110
Argentina.	164	157
Paraguay	108	105
Chile.	93	88

Source: Economic Commission for Latin America, *Comparative Prices and the
Purchasing Power of Currencies in Selected Latin American Countries* (E/CN.12/589),
pp. 43, 47.

[1]The figures for each country represent the cost of an assortment of investment
goods expressed as a percentage of the cost of an assortment of consumption goods.
The respective assortments are the same for each country; and, on the average for
the nine countries, the cost of the assortment of investment goods is equal to that
of the assortment of consumption goods.

[2]As computed in source.

TABLE 23

RATE OF INFLATION AND INVENTORY INVESTMENT, 1950–60
(Based on Data in Current Prices)

Year	Philippines A¹	Philippines B²	Ecuador A¹	Ecuador B²	Colombia A¹	Colombia B²	Mexico A¹	Mexico B²	Peru A¹	Peru B²	Brazil A¹	Brazil B²,³	Chile A¹	Chile B²
1950.........	..	..	..	..	..	..	..	..	11	15	7	–3	..	..
1951.........	9	14	11	17	..	..	..	..	10	16	5	10	22	6
1952.........	–6	14	2	12	..	..	15	..	7	9	22	25	21	–9
1953.........	–4	18	1	26	8	–9	–2	–3	9	7	22	15	25	37
1954.........	–1	28	3	18	9	–1	5	29	5	10	18	19	77	–20
1955.........	–1	26	2	17	–1	—	16	20	5	9	19	8	74	–2
1956.........	2	12	–5	14	6	7	5	18	5	7	22	8	58	21
1957.........	2	16	2	16	15	34	5	17	8	9	20	15	25	–7
1958.........	3	10	—	17	14	16	11	17	8	11	16	—	27	–3
1959.........	–1	9	—	11	7	12	3	17	13	16	37	—	38	5
1960.........	5	4	2	15	4	13	6	14	..	..	..	..	12	5
Average.......	1	15	2	16	7	9	7	14	8	11	19	10	38	3

Sources: Based on data in United Nations, *Yearbook of National Accounts Statistics* and *Statistics of National Income and Expenditures; IFS.*

¹Rate of inflation, that is, percentage change in annual average of cost of living index.
²Inventory investment as percentage of gross domestic investment.
³Excluding stockpiling of coffee and cotton by the government.

TABLE 24

Volume of Major and Minor Exports, Selected Countries, 1958–59

(*1953–54 = 100*)

Countries	Major Exports[1]	Minor Exports
Stable countries[2]	**118**	**139**
Malaya	107	153
Philippines	110	181
Central American Republics[3]	126	181
India	102	120
Ghana	100	138
Australia	131	135
Sudan	175	114
New Zealand	121	124
Strong inflation countries[2]	**110**	**100**
Turkey	93	79
Uruguay	67	57
Argentina	125	104
Brazil	115	112
Indonesia	92	84
Chile	128	116
Bolivia	66	70

Source: Based on data in Gertrud Lovasy, "Inflation and Exports in Primary Producing Countries," *Staff Papers*, Vol. IX (1962), pp. 65, 66.

[1]The major exports for each country are identified in the source.
[2]Averages are weighted by 1959 export values.
[3]Costa Rica, El Salvador, Guatemala, and Nicaragua.

TABLE 25

DOMESTIC PRICES, EXPORT PRICES AND VOLUMES, AND EXCHANGE RATES,
SELECTED COUNTRIES

Countries	Cost of Living, 1959[1] (1953 = 100)	Export Prices, 1959[2] (1953 = 100)	Export Volume, 1958–59[3] (1953–54 = 100)	Exchange Rates, 1959[4] (1953 = 100)
Stable countries[5]	**109**	**95**	**124**	**100[6]**
Malaya	92	131	126	100
Dominican Republic . . .	102	92	115	100
Ecuador	102	94	150	100
Ceylon	104	107	104	100
Philippines	104	94	132	100
Guatemala	105	76	127	100
Portugal	107	96	127	100
El Salvador	107	74	162	100
Ghana	112	116	106	100
Costa Rica	113	84	120	101
India	115	100	111	100
Sudan	115	90	149	100
Australia	116	74	132	100
Nicaragua	116	82	164	100
Ireland	117	104	111	100
New Zealand	124	98	124	100
Mild inflation countries[5] . .	**143**	**90**	**119**	**164**
Thailand	119	86	114	116
Iceland	130	105	123	. .
Finland	130	95	132	139
China (Taiwan)	150	85	136	208
Spain	150	92	108	152
Peru	152	91	143	164
Mexico	154	. .	127	145
Colombia	162	80	95	273
Strong inflation countries[5]	**500**	**84**	**106**	**800**
Turkey	217	88[7]	86	. .
Paraguay	240	95[7]	110	400
Uruguay	244	70	65	. .
Indonesia	311	105	90	500[7]
Brazil	325	64	114	600
Argentina	464	75	116	1,000
Chile	1,040	. .	125	1,350
Bolivia	2,990	92	67	6,250

[1] Based on data in *IFS*.
[2] Based on U.S. dollar price indices in *IFS*.
[3] Based on data in G. Lovasy, *op. cit.*
[4] For countries with multiple currency systems, the degree of exchange depreciation was computed by dividing the change in the domestic currency value of imports, recorded in *IFS*, by the recorded change in the U.S. dollar value of imports.
[5] Averages are weighted by 1959 export values.
[6] Changes in fluctuating rates within the limits of the Articles of Agreement of the International Monetary Fund have been ignored.
[7] Estimate.

TABLE 26

HOLDINGS OF SOME FINANCIAL ASSETS BY PRIVATE SECTOR, 1950–62

End of Year	Brazil (Billions of Cruzeiros)						Argentina (Billions of Pesos)		
	Money	Quasi-Money	Govern-ment Securi-ties	Life Insur-ance[1]	Total Current Value	1951 Value[2]	Money	Quasi-Money	Govern-ment Debt
1950........	..	..	..	..	...	...	22	11	3
1951........	91	20	8	8	127	127	27	11	1
1952........	104	21	8	10	143	117	30	12	2
1953........	124	22	8	11	165	111	38	15	3
1954........	151	25	8	13	197	112	44	18	3
1955........	178	24	8	14	224	107	52	20	4
1956........	217	25	7	17	266	104	60	29	2
1957........	291	29	6	19	345	112	68	30	1
1958........	353	33	8	25	419	118	99	41	1
1959........	501	39	11	28	579	119	142	45	1
1960........	692	57	12	32	793	121	179	60	3
1961........	1,042	67	..	..	...	130[3]	205	75	3
1962[4].......	1,368	73	..	..	...	75[3]	...	..	..

Sources: Brazil—from *IFS*. Argentina—money and quasi-money, from *IFS;* government debt prior to 1957, estimates by the author; subsequently, from Banco Central de la República Argentina, *Boletín Estadístico.*

[1] Total assets of life insurance companies.
[2] Current value divided by cost of living index (base, 1951 = 100).
[3] Estimate.
[4] September.

TABLE 27

AVERAGE ANNUAL CHANGES IN REAL WAGES,[1] SELECTED
COUNTRIES, SELECTED YEARS[2]

(*In Percent*)

Countries	Change
Stable countries	2
Vietnam	1
Australia	1
Burma	1
Philippines	2
Ceylon	4
United Arab Republic	5
Honduras	−3
India	2
Costa Rica	3
Pakistan	..
New Zealand	1
Guatemala	3
Mild inflation countries	2
Finland	3
Mexico	2
Strong inflation countries	1
Peru	2
Brazil	1
Argentina	−1

Source: Based on data in *IFS*.

[1]Average annual change in money wage rates divided by average
annual change in cost of living index.
[2]See page 69 for description of "Selected Years."

TABLE 28

CHANGES IN COST OF LIVING AND IN SHARE OF WAGES AND SALARIES* IN
NET DOMESTIC PRODUCT

Countries	Average Annual Increase in Cost of Living Index,† 1950–57	Change from 1950 to 1957 in Percentage Share of Wages and Salaries in Net Domestic Product‡
Stable countries................	2	−1
Ceylon.....................	1	−4
Costa Rica.................	2	−1
Canada....................	3	1
Mild inflation countries..........	7	..
New Zealand................	6	1
Colombia...................	6	1
Finland....................	7	..
Australia...................	8	−3
Strong inflation country		
Brazil.....................	18	2

*Including income of unincorporated enterprises (for example, farmers) as part of wages and salaries.

†Calculated from *IFS*.

‡From E. H. Phelps Brown and M. H. Browne, "Distribution and Productivity Under Inflation, 1947–57," *Economic Journal*, December, 1960, p. 732.

TABLE 29

COMPARISON OF INDICES OF GENERAL WHOLESALE PRICES AND OF PRICES OF
BUILDING MATERIALS, SELECTED COUNTRIES, 1959

(1953 = 100)

Countries	General Wholesale Prices (1)	Building Material Prices (2)	Col. 2 ÷ Col. 1 (3)
Stable countries...............	107	105	99
United Arab Republic.........	117	109	93
Guatemala..................	102	107	105
Venezuela..................	104	98	94
Thailand...................	115	103	90
Iraq......................	106	107	101
Syria.....................	101	104	103
Lebanon...................	102	108	106
Mild inflation countries..........	157	175	113
Iran......................	123	168	137
Spain.....................	149	155	104
Mexico....................	143	161	113
Colombia..................	187	203	109
Peru......................	181	187	103
Strong inflation countries........	470	478	102
Excluding Paraguay............	*528*	*573*	*114*
Paraguay..................	297	193	65
Turkey....................	227	278	122
Brazil.....................	305	354	116
Chile.....................	1,053	1,086	103

Source: Columns 1 and 2 are from A. S. Shaalan, "Impact of Inflation on the Composition of Private Domestic Investment," *Staff Papers*, Vol. IX (1962), Table 5, p. 259.

b. INFLATION AND GROWTH: THE HEART OF THE CONTROVERSY[1]

Dudley Seers

This is not just a technical issue in economic theory. At the heart of the controversy between "monetarists" and "structuralists" are two different ways of looking at economic development, in fact two completely different attitudes toward the nature of social change, two different sets of value judgments about the purposes of economic activity and the ends of economic policy, and two incompatible views on what is politically possible. Rather than repeat here a historical analysis of the inflationary forces in Latin America, or outline again a general theoretical explanation,[2] it may be useful to review in their historical perspective the basic theoretical issues underlying this clash of ideas.

It is only fair to recognize that monetarism is far more than an emphasis on monetary causes of inflation and on the need for restricting the expansion of the quantity of money if inflation is to be ended. A stable price level and a stable exchange rate are considered necessary conditions for growth. Where these are to be found, savings will be encouraged; it will be easier to promote exports; foreign capital will be attracted (and domestic capital will not flee abroad); investment in long-term projects will be greater. The really essential thing on this line of argument is to create an atmosphere in which growth will take place spontaneously, as a result of private enterprise responding to opportunities of profit. What the authorities should do, therefore, is to keep the budget balanced and low, avoid a big credit expansion, and maintain a freely convertible currency at a single and steady rate of exchange, giving the price system an opportunity to work.

The implied value judgments are in favor of a stable society,

---

[1] I am grateful for comments by Sr. Andres Bianchi, Professor Joseph Grunwald, Professor Charles Kennedy, and Mrs. Joan Robinson, which helped me to revise this paper.
[2] These can be found in the ECLA study, "Inflation and Growth in Latin America," which contains a general regional analysis, statistics for the main countries going back to 1929, and country studies of Argentina, Brazil, Chile, and Mexico.

where one knows the "rules of the game" because these are not changed overnight by bureaucrats, and where one does not have to worry constantly about how to safeguard one's business and one's family against the effects of inflation. It is a preference for *not* having to bother about the rate of exchange or the disposition of customs officials. More profoundly, it is a preference for the security of a framework, rather than an unsettled society where speculators and political hangers-on flourish.

There is good historical evidence on the side of this attitude to the process of growth. The nineteenth century, when the United Kingdom, the United States, and western Europe emerged as major industrial areas, was a century in which government action (and inaction) followed broadly this prescription. Prices were steady and currencies solid, and the recovery of West Germany since the war has taken place under more or less the same conditions.

There is also a respectable and elaborate body of theory to support this attitude. No Englishman could deny the authority of the classical school, which not merely provided us with the main categories of economic analysis, but also (and this was its great intellectual appeal) attempted to explain economic development as a total process covering all aspects of human affairs.

To summarize (very drastically indeed) the essential points in the doctrine of the classical school: (1) If people are free to seek their self-interest, the working of the price system will insure that resources will be automatically mobilized for the satisfaction of society's needs (Adam Smith's "invisible hand"). (2) If these wants are not adequately expressed by the existing distribution of purchasing power, it is nevertheless dangerous to tamper with this distribution because one might impair incentives (and, in the view of some, reduce savings and cause unemployment). (3) Internationally, freedom of trade would lead to each country specializing in lines of output where it enjoyed comparative advantages, and all countries would benefit. (4) There is little need for economic policy as such, the important thing being for governments to maintain stable currencies by balancing their budgets (and, in later versions, by curbing the expansion of bank credit); disturbances will be automatically corrected and growth will take place spontaneously.

The counterpart in politics of this economic doctrine was parliamentary democracy, with the individual free to express his views by voting; in law, the sanctity of contract and property rights, but with equal access to justice; in international affairs, the right to self-determination and thus sovereignty. Such in brief was the classical liberal school.[3]

Before we try to assess the relevance of this doctrine to Latin America today, let us first ask ourselves why it has ceased to be widely held, at least in this form, in the industrial countries, especially the United Kingdom and the United States. Classical liberalism is of course very much alive in Latin America, and forms the ideological core of monetarism. The reasons for its modification and partial rejection abroad may give us some clues on the ways it should be modified (or why it should be rejected) here.

THE DECLINE OF CLASSICAL LIBERALISM IN DEVELOPED INDUSTRIAL ECONOMIES

The erosion of the doctrine had two causes. The implicit assumptions ceased to be valid (perhaps they had never had been fully valid), and the implicit value judgments ceased to be politically acceptable.

The Invisible Hand

It became clear, as analysis was developed and made more rigorous, that the classical doctrine rested on certain factual assumptions which could be tested—in brief, assumptions that the markets for products and factors are fully competitive. Perfect competition is not merely desirable but necessary as a condition for the successful operation of the price system as an allocator of resources and a maximizer of welfare. But theoretical and empirical work has revealed considerable imperfections—brand names, patent rights, size of firms, and cost of entry are used to protect business from the full force of competition, where there are not outright monopolies or cartels.[4] Many would also include labor organization as a serious rigidity hindering the free play of economic forces. Theoretical work in the economics of welfare showed that the use of taxes and subsidies could make the price mechanism reflect more adequately social needs and costs. On the other hand, wartime experience (and a glance at countries where planning was being used) showed that

---

[3]This is of course not to be confused with what is called "liberalism" in North America, a very different system of ideas.

[4]"The principle of free and unfettered competition working in a perfect market has suffered severe erosion over the years, often at the hands of those who have lavished greatest praise on it as an idea." B. Ralph Stauber (Official, U.S. Dept. of Agriculture) in *Problems of United States Economic Development*, Vol. II. published by Committee for Economic Development, New York, 1958.

there were other ways of mobilizing resources, ways which, with
all their wastage and political drawbacks, did work to raise the
national product.

The Existing Distribution of Income

The distributional tenets of the school have never been very
attractive to the poor. It is difficult to convince people who see little
hope of escaping from poverty in their lifetime that they need ac-
quiesce in this state of affairs, particularly when they start to ap-
preciate the possibilities of political action. One plank in the platform of the liberal school, political democracy, has proved incompatible with another, a limited national government. Not merely
has there been a growing tendency for governments to mitigate
the exploitation of unskilled labor and to provide social services by
progressive taxation; they have also intervened to subsidize particular economic sectors (agriculture, mining, transport), in these
ways further impairing the ability of the system to change in response to price signals. On the theoretical side, there was growing
support for the view that the government should use its fiscal power
to modify the initial income distribution if welfare was to be
maximized.

International Free Trade

Similarly, while the emphasis on freedom of trade appealed
strongly to the then pre-eminent British manufacturers, it did not
seem at all attractive to the more backward industrial countries,
who would have found it very difficult to overtake the United Kingdom without some form of protection. German economists, in particular, devoted themselves to attacks on this part of the liberal doctrine, but there was support from other industrialized countries, including the United States. Eventually it became increasingly widely
accepted that it was theoretically possible for any one country to
improve its trade balance and to raise its national income by protecting its industries. The school's emphasis on national sovereign
rights turned out not to be compatible with its advocacy of freedom
of trade, and this has, as time passed, ceased to be anywhere near
accurate as a description of relations between the industrial countries. Even in the United Kingdom (and later in all industrial countries), there was a strong and increasingly effective pressure from
sectors which could not resist foreign competition (especially farmers) for some shelter from its full force. Though at times there has
been some lowering of barriers, the general trend has been away

from the fairly free international system of the 1870's, and this process has been hastened at other times by wars and recessions.

Sound Finance

The biggest blow to classical liberalism was, of course, the slump of the 1930's. Up to then it had been feasible to argue that a fall in employment (by lowering the price of labor) would prove only temporary, and that a decline in foreign trade could be corrected, provided the rules of the gold standard were followed, because a mild recession would reduce imports and stimulate exports, through a reduction in costs and a lowering of home demand. Indeed, full employment was assumed as the normal condition of economic life, and this assumption was a central one (for example, to justify thrift). Henceforth it was academically difficult, and politically impossible, to deny that the government had some responsibility for avoiding large-scale unemployment. This implied a much more active fiscal and mometary policy than previously.

Controversy naturally focused on the status of the quantity theory, since this had emerged as the central theoretical justification for "sound finance." The present position generally accepted in the profession seems to be approximately as follows: Some association between a change in the quantity of money and the price level is not denied; whatever increases the money supply (for example, a budget deficit or an extension of bank credit) may well raise demand too, both directly through its effect on purchasing power, and indirectly because of changes in the asset structure. But the effect on prices depends on the conditions of supply. The "theory" is therefore of not much use as a direct causal explanation. The velocity of circulation is a focus of many influences, and lacks the stability that would be needed if one wanted to predict the rate of inflation from changes in the supply of money.

Monetary fundamentalism has therefore fallen out of favor in academic circles in the Northern Hemisphere (except perhaps for Chicago and the universities of the Soviet bloc). It is felt to be misleadingly facile, and the emphasis is now primarily on income flows.[5] Many who regard themselves as belonging to the classical tradition have abandoned pre–1929 monetary orthodoxy, which turns out not to be essential to the traditional liberal doctrine.[6]

---

[5]One qualification here is the renewed interest in some circles in the effects of changes in the real value of liquid or near-liquid assets on both investment and consumption.

[6]Though the traditional liberal doctrine is essential to monetarism.

However, the quantity theory remains the favorite economic heresy of laymen, including bankers and politicians. It is simple; it is plausible; it is at least broadly compatible with historical evidence, especially in the long term; and it satisfies the puritanical conscience. Policies of monetary restraint were widely adopted in the 1950's, in the attempt to check price increases. But since this decade turned out to be one of slow growth in several industrial countries, notably the United Kingdom and the United States, and since (moderate) price rises continued anyway, disillusion with monetary policy spread.[7] Among the criticisms levied were that it could only cure inflation and payments deficits at the cost of unemployment and semistagnation, if there were upward pressures on costs, especially from trade unions, and conventionally rigid profit margins in industry. It was a blunt weapon, even with all the subtle variations in policy possible in complex money markets, and it might well not merely lower investment but also change its composition in ways unfavorable to growth.

RELEVANCE TO THE ECONOMIES OF LATIN AMERICA

Since all these modifications in the classical doctrine, especially in monetary theory, have been so widely accepted in developed economies, it is somewhat surprising to see it reappearing in Latin America like a handed-down suit that no longer fits the original owner. Even the brief and oversimplified sketch above of the reasons for these modifications immediately suggests that even more far-reaching qualifications are needed if one is considering applying this doctrine to the case of Latin America.

First it is necessary to recall in note form some salient features of Latin America, and the most important trends in the past decade which distinguish it from North America and western Europe.[8]

Foreign Trade. Each country relies on exports of primary products for practically all its foreign exchange, usually exports of goods for which the home market is very limited. Its imports consist largely of manufactures, many of which are types of goods the country concerned does not yet make.

---

[7]See *Report on Employment, Growth and Price-Levels,* Joint Economic Committee, U.S. Congress, and *Report of the Committee on the Working of the Monetary System,* a committee set up by Her Majesty's Government. Both reports were issued in 1959. The success of French experience with a rather expansionist policy and some central planning of investment also played a part.

[8]These bold statements are documented (and duly qualified) in the ECLA Study on Inflation and Growth, especially chaps. ii, on external characteristics and trends and iii, on internal characteristics and trends.

Factors of Production. The majority of the population in most countries, though not all, is rural and illiterate. Land is the most important form of private property, and it is very unequally distributed. Capital markets are fragmentary; local firms finance their expansion mainly by reinvesting profits; foreign ones either do this or bring funds in from abroad. Another big source of capital is government assistance—via development banks. Stock exchanges are small and bond markets hardly exist at all.

Productive Sectors. Transport facilities are meager and often overloaded. Agriculture (except in export crops) is usually far from efficient or progressive. Manufacturing is highly monopolistic, partly because of the limited size of markets.

Population Trends. The population has been growing at a rapid rate (probably at not much less than 3 percent a year for the region as a whole). City populations are growing even more quickly.

Mounting Political Tensions. Discontent over poverty and unemployment is becoming increasingly vocal, partly because of the example of the Cuban revolution.

Commodity Markets. Commodity markets have been generally weak since the Korean War, and exports have not risen much. Most countries are by now in a severe balance of payments crisis.

The social characteristics of Latin America mean that economic development has been and is urgent. With the population rising at this pace, the national product has to grow at a rate of at least 5½ percent a year, if living standards are to rise significantly and unemployment to be contained. The demand for manufactures grows faster than the product. Yet the capacity to import does not rise as quickly as this.[9] Consequently, local manufacturing has to grow much more rapidly than 5½ percent and this now means increas-

---

[9]As a statement of present prospects, this requires more elaboration. How will the Alliance for Progress affect the trend? The Charter of Punta del Este speaks of $20 billion over ten years, which is apparently supposed to be the gross inflow of long-term capital from all sources, that is, $2 billion a year. Since it has been flowing at about half that rate, the net increase (if the Charter is fulfilled) would amount to about $1 billion compared to the 1950's or rather under 10 percent of foreign exchange receipts. Of course, presumably capital inflows will rise year by year, but they could hardly show an average upward trend of more than $200 million a year (given the total for the decade). This is equivalent to a rise of less than 2 percent a year in the capacity to import. However, it seems unlikely that exports will rise by enough to provide a further 3½ percent (making 5½ percent in all) and no allowance has been made for the increasing outflow of private capital, or for the fact that most countries (especially Brazil) have been maintaining their imports only by running down reserves and incurring short-term debts on a scale which can hardly continue. Financial assistance of the magnitude contemplated by the Charter of Punta del Este can certainly be of great help, because it gives the region more time to solve its problems, but it is not in itself by any means a complete solution.

ing emphasis on heavy industries, where expansion is particularly hard to achieve.[10]

Thus a more rapid structural transformation is needed than was carried out in the nineteenth century in the countries that are now industrialized, and the successes of western Europe and North America are not necessarily relevant examples. The countries of western Europe could expand their exports, in fact exports of industrial products, for which they had ready markets, as the economy grew; and the income elasticity of demand for imported luxuries must have been much lower.[11] At least toward the end of the century, the terms of trade were turning in their favor. Moreover, the structural position was different: trade unions were weak and military expenditures were low.[12] The task facing Latin America is more like that of Russia in 1917, and the problem might be put as one of achieving a comparable pace of economic development without going through a period of Stalinism.[13]

The Invisible Hand

It is a strain on the price system to carry out this transformation, particularly in view of the structural features noted above, for these imply that factor and product markets are still more imperfect than those in the industrial countries. Moreover, the biggest shifts that have to occur are not *within* sectors, but from one sector to another. The labor shift is usually a geographical move as well, and, while migration from the countryside occurs almost spontaneously, the newcomers to the cities are not necessarily adequate as recruits to the labor force; there is a perpetual shortage of skilled and supervisory grades, which means high costs of production.[14]

---

[10]This highly compressed account is elaborated in the author's "A Theory of Growth and Inflation Based on Latin American Experience," *Oxford Economic Papers,* June, 1962.

[11]There were no films or television programs showing the masses in other countries how the upper classes lived in the United Kingdom.

[12]These were also, apart from a high educational level and familiarity with industrial processes, factors in the fast postwar recovery of West Germany.

[13]This is also basically what Cuba is attempting to do, though in a different way, which is one reason why Cuba's experience in the coming years will be of the greatest interest.

[14]As Mr. Marcus Fleming points out: "The overall elasticity of the labour supply is likely to be low, and the ease with which labour can be transferred from agriculture to non-agricultural industry, where the opportunities for economies of scale are greater, has frequently been exaggerated. As to capital, the domestic supply is likely to be practically inelastic within any short period of years." "External Economies and the Doctrine of Balanced Growth," *Economic Journal,* June 1955.

Profit margins in industry are also high, as they have to be to attract capital from the relatively secure distributive trades, yet being high they draw political criticism. Entrepreneuers are not easy to recruit in those countries where social prestige still attaches mainly to owning land (and livestock),[15] and where the necessary rates of profit bring social odium.

For these reasons the transformation of the economy, which is forced by the shortage of imports, involves a structural upward pressure on prices, if price movements are the main means of achieving this change. One further complication is that food deliveries to the cities may not rise as fast as the urban proletariat grows, which would augment any inflationary tendencies. Another is that development, especially when it is accompanied by rapid industralization, requires a big increase and improvement in transport facilities, power supplies, communications, etc. If capital is directed to these sectors, there are dangers of excess demand; if not, and these sectors lag, this will also tend to raise costs and prices; since political and trade union forces try to prevent declines in real income, any price rise becomes generalized.

The Existing Distribution of Income

Where land is highly unequally distributed, and other forms of private property are relatively less important (yet they too are concentrated in very few hands, often the same as those that own most of the land), and where there are large numbers of unemployed and unskilled laborers, personal income will also be very unevenly distributed. This situation is not significantly modified in Latin America by direct taxes. Consequently, the distribution of effective demand bears little relation to real need. Effective demand is high for imported luxuries; the region's most urgent needs are that large numbers of people should be properly fed and housed. Even if the present inequalities are not morally offensive, they appear to be politically intolerable. They do not even have the economic justification that they promote thrift, since the upper income groups do not contribute significantly to savings.

Granted that the basic assumptions of classical liberalism are so much at variance with reality, it clearly may be unwise to concentrate one's efforts on creating a framework within which the

---

[15]"The human traits which have kept capitalists in the less-developed countries from becoming entrepreneurs are well known. Real-estate-mindedness, mistrust of industrial ventures, remnants of a feudal past, have all contributed" (Henry Wallich, "Some Notes Toward a Theory of Demand Development," 1952).

price system would work. In Latin America, the actual disparities in living standards are usually less than those in money incomes. This is partly because luxury taxes are high, but also because imports of luxury goods are subject to special exchange rates, high tariffs, prohibitions, quotas, advance deposits, etc., and are thus made very dear or even unobtainable. Foreign exchange is preserved in a measure for the capital equipment needed for development. A discriminatory import regime therefore makes up in some degree for the inadequacy of direct taxation. Consequently, a policy of dispensing with devices of this kind, in the name of economic liberalism, in order to make prices more "realistic," may simultaneously impair the process of development and raise political tensions.[16]

International Free Trade

This is the part of the doctrine which is perhaps most obviously unacceptable in Latin America.

To start with, the possibility of general free trade does not exist for Latin America. The region's exporters face a world full of restrictions. All the industrial countries protect their own farmers from imports of livestock products, cereals, and sugar (meat, other than certain processed products, is virtually a prohibited import into the United States). The United Kingdom and France discriminate by tariff preferences and quotas, in favor, respectively, of British Commonwealth countries and most former members of the French empire. The arrangements agreed upon for achieving economic integration in Europe compel other west European countries, notably West Germany, to offer similar special treatment to primary producers which are competitors of Latin America (affecting especially bananas and coffee), as well as to each other's farmers. The United States applies quantitative restrictions on imports of petroleum, lead, zinc, sugar, and wool and uses subsidies and/or tariffs to help domestic producers of these and a number of other items, for example, cotton and copper.

It is intellectually possible (though I think mistaken) to argue that Latin America could benefit from a freely competitive international system. But there is no chance of such a system being created, and in the circumstances to insist on multilateralism, free trade, and currency convertibility is to advocate that Latin America alone open its doors to the full force of international competition.

---

[16]See a paper by T. Balogh in *Economic Bulletin for Latin America* (ECLA, February, 1961) on the imperfections in Latin-American economies, and their influence on inflation.

Apart from hindrances on product flows, there are also international restrictions on the movement of labor; moreover, political uncertainty has meant that private capital expects a much higher return in Latin America than in the industrial countries. Consequently, factor mobility, which might be expected to mitigate international differences in living standards, is, on the classical scheme, hardly significant.

Finally, the existence of chronic unemployment, continually swelled by the flood of new recruits to the labor force, means that the classical doctrine of comparative advantage cannot be applied, at least without considerable modification. (Labor has to be considered very much cheaper than is suggested by current wage rates.)

Since the international implications of liberalism have always been an indispensable element in classical economics, these qualifications make it really quite out of the question for a Latin American economist to be a thoroughgoing member of the classical school. This greatly weakens the appeal of other parts. As was pointed out above, one of the school's great attractions was that it provided an integrated view of the whole of society with a comprehensive guide to policy in all fields.

Sound Finance

The description of the social and economic characteristics of Latin America implies that monetarist policies are insufficient to insure that economic growth and transformation will take place at a fast enough pace. The question is not whether inflation is helpful to growth or otherwise. There is no need to list the distorting effects of inflation in the longrun—it discourages personal savings; attracts capital to investment projects where the money return is flexible (like luxury apartment blocks), and may well in itself make the distribution of income still more unequal.[17] We can surely take it as common ground that it is better to combine stability and growth, if that is possible, and the *other things being equal,* stability favors growth. We need not argue this point, or dispute what is obvious, that governments have often been far too expansive in monetary policy.

Visitors to Latin America naturally have difficulty in switching

---

[17]In passing we might note that one can also see low savings, luxury investment, and unequal income distributions in Latin-American countries where there was a stable price level over most of the 1950's (for example, the Central American republics, or Cuba and Venezuela in the decade 1948 to 1958). I owe this point to Sr. Pinto.

to a different plane of argument. The question of whether inflation causes or hinders growth, or whether inflation is cost-induced
or demand-induced, or how much inflation can be afforded, are
really irrelevant questions, derived from foreign, not Latin American, experience. It is more fruitful to ask whether rapid growth
can take place in this region without price rises, unless export
markets are booming. The qualification is important: Venezuela
and Ecuador enjoyed rapid growth without price inflation for several years (three decades in the case of Venezuela), but not every
country has a petroleum pool like that under Lake Maracaibo, and
not every country can multiply its banana exports several times.
Structural change could only have been avoided in Latin America
in the 1950's (that is, growth could only have taken place at a rate
of 5 percent a year without the share of manufacturing in the national product rising) if the whole region's exports had risen by
more than 5 percent a year (with stable terms of trade), probably
much more than 5 percent. Yet the real imports of the industrial
countries, especially the United States, were simply not rising at
that rate (apart from petroleum), even if one does not adjust for
changes in the terms of trade.

So income had to grow more quickly than export. Yet there has
been no case in Latin America (in the past three decades), so far
as the statistics go and can be trusted, of the national product growing significantly faster than exports without a least a moderate degree of inflation.

Suppose it really is hard for structural change to occur, in a
given political context, without price rises: then the attempt to
suppress inflation by financial policy can only succeed if it is carried to a point where structural change and thus development, too,
is slowed down. This is a terrible price to pay in an underdeveloped country.

The dilemmas facing policymakers are severe. The monetarists
advise balancing budgets and using banking regulations (especially
reserve requirements) to stabilize prices. But the attempt to carry
this program out rapidly may mean a serious increase in social
problems, leading to political unrest, possibly ending only in the
suspension of constitutional procedures and the establishment of
military or quasi-military regimes. In view of the recent history of
Latin American, there is no need to labor this point.[18]

---

[18]*New York Herald Tribune* (editorial of March 2, 1962). "President Frondizi
was a victim of orthodox economic planning. His goals, charted by the International Monetary Fund . . . were politically unpopular and, as we now see, al-

If deep structural problems exist, global financial policies are clearly inappropriate. So the monetarist has two alternatives: he can argue either that structural problems are not important, or that they can be cured rapidly. Whichever his view, a detailed analysis of the problems of any economy's productive sectors, and some conclusion as to how these problems might be solved, constitute essential steps before recommendations are made about fiscal and monetary policy. There can be no general rule, such as balancing budgets, that can be applied in all countries and all circumstances.

For the reasons given above, it is difficult to argue that structural problems are negligible in most of the large countries of the region (or that they would remain so in the smaller countries of the region if development were pressed). There is of course nothing to stop a monetarist from advocating rapid structural change and this would seem to be a logically indispensible part of the monetarist program. A big increase in direct taxes would help check the growth of consumer demand for nonessentials, and thus reduce the pressure to import or produce them. More fundamentally, educational advance and land reform (that really redistributed property) would unify the economy and make it more flexible in response to price changes. But to demand this is in effect to demand a change in the social order. Only in a quite different type of society would the price system have any hope of acting as an efficient allocator of resources. Monetarists somehow do not always push the classical conditions for the effectiveness of monetary policy into the forefront.

It may be held that, whatever may be their effects on growth, sound financial policies are essential to eliminate intolerable deficits in the balance of payments. The balance of payments is in fact the main concern of the International Monetary Fund, which has played a big part in inducing governments to accept stabilization programs; after a certain level is reached, aid is made conditional on these programs being accepted, and public and private banks in the United States and western Europe have often waited to see whether the IMF's conditions were accepted before they made loans themselves.

I think we should hesitate before judging the IMF too harshly. After all, it is in a rather unfortunate position, perhaps more unfortunate than it realizes, for it is an agency to help countries in balance of payments difficulties, which are assumed to be temporary

---

most impossible." This is somewhat of an oversimplification, of course, and therefore rather unfair to the IMF, but nevertheless it contains a grain of truth.

and readily soluble.[19] It is not wholly implausible to argue that industrial countries can enhance their balance of trade, at least in the short run, by financial policy if demand for motor cars falls slightly at home, there will be more pressure to export them and the elasticity of foreign demand is doubtless fairly high (small cars like Volkswagens, Fiats, Renaults and Morrises are all in the same price bracket, so a price reduction should noticeably stimulate exports). Similarly, many imports are nonessential, and can be reduced or eliminated easily and without great harm. Moreover, capital flows between industrial countries seem quite sensitive to changes in short-term interest rates.[20]

In the case of underdeveloped economies like Latin America's, however, the reaction of foreign trade to domestic policy is very much more sluggish. If home demand declines, the effect on exportable supplies is not very significant in the case of coffee, sugar, bananas, petroleum, or metals (though it may be more considerable for livestock products and cereals), because they do not absorb a large proportion of total local demand. Moreover, except for petroleum, the income elasticities of demand for primary products are not large. In most of the large countries in the region, the margin for compressing imports has become so small that mere financial devices are unlikely to affect foreign payments greatly. Where staple foods, equipment, spare parts, fuel, and materials account for the great bulk of imports—as they do in Argentina and Brazil, for example—the demand for foreign exchange is not going to prove very responsive to changes in prices and the level of activity, unless of course financial pressure is carried to the point of causing a fall in investment.

Yet if the payments crisis of a country is not a *temporary* problem but a chronic one, in fact an inevitable feature of the present period for most developing countries, then there can be no question of righting it by mere monetary restriction or devaluation; indeed if such measures succeed in lowering investment, they will postpone the day when the economy will be viable in foreign trade. So the IMF is really grappling with a problem that cannot be solved within its terms of reference.[21]

---

[19]It was set up, in fact, to help industrial countries meet such temporary difficulties (so that they would not have to indulge in policies of financial deflation!). Its role in the economies of development was never envisaged.

[20]Though the consequent movements in reserves are somewhat misleading.

[21]Unless, which seems quite plausible, it allows that there can be a "fundamental disequilibrium" of a sort that cannot be cured by adjusting exchange rates.

It should not be concluded from these remarks that budgets ought to be left unbalanced, or credit should be liberally given away. On the contrary, *ceteris paribus,* surpluses are needed to finance the heavy investment of public corporations. The economic prospects of most Latin American countries would be considerably better if twice as much was collected in direct taxes and if credit was restricted for nonessential purposes. Nor do I want to imply that the problem can be solved merely by government controls; these might strain administrative capacity. Clearly there is no quick and easy solution to a socioeconomic crisis of such gravity. The only overriding principle is that financial policy should be as restrictive as is compatible with rapid development.

The charge that can be made against the monetarist school is that it directs attention away from the fundamental problems of economic growth, and so discourages the search for political strategies and economic plans to solve these problems. It puts forward instead a panacea, irrespective of social reality. (Does a monetarist adjust his advice if the population increase accelerates from 2 percent a year to 3 percent—and by what theoretical path does he do so? How does he propose to maintain economic growth during an export recession?) Consequently, overemphasis on monetary measures involves serious risks. The paradox is that though the monetarist is normally far from a revolutionary, and his preference is for peace and quiet, his policies may lead to social disorder and eventually regimentation of one form or another. His nostalgic wish for a re-establishment of nineteenth-century security is unattainable, and by pursuing it he may hasten the current dissolution.

There is doubtless much to be said for the Nietzschean precept, "Live dangerously," but in the twentieth century life is quite dangerous enough without taking on additional social gambles. Perhaps we are best advised to proceed empirically rather than dogmatically, testing the local political framework before we throw on it the full weight of policies derived from a doctrine which was developed for the needs of another century and another part of the world.

c. COMMENT
Carlos Massad

I do not think anybody disagrees with the proposition that it would be better to have growth without inflation. I am no exception to this rule and, obviously, neither is Mr. Dorrance. However, his paper goes far beyond it, to argue that inflation slows down the rate of increase in per capita income by reducing investment and by inducing a misallocation of resources. To support this view he presents a set of tables wherein different countries in different periods are classified under three groups according to the rate of inflation experienced, the rate of inflation for each of the groups being compared successively with several other variables, one by one.

This procedure is, in my opinion, highly dangerous. First, it implicitly assumes from the start that the rate of growth is mainly a function of the rate of inflation. The alternative approach, that is, the rate of inflation as a function of the rate of growth, was not even tried. Inflation is here the independent variable. Second, all other factors are eliminated from the comparison and inflation is blamed for the observed results. Third, in each table different countries are included, and for different periods, thus aggravating the defects previously mentioned. Fourth, no attention is given to what happened within the periods considered, emphasis being thrown on the average results.

There has been an extended discussion on the problem of inflation and growth. Several hypotheses about inflation link it to the growth process, either through prices of wage goods or through downward rigidity of prices that forces changes in the price level when some bottleneck appears, or in other ways. Even though these hypotheses, and others, have not been tested to the satisfaction of the economic profession, they cannot be easily dismissed. However, the procedure used in Mr. Dorrance's paper implies the opposite. There is only one phrase where an alternative position is taken: ". . . rapid economic development is likely to provoke inflationary pressures." An exploration of the analytical content of this phrase is, I suppose, crucial in order to determine whether the anti-inflationary measures usually put into operation may be applied without paralyzing the process of growth.

In the same way in which at times everything conceivable is

taken as a cause of inflation, Mr. Dorrance blames inflation for all the evils of the countries studied. I really wonder whether such a conclusion is justified. In the case of Chile, for example, a country that appears to have strong inflation and no growth, the story is much more complex; but one could say that the stagnation of the growth process in the Chilean economy during the late fifties has much more to do with the efforts to curb inflation than with inflation itself. The annual rate of price increases was brought down from 70 percent plus in 1954 and 1955 to around 40 to 30 percent in the following years. As a consequence of anti-inflationary policy, real GNP per capita dropped more than 8 percent in 1956, and by 1960 it had not recovered even half of that drop. Unemployment grew steadily from 1956 to 1959. For Chile, at least, the blame is not to be placed on inflation but rather on the particular measures which were adopted to stop it. There is a possibility that the same situation obtains in other countries.

On the other hand, a crucial element in the Chilean case has been foreign trade. The acceleration of inflation in 1954 and 1955 is closely related to a sharp drop in the value of Chilean exports and imports. One finds that in the period of acceleration of inflation investment dropped somewhat, and that it increased afterward when the rate of price increase was brought down. But most of this change in investment can be explained by changes in imports induced by fluctuations of international markets; so that, doubtless, foreign trade is an important element in explaining both the acceleration of inflation and the decrease in investment, while a one-to-one comparison suggests only a relation between inflation and investment. One can say at least that it is not easy to determine how much of the change in investment is due to changes in the rate of inflation and how much is due to changes in foreign trade.

This leads to a closely related problem in the procedure used. By taking averages of five- or six-year periods, some very crucial elements disappear from the picture. Let me illustrate, again using the case of Chile. The average rate of inflation will not be very different if one takes the periods 1950–54 or 1954–59. However, in the former the rate of inflation was more or less stable, around 20 percent, until 1953, but then it increased sharply in 1954. In the latter period, the rate was over 70 percent in 1954 and 1955, and dropped sharply afterwards. In 1950–54 real GNP per capita increased by more than 15 percent; in 1954–59 it decreased by 5 percent. Now, if the rate of inflation were constant, many of the evils mentioned in Mr. Dorrance's paper would probably disappear. If the rate changes appreciably, a different result is obtained. It may be more important to consider the changes in the rate of inflation rather than the average rate over a period, particularly when emphasis is placed on the elements of uncertainty introduced by inflation.

The Chilean experience, then, suggests that the method used by Mr. Dorrance is somewhat inadequate, and that one cannot avoid studying in detail the events in specific countries rather than lumping them together under broad categories.

Let me assume, however, that the analysis made by Mr. Dorrance is correct and that the empirical evidence presented leads to the conclusions at which he arrives. We would know, then, that inflation produces many evils and that it would be well to stop it. Now, two additional questions come to mind. First, how to stop it, and second, once it has been halted, will the rate of economic growth increase noticeably?

The first question cannot be answered intelligently unless the process of inflation and the elements that provoke it are well understood. The policy prescriptions will be different if one is facing an inflationary situation that is essentially demand-induced, or is mainly a reflection of a cost push-type process, or both intermixed in a kind of structuralist model. In the first case, a restrictive monetary policy probably will be able to do the trick without very much unemployment and, if some unemployment is generated, the transition period will not be very long unless inflation has been present for a decade or more. In the second and third cases, a restrictive monetary policy will also do the job, but at a much higher cost in terms of the magnitude of unemployment and in terms of time. As a matter of fact, a very tight monetary policy may in this case endanger the existence of a democratic system of government.

It seems to me, then, that in cases where inflation has been present for a long time, or in the second and third cases mentioned above, a better policy prescription would be not to attempt to stop it drastically, but rather to announce a policy of gradually increasing monetary tightening parallel to the enforcement of other measures directed against the basic causes of inflation.

This question of diagnosis was not tackled in Mr. Dorrance's paper, partly because, as is obvious, a paper cannot cover all subjects. Also, I think, he considers inflation as policy, a wrong one but still a policy, rather than as the consequence of a process of growth or of other factors in the economy. Probably one can find both things in the world, but it would be rather dangerous to act as if only one of them existed. It would imply, at least, taking a firm stand on an unsettled issue.

The second question, whether the rate of growth will increase noticeably once inflation has been halted, has at least two angles. One refers to the problem of whether it is possible to control inflationary pressures without incurring too high a cost in terms of growth; the other relates to the possibility of carrying out without inflation some basic changes needed for increasing the rate of growth in Latin-American countries.

The first angle is really a question of magnitude. What rate of inflation can be accepted, if any? Chilean experience indicates that a rate of increase in prices of 10 to 15 percent per year does not worry anybody; so that efforts to reduce it very much under that level may imply a cost with no appreciable benefit. This rate, as a matter of fact, existed during the period of fastest development after the Great Depression, from 1940 to 1950, and is also the rate observed during 1961, the best year in terms of growth of GNP since 1954. However, according to Mr. Dorrance, this would be a strong inflation.

The second angle of the question, the possibility of carrying out some basic changes needed to step up the rate of growth, leads one to think in terms of price flexibilities and mobility of resources. Any basic change, like a land reform or a redistribution of income, is bound to change rather rapidly the pattern of demand, and the adjustments to it may require a long time. Given that prices are inflexible downward, these changes will produce inflationary pressures which, if attacked with tight monetary policies, will generate unemployment and add to the inevitable social tensions of the process. Since these changes cannot be planned perfectly and carried out smoothly, the question is not, as Mr. Dorrance puts it, whether attacks on such problems are likely to be more feasible in an atmosphere of financial stability, but rather whether they can be carried out at all without inflation.

d. COMMENT
Mario Henrique Simonsen

The purpose of the following remarks is to suggest a general method of analysis of the controversy between monetarists and structuralists. Professor Dudley Seers's paper on the "heart of the controversy" will be taken as a representative standard of the struc-

turalist position. Professor Graeme Dorrance's paper on inflation
and growth will be taken to represent a synthesis of the monetarist
thought. Both papers constitute very brilliant defenses of two opposite points of view and I wish to congratulate their authors. It
seems to me, however, that a nonemotional appraisal of the controversy will lead most economists to less extreme positions.

First, a value judgment. I will assume throughout my comments
that growth is more important than price stability, as structuralists
emphasize, and I am sure that every "human" economist will agree
with me. Of course, this does not prove anything unless we show
that stability and growth are incompatible.

Second, a matter of definition: what is a monetarist? what is a
structuralist? Professor Seers, in the first page of his paper, associates monetarist thought with the assumption that "monetary stability is a necessary and sufficient condition for growth." From my
point of view this is quite an extreme definition. No economist
well acquainted with statistical data will assume that price stability
is either a necessary or a sufficient condition for growth, since there
exist unstable and growing economies as well as stable and stagnant economies. (There also exist unstable and stagnant as well as
stable and developing countries.) On the other side, what is structuralism? Up to now, I did not find any brief definition and I am
afraid that some extreme monetarist—someone who believes that
price stability is a necessary and sufficient condition for economic
development—would define structuralism as a school of thought
which tries to exempt Latin-American governments from any responsibility for inflation by throwing it to the mystical class of the
structural price pressures. I am sure that Professor Seers would
never be classed in this extreme position since he explicitly says,
"There is no need for us to dispute, what is obvious, that governments have often been far too expansive in monetary policy." In
any case, it seems useful to make some clear definitions.

It seems to me that the simplest and also probably the best definition of the conflicting views lies in the expected sign of the correlation between inflation and growth. Monetarists believe this correlation is a negative one; structuralists believe in a positive regres-
sion coefficient.

This suggests a problem of measurement. There is no reason for
us to assume that the relation between inflation and growth (if it
exists) has a linear shape, and, actually, this would be quite a
strange assumption, especially if we adopted the structuralist views.
That is to say, the controversy has no meaning unless we point out

at every step the inflation rate under discussion. One can be a structuralist at a 5 percent a year inflation rate and a monetarist when prices are increasing at 50 percent per annum.

The lack of quantitative reasoning seems to be the main weakness of structuralist thought. If I have well understood the structuralist theory, its main issue is that underdeveloped countries facing stagnant or slowly rising exports cannot grow without some degree of inflation. This happens because economic development under these conditions requires structural changes. Because of the rigidity of certain supplies, because of the very limited capacity to import, and because of the need for import substitution, these structural changes are likely to require some modifications in the relative price system. Since money prices hardly could be expected to fall, relative price falls can only come about as required if the general price level goes up. A blind stabilization program, with no regard to this peculiar feature, could only stop prices from rising by slowing down the process of structural change and, therefore, by hindering economic growth.

I have no doubt about the sound theoretical quality of these arguments, although I think that structuralists usually overemphasize certain points. Bottlenecks in Latin-American countries are not completely autonomous, as some structuralists seem to believe, but many of them have been caused, at least partially, by inflation. To give an example, it seems quite plausible to assume that Brazilian exports could hardly have increased so as to eliminate the need for structural changes. But one can be sure that Brazilian exports have been hindered by an artificial exchange policy under inflation. Another point one should remember is that the downward rigidity of sectoral prices could be at least partially offset by increases in productivity. Notwithstanding these qualifications, it seems plausible to assume that upward price pressures are difficult to avoid when structural changes are rapid enough.

The main question, however, concerns the quantitative relevance of these arguments: which rate of inflation can be accepted as an inevitable result of the structural price pressures? This seems to be the really important point of the discussion. Inflation is a multipurpose word which serves indistinctly to qualify a 5 percent or a 50 percent a year price rise, but if we don't want to lose ourselves in semantic traps, we should remember that there is a much sharper difference between a 5 percent and a 50 percent a year inflation rate than between stability and a 5 percent a year price rise. This is why I think it indispensable for the structuralist school to be more quantitative-minded and to try to measure the rates of inflation that can be attributed to structural pressures. Of course, there will be a different answer for each particular country. It seems to me, however, that these ideal rates of inflation will be considerably smaller than the ones which have been observed in most of the Latin-American countries. In the specific case of Brazil, there can be no doubt that only a very mild inflation could be considered a necessary result of structural changes. Since we are now facing a 50 percent a year inflation, it would be meaningless to concentrate our emphasis on a theory which just explains a very small fraction of the price increase in the country.

There is a way of transforming the structuralist theory into a meaningful approach for countries like Brazil. This is to include the government deficits among the structural causes of inflation. Latin-American governments have shown a propensity for budgetary deficits. This can be easily explained by the following: (1) it is extremely popular to increase budgetary expenditures; (2) it is highly unpopular to raise taxes; (3) most of the people do not grasp the correlation between government deficits and inflation. If budgetary deficits, however, are accepted as an outstanding "structural" cause of inflation, the controversy between monetarists and structuralists is reduced, at least in part, to a simple game of words, for monetarists also point out the deficits as the main cause of inflation. The structuralist advocate could argue that the word "structural" plays an important role in the explanation, since it is not enough to observe that government deficits exist in Latin-American countries, which is obvious, but one should look at the political and sociological roots of these deficits. This, however, is obvious too.

Now, a few words about monetarism. I do agree with the basic idea that a violent inflation like the Brazilian should be fought for two main reasons: (1) because inflation is socially bad; (2) because any development rate achieved along with inflation would have been compatible with a convenient stable price policy, except for mild upward price pressures. The latter, however, cannot be proved as a scientific law. It is a working hypothesis, which appears to me quite reasonable, but which is not based on sufficient empirical evidence to dispel any doubts about its validity. What seems to be wrong with monetarists is that they believe in a simple negative correlation between inflation and growth with the same confidence they accept the gravitation law of mechanics.

Actually, I have some very serious doubts about the scientific merits of any attempt to correlate inflation and growth in general terms. First, inflation and growth are multipurpose words: there are many kinds of inflations and several types of growth. Second, growth depends on many other variables, probably more important than the inflation rate. General statements regarding inflation and growth as univalent phenomena and assuming a nonexistent *ceteris paribus* are scientifically loose and, with some skillfully selected statistics, may lead us to any a priori established conclusion.

In the same way, it seems to me that monetarists should be more careful when discussing stabilization policies. I share the opinion that price stability is an important goal, but I think we should never be unmindful of the internal composition of the stabilization policies. Once again, stabilization is a multipurpose word. There are different paths leading to stable (or almost stable) prices and we cannot disregard the problem of selecting the best one. If we take into account the sectoral details of the economic system, the optimal choice of a stablization program is far from being an obvious one, and we should come to the conclusion that there are good as well as bad stabilization policies. To assume that they are all good is almost as naive as to believe that price stability is a sufficient condition for growth. The economist should remember that it is not enough to use the quantity theory equation in order to formulate a good stabilization program, and that people may even be nostalgic about inflation if they are submitted to an awkward anti-inflationary policy.

4. STATISTICAL PROBLEMS

a. STATISTICS FOR ECONOMIC DEVELOPMENT WITH SPECIAL REFERENCE TO NATIONAL ACCOUNTS AND RELATED TABLES[1]

Roger Messy and Hans Pedersen

INTRODUCTION

The present note is part of an effort to work out a consistent minimum program for statistics required in the formulation and implementation of a plan for general economic growth.

Many statistics are needed to guide efforts toward economic development. The statistical program outlined below refers to the most essential priorities and is not an exhaustive list of statistical activities. It is extremely difficult to define a list of basic statistics, because of the multiplicity of their uses. The "Basic List of Statistics for Economic and Social Development"[2] prepared by the Statistical Commission of the United Nations is a great effort in this direction. In many respects the present paper differs much from the above-mentioned list because it includes and puts the stress on national accounts tables and related statistics, which are needed in the formulation and implementation of a plan and for the checking of economic policies linked to it. On the other hand, it does not deal with some of the detailed series included in the United Nations document.

---

[1]The substance of this note is part of a wider effort undertaken by the Secretariat of the Economic Commission for Latin America to define a minimum statistical program with special reference to the specific problems of Latin-American countries. The authors, as members of the Secretariat, are under obligation to ECLA as a whole and particularly to their colleagues engaged in planning activities for their advice and positive suggestions. However, the conclusions, opinions, and other statements in this publication are those of the authors and not necessarily those of ECLA.

[2]United Nations Statistical Commission, documents E/CN.3/248 and E/CN. 3/L.41.

In defining a minimum statistical program of this sort, it is of great advantage to use a framework of national accounts, since this permits a rigorous and consistent approach in the selection of the statistical series needed. It would be quite insufficient, however, to limit the statistical program to national accounts only, since many other statistics are needed for an analysis of changes in the main aggregates. Special emphasis is also placed on statistical instruments for short-term economic policies, intended to check distortions which may arise during the course of the plan, which call for economic indicators in advance of national accounts data relating to the same period of time. A consolidation of all requirements into a single basic list is attempted.

In most Latin-American countries the statistical system is deficient and not sufficiently elastic to meet the increasing demand of economic policies. The present program intends to help the countries make the best use of existing resources, but an increase in these resources is also needed even for obtaining the most essential information. It will be necessary, of course, to develop the statistical system further, once this first stage has been reached.

In the first section, statistical needs are defined from the viewpoint of the users, while the second section refers to methodological aspects and basic material needed in the preparation of final tables.

DEFINITION OF STATISTICAL NEEDS
National Accounts and Related Tables

Purposes for Which These Statistics Are Needed. Experience over the last twenty years has shown that an arrangement of basic economic data within the conceptual framework of national accounts estimates provides an extremely useful tool for macroeconomic analysis and economic policy and planning. Since they gave a comprehensive picture of over-all economic developments and the interrelationships between strategic magnitudes, these estimates are indispensable for economic analysis, over shorter as well as longer periods. National accounts statistics are also of great use to governments in the diagnosis of present economic situations necessary before appropriate policy measures can be taken and in the formulation and implementation of development plans.

Economic development plans of the medium or long-range type have already been formulated in at least ten Latin-American countries. In several other countries of the region, the first steps have been taken to introduce such plans. The formulation of the plans has met with great difficulties because of lack of statistical data, particularly of the national accounts type. This lack of data is even more serious for the implementation of the plans—a stage which is now approaching.

To formulate a consistent and workable development plan, a fairly detailed picture of the economic situation in the base year and of past developments during a reasonably long historical period is needed. A quantitative assessment of general economic growth during past years and of the contributions of the various industries and factors of production to this growth is required to reveal basic weaknesses and strong points in the economic structure and to show to what extent a balanced development has so far been achieved. To obtain an idea about the investment effort necessary for an increase in the product of a given magnitude it is also necessary to know the share of total resources which in recent and past years has been devoted to the building-up and renewal of the capital stock. The more detailed such an analysis could be made, the more significant it would be, and, to achieve a reasonably detailed analysis, at least some information about investment by main sectors of the economy is needed.

At the stage of implementation of the plans it is necessary to make frequent checks of their progress so that the direction of the effort may be changed or the targets modified, if need be, in the light of developments during the plan period. Without intermediate projections and reliable and up-to-date estimates of national accounts, such checks cannot be made.

National income and national accounts estimates furnish the raw material for the construction of balances of total demand and supply by main components, which are indispensable in revealing the existence and sources of inflationary pressures or pressures on the balance of payments. The existence of such balances makes it possible for the planners to take measures which may prevent future monetary disequilibrium or a balance of payments crisis during the implementation of a plan.

National budgets, or one-year economic plans, which present as complete a picture as possible of the likely development of the economy in the year to come and are intended to form a consistent framework for short-term economic policy, have been found useful in many countries. The national budget is usually presented to parliament together with the government budget or as a supplement to it.

In addition to their primary purpose of facilitating short-term policy decisions, the rational budgets could also be, of course, very useful instruments in connection with the implementation of long or medium-term plans. The information required to make up national budgets is essentially the same as that needed to make short-term projections of the national accounts.

No Latin-American country so far prepares a national budget of this sort, but the need for such a tool is evident. Several countries are in the process of changing their budgetary procedures by adopting program and performance budgeting and more analytically meaningful economic-functional classifications of their government budgets which could be directly fitted into a national budget. No doubt the main reason why complete national budgets have not yet been formulated is the lack of statistics on which to base them. For national budgeting, up-to-date, reliable, and fairly detailed national accounts data are indispensable.

Types of Data Needed. Basically, the same set of national accounts data is needed for economic analysis, planning, and national budgeting. The requirements with regard to the accuracy and timeliness of the data are, however, considerably greater for planning than for general economic analysis. For the latter purpose, relationships based on orders of magnitude only may sometimes be useful, while for planning, particularly over the short term, figures with too large a margin of error may lead to erroneous and harmful policy conclusions.

To serve the purposes mentioned above the national accounts data listed under points 1–9 below should be made available in a provisional, if necessarily incomplete, but relatively firm form about six months after the end of the year to which they refer. Final estimates should appear one year later. In addition, historical series covering at least a decade are required. Elaboration and improvement of the current data should, however, be given first priority.

To make possible the formulation of a national budget, and for planning purposes in general, preliminary estimates made available before the end of the year to which they refer are also required. Such estimates, which necessarily have to be based on incomplete data covering only part of the year, are more in the nature of projections than ex post estimates. It is all the more necessary that the figures for the last year for which a complete estimate is available are as reliable as possible, so that they may serve as a firm basis for these semiprojections.

A number of national accounts series are listed below which may be considered the minimum requirement for purposes of long and short-term planning and economic analysis. A less complete set of estimates would still be useful for some purposes, but without the series mentioned under point 1, 2, 3, 6, and 7 below, even rudimentary planning and economic analysis would be difficult. With regard to detailed breakdowns of the series listed below, reference is made to *A System of National Accounts and Supporting Tables (Studies in Methods*, Series F, No. 2, Rev. 1, United Nations, New York, 1960 [hereafter called SNA]).

1. *Gross domestic product by industrial origin, at current and constant prices, with a sector breakdown at least as detailed as the main groups recommended in SNA.* Further detail than the main groups would be very useful, particularly for agriculture (where crop and livestock production, forestry, and fishing may be separately shown) and manufacturing (where not only the main industries may be separately shown, but also small-scale and handicraft industries as distinguished from large-scale industry).

2. *Expenditures on gross national product at current and constant prices, classified by main items as recommended by SNA.* Although many countries at present find it difficult to make constant price estimates for the expenditure side which are consistent with those for the product side, such estimates are essential and every effort should be made to provide them. As far as semiprojections for the most recent year are concerned, these estimates, if they are possible at all on the basis of the data available, are easier to make at constant than at current prices, particularly for countries which experience considerable price increases affecting the various parts of the economy to different degrees. This goes for estimates of product by industry as well as for national expenditure. Similar estimates at current prices should, however, also be made, if at all possible, since they are essential in analyzing the prospects of financial disequilibrium.

3. *Breakdowns of gross fixed capital formation by type of capital goods, by public and private and, if possible, by industry of use, at current and constant prices and with details as recommended in SNA.* Since it may be expected that many countries would not be able to work out a breakdown of gross fixed capital formation by industrial use per se, an attempt may be made to obtain a partial substitute by making the breakdown by type of capital goods as detailed as possible. Dwelling construction and other "social investments" should in any case be separated from "economic investments" and, in addition, capital formation in machinery and equipment might be split between agricultural, transportation, and other equipment. It may also be possible to achieve separate estimates for

capital formation in machinery and equipment in the manufacturing and construction industries. Construction expenditures, on the other hand, are very difficult, if not impossible, to allocate by industry (aside from dwelling construction), except by direct investigation.

4. *A breakdown of private consumption by main groups, according to SNA, at current as well as constant prices.* If at all possible, such a breakdown, which is of great interest both for analytical and planning purposes, should be made available annually. To be of maximum usefulness it should be a genuine direct estimate and not a breakdown of a total obtained as a residual. For bench mark years, a classification in greater detail, at least corresponding to the subgroups recommended by SNA, should be worked out.

5. *Distribution of national income at current prices according to the main items recommended in SNA.* The most important components of this distribution are independent estimates of wages and salaries and of the savings of corporations. Some of the other items it contains could be obtained from the statement on government expenditures, mentioned under point 6 below. Direct information on income from unincorporated enterprises and property income of households would not be available in several countries of the region, and the sum of these items would have to be obtained as a residual.

6. *Breakdown of general government incomes and current and capital expenditures by economic and functional categories.* Considering the importance of the government sector for planning, as much information as possible is needed about the composition of its incomes and expenditures. A breakdown which contains the elements of the general government revenue and expenditure account of the SNA, but is more comprehensive in that it also includes capital expenditures and a classification by functional categories, is recommended in *Manual for Economic and Functional Classifications of Government Transactions.* (United Nations, New York, 1958 [hereafter called the *Manual*]) and has later been amended by several United Nations Workshops on Budget Reclassification and Management. Particularly for short-term planning, an arrangement of government income and expenditure data within this framework would be very useful.

7. *A statement of international transactions.* Information about transactions with the rest of the world is needed in the full detail recommended for the supporting table "International Transactions" in SNA.

8. *A system of national accounts.* Both for economic analysis
and planning, a set of formal national accounts is needed. The construction of such a system of accounts requires the arrangement in
systematic form of selected items from the breakdown listed above
in addition to supplementary information on a number of points.
The system of national accounts recommended in SNA may on
some points be too detailed for the purposes of the countries of the
region (as, for instance, with regard to the inclusion of capital reconciliation accounts) and on other points it may not be detailed
enough. An extension of the system by incorporating production accounts for the various industries, as well as balances of supply and
demand by commodity group for selected years, may be desirable.
Such balances would be very useful for planning purposes and are,
as a matter of fact, almost indispensable for locating bottlenecks
which may arise in the supply of the products of specific industries.
An interesting proposal for an intermediate system of national accounts within the framework of SNA which includes extensions in
the directions mentioned has recently been worked out for Africa.[3]
This system also extends the SNA on other points, by introducing a
separate account for agricultural households and an appropriation
account for the corporate sector. In the second section a more detailed description of the system will be given.

9. *Input-output table.* An input-output table for a recent year
would be very useful both for economic analysis and for planning.
The concrete form of the input-output table required for planning
purposes depends on the planning model used. Some types of input-
output tables enable the planners to derive the probable effects on
imports of a given short-term development of the product as well as
the longer-term effects of import substitution. For the purposes of
analyzing the effects on domestic production of an expansion of
specific sectors of the economy, it has been found that even tables
which cover a limited number of industries, with heavy concentration on the manufacturing industries, are useful.

Specialized Statistics

Although there are many differences in concept and coverage between aggregates of national accounts and detailed sectorial statistics, the latter are frequently used for analysis of changes over time
of components of each aggregate. These specialized statistics serve
the double purpose of helping us to understand the changes in na-

---

[3]"Proposals for an Intermediate System of National Accounts in African
Countries," by Philippe Berthet, E/CN.14/NAC 7, August, 31, 1962.

tional accounts data and of providing the necessary statistical instruments for a specific analysis of each individual sector. For this reason, no attempt is made to distinguish between statistical requirements for each of these two sets of uses.

Population and Labor Force. Data on population are needed for a number of purposes, notably for the determination of final demand and also for making an inventory of human productive resources. Although some coefficients, such as birth and death rates, do not have important annual fluctuations, it is preferable to dispose of a set of annual data for all series concerned.

Apart from total population for the whole country, estimates for the various parts are needed for a regional development policy. Population data by age groups and sex and by rural and urban areas are required. Rates of births, deaths, and natural increase should be accurately known. Because of the rapid urbanization in Latin America and the importance of the problems it raises, it is essential to have good data on the population in the main cities.

Data on the labor force are essential for economic planning. It is not sufficient to obtain some of these data as by-products of establishment surveys on mining and manufacturing, but an inventory of employment by main sectors of economic activity is needed because of the primary importance of shift in employment from low to high productivity sectors.

Census data should be supplemented by annual indicators of employment by broad sectors. Data for mining, manufacturing, and public or semipublic services should have a large coverage, while those for other activities could be more fragmentary.

It is difficult in countries in which underemployment is large to have meaningful measurement of unemployment. It would be useful, however, to know about unemployment of people who had previously been employed in industry.

Agriculture, Forestry, and Fishing. For most Latin-American countries this is still the sector of economic activity with the largest employment and, for some of them, its contribution to GDP is also larger than that of any other sector. This in itself would justify a comprehensive set of statistical data.

In addition, agriculture plays a key role in the industrialization process because it has to supply the expanding sectors with part of their manpower, to deliver to urban areas increasing quantities of food, and to maintain the competitiveness of the countries' agricultural exports. Under these conditions, it is essential to have good statistics of production and factors of production in the sector.

Annual balances for commodity groups of food and agricultural raw materials are needed for a good analysis of availabilities of the main products. When compared with estimated requirements, these data would help much in anticipating the needs for imports and availabilities for export.

More specialized data are needed about the land and the means of production (cleaning of virgin land, improvements in irrigation, number of tractors, etc.); the uses of land, the main inputs, the yields for main crops, and prices paid to farmers.

Mining, Manufacturing, Construction, and Energy.   In the process of industrialization, these activities, together with transportation, should be the expanding sectors. The importance of having good statistical instruments for them is obvious.

Mining is still the main source of foreign exchange for several countries in the region. It is also a key sector for industrialization as far as extracing of petroleum and iron ore is concerned. Production statistics are generally of an acceptable quality, although small mining escapes good measurement. Better statistics are needed for employment, consumption of energy, capital formation, and also national income derived from the activity of the large foreign companies.

A continuous and harmonious expansion of manufacturing is generally a main target of an economic development policy. It is therefore a sector which calls for a considerable effort in quantitative measurement. Planning for the manufacturing industry requires much detailed information, obtained from general industrial surveys and censuses, completed by special inquiries. The information should be detailed enough to make possible the construction of input-output tables for selected years. Since the targets are a substitution of imports of manufactured goods and an increase in their national consumption, called for by a rise in income per capita, it is necessary to have a comprehensive set of indicators for keeping under control the whole process of industrialization. Particular attention should be paid to statistics of production and requirements for intermediary products, because bottlenecks at this level can arise which would significantly affect the consuming industries.

Although construction does not represent a high percentage of GDP, it is essential to measure it carefully for a number of reasons. Because of the large urbanization which is linked to industrialization, there is a great need for planning of housing and other construction. It is essential to know about the supply of new dwellings and private houses, as well as schools and other social investments.

Construction is also a very meaningful indicator of the current trend in the economy as a whole. It must be noted that in industrial countries, a considerable part of private construction would escape measurement if data were collected only through an industrial survey, because, contrary to what happens it is current practice that individuals take direct care of the construction of their own houses, employing only a small number of workers (below the limit used in the survey).

Energy has frequently been a bottleneck sector in the industrialization process in Latin-American countries, domestic production being unable to meet the demand, so that imports of fuel have taken too much from foreign exchange availabilities. This was partly due to a lack of good information about the structure of actual demand as well as of a forecast of future demand. Much better statistics regarding the natural resources, production by types, and a sectorial detail of uses of energy are called for.

Transportation. This sector is also a frequent bottleneck in Latin-American economies. It is a well-known fact that the lack of integration between the various regions within these countries is due to inadequate means of transportation and that important structural changes of the system are needed. Otherwise the efforts of the other sectors would not serve the economy fully; food and raw materials, for instance, would not be carried to the users in time. Expansion in this sector has to be planned with great care, as the infrastructure is very costly and the vehicles are generally imported. Detailed data are needed on the equipment, the transportation by types of goods, and for passengers.

Private Services.[4] This is a large and heterogeneous sector which has a considerable share in employment and GDP of Latin-American countries. Although its output is not of primary concern in a development policy, it is very important to know, not only about income generated in this sector, but also about employment, gross margins of the distributive trades, etc.

Money, Finance, and Prices. It is essential to have up-to-date information on foreign exchange reserves and the external debt. Balance of payments data should be obtained with minimum delay.

All the statistical instruments for an intelligent credit policy should be quickly available.

Requirements for price data will depend much upon the degree

---

[4]Government services are reviewed in connection with the treatment of national accounts.

of price control used in the country. In any case, however, it will be necessary to collect prices at the various stages of production and distribution. Such data are also very relevant indicators of distortions in the economy and will help to detect bottlenecks.

External Trade. Because they are from an administrative source, external trade data can easily satisfy the following requisites: large coverage, presentation in great commodity detail, and availability within a reasonable time. They are not only of great interest in themselves, but also represent a mine of information which can be used as short-term indicators for activity in the various sectors. A great effort should be made to obtain foreign trade statistics of a high quality, because of the numerous purposes they serve.

Apart from the usual commodity breakdown for tariff or statistical uses, data should also be tabulated according to "economic" classifications, such as by industry of origin, sector of final use, stage of processing, etc.

Existing Series and Main Gaps

The availability of statistics in the various Latin-American countries depends much on their degree of economic development. For this reason, no reference will be made to individual countries, and the general considerations presented below will have some arbitrary character, due to the variety of situations.

It can be said, however, that statistics are generally deficient, given the heavy strain placed on them. It is a widespread opinion among professional circles of the region that a great effort has to be undertaken for raising the quality of statistical instruments so that they may adequately serve suitable economic policies.

The following gaps seriously limit any quantitative economic research:

Agriculture. Data cover only the main products. Little or no annual information is available on farm consumption and inputs. Prices paid to farmers are available only in a few cases.

Mining. One of the best sectors for statistics. It has still to be improved regarding quickness of information, inputs, and wages.

Manufacturing. Suffers much from nonresponse in industrial inquiries, as well as from lack of adjustment for new establishments in samples.

Construction. Only indirect measures, such as building permits for the main cities, are available.

Energy. "Commercial energy" is sufficiently known, while information on self-produced energy is generally lacking.

Transportation. Only railways are relatively well covered, while air and (especially) road transportation are very badly investigated.

External Trade Statistics. These should be a mine of essential data for industrializing countries but are too conventional and not sufficiently analytical.

Prices. Retail price collections do not have a sufficient coverage. Consumer price indexes are weighted according to very obsolete patterns of consumption.

As a consequence of this situation, sufficient basic data to make reliable national accounts estimates are often lacking.

Capital formation is generally etsimated on the basis of imports of capital goods estimated (imperfectly) at prices of the end users; plus domestic production of equipment; plus construction, very roughly measured.

Private consumption is obtained as a residual, generally without any indication of its components.

Government accounts, which are essential in an effort to guide the whole economy, are sometimes badly classified and public capital formation is not accurately known.

In conclusion, it can be said that, because of lack of resources, statistics in the region are generally not ample and reliable enough to meet the needs of policymakers.

BASIC MATERIAL AND METHODOLOGY

In the first section, "final requests" on the part of the users of statistics have been reviewed in general terms. Now, an inventory will be made of the basic material required by these statistical elaborations, part of it no more than an "intermediary demand" for statistics which have to be further elaborated.

For national accounts and other macrostatistics, the needs for basic material depend on the method of estimation which is recommended. Different sets of statistics are required for an "income" or a "commodity flow" approach.

In the first part of this section, the methodology recommended for national accounts will be described, as well as its implicit statistical requirements.

In a second part, basic material by sectors and methods of collecting data will be reviewed, taking into account all needs.

Basic Material for National Accounts and Related Tables

General Remarks about the Present Method of Estimation. In the first section of this paper a short review was given of the purposes for which national accounts statistics are needed and of the types of data required as a minimum to serve these purposes. In the present section, an attempt will be made to indicate how the methods of national accounts estimation in the countries of the region may be improved so that the estimates can more adequately serve these purposes and to show which basic statistics are required for improved methods.

Being derived statistics, national accounts estimates of a sufficient degree of reliability can only be developed in close conjunction with basic economic statistics. As has been seen from the discussion above, these statistics suffer from many weaknesses in the region. In particular, the lack of sufficient and up-to-date information is a source of constant frustration for national accounts statisticians.

Most countries of the region proceed in the following way in estimating their national accounts: a total for domestic product is first arrived at by means of the so-called "value added" method, that is, by summing up estimates of gross production values less inputs, industry by industry.[5] This total forms the central part of the whole national accounts structure. Breakdowns by expenditure categories, income shares, etc. are subsequently arrived at by utilizing whatever further information is available—most important, social security, wage and employment records, government accounts, foreign trade statistics, and balance of payments. A number of important items, such as personal consumption, savings, income of households, and unincorporated enterprises, are generally obtained as residuals.

This method of estimation is not in itself objectionable. In its practical application, however, the national accounts statisticians, faced with the fact that a sufficiently broad basis of economic statistics is lacking, are often forced to stretch their imaginations and apply their ingenuity to a large extent. For years for which censuses of manufacturing or agriculture are not available, the value added of these industries has to be obtained by extrapolation of benchmark year estimates, by means of often dubious indicators, or has to be estimated on the basis of incomplete and sometimes fragmentary data. For most other industries, even relatively reliable bench-mark year estimates are lacking. As a consequence, experience in several countries has shown that the estimates of domestic product by industry are subject to repeated and substantial revisions both as to levels and movements, not only for the most recent years, but often over periods as long as a decade. Repeated and violent revisions of the figures for a series of years tend to discredit the estimates and

---

[5]A few countries use an income approach in building up value added, that is, they estimate each of the factor shares—wages and salaries, interest, etc.—industry by industry. At least one country obtains the basic data for estimating value added by industry, as well as some of the components of other breakdowns, from an annual survey especially designed for the purpose.

should not be necessary if the first calculations were carefully made and enough basic statistics were available to produce them at all. Another point is that periodical revisions, for instance, in the wake of a new census of agriculture or manufacturing, are both justified and necessary. New censuses provide the basis for new bench-mark year estimates and may require revision of the data for previous years to maintain a homogeneous series.

There is a very real danger that the breakdowns, aside from product by industry, may be seriously distorted and inconsistent. The items estimated as residuals absorb the unknown, but presumably considerable, errors in the independently estimated items. The residuals are, of course, also influenced by the relative reliability of the independently estimated items and the total obtained from the product side.

The estimates are, in the majority of the countries, first made at current prices. Because of the basic inconsistency of the various breakdowns and the extensive use of residual estimates, it has proved impossible in most countries to arrive at data at constant prices which even maintain the formal consistency of the current series. Most countries, therefore, present constant price estimates for product by industry only. Of the few countries which also include expenditure data at constant prices, some have achieved formal consistency simply by deflating all the items of one breakdown by the implicit price index of the total for the other breakdown, or they have applied the cost of living or wholesale price index to all items of both breakdowns.

As a means to achieve consistency between the estimates of product by industry and by expenditure categories, it is suggested that the so-called commodity flow method could with advantage be applied by the countries of the region.

The Commodity Flow Method. This method consists essentially in a careful analysis of all existing data on imports, exports, and domestic production, following each item or group of items from origin to final destination as inputs in domestic industries, or as consumption, capital formation, or exports. Appropriate trade and transport margins obtained by means of surveys are added to the original CIF or exfactory values and the items valued at purchaser prices are allocated by final destination, taking account of the nature of the commodity. A number of more or less arbitrary decisions are involved, both in deciding the markups and, particularly, in the allocation of the various items by final use.

The commodity flow method is already being widely applied in the region for estimating capital formation in machinery and equipment. A few of the statistically more developed countries apply the method also to obtain a check on the residual estimate of private consumption. It is of interest to note that, in addition, it has been found possible to construct input-output tables in some detail for several of the countries for years in which manufacturing censuses were taken. Such tables can only be established if even more detailed basic data are available than are required to apply the commodity flow method for national accounts estimates.

The aim should be, however, to extend the basis of current statistics to such an extent that the commodity flow method can be generally adopted for annual national accounts estimates. This would insure a higher degree of systematization of the work and make possible a simultaneous estimation of domestic product from the product and expenditure sides. The construction of input-output tables and commodity balances for selected years could then also be easily fitted into the scheme.

To apply the commodity flow method successfully, the countries need to analyze all existing data on exports, imports, and domestic production in as great detail as possible. One of the reasons why the method is a forceful tool for national accounts estimation is precisely that, if effectively applied, it forces the statisticians to utilize to the full all available data in these fields. Furthermore, it centers attention on a critical survey of these data, which are of fundamental importance, not only for national accounts estimation, but are indispensable in themselves as the basis for economic policy and planning.

For the commodity producing sectors, and as far as possible also for the service sectors, it is essential to have data on imports and exports and on individual commodities or commodity groups in sufficient detail to enable the estimators to make a rough distribution by final use from the nature of the products. For the purposes of estimating product by industry and by expenditure categories, using the commodity flow method, it is sufficient to be able to assess the total value of inputs in each industry, as well as the part of total production of a commodity or commodity group which is used for inputs in all industries together, and for capital formation, increase in stocks, and exports.

Since most products may, at least to some extent, have multiple uses, the nature of a product is rarely sufficient to determine its final use. More or less arbitrary assumptions therefore often have to be made by the national accounts estimators in order to split uniform products between different end uses. In making this allocation, any available information on inputs of goods and services in the various industries is of great help. To utilize the information on inputs as effectively as possible, it is very helpful to arrange the data in matrix form, similar to the upper left-hand quadrant of an input-output table. Each square of this matrix can then be filled in, either by using information on inputs in the various industries, by referring to the nature of the product, or by rough allocation. Since it is only the sum total of each line and each column which will finally be used by the national accounts estimator, errors in the detailed allocation of inputs may be expected to outweigh each other to some extent.

Furthermore, if this procedure is applied, the essential framework for input-output calculations has already been established. For years with particularly ample basic statistics, the additional detail available will make possible the expansion of the estimate into a full-fledged input-output table. For this purpose, of course, each square of the table has to be estimated to a higher degree of accuracy than necessary for estimating the national accounts.

The specific basic data needed to apply the commodity flow method are, in broad terms, the following:

1. Annual statistics on exports and imports, classified in sufficient detail to enable the national accounts estimators to group commodities with similar uses together, are required. Detailed end-use classifications built into the foreign trade statistics themselves would be of very great help in this respect.

2. Annual production statistics for agriculture, mining, energy, and manufacturing, classified in similar detail, are essential for combining data on domestic production with imports and exports data, to arrive at total availabilities of the various commodities or commodity groups.

3. Special annual information on the value of the output of the construction industry is needed, as it is not possible to arrive at reliable figures for construction expenditures by means of the commodity flow method. These data should make possible separate estimates of dwelling construction, other building, and other construction, including constructions and works by farmers.

4. Annual data on the value of services rendered by commerce and transportation, the latter divided between passenger and freight transport, is needed to estimate value added of these sectors and as a check on total markups added to CIF and ex factory values in order to arrive at amounts paid by the final purchasers. To establish these markups themselves, direct information is needed on average trade margins, transport, and installation costs incurred for various types of commodities from the border or the factory till they are put to their final use.

5. An annual estimate of total rents paid is needed as a measure of the value of housing services rendered.

6. Annual statistics for banks and other financial institutions sufficient to estimate the value of paid and imputed services rendered by these institutions are also required.

7. Very little statistical basis exists for estimating the private part of personal services (educational, medical, recreational, and professional). More statistical information for this sector is therefore urgently required.

To the extent that both values and quantities of the various goods and services can be derived from the basic statistics, the commodity flow method is equally applicable to estimates at constant and at current prices. Constant price estimates can be obtained simply by valuing the various quantities at base year purchaser prices, derived by comparing base year values with base year quantities, commodity group by commodity group.

Like any other method of national accounts estimation, the commodity flow method is applicable to only part of the total set of estimates needed. Other important sections of the estimates always have to be obtained by other than the main methods. A particularly important source for this part of the estimates is the consolidated accounts for all levels of government.

The Government Sector. Since statistics on government finances are not dealt with in the section on specialized statistics, the government sector is given a somewhat fuller treatment below than is strictly required from a national accounts point of view.

The product of the sector of public administration and defense is defined as wages and salaries paid to government civil servants in these occupations, and therefore has to be estimated independently of the commodity flow method. Similarly, the estimate of government product in the educational, medical, and other service sectors also has to be made on the basis of data extracted from the government accounts. Other important items on the various national accounts which have to be derived from the same source are: public consumption, indirect taxes and subsidies, direct taxes on corporations, government income from property and entrepreneurship, transfers to and from the government sector, and government savings. The value of government construction may also be obtained from this source.

If the commodity flow method is used, production and input of government enterprices is estimated together with the same items for private enterprises in the same branch of activity. Any information available in special accounts for the government enterprises, of course, has to be utilized for the purpose. This is, however, a somewhat different problem from that dealt with here, which refers to the extraction of items from the accounts of general government only.

Government budgets and accounts traditionally have primarily served the purposes of fiscal control by parliament and have only recently been conceived as instruments of economic policy. The classifications of incomes and expenditures in the government accounts of most countries of the region still reflect the traditional purposes of the documents and focus attention mainly on an itemization by administrative unit rather than by economic significance. The items required to fill in the national accounts cannot be obtained from a traditional government account without reclassification and, to some extent, arbitrary splitting of the original items. This is a formidable task if carefully done, particularly since not only central government accounts, but also the accounts of provinces, municipalities, and extrabudgetary funds have to be reclassified to achieve full coverage.

In some of the countries the task of extracting the items they need from the government accounts is undertaken by the national accounts statisticians themselves. Since they are pressed for both time and resources they have to concentrate on the best possible approximation of the items needed to fill in their national accounts (usually the items mentioned above and the main items shown on the government revenue and expenditure account of the SNA). Although a full reclassification of the accounts for all levels of general government is, in principle, necessary for this purpose, in practice the results often suffer from shortcomings both with regard to coverage and details.

A better solution, which would both relieve the national accounts statisticians from a difficult and time-consuming task and insure a more complete and exact result, is to have the reclassification work in connection with the working out of budgets and accounts done in the ministries of finance themselves. Since the importance of government budgets and accounts as instruments of economic policy and as integral components of economic development plans has been realized, several countries of the region have, as a matter of fact, adopted this procedure. Rather than basing their reclassification work on the more limited detail recommended in SNA, these countries follow the recommendations of the United Nations *Manual*. In addition to the countries which undertake supplementary classifications on this basis, no less than five countries of the region have worked the classification system of the *Manual* directly into their budgets and accounts.

Application of the classification system of the *Manual* makes possible the inclusion of a combined economic and functional classification of all government transactions instead of the less detailed classification of government consumption expenditures recommended in SNA. Additional useful information would be provided by including this more detailed account.

The two most serious problems met by the countries in deriving figures for the government sector in their national accounts are the difficulty of obtaining up-to-date information for local government and the fact that budget data often have to be used instead of realized amounts for a number of years. The best way of obtaining as recent and complete information as possible on local government is probably to centralize the reclassification work for all levels of government in the ministries of finance. Even so, because the basic information for local government bodies, like municipalities, can only be obtained with some delay and takes considerable time to compile because these bodies are so numerous, extrapolation by means of incomplete information will be necessary for the most recent years.

For use in the national accounts, budgetary data ought as far as possible to be avoided, since experience shows that budget estimates always differ considerably from realized amounts and this difference varies much from item to item. Budgetary figures for the most recent years, therefore, ought to be replaced by realized amounts as soon as the latter become available. However, for short-term economic policy and the formulation of national budgets and development plans, budget figures for the consolidated government sector for one or more years into the future are of the greatest interest in themselves. A reclassification of the budgets by economic and functional categories is therefore necessary as soon as they appear.

Another type of information about government finances, not directly connected with national accounts estimates, but of great importance for the implementation of national budgets and plans, refers to quarterly and monthly data on government incomes and expenditures. These data, which necessarily must be partial, still ought to be tied in as closely as possible with the concepts and classifications adopted for annual budgets and accounts. The main difficulty in this respect is to reconcile the current data, which are shown on a cash basis, with the annual figures, which conform more closely to an accrual basis.

Other Data Needed to Complete the System of National Accounts and Related Tables. The commodity flow method is applicable only to estimates of domestic product by sector of origin and by expenditure categories, and government accounts provide only part of the additional information needed to complete a system of national accounts and supporting tables. For the third "traditional" breakdown, referring to national income by factor shares, information is first of all required on wages and salaries, including social security contributions and income in kind. Part of this information may be obtained from social security records, but direct surveys would be needed to obtain the data for the agricultural sector and to supplement the data obtained from the social security systems.

A number of the other items needed for the breakdown of national income by factor shares according to SNA may be obtained from government accounts. An independent estimate of corporate savings is, however, necessary. This could be derived as the balancing item on a special appropriation account for corporations. Such an account could be built up from the individual profit and loss accounts of corporations, which should be generally available. To complete the breakdown, income from unincorporated enterprises and income from households may be obtained in one sum as a residual.

Several statistically well-developed countries in various parts of the world have found economically meaningful depreciation estimates to be practically impossible and therefore present their data on a gross basis only. Although net figures would be useful for some purposes, it is doubtful that depreciation estimates for the countries of this region can be sufficiently firmly based to yield results which are significant. If it is felt that depreciation cannot be estimated on a reliable basis, national income, savings, etc. may be presented as gross concepts.

Up-to-date balance of payments statistics are needed and are also generally available in the region. A breakdown in the detail recommended in SNA should be shown, and such detail is generally available in the balance of payments statements. It would be an advantage to show separately how the surplus or deficit on current accounts has affected foreign reserves and net foreign lending and borrowing.

Special information on the increase in inventories is needed in order to check the necessarily arbitrary allocation of goods to this item by the commodity flow method. This is one of the most difficult items to estimate in the national accounts of any country. In this region, information would probably be confined to main export items while the rest of the inventory change would have to be included with consumption or as part of a statistical discrepancy.

The System of National Accounts. In the preceding, some indications were given of methods that may be applied and basic material which is needed to improve and extend the national accounts data of the region. The stress was placed on how to estimate the "traditional" breakdowns of national income and product and it was more or less tacitly assumed that the system of national accounts which may be established by rearranging these data and adding some supplementary information would be the system recommended in SNA with some modifications.

These modifications correspond more or less to those proposed for Africa in a recent United Nations document. It is realized that a national accounting system suitable for the Latin-American countries would in many respects have to differ from one suitable for Africa. Proposals for such a system have yet to be worked out. The proposed African system, however, contains a number of features which could be of practical use, regardless of how the national accounts are arranged in detail. A short description of the system follows.

The proposed intermediary system for Africa contains a number of simplifications compared to SNA, but also extends the SNA on important points. The criteria which governed the choice of tables included in the system were (1) simplicity of compilation, (2) feasibility, and (3) the needs of the planner for a general assessment of the structure and growth of the economy. All main tables which represent necessary intermediate steps in the compilation of the entire set of accounts have been included. The emphasis is placed on a low, rather than a high, level of aggregation of economic flows as being better adapted to the treatment of statistical series of uneven quality.

The main simplifications compared to SNA are: the capital reconciliation account of households and private nonprofit institutions has been omitted (the only SNA account or table entirely omitted from the system); depreciation estimates are not required; national income by factor shares has been shown before final appropriation of interest, dividends, and corporate transfer payments; consumer debt interest has been omitted; all transfers have been treated as current transfers.

The SNA system has been extended by the inclusion of five extra tables and accounts, namely, an account of uses and resources by commodity group; an appropriation account of corporations; an agricultural rural household account; a combined economic and functional classification of general government current and capital expenditures; and, finally, an inventory account of human resources.

The account of uses and resources by commodity group is a central feature of the system. Document E/CN.14/NAC 7 states that this account "provides a logical framework within which to balance the various uses and resources of each commodity or group of commodities, both in terms of quantity (when relevant) and values." Such a commodity analysis "is a quick and logical way of obtaining, through the reconciliation of the product and expenditure approaches, an overall picture of the economy, including the main aggregates of production, consumption and capital formation". Also, "these accounts of uses and resources by commodity, used in conjunction with inventories of available human and material resources, can be of great help to the planner in establishing production targets."

The analysis of the domestic product by industrial origin is considered as absolutely essential and is therefore built into the main part of the system, while it is treated as a supplementary table in SNA. The account for domestic product by industry is closely connected with the account for uses and resources by commodity group, since gross production values and inputs necessary to derive value added in the former account are derived from the latter account.

The appropriation account of corporation which is added to the SNA accounts in the system is "justified by the fact that it forms a logical part of a fully articulated system of appropriation accounts." It is stated that it "is already or will be in not too distant future within the reach of many African countries. The sources of information would be income tax returns, special enquiries concerning enterprises in the form of (1) censuses of agriculture, industrial production and distribution, and services, (2) special returns calling for information on business profits and losses and appropriation accounts." A similar account could probably with advantage be included in an eventual national accounting system adapted to Latin-American conditions.

The agricultural rural household account is also an addition to the accounts presently included in the SNA. This account contains the bulk of imputations required for estimating the value of subsistence activities within an economy. Such an account could also be usefully included for the countries of this region. A considerable

amount of information referring specifically to the economic transactions of rural households would, however, be necessary to fill it in
and this should be taken into consideration in planning rural household surveys in the various countries.

The system includes three accounts for the general government
sector, because of the great role played by government transactions
in the economies. The current part of the general government account of SNA is left unchanged, while the capital reconciliation part
of the account is expanded into a separate capital and financing account, which for general government gives information which could
later be expanded into a full analysis of financial transactions. In
addition, an economic and functional classification of all government transactions is included, based on the recommendations of
the United Nations *Manual* as amended by various workshops on
Budget Reclassification and Management. The basic material
needed to fill in similar accounts is also available for the countries
of this region.

List of Basic Statistics

It is impossible to make a standard list of statistical series applicable to all countries of the region, because the relative importance
of the producing sectors will determine the order of urgency for
the various parts of a statistical program and the use of statistical
resources. As an illustration, Haiti will have to make a great effort
in the field of agricultural statistics, while Argentina should take
great care with manufacturing statistics.

Several tentative efforts to draw up a basic list of statistics applicable to countries just embarking on economic and social development have been made, notably by the United Nations. The present
paper will try to adapt such a list to the special conditions prevailing in Latin-American countries, because the institutional context,
the level of income, and the structure of production may differ from
those of areas generally considered as underdeveloped.

As the quality of data depends on the way they are obtained, a
brief description will be given of the methods of estimation which
seem most appropriate, although the choice will be determined by
administrative practices and other factors which characterize a
given country. Needless to say, reference to the methods is only in-
dicative, as they should have to be dicussed in greater detail. In
each field the standards approved by the U.N. Statistical Commission will be used.

Population and Labor Statistics. The following data are needed for each year:[6]

1. Estimates of total population.
2. Estimates of total population by major territorial divisions.
3. Estimates of population by age groups.
4. Number of births and deaths by sex (and age for deaths).
5. Number of international migrants (only when it is important).
6. De facto population in large cities.
7. Estimates of rural and urban population.
8. Estimates of economically active population by large sectors (agriculture, mining, manufacturing, construction, transportation, government services, and other services).
9. Number of unemployed people.

Methods. If the registration of births and deaths is reliable and if international migration is adequately measured (or negligible), it must be possible to estimate 1, 2, and 3 by an extrapolation of census data.

If the registration is deficient[7], 1, 2 and 3 may be estimated in a cruder way, according to assumptions made regarding the rates of fertility and mortality. It is important to register the population in large cities because of its great interest in measuring the trend of urbanization.

A sampling survey on population by economic activity, as distinct from establishment surveys, will help in the estimation of employment by large sectors, as well as for an estimate of unemployment.

Agriculture, Forestry, and Fishing. Apart from data requirements mentioned elsewhere (employment, capital formation, loans, etc.) the following intercensal data are needed for each year:

1. Land improvements by areas cleared, newly irrigated, etc.
2. Estimates of the number of agricultural tractors, by power, size, etc.
3. Estimates of consumption of main inputs: seeds (by product), energy, pesticides, packing material, etc.
4. Quantities produced by main crops, increase in livestock, slaughtering of animals, and production of milk and dairy products.
5. Areas sown and harvested and yields for main crops.
6. Prices paid to farmers for main products and prices paid by farmers for main inputs and investments.

---

[6]It is assumed that decennial censuses are taken as recommended in *1960 World Population Census Programme. Draft International Recommendations,* Statistical Office of the United Nations.

[7]Obviously, in that case, an improvement of the registration system should be undertaken. However, it would probably take several years to reach an acceptable degree of accuracy.

7. Estimates of average wage rates for agricultural workers (by region if there are large regional differences).

8. Volume of sawn wood removals by coniferous and nonconiferous.

9. Landing of fish, by kind.

Statistics for this sector are extremely difficult to collect, because of the large number of producers, the wide range of products, the fact that small producers consume a relatively large part of their products, and also because they are very reluctant to fill in questionnaires. An additional difficulty regarding inputs is that most of them do not constitute a more or less constant proportion of the gross production due to the wide annual fluctuations of yields.

When purely administrative statistics are collected by the way of questionnaires filled in by local civil servants, data suffer much from the crude character of these estimates and the apparent advantage of having a large coverage is of limited help when the basic data are not sufficiently reliable.

It has been found in many countries that meaningful agricultural statistics can be collected at a relatively low cost by using sampling techniques. This will provide more specific data regarding yields, inputs, wages, farm consumption, etc. The statistics so obtained can, of course, be supplemented or checked by those from other sources.

The quality of forestry statistics will depend much on the grade of concentration of the production, as well as on the system of data collection. This is equally true for fishing statistics, for which only deliveries to markets or factories can be measured.

Mining, Manufacturing, Construction, and Energy. The following data are needed (at least annually):
Mining:

1. Production of main minerals (quantities); for metallic minerals, quantities in metal content for the various classes of minerals (monthly or quarterly).

2. Gross value of production for each important mineral and industry.

3. Value of inputs (with some detail).

4. Value added, for each industry.

5. Employment, man-hours worked, wages and salaries, for each industry.

6. Fixed capital formation and value of stocks by type, for each industry.

7. Prices for main products (monthly).

When most of the production is exported, the statistician is tempted to rely on export statistics for his production figures. These, however, do not provide all details required and are conceptually different from production data. An establishment survey should be taken annually, covering all the larger production units.[8]

Manufacturing. Data required for manufacturing are numerous and some of them are of a complex nature. A full list of statistics recommended for publication is given in a UN statistical document, *International Recommendations in Basic Industrial Statistics,* which can be summarized as follows:

8. Employment, man-hours worked, wages and salaries, for each industry.
9. Fixed capital formation and value of stocks by type, for each industry.
10. Value and quantity of inputs, by type, for each industry.
11. Gross value of production, quantity and value of individually important products, for each industry.

Construction. The same kind of data as for manufacturing should be gathered for construction through an establishment survey. This will provide data of special interest for inputs, wages, and capital formation in construction industry. However, it will not have a sufficient coverage as far as construction by type is concerned. Apart from 8, 9, 10, and 11, the following data are needed:

12. Completion of dwellings (number, area, and value).
13. Completion of nonresidential buildings by type: private or public, industrial buildings, schools, etc. (number, area, and value).
14. Completion of other construction by type (area and value).
15. For 12, 13, 14 work in process.
16. For 13 and 14 building permits (number, area, and estimated value).

Administrative statistics may be used for this kind of data when the construction activities are subject to sufficiently strict regulations. For public construction, a centralized agency may exist in the country and, in combination with government accounts, would be the most adequate source of information.

Energy. The production of petroleum, gas, and coal, and their processing, will be covered either by the mining or the manufacturing surveys, so that production data should be collected only for electricity. In addition, data are needed for a balance of energy by types of products and by main sectors of use.

17. Maximum capacity and average production of electric plants by type (and also for the public system and self-producers).
18. Monthly electricity production of the public system by type.

---

[8]For the methodology, see *Industrial Censuses and Related Enquiries,* United Nations.

19. Consumption of fuels by electricity plants.
20. Consumption of electricity by sector of economic activity.
21. Fixed capital formation of electricity plants by type.
22. Annual balance of energy by type of final energy and consumption by main sectors.

Data for the public electricity sector should be gathered through an establishment survey. For self-producers the data would have to come from establishment surveys covering the various sectors which produce part of their energy.

Transportation. The main requirements for water, railway, road, and air transport, separately, are as follows:

1. Length of railways by gauge and length of roads by type; both given for each major administrative division (annually).
2. Number, power, capacity, etc. of vehicles (annually).
3. Tonnage of goods loaded and unloaded in domestic and international traffic, by commodity class (monthly).
4. Number of passenger—kilometres in domestic and international traffic (monthly).
5. Gross capital formation by type (annually).
6. Employment, wages, and salaries (annually).
7. Gross value of services performed during the period (monthly).
8. Consumption of energy by type (annually).

For water, railway, and air transport it should be possible to rely on administrative sources of data. This, however, may require some reorganization of administrative practices. For road transport, series 1 and 2 should also be available easily, while exhaustive data on traffic would be nearly impossible to collect. It is recommended that sampling surveys be used for obtaining these latter data for the transportation of goods and passengers by private road transport.

Private Services. For all other sectors it has been assumed that bench-mark data are available as a result of at least decennial censuses. For the various types of private services, most countries of the region have not yet taken any census and are not intending to do so in the near future. Annual indicators for this field are extremely scarce and weak, so that an estimate of the product is extremely difficult to make.

It is sometimes said that because these statistics are not of first priority, statistical resources should not be "wasted" in expensive surveys on trade and other private services. In most cases, however, it seems necessary to take special surveys for a sample of establishments, because census or current data on employment and estimates of markups based on price statistics cannot suffice for estimating even the order of magnitude of the sector product. Depending on the country, social security statistics could be used for estimating employment and wages and salaries. Other types of income, however, should be investigated independently. In some cases, such as banking, annual statements of accounts of the establishments could be used.

Prices and Finance. Prices should be collected for each of the main items of input and output of goods and services for each sector. Such prices could, in many cases, be derived from values and quantities of gross production or trade. However, these "unit values" are not sufficient for an analysis of price changes and a number of price surveys for well-defined items should be conducted.

Consumer price statistics are of special importance as an indicator of inflationary pressures and also as an essential measure of the purchasing power of the currency. This type of statistics should be collected, not only in the capital city, but also in various parts of the country.

When computing price indexes, the weighting should correspond to the use which will be made of the data. The commodity structure used as weights should normally be available as a by-product of statistics listed in this section. For consumer price indexes relating to specific types of consumption patterns (for example, for wage earners), the weighting should be based on data collected through household surveys.

The availability of financial and monetary statistics depends much on the institutional aspects of the banking and monetary sector. In all cases, great effort should be made to obtain the following information:

1. Balance of payments according to the standards defined by the International Monetary Fund (annual).
2. Account of operations in foreign exchange (quarterly).
3. Gross foreign exchange reserves of the central bank (gold *plus* foreign exchange assets available on demand during the next 12 months).
4. Net foreign exchange reserves of the central bank (gold *plus* foreign exchange assets *less* foreign exchange liabilities available on demand during the next twelve months).
5. 3 and 4, if possible, for the main commercial banks.
6. Current position of the central bank (quarterly).
7. Amount of the external public debt classified according to maturities (twice a year).
8. Amount of long-term loans by functional type (annual).
9. Amount of short-term loans by institutional type, that is, according to the economic activity of the recipients (twice a year).

External Trade. The following data should be made available with a minimum of delay:

1. Total imports and exports (monthly).
2. Commodity composition of imports and exports according to SITC items (monthly).
3. Breakdown of imports and exports according to "economic classifications" (annually): by industry of origin, by end user sector, by stage of processing.
4. Indexes of quantum, unit value of imports and exports, and terms of trade (monthly).
5. Trade by countries of origin and destination (monthly).
6. Trade by countries of origin and destination and by SITC commodity groups (annually).

Trade data suffer much from errors in declared values, owing to the large number of factors in the assessment or to declarations deliberately falsified. Quantities may also be distorted due to the use of a conventional unit weight instead of the actual weight. The countries should quickly improve their trade statistics, not only because of the excise duties, but also because of their great interest for economic policy.

Large improvements are necessary to shorten the delay in tabulation. Most data should be available no more than two months after the period to which they relate.

In the tabulation by "economic classifications" a number of assumptions have to be made regarding the final destination of the goods or their origin, etc. This should not, however, inhibit the statistician.

New Statistical Activities

Although this paper is not intended to review the organizational aspects of the national statistical offices, a number of specific statistical activities, such as sampling, which would require a certain amount of new statistical resources and some administrative reorganization, have been referred to.

In most countries, censuses of population, housing, agriculture, mining, and manufacturing are taken at more or less decennial intervals. Tremendous efforts have to be made for the technical preparation of these censuses, the training of enumerators, the tabulation of data, etc. Unfortunately, the amount of experience acquired in that way is not fully capitalized upon because many of the persons engaged in a particular census do not participate in the following ones, due to the long interval of time between them. This is an inherent weakness of censuses, as far as improvement in statistical knowledge is concerned.

On the contrary, the collection of data and the statistical elaborations required by the continuous series listed above will quickly produce a great improvement in knowledge and experience of the statistical staff engaged in this work. It will be necessary, of course, that acceptable salaries and other working conditions be offered to qualified statisticians in each national office. The pressure of requests from the planning office for good and readily available statistics would help the statistical office to build up an efficient statistical system, provided the political decision to make the necessary investments in statistics is taken. This latter condition is, of course, determinant.

A high grade of centralization is needed in statistical activities, because it is a necessary condition for obtaining consistency of data in the various fields, a flexible use of scarce specialists (such as in sampling) and a good coordination between the primary collection of data and their processing. In cases where data come first as a by-product of an administrative registration (foreign trade, population registry, etc.), and then are further processed by the central statistical office, this coordination will be essential, and facilities should be given to the statistical office for introducing appropriate innovations in purely administrative data collections.

The consistency of data regarding basic concepts and classifications is of special importance when figures from various sources have to be assembled in macroeconomic tables, such as national accounts. It will be essential, for instance, to have a common classification of goods for production and foreign trade if such data should be used according to the commodity flow method for an estimate of expenditure and of balances by commodity groups.[9]

Sampling techniques have been referred to in many parts of this paper, especially when other techniques could not be used in Latin-American countries because of the formidable task they would imply. This is the case for a large number of fields, such as employment and unemployment, agriculture (crop and livestock production, yields by crop cutting, prices paid and received by farmers),

---

[9]As an attempt to solve this problem of common classification, the Statistical Division of ECLA has prepared a draft list of all industrial activities for groups 201 to 399 of the *International Standard Industrial Classification* with a key for the classification of the main products according to the *Standard International Trade Classification*. In spite of many conceptual and practical difficulties, it is hoped that this attempt might be of use in solving the kind of problem mentioned above.

fisheries, household industries, construction, road transport, household surveys, private savings, nutrition, housing conditions, etc. They can also be used for pretabulation of large censuses.

Because of these numerous purposes, it is essential to have in each country a permanent team of sampling specialists and interviewers. Such investment would produce, at a relatively low cost, an immediate improvement in a large number of essential statistical series.

b. COMMENT
Raymond Goldsmith

The brief remarks which I am going to make will deal only parenthetically with the paper of Messy and Pedersen. The reason for this is that the paper says hardly anything on the statistics which are specifically relevant to the analysis of inflation. Everybody, no doubt, will endorse the authors' statement that "all the statistical instruments for an intelligent credit policy should be quickly available," but these two lines are hardly sufficient, without considerable elaboration, to help us in deciding what statistics we need to analyze the inflationary process in Latin-American countries or how we can get these figures or the least objectionable substitutes for them. I shall, therefore, limit myself to two comments, one negative and one positive. The social accounting system suggested by Messy and Pedersen, while of some merit as an ultimate goal, is in many directions much too ambitious to serve as a guide for improvements that can and should be made in the national accounts of the Latin-American republics during the next few years. On the other hand, I regret the limitation of the paper to the income and product account once one is as ambitious as Messy and Pedersen, and would have liked a discussion of the problems and possibilities of a comparatively integrated system of national accounts for Latin-American countries. On the positive side, I should like to endorse two suggestions made by Messy and Pedersen: the development of statements of material balances, Soviet style it must be admitted; and the greater emphasis on sampling as a source of data. I hope these two suggestions will receive in the discussion the attention they deserve.

The main point I want to make concerns the development of a

system of financial statistics which will provide both the operating authorities and academic observers with reasonably reliable information on the essential features of the process of inflation. There is not time, of course, to discuss in any detail exactly what data are needed, how they can be obtained, and into what statistical framework they should be fitted.

In the long run, the goal undoubtedly is an integrated and comprehensive system of financial accounts covering both flows and stocks. The difficulties certainly are formidable. Nevertheless, such a system appears less utopian in a situation such as prevails in most Latin-American countries than it does in the nonfinancial field. In finance, the sources of information are more concentrated—primarily in the central bank, the commercial banks, and the treasury—and may be presumed to be more inclined to cooperate with the statistical authorities than is the case in many other sectors of the economy. One of the most serious problems is the lack of adequate records of capital movements across boundaries. The beginning in the construction of such a system of financial statistics has been made in a few Latin-American countries—I am aware of such attempts in Mexico and Venezuela—and continued experimentation and gradual expansion should be encouraged.

For the immediate future, however, we shall have to be less ambitious in most countries. One possibility here is to arrange the statistical data around the main terms of the quantity equation (or identity). The minimum of information needed concerns the volume and velocity of the main types of money, the volume and prices of the main components of output; the latter, of course, constitute part of the statistics of national product. I shall, therefore, refrain from specific suggestions except to stress the need for much better information on changes in inventories in both industry and trade.

Every country has some information on the volume of money, but the need is for much more detailed figures than are usually available on the distribution of currency and bank deposits among the relevant economic sectors, and on the velocity of turnover on these deposits. In addition to these basic components of the quantity equation, we need, at least, a breakdown by borrowing sector and size of credit, of bank credits and of credits extended by other financial institutions. In an inflation of the intensity experienced in many Latin-American countries, credit is close to subsidies. It is, therefore, very important to know the immediate beneficiaries of inflationary expansion. We also need much better current data on business profits. Such data should not be beyond reach in the sectors dominated by a few firms. They will encounter considerable difficulties in other sectors, difficulties to be overcome, if at all, only by the judicious use of sampling.

The exact character of the data will vary from country to country, depending on the structure of financial institutions and the maturity of the country's statistical organization. What is important is that a reasonable comparability among countries be kept in mind. I hope and trust that the IMF will continue, and even intensify and accelerate, the efforts it has been making in this direction.

My experience in a few Latin-American countries, short as it has been, has convinced me that what will decide the success or value of any attempt to improve the statistics needed for the analysis of inflation are not so much technical problems—we know from experience elsewhere how to solve these—as the interest shown in these figures by the top level authorities. I would go so far as to say that, under Latin-American conditions, unless the president of the central bank, or better still, the president of the republic, really wants these figures, we will not get them. The influence of the civil service, which may suffice for such purposes in Europe and North America, is not strong enough in Latin America to overcome the obstacles—whether lethargy, obscurantism, or cost—which will be raised not only by the financial institutions that must furnish most of the data, but also by the old-line statistical organizations themselves.

So far I have dealt only with the future. But as an academician, I am also interested in the history of inflation in Latin America. Indeed, I doubt that we will be able to understand the inflationary problems that are facing Latin America in the years to come unless we know much more about past course, present course, and future effects of inflation in Latin America, and unless we are able to make truly comparative studies on inflation and economic growth in a number of Latin-American countries back to at least the turn of the century. I would, therefore, like to close with a concrete suggestion that would provide at least a starting point for such an analytical history of inflation in Latin America. I suggest that for each Latin-American republic, or at least the dozen larger ones, there be prepared an abstract of the main financial data and other statistics that are relevant to the analysis of an inflation. Each series should be carried as far back as information is available. It should be accompanied—and this is a very important aspect—by sufficient comments on content and sources to enable the reader to appraise each series' reliability and consistency over time and its comparability with similar data in other Latin-American countries. The relevant sections of *Historical Statistics of the United States* are a good example of what I have in mind, although the number of series included for each country would be only a fraction of what we have in the United States, and the length of most series would be considerably less. This, of course, would have to be a cooperative project because in general only the domestic government or academic statistician will have the required detailed familiarity with the figures. However, central direction will be needed to develop the framework; to select the series needed; to insure a reasonable degree of comparability among countries; and to evaluate critically the quality of the data. Is it too much to hope that one of the international or regional economic organizations will interest itself in this project?

c. COMMENT

Charles F. Schwartz

NOTE TO READER: For this Comment, turn to Appendix A at the end of the book.

5. ORGANIZATIONAL PROBLEMS

a. ORGANIZATIONAL REQUIREMENTS FOR STABILITY AND GROWTH

Luis Escobar C.

I. INTRODUCTION

I apologize to my readers for the possible disjointedness of some parts of this paper, a result of the lack of time for greater refinement in preparation. The heavy tasks that fall upon the Minister of Economy in an underdeveloped country leave only a narrow margin for academic activities. Likewise, I apologize for the discrepancies between what I could have stated as a professor of economics free from political responsibilities, and the ideas which follow, heavily influenced by experience in the exercise of the follow, heavily influenced by experience in the ministry of economics.

In the following discussion, I want to stress that the frame of reference corresponds to a "mixed economy" where both the private and public sectors own means of production and are entrepreneurs; where a democratic political system prevails, with political parties, labor unions, and other organized "pressure groups" which influence economic and political decisions.

II. THE BACKGROUND OF THE PROBLEM

We understand that the present paper need not justify the necessity to accelerate economic development. On the contrary, we take it for granted.

To answer the fundamental question which we have posed requires, however, that we answer another one first: what is meant by economic development with stability? We will understand it as a process of development at a rate faster than the historical one achieved until now, which should be accompanied simultaneously by: (1) full employment, (2) sectorial and geographical harmony, (3) monetary stability, and (4) foreign trade stability. Sectorial and geographical harmony should be interpreted in the sense of avoiding sectorial bottlenecks, shortages of capital or human factors, or

146

the lagging of any geographical region too far behind the rest of the country.

We consider any process of development not complying with the aforementioned requisites as one inherently containing germs of instability. For example, the appearance of an unemployment situation obliges the withdrawal of financial resources which were reserved, or could have been reserved, for the execution of specific investment programs whose interruption or postponement could damage the overall rate of development in the country. If one sector of production, say agriculture, lags behind, this also introduces elements of instability into the economic process.

It is convenient, perhaps, to expand on the last point. Economic growth is, in general, regarded as progress primarily in industrial activities and as an increase in general services. This implies that income increments mainly benefit urban sectors of the population.

Since in underdeveloped countries per capita income is quite low, the population allocates a very high and almost constant proportion of its income to the consumption of agricultural products. The demand for these products therefore increases secularly, whereas their supply increases more slowly (agriculture lags, relatively). The opposite takes place with nonagricultural products. Hence, a secularly increasing trend prevails in prices of agricultural products. As these prices have a very heavy weight in the cost of living index, the process implies also a chronic upward trend in that index. And as this is the point of reference for negotiations on the levels of wages and salaries, workers demand periodic adjustments in their compensation which frequently exceed normal increments in productivity. Industrial enterprises and the government cannot escape the demands of these sectors of the population. The result is that, in view of the fiscal impossibility of subsidies for those enterprises and of increased tax revenues for the government, the latter is compelled to get additional resources through a budget deficit financed by the central bank. Thus the internal price level is raised for the whole economy, reconciling thereby the final level of real wages with that allowed by normal increments in productivity.

III. ORGANIZATION FOR DEVELOPMENT WITH STABILITY

The National Development Plan

Rather than extend the preceding discussion for each of the sources of instability mentioned, we prefer to leap immediately to the statement of a thesis: the free operation of market forces guarantees neither faster economic development, nor stability, nor both at once.

As we see it, it is irrelevant to discuss whether, in the past, market forces have been free to operate. Perhaps in no Latin-American economy has there been a case of a free market economy during a period long enough for the fruition of the benefits of such systems. Economists have never clarified just how much time a free market economy requires to demonstrate its merits. It is our impression that, in the Latin-American countries, impatience for progress more rapid than that guaranteed by such a system has led to open state intervention.

This impression contains a scorn for the promises of a free market economy, because the progress achieved by Latin-American communities from the last century until today is far from the spectacular results achieved in the European countries or in North America from the industrial revolution until now. The pressure felt in an underdeveloped country to achieve higher consumption levels is extremely strong, not only as a result of prevailing low standards of living, but also from the powerful impact of the "demonstration effect," both domestic and international, upon the expectations of the majority of the population.

Nevertheless, we insist that it is irrelevant to argue whether the free market economy has had its opportunity in the past, because there is no reason to think it will have it in the future. The prevailing impression, which sustains our own convictions, is that in countries with one main product, as the Latin-American countries, it is impossible for the state to remain passive. The most varied decisions taken by companies, or even just one firm, or by a labor union, at times one whose membership is very small, have repercussions throughout the national economy. This situation obliges us to seek other systems of economic organization to accelerate growth and to guarantee its achievement with stability. As an answer we find planning.

We shall interpret a national plan for economic development to mean a coherent and detailed system of economic policy, resulting from an objective examination of the possibilities for accelerating the progress of a country. In the planned economy, delicate questions come up as to organization; for example, who shall prepare the plans? Who accepts or rejects the national plan? What ought to be in the plan? How far shall the intervention of the state go? How shall the plan be put into practice?

In the process of formulating the development plan, the needs for investment in physical and human capital are identified and evaluated in order to expand the stock of existing capital and to decide its best allocation, with the object of achieving a higher level of incomes. With present income and habitual consumption, the margin of savings appears insufficient. Investments in excess of present savings levels could be financed by (1) freezing present per capita consumption levels as income rises, (2) incurring external indebtedness, or (3) incurring a greater external indebtedness and permitting a small secular increase in per capita consumption.

In the formulation of a plan a rate of economic growth is chosen that is consistent with the full employment of productive factors, with a determinate standard of living for the population in the short run, and *very important,* with a certain distribution of national income.

Obviously, these and other decisions not mentioned are of profound political significance. Thus, *who* plans appears to be a substantial problem in organization for development. In my judgment, there are two alternatives: (1) the plan may be prepared by a specialized technical organization similar to a research institute, or (2) it may be prepared by a technical group including representatives or delegates of the diverse sectors, public and private, that will be in charge of the realization of investment programs.

Alternative (2) has the advantage of relating those who formulate the plan with those who will have to make it a reality, and therefore appears preferable in theory. Nonetheless, we must abide by the reality of the vast majority of underdeveloped countries. What is this reality? As we see it, one of its principal characteristics is the acute shortage of specialists in the various subjects requiring —let us say—good scientific and technical university training. Thus it is exteremely difficult to arrange for the leading executives, both in the private and the public sector, to have time to dedicate themselves exclusively to the study and preparation of a plan as well as to the normal direction of their organizations. These executives have little time to think in terms of national planning. I realize that many of my colleagues from European countries or from North America will consider this assertion highly debatable, but I am certain that my colleagues from Latin-American countries will easily understand what I am trying to explain. This is the main reason that in Chile, as in other countries, the decision was for alternative (1).

Alternative (1) signifies that the countries must have an *ad hoc* group to prepare and formulate the plan, with the aid of foreign advice. This group must maintain contact with, and know the aspirations of, the diverse sectors, geographic zones, and significant economic organizations of the nation. This group will take transcendental decisions of the sort we mentioned above, and will establish priorities with criteria that will not necessarily coincide with those which the government has had or has at present.

For this reason, when alternative (1) is applied, once the plan is formulated a second stage consists in explaining it to the political authorities of the government and to the principal groups of the private sector, all of whom have been heard during the formulation stage. As a result of this second stage, it may be necessary to reformulate the plan. Once approved by the government, the plan becomes the definitive program, subject to periodic revisions that may be necessary.

From what has been said before, it is clear that we consider that it is the executive branch of the government that must approve the plan: the President of the Republic and his ministers. It is these authorities, principally, upon whom lies the responsibility for progress in the community and for exhausting all available means and efforts to achieve it. This is as natural as is the responsibility of the legislative power, for example, to control the actions of the executive and to be sure that the latter does not exceed his powers. Thus, the approval of the plan by congress, should it be judged necessary, would not be more than a formality, more or less politically important, regarding a decision taken by the government.

To insure speed in the implementation of the plan, in the control of its development and its explanation to the citizenry, and in domestic and international negotiations for its financing, it must be copiously backed up with specific projects. The plan without such backing is no more than an argument, objectively documented, as to the progress which could be achieved if economic activity were to be conducted along the lines suggested by the plan. Such an argument should be understood, however, as an emphatic suggestion for the preparation of specific projects within the limits of the plan. Thus an unavoidable responsibility and function of organization for planning is the recognition of the necessity of complementing the plan with projects, and of guaranteeing the existence of resources and institutional mechanisms such that these projects can appear promptly and in satisfactory quality and quantity.

In the organization for planning, one must never forget that one of the worst bottlenecks that can appear in the realization of the plan is the lack of specific projects in the various investment categories contemplated by the plan. These projects should be prepared in such a way that it will be simple to verify their harmony with the plan, their internal justification, and their conformity with the requirements of international organizations (to the extent that external financing is required).

Each country will resolve this problem according to its own characteristics; nonetheless, several general observations might be in order. It may be desirable that the projects be prepared in the very institutions that subsequently will be responsible for carrying them out. Briefly, the alternative is to prepare them in a decentralized form or, on the contrary, to create a central office in charge of project preparation. We believe that a good solution is to give this responsibility to a national economic committee, which can delegate these functions to its technical secretariat or to the organization preferred in each country for its location and rank in the public administration, and for its technical competence. This committee should stipulate general norms to all public offices, according to which each office will prepare the investment projects for which it will be responsible.

Each ministry or institution should therefore have a project office, with the necessary staff to prepare not only those investment projects already contemplated in the plan but, gradually, a larger number of projects which will document and back up successive revisions of the plan. This arrangement will resolve the problem so far as the public sector is concerned. All developing countries that want to have an adequate number of projects will probably need foreign consultants, for lack of sufficient number of specialized personnel. These advisers should be located in the institution corresponding to their specialities.

The private sector also needs attention and help. The central organization in charge of this responsibility ought to provide the private sector with technical assistance, both national and international, for the preparation and evaluation of projects. In addition, it ought to make loans to finance their cost. In many cases, it may be advisable for the government itself—through this central office—to prepare and evaluate a set of projects which can be turned over to the private sector for implementation. Obviously, various formulas could be discussed for the financing of the cost of such studies.

The National Economic Committee

Starting the plan demands discipline on the part of the various organizations that will have to submit to its guidelines. This requires coherence among monetary, credit, financial, tax, and foreign exchange policy; internal and external coherence, in prices and remunerations; coherence in the investment policies of various public and private organizations.

Who, then, must take the decisions to assure the satisfaction of these requisites?

It can be seen that putting the plan into practice involves matters within the competence of different ministries and of public corporations which enjoy certain degrees of autonomy. It can also be seen that the discipline required by the plan makes it necessary that the decisions come from the highest level of authority. Thus; the existence of a national economic committee appears highly desirable. The committee includes the ministers of state whose portfolios belong to what we might call the economic sector, as well as the top authorities of those semiautonomous corporations whose field of action is also important in the economic sector. This committee should meet weekly to discuss current problems whose solutions must be accepted jointly by distinct ministries or corporations, as well as to report periodically on the progress of the plan within the field directed by each member of the committee. The president of this committee should be that minister with the greatest responsibility, after the president of the Republic, for the execution of the plan—that is, the Minister of Planning.

The Ministry of Planning

It appears to us, then, that just as there is a Ministry of Agriculture, of Public Works, of Finance, etc., there must be a Ministry of Planning whose head, the Minister of Planning, ought to be a public functionary with very few routine administrative obligations, so that he can dedicate himself completely to the discussion of the nature of those changes which periodically must be made in the national plan, to the control of its functioning, and to decisions as to the measures which must be adopted to resolve unforeseen contingencies during the application of the plan. The Minister of Planning should preside at meetings of the national economic committee. In order that he might have a maximum of stability in his function, although he would be named by the President of the Republic, the President should be able to remove this minister only if the dismissal is ratified by the senate.

In our opinion, based on experience acquired during the exercise of an important public function, this Ministry should have four major divisions:

1. The Bureau (*Dirección*) of Budgets
2. The Bureau of Planning
3. The Bureau of External Credit
4. The Bureau of Statistics.

The Bureau of Planning should be the body in charge of preparing national plans, of maintaining necessary contacts with the public and private sectors, and of popular explanation of the national plan.

The Bureau of Budgets would be the organization in charge of assigning public funds and budget resources in accordance with the requirements of the plan. The Bureau of Budgets thus appears as the organization responsible directly for the execution of the plan.

The Bureau of External Credit would be in charge of the coordination of external financing for the various investment projects in which the public sector participates, directly or indirectly, and would maintain appropriate contacts between the government and the international financial institutions.

The Bureau of Statistics, as its name indicates, would be in charge of collecting, centralizing, tabulating, interpreting, and publishing the statistics of national interest, and especially those necessary for the preparation of plans and for the control of their execution.

Regional Planning Committees

A necessary complement to this scheme is the existence of regional planning committees, each corresponding ideally to an economic region in accordance with the economic geography of the country. The corresponding organization may, however, run into grave difficulties whenever the regions distinguished by the political administration of the country (provinces, departments, states, counties, etc.) do not coincide with these regions as distinguished economically. It is highly probable that such difficulties would occur frequently. As each region has its political authority, and each regional planning committee also would have its own authority, difficult problems of subordination, power, and hierarchy would present themselves in every case in which the regional planning committee included more than one political region, and/or parts of them. In these cases, we believe that, unless there were willingness to restructure the entire political-administrative organization of the country, it would be preferable to recognize the supremacy of the present administrative structure and to create local committees, in accordance with it, leaving the full reform mentioned until later.

The regional planning committees should include representatives of both the public and the private sectors. Their function should be that of studying specific problems of economic development in their respective regions, suggesting solutions to the Bureau of Planning, collaborating with the latter in checking on the physical and financial progress of the tasks of the public sector in each region, and collaborating with the Bureau of Statistics in its respective tasks at the regional level. These committees should also be responsible for communicating to the Minister of Planning those regional problems which, though not contemplated in the national development plan, require government action for their solution.

In accordance with the organization so briefly described, it is possible to solve problems of formulating a national development plan with counterparts at the regional level, as well as the corresponding regional administrative problems.

Policy as to Remunerations

No mention has yet been made of one of the instability factors named above: that of the remuneration of factors of production, which is intimately linked with the distribution of the national income. In our countries, we are witnessing a competition within and between capital and salaried sectors to maximize relative shares of the national income, as well as to raise incomes. They apply pressures via prices and via salaries, respectively.

This struggle introduces monetary, social, and political instability into the economic system and thus, to economic development. To the extent that such competition worsens and dominates the political scene, uncertainties are introduced for investors. This depressing element restricts entrepreneurial initiative and harms the growth rate. We say that it introduces political instability, for it drags down political representatives, congressmen, city councilmen, etc., who must answer to electoral groups that are structured, roughly, into groups of either hired workers or businessmen, whose interests appear to be in conflict. Every time congressmen succumb to the pressure of small groups, either of workers or of businessmen, their attitude may damage the national interest. If the wage policy or the price policy were the subject of congressional initiative, the pressure groups would win because congressmen are afraid of falling into "electoral unpopularity."

We have said that this competition introduces monetary instability as well. The firms that cannot resist the pressure of the labor unions yield, but on condition that the government—fearing un-

employment—concede subsidies to the firms. Improvised and volum-
inous subsidies make an impact on the fiscal treasury. Fiscal revenues are already obligated for operating costs which are difficult to
reduce, for other subsidies whose elimination would provoke disturbances equal to those which it is now sought to avoid, and for
investment outlays whose reduction would, in turn, provoke unemployment.

Congressional approval of laws for new or higher taxes is slow,
and their yield, moreover, reaches the treasury much later. Worse
still, the congressmen themselves defend the taxpayer against higher
taxes. Therefore, within the present political and constitutional
organization, and in order to respect their investment programs,
our governments wind up with the monetary resource through
which the central bank creates an emission for the exchequer, providing the financing for the subsidy mentioned above. Thus, finally,
the price level rises, real wages are not improved as much as the
workers originally desired, employment and public investment are
protected, but monetary stability collapses—or, at least, is threatened.

Our political system conceives of the solution of money problems
between labor and business by backing the right to strike and out-
lawing the lockout. Coldly considered, the institution of the strike
is indisputably reactionary. Who can hold out longer in a strike?
As a result of imperfections in the capital market or, if you like,
as a result of norms that outlaw slavery and that consistently con-
secrate the human person (source of labor services) as unattachable,
it is clear that those who have material assets and thus have access
to credit—the businessmen—are the ones who can wait out a strike.
The workers cannot finance the waiting period because they have
no collateral or security to offer lenders. Economic cohesion among
wage earners themselves is poor; the monetary aid of those who
are working for those on strike is distributed, besides, with political
and personal favoritism. On the other hand, union funds—in relatively poor countries—are of no real importance.

Strikes impose high social costs. Moreover, the interruption of
certain productive operations can damage all activity in the country,
which is especially serious in countries with single product or single
export product structures.

The existence of a national organization to arbitrate these problems thus appears desirable: a national tribunal of conciliation. It
should include representatives of the wage earners, of employers,
and of the state (executive branch), with a majority of the latter.

The appointments of its members should permit a partial replacement of the tribunal from time to time. This tribunal would be the final arbiter in any dispute between workers and employers, in questions of prices, etc., and it would decide questions in accordance with the price and remunerations policy of the government. This policy, as we indicated earlier, must be explicit in the national development plan. Naturally, the decisions of the tribunal should be binding upon all sides.

I deliberately throw this problem out for debate because, to guarantee its effectiveness, any jurist would want to define in advance the punishments that would fall upon the litigants should they fail to comply with a decision of the national tribunal of conciliation. If the firm involved does not heed the ruling of the tribunal, how can the government force it to do so? If the union refuses to accept the ruling of the tribunal, will we be willing to dissolve it? Or to jail the necessary number of union leaders? I believe I have put a finger on a very important point in our political, social, and economic organization. As I see things, there is an incompatibility between development with monetary stability and the judicial, constitutional, and organizational pattern which governs our collective life and, especially, the relations between capital and labor.

IV. THE EXISTING SITUATION IN CHILE

As described above, we have established in Chile an organization for planning which includes as the group highest in the hierarchy for this area, something called COPERE (Comité de Programación Económica y de Reconstrucción, or Committee for Economic Programming and Reconstruction). This committee includes the Minister of Economy, Development, and Reconstruction, who presides at its meetings, as well as the ministers of Finance, of Public Works, of Lands and Colonization, of Agriculture, and of Mines. It also includes the Executive Vice-President and the General Manager of the Development Corporation (CORFO), the Executive Vice-President of the Housing Corporation (CORVI), the President of the Central Bank, the President of the State Bank, and the Director of the Budget.

Thus, the ministers of the "economic sector" and the highest executives of the financial and economic institutions of the state are represented in COPERE. The importance of this organization, as coordinator of economic policy and as the controller of the realization of the plan, induces the majority of the cabinet to attend its meetings, and the President of the Republic requests the opinion of COPERE in order to take important decisions in economic and financial matters.

The technical secretariat of COPERE is the Development Corporation (CORFO), an autonomous institution whose departments include the Bureau of Planning (the organization in charge of formulating the national plans). To assure compliance with the decisions taken in COPERE, not forgetting that "He who pays the piper calls the tune," a mechanism has been established that relates the delivery of fiscal funds to the various governmental departments to the fulfillment of the investment programs in the national development plan, programs which have been approved by the same COPERE.

Legislation in Chile orders that all capital budgets of the public sector be signed by the appropriate minister and also by the Finance Minister, the Minister of Economy, and the President of the Republic. COPERE has agreed that the ministers of Finance and Economy and the President will sign only with a previous approval of the Budget Director, who for this purpose has been named coordinator of the National Development Plan. The Budget Director has begun, in 1962, to institute a system of program budgets which will permit, in 1963, a control of each program; he will authorize drawings on fiscal funds in accordance with the progress of each program.

In his role as coordinator, the Budget Director works with a small team of experts, sectoral coordinators continually concerned with watching and pushing compliance with the plan within their respective sectors.

The integration of national and regional planning has been achieved with the creation of the Provincial Development Committees, as consultative organs of the central government. Their fundamental objective is the incorporation of the provinces in the study and analysis of the development plans and supervision of the fulfillment of the state investment programs. They thus constitute an extension to provincial level of the administrative and coordinating action of COPERE. In them, in addition to the technical advisers of CORFO, there are members named by the government, by the labor unions, and by associations of businessmen. The executive secretary function of the Provincial Committees is also in the hands of CORFO.

The Provincial Committees have also been assigned to the popular dissemination of the national development plan, explaining to

the country, and especially to their provinces, what the plan signifies.

In instituting the Provincial Committees we have preferred to
begin regionalization by identifying the economic division with the
existing political division, because of the advantages pointed out
earlier.

b. GOVERNMENTAL ORGANIZATION FOR GROWTH AND STABILITY

Harvey S. Perloff[1]

Whatever assumptions one may make as to the proper policies
for achieving self-sustaining economic growth without disruptive inflation, one element is inevitably present: a large and difficult role
for government. Therefore the nature of this role and the way in
which governments are organized to handle it become questions of
some importance.

Experience in various parts of the world has provided some valuable guidelines for managing economic affairs in countries seeking
rapid development, and practical men can readily find lessons for
application in setting up organizational arrangements and administrative processes in government. Learning from the successes or failures of other countries certainly makes good sense, but, in applying
experience from elsewhere it is extremely easy to miss the mark. It
is particularly easy to borrow ideas about organizational *form*—this
is often done under the heading of applying so-called "sound principles of administration"—and to overlook the question of *content,*
or the inherent rationale behind given arrangements which made
them effective in the first place in achieving the desired economic or
social objectives.

---

[1] I wish to express my thanks to a number of generous individuals who went
over an earlier draft and provided many valuable suggestions for improvements:
Robert E. Asher, H. Field Haviland, Jr., Felipe Pazos, Benjamin Hopenhayn,
Dankwart Rustow, Hiram S. Phillips, Jack Koteen, Gerhard Colm, and Albert
Waterston. Of course, they are not to blame for any of the shortcomings of this
paper.

The "Self-Sustained Growth" and "Nondevelopment" Models

A suggestive framework for viewing organizational requirements in government can be evolved by the use of what is known as an "ideal type" approach, applied selectively to the question of the appropriate role of government, the center of our concern. This approach, characterizing different states of being in more or less black-and-white terms, helps to bring into focus the essential differences and, therefore, the critical change factors in going from one state to another.[2]

The "ideal types" we want to compare are (1) the country characterized by nonself-sustaining economic growth, or the "nondevelopment model"; with (2) the country characterized over a substantial period of time by relatively rapid, self-sustaining development without disruptive inflation, or the "growth-stability model,"[3] both as representative essentially of twentieth-century situations.

Three elements would seem to be central to the governmental role in each case: the nature of the government services rendered, the approach to the reconciliation of conflicting interests, and the approach to international relations.

The first (or nondevelopment) situation is typified by the following roles of government: (1) the provision of limited (minimum) government services in response to the more powerful political pressures, (2) the reconciliation of conflicting interests around the existing economic structure and income distribution pattern, and (3) in international relations, the maintenance of prestige, the prevention of conquest, and the obtaining of help in intermittent international crises.

In a nondevelopment situation, the government is expected to provide at least a minimum of essential public services, including not only police and fire protection but also such services as educa-

---

[2] This is appropriate only when the variations are more of kind than of slight degree, as is the case here, otherwise we could not talk about "developed" and "underdeveloped" countries or "self-sustained growth" situations as against "nondevelopment" situations. Since an "ideal type" *represents* a situation, rather than describes it, broad generalizations are permissible and one need not get bogged down in the many variations and mixes which are typical of the actual conditions. The very term "ideal type" suggests that a perfected (idealized) version rather than a typical case is provided. The "real world" situations are, of course, anything but black and white in character, but for present purposes there are gains in clarity to be had by the use of this technique (as long as the objectives—and limitations—are kept in mind).

[3] The terms "over a substantial period of time" and "self-sustaining development" are important here in order to contrast this situation with one characterized by a spurt of rapid economic growth which is not sustained. The reader will be able to think of a number of cases to which the latter can be applied.

tion, health, transportation, and possibly even social security of sorts. These tend to be provided in response to the "loudness of the squawk" (politically effective pressure). In addition, certain minimum requirements of economic policy must be met, as in regard to exports, imports, and foreign exchange, or in regard to money supply.

In the provision of public services and the design and execution of economic policy, the government must necessarily reconcile the more significant internal interests, which inevitably will be in conflict on certain scores. It will do this normally while supporting a dominant interest, such as the land owners. The ability to get into power, and stay in, is of course closely tied up with this role. Typically, in the nondevelopment situation, the reconciliation will take place within the framework of the existing economic structure and along the lines of the existing "division of the pie," with only limited modifications contemplated. A significant change in either normally calls for a drastic change in the governmental power structure. Once this takes place, the reconciliation role remains but is turned now to a new dominant interest.

In international relations, the classic role of providing for defense and maintaining prestige dominates the picture. Economic relations will normally center on protection of the balance of payments situation, including borrowing and at times some assistance to the exporters of the major export products (often representing the dominant internal interest group).

Now let us examine the (abstracted) characteristics of the "growth-stability model" in terms of the same three governmental roles. It is immediately apparent that rapid, self-sustaining growth, with a reasonable amount of stability, is an extremely demanding objective, putting great burdens on the government. The governmental roles under such conditions are: (1) to design and carry through consistent developmental policy and to channel substantial capital investment along predetermined lines; (2) to reconcile conflicting interests around future or anticipated gains; and (3) to work out international relations so as to advance the internal developmental goals, while providing at the same time for the defense and prestige functions.

Government, in a growth-stability situation, has to accept the responsibility for fostering development measures—whether directly or quite indirectly—to encourage a large volume of savings and productive investment and advanced modes of farming and working generally. It also has to provide a wide range of infrastructure facilities and services—of the right kind, in the right place, at the right time. Even the older traditional government services, such as education and health, now have to meet the developmental requirements. It is no longer a question of providing minimum services demanded by politically important groups but of meeting productivity and related objectives as well. Thus, there is now a "developmental government" rather than a "minimum-services government."

Equally drastic are the differences in the second role. Conflicting interests are no longer reconciled around the existing economic situation—the present pie—but around the future size of the pie, as well as its distribution. This calls for a general acceptance of the overriding importance of the goal of rapid economic expansion. The hauling and pulling thus takes place within restricted bounds, those set by the demands of rapid economic growth with stability. Pure strength is no longer the sole arbiter. Considerations of investment incentives, competitive pricing, greater internal purchasing power, and the like, enter into the "dialogue." *Social discipline* and *public responsibility* on the part of all the actors involved become key requirements; this is true for the political parties and the conflicting economic groups, as well as for the government itself.[4]

Discipline and responsibility are at the very heart of the matter, possibly more central to the growth-stability model than any other feature. A critical test is whether each group simply asks: "How can we further our own immediate ends?" or whether the form of the question is, "How can we best further our basic interests within the limits of what it takes rapidly to increase total national productivity?" Interest groups will adopt such a forward-looking posture for a variety of reasons; but whatever these are, the important thing is that the terms of the struggle are basically compatible with the goal of development. Thus, farmer associations would be as concerned with the full use of cultivatable land and individual farm productivity as any planner within the Ministry of Agriculture. (The history of, let us say, the Danish farm groups would be very instructive in this respect.) Business groups would be sensitive to

---

[4]Political aspects of development are treated usefully from various points of view in the Social Science Research Council's volume, Hugh Aitken (ed.) *The State and Economic Growth* (New York, 1959). Social discipline and public responsibility are elements deeply rooted in the culture, so that they involve difficult questions of cultural change.

the requirements of making basic investments and would approach labor negotiations with an appreciation of the implications for the purchasing power base and worker incentives (and not only to maintain the lowest possible money wage cost). In the same light, labor union leaders could be expected to set demands within a range not too far removed from productivity increases. Equally important is the discipline and sense of responsibility accepted by the policial parties vis-à-vis national economic development and the requirements of consistent economic policy necessary to achieve it. For all of these key groups, it is a matter of gearing activity to *expectations of long-range gains with short-term down payments,* as against an open struggle for immediate gains.[5]

On the part of government, the requirement is for a special approach to the reconciliation of conflicting interests, an approach determined by the severe demands of rapid development. This includes the setting up of new rules of the game for the chief actors and tough enforcement of the rules. It also involves a "new politics" geared to maintaining the balance among interests by fostering a sense of fairness or equity, as through the carrying out of far-reaching land and tax reforms.

Where there is a national plan for development, a ready test of the crucial discipline requirement exists: Does the government exert the political discipline necessary to carry out the core elements of the plan? Where there is no plan designated as such, the same test applies to the discipline involved in carrying out key developmental policy. (Here the developmental history of countries like Japan comes readily to mind.) Discipline always involves political risks, so this requirement for the government is every bit as demanding as that imposed on the nongovernmental groups.

The international relations role in the growth-stability situation is also significantly different from that of the other model. Extensive activities on the part of government are called for, particularly with regard to economic matters. Thus, the government has to be directly concerned with foreign trade, for example, by assisting private businesses in marketing operations and in other ways encouraging exports, protecting economic interests overseas, helping to develop regional market arrangements, taking part in international trade agreements, maintaining the nation's credit, and the like. Under present conditions, it also involves obtaining external financial as-

---

[5]See Karl Deutsch *et al., Political Community and the North Atlantic Area* (Princeton, N.J.: Princeton University Press, 1957).

sistance for essential investments. Developmental objectives and the longer-run interests would tend to dominate the nation's external relations and would even color the traditional defense and prestige functions.

Generalization and Reality

In examining these generalized characteristics of the two "ideal types" as against the real world, all sorts of differences quickly come to mind. One can think of "nondevelopment" countries that have made extensive development expenditures beyond the scope of "minimum services," or have carried out a rather aggressive overseas economic policy. One can think of "growth-stability" countries where the governmental reconciliation of conflicting interest groups would not seem to be especially characterized by a sense of public responsibility or long-term-mindedness on the part of such groups. However, even after such an exercise, the closeness of the fit between the generalizations and the reality remains evident. Just as a person can enjoy good health without being perfectly healthy, so a nation enjoying rapid growth with stability can fairly readily be characterized as such even though it may fall short of the "ideal type."

What such a "bare bones" look particularly suggests—and this is something that can get lost when we get bogged down in the endless details of "real world" variations—is that there are certain requirements that must be met in terms of governmental role if sustained development is to be achieved. Of course, this alone is not enough; an appropriate governmental approach to development is not by itself a sufficient condition for sustained growth with stability. But the point is that our current knowledge, plus a side glance at history,[6] suggests that, like a few other core elements, this is a necessary condition of, as well as a vehicle for, sustained development. It is not enough for a government merely to say that it wants to help achieve sustained growth and to go through certain limited measures, such as launching miscellaneous public works programs and preparing a national plan. If it is to be successful, stage by stage it must begin to meet all the essential elements suggested by the development model. In this light, it can be seen that

[6]As regards history, not only is it worth noting the continuing, if erratic, Hamiltonian spirit behind United States development, but, more pertinently, the more recent evidences from the development of Australia, Canada, New Zealand, Japan, and, to some extent, Israel and Puerto Rico. In each of these cases, the growth-stability model accurately characterized their governmental functions from the earliest stages of modern development.

many underdeveloped countries have not yet really begun to fashion this important vehicle for development.

Against this background, the subject at hand can be brought into proper focus. That is, the logic of the situation suggests that the governmental organization and administration requirements for growth and stability are essentially the operational counterparts of the sociopolitical-economic requirements outlined earlier. In the remainder of the paper, we will focus on the specifics which would seem to deserve special attention, following the lines of the three key governmental roles which we have identified as particularly important.

Development as a Key Task of Government

The change from the provision of minimum government services to a developmental approach, where all sorts of new investments have to be made and new arrangements brought about, is of course a highly significant one. While the former can be handled quite effectively by a legislative body loosely held together by a chief executive, the latter calls for positive executive leadership. This is so for many reasons. Thus, normally only the chief executive can represent the national interest as against specific provincial interests; a strong executive hand is needed to evolve and carry out a system of priorities among public investments; and positive executive leadership is needed to push through politically distasteful measures, of which there are inevitably many when a nation seeks to achieve self-sustaining growth with stability.

The first organizational requirement, then, is for a relatively strong executive. This can be achieved through a variety of organizational forms, as shown by the experience of the already developed countries. But whatever the form used, it implies not only a strong constitutional position but an effective executive branch—that is, line ministries that are the operational arms of the chief executive, as well as staff offices which can provide the executive with the expert knowledge and staff assistance that he needs. This does not in any way suggest the requirement of a weak or disorganized legislature as the counterpart of a strong executive. (The history of Great Britain, the United States, and other countries should make this evident.) In fact, a strong legislature can be a valuable asset for a democratic country seeking development. The main point here is that while a weak executive arrangement is consistent with the nongrowth model, it is essentially incompatible with the requirements of rapid development, at least under current conditions.[7]

A second requirement is for the organizational ability to design *and* execute a consistent middle- or long-term development strategy. This, in turn, must be backed by appropriate economic policy, a (detailed) public and (general) private investment program, a plan for implementation including direct and indirect aids to private groups, and similar tools. A consistent and known development strategy can contribute in many ways—in generating an appropriate "ambiente" for encouraging private saving and risk-taking investment, in serving notice that public operating expenditures cannot climb beyond certain levels because of the specified requirements for public savings, in providing a coordinating framework for the policies of diverse ministries and their day-by-day administration, and, more generally, in laying out the essential pathways of development.

A development strategy, with its various elements, can be organized formally through a planning operation, or handled informally (but with continuing central guidance). While it is evident that the latter might well suffice under unusually favorable circumstances, there are certain clear-cut advantages in the more formal planning arrangements. Thus, for example, planning imposes a more definite kind of discipline than does reliance on general policy guides alone. This is true of the choice of goals, since under planning the quantitative targets must be compatible with a realistic appraisal of resources, and it is eminently clear that tough choices have to be made among an endless list of attractive possibilities. Without the discipline of planning (always assuming that it is effectively done), it is only too easy to try to do too many things at one time and to lose a strict sense of priorities. Such discipline is particularly important in keeping a lid on government operating expenditures, vis-à-vis the anticipated public resources, to maintain an adequate level of public savings for investment purposes, and to prevent the aggravation of inflationary forces. On the positive side, the detailing through planning of needed investments of specified categories (even if fairly broad) encourages appropriate production scale and production linkages which tend to be critical for the achievement of ambitious growth goals, while

---

[7]However, it does not necessarily follow that *any* strong executive is invariably an asset to national development. The many dictators and "strong men," as well as the autocratic regimes, of the past decades have amply proved this.

the detailing of the flow of funds provides a strong weapon in any struggle for monetary stability.[8]

The design and execution of a consistent development strategy, especially if the more formal approach of planning is employed, call for organizational arrangements specifically geared to this demanding and complicated task. From what has been said to this point, it should be evident why persons who have studied planning experience under various kinds or arrangements should stress so strongly the need to have the planning agency directly tied to the chief executive. For it is clear that the chief executive's prestige and power must be totally behind the choice and the implementation of the development strategy if it is to be at all successful. Also, from the nature of the task involved in controlling both the capital and operating expenditures of government and in achieving an appropriate balance between public outlays and receipts, it follows that planning and budgeting must be closely tied together. The ineffectiveness of much of the planning done today is due precisely to this shortcoming: the budget is not the detailed financial implementation of the plan in the public sphere that it must be if the development strategy is to be designed and carried out properly. What is called for clearly is not only a formal coordination at the top staff agencies, but an integration of planning and budgeting throughout the whole governmental organization.

Also, given the nature of the subjects that developmental planning must deal with, ranging from a host of aggregates, such as population, labor force, national income, balance of payments, cost of living, and the rest, all the way to the details of government programs, such as the potentialities of given crops and the problems of specific industries, it is evident that *information* is the life blood of planning. It takes full consciousness of this fact, plus a strong informational apparatus, to provide an adequate base for effective planning. Where statistics are not easy to come by, special arrangements are needed to make the most of the data collected by the governmental agencies in normal operations. Even then, substantial funds have to be appropriated for key series, and kept up to

---

[8]For a suggestive discussion of the advantages and limitations of the planning approach, see OAS Official Records, "Consultas sobre Planificación del Desarrollo Económico y Social—Febrero—Marzo de 1962" (OAS Reference Document No. 1, July 1, 1962).

See also the excellent statement on development planning by Gerhard Colm and Theodore Geiger, "Country Programming as a Guide to Development," in *Development of the Emerging Countries: An Agenda for Research* (Washington, D.C.: The Brookings Institution, January, 1962), pp. 45–70.

date as a basis for planning decisions and for evaluation purposes. To mention only one item, it is anything but easy to handle inflationary pressures effectively if current data are not available on prices, wages, private investment including inventories, flow of funds, and other key items. Without adequate information for economic management, it is like trying to drive a car blindfolded.

Plans that remain on paper can only give aesthetic satisfaction to technicians. The real payoff is in the execution of the development strategy. The administrative requirements for effective implementation are, therefore, of primary importance. The achievement of a modern executive machinery of government obviously must be the aim of any nation that seriously aspires to rapid development. But not all administrative elements are equally essential. Special importance attaches to two items—men and money; that is, the development of a modern career personnel system (which has a continuing training process built into the system) and the evolution of an effective tax administration. Simply put, a government cannot carry out a development strategy calling for great changes and a disciplined channeling of effort and resources without able full-time personnel (possessing the necessary technical skills) and without adequate funds.[9]

Among the many other items that might usefully be discussed under the rubric of development as a government task, I would like to touch on only one other, the question of administrative centralization and decentralization. Under the nongrowth situation, with government typically providing only a minimum of public services, there is a strong tendency to centralize much of what is made available in services within the capital city. The capital grows rapidly, in part precisely because people crowd into it to take advantage of such services as are provided, and by this very crowding make necessary additional services, as for instance sanitation and health, thus using up a large share of the limited public budget available for services. A development push, by contrast, calls for careful attention to all sections of the nation—to the exploitable natural resources in every part of the country as well as for the fastest possible improvement in the nation's human resources wherever they may be located. This, in turn, suggests the advantages of a fairly substantial amount of administrative decen-

---

[9]The extent to which poor public administration can hamper the achievement of development goals is discussed in Fred Riggs, "Public Administration: A Neglected Factor in Economic Development," *Annals of the American Academy of Political and Social Science,* Vol. 305, May, 1956, pp. 70–80.

tralization, among other reasons, to deeply root the development programs and provide a training ground for leadership. Here strong centralization traditions can be a great hurdle and a determined effort on the part of the governmental leaders to build up effective centers of administration throughout the country is a minimum requirement.

Ideally, regional and local planning should be seen as essentials of the total planning picture, so that development programs are evolved at least as much from the "bottom up" as from the "top down." Attention must be given continuously not only to the nature of public services but to the extent of such services—that is, the extent to which the governmental services reach the people of the nation and provide a developmental impetus.

Reconciliation of Conflicting Interests

It was suggested earlier that a key element in the achievement of growth with stability was the resolution of conflicting claims within the restraints imposed by the requirements of across-the-board economic expansion. This means that the nation must evolve a *politics of development,* as well as an economics of development, characterized by a relatively high degree of social discipline and public responsibility.

A number of implications for organization and administration follow from that requirement. If acceptance of development objectives is not to be imposed by force—and, by definition, a democracy cannot follow such an approach—then it is evident that the groups representing the main social, political, and economic forces in the nation must take a direct part in the preparation and carrying out of the development strategy (in the planning, if planning is used), so that it represents their views and plans and not those of the government alone. Such direct involvement is essential to a sense of commitment on the part of the major national interests, and such commitment, in turn, is crucial if the struggle among conflicting interests is to be kept within nondisruptive bounds.[10]

---

[10]Such bounds would seem to be fairly broad and elastic, as suggested by the political history of the developed countries. The major requirement would seem to be that group demands not be such that the forward movement of the economy is blocked, either by imposing stagnation (for example, the insistence on being permitted to hold on to unused land) or by imposing disruptive continuing inflation (for example, by forcing large end-on-end government budget deficits). The elasticity of this requirement is fortunate because the organizing of economic and political groups adequately to effect genuine participation is extremely difficult.

The organization of the planning should be such that the farm, labor, business, professional, and other important groups take a direct part at every stage. (A possible technique, where applicable, is the one currently being evolved in France and Japan.) For the same reasons, it is important that the legislature vote on major planning decisions, so that such decisions may be representative. However, at this point it is well to note that leaders will be able to follow a nondisruptive course in the struggle for group advantage only if the general public itself becomes involved in the development process and increasingly understands, and enthusiastically backs, the development strategy—at heart a strategy of change, modernization, and improvement, whatever other trappings it may have.

The importance of this has been stressed time and again in the literature. It is often taken to be the most critical factor in development. Yet, where it does not come about more or less automatically from forces deep in the culture (as has been the case in, say, western Europe), this requirements imposes for a democracy one of the severest problems in organization in the whole economic growth picture. Valuable beginnings have been made with the evolution of the "community development" idea, the process of people becoming involved in modernization by way of self-help programs in communities. (India has put a great deal of effort along such lines.) It has also been argued that a judicious provision of certain popular social services such as public housing, which demonstrates what development can mean in the longer run, can generate enthusiasm for development generally. Education, including adult education, can of course be a great weapon in providing a base of understanding of the development requirements, as well as a direct force in development itself. Possibly most important of all is the sense of involvement in the process of development that is generated through the use of economic incentives. (Farmers who have been helped to achieve higher prices through governmental marketing and road-buliding programs, or storage to equalize supplies, can become "sold" on economic development without any preaching.)

While all of these are undoubtedly useful, it is well to recognize that not too much is known about the process of involvement. At this stage in the world's knowledge, the achievement of the crucial objective of broad participation clearly calls for the organization and testing of all sorts of experimental approaches.

The problem of discipline and responsibility on the part of the key groups in the society is particularly difficult as regards the political parties and the military. This remains one of the unsolved problems in democratic development. It is easy enough to predict, on the basis of both logic and history, that rapid development with stability is not likely to be achieved unless both the military and political parties are willing to accept the requirements of discipline and responsibility in their relationships with the other groups in the nation. It is another matter to try to understand how this objective can be achieved in a positive manner. Certainly it deserves the deepest study and best thought of which we are capable.

In an effort to bring key groups in the society into the design and execution of the development strategy—in order to get them committed to the longer-run view—the more formal planning approach has certain advantages over the purely informal "economic policy" approach. For planning shows in a specific and dramatic way what the gains for the whole society will be from restraint—the size of the future pie—so that the struggle for the division of the present pie can be somewhat mitigated. Planning also helps to make specific the items that are critical for rapid growth with stability, so that it is easier to post the "off limit" signs in the group struggles.

On the side of the execution of plans, it is evident that a "developmental government" (as against a "minimum-services government") inevitably must restrain the various interest groups through measures that are likely to make one or another of these groups terribly unhappy. It follows, then, that in a democracy the more indirect the restraints and the less visible the government's hand, the greater are the chances of avoiding unduly high political costs and weakening of the government's developmental role. This suggests that a government, seeking to achieve progress along a broad front, must weigh certain political disadvantages of direct productive operations against the anticipated gains. In many instances indirect assistance and subsidy, joined with indirect controls of various types, can normally accomplish even ambitious objectives if the development strategy is genuinely sound. But even where government ownership and operation of an enterprise is desirable for one reason or another, a strong case can be made for the avoidance of arbitrary pricing for immediate political ends when rapid growth is the key objective.[11]

---

[11]The nature of the problem can be seen by taking the example of the government's setting administered prices for publicly or privately-owned utilities. Once it gets away from prices determined on the basis of demand and cost fac-

International Relations and External Financing

The organizational and administrative requirements associated with the international tasks of a "developmental government" are particularly demanding and difficult to meet. To some extent this is exemplified in the fact that it is often difficult to get a ministry of foreign affairs to be development-minded. And yet foreign affairs must be just that if the growth-and-stability goals are to be achieved. Some of the key elements in economic growth are basically international in scope: the extension of foreign markets for the products of the nation, the speeding of regional integration, the need for commodity agreements to stabilize certain of the commodity prices, the requirements of external financing and assistance, and many related elements. As a matter of fact, it may well be that under modern conditions very few countries can achieve the goal of growth-with-stability without a great deal of help from outside and without an effective strategy for international relations. One of the main tasks of developmental planning is to provide for both of these.

A starting point is a careful estimation of how much foreign financing is essential to carry out the plan goals. This is no cut-and-dried exercise but involves difficult estimates of such key items as export earnings and import requirements (including those flowing from the multiplier effects of the first-round investments), as well as of the nation's debt capacity. It also involves the results of decisions of great moment, for example, how much of a tax burden the nation can, and is willing to, maintain. Here again, the more formal planning approach has an advantage in making all of these elements explicit and thereby forcing the hard decisions that have to be made (or if not, at least the awareness that the development goals are not likely to be achieved).

What also becomes apparent is the need to evolve strong institutional weapons to cope with the external aspects of development. Thus, the government should be equipped to help export industries (actual and potential) in their marketing efforts, through information, representation, international trade agreements, and any other means that might be called for. The same holds for assistance

---

tors, it must inevitably box itself in politically. It cannot meet the developmental requirements of insuring adequate utility facilities and services and preventing low-priority use of such services if it maintains below-cost prices. Once it establishes the fact that all utilities are to be on a genuine price-system basis, it takes them out of the realm of political maneuver—a single political cost as against a continuing political problem.

in purchases from outside, particularly since exports and imports are, under certain circumstances, tied together through foreign exchange restraints.

Under the conditions prevailing in Latin America, a development-minded government can be expected to contribute in important ways toward speeding the evolution of regional economic integration and sensible commodity arrangements aimed at achieving some stability in export earnings. These are critical for rapid growth without inflation in most Latin-American countries, particularly those with limited internal markets.[12] Problems of this nature should be a major continuing responsibility of a strong agency, and, given the many unknowns surrounding them, should be the subjects of continuing high-level research within such an agency (as well as at universities).

An element of great importance in external matters is the efficiency with which the government carries out export, import, and foreign exchange controls when these are required. Two interrelated problems are involved here—actually, two sides of the same coin: on one side, the problem of designing such controls so that they are not more complicated than government agencies can handle expertly; and, on the other, the problem of strengthening (mainly through higher-level personnel) the control agencies so that the objectives are actually realized and the controls are not merely an exercise in red tape, as is so often the case today.

In modern times, among the most important parts of the governmental structure of a developing country are the units with the responsibility for arranging external financing and other forms of assistance. The availability of substantial external financial assistance is clearly one of the major weapons in the hands of any government seeking rapid growth. However, the full use of this weapon calls for as much organizational and administrative strength as any element in the developmental picture.

Here, once again, the caliber of the planning is a key factor. While the international lending agencies and the aid agencies of the richer countries might be willing to provide financing for specific isolated projects, when justified through feasibility studies, they cannot be expected to provide large-scale, long-term financing on favorable terms without a sound total development plan to back up such extension of credit. At the same time, long-term plan-

---

[12]On this point, see the valuable study by Victor L. Urquidi, *Free Trade and Economic Integration in Latin America* (Berkeley and Los Angeles: University of California Press, 1962).

oriented financing does not mean that individual projects are no longer the focus of attention. Project studies have to be carried quite a distance in economic and engineering terms if the investment program projections are to be at all meaningful, rather than pure guesses, and lending agencies naturally insist on fairly firm estimates. In addition, they want to see, in the cases of certain sectors such as transportation and power, how the individual projects fit together to make the network total. Thus, the extent to which a country is equipped to prepare sound plans *and* projects—as well, of course, as sound economic policy—will be a determining factor in its ability to get external financial assistance in the amount it needs.

A development-conscious country will also want to take advantage of other forms of assistance, such as technical assistance, surplus food, and the like. All this adds up to the logical requirement that the country be well equipped to take full advantage of all forms of aid available. It needs strong offices with responsibility for the aid programs, manned by persons well versed in these complicated matters, and prepared to work with neighboring countries or on a regional basis where joint efforts can be more effective.

Present Inadequacies and Potentialities

We know from history that economic progress can be made under organizational arrangements and administrative processes that are far from ideal. Nevertheless, rapid growth without disruptive inflation is a demanding objective and a country must be heading in the directions specified above if it is to achieve this objective. The disturbing fact is that, viewed in terms of the outlined requirements, the organizational structures in the great majority of Latin-American countries can be seen to be inadequate for the job of development.

While the situation varies greatly from country to country, certain weaknesses and gaps are quite common.

There are only a few countries which can be said to have a well-established developmental strategy and fewer yet where such strategy is backed by relatively effective executive machinery. Even where rapid development has been set officially as a national objective, government organization is much closer to the traditional minimum-services approach than it is oriented to development.

Very few countries have yet seriously tackled the difficult task of generating, step by step, a sense of social discipline and public responsibility on the part of the major economic and political groups. In most places, there is still the illusion that development can be fostered even if every group holds on to its cherished special privileges—low tax payments by the rich, great land holdings that are neither used nor taxed, money sent out of the country at the slightest economic disturbance, leaders in labor-management relations handling their affairs through bribery and force, and the rest of it. With a few important exceptions, arrangements have not yet been worked out to encourage disciplined and responsible actions through various types of inducements, education, and governmental controls.

In international relations, progress has been somewhat more encouraging. But even here the painfully slow progress of ALALC and the very few coordinated efforts that have been made to strengthen marketing arrangements overseas suggest that the Latin-American countries in most cases have a long way to go.

The organizational weaknesses are particularly apparent where national planning efforts exemplify the government's approach to development, for then the shortcomings are more sharply focused. Thus, a look at the existing planning efforts shows the following: planning organizations are weak and inadequately staffed; planning ties to budgeting are tenuous or nonexistent; there is very little sector planning (for example, for agriculture or education) going on in the ministries (if done at all, such planning is done largely within the central planning organization); statistical and other informational efforts are extremely limited; government planning is not related effectively to the needs and plans of the private sector; and the institutions and techniques for involving the general public in the development efforts are particularly weak, so that such efforts are not at all deeply rooted.[13] This is only a partial list. Actually, serious weaknesses are to be found at almost every point highlighted in the previous sections as being required for rapid growth with stability.

How are these weaknesses to be overcome? Clearly, each country that genuinely wants rapid development will have to seek to meet the major organizational and administrative requirements in its own way. While on the negative side there is the disturbing fact that most of the countries are starting from extremely low levels

---

[13]Analyses of present weaknesses and some suggestions for overcoming them are to be found in the OAS document referred to in footnote No. 8 and in Albert Waterston's *"Planning the Planning" Under the Alliance for Progress*, a paper presented on April 30, 1962 at Syracuse University (mimeo); the step-by-step pragmatic approach suggested may well have broad application to the introduction of administrative improvements in general.

administratively, there are also unusually favorable elements in the present situation. Outstanding among these is, of course, the whole Alliance for Progress program—the most comprehensive cooperative program for development ever conceived.

Conceptually at least, the Alliance program is designed to be helpful to the developing country at most points which have been identified in this paper as particularly critical: (1) the preparation of development plans and policy (the help here is through technical assistance and various training programs) and the evaluation of their inherent soundness (through the mechanism of the Committee of Nine); (2) the contribution to the evolution of a sturdy social and political, as well as economic, base for progress through emphasis on land, tax, and administrative reforms, social projects such as those in housing, education, health and sanitation, and related measures; (3) the provision for concerted efforts to bring about regional integration and commodity stabilization; and finally (4) the assurance of substantial United States financial assistance over a decade which, joined with the assistance of the international agencies and other economically advanced countries, can provide a critical part of the resources needed to finance programs aiming at rapid economic development. Possibly the most significant aspects of the Alliance are the open-ended possibilities inherent in the joining of forces on a regional and international basis. Even the limited experience to date suggests that many of the requirements which are so difficult to meet on a purely national and isolated basis can be met more readily with the backing of regional cooperation and external assistance.

At the same time, we have to face the fact that at this stage the Alliance is young, itself not very powerfully organized, and that it has not yet developed a concept of appropriate scale. Thus, it seems evident that we need training facilities with capacity several times the existing one for administrators, planners, economists, statisticians, civil engineers, and many others essential to the workings of modern government. These people are needed not only as technicians but as carriers of the "spirit" of development and modernization. There is need for technical assistance programs of an entirely different order of excellence than the present ones. And there is need for a substantial improvement in the Alliance machinery.[14]

---

[14]These requirements are analyzed in Organization of American States, *Informe de la Nómina de Nueve al Consejo Interamericano Económico y Social* (OEA/Ser. H/X.3, September, 1962).

The major question, however, concerns the capacity and willingness of the various nations to undertake with vigor and speed the basic measures outlined in the Charter of Punta del Este. The charter, it is well to note, specifically points to the need for each country to provide organizational and administrative tools designed for, and capable of coping with, the demanding tasks involved in achieving rapid economic development.

Thus, this paper is essentially an attempt to spell out in some detail the implications of the section of that remarkable document forged at Punta del Este which deals with "the basic requirements for economic and social development."

c. COMMENT
Neil Chamberlain

Before commenting, I should like to enter a disclaimer. My familiarity with the Latin-American scene derives solely from secondary sources rather than firsthand experience, so that any value which attaches to my remarks comes from some knowledge in the subject area of planning rather than from planning applications in a particular geographical region.

I am quite in agreement with Mr. Escobar that the element of impatience is a significant economic ingredient which is driving most of the underdeveloped economies toward a reliance on planned outcomes rather than longer-run market adjustments. There are other reasons for the currently strong tide running in favor of planning, even in the industralized countries, such as the need for coordinating responses to more rapidly changing economic variables, but certainly impatience to achieve wanted results by will rather than by wait is one of the most important.

But my agreement with Mr. Escobar's basic premise does not extend to his more specific mechanisms for planning. As I read his proposal, he would have a ministry of planning which would

1. Set a growth rate.
2. Formulate a broad plan to achieve it.
3. See that projects are devised to carry it out.
4. Follow it through to completion.

The Minister of Planning would be appointed by the President, but could be dismissed only by consent of the Senate.

This program would, I fear, involve both excessive centralization and excessive diffusion of political responsibility. Let me consider first the matter of centralization.

Although Escobar suggests that private economic groups should be consulted in the planning process, he maintains that the Ministry of Planning should itself produce the broad program, assuming central responsibility for it. But this perpetuates the present unfortunate position in which many governments find themselves, of providing a target for the economic demands of major pressure groups, one following on the heels of another, and of finding difficulty in saying "No" to each in turn, partly out of political necessity and partly on grounds of equity. (If one group has been given concessions, how can concessions be denied to other interests?)

Obviously, this kind of chain reaction is nothing that can be changed quickly. In some countries, it would seem, it has become standard operating procedure. But a start might be made in the direction of breaking the chain by attempting to involve the major centers of private economic activity in the over-all economic planning process. If the major interest groups can be involved, all at the same point in time and with a focussing of public attention on their roles in the economy, their inescapable responsibilities may be dramatized in a way that encourages their fulfillment. The involvement of these groups in the over-all planning process may help to break the present chain of sequential pressures and give greater assurance to such groups that their rightful claim to equitable treatment will be honored, since all jointly participate in hammering out the terms of the program on which they agree to collaborate.

Perloff, who likewise asserts the need for economic planning, stresses the importance of such involvement, and I strongly support his position. But the answer which Escobar would presumably make is that, as desirable as such involvement may be in theory, in practice the number of "highly qualified economists" who are to be found in the employ of the interest groups and organizations is very limited, and great demands are made on their time, so that they would scarcely be available for additional assignments in a planning program. I sympathize with the difficulties attending a shortage of expertise—this is something that every country, at every stage of development, confronts—but I am inclined to believe that Escobar exaggerates the degree of economic expertness

which is required of private representatives. The main objectice is
to secure their assent to what they believe is a meaningful, practical, and equitable program, and this does not require a fine knowledge of economics. Moreover, it is hard for me to believe that this
participation is not of sufficient importance to the total economic
framework within which government and private groups alike
must operate, that use of their limited time for this purpose
should not supersede some other present uses of their time.

There is the further question of whether such participation is
compatible with a cultural milieu which emphasizes strong governmental leadership, but this is not an issue which disturbs me
greatly. To be sure, the notion of a concurrence of private views
as the effective motivational force in getting the plan to work may
be something strange to the present scene, and therefore difficult
to accomplish. But this does not necessarily argue against it. While
it is true that we must all learn to operate within a given cultural
framework, it is also true that the results we seek must involve
conscious effort to modify that framework.

The problem here is basically one of motivation—how to get
all the parts of the economy pulling together—and this brings me
to the question of the objectives of the plan.

Escobar suggests that the objective should be a growth rate.
Of course we all understood that this is simply a shorthand expression, but its use may have the unfortunate effect of hiding
what it stands for—the *parts* of the economy where growth can be
expected and where it is most wanted. The latter is especially important to motivation. I hurry along, making only two brief comments on this point.

1. In every plan there might be some overriding objective
which would arouse and focus the national imagination and thus
help to impose responsibilities on the cooperating private interests in realizing it. We have here heard repeated testimony to the
importance of extending educational achievements in the Latin-
American societies. Perhaps specific announced, and realistic, objectives along these lines (such and such results to be achieved
within a one, three, and five-year term) would serve as far more effective motivation than a projected over-all growth rate of a certain
percent, which the average person can scarcely translate into anything concrete and personal.

2. There is an obvious need for a detailed survey of the available resources, both manpower and capital, and their expected and
possible uses. This is not with the intent of *directing* their use along

particular lines but of permitting an exploration of alternative uses, and of helping to make their use more effective and more certain.

In connection with this last point I shall make two other short comments:

First, the need for more, and more reliable, statistical information on resources in the Latin-American economies is patent. This has been emphasized by Seers, Schwartz, Perloff, and Escobar, among others.

Second, there would also be great value in stressing, by way of public education, one of the simplest but most powerful of economic concepts—opportunity cost. What is being foregone by using resources in one way rather than another, or by not using resources rather than by using them, or by developing resources for more effective later use rather than putting them to immediate use?

In any event, as I see it the projected growth rate is a result of the ways in which it is planned to use resources, and not itself a target to which the plan is addressed. The objectives, over the years, are not rates of growth but states of growth, concrete objectives which can stimulate responses, rather than percentages which are meaningless and mysterious to many people.

Now it is time for me to turn to the second line of disagreement with Escobar's planning mechanism, my belief that it represents excessive diffusion of responsibility. For any program so important to an economy—to a society—as a whole, leadership cannot be devolved upon a minister of planning. Leadership must stem directly from the chief executive of the state. The plan is presumably directed not simply to a random assortment of production advances, which collectively add up to some rate of growth, but stands for desired achievements in specific areas, some more important than others. The question of priorities is basic to the program, and it can receive its appropriate answer only from the chief executive, who alone has the authority and influence adequate to win agreement on them and cooperation in achieving them. Insofar as the parts of the economy can be induced to pull together to realize defined goals, it will be through his prestige and position, playing on the desires of the people. Is any other function of his office more important than this?

I have time to deal only lightly with Escobar's proposed national tribunal of conciliation, which is really an arbitral body, and which, I feel sure, would be subject to the same pressures as the central government is now. If the problem is, at least in part, one of the power of private groups to intimidate or control the state, for fear by the political leaders of retaliation, so that the government says "Yes" to every pressure group, there must be some way of meeting this problem more effectively than by subjecting a new body to the same pressures. Here I repeat myself. This is the reason for the attempt to involve all major private interest groups in the planning process. As long as they can approach the government seriatim, political realities will involve the government in a sequence of acquiescences to a continuous inflationary policy. As I have suggested, it may be possible to go at least part way toward meeting this problem by some simultaneous understanding on income shares as part of an over-all plan, giving each group some assurance of (1) betterment and (2) equity, within a framework of commitment to national goals. In this, the sense of *national* objectives is important. In any event, to think of punitive measures against major sectors of society as a means of enforcing an income policy seems to me unfeasible and undesirable.

If the kind of programming effort I have suggested can be made to work—

Planning carrying the imprint of the highest political authority
Directed toward generally accepted national objectives
Involving all major private economic interests

—then the resulting mechanism may help to avoid any *contest* between inflation and growth. The same mechanism may serve as a stimulant to growth and a control element with respect to inflation.

In conclusion, I should like to point out the remarkable areas of agreement between these two papers. I have perhaps stressed degrees of differences more sharply than they exist, or have placed emphasis where it was not intended. If so, I offer my apologies to the authors. But in general, I feel inclined to say, the policy prescriptions of these two papers point in the right direction.

d. COMMENT

Benjamín Hopenhayn

There is a wide area of agreement between the basic views of Professor Escobar and Dr. Perloff, as set out in their papers, and my own. This opens the way for a constructive discussion, although it undermines the possibility of a lively and ingenious debate.

The two papers focus upon the question of organizational requirements for growth and stability in underdeveloped countries as a fundamental institutional problem, rather than as a matter of administrative techniques. These authors recognize an acute social imbalance which poses insurmountable rigidities to the use of formulae which have not been entirely unsuccessful elsewhere, but which have failed almost without exception in Latin America.

Both authors hold that in this part of the world it is not possible to achieve a high rate of development with a relative price stability unless the public sector plays a very active part in the process, directing, orienting and limiting to a great extent the "free play of the market forces." This shift from a traditional, rather passive type of government toward what is sometimes called an "interventionist" government would reflect the adjustment of the administrative processes and machinery to changes in the socioeconomic infrastructure. In other words, the organization of the state must adapt itself dynamically to the organization of the respective national society. Or, as Dr. Perloff states, ". . . the governmental organization and administration requirements for growth and stability are essentially the operational counterparts of the sociopolitical-economic requirements." You cannot maintain or reestablish in the second half of the twentieth century in Latin America a type of government conceived to fit the needs of mid-nineteenth century in Europe. It does not work.

Luis Escobar, in turn, stresses a fact unknown to, or often forgotten by, economists and social scientists from abroad who look at our problems of development and—in general guided by the best intentions—advise Latin-Americans to adhere to certain policies and procedures. "I want to stress," states Escobar, "that the frame of reference corresponds to a 'mixed economy' where both the private and public sectors own means of production and are entrepreneurs. . . ." And further on he mentions, ". . . it is irrelevant to argue whether the free market economy has had its opportunity in the past, because there is no reason to think it will have it in the future."

What pattern of economic organization does Professor Escobar propose to substitute for the existing one? A national planning system, which he sets out to describe in some detail in his paper. Toward the end of this description he reaches the question of wage policies—one of the two culprits in the "devilish" spiral of wages and prices. There he reaches an apparent canyon which leads him to the conclusion that "there is an open incompatibility between development with monetary stability and the judicial, constitutional, and organizational pattern which governs our collective life and specially, the relations between capital and labor."

I fully agree that a process of comparatively fast growth with stability will only be possible in Latin America if the present organization of society undergoes fundamental changes. The daily agitation in these turbulent countries is mainly caused by the stubborn survival of an anachronistic social organization. This is the source of a "climate" of permanent conflict, flaring more and more into the open.

To come back to inflation, as we always must in this conference, the condition prevailing in Latin America could be described as a struggle of high income groups to maintain their privileged share of national income, mainly through the price mechanism, in the face of growing pressures of the other social groups, exerted mainly through wage and salary claims. Thus, the price-wage spiral is only the effect or manifestation of an acute socioeconomic imbalance which is lasting far beyond an acceptable period. Why is this happening? Arthur Lewis—neither a monetarist nor a structuralist, but a "politicist"—explains that it is basically because "Latin America is the most politically reactionary of all the continents," and because "the wage spiral in Latin America is fundamentally political, and cannot be eliminated without fundamental political change." And the failure of the stabilization dies stamped on some countries in this area is undoubtedly due to the fact that they try to re-establish —sometimes inadvertently—a socioeconomic pattern long overdue. Consequently, tensions are often more acute, the imbalance more unruly and violent.

This path of reasoning leads, unfortunately, to the dangerous swamp of political speculation, where honest economists trying to escape the limitations of quantitative techniques have drowned or come out tarnished. It would, therefore, be wiser to stop here in this broad diagnosis of the social disequilibrium and devote our efforts to exploring in more detail its relation to the stampeding inflation and low rate of growth affecting Latin America as a whole. We believe, however, that intellectuals have a responsibility at least to stimulate the theoretical search for an organization of society which could be both fit and feasible for the implementation of policies apt to achieve a high rate of growth with a reasonable price stability. This amounts to looking for an exit to the spiral of institutional disequilibrium through achieving and maintaining an open society, capable of reaching through successive approximations a high rate of economic and *social* development, as pointed out by Celso Furtado in his lucid and admirable essay on the "Brazilian Prerevolution."[1]

Before making some preliminary suggestions on the new organization of society which we feel could improve considerably the conditions prevailing in Latin America, let us glance over some features of the present situation in the area: acute political and institutional instability, average per capita GNP of about $300 per year, very unevenly distributed; over 40 percent of the population under 15 years of age; 54 percent of the total population living in rural areas; high level of unemployment or underemployment, etc.

As policy decisions are previous to organizational decisions, and policies for growth and stability are dealt with by others in this conference, let us simply assume that a clearly defined and continued development policy is adopted. The organization suitable for the development effort must be consistent with the policy chosen. Such organization should politically allow the active participation of all groups willing to contribute to the development process; socially, maximize equality of opportunity; and, economically, facilitate the achievement of a continuing high rate of growth, income redistribution, and diversification of economic activity through a high rate of capitalization, expansion of domestic markets, diversification of exports, and so on.

The most rational way to achieve these goals—provided that all other essential conditions are met—is through a national development plan with explicit built-in policies, geared, among other things, to change the economic and social structure of the country and remove existing obstacles to further growth. The plan should be much more than a macroeconomic blueprint for development. It should, in fact, be implemented through a national planning system—and this, in our view, is a basic organizational prerequisite—directing the activities of the public sector and orienting those of the private sector toward certain clearly defined goals through a clearly defined strategy.

In order to achieve these objectives, the political life of the hypothetical country in question should insure the following essential conditions: (1) continuity of adopted development policies; (2)

---

[1]Celso Furtado, "Reflexiones sobre la pre-revolución brasileña," *El Trimestre Económico*, No. 115, July–September, 1962.

ample and active participation of the largest possible majority of the population; and (3) a normal institutional life for the country. Social prerequisites, on the other hand, should be to achieve the highest degree of social mobility through the greatest equality of opportunities at the same time, through the inspiration of a vigorous "development mentality" or mystique. Education will play a basic role in creating this spirit, provided it gives the younger generations the ability to absorb modern technology and to apply it to the struggle against underdevelopment. Massive technological training at all levels will no doubt contribute considerably in achieving such "development mentality", that is, the self-reliance of Latin-Americans on their own capacity to create a better world for themselves.

If the political, social, and economic life of the countries in this troubled area is mobilized toward the realization of such national goals of economic and social development, a more vigorous will to attain them and, at the same time, a more strict self-imposed discipline should characterize the activities of entrepreneurs, labor and, government. Thus, a rational and feasible alternative to existing disequilibrium will be in force, and, consequently, a road will be followed which offers a much greater probability for a balanced, sustained high rate of growth.

e. COMMENT

Kalman H. Silvert

Messrs. Escobar and Perloff have done us the invaluable service of introducing the political factor into our debates. The former, in choosing to present some administrative solutions fitting to the Latin-American experience, has also subtly implied the nature of some of the important limitations on political activity. Mr. Perloff has shown himself to be concerned with the political process but he, too, is not hypnotized by mere governmental mechanisms and gimmicks. The two papers lead us toward very important generalizations concerning the powers of Latin-American governments and suggest how important the heuristic device of the typology can be for an understanding of the fitness of proposed policy measures. But I should like to apply myself directly to a broader look at the sociopolitical aspects of Latin-American development, with some thought for their specific operational relevance to the problem of inflation.

As an alien to the fraternity of economists, I have been bemused by the flexibility evidenced by the practitioners of what is supposed to be the most exact of the inexact sciences concerning what is a "proper" or "safe" or "desirable" rate of inflation in developing countries. Some talk of 5 percent, others of 10 and 15 percent, and yet others of even more, tempting me to the comment that my taste runs to 7.6 percent per year. I should like to suggest that greater precision in determining, within a particular country, when inflation becomes incompatible with growth is a problem in multiple correlation, and that we shall have to look beyond the strictly economic for the elements adequate to the appropriate analysis.

That very high rates of inflation have sometimes accompanied continued high rates of capitalization is part of the indisputable historical record of Latin America. Nevertheless, this combination of occurrences has so far persisted only in the short run, or, at best, in a truncated intermediate run. But not much more can be said of the industrial developmental process as a whole in Latin America, for no country has as yet demonstrated the long-run ability to press forward into relatively assured self-sustaining industrial development. The old economic leader—Argentina, Chile, and Uruguay—have all faltered and stalled, and Argentina is even, indeed, "undeveloping." Warnings are continually heard about Mexico and Brazil, the next two on the line, and there are some excellent noneconomic reasons for suspicion about the course of their future transition into the patterned institutionalization of change characteristic of truly modern polities. I strongly suspect that the inabilty of such countries as Chile and Argentina to continue economic development is closely linked to their monetary difficulties—not that the latter cause the former, but that both are reflections of the same malaise.

The emphasis I have been putting on the time factor leads me to advance the following hypothesis: a sharp rate of inflation will *in the long run* either inhibit or absolutely prevent *sustained* development. The reasoning behind this suspposition may be summarized as follows: (1) secular inflation involves an income redistribution from the social bottom and parts of the middle to the top; (2) after the initial reshuffle of the beginning phases of an inflation, the process settles down to the ratification of new, as well as old, power differences; (3) social distance thus grows greater between the several layers of the stratification system, mobility becomes more difficult, and feelings of alienation find vent in political unrest and lowered productivity, as in the case of Argentina today; (4) the immediate economic effect is a restriction of effective demand and a closing down of market opportunities, thus making further investment in many areas an economic irrationality; and (5) in the political area the civic market place also becomes inhibited, reducing or containing the area of consensus and thus preventing that application of public power needed to build legally guaranteed continuity and predictability into the complexity of modern industrial organization. Inflation, then, if sharp and long drawn out, becomes one of a multitude of factors contributing to particularism when development demands national universalism, to class conflict when cooperation and open mobility paths are needed, and to untoward concentrations of power when a dispersion of responsibility is demanded by the interdependencies created by a higher order of specialization.

These concepts can be operationalized, toward the end of deciding when an inflation is "good" in the sense that it promotes growth and "bad" in the sense that it inhibits it—for indeed both can happen, even if in different time periods, depending on the rate involved. Certainly, if some distributional balance is maintained, even during sharp periods of inflation, and if the price rises at the same time add a sufficient disguised profit increment to foment continued private investment, then reasons for worry concerning the domestic economy are not well taken, even though foreign exchange and related external problems will of course, remain. It is only when internal flexibility of response to the inflation fails that its general developmental reason for being becomes self-defeating.

I submit that the standard cures for inflation applied recently in Latin America have failed—as indubitably they have in all cases—because they treat inflation as though it were a primary cause, or at least as though monetary manipulation can lever profound economic and political change into being. Many economic advisers working in Latin America abstract their policies from the experiences of the developed nation-state systems of the modern world, yet apply their advice through governments of prenational stripe. Such advice is as useful as asking the mother bear to give birth to an astronautical chimpanzee. Power and technique are required for the application and administration of austerity programs, but the nearly universal consensus which is the wellspring of the power of developed, broadly participant states can be counted on by no Latin-American government. The matter is worsened by the fact that inflationary control programs call in the short run for a deepening of those very social divisions which halting the inflation is supposed to mitigate in the longer run. Naturally the resultant heightening of social tension demands more power for its containment at the same time as the government inevitably becomes further weakened. Limited power, unconvinced economists and administrators, and bureaucracies of traditional mold combine to make impossible the socially incongruous inflation control programs usually suggested.

We think we know what a developed economy is. We must also think about the shape of the modern polity which must accompany economic development. Among all the world's emergent areas, Latin America is by and large economically the most advanced. This elementary truth forces us back into the experience of the already advanced societies, to our baseline notion of the total complex of development, so that we may see why Latin-American economic advance has not "automatically" led to continued development. We find in all modern nations that social class differences are sunk back or at least canalized, contained within a set of rules permitting some degree of rationality in the mobilization of human resources, and promoting it by such appropriate institutions as the educational system. We also see some means of assuring equality before the law and the ordering of dispute by a secular governmental system applying socially relativist, not absolutist, criteria of judgment. A relatively broad base of social participation creates that social "engagement" required for law to have effect through anticipatory acceptance, instead of depending largely upon the application of direct sanction. These factors are what give truly national governments great strength and explain why every developed society has also defined itself within the social, as well as geographical, confines of a nation-state. In this sense every Latin-American government is more or less weak, and thus unable to make fully effective those "leakproof" laws needed for the "rapid purgative medicine" of the austerity program. The result that flows from this weakness is that measures depending for their very effectiveness upon speed become transmuted through time into instruments for economic stagnation rather than economic sanitation.

The papers of Escobar and Perloff are crucial to these discussions, as they imply the political differences dividing the Latin-American experience from that of the developed world. If the German and British governments are different from those of Bolivia and Argentina, so, too, are the several reasons for their differing inflations, the relationships between their monetary instability and continued economic growth, and the measures which the responsible social scientist should propose to responsible political agencies. There is no theoretical or technical reason to prevent our operationalizing the concepts needed for research into the question of inflation and growth. But the first step, as in all scientific endeavor, is to cast aside inhibiting ideology.

6. COMPARATIVE ANALYSES OF THE EXPERIENCE OF NON–LATIN-AMERICAN COUNTRIES

a. POSTWAR EXPERIENCE OF INFLATION IN THE INDUSTRIAL COUNTRIES[1]

Sidney Dell

It is a remarkable fact that, 17 years after the end of the war, the governments of the industrial countries still have not succeeded in finding a satisfactory relationship between the goal of price stability and the various other possible targets of public policy.

This is partly the fault of economists, who have themselves given too little attention to the question: how important is price stability in relation to the other goals of economic policy? What does one gain and what may one, perhaps, lose through price stability, and how much of something else is it worth giving up for the sake of price stability? Such is the fear of inflation that the target of price stability is usually treated in the literature as an end in itself, not to be questioned or even thought about, rather than as a means to some other end.

This absolutism about price stability is reflected in many ways. Not merely does it distort much of the theoretical work in this field, but it even gives rise to flat assertions about the nature of the empirical evidence that simply do not accord with the facts. Consider the following passage from the concluding note of *The Problem of Rising Prices,* a study prepared for the OEEC by six most distinguished economists of international reputation[2] (whom we may, for brevity, call the Six):

---

[1]The author gratefully acknowledges helpful comments received from his colleagues G. Arsenis, T. C. Chang, K. Saramo and N. T. Wang. The views expressed in this paper are those of the author alone, however, and do not necessarily represent those of the United Nations Secretariat, to which he belongs.
[2]William Fellner, Milton Gilbert, Bent Hansen, Richard Kahn, Friedrich Lutz, Peter de Wolff.

We have concentrated in this report on the problem of price stability, in accordance with our mandate. This does not imply that we wish to put a lower priority on economic growth, and we know that such was not the intention of the Council in formulating our mandate. It is, rather, that rising prices are not compatible with steady growth.

One must admire the Six for the directness and simplicity with which they were able to formulate the conclusion in the last sentence cited, unencumbered by qualifications of any kind. Notice, for example, that they were not arguing that *excessively* rising prices are incompatible with steady growth, or that rising prices are incompatible with steady growth over a prolonged period.

Two sets of evidence may be cited as having a bearing upon the statement of the Six. In *World Economic Survey, 1957,* published by the United Nations, data on industrial production and prices during periods of rising output were presented for ten European countries and the United States, for series of years going back to 1870. The data, which are reproduced in Table 1, show that since 1870 rising production has more often than not been accompanied by rising prices.[3]

Secondly, the staff of the Joint Economic Committee of the U.S. Congress, in a study entitled *Employment, Growth and Price Levels,* used the data reproduced in Tables 2 and 3 in reaching the following conclusion:

> The historical record, which is summarized in tables [2] and [3], casts considerable doubt on the view that inflation and growth are incompatible. . . . The data in both tables point to a single conclusion: there is no simple relationship between changes in output and changes in prices. Rapid economic growth has at different times been associated with rising, constant, and falling price levels, just as periods of slow growth, or, indeed, of no growth, have been marked by every manner of price behavior.[4]

This being the case, how does one account for the uncompromising statement by the Six that "rising prices are not compatible with steady growth?" Perhaps they would not accept any of the data cited above as being in any way relevant to the issue. After all, economic growth has almost always proceeded in fits and starts, periods of massive upsurge alternating with equally intense downswings; consequently growth has been anything but "steady." In other words, it may be held that historical evidence does not dis-

---

[3] United Nations, *World Economic Survey 1957* (New York, 1958), pp. 19–21. (Referred to subsequently as *Survey 1957.*)

[4] *Staff Report on Employment, Growth and Price Levels* (Joint Economic Committee, 86th Cong., 1st Sess.) (Washington, D.C.: U.S. Government Printing Office, December 24, 1959), pp. 11–13. (Referred to subsequently as *Staff Report.*)

TABLE 1

INDUSTRIAL PRODUCTION AND PRICES DURING PERIODS OF RISING OUTPUT,
BY COUNTRY

(*Average Annual Percentage Change*)

Country and Period	Production*	General Whole-sale	Raw Materials	Manu-fac-turing†	Consumer Total	Food
Federal Republic of Germany						
1880–91	6.8	0.2	...	...	...	...
1892–99	9.0	0.6	...	...	...	...
1901–7	6.1	3.2	2.9	...	2.4	2.5
1908–13	6.4	1.5	2.5	...	2.0	1.7
1924–29	9.8	—	−1.9	...	4.1	2.7
1932–38	20.4	1.6	1.2	2.1	0.8	0.9
1952–57	11.6	0.4	0.2	0.5	0.9	1.2
France						
1879–83	6.7	−1.5	−0.3	...	...	−2.8
1886–90	6.0	1.3	2.0	...	...	0.2
1895–1900	4.6	3.3	6.1	...	...	−0.2
1902–7	4.3	3.2	4.3	...	...	1.9
1908–13	6.2	3.0	3.5	...	3.0	2.3
1923–29	8.5	7.6	7.0	...	13.4	...
1932–37	4.0	7.6	5.4	4.7	4.4	...
1952–57	8.5	0.6	0.2	—	0.8	−0.2
Sweden						
1870–76	12.3	1.1	...	...	...	...
1879–85	9.1	−1.5	...	...	...	...
1888–98	18.6	−0.4	...	...	...	...
1901–7	5.0	2.0	...	...	1.7	...
1909–13	7.2	3.1	...	...	1.3	...
1923–29	9.8	−2.2	−2.3	−2.4	−0.7	−1.3
1932–37	14.1	5.1	4.4	4.4	0.6	1.9
1952–57	3.8	0.4	0.4	0.6	3.1	3.3
United Kingdom						
1870–74	3.9	1.6	−2.0	1.2	1.1	...
1879–83	7.9	—	0.2	−0.6	0.4	...
1886–90	5.2	0.9	1.6	2.0	—	−0.3
1893–99	4.1	—	1.4	−0.4	−0.6	−0.6
1904–7	4.0	4.4	6.5	4.0	1.1	1.1
1908–13	6.2	3.3	4.5	1.5	1.9	1.5
1923–29	2.7	−2.4	...	2.7	−0.8	−1.2
1932–37	8.5	5.3	11.2	4.0	1.4	2.0
1952–57	4.3	...	−0.6	1.8	3.7	1.9
United States						
1876–82	12.0	−0.3	...	...	...	...
1885–92	10.0	−1.5	...	...	...	...
1896–1903	11.0	4.0	...	...	2.2	...
1904–7	9.9	3.1	...	...	3.2	...

(*Continued on next page*)

Inflation and Growth in Latin America

TABLE 1—Continued

Country and Period	Production*	Prices			Consumer	
		General Whole-sale	Raw Mate-rials	Manu-fac-turing†	Total	Food
United States —Cont'd						
1908–13........	9.8	2.2	...	...	2.4	...
1924–29........	7.0	−0.6	...	−0.4	—	1.6
1932–37........	20.0	6.6	10.8	4.8	1.0	4.3
1954–57........	5.0	2.2	−0.3	2.3	1.5	0.5
Belgium						
1923–29........	8.0	11.8	...	...	16.3	...
1932–37........	7.6	5.7	...	...	1.3	1.6
1953–57........	5.6	1.9	...	...	1.5	1.7
Canada						
1924–29........	10.0	−0.8	...	...	0.4	...
1932–37........	13.6	5.3	10.6	2.4	0.4	...
1954–57........	5.8	1.6	0.8	2.0	1.5	1.8
Denmark						
1923–29........	4.0	—	...	...	−2.7	...
1932–37........	9.1	8.3	...	...	3.3	4.8
1952–57........	4.0	—	−0.7	0.6	2.6	2.3
Italy						
1923–29........	6.6	−2.2	...	...	1.7	...
1932–37........	9.7	5.5	...	...	1.8	...
1952–57........	10.2	0.5	0.2	−0.2	2.9	2.4
Netherlands						
1923–29........	10.4	1.0	...	...	−0.5	...
1933–38........	7.0	2.8	4.0	1.6	−0.1	...
1952–57........	8.2	1.0	1.4	1.0	2.4	3.2
Norway						
1923–29........	4.6	−5.7	...	...	−4.1	...
1932–37........	7.8	5.6	8.6	4.0	2.2	2.5
1952–57........	6.5	2.3	...	...	2.9	2.9

Sources: World Economic Survey, 1957. Production data for years before 1900, League of Nations, *Industrialization and Foreign Trade* (Geneva, 1945); production data for 1900–37, Organization for European Economic Cooperation, *Industrial Statistics, 1900–1955* (Paris, 1955); Federal Republic of Germany: Bremen Committee for Economic Research, *Wirtschaftsdaten, 1956* (Bremen) and current official sources; France: Statistical Office, *Annuaire Statistique de la France, 1956* (Paris) and National Institute of Statistics and Economic Studies, *Bulletin de la statistique générale de la France* (Paris); Sweden: Central Bureau of Statistics, *Statistisk Arsbok för Sverigue*, 1921, 1922, and 1938 (Stockholm) and current official sources; United Kingdom: *Nineteenth Abstract of Labour Statistics*, Cmd 3140 (London, 1928); Werner Schlote, *British Overseas Trade from 1700 to the 1930's* (Oxford, 1952) and current official sources; United States: Department of Commerce, *Historical Statistics of the United States, 1879–1945* (Washington, D.C., 1949) and current official sources; all other countries: League of Nations, *Statistical Yearbook* (Geneva) and current official sources. Data for the various periods shown refer to the territorial boundaries then in existence in each country, except that data for the Federal Republic of Germany for 1938 relate to the 1937 boundaries.

*From 1900 to date, total industrial production; for earlier periods, manufacturing production; in the United States, manufacturing production up to 1903.

†United Kingdom: export unit values for manufactures.

TABLE 2

GROWTH OF OUTPUT AND CHANGES OF PRICES, SUCCESSIVE DECADES,
IN SOME ADVANCED COUNTRIES*

Change from Preceding Decade†	Output Growth (percent)	Price Change (percent)
United States		
1879–88	88.0	−19.5
1889–98	38.2	−12.9
1899–1908	56.4	9.3
1909–18	35.5	34.6
1919–28	39.2	46.3
1929–38	6.2	−18.0
1939–48	71.7	34.2
1950–54	29.0	34.5
United Kingdom		
1875–84	21.2	....
1885–94	37.6	−15.0
1895–1904	29.2	−.9
1905–14	16.5	9.6
1915–24	−.8	106.0
1925–34	21.1	−16.6
1935–44	30.2	17.1
1949–53	22.7	51.3
Japan		
1892–1902	64.8	35.4
1903–12	34.7	38.2
1913–22	45.3	86.5
1923–32	67.4	−7.1
1933–42	52.1	28.6
1950–54	10.6	1,856.3
Norway		
1909–18	33.0	71.9
1919–28	29.1	60.8
1929–39	38.1	−37.5
1950–54	33.5	174.6
Netherlands		
1914–23	25.1	58.3
1924–33	40.1	−12.7
1934–43	.2	−7.1
1950–54	33.7	145.4
Italy		
1874–83	4.2	13.1
1884–93	19.4	−.87
1894–1903	11.8	−2.6
1904–13	30.7	11.4
1914–23	9.3	260.0
1924–33	40.6	35.0
1934–43	8.8	18.5
1950–54	23.9	4,442.4

(*Continued on next page*)

TABLE 2—Continued

Change from Preceding Decade†	Output Growth (percent)	Price Change (percent)
Sweden		
1874–83	30.6	7.5
1884–93	21.7	−12.0
1894–1903	40.5	2.7
1904–13	40.3	13.9
1914–23	25.1	99.2
1924–33	23.2	−11.3
1934–43	36.3	13.0
1950–54	60.1	62.4
Denmark		
1884–93	24.3	−6.2
1894–1903	38.4	——
1904–13	41.9	3.5
1914–23	35.8	126.5
1924–33	36.7	−26.7
1934–43	16.1	25.6
1950–54	28.5	119.3

Sources: *Joint Economic Commit'ee*, U.S. Congress, *S'aff Report on Employment, Growth and Price Levels*, computed from data appearing in S. Kuznets, "Quantitative Aspects of the Economic Growth of Nations," *Economic Development and Cultural Change*, Vol. V, No. 1.

*No sign indicates increase; minus indicates decrease.
†Last figure for all countr:es is not a decade-by-decade comparison.

prove the contention of the Six, because there never was a period of "steady growth," at any rate up to the second world war. If this is the argument, however, it is equally plain that historical evidence cannot support the views of the Six, either. In short, either historical evidence up to 1940 is relevant to the point under discussion, in which case the Six appear to be wrong, or it is not relevant, and cannot therefore either contradict or sustain the views of the Six.

But what of the postwar evidence? Economic growth since the second world war has probably been about as steady as could reasonably be expected in a world of rapid technological change and severe political tensions. Is this growth also doomed by rising prices? There seems to be no evidence that it is. Growth rates do indeed seem to have been falling in the industrial countries in recent years, but it could hardly be said that this is due directly or inherently to the fact of rising prices. It is true that governments seem to have felt the need to press the attack on rising prices almost to the point at which growth would stop. But to suggest that this is the reason why growth and rising prices are incompatible would be to give a rather strange significance to the views put forward by the Six.

TABLE 3

AVERAGE ANNUAL CHANGES IN PER CAPITA OUTPUT* AND PRICES,†
BY COUNTRY, 1949–58

(*Percent*)

Country	1949–58	
	Output	Price
Austria...............................	6.5	7.2
Federal Republic of Germany............	6.3	3.3‡
Italy.................................	5.5	2.9
France...............................	4.0	7.0
Switzerland...........................	3.5	1.2§
Netherlands..........................	3.2	4.3
Belgium..............................	2.6	2.5§
Sweden...............................	2.5	5.1
Norway...............................	2.5	5.4
Denmark..............................	2.1	4.0
United Kingdom.......................	1.9	4.5
United States........................	1.9	2.4

Source: Joint Economic Committee, U.S. Congress, *Staff Report on Employment, Growth and Price Levels,* based on data cited in M. Leiserson, *A Brief Interpretive Survey of Wage-Price Problems in Europe,* (Washington, D.C.: U.S. Government Printing Office, Study Paper No. 11), p. 36.

*Real gross national product per capita.
†Price indexes of gross national product.
‡1950–58.
§1949–57.

We must conclude, it seems, that whether or not there is any historical evidence supporting the belief that steady growth is compatible with rising prices, there is certainly no evidence whatever showing that stable prices are indispensable for steady growth. Such a view can be based only on a priori considerations. And presumably an a priori defense of the Six would have to rely mainly upon the contention that increases in prices, if continued long enough, are inherently explosive in character. As Lipsey has shown, however, even sustained inflations are explosive only if public reaction in adjusting to any given rate of inflation is such as to cause a further increase in prices equal to or greater than the previous increase. The inflation will, on the contrary, reach a steady rate if public reaction, in adjusting to any given rate of inflation, is such as to cause a further price increase that is less than the previous increase. As Lipsey has also shown, moreover, there is no reason why the acceptance of steady inflation should cause people to hoard commodities, provided that the rate of interest is adjusted to the inflation; and while steady inflation may lead to some reduction in desired cash holdings, it will not necessarily lead to a cumulative flight from cash any more than a rise in the interest rate would.[5]

Admittedly, there is no more reason, a priori, to assume that the public will react to steady inflation à la Lipsey than in a manner tending to generate hyperinflation. But in that case, we are back at the question of what the empirical data show about the nature of the public's reaction; and here, as we have seen, there is no comfort for the Six at all. As a matter of fact, Lipsey himself does examine the facts for 40-odd countries and finds that inflations of quite large magnitude have been maintained for long periods without showing any explosive tendencies, while a more detailed study of 20 of these countries indicates no general tendency for rates of inflation to accelerate from one year to the next.

If we now turn to the postwar experience of the industrial countries with inflation, the thing that we find most striking is how mild the adverse economic effects of the inflation seem to have been.

In the first place, there seems to have been no tendency for the inflations in western Europe or North America to get out of hand, despite the fact that the public was widely thought to have accepted the idea that inflation would last indefinitely. It is true that tight money policies were employed quite widely as a device to arrest inflation by restraining aggregate demand. The effectiveness of the restrictions actually imposed is subject to question, since in virtually all countries the gross national product rose considerably more than the supply of money. In other words, the impact of the restrictions was offset in whole or in part by economies in the use of money. This assessment remains valid even if, for this purpose, we include the near substitutes for money within the definition of money, despite the increased use of the former induced by restrictive policies.[6]

However, even if we were to conclude that the postwar inflations in the industrial countries were kept within bounds only by virtue of tight monetary policies, that very conclusion would itself imply that there was little real danger that the inflations would get out of hand.

Adverse effects on the allocation of resources are also not much in evidence. There seems to have been no excessive hoarding of

---

[5]R. G. Lipsey, "Is Inflation Explosive?," *The Banker*, October, 1961.

[6]See *Survey 1957*, p. 52, Footnote 48; and A. E. Holmans, "The Quantity of Money, Gross National Product and the Price Level," *Scottish Journal of Political Economy*, February, 1961, Table III.

commodities except during certain isolated periods of uncertainty, such as immediately after the outbreak of hostilities in Korea. Nor does there appear to have been any abnormal growth in luxury consumption. Even in the countries experiencing the highest rates of increase in consumer prices during the 1950's, such as Sweden and the United Kingdom, the proportion of personal disposable income saved rose steadily. Investment in the expansion and modernization of productive capacity was sustained at relatively high rates over a much longer period than had been customary in the past.

Nor have the major shares in the distribution of income been affected very much. In particular, the evidence does not suggest any considerable shift from wages to profits such as might be expected as the result of inflation. Phelps Brown and M. H. Browne found a remarkable stability in postwar shares of pay and property incomes in net domestic product in 25 countries for which they examined the data available. As they themselves conclude: "Over the whole field, what is remarkable is the absence of any general distributive change in the presence of general inflation."[7]

Some minor income groups possessing relatively little bargaining power have undoubtedly fallen behind. In the United States, for example, the major lagging groups have been employees of government, educational institutions, and religious and charitable organizations, and, above all, retired persons dependent on fixed income payments.[8] It would have been quite possible to avoid these consequences of inflation had there been sufficient public *esprit de corps* to compel the necessary action to be taken.[9]

There remain the effects of inflation on the balance of payments. Here, of course, one cannot speak of general effects throughout the group of industrial countries. Balance of payments pressures may arise in particular countries experiencing more intense rates of inflation than their trading partners; but external disequilibrium may just as well result from differential rates of decline in prices in various countries as from differential rates of increase. And even a situation of stable prices all round may be accompanied by severe

---

[7]E. H. Phelps Brown and M. H. Browne, "Distribution and Productivity under Inflation, 1947–57," *Economic Journal*, December, 1960, p. 745.

[8]*Staff Report*, pp. 110–12.

[9]For example, Amotz Morag has put forward the idea of escalating all contractual payments in relation to a price index agreed upon for the purpose. See "For an Inflation-Proof Economy," *American Economic Review*, March, 1962, p. 177.

balance of payments disequilibria if incomes rise at very different rates in various countries, or if given rates of increase in income in various countries are associated with widely divergent rates of increase in imports or exports. While, therefore, it is customary to refer to certain cases in which balance of payments problems of particular industrial countries are thought to have been associated with domestic inflation, it could hardly be said that postwar balance of payments disequilibria among these countries as a group have been made especially severe by inflation. On the contrary, such disequilibria have probably been less acute than those of the inter-war period.

Before reviewing the causes of postwar inflation in the industrial countries, it may be helpful to get out some price indices that will indicate the order of magnitude of the problem under something reasonably close to normal conditions. In Table 4 consumer price indices are shown for 1961, taking 1953 as the base. Thus the indices abstract not only from the abnormal developments immediately after the war but also from the immediate impact of the outbreak of hostilities in Korea in 1950. The cumulative annual rates of increase in prices during this eight-year period ranged from 1.2 percent in Switzerland to 3.1 percent in Sweden; in France the rate was as much as 4.1 percent per annum, but it has to be borne in mind that the franc was devalued by nearly 30 percent in the course of the period.

These rates are, of course, very low by Latin-American standards. The very fact that they are so low raises serious problems of statistical interpretation. As Ruggles has pointed out:

> There is, thus, an upward bias in the price indexes for almost every category of expenditures. For commodities it exists because quality changes and new products cannot be adequately integrated into the price data. For services it exists because by and large the value of services is assumed not to increase, although there is strong evidence that it does. By ignoring the upward bias of the price indexes we are likely to be basing our policy on a mistaken impression. Since we are forced to use inflexible and inadequate assumptions to arrive at specific price indexes, we may create indicators which are more the result of our assumptions than of the real world.[10]

It will be obvious that, particularly for those countries that appear near the bottom of Table 4, it would not take much in the

---

[10] Statement submitted by Professor Richard Ruggles, Yale University, to the U.S. Senate Judiciary Subcommittee on Anti-Trust and Monopoly, on Bill S.215, requiring advance notice of price increases.

way of adjustment for the factors listed above to eliminate all indication of consumer price inflation. Indeed, the Ruggleses have posed their famous Sears Roebuck conundrum to emphasize the point. Assume, they say, that a consumer were given $1,000 which he was free to spend either wholly on items from the 1948 Sears Roebuck catalogue or wholly on items from the current catalogue.

TABLE 4

CONSUMER PRICES, 1953 TO 1961*

	Index in 1961 (1953 = 100)	Average Annual Percentage Increase from 1953 to 1961 (percent per annum)
France...................	138	4.1
Sweden...................	128	3.1
United Kingdom..........	125	2.8
Norway.................	124	2.7
Netherlands.............	123	2.6
Japan...................	120	2.3
Italy....................	118	2.1
West Germany...........	114	1.7
Canada.................	112	1.4
United States...........	112	1.4
Belgium................	111	1.3
Switzerland.............	110	1.2

Source: United Nations, *Monthly Bulletin of Statistics*, April, 1962.
*Countries listed in descending order of the indices.

It is by no means obvious that he would prefer the 1948 catalogue, despite its apparently "lower" prices. If, however, he did choose the current catalogue, in what sense could it be said that prices had risen since 1948?[11]

Since there is no way of determining what allowance to make for the upward bias in the price indices, we shall have to assume, at least for the sake of argument, that any such allowance would still leave something in the way of inflation to be accounted for. We may have our own views as to whether the adjusted rates of increase in prices could be such as to warrant the extraordinary efforts that have been made to damp them down—efforts that have not stopped short, in some countries, of bringing the whole process of economic

---

[11]Professor Richard Ruggles and Dr. Nancy D. Ruggles, *Prices, Costs, Demand and Output in the United States, 1947–1957*, Statement for the Joint Economic Committee Hearing on The Relationship of Prices to Economic Stability and Growth, May 15, 1958.

growth almost to a halt. However that may be, it is still necessary
to determine the factors that lie behind these price increases.

There seems to be a growing measure of agreement among economists about the nature of the inflationary process in the industrial
countries. It is still not uncommon to meet economists, both young
and old, who will maintain quite cheerfully and without the slightest apparent qualms that there is only one kind of inflation—the
kind that is due to excess demand; this may or may not be coupled
with emphasis on the supply of money as the key factor in generating excess demand. But it appears that this can no longer be
regarded as the dominant view.

Traditional economic theory gave no basis for anything but a
one-track analysis of inflation. In the world of perfect competition,
with infinitely mobile factors of production and infinitely flexible
prices of both commodities and factors that were continuously adjusted to clear the market, there was no room for any sort of inflation other than that brought about by an over-all excess of demand.
Not until economists recognized the existence of structural rigidities did they begin to see the possibility that factors other than excess demand could set off an upward movement in prices.

The correct diagnosis of the nature of inflation in any particular
country is, of course, an indispensable requirement in deciding what
anti-inflationary policies to pursue. If all inflations are simply the
result of excess aggregate demand, anti-inflationary policies must
concentrate upon reducing aggregate demand. If, on the other
hand, there are inflationary processes that do not involve an excess
aggregate demand, attempts to deal with them through the curtailment of such demand are bound to create unemployment without
even any assurance that the unwanted price increases will be prevented.

A considerable step forward from the traditional view of inflation
is reflected in the report of the Six. They came to the conclusion
that there were four main groups of factors accounting for rising
prices, which they listed as follows:

1. special or temporary factors
2. excess demand for goods and labor
3. excessive negotiated wage increases as an independent force
4. monopolistic pricing

The special or temporary factors need not detain us long. They
include increases in indirect taxes, advances in import prices, and
the effect of derationing or decontrol. Sweden, particularly, would

have appeared in a much lower position in Table 4 but for the effect on prices of considerable increases in indirect taxes during the period.

On the whole, import prices appear to have been stable or to have fallen slightly in most industrial countries since 1953. There was, however, a marked upward movement from 1955 to 1957 which probably had a significant impact on final prices. And while there was a subsequent import price decline, the usual "ratchet" effect may have come into play, so that the net impact of import prices on the general price level may well have been inflationary, taking the period since 1953 as a whole.[12]

Changes in administered rents are among the most important of the third category of "special" factors listed above for the industrial countries as a group. In addition, in the case of the United Kingdom, part of the increase in consumer prices during the early part of the period since 1953 reflected the much slower decontrol of food prices in that country after the war than in the other countries of the industrial group.

Apart from the above, the Six refer to the upward pressures on prices that may result from accidental factors, such as poor harvests, or from an event such as the Suez crisis.

None of these various sources of pressure on prices was the result of excess demand, and it would therefore have been a policy error to attempt to prevent price increases by measures of monetary or fiscal contraction. Reference has already been made to the upward bias that exists in our price indices. It will now be further apparent that, after making additional allowance for the impact on prices of the special factors described above, the residual price increases to be attributed to all other influences, including both demand and cost pressures, become even smaller.

The second main source of price increases listed by the Six[13] is excess demand which they define as:

. . . a volume of aggregate monetary demand which cannot be met at existing prices without exerting undue pressure on productive resources.

---

[12]The justification for including movements in import prices among the "special" factors lies in the fact that for all of the industrial countries individually, except possibly the United States, import prices may be regarded as exogenously determined. For the group as a whole, on the other hand, movements in import prices would have to be considered as reflecting changes in domestic demand as well as in external supply.

[13]One of the Six—Professor Kahn—dissociated himself from the analysis of inflation in terms of "excess demand." The strictures that follow in the above discussion do not therefore apply to Kahn.

The direct chain of causation from excess demand to rising prices is well known: pressure is put on productive resources as more and more goods are demanded, capacity becomes strained, a general labour shortage develops, and prices and wages are bid up by buyers and employers competing for the scarce supplies.[14]

This definition is, perhaps, not fully satisfactory as it stands because it does not clearly indicate the essential element that causes an initial rise in prices to be transformed into a cumulative process of inflation. That essential element is the reaction of those social groups whose real incomes are depressed by the initial rise in prices. If there is no reaction from these groups, equilibrium between demand and supply is restored at a higher level of prices and lower level of real wages. It is usually the attempt of wage earners to regain their share of aggregate real income that sets off a cumulative spiral of wages and prices.[15]

The Six consider that there was excess demand, in their sense, in most of the industrial countries from 1955 to 1957, as a result of a boom in industrial investment superimposed upon a strong upward trend in consumer demand, particularly for durable goods, and a high level of housing outlays.

It is open to question, however, whether the Six were correct in attributing the price increases of this period to excess aggregate demand. The point is of some importance because if the Six have made a valid diagnosis, the countries concerned were right, or would have been right, in seeking to combat the prevailing inflation through the usual global measures of fiscal and monetary contraction. If, on the other hand, the Six were wrong, it is possible that measures of a quite different type were really needed. Since the present conference is oriented toward the problems of Latin America, and since some of the difficulties in dealing with inflation in Latin America have been the result of incorrect diagnosis of the malady, this matter may repay more detailed examination.

The difficulty arises because the Six failed to distinguish a fifth factor which, it would seem, was one of the most important, if not the most important, in the price increases that occurred in the industrial countries during the 1950's. This factor was what we called "excess sectoral demand" in *World Economic Survey 1957*:

> In a second type of inflation the essential common element is a shortage of certain specific items; the prices of these items rise and thereby exert

---

[14]Organization for European Economic Cooperation, *The Problem of Rising Prices* (Paris: May, 1961), p. 33. Referred to subsequently as *Rising Prices*.

[15]As indicated below, excess aggregate demand is not an indispensable prerequisite for a wage-price spiral.

pressure on the prices of other goods. The most characteristic situation of this type is that in which supplies of raw materials respond sluggishly to a general advance in demand.

The basic difficulty here is not, as in the first case, that supply in general falls short of aggregate demand at existing prices. It is rather that the pattern of supply is ill adjusted to the pattern of demand; or, to put the same point in another way, that the typical elasticities of supply of various commodities are widely different, depending upon whether they are products of agriculture or industry, whether the time taken to produce them is long or short, whether there is excess capacity—and so forth. As before, the rise in prices becomes cumulative because of its tendency to affect the level or distribution of real income, and because of the resistance offered to this tendency by those adversely affected. This second type of inflation, which may be attributed to 'excess sectoral demand,' can occur under conditions in which resources in general are far from fully employed; experience during the economic recovery of the nineteen thirties provides an ample illustration.[16]

As is well known, prices of raw materials and certain other items may rise quite sharply even near the low point of a depression because of a short-period inelasticity of supply in the face of expanding demand. Such price increases in certain sectors push up the costs and hence the prices of other sectors, and in this way upward pressures on prices may spread throughout the economy, becoming cumulative and self-sustaining *even though aggregate demand remains well below the full employment level.*[17]

Even in situations that may correctly be characterized as situations of excess aggregate demand, it is important, in determining appropriate anti-inflationary policies, to be able to identify pockets of excess sectoral demand, since these in any event require special treatment. For example, the immediate postwar inflations in western Europe were the result of the overall pressure of pent-up demand on the part of both producers and consumers, who had at their disposal large volumes of liquid assets that they had accumulated during the war. This situation of excess aggregate demand was, however, complicated by shortages of food. In this respect the im-

---

[16]*Survey 1957*, pp. 22–23. See also pp. 29–33.

[17]In this connection, the Six appear to confuse an excessively high *level* of demand with an excessively high *rate of increase* in demand. Having defined excess demand in the manner referred to above, they proceed to document their belief that there was excess demand during the period 1955–57 by stating that:

> . . . in the United States, expenditures on new plant and equipment for the year 1957 were 23 per cent higher than in the year 1955—already a substantial increase. But between the first quarter of 1955 and the first quarter of 1957 the increase, at 60 per cent, was nearly three times as great.

This evidence, however, cannot in itself even establish an excessively high *level* of demand in the engineering sector of the economy, let alone an excessively high *level of aggregate demand.*

mediate postwar inflations in the industrial countries bore certain striking similarities to some of the inflations that have occurred in underdeveloped countries, where food shortages have likewise been crucial.

Food is, of course, a particularly strategic item in consumption, and global measures of monetary or fiscal contraction may therefore not have any marked impact on the demand for food unless they are pushed to the point at which they cause substantial unemployment. It was partly for this reason that governments relied on direct controls on the distribution of food during and after the war: the controls held down the prices of food as well as insuring equitable distribution of available supplies.

Sectoral pressures were also important in the upsurge in prices associated with the outbreak of hostilities in Korea, in 1950–51. In fact, although it is widely believed or assumed that the industrial countries experienced a wave of excess aggregate demand during that period, the available evidence does not give unambiguous support to this view, at any rate for all countries. It is true that there were significant increases in government defense expenditures and associated private investment outlays. But stiff anti-inflationary measures were adopted at the same time, and the crucial point is that these measures were based on the expectation of a much larger rise in military expenditure than actually occurred. What happened was that in practice rearmament programs were stretched out over much longer periods than had originally been intended. Consequently the anti-inflationary measures tended to overcompensate for the growth in demand, with the result that seasonally adjusted industrial production indices leveled off or declined before the end of 1951 in all the industrial countries.[18] Certainly there was little sign in most countries of some of the usual features of a classical inflation, such as a shift to profits; in most countries, moreover, the ratio of consumption to personal disposable income actually declined in 1951. Thus the fact that prices rose considerably was probably due much less to the pressure of aggregate demand than to the impact of the business expansion upon the prices of primary products, supplies of which did not respond readily to the sudden growth in demand. This sectoral increase in prices spread rapidly throughout the economy.

During the period of expansion in the industrial countries from 1955 to 1957, the principal sectoral bottlenecks were to be found

---

[18]*Survey 1957*, pp. 25–26.

not in raw materials or in foodstuffs but in the industries producing durable goods. A high level of business demand for machinery and equipment was accompanied in several countries by a boom in purchases of consumer durables. This led to severe pressure of demand upon supply in the engineering sector of the economy. Meanwhile, in other sectors of the economy demand was generally below capacity levels. As we indicated in *World Economic Survey 1957:*

> What happened, in effect, was that the pattern of demand for consumption and investment was substantially different from the pattern of supply of consumer goods and investment goods made possible at full employment by the existing distribution of productive resources. In other words, the community was demanding more durable goods than could be supplied, and could have supplied more by way of other goods than was being demanded.[19]

As a result, prices rose sharply in the coal, basic metal, and engineering industries, and these prices then spread throughout the economy. The key importance of the steel- and machinery-producing sectors in the inflation may be illustrated by the data for the United Kingdom and the United States shown in Table 5.

TABLE 5

WHOLESALE PRICES IN 1957

(1955 = 100)

	All Finished Goods	Steel	Machinery
United Kingdom..........	107	142	112*
United States............	107	115	116

Source: United Nations Statistical Office and national sources.
*Export unit value.

In order to focus the discussion a little more sharply it may be worth-while to dwell for a moment on at least one of the specific examples of excess aggregate demand cited by the Six. According to the Six, the United States was in a situation of excess aggregate demand from "late 1955 to early 1957."[20]

First of all, U.S. unemployment averaged 4.2 percent of the labor force in 1956, as against 4.4 percent in 1955: both figures are much higher than the frictional minimum, and considerably higher than,

[19]*Survey 1957*, p. 60.
[20]*Rising Prices*, Table 4, p. 35.

say, the 2.9 percent average for 1953—not a year of excess demand according to the Six.

Secondly, the output of all manufacturing industries rose only 1 percent from the fourth quarter of 1955 to the fourth quarter of 1956. Since manufacturing capacity is estimated to have risen by at least 5 to 6 percent during this period[21] it will be quite apparent that the pressure of demand upon capacity must have slackened considerably. Even at the end of 1955, in fact, the rate of utilization of capacity in manufacturing was considerably less than in mid-1953,[22] and by the end of 1956, of course, the rate of utilization was even lower.

Even in the durable goods industries alone, the rate of utilization of capacity must have been significantly lower at the end of 1955 and in 1956 than in mid-1953. It will be seen from Table 6 that durable goods output in 1956 averaged only 1 or 2 percent higher than in the second quarter of 1953, immediately before the 1953 recession. Data on fixed investment in the durable goods industries suggest that capacity must have grown much more than this during the intervening period.

Table 7 shows further that the hardest-pressed industries did not produce much more in 1956 than they had in the second quarter of 1953; indeed the primary metals sector produced at about the same rate in the two periods, while output in the fabricated metals, non-electrical machinery, and motor vehicle industries was actually lower in 1956 than it had been three year earlier.

It is very difficult to reconcile this evidence with the assertion that there was excess aggregate demand in the United States in 1956. Strangely enough, moreover, the Six were themselves fully aware of these facts, as they indicate in their own discussion of the matter. After describing the boom in industrial investment in the United States in 1956, they go on to say:

> In view of the limited extent to which resources can be switched from one sector to another and in view of the manner in which inflationary developments tend to be transmitted to others where perhaps no disequilibria exist, fluctuations in fixed investment demand of the magnitude experienced in the period 1955 and 1956 would appear to be virtually impossible to reconcile with financial stability and a steady rate of growth at high employment levels.[23]

---

[21]See "Business Plans for New Plant and Equipment," *11th Annual McGraw-Hill Survey*, April 18, 1958, Table VI.

[22]*Survey 1957*, Table 63, p. 163.

[23]*Rising Prices*, p. 38.

This being the case, how is it that the Six believed that there was excess aggregate demand in the United States in 1956—a judgment carrying with it the implication that global measures of restriction are an appropriate weapon for dealing with immobilities of the type referred to in the quotation cited above? It is not easy to answer this question, except perhaps by saying that since the Six did not recognize a distinct category of inflation associated with excess sectoral demand, they chose the category which seemed nearest at hand.

TABLE 6

UNITED STATES: INDEX OF MANUFACTURING, SEASONALLY ADJUSTED

(1957 = 100)

Year and Quarter	Total	Durable	Nondurable
1953 II................................	94	99	88
1955 IV................................	100	101	98
1956 I.................................	99	100	98
II................................	99	100	99
III................................	100*	101*	99
IV................................	101	102	100
1957 I.................................	102	103	100

Source: Board of Governors of the Federal Reserve System, *Industrial Production 1959 Revision* (Washington, D.C.: U.S. Government Printing Office, 1960).

*August–September only. Production in July was affected by a steel strike.

Perhaps they also subscribed to the position taken by Wilfred Beckerman, the secretary of the group, who in an appendix to the report argued that:

> Thus, towards the second half of 1955, the level of demand was sufficiently heavy in important sectors or regions of the United States for it to have been generally in excess. . . [24]

When not all sectors of an economy are affected by excess demand, it may admittedly become a question of judgment to decide exactly where sectoral inflation ends and general inflation begins. But such a question could hardly arise in the instance under discussion. The basic metal and engineering sectors together accounted for only 16 percent of the national income of the United States in 1956, so that to argue that pressure in this sector was equivalent to pressure on the whole economy would seem to be a case of the tail

---

[24]*Rising Prices,* p. 208.

wagging the dog.[25] Moreover, as is apparent from Table 7, it was only certain of the engineering industries that can have experienced really severe pressure of demand against capacity. That there was little or no pressure on consumer goods industries in 1956 is confirmed by the sharp drop in the ratio of consumption to personal disposable income in 1956, following the increase in 1955 which had resulted from an exceptionally high level of sales of passenger cars. So far from there being excess aggregate demand in 1956, the ratio of consumption to personal disposable income in that year was well below the average for the decade of the 1950's.

TABLE 7

UNITED STATES: INDEX OF OUTPUT OF DURABLE MANUFACTURES, SEASONALLY ADJUSTED

(*1957 = 100*)

	1953 Second Quarter	1955 Fourth Quarter	1956 Year	1957 First Quarter
Durable manufactures				
Total..........................	99	101	100	103
Primary metals...............	104	111	104	106
Fabricated metals.............	102	100	97	100
Machinery....................	99	98	103	105
Electrical...................	94	96	102	103
Nonelectrical................	104	99	103	106
Motor vehicles and parts.......	95	118	92*	104

Source: Board of Governors of the Federal Reserve System, *Industrial Production 1959 Revision* (Washington, D.C.: U.S. Government Printing Office, 1960).

*Index for 1955: 118.

The term "excess aggregate demand" ought, it seems, to be reserved for those situations in which the pressure of consumer de-

[25]Beckerman suggests that capacity was fairly fully extended in the motor vehicle and other consumer durable industries as well as in certain industries producing materials. It is true that the motor vehicle industry was fully extended in 1955, but in 1956, which is the year of alleged over-all demand inflation, there was a sharp decline in consumption of durables, particularly motor cars. There was also a considerable drop in residential construction. As regards the industries producing basic materials, these were operating in the second half of 1955 and in the first half of 1956 at rates of capacity utilization little or no higher than in the first half of 1953, and much lower than in 1951. This was just as true of the basic metal industries as of other materials-producing industries. The textile materials industries were operating at only 80 percent of capacity in the first half of 1956. In the second half of 1956, rates of utilization declined considerably in all industries. See *Survey 1957*, Table 60, p. 159.

mand upon supply causes widespread shortages of major items of consumption. Such pressure of consumer demand may be the result either of efforts by the government or business sector to appropriate major additional real resources for public expenditure or private investment, under conditions of full employment; or it may be associated, under the same conditions, with a sharp increase in the proportion of personal disposable incomes spent. The appropriate remedy in these cases, as already noted, would be measures of global fiscal and monetary contraction.

But if the overwhelming majority of the economy producing consumer goods is operating well within its capacity limitations, measures to restrict total demand will not only ease the load on the hard-pressed sectors but will further depress the slack sectors as well. And this is, of course, exactly what happened both in the United States and in the United Kingdom from 1955 onward.

Thus far it has been implied that if we want to curb sectoral inflation, we should do so through measures that are selective in their impact and do not penalize the whole of the economy because of the pressures experienced by a small part of it. The next question one might ask, however, is—do we necessarily want to curb sectoral inflation in all circumstances? Suppose, for example, that a government decision had been taken to raise the rate of growth substantially and that this involved an increase in the rate of investment sufficient to create serious bottlenecks in the investment goods industries—serious enough to lead to price increases. It has to be borne in mind that such price increases are the signal, in a market economy, for business enterprise to create new capacity in the sectors where shortages have arisen. If the government always acts to prevent such price increases, the incentive to private business to overcome the shortages may be greatly weakened, especially if government policy goes so far as to bring about a general economic slowdown. In such circumstances, the rate of growth of the economy as a whole may come, in effect, to be limited by the existing bottlenecks to higher production; and the fear of price increases may thereby lead to a vicious circle of unbalanced production and government anti-inflationary restrictions. Government policies to deal with sectoral inflation should therefore concentrate on measures to increase sectoral supplies, and should not undertake to curb even sectoral excess demand without carefully weighing the consequences.

We come finally to the last of the causes of postwar inflation—namely autonomous tendencies for factor incomes to rise faster than productivity. Inflation of this type may be touched off even in the absence of excess aggregate or excess sectoral demand. All that is required is that demand should be sufficiently buoyant to permit entrepreneurs or workers to press successfully for higher profit margins or higher wages: in either case the effect may be to initiate an upward spiral of wages and prices.

It appears that there are certain structural features of the relationship between wages and productivity that predispose the whole economic system toward cost inflation once anything happens to start an upward spiral going. The essence of the matter is that while there are strong influences tending to bring about parallel movements in earnings in all industries, productivity usually rises very much more in the rapidly expanding industries than in the rest of the economy. The evidence for this conclusion was set forth in two tables in *World Economic Survey 1957,* which are reproduced in part as Tables 8 and 9 in the present paper. From Table 8 it will be seen that while there were considerable differences between countries in the interindustry dispersion of wage increases

TABLE 8

INTERINDUSTRY VARIATIONS IN HOURLY EARNINGS AND PRODUCTIVITY IN
MANUFACTURING, 1950–56

(Percentage)

	Coefficient of Variation†		*Average Annual Percentage of Unemployment*
Country*	*Average Hourly Earnings*	*Output per Man-hour*	
Italy‡............................	22	76	9.5
Belgium........................	21	. . .	10.1
Canada........................	19	118	3.5
Denmark§....................	19	89	9.8
United States................	18	95	4.1
Netherlands‖.................	13	99	2.1
Federal Republic of Germany......	12	38	7.3
Sweden¶.......................	11	62	2.4
United Kingdom...............	10	81	1.5
France‖........................	9	88	. . .
Norway‖.......................	9	86	1.2

Source: United Nations, *World Economic Survey 1957.*

*Countries ranked in descending order of the relative dispersion of percentage changes in earnings.

†Coefficient of variation is the standard deviation expressed as a percentage of the mean change. It measures the extent to which percentage changes in hourly earnings and output per man-hour in various industries are clustered about the mean percentage change for all manufacturing industries.

‡1951–55.
§1951–56.
‖1950–55.
¶1952–55.

from 1950 to 1956,[26] the dispersion was in all cases very much smaller than the corresponding dispersion in productivity gains.

Again, from the data in Table 9 it emerges that the upper quartile of industries recording the greatest expansion of output

TABLE 9

DETERMINANTS OF WAGE COST IN MANUFACTURING, BY COUNTRY*

Country and Item	Average Annual Percentage Change, 1950–56†			
	Output	Output Per Man-hour	Average Hourly Earnings	Wage Cost Per Unit of Output
Canada				
Average of highest quartile.....	10.1	6.8	8.1	0.9
All manufacturing............	4.2	2.4	7.7	4.7
Denmark				
Average of highest quartile.....	7.0	3.5	4.5	0.8
All manufacturing............	2.2	1.5	4.7	3.0
Federal Republic of Germany				
Average of highest quartile.....	28.4	7.0	8.6	1.1
All manufacturing............	16.5	6.7	8.9	1.5
Netherlands				
Average of highest quartile.....	11.3	4.8	6.4	1.3
All manufacturing............	7.0	2.6	6.8	3.8
Norway				
Average of highest quartile.....	9.5	5.1	9.3	3.4
All manufacturing............	5.6	3.0	9.5	5.7
Sweden				
Average of highest quartile.....	7.8	6.4	15.6	7.0
All manufacturing............	2.8	2.8	14.0	9.8
United Kingdom				
Average of highest quartile.....	5.6	1.7	9.5	7.2
All manufacturing............	3.5	1.2	9.1	7.4
United States				
Average of highest quartile.....	8.7	3.0	6.0	2.6
All manufacturing............	4.7	2.3	5.8	3.1

Source: United Nations, *World Economic Survey 1957.*

*Based on industrial censuses.
†For Denmark: 1951–55 and 1953–55; for the Netherlands, Norway, and Sweden: 1950–55 and 1953–56.

[26] As discussed below, the interindustry dispersion of wage increases seems, with some exceptions, to have been smallest where the labor market was tightest, as reflected in unemployment percentages.

from 1950 to 1956 also generally enjoyed the greatest advances in productivity; and this in turn was usually associated with a somewhat smaller rate of increase in wage costs per unit of output in the upper quartile of industries, even where average hourly earnings rose more rapidly than in manufacturing industry as a whole. Productivity increases were, in fact, greatest in the rapidly growing metals and engineering industries, and least in the relatively stagnant or slow-growing textile and food processing industries.

The implication of the above pattern of relationships is, of course, that workers 'in rapidly growing industries have only to demand and secure wage increases that exceed the average productivity advance of the economy as a whole (though not necessarily that of their own industries) for a general upward pressure on costs and prices to develop. For while wages in other industries will then move more or less in sympathy with wages in the most dynamic industries, productivity increases will be much lower. Thus costs and prices might rise for the economy as a whole even though productivity remained in step with wages in the most dynamic sectors. A fortiori, if the concentration of heavy pressure of demand in a particular sector (such as the basic metal and engineering sectors in 1955–57, as we have seen) led to an increase in wage costs in that sector, the interindustry wage-productivity relationships described above would cause the increase in costs to spread to other sectors, even though the latter might be operating below full capacity.

Some economists have suggested that the increases in wages that took place during the 1950's were simply the result of excess demand manifesting itself in the labor market through the bidding up of wages by employers. In this view, in fact, the role of the trade unions must have been illusory, since wages would in any case have risen to the extent that they did under the influence of market forces. This sort of analysis is, however, difficult to reconcile not merely with such observed facts as the overt struggles between employers and workers over the issue of higher wages but with the very low interindustry dispersion of earnings shown in Table 6. Clearly, interindustry differences in the rate of growth of demand must have been much greater than corresponding differences in the rate of increase in average hourly earnings. But in that case, how could one account for the relatively large wage increases in the slack industries except in terms of autonomous forces such as trade union action?

It is true that the degree of dispersion of increases in earnings appears to be related to some extent to the level of unemployment.

In other words, the uniformity of wage movements was greatest, on the whole (and with some exceptions) where there was the greatest overall pressure of demand in the labor market, namely in the Netherlands, Norway, Sweden, and the United Kingdom; and uniformity was least where unemployment was relatively high, namely in Belgium, Denmark, and Italy. This could, perhaps, be interpreted as meaning that as demand pressures increase and become more and more pervasive throughout the economy, excess pressures in the labor market also become more widespread, so that earnings tend to move more closely in line. There may be something in this, but such an analysis would still not explain why wages and prices rose even in countries where unemployment percentages were as high as 9 or 10.

By the same token, the fact that average increases in wages have responded to some extent to business cycle fluctuations does not mean that wage advances have always been the result of excess aggregate demand. The state of demand may indeed affect the wage bargaining process not only directly, through the market for labor, but also indirectly through its effect on the positions taken by employers and workers at the bargaining table. But this does not mean that there is any simple relationship between the level of demand and the rate of increase in wages. Certainly wages have risen considerably even during periods of recession, so that whatever there is between wage increases and demand must, at the very least, involve significant time lags.

It is also important to bear in mind that it is not only wages that respond to business cycle fluctuations but productivity as well. We have already noted that productivity has generally risen most rapidly in the fastest expanding industries. It may now be observed that postwar business cycles in the industrial countries have been marked by rising overall productivity during periods of growth and by stagnant or falling productivity during periods of slack demand or recession. Thus a reduction in the pressure of demand below the full employment level may contribute to a slowing down in the rate of increase in wages without thereby restraining advances in wage costs per unit of output, simply because of the adverse impact of slack demand on productivity. In fact, in the United States from 1957 to 1961 labor cost per unit of output seems to have risen during periods of falling production and to have declined during phases of recovery, because the adverse effect of falling demand on productivity was much greater than the "favorable" effect on wages, and vice versa.[27]

---

[27]See United Nations, *World Economic Survey 1961*, pp. 137–38.

Thus a policy of attempting to control wage increases through curtailment of the volume of demand can prove to be entirely self-defeating. In fact it may accelerate increases in wage costs instead of slowing them down. No policy can be regarded as satisfactory in this field which does not take the effects on productivity fully into account.

Despite this, much of the discussion of wage policy seems to assume that productivity can be taken for granted. This is true not only of those who believe that changes in wages result exclusively from variations in demand but also of those who subscribe to the possibility of autonomous shifts in wages and profits. For example, the Six expressed themselves on the need for a wage policy as follows:

> By having a wages policy, we mean, first of all, that the authorities themselves must have a reasonably precise view, estimated by the best means which they can devise, of the average increase in wages that is appropriate to the economic situation and consistent with stability of the price level. This view will necessarily depend primarily on experience and expectations regarding the longer-run rate of productivity increase in the economy.[28]

But what "expectations regarding the longer-run rate of productivity increase" should one have? Rates of productivity increase in manufacturing in the industrial countries shown in Table 9 vary from 1.2 percent per annum in the United Kingdom to 6.7 percent per annum in western Germany; for Italy the corresponding figure would be 8.9 percent and for Japan something even higher. Is it likely that a trade unionist in a slow-growing country would be prepared to take for granted, for wage-setting purposes, a rate of increase in productivity that he suspects is at least partly the result of misguided government policies?

Even more important are the considerations advanced by Kaldor in this connection. As he points out, given a slow rate of growth in productivity and total production, a certain degree of inflation can scarcely be avoided except at the cost of jeopardizing the modest annual improvement actually attained:

> . . . it is dangerous for a weakly-progressive economy to aim at a regime of stable prices (let alone at a regime of falling prices) since when the rate of growth of production is low (on account of a stagnant working population, a low rate of technical progress, or both) stable prices are only consistent with low rates of profit which may be insufficient to maintain the inducement to invest. . . . In the light of this the objective of stable

---

[28]*Rising Prices*, pp. 57–58.

or falling prices may well be regarded as a luxury which only fast-growing economies can afford.[29]

In other words, the first target of any policy designed to maintain price stability in the industrial countries should be *to secure an adequate rate of growth of output and productivity.* If experience of inflation in the industrial countries during the 1950's has taught anything, it has taught this.

Before ending this review of postwar experience of inflation in the industrial countries, it should, perhaps, be emphasized that conclusions drawn from the experience of moderate inflation in these countries cannot be mechanically extrapolated so as to apply to underdeveloped countries, particularly those where inflation has been rapid. Moreover, nothing in the present review should be regarded as justifying a passive or indifferent attitude to inflation. Inflation has little merit as a policy for economic development. Indeed, inflation may be regarded as a result of the *lack* of a genuine development policy caused, usually, by unwillingness or inability to face up to all the political, social, and economic implications of such a policy. On the other hand, any attempt to deal with inflation through stereotyped procedures that do not go to the heart of the development problem is bound to fail and may, in failing, bring about a situation even worse than that which already existed.

Let us now briefly recapitulate the main lessons of postwar experience of inflation in the industrial countries:

1. Postwar experience in the industrial countries yields no evidence that all inflations are inherently explosive in character.

2. Postwar economic growth has been associated both with stable and with rising prices, depending on the country and time period involved.

3. At moderate rates of inflation, adverse effects on the allocation of resources and the distribution of income may be relatively small.

4. Since there is more than one kind of inflation, a correct diagnosis of the type of inflation prevailing is an indispensable prerequisite in devising a sound anti-inflationary policy.

5. In particular, it is essential to distinguish between excess aggregate demand, excess sectoral demand, autonomous factor income inflation, and inflation due to special factors such as poor harvests, increases in import prices, and so forth. It is also important to select only those anti-inflationary measures that are appropriate for the particular type of inflation encountered.

6. The first element of any sound anti-inflationary program is a policy for achieving adequate rates of growth of output and productivity.

---

[29]Nicholas Kaldor, "Monetary Policy, Economic Stability and Growth," a memorandum submitted to the Committee on the Working of the Monetary System, HMS, 1960.

b. INFLATION AND GROWTH: THE EXPERIENCE OF EASTERN EUROPE[1]

John M. Montias

I. RETROSPECT

During the Soviet Union's great industrialization drive beginning in 1929, the Soviet economy suffered severely from inflation. In order to hold down prices in state and cooperative stores, the government found itself forced to introduce consumer rationing. The excess purchasing power of the rapidly rising urban working force was spent on the free collective farm market, where prices rose by fifteen- to twentyfold from 1928 to 1933, and in state-run "commercial stores," which charged prices many times higher than consumers paid for their rations.[2] After rationing had been gradually abolished in 1934, prices in state and cooperative stores were unified at a level about seven times higher than in 1928. In spite of rapidly rising costs in industry, due to the upward trend of wages, the government maintained prices of industrial producer goods, except for petroleum products, approximately at 1928 levels by meting out lavish subsidies to these basic industries. This policy lasted until 1936, when prices were raised by approximately 50 percent and brought more or less into line with average production costs.[3]

The partially successful efforts of the financial authorities to curb inflationary pressures were interrupted by the war, when rationing had to be reinstated and collective farm prices were bid up to exorbitant levels. Following the monetary reform of December, 1947, in which the Soviet authorities confiscated nine tenths of the currency holdings of the population, the government was

---

[1]I am grateful to Professor Raymond Powell for his expert advice on many of the points raised in this paper. Mr. Sylvester Berki kindly helped me with the translation of the Hungarian statistical material used in Part IV. I am also indebted to Dr. Israel Borenstein and Dr. Andrzej Korbonski for their help in locating Polish and East German sources.

[2]A. Baykov, *The Development of the Soviet Economic System*, (Cambridge and New York: Cambridge University Press and the Macmillan Book Co., 1947), pp. 233–50.

[3]All price trends are cited from F. Holzman's "Soviet Inflationary Pressures, 1928–58: Causes and Cures," *The Quarterly Journal of Economics*, (May, 1960), Vol. 74, No. 2, Table I.

able to resume its stabilization policy and succeeded in pressing toward its industrialization targets without releasing a new inflationary spiral. From 1947 on, wages rose very slowly, their increase falling far short of productivity gains. The trend in collective farm prices, the most sensitive indicator of monetary disequilibrium, remained steady; and prices in state stores were actually reduced on several occasions.

Just when the Soviet authorities had begun to get on top of their financial problems, their East European allies,[4] equipped with a complete panoply of Soviet institutions to carry out their own industrialization policies, were engaged in a losing battle against inflation. It took the satellite states a few years before they learned their lesson, but by the mid-1950's they also had begun to exercise a reasonable degree of control over their monetary and financial variables. It is this experience that I propose to relate. But before doing this, I wish to consider in some detail the policy objectives of the financial authorities and the instruments at their disposal to accomplish their tasks.

II. POLICY OBJECTIVES

1. The primary task of financial planning is to facilitate the fulfillment of the state's growth objectives as they are formulated in the yearly plans.[5] Insofar as the full consequences of the plans, expressed in natural units or in conventional value aggregates, may only become apparent when the financial balances have been analyzed, the physical plans, in the early stages of the yearly planning process, may also be subject to revisions in the light of the results of aggregate analysis. But once the state plan for the year has been promulgated, the National Bank and the Ministry of Finance must see to it that the production activities of socialized enterprises, the investment program of the state, the foreign trade plan, and any other tasks contemplated in the plan are carried out without financial impediments.

2. Prices of consumer goods, and particularly of essentials, should be constant or should decline over time, both in the state retail network and on the free market.

---

[4]This group now includes Poland, Rumania, Czechoslovakia, East Germany, Hungary, and Bulgaria. It also included Yugoslavia until 1948 and Albania up to approximately 1960.

[5]With the exception of Czechoslovakia and East Germany, which in recent years have begun to draw up long-range financial balances, the scope of financial planning has always been confined to yearly and quarterly plans.

3. Direct subsidies to socialized enterprises unable to cover their production costs should be kept to a minimum.

4. Transfer prices used in transactions among socialized enterprises should be revised as seldom as possible, to avoid the planning and accounting complications attending these revisions. A corollary objective to 3 and 4 is that wage increases must be kept short of productivity gains to prevent rising labor costs and the emergence of financial deficits in industries where prices barely cover costs.[6]

5. There must be no "spontaneous" (unplanned) redistributions of incomes or assets between the different classes of the population. "Speculative" or black market activities, which bring about these redistributions, must be discouraged by financial pressures and by the avoidance of monetary disequilibria stimulating these illegal activities. Abnormally heavy purchases by the urban population on the free collective farm or peasant market should also be held in check, as they are likely to cause politically undesirable transfers of wage earners' incomes to the peasantry. (Such purchases, by raising prices, will also conflict with the second objective stated above.)

Two secondary objectives designed to help accomplish the basic objectives already listed may be described as follows:

First, the currency holdings of households should be limited to the amounts required for normal transaction demands. The population is urged to deposit unspent income, in excess of minimum currency balances, in savings institutions. (These savings are alleged to be less volatile than currency holdings and are not considered as dangerous a potential source of market disequilibrium.)

Secondly, enterprises must be allowed to keep only negligible currency holdings and minimum deposit balances with the National Bank and with the specialized banks, so as to discourage them from making payments on transactions not foreseen by the plan.

III. INSTRUMENTS OF MONETARY POLICY

The starting point for this analysis of the instruments of monetary policy is a balance of "total disposable product," which, although it is not itself used as a planning document, subsumes several of the operational plans and will serve to show how these plans are interrelated.

---

[6]In principle, prices of producer goods in Soviet-type economies are set at a level covering the average production costs of the industry plus a small profit margin, expressed as a percentage of costs.

This balance, expressed in value terms, may be written:

1. $$M + P = AP + C + I + E$$

where M stands for total imports, P for domestic production, AP for the costs of materials and other current inputs used in domestic production, C for total (private and social) consumption, I for gross investments, and E for exports.[7] Gross national product equals the right-hand side of the above balance (omitting input costs AP) minus imports. "National income produced" in Soviet and eastern European accounting may be derived from this same gross national product by subtracting depreciation and "nonproductive services" (the nonmaterial costs of administration, defense outlays, social services, *et al.*).

Three breakdowns of national income excluding nonproductive services are normally prepared for planning and for analytical purposes in the Soviet-type economies: (1) A breakdown by economic sector of national income produced; (2) a breakdown by factor payments (wages and salaries plus the net income of the government and of enterprises); and (3) a division of national income into consumption and "accumulation," which is defined as increases in fixed capital, minus depreciation, plus increases in inventories and reserves, plus the net foreign balance (or $I_f - D + I_i + E - M$, where I_f is gross investment in fixed capital, D is depreciation, and I_i the rise in inventories and reserves).

One of the key decisions taken toward the beginning of the planning period, around March or April of the year preceding the plan year, is the setting of a target proportion between accumulation and national income. This proportion usually varies anywhere between 15 and 25 percent. The upper limit is often exceeded in the course of executing the plan, owing to such causes as unplanned excesses in inventories and shortfalls in the production of consumer goods.

The other synthetic balances, such as the balance of incomes and outlays of the population, the government budget and the financial program of the state, register income flows, capital transactions and changes in intersectoral claims. They essentially represent total sources and uses of funds. These accounts, inasmuch as they in-

---

[7]Instead of value sums, the symbols M, P, C, I, and E may also denote vectors of commodities and services produced and consumed in the economy. In that case A would represent a matrix of technological coefficients (a_{ij}) for the n commodities and services, where a_{ij} stands for the input of item i per unit of output of item j. If the a_{ij} elements are expressed in value terms, then their column sums would be the material and service costs per unit of output of each of the n items.

clude nonproductive services, cannot be mechanically fitted into the official national income accounts. They will be related, however, to the more comprehensive accounts of equation (1).

The four sectors into which the economy is divided for purposes of financial and monetary planning are the following: (1) A "private sector," made up of households, private enterprises, and cooperative farms; (2) an enterprise sector including state enterprises and nonagricultural cooperatives on cost accounting; (3) a government sector;[8] and (4) the banking system.[9]

The "balance of incomes and outlays of the population" registers the planned sources and uses of funds in the private sector:

2. $$Y^P - T^P + L^G = C^P + I^P + N^P + S^P$$

In the equation,[10] Y^P refers to the total money incomes paid by the remaining three sectors to the private sector, including purchases by the government of private and collective farm production. Net payments by the private sector to the government (direct taxes and other fiscal payments minus transfer payments to households from the government) are denoted by T^P. L^G stands for the net increase in government loans to the private sector, to finance agricultural investments, private residential construction, and consumer credit. C^P and I^P refer to private consumption and investment embodied in goods purchased from other sectors. N^P is the increase in currency holdings in the private sector; S^P denotes increases in private deposits in the savings bank together with purchases of state obligations.

---

[8]The government sector is composed of the Treasury and of "units on budget account," administrative entities, which, unlike enterprises on cost accounting (*khozraschet*), do not draw up a balance sheet and must remit to the Treasury surpluses of current incomes over expenditures.

[9]The State Bank (*Gosbank* in the Soviet Union, *Narodowy Bank Polski* in Poland, *et al.*), at which enterprises hold their current accounts and which, by crediting and debiting current accounts, effects the bulk of payments between enterprises as well as payments to households and to the private sector; the Savings Bank, whose branches accumulate private saving deposits; the Investment Bank, which channels budget grants to investors from which construction enterprises are paid for their services, and finances the current operations of construction enterprises; and the Agricultural Bank, financing investment activities and current operations in agriculture and forestry. This system has been virtually identical since 1949–50 in the various countries of the Soviet bloc, except that, in recent years, several countries have eliminated one or another of the specialized banks. (The Investment Bank has been liquidated in Czechoslovakia and the Agricultural Bank in Czechoslovakia, Hungary, and Rumania. Their functions have been taken over by the State Bank.)

[10]Superscripts in this, as in later equations, designate the sector responsible for an item of expenditure or for the acquisition of a claim on another sector.

The balance of incomes and outlays does not cover the portion of the private sector's production that is not purchased by other sectors. A balance of this remainder, which may be sold within the sector or consumed in kind by the producers themselves, has been prepared in some of the eastern European economies in recent years.[11] This balance is then called part B to distinguish it from part A summarized in equation (2).

It reads:

3. $$Y_k = C_k + I_k$$

where Y_k refers to income from goods and services produced and consumed within the sector, and C_k and I_k represent consumption and investment by members of the sector of products originating in the sector. A large part of Y_k is of course income in kind directly consumed by farmers.

The balance of incomes and outlays is usually prepared by the planning commission in conjunction with the yearly national development plan. The State Bank draws up quarterly "cash plans" recording the total currency receipts and expenditures of the budget and of enterprises. Receipts include all sales of goods and services to the public by socialized entities, proceeds from which must be deposited at a local office of the bank as soon as physically possible, together with direct taxes (other than those on wages and salaries), and various budgetary receipts from the population. The expenditures recorded in the balance are wage and salary payments by socialized entities, net of direct taxes on incomes, purchases from the farm sector, transfer payments, and loans to the private sector, all such disbursements being effected through the State Bank. Except for the fact that wages and salaries are recorded on a net basis, the cash balance is obviously a counterpart to part A of the balance of incomes and outlays. The cash outlays of the population are the receipts of the state, while state expenditures for services rendered and goods sold by the private sector constitute the incomes of that sector. Increases in currency in circulation and in the population's savings deposits are also the equilibrating items in the cash balance, where they appear as items of state receipt.

The state budget summarizes the accounts of the government sector:

4. $$T^P + T^s - S^g - S^\kappa + S^P = L^g + I^g{}_f + I^g{}_i + C^g$$

---

[11]The German Democratic Republic is the only country where a single balance is constructed for all incomes of the private sector including income in kind and income from sales within the sector (*Finanse*, No. 10, Warsaw, 1961, p. 63).

In this equation, T^{z} is net government income from enterprises (the sum of profit levies, turnover taxes, and net profits on foreign trade,[12] minus operating subsidies), S^{a} is the budget surplus deposited to the treasury account at the State Bank, and S^{K} is the increase in the banks' own capital financed from budget surpluses. On the expenditure side, I^{a}_{f} and I^{a}_{i} denote fixed investments and inventory accumulation financed from budget grants; C^{a} is social consumption, including defense, government services, and administration. The funds borrowed from the government by the private sector (L^{a}), which were recorded as resource in balance 2, now appear as a use of funds in this equation. S^{p}, which includes increases in private savings deposits in addition to purchases of government bonds, appears as a source of funds for the state because savings bank deposits of the public are deposited at the state bank, where, in most of the east European countries, they are normally credited to treasury account.[13]

A balance may also be written for the sources and uses of funds by state and cooperative enterprises. This balance, which, in the Polish and Czechoslovak accounts is consolidated by ministries, reads as follows:

5. $$R + I^{a}_{i} + I^{a}_{f} + C^{B} = K + I_{f} + I_{i} + T^{E} + S^{E}$$

where R stands for the gross receipts of all enterprises and nonagricultural cooperatives, C^{B} for the net increase in short-term and long-term credits extended by the banks to enterprises, S^{B} for increases in enterprise bank deposits, mainly at the State Bank. (Currency holdings by enterprises are very small and may be neglected in this analysis.) K represents the total production costs of enterprises. The remaining symbols have already been identified.

We now come to the credit plan,[14] which records the banks' sources and uses of funds:

6. $$N^{P} + S^{a} + S^{B} + S^{K} = C^{B}$$

The left-hand side shows increases in the liabilities of the banks, matching the net increase in loans outstanding, representing the banks' assets.

---

[12]Net profits on foreign trade represent the difference between "positive budget differences" and "negative differences." The former accrue chiefly in importing consumer goods while the bulk of the latter represent export subsidies.

[13]The surpluses shown in the closed budgetary accounts include revenue from the sale of bonds and increases in private savings deposits.

[14]The magnitudes entered in the operational credit plan are beginning- and end-of-year totals. Equation 6 represents the yearly increments in the credit plan rather than the plan itself.

It is evident from the credit plan (equation 6) that if an unintended expansion in the monetary supply is to be avoided, an increase in bank credits from one year to the next must be matched either by a budget surplus or by a rise in enterprise deposits S^B. But the latter is ruled out as a source of finance of any major expansion in credits, since it conflicts with the objective of reducing enterprise liquidity to minimum requirements. (Enterprise deposits in excess of approved requirements will not remain idle: the larger part will be used to purchase extra materials or labor and will reappear as unplanned increments in currency holdings.) Only a budget surplus can serve to offset a significant expansion of credits without releasing inflationary pressures.

By adding balance equations (4), (5) and (6), we obtain what the Soviets call the "consolidated financial plan" *(Svodny finansovy plan)* and the Poles the "state financial program:"

7. $$T^P + R - K + S^P + N^P = L^G + I_f + I_i + C^G$$

Net budget income from the private sector plus gross profits of enterprises plus increments in private saving, including increases in monetary circulation, equals investment and inventory accumulation by enterprises plus loans to the private sector plus social consumption.

The gross national product accounts emerge when parts A and B of the "balance of incomes and outlays of the population" are added to equation (7):

8. $$Y^P + Y_k + R - K = I_f + I_i + I^P + I_k + C^G + C^P + C_k$$

The left-hand side represents the factor incomes into which gross national product on the right may be resolved: Private incomes from all sources, including intrasector sales of goods and services, plus gross profits of enterprises, including indirect taxes, equal total private and state investments (gross) plus private and social consumption. It should be noted that net profits on foreign trade transactions $(M - E)$ in equation (1) are tucked away in the gross profits of enterprises $(R - K)$. If the foreign balance in terms of national currency is negative, then gross national product available for distribution, which has been recorded in equation (8), is larger than gross national product domestically produced. By subtracting profits on foreign trade from both sides (that is, by adding $E - M$ on both sides), we finally derive gross national product corresponding to the elements of income in equation (1).

This accounting framework put into place, we are ready to

analyze the impact on monetary equilibrium of alternative development policies and of discrepancies arising in the course of fulfilling
the plans. We shall start with a fully balanced set of financial plans,
such that the aggregate supply of consumer goods equals the aggregate demand for these goods at fixed prices, given a satisfactory
ratio of inventories to sales. (Neither formal nor informal rationing
prevails in the consumers' market.) The plan assumes that households have fully adjusted the level of their currency balances and
bank savings to their personal incomes. Now, consider a single
deviation from this balance, which tends either to reduce the output of consumer goods or to increase personal incomes or both.
This deviation may be due to a decision on the part of the planning
authorities to raise the ratio of fixed investments to national income at the expense of consumption; or it may arise from a discrepancy arising in the execution of the plan, such as an excessive
disbursal of wages, a failure of labor productivity to rise according
to plan in a consumer goods industry, or an unforeseen shortage of
imported raw materials that forced consumer goods industries to
cut back their output.

So far we have made no behavioral assumptions about any of the
variables in the system. Our first assumption is that private saving,
consisting of additions to currency balances (N^p) and to private
bank deposits (S^p), is an increasing function of personal incomes
(Y^p). (Other variables affecting private saving will be introduced
later.) If the deviation from the initial set of balances consists exclusively in a drop in consumer goods output, leaving Y^p unchanged,
there should be no change in private saving or, for that matter, in
any of the elements in the balance of incomes and outlays of the
population in equation (2). Inventories of consumer goods must
then fall by the extent of the drop in the output of these goods. If
incomes rise, so will private saving, and the fall in inventories will
equal the increment in income minus the increment in saving. But
as the over-all volume of inventories declines and retail stores begin
to run short of an increasing number of items, some form of rationing must come into play. These deficits cause consumers to hold on
to a larger part of their incomes than they would otherwise. Saving
is then an inverse function of the level of inventories as well as an
increasing function of incomes. Hence, deviations of the type considered must generate some expansion in monetary circulation or
in savings deposits.

At this point, we may introduce another behavioral assumption,
namely that the volume of credits extended by the banks varies

with the level of inventories.[15] In the above case, a fall in inventories will cause a contraction of credits. Referring to the credit balance of equation (6), we see that both the assets and the liabilities of the banks must decline. But we have already concluded that the deviation from the initial plan was likely to bring about an increase in monetary circulation simultaneously with the shrinkage of inventories. The deposits of the treasury and of enterprises and the banks' own capital must fall by an amount equal to the decline in the volume of credits plus the increase in currency in circulation.

What forces will bring about the adjustment? This depends on the exact nature of the disturbance. If the initial level of consumption is reduced, because of a sudden acceleration in the investment program financed by the state, then the budget in equation (4) must show a smaller surplus (or larger deficit) than had been at first scheduled. Treasury deposits or funds allotted for increases in the banks' capital must then decline, or at least fall short of the original target. On the other hand, if wage payments, rather than investment outlays, exceed approved limits and raise the costs of enterprises (K) above plan, then, assuming a parallel decline in credits (C^B) and in inventories (I_i), we may conclude from equation (5) that enterprise deposits (S^E) will have to be curtailed. But since the deposits of most enterprises are small to begin with, they are likely to be exhausted before a full adjustment has been achieved. To avoid the serious crisis that would result from the exhaustion of enterprises' means of payment, either the budget would have to meet at least part of the above-plan rise in labor costs by granting larger subsidies to enterprises, or the banks would have to finance a larger proportion of enterprises' inventories, in which case C^B would decline less than I_i. Which of these alternative policies will be adopted in practice will depend in essence on the relative willingness of the banks and of the fiscal authorities to deviate from the "sound" fiscal or banking principles to which they normally adhere. We shall return to these alternatives when we come to discuss the Polish experience of 1956, when a situation similar to the one just described actually occurred.

The successive adjustments we have tracked down so far still leave the economy with an abnormally low level of inventories. To restore equilibrium in the consumer market, by which we understand a return to the initial inventories-to-sales ratio, the

---

[15]Short-term loans, which make up the bulk of credits in the centralized economies are, for the most part, secured by inventories.

authorities may resort to any of the following tactics. They may
(1) confiscate some of the excess currency balances by a monetary
reform; (2) raise prices of consumer goods until they equilibrate
demand at the new level of output; (3) increase direct taxes; (4)
depress the personal incomes of the farmers by confiscating a larger
part of their produce by compulsory deliveries or by imposing lower
prices for the amounts collected; (5) pare down urban incomes by
tightening work norms or by other means; or, finally, (6) offset
the initial deviation by reducing the ratio of investments to national
income in the next period. At one time or another, all six of these
policies, alone or in concert, have been tried out in eastern Europe.
In recent years, however, political developments in the area have
prompted changes in the relative importance of these various
remedies. This will be brought out in the next section, which
summarizes the monetary experience of the East European countries of the Soviet bloc since World War II.

IV. THE EXPERIENCE OF INDIVIDUAL COUNTRIES

Analysis of East European inflationary problems is greatly hindered by the absence of comprehensive financial and monetary data.
Only three countries—Poland, East Germany, and Hungary—have
released statistics of currency circulation, but, whether by design
or by unfortunate coincidence, they publish no regular statistics on
credits extended to state enterprises. Only occasional data for the
early 1950's have been found to fill this gap. Bulgaria is the only
country to publish credit statistics regularly; Rumania and Czechoslovakia, which are most secretive about their financial affairs, have
released credit data for scattered years and little else. Information
on the retained profits of enterprises and on the size of their bank
deposits is only available for Poland. At least partial data on personal incomes and on sales of goods in state and cooperative stores
can be found or estimated for all countries under consideration,
but they usually do not provide a sufficient basis for calculating
changes in currency circulation (because of the lack of estimates
on services sold to the population, gaps in personal incomes, and
incomplete information on net fiscal payments by the private sector
to the state).

We proceed now to a discussion of monetary developments in
eastern Europe, with special emphasis on the Polish experience of
the 1950's, which can be more fully documented than that of any
other country.

Developments in eastern Europe can be divided into five periods:

(1) reconstruction and gradual socialization of the East European economies, from 1945 to 1948; (2) the imposition of Soviet economic institutions, the initiation of long-term development plans, rapid progress toward industrialization, urbanization, stagnant or declining real wages, and inflationary pressures, from 1949 to mid-1953; (3) consolidation of previously made gains, increases in real wages, a more cautious expansionary policy and subsidence of inflation from 1953 to mid-1956; (4) severe disruptions in development plans and renewed inflationary tendencies in the aftermath of political events in Poland and Hungary from 1956 to 1958; finally, (5) a new upsurge in investments accompanied by rapid growth from mid-1958 to the present, interrupted by occasional *crises de croissance* such as occurred in Poland and Hungary in 1959, in Bulgaria in 1960, and in Czechoslovakia in 1961–62.

Until the end of the first period, monetary circulation and retail prices rose apace. The currency refundings that occurred in Czechoslovakia and Poland in 1945, in Hungary in 1946, in Rumania and Bulgaria in 1947, slowed down but did not check this inflation.

However, by early 1949 monetary equilibrium had been sufficiently restored in Poland and Hungary to abolish consumer rationing. In Rumania, on the other hand, which had to pay heavy reparations to the Soviet Union, rationing continued without interruption until the end of 1954.

Replicas of Soviet economic institutions were implanted from 1949 to 1951 in all the "Peoples' Democracies." Enterprises were placed on cost accounting (*khozraschet*) and henceforth effected their payments to other enterprises exclusively through bank transfers. They received a norm of working capital to cover their minimum needs and were enjoined to apply for short-term credits to the State Bank to finance their seasonal requirements and their goods in transit. Long-term credits were basically eliminated and supplanted by nonreimbursible budget grants. Turnover taxes levied on consumer goods became the chief item of government revenue. In 1951 and 1952 the planning commissions of the different countries began to construct interlocking synthetic balances, such as were described in section II, and to coordinate these yearly financial plans with the quarterly cash and credit plans prepared by the State Banks.

It was easier to accomplish this formal alignment than to take advantage of the considerable experience that had been built up in the U.S.S.R. in the 1930's in the course of operating these institutions. Indeed, the ambitious long-term plans launched in

1949 and 1950 in Czechoslovakia, Poland, Hungary, and Bulgaria and, a year later, in Rumania soon released new inflationary pressures, due, in part, to the failure to provide for budgetary surpluses, but also to the excessive optimism of the planners with respect to labor productivity increases and to the output and marketed share of farm products.

In the course of executing these plans, the authorities enforced a system of priorities, which, by discriminating against consumer goods industries, tended to magnify the inflationary impact of initial errors in the plan. When shortages occurred, allotments of raw materials and other inputs were diverted from consumer goods industries to heavy industry; as a consequence, failures to hit production targets were concentrated mainly on industries producing for the retail trade network, whose sales were initially supposed to absorb the disposable incomes of households.

TABLE 1

The Second Wave of Monetary Reforms

	Number of Units of New Currency Exchanged for 100 Units of Old Currency			
Categories	Poland (October, 1950)	Rumania (January, 1952)	Bulgaria (May, 1952)	Czechoslovakia (May, 1953)
Prices, wages, and state funds.	3	5	4	20
Currency balances				
lower portion..............	1	1	1	20
upper portion.............	1	¼	1	2
Savings deposits				
lower portion..............	3	2	3	20
upper portion.............	3	½	1	3–10

Source: N. Spulber, *The Economics of Communist Eastern Europe* (Cambridge; 1957), p. 128.

Within one to three years after the initiation of the long-term plans, the monetary situation had gotten so out of hand that a second refunding operation which confiscated the bulk of the currency holdings of the population became necessary.[16] The basic elements of this reform are shown in Table 1.

Although no monetary reform took place in Hungary in this period, the official index of the cost of living, dampened as it might

---

[16]For details, see Edward Ames, "Soviet Bloc Currency Conversions," *American Economic Review,* June, 1954.

be by price controls, indicates that inflationary pressures also developed in that country: by 1952 the over-all index stood at 179 percent of the 1949 level and the food component at 220 percent.[17]

Virtually no data have been released concerning the period immediately before or after each of the reforms in the Peoples' Democracies. We can form some idea of the circumstances of the Polish reform, whereby approximately two thirds of the population's currency holdings were confiscated, by comparing, in Table 2, the monetary situation ten months before the reform and at the end of 1951.

TABLE 2

Total Credits Outstanding, Currency in Circulation, Savings Banks Deposits, Government and Enterprise Deposits, Average Wages, and Prices Indexes in Poland, 1948–52

(Billions of Postreform Zlotys, December 31 of Each Year, Except as Indicated.)

	1948	1949	1950	1951	1952
Total credits outstanding (short- and long-term)..	13.8	16.6†	28.3	34.6	44.8
Currency in circulation...	3.9	5.3	10–15‡	5.22	6.23
Savings bank deposits (all banks)..............	0.05	0.07	0.15	0.36	0.55
Government deposits (at all banks)............	2.76*	6.0*	n.a.	11.5	23.6
Current account deposits of enterprises.........	4.2*	3.1*	n.a.	5.5	7.5
Budget surplus (+) or deficit (−)...........	1.35	0.69	—§	12.0	9.2
Index of retail prices.....	96	100	107.5	117.7	134.8
Food prices on peasant markets..............	n.a.	100	121	157	240
Average wages (net, zlotys per month)...........	n.a.	447	541	592	644

Sources: W. Jaworski, *Zarys rozwoju systemu kredytowego w Polsce Ludowej* (Warsaw; 1958) pp. 118, 122–23, 178–79; *Rocznik statystyczny 1949*, p. 167, *1957*, p. 238; *Ekonomista*, No. 3, 1961, pp. 684–85; *Finanse*, No. 9, 1961, p. 12.
*Estimates.
†At the end of 1949, 18.7 billion zlotys of long-term credits outstanding (not included in the figure in the table) were converted into nonreimbursible grants to socialized enterprises.
‡Estimate for September, 1950 (before the monetary reform).
§The plan called for a balanced budget. The results are not known.

Interviews with Polish bank officials reveal that there were considerable divergences of opinion as to the necessity of the reform. Some influential officials urged, instead, that prices in socialized trade should be allowed to rise to absorb the surplus purchasing

---

[17]Central Statistical Office, *Statisztikai évkönyv 1959* (Budapest, 1960), p. 275.

power. The Polish population might have been less alienated by another dose of inflation than by the outright confiscation of most of its currency holdings. But this argument overlooks the class bias that was probably uppermost in the minds of the politicians ultimately responsible for the reform. The confiscation hit, first of all, the "petty capitalists" who had not yet been eliminated by the socialization campaign of the preceding three years and, secondly, the peasants who normally hold large balances—particularly in the late autumn when they are cashing in on their harvests. To raise prices in state and cooperative stores with a view to absorbing surplus purchasing power would have been especially hard on urban workers and employees, who, in the eyes of the Communists, were already paying more than their share of the costs of industrialization.

Those who opposed the 1950 reform may have gotten some satisfaction out of the fact that the operation was unable to check the inflationary tide. Despite the flotation of a large government bond issue in 1951, which absorbed some of the surplus purchasing power, rationing had to be reintroduced later on in the year to supply the urban population with minimum amounts of essential commodities at stable prices.[18] This failure is all the more striking in view of the sedulous efforts of the government to pile up large budgetary surpluses to offset the rapid credit expansion.

The East European inflations of the period of the first long-term plans had a characteristic feature, of special interest to the study of inflationary phenomena in developing countries: the terms of trade between agricultural and industrial products, instead of shifting in favor of the still uncollectivized farm sector, as rapid urbanization and the attendant pressure on a more or less constant food supply might have led one to expect, turned strongly against farmers. This was not, of course, the result of free market forces but of the government's price policy with respect to agricultural procurements. The government paid for compulsory deliveries of farm produce at exceedingly low prices; it also bought most of the surplus above these quotas at prices that were significantly inferior to those obtained on the free peasant market. The following trends shown in Table 3 shed light on the Bulgarian government's success in enforcing this policy.

---

[18]The disastrous drought of the spring and summer of 1951 caused a failure in food supplies which could not have been foreseen at the time of the reform. This failure certainly compounded such errors as the monetary authorities may have made in designing the reform.

The Bulgarian index of industrial consumer goods prices rose—although at a decelerating rate—from 1949 to 1952, whereas agricultural procurement prices followed a steady downward course. The rising trend in industrial prices was stemmed after the successful monetary reform of May, 1952, but it was not until after the death of Stalin that the downward trend of agricultural prices was finally arrested.

TABLE 3

INDEXES OF PRICES OF INDUSTRIAL AND AGRICULTURAL PRODUCTS IN BULGARIA,
1939, 1945, 1949–52

	Index of Prices of Industrial Consumer Goods (1939 = 100)	Index of Procurement Prices for Agricultural Produce (1939 = 100)	Index of Percentage Ratio of Industrial to Agricultural Prices (1939 = 100)
1945............	573.7	553.7	102
1949............	697.4	654.6 (821)	106.5 (85)
1950............	919.2	n.a. (742)	n.a. (124)
1951............	1.063.5	n.a. (694)	n.a. (152)
1952............	1.085.8	n.a. (483)	n.a. (224)
1953............	1.010.9	388.9 (444)	259.9 (228)

Note: Figures in parentheses refer to grain prices only.
Sources: G. Kostov, "Zakon za stoinostta i tsenite na selskostopanskite proizvedenia" (The law of value and prices for agricultural products), *Trud i tseny* (Sofia), No. 6, 1961, pp. 45–46.

In Rumania the pressure of the government on farm prices was at least as powerful as in Bulgaria. By 1952, Rumanian farmers could buy only one fourth to one half as much for their products as in 1938, when the parity index was already much more disadvantageous to them than before World War I.[19]

The death of Stalin marked a turning point in the policies pursued by the Communist leadership in the European satellites of the Soviet Union. State investments in fixed capital were either reduced in 1953 and 1954 or at least their rate of increase slowed down considerably by comparison with the preceding years of head-

---

[19]The estimated averages of farm prices (including sales on the free market) have, if anything, an upward bias. They have been compared with the "commercial" (higher) prices of industrial products, since peasants were not issued ration cards and had only very limited opportunities of buying at the lower prices. Commercial prices of textile fabrics and shoes were about twice as high as rationed prices; the ratio for sugar was a little over three to one. (*Hotarirea consilului de ministri cu privire la intocmirea si publicare cataloagelor de preturi* [Decision of the Council of Ministers concerning the promulgation and the publication of price catalogues], Bucharest, 1952.) Price quotations are taken from *Probleme economice*, No. 9, 1954, p. 93; No. 5, 1955, pp. 81–83; No. 9, 1955, p. 73; and No. 3, 1957, p. 89.

on industrialization. Inventories rose at a slower rate after register-
ing a discontinuous upsurge in 1953, probably due to the dislocation
in production schedules that resulted from this sharp turn in
economic policy. The growth of employment in the socialized
economy, which had been extremely rapid in the last few years,
declined, and, in some countries, was actually brought to a halt
(Rumania and Hungary). Rates of growth of industrial production
in the area, which had been of the order of 15–25 percent per year
from 1950 to 1952, now fell below 10 percent.[20]

TABLE 4

SELECTED MONETARY INDICATORS, POLAND, 1952–55

(*Billions of Zlotys, End-of-Year Data, Except Where Indicated*)

	1952	1953	1954	1955
Currency in circulation................	6.23	8.5	10.1	11.6
Savings deposits.....................	0.55	0.96	1.53	2.37
Total credits (all banks)..............	44.8	59.8	62.5	62.7
of which, short-term credits of National				
Bank...........................	43.3	n.a.	61.9	60.4
Working capital of socialized enterprises*.	63.3	87.4	94.3	103.6
Treasury deposits (at all banks)........	23.6	n.a.	29.2	27.7
Banks' own capital...................	3.1	n.a.	7.1	7.3
Current account deposits of enterprises				
(all banks).......................	7.5	n.a.	11.3	12.4
Budgetary surplus for year ("cash sur-				
plus")	9.2	6.6	0.3	1.1

Sources: W. Jaworski, *Zarys rozwoju systemu kredytowego w Polsce Ludowej* (Warsaw; 1958),
pp. 178–79, 199; Z. Pirozynski, "Budżet państwowy Polski Ludowej wokresie uprzemystowienia,"
Finanse, No. 9, 1961, p. 12; A. Zwass, "Szybkość obiegu pieniądza gotówkowego w Polsce, N.R.D.
i Jugostawii," *Finanse*, No. 9, 1960, pp. 48, 55; *Ekonomista*, No. 3, 1961, p. 684.
*Value of inventories plus reserve funds for future payments.

The analysis of the monetary effects of the "New Course" in
Poland is complicated by the incidence of two crucial price reforms
that preceded the death of Stalin by a few months. On January 1,
1953, the transfer prices of most raw materials and semifabricates
consumed by socialized enterprises were raised by anywhere from
20 to 80 percent, while prices of finished products, including proc-

---

[20]A carefully constructed index of Polish industrial production shows that the
increases in output declined from 15 percent in 1950 to 8.5 percent in 1955
(M. C. Ernst, "Measurement of Polish Industrial Growth, 1937, 1946–1955,"
unpublished Ph.D. dissertation, Columbia University, p. 100). The Hungarian index of net output, which is thought to be fairly reliable, chalked up gains of 15 to
20 percent from 1949 to 1952, then subsided to 10 percent in 1953, 0.5 percent in
1954, and 7 percent in 1955 (*Statisztikai évkönyv 1959*, p. 69). In Rumania, the decline was from an average 25 percent a year from 1948 to 1952 to 8 percent per year
from 1952 to 1955.

essed chemicals, rubber goods, and many machinery items, were reduced by 20 to 50 percent. Two days later the government decreed a general increase in the prices of consumer goods in socialized shops of a little over 40 percent, simultaneously abolished rationing, and raised wages by an average of around 25 percent. By the end of 1953, however, the upward drift in wages had caused the average wage to catch up with the rise in prices of January 3rd and had wiped out the initial loss in real wages.[21] The increase in monetary circulation for the entire year shown in Table 4 probably occurred mainly in the second half.[22]

The data in Table 4 are relevant to the factors underlying the money supply. What happened to the demand for currency may be inferred from the growth in the incomes and outlays of the population and from the evolution of inventories in domestic trade, as shown in Table 5 below:

TABLE 5

Selected Indicators Related to the Demand for Currency, Poland, 1952–55

	1952	1953	1954	1955
Money incomes of the population (billions of zlotys)	79.0	118.9	130.6	140.9
Money expenditures of the population (billions of zlotys)	78.4	116.6	128.9	139.4
Inventories in domestic trade (billions of zlotys)	24	33	35	42
Income velocity of currency in circulation (ratio)	13.9	17.0	14.4	13.6
Marginal income velocity of currency in circulation*	n.a.	30.3	5.57	7.9
Marginal income velocity of the sum of currency holdings and bank savings of population†	n.a.	23.3	4.4	4.8
Index of retail prices (preceding year = 100)	115	143	94	98
Index of food prices on the peasant market (preceding year = 100)	153	112	99	106

Sources: A. Zwass, "Szybkość obiegu pieniądza gotówkowego w Polsce, N.R.D. i Jugostawii," *Finanse*, No. 9, 1960, pp. 48, 50; W. Jaworski, *Zarys rozwoju systemu kredytowego w Polsce Ludowej* (Warsaw; 1958), p. 200; *Rocznik statystyczny 1957*, p. 228.

*Increase in money incomes of the population divided by the increase in the average volume of currency in circulation during the year.

†The ratio of money incomes to average currency holdings plus end-of-year bank savings.

[21]J. M. Montias, *Central Planning in Poland* (New Haven and London: Yale University Press, 1962), pp. 226–27; *Rocznik statystyczny 1957*, p. 267.

[22]The average volume of currency in circulation was 5.7 billion zlotys in 1952 and 7.0 billion in 1953. The corresponding end-of-year figures were 6.23 and 8.5 billion zlotys. If circulation in 1953 had developed on the same monthly pattern as in 1952, the end-of-year circulation should have been around 7.7 billion instead of 8.5 billion.

The increase in velocity in circulation in 1953 is evidently related to the reduction in households' idle currency balances, which could not easily be spent during the period of rationing. At least during the first half of the year, the urban population, which was hit more severely by the price reform than the peasantry (food prices in retail shops rose more than industrial consumer goods), had to curtail their balances—or at least the ratio of their balances to their income —to maintain anything like their customary living standards. Later on, as unplanned wage increases began to swell purchasing power, the demand for monetary holdings on the part of the urban population probably resumed its expansion.

The relative stabilization of the currency supply (linked to the very moderate expansion of short-run credits) appears to have been an area-wide phenomenon in the 1950's. Efforts were made to keep increases in monetary circulation proportional to the planned volume of retail trade and services. To finance increases in their working capital, enterprises were allowed to keep a larger share of their profits. This reduced the need both for credit expansion and for budgetary surpluses. Those countries which were most successful in holding down the volume of credits seem also to have done best with regard to price stability. Thus, in Czechoslovakia, where the volume of short-term credits actually fell by about one fifth between 1953 and 1957, the official index of the cost of living declined by over 15 percent. In Bulgaria credits remained about level between these same dates, and retail prices dropped by 23 percent. On the other hand, in Rumania credits went up by 60 percent and retail prices by 20 percent.[23]

A crucial test of stability is whether stability can be maintained during periods of accelerated growth. There is some evidence that all three countries just listed were subject to inflationary pressures after they stepped up their rates of investment at the end of the 1950's.[24] In Bulgaria, total credits, which had been running at 11 or

---

[23]*Bulgaria: Statisticheski godishniak na N.R.B. 1961*, pp. 320, 324–25; St. Vasilev, "Vzaimootnoshenia mezhdu finansovite planove v N.R.B.," *Izvestia na ikonomicheskia institut*, No. 18, 1959, pp. 105–06, 127. *Czechoslovakia:* Z. Kodet, *Oběžne prostředky v prumyslu a cesty zrychlováni jejich obratu*, Prague, 1960, p. 38; *Statisticka ročenka CSSR 1960*, pp. 26, 36, 482. *Rumania:* Institute of Economic Research of the Academy of Sciences, *Economia Rominei intre anii 1944– 1959*, Bucharest, 1959, pp. 540–42 and *Dezvoltarea Economiei R.P.R. pe drumul socialismului 1948–1957*, Bucharest, 1958, pp. 348–53; *Anuarul Statistic al R.P.R. 1961*, Bucharest, 1961, pp. 306, 322–23.

[24]In Rumania, for example, net accumulation was held down to about one fifth of national income, excluding services, from 1955 to 1959. In 1960 and 1961, this share probably exceeded one fourth. The equivalent shares for Bulgaria were 20.8 percent in 1955, 14.2 percent in 1956, 20 percent in 1957, 19.4 percent in 1958, 29.9 percent in 1959, and 27.4 percent in 1960 (*Statisticheski godishniak*

12 billion Levas from 1953 all the way to 1957, now jumped to 20.9 billion in the next three years. Budget surpluses for the years 1958, 1960—which totaled less than 2 billion—were certainly insufficient to offset the increase in credits.[25] Considering the very swift rise in retail trade sales (at constant prices) from 1958 to 1960, it is at least conceivable that the transaction demand for cash absorbed a large part of this putative currency issue. In any event, prices on the co-operative market, which had been on the downgrade from 1954 to 1958, showed a slight tendency to rise in 1959 and 1960. In 1961 and 1962 the situation manifestly deteriorated. Prices on the cooperative market in the second quarter of 1962 were already 26 percent higher than in the previous year.[26] A monetary refunding took place on January 1, 1962, on the recent French and Soviet patterns, which in effect raised prices in state stores by a few percent. Later in the year, the Bulgarian government found itself compelled to boost the prices of foodstuffs in socialized trade to avert queues and shortages. It is not possible with the evidence at hand to sift out the effects of short-falls in the agricultural plans from the purely monetary antecedents of the crisis.

In Rumania, where credits also must have expanded rapidly,[27] prices began to rise on the peasant market in 1960. Severe shortages of meat all over the country and of bread in the villages had developed by the spring of 1962. It was clear by then that there was a surplus of purchasing power in circulation, but the government had taken no action to absorb it, either through price increases or through a monetary reform, at the time of writing.

The disturbances that afflicted the economy of Czechoslovakia from late 1960 to 1962 were also due to overoptimistic planning—particularly with regard to the growth of labor productivity—but they were compounded by the far-reaching administrative decentralization that took place from 1959 on. The shortfalls in labor productivity brought on unplanned wage disbursals, which might have been neutralized by credit restrictions or by reducing less essential investment projects if it were not for the decentralization that had seriously curtailed the maneuvering power of the financial authorities.

To take remedial action in face of these inflationary pressures, the Ministry of Finance would have had to curb decentralized invest-

---

1961, p. 96). In Czechoslovakia, the same share rose from 14 percent in 1955 to 19 percent in 1959 and 1960 and 22 percent in 1961 (*Politicka Ekonomia*, No. 6, 1963, p. 443).

[25]*Statisticheski godishniak 1961*, pp. 320, 324.

[26]*Statisticheskia izvestia* (Sofia), No. 3, 1962, p. 44.

[27]For indirect evidence of this, see *Revista de statistică*, No. 3, 1962, pp. 47–48.

ments, making up over 50 percent of total investments in 1960 and 1961, but this was contrary to the principles of the 1959 reform, which was supposed to insure the stability and the maximum possible freedom from outside interference of enterprises' long-run (five-year) financial plans. On the other hand, the authorities were reluctant to cut back on the centralized plan, which represented the hard core of the state's development program. When the state finally resolved to clamp restrictions on the financial autonomy of enterprises and to restructure the development plan, inflationary tendencies had already become manifest in food shortages and in lengthening queues before retail stores. Unfortunately, we have no financial statistics pertaining to monetary circulation or to credits extended that would give us an objective measure of the gravity of the situation.

The dearth of financial statistics also complicates the task of relating the experience of the three countries—Poland, Hungary, and East Germany—that in one way or another were most strongly affected by the political events of 1956.

The inclusion of East Germany in this group is perhaps questionable in view of the absence of any dramatic evidence of political disturbance in 1956. My only justification for doing so is that the Pankow regime, after several years of monetary stability probably unparalleled in eastern Europe, found itself obliged to carry out a second monetary reform in October, 1957, in part to syphon off the excess currency it had released in the preceding year, in part also to confiscate the West German holdings of its bank notes. The figures below bring out the progressive deterioration that occurred from 1955, a year of great stability, to 1958:

MONTHLY AVERAGES OF CURRENCY IN CIRCULATION

Millions of Deutsche Marks

1955	January	4,464
	December	4,388
1956	January	4,311
	December	4,824
1957	January	4,698
	June	5,227
	September	5,480
1958	January (postreform)	3,709

Source: *Statistiches Jahrbuch der D.D.R. 1961* (Berlin, 1961), p. 245.

The monetary expansion resumed its course almost immediately after the reform. Currency in circulation had already risen to 5 billion DM. by December, 1960. The inflation was fed by unplanned wage increases: from 1958 to mid-1961, the disposable cash income of the population rose by 10.6 billion Deutsche Marks, or 2.6 billion more than had been planned. A recent pronouncement by a high official of the Planning Commission explained that these excess disbursements were the unavoidable consequence of developing an economy with an "open border."[28] Too little time has elapsed since the closure of the Berlin border in August, 1961 to tell whether the government is now in a position to resist the population's pressure for higher wages and salaries.

Hungary, of all the European satellites, had the most difficulty overcoming the legacy of structural disproportions and misdirected investments left over from its first long-term plan. According to official estimates, Hungarian national income in 1955 exceeded its 1953 level by only 4 percent (compared to increases ranging from 8 to 25 percent in the other countries).[29] Deep cuts in state investments and an increase in foreign indebtedness[30] had made it possible, despite the overall stagnation of national income, to raise retail sales by about a quarter and real wages by about a third in the two years following Stalin's death. Retail prices were officially reported to have undergone a slight decline. The year 1956 was to have inaugurated a more vigorous investment policy, which would have permitted a resumption of the interrupted growth in national income. State investments indeed picked up enough to register a gain for the entire year, despite the virtual standstill in economic activity from late October to December.

From June, 1953 to June, 1956, four months before the revolution got under way, monetary circulation had gone up by 85 percent, from an estimated 2.8 billion to 5.2 billion forints.[31] Most of this increase took place in 1954, when circulation rose by 51.2 percent compared to 1953. Neither the growth in money incomes nor the expanded volume of retail sales can account for this large increase in the demand for currency holdings. It is reported that much of the hoarding was done by peasants, apprehensive of forced collectivization, who wished to keep their assets as liquid as possible in the face of this eventuality.

Savings deposits only increased from 403 million in 1953 to 722

---

[28]B. Leuschner, in *Neues Deutschland*, December 3, 1961.

[29]United Nations, *World Economic Survey 1957*, p. 126.

[30]Short-term external indebtedness rose by 83 percent (by 1.4 billion forints) from 1953 to 1956. (S. Ausch and T. Gerö, "Az inflácio veszélyéröl" [The danger of inflation], *Közgazdasagi szemle*, November–December, 1956, p. 132.)

[31]*Ibid.*

million in 1955, when they amounted to a mere 13 percent of the total holdings of the population. These figures, together with data on currency in circulation and savings for other years, are brought together in Table 6 below:

TABLE 6

Savings Deposits and Estimated Currency in Circulation in Hungary, 1953 to 1960

(*Billions of Forints*)

	1953	1954	1955	1956	1957	1958	1959	(End of Year) 1960
Savings deposits......	403	581	722	573	1,338	2,327	3,895	5,480
Currency in circulation..............	2,940	4,445	4,716	6,467	6,519	6,902	8,172	8,287
Total monetary holdings of the population	3,343	5,026	5,438	7,040	7,857	9,229	12,067	13,767
Percentage of savings deposits to total money holdings.....	12.1	11.6	13.3	8.1	17.0	25.2	32.2	40.0

Source: W. Przelaskowski, "Oszczedności pienięźne ludności na Wegrzech i w Polsce," *Finanse* No. 9, 1962, p. 59.

The revolution of the fall of 1956 touched off a general strike that lasted about two months. During this period, despite the production breakdown in the socialized sector of the economy, wages and salaries were paid as if normal business were going on.[32] The impact of this disjunction on the performance of the economy during the entire year is set in relief by the figures in Table 7.

The immediate effects of the 1956 events are most clearly discernible in the decline in industrial output and in the collapse of inventories. More detailed analysis shows that inventories of goods in process actually increased during the year (because of the dislocation of production that accompanied the frequent changes in plans and allocations effected) so that the entire burden of adjustment rested on inventories of finished goods, especially on those held by the trading network. In fact, retail inventories fell by over five billion forints during the course of the entire year.[33] By December 1, 1956, the value of finished goods inventories had sunk to 40 percent of their prerevolutionary level. The ratio of inventories to currency in circulation, which had been 2.2 in October, was now

---

[32]From October 1 to November 30, 1956, the National Bank of Hungary credited enterprises with 600 million forints for wages and salaries *in excess of plan.*

[32]Central Statistical Office, *A nemzeti es a lakosság jövedelme 1958—ban* (Budapest, 1959), p. 23.

down to 0.75. Most flannel and cotton goods, better quality woolens, and a wide range of durable goods, including bicycles, radios, and stoves, were completely sold out.[34]

It so happened, however, that the initial volume of inventories and its composition were just sufficient to cushion the impact of the drop in production. The increase in circulation was held to about 1 billion forints, or less than 20 percent above the October level. Retail prices remained steady. By late November, the volume of circulation had slid from its peak level and settled at around 7 billion forints, a remarkably prompt stabilization for such a powerful disturbance.[35]

TABLE 7

INDUSTRIAL PRODUCTION, LABOR PRODUCTIVITY, FIXED INVESTMENTS, INVENTORIES, PERSONAL INCOMES, AND RETAIL PRICES IN HUNGARY, 1955 TO 1958

(Indexes, Preceding Year = 100, Except as Indicated)

	1955	1956	1957	1958
Net industrial output	108	90	117	112
light industry	108	83	123	109
food processing	107	96	110	100
Net industrial output per worker (state industry only)	107	88	114	109
Gross fixed investments (constant prices)	96	103	96	123
Cost of living index (workers and employees)	99	100	102	100
Changes in total inventories (billions of forints, constant prices)	+ 8.0	− 5.6	+14.4	+ 5.1
Personal incomes from wages and salaries in productive sectors (billions of forints)	28.9	30.9	33.9	36.5

Sources: Central Statistical Office, *Statisztikai évkönyv 1959* (Budapest; 1960), pp. 47, 85; *Statistical Pocket Book of Hungary 1960*, pp. 32, 37, 136; and *A nemzeti jövedelem és a lakosság övedelme 1958-ban* (Budapest, 1959), pp. 22, 25.

Even though personal incomes rose by 2 billion forints in 1956, total national income at current prices fell compared to 1955—from 93.1 billion to 83.1 billion forints—due to a decline of 12 billion in state and enterprise incomes, including indirect taxes, social insurance, and profits of enterprises. In terms of the consolidated financial plan of equation (7), the deviations from plan that probably occurred during the year were of the following magnitudes:[36]

---

[34]Ausch and Gerö, *op. cit.*, p. 1323.

[35]*Ibid.*, pp. 1322–23.

[36]The planned figures with which actual performance was compared are based on the percentage increases in the United Nations, *Economic Survey of Europe in 1956*, p. 15 and on the data for 1955 in *A nemzeti jövedelem*, p. 25.

ESTIMATED DEVIATIONS FROM FINANCIAL PLAN IN 1956

(*Billions of Forints*)

Gross Income of Enterprises	Monetary circulation Plus Personal Saving	=	Gross Investments	Change in Inventories	Social Consumption*
−15	+1		−1	−12	−1

*The decline in social consumption, including defense expenditures, which occurred in 1956 was calculated from a comparison of the index of "total consumption" with the index of "total consumption of the population" in the national income accounts and from an estimate of the percentage that the plan for 1956 provided for the same increase in social consumption as in private consumption.

Many Hungarian economists predicted in late 1956 that the inflation had only been postponed by the drop in inventories, that it would burst out in the open as soon as inventories were repleted in the coming year. A prediction along these lines would have been reinforced had one known that "the shortage of working capital [caused by the revolution] was made good by bank credit" and that the ratio of credit to the total working capital of enterprises was rising continuously from 1955 to 1958.[37] Yet this prediction was wide of the mark. The balance of incomes and outlays of the population for 1957, which was published by the Central Statistical Office of Hungary, shows that the total of currency in circulation plus private bank savings rose by only 596 million forints during the year compared to total cash incomes of 68.4 billion forints (net of direct taxes and fiscal payments).[38] Although an official of the Hungarian National Bank conceded that a "significant portion" of this increase was in the nature of "forced saving," the small amount involved strongly mitigates this statement.[39]

The inflation in 1957 was avoided, despite an increase in total inventories of 14.4 billion forints,[40] as a result of a moderate reduction in the level of fixed capital investments—by about 4 percent compared to 1956—and of substantial external aid. During the course of 1957, national income consumed exceeded national income

---

[37] The ratio rose from 37.9 percent in 1955 to 49.7 percent in 1958. (V. Bochkova, *et al.*, *Banki i kredit v stranakh narodnoi demokratii* [Moscow, 1961], p. 118.)

[38] This increase is an average for the entire year and is not comparable with the end-of-year data in Tables 6 and 7.

[39] As reported by S. Michalski in *Wiadomósci Narodowego Banku Polskiego*, No. 9, 1958, p. 420.

[40] *A nemzeti jövedelem*, p. 22. This figure covers all sectors of the national economy including agriculture, but apparently excludes the change in animal herds.

produced by 4.8 percent,[41] thanks mainly to a credit of 250 million dollars extended by the Soviet Union in February, 1957.[42] The proceeds from increased imports boosted budget incomes (on account of the overvaluation of the forint), and helped build up what must have been a large budget surplus for that year. Besides, the 3 percent increase in the prices of foodstuffs, which was the main factor behind the slight registered increase in the over-all index of the cost of living in 1957, also helped to blot up surplus income.

In 1958, the gap between the money incomes and outlays of the population widened slightly—to 1.4 billion forints—but in view of the steadiness of the price index and of the fact that nearly a billion out of this 1.4 billion increase in the assets of the population was deposited in savings banks, it is doubtful that forced saving was involved to a considerable extent.

In Hungary, as everywhere else in eastern Europe, state investments increased sharply in 1959. With a 41 percent increase over the previous year, Hungary led all the other members of the eastern European bloc, except for Bulgaria, in this respect. Such a discontinuous acceleration of investment effort could not easily be carried off without inflationary pressures. The 31 percent rise in the monetary holdings of the population shown in Table 6 for 1959 testifies to a significant degree of imbalance in the money market. In 1960, by contrast, when the rise in state investments over the previous year was held to 11 percent, the amount of currency in circulation was nearly stable, and the entire increase in monetary holdings, amounting to 14 percent, was confined to a change in the public's savings deposits.

The Polish experience of 1956 offers a most interesting contrast to the Hungarian. The disturbance in this case lay in excessive wage disbursals rather than in a shortfall in deliveries of consumer supplies to the trading network as in Hungary. For the year 1956 as a whole the wage fund was overexpanded by 11.7 billion zlotys, or by 12 percent; in addition, government disbursals for farm procurements were 5 billion zlotys in excess of plan, about half of which was due to unanticipated increases in average purchase prices.[43] As in Hungary, prices both in socialized shops and on the free market

---

[41]*Ibid.*, p. 15.

[42]*United Nations*, Economic Commission for Europe, *Economic Survey of Europe in 1956*, p. 19. Geneva 1957.

[43]Economic Council of the Council of Ministers, *Przeglad bieżacej sytuacji gospodarczej kraju i zadania stojace przed polityka gospodarcza* (Warsaw, 1957), pp. 10–11.

remained remarkably steady, but in this case it was not so much trade inventories as monetary circulation that adjusted to the initial disturbance. True, trade inventories rose far less than in the preceding year (1.4 billion in 1956 versus 4.6 billion in 1955), but, since there had been a more than adequate accumulation of inventories in 1955, the actual rise in 1956 may not have fallen far short of plan.[44] The deterioration that did occur in the ratio of inventories to retail sales, particularly in the last quarter of 1956 and in the first quarter of 1957, the period during which "wage discipline" was at its loosest, is brought out in the figures below:[45]

RATIO OF INVENTORIES TO RETAIL SALES

(Corresponding Quarter of Preceding Year = 100)

	1956	1957
Second quarter	103.2	78.4
Third quarter	99.5	80.4
Fourth quarter	86.7	84.0

Currency in circulation jumped from 11.6 billion on December 31, 1955, to 17.4 billion on December 31, 1956, and then to 19.0 billion in June, 1957—a 64 percent increase in 18 months. Total savings deposits at all institutions also doubled during this period.[46] The explanation that workers and farmers did not have time to spend their newly acquired earnings and held on to their incomes is not satisfactory when one attempts to trace "where the money ended up." According to a balance sheet prepared in the chief statistical office, the increase in currency holdings and in bank savings from 1955 to 1956 was divided as follows:[47]

	Billions of Zlotys
Wage and salary earners	+1.3
Farmers	+4.4
Others (free professions, private trade, etc.)	+1.0
	6.7

Most of the excess wage and salary payments were apparently

[44] *Total* inventories rose by 6.7 billion zlotys in current prices, compared to a planned increase of 4.1 billion. *(Wiadomości Narodowego Banku Polskiego*, No. 6, 1958, p. 254, and No. 7, 1960, p. 314.)

[45] M. Kucharski, "Sytuacja finansowa kraju", *Finanse*, No. 2, 1958, p. 9.

[46] *Rocznik statystyczny 1961*, p. 409; *Ekonomista*, No. 3, 1961, *Wiadomości Narodowego Banku Polskiego*, No. 5, 1958, p. 211.

[47] L. Zieńkowski, *Jak oblicza sie dochód narodowy*, Warsaw, 1959, Table I, annex.

spent. It is rather to the farmers and to the "petty capitalist elements" in the cities that we must look in order to account for the sudden surge in currency hoarding. This is consistent with the analysis of the year's events prepared by the economic council attached to the Council of Ministers, which suggested that the hoarders were mainly: (1) peasants saving to buy land, build structures, or purchase machinery (to take advantage of the more liberal attitude of the regime toward private farming) ; (2) small merchants, operators of handicraft shops, and artisans laying aside funds to expand their operations; and (3) white-collar workers threatened by administrative retrenchments who saved with a view toward supporting themselves during a temporary period of unemployment.[48]

During the first six months of 1957, however, as the supply of attractive goods in state stores dwindled, the city population began to displace the farm population as the principal agent of monetary hoarding.[49]

On the supply side of monetary operations, we have just enough data to trace the general course of events. The total volume of credits outstanding increased from 63 billion zlotys at the end of 1955 to an estimated 77 billion at the end of 1956. It then rose to 86 billion by June 30, 1957 and reached 95 billion at the end of the year. During this two-year period, enterprise deposits went up by 13 billion, while the budget surpluses accumulated in 1956 and 1957 were reflected in a rise in treasury deposits at the National Bank of 11 billion. These changes in the banks' liabilities offset about two thirds of the increase in assets corresponding to the credit expansion and helped limit the rise in monetary circulation—defined to include only currency in the hands of the public—to 14 billion zlotys.[50]

Why was such a large part of wage disbursals in 1956 financed by credit expansion? These wage expenditures raised production costs and reduced enterprises' gross profits ($R - K$ in the consolidated financial plan of equation [7]). This in turn diminished government revenue. Instead of a planned budget surplus of 4.6 billion zlotys, the state, after curtailing its expenditures by 2.8 billion short of the amount it had originally budgeted, still only showed a 1.7

[48]Economic Council, *Przeglad biezacej sytuacji gospodarczej kraju i zadania stojace przed polityka gospodarcza*, p. 14.
[49]*Wiadomości Narodowego Banku Polskiego*, No. 5, 1958, p. 211.
[50]These estimates are based (1) on a flow of funds matrix for the first half of 1957 (*Wiadomości Narodowego Banku Polskiego*, No. 5, 1958, pp. 210–11), (2) on monetary circulation figures in *Rocznik statystyczny 1961*, p. 409, and (3) on W. Jaworski, *Kreditnaya sistema Narodnoi Polski*, Moscow, 1961, pp. 101–2.

billion surplus.[51] To keep a lid on credits, the state would have had to increase its subsidies to the national economy, at the cost of a budget deficit and of a decline in treasury deposits at the National Bank. The monetary consequences of such a policy would probably have been the same as for the one that was actually chosen, but administrative convenience and the possibilities of exercising firmer control on reimbursible bank funds than on subsidies apparently predisposed the authorities toward the issuance of credits.

The squeeze on gross profits and on state revenue which tended to reduce the income side of the state's consolidated financial plan might have been offset by a decline in fixed investments or in inventories. Actually, state investment went up almost as much as the 8 percent increase targeted. As we have already seen, inventories also continued to rise, though at a somewhat slower pace than had been originally contemplated. Moreover, the expenditure side of the program was weighted down by unanticipated outlays on credits to the population (L^a in equation [7]). There was no option but to increase monetary circulation to "finance" expenditures, at least as long as direct taxes could not be raised on short notice.[52]

The reader familiar with Soviet financial practice might well ask what sort of assets the National Bank pegged its credit expansion on, considering that inventories rose by somewhat less than plan and that the bank is not normally expected to lend on anything except tangible assets. This argument in any case does not apply to the new loans extended to the farm sector—about 10 billion zlotys from the end of 1955 to 1957—which normally have no counterpart in inventories. But even in the case of industry and trade, a given volume of inventories may serve as security for a varying amount of lending, since enterprises can delay repayments of their credits and use the funds they earmarked for repayment for other purposes. Overdue credits already came to 7.3 billion, or 11.7 percent of total credits at the end of 1955. They were 94 percent greater than in July of 1955 by the end of March, 1956,[53] and they probably con-

---

[51]On the original budget, see *Trybuna Ludu*, No. 115, 1956. On the actual surplus, *Finanse*, No. 9, 1961, p. 12.

[52]The following percentage breakdowns have been published of the income side of the consolidated financial plan for 1955, 1956, and 1957:

	1955	1956	1957
Financial accumulation ($R - K$)	84.0	79.3	81.3
Taxes on the nonsocialized population (T^P)	13.8	13.7	13.8
Increase in the population's monetary holdings	2.2	7.0	4.9
of which: in banks (S^P)	0.5	0.9	3.1
in currency (N^P)	1.7	6.1	1.8

(M. Kucharski, "Sytuacja finansowa kraju," *Finanse*, No. 2, 1958, p. 11.)

tinued to climb during the year. Credits on overdue accounts payable doubled during the course of 1956 and added another half-billion zlotys to the working capital of hard-pressed firms. Greater liberality on the part of banks in defining "good" inventories susceptible of being credited probably accounts for the rest of the unplanned expansion.

The inflationary forces released by the 1956 crisis were more or less spent by the middle of 1957. The increase in credits and in monetary circulation were fairly normal in 1958, although inventories rose a good deal more than had been planned in the second half of the year. In 1959, however, a combination of adverse circumstances upset the delicately poised financial balance for the second time in three years. On this occasion it was an overexpenditure of investment funds, combined with a failure of agricultural procurement, that set off the disturbance. The situation was harder to bring under control than in former years because, as in Czechoslovakia, a significant part of investments had been decentralized and was escaping direct bank controls.[54] Currency in circulation went up again, this time from 22.6 billion zlotys on December 31, 1958 to 26 billion zlotys on June 30, 1959.

When both employment and average wages in the construction industry rose above plan in the first half of 1959, excess purchasing power was released which spilled into the food market, where it converged on a declining supply of meat (due to procurement failures). By the end of the summer, the government had resolved on two rapid and effective means for combating the incipient inflation: (1) A rise in prices of meat products averaging 20 to 25 percent, and (2) layoffs in the construction industry to reduce employment to the preboom level. Before the end of the year, currency in circulation had fallen by three billion compared to its peak 1959 volume and had reverted to its December, 1958 level.

A significant aspect of this cycle of events was that the authorities were prompt to trim investments, even though they were part of the approved centralized program. They did so in order to re-establish financial equilibrium, thus marking a departure from the practices that used to prevail in the early 1950's, a time when inflation seemed a reasonable price to pay for a high and accelerating rate of growth.

---

[53]Jaworski, *Zarys rozwoju*, p. 196.

[54]However, the proportion of decentralized to total investments was a little less than one third, as against 50 to 60 percent in Czechoslovakia. For a more comprehensive description of this crisis, see J. M. Montias, *op. cit.*, pp. 315–19.

Although this attitude evidently reflects the regime's more liberal stamp, the avoidance of inflation is more than just a matter of placating the consumer: the authorities also wish to maintain at least a moderate degree of decentralization in managing the economy. For this they need fairly stable prices and costs to guide managers and to facilitate central financial controls. They have had enough experience with inflation to learn that wage drift and creeping costs are substantially incompatible with efficient profit-oriented managerial decisions.

V. CONCLUSIONS

In the first years of existence of the centrally planned systems, the planners had neither the knowledge nor the control over economic agents necessary to construct accurate financial plans. They were insufficiently familiar with an economy in constant flux; their statistics were inadequate; their forecasts of labor productivity and agricultural output, matters that partially escaped their controls, were often little better than guesses. In conditions of political precariousness, such as prevailed in eastern Europe after World War II, these guesses were necessarily colored by a heavy dose of official optimism. Finally, they lacked the technical experience with the manipulation of financial variables in a new institutional framework that might have compensated for their errors. It took the fledgling planners of eastern Europe several years—until 1951–52—to master elementary financial techniques, such as the running of budgetary surpluses to offset the expansion of credits. But it was not until the breathing spell associated with the New Course (1953–54) that they even approached their monetary objective of price stability without excess liquidity. Yet, when it came time to raise the investment rate —in early 1956 and again in 1959—several of the economies in the area again ran into inflationary pressures.

The varying degree of susceptibility to inflation exhibited in the last decade by the centrally planned economies cannot be explained merely on the basis of differences in the quality or the experience of their financial planners. For one thing, the financiers have had to suffer the consequences of the mistakes made by their colleagues in the planning commissions who overstrained their manpower and material balances and were to blame for the excessive wage disbursals and the unplanned accumulation of unfinished inventories that eventually had to be credited with inflationary effect. For another, they were not responsible if the political decision makers preferred to let the inflation unfold rather than cut back state invest-ments or other items of budget expenditure as they frequently did, especially before 1953.

In addition to the differences in the proficiency and maturity of planners, a number of other factors may be singled out that tend to make a centrally planned economy more or less inflation-prone. Among these we may distinguish between factors bearing on the supply of, and the demand for, currency.

On the supply side, we should mention first of all the varying degree of social and political control that the Communist authori-ties are capable of exercising. This is essentially what is involved in "wage discipline": the ability to resist spontaneous wage demands, and the forcefulness with which revisions of "work norms" are periodically imposed. When controls break down, as they did in Poland in the second half of 1956, inflation ensues. The ability of the administration to bludgeon the peasants into delivering their compulsory quotas of agricultural produce despite poor harvests or other hardships also influences the maintenance of equilibrium, since these quotas make up an important part of the planned food supplies necessary to "close" the balance of incomes and outlays. In Rumania, the authorities had little trouble extracting the surpluses of a submissive peasantry; in Poland, on the other hand, not only were the peasants more recalcitrant, tending to fall behind in their deliveries, but they also reacted perversely by cutting back the acre-age they cultivated and by restricting their production of meat and other animal products. The inability of the regime to force collec-tivization through in the face of peasant opposition foreclosed a possible issue to the dilemma. A free agriculture makes Poland ap-preciably more sensitive to inflationary pressures than the other countries of the Communist bloc, where collectivization has been nearly completed in recent years.

The experiments in decentralization conducted in Czechoslovakia and Poland since 1958–59 have greatly complicated financial plan-ning, just at a time when stability appeared to be an essential condi-tion of the success of these innovations. Enterprises, keeping larger liquid balances, can more easily shift their funds from working-capital accounts to investments or capital repairs, and are generally less predictable in their financial decisions than they were before they received their new prerogatives. The wider role played in the in-vestment field by local authorities (for example, by the National Committee in Czechoslovakia) also makes it harder for the planners to anticipate effective demand, because these local decisions cannot easily be tracked down and controlled from any central source of authority.

Finally, a couple of technical points may be put forward regarding the credit policy of the State Bank which of course influences directly the money supply. Soviet credit policy by all accounts is distinguished by an extremely conservative attitude toward the nature of "bankable assets."[55] Yet confining loans to inventories and goods in transit will not guarantee monetary stability, since enterprises' needs for liquidity depend on the synchronization of receipts and payments, which is not simply correlated with the size of their inventories. About all that can be said in favor of this crediting policy is that, if strictly carried out, it should be able to prevent a credit expansion in excess of inventory increases (assuming that goods in transit move in close relation with inventories). Thus strict adherence to Soviet precepts in Hungary and Poland might have placed a significant obstacle in the way of inflation in 1956. However, the government preferred to expand credits rather than to suffer budgetary deficits, and the banks were obliged to fill the gap in enterprises' receipts created by the government's wage policy. In Poland they financed unplanned wage increases; in Hungary they credited at least a part of the wages and salaries that the government decided to continue paying out in October and November, 1956, even though receipts from sales of industrial products to the trading network had dwindled to practically nothing. The scattered statistics so far released suggest that the proscriptions on unsecured assets were loosened to accommodate the government's policy. In general, if the banks rather than the budget are forced to adjust to discrepancies from plan, differences in the stringency of the various state banks' lending policies will only have a marginal effect on credit. Stringency may cause enterprises to reduce their bank deposits in order to finance their own working capital needs, as happened in Poland in 1958–59, but the small size of these deposits imposes narrow bounds to the success of such tightening measures.[56]

---

[55]On January 1, 1956, 90.4 percent of bank loans were "secured" by raw materials, material supplies, and finished goods, as well as goods in transit (D. Hodgman, "Soviet Monetary Controls Through the Banking System," *Value and Plan* [G. Grossman, ed.], p. 118).

[56]In Poland, stringency has at times led to considerable interfirm crediting: the accounts payable of enterprises rose from 26 billion zlotys on June 30, 1958, to 32 billion a year later, of which overdue bills amounted to 5.8 billion in 1958 and 10 billion in 1959. (*Wiadomości Narodowego Banku Polskiego*, No. 11; 1959, p. 544.) This deterioration in enterprise finance was accompanied by a sharp reduction in enterprise liquidity, the combined deposits and currency holdings of

Factors underlying the demand for currency account for most of the difference between the Hungarian and the Polish experiences of 1956. Essentially, in Poland there were valuable opportunities to look forward to and to save for, which caused farmers and self-employed persons to build up their cash hoards and their savings deposits, while the best the Hungarians could do—if they were not taking an active part in the revolution—was to raid the stores, fill their closets, and wait out events.[57]

To conclude, it may be useful to speculate on the ultimate strengths and weaknesses of financial planning in a centralized economy.

A rapid rate of economic growth is not an insuperable obstacle to monetary equilibrium. Neither is a high but sustained "rate of accumulation." There are two basic problems: the first is to adjust the system to discontinuous increases in the share of investments in national income when production costs have not declined sufficiently to finance the new investments. This is essentially the problem that occurred in most of the economies of eastern Europe in 1959 and which the authorities resolved by letting monetary circulation expand (instead of raising direct or indirect taxes to absorb the excess purchasing power of the population). The second is the inability of the planners to predict with exactitude the changes in the level of inventories in marketed food supplies, in labor productivity, and in the foreign trade balance corresponding to the growth they have targeted, and their unwillingness to provide for sufficient budgetary reserves to offset excessive inventory accumulation, unexpected deterioration in the terms of trade, or failures to hit productivity targets.[58]

In countries, such as Czechoslovakia and Poland, that have launched far-reaching programs of administrative decentralization and that have significantly widened the financial latitude open to socialized enterprises, the maneuvering power of the central authorities has been so narrowed during the course of execution of the

---

socialized industry and trade falling from 15.1 billion at the end of 1958 to 11 billion at the end of 1959 (*Rocznik statystyczny 1960,* pp. 431–32).

[57]Differences in the inventory-to-sales ratio in Poland and Hungary before the events of 1956 are too slight to explain why inventories acted as a much more resistent barrier to the inflation in Hungary than in Poland.

[58]Eugeniusz Szyr, one of the top Polish planners, recently conceded that it would do more harm than good to try and set a hard-and-fast limit on inventory accumulation. "All errors in the plan and in its execution find their outlet in increases in inventories"; there is too little elasticity in other items of the enterprise's plan to allow it to adapt to discrepancies, except through these unplanned changes in its inventories (*Zycie gospodarcze,* No. 42, 1962 p. 4).

plan that their only realistic way of adjusting to adverse deviations from plan consists in cutting back centralized investment *ad hoc* to preserve macroeconomic equilibrium. The Poles, after the embarrassing episode of the summer of 1959, when meat prices had to be jacked up to absorb the surplus purchasing power generated by excessive investment spending, have shown greater flexibility than their neighbors in adapting the rate of expansion of their economy to satisfy current monetary constraints. Judging by the crisis that developed in Rumania, Bulgaria, and Czechoslovakia in 1962, the more authoritative of the Communist regimes seem less eager to give up increments in growth for the sake of averting consumer hardships or inflation.

In the present stage of development of the centralized economies, the planners' degree of success in achieving their monetary objectives still seems to depend essentially on the scale of priorities governing the allocation decisions made in the course of the year to correct discrepancies from plan.

c. EXPERIENCE OF INFLATION AND GROWTH IN SELECTED ASIAN COUNTRIES[1]

Tun Thin

I

The present paper is intended to bring out the experience of some selected countries in Asia[2] with respect to inflation and growth so that a comparative analysis may be made with that of the Latin American countries. The word "inflation" is here taken to mean a condition of rising prices. In general, reference will be made to the level of consumer prices as an indicator of inflation.

---

[1]The author wishes to express his indebtedness to his colleagues in the Asian Department of the International Monetary Fund for their considerable assistance. Needless to say, any errors in this paper are those of the author, and he takes the responsibility for the views expressed and interpretations made. They do not necessarily represent the views of the IMF, of which the author is an official.

[2]Selected Asian countries are Indonesia, China (Taiwan), Korea (South), Burma, Thailand, Japan, India, Philippines, Ceylon, Federation of Malaya, and Vietnam (South).

Cost of living indices do not, of course, provide a strictly accurate and comparable measure of inflation. They do not generally reflect the inflationary experience of the country as a whole, as they usually relate to the cost of living for a class of wage earners and cover only a limited range of commodities. Moreover, in some countries, governments exercise control over prices of certain food items and rent which are fairly heavily weighted in the consumer price indices, so that the indices become misleading. Nevertheless, the cost of living indices provide an approximate measure of the varying degrees of inflation which different countries have experienced over a number of years.

As a measure of inflation, these indices reveal a great diversity of experience (Tables 1 and 2). At one extreme, countries such as Ceylon, Malaya, Dominican Republic, El Salvador, Guatemala, Haiti, Honduras, and Nicaragua have exhibited a high degree of stability between 1953 and 1961. At the other extreme, the price levels of such countries as Bolivia, Chile, and Indonesia have shown a high degree of inflation. For the first group of countries, a price increase of 2 or 3 percent per annum may appear inflationary, and for the second group, a price rise averaging 10 percent a year would amount almost to stability. Partly because of these differences among the countries and partly because the price indices lack both accuracy and full coverage, as mentioned above, countries are classified over three broad ranges of rates of increase in the cost of living indices. Thus, in Tables 1 and 2[3] countries are classified under three headings: group A, high inflation (average over 10 percent per annum increase in cost of living index) ; group B, high to moderate inflation (5 to 10 percent); and group C, moderate inflation to stable (under 5 percent).

For the measurement of growth, economists have suggested various yardsticks, for example, the rate of capital accumulation, the rate of growth of national product or income, the rate of growth of per capita product or income, and that of consumption levels. Each of these has its own weaknesses, arising from the difficulties of defining, measuring, and interpreting it. International comparisons of growth, of course, involve more problems, as different

---

[3]Tables 1, 2, and 3 give average annual percentage changes for 1954 and 55, 1957 and 58, and 1960 and 61. These periods have been taken in order to avoid the years 1956 and 1959, when Bolivia and Argentina adopted fluctuating exchange rates. For classification of countries into three groups according to degree of inflation, averages of 1957–58 and 1960–61 have been taken to show recent trends.

TABLE 1

SELECTED ASIAN COUNTRIES: CHANGE IN COST OF LIVING AND MONEY SUPPLY

(Average Annual Percentage Change)

Rate of Increase in c.o.l. Index During 1957–58 and 1960–61 (column 4) / Country	Cost of Living				Money Supply			
	(1) 1954–55	(2) 1957–58	(3) 1960–61	(4) Average (2) & (3)	(5) 1954–55	(6) 1957–58	(7) 1960–61	(8) Average (6) & (7)
A. High (over 10 percent) Indonesia..............	21	30	33	32	32	60	48	54
B. High to moderate (5 to 10 percent) China (Taiwan)........	6	7	13	10	24	27	15	21
Korea (South).........	65	9	9	9	105	28	27	28
C. Moderate to stable (below 5 percent) Burma...............	—	—	8	4	24	−1	—	—
Thailand............	3	6	3	4	11	5	11	8
Japan...............	2	2	5	3	10	9	20	15
India...............	−5	5	2	3	10	4	7	6
Philippines.........	−1	3	3	3	5	8	10	9
Ceylon.............	—	2	—	1	15	−2	4	1
Federation of Malaya...	−5	2	—	1	12	−2	3	—
Vietnam (South)......	12	−6	2	−2	...	−4	8	2

Source: International Monetary Fund, *International Financial Statistics*.
General note for all tables: (...) indicates nonavailability of data, and (–) indicates nil or negligible.

TABLE 2

LATIN-AMERICAN COUNTRIES: CHANGE IN COST OF LIVING AND MONEY SUPPLY

(Average Annual Percentage Change)

Rate of Increase in c.o.l. Index During 1957–58 and 1960–61 (column 4)	Country	Cost of Living				Money Supply			
		(1) 1954–55	(2) 1957–58	(3) 1960–61	(4) Average (2) & (3)	(5) 1954–55	(6) 1957–58	(7) 1960–61	(8) Average (6) & (7)
A. High (over 10 percent)	Bolivia	151	61	10	35	120	25	14	20
	Brazil	20	19	43	31	22	30	54	42
	Argentina	9	32	22	27	19	32	22	27
	Paraguay	24	11	:	:	33	12	15	14
	Uruguay	11	17	35	26	7	20	25	23
	Chile	101	30	10	20	70	36	30	33
	Colombia	4	16	6	11	12	18	18	18
B. High to moderate (5 to 10 percent)	Peru	5	8	7	8	8	6	16	11
	Mexico	11	9	3	6	17	7	8	8
C. Moderate to stable (below 5 percent)	Costa Rica	3	3	1	2	9	8	—	4
	Ecuador	3	1	3	2	5	2	6	4
	Dominican Republic	−1	2	−3	—	15	16	7	12
	El Salvador	3	—	1	—	7	−3	−5	−4
	Guatemala	2	—	—	—	7	—	−2	−1
	Haiti	3	—	—	—	13	−12	10	−1
	Honduras	7	—	—	—	1	−4	—	−1
	Nicaragua	12	—	—	—	8	−3	4	−2
	Venezuela	—	1	:	:	8	23	−2	10

Source: International Monetary Fund, *International Financial Statistics.*

countries employ different concepts, have different social systems, and are at different stages of growth. In the *Economic Survey of Asia and the Far East*,[4] an attempt has been made to use several indicators in the assessment of the dimension of growth. However, in the present paper, if for no other reason than shortage of time and labor, growth in aggregate real product has been employed as the indicator of growth.

II

Among the Asian countries, Indonesia is the only country in the high inflation group (Table 1) and China (Taiwan) and the Republic of Korea are the two countries in the high-to-moderate-inflation group; while the growth rates of Indonesia and Korea have been low, the growth rate of China (Taiwan) has been quite high (Table 3). We shall now proceed to study these three countries to find out what circumstances have led to the absence of any uniform pattern in the relationship between inflation and growth.

Indonesia suffered heavy economic damage during the war and much capital was destroyed. The struggle for independence in the 1945–49 period delayed the task of reconstruction. During the period 1950–57, while Indonesia was rehabilitating and expanding prewar production capacity—especially in the manufacturing sector—the economy achieved appreciable growth even though political instability and fluctuation in export earnings disturbed the steady pace of development. However, since the beginning of 1958, economic growth has practically stopped. This was brought about mainly by two developments. First, with the rebellion in the Outer Islands and the sharpening of the long dispute with the Netherlands over West Irian, high military expenditures caused a substantial drain on resources and an acceleration of inflation. Secondly, this period was marked by fundamental changes in the institutional structure of the economy: Dutch enterprises were taken over by the government in 1957; the government share of total import trade was extended to cover almost 80 percent; and a large part of the retail trade, formerly carried on by the Chinese, was given over to cooperatives and shops supervised by the government. But the government lacked experienced and skilled personnel to run these enterprises and consequently the production and distribution sectors suffered.

The Indonesian budget has been in chronic deficit since 1952.

---

[4] *ECAFE*, 1961.

TABLE 3

SELECTED ASIAN COUNTRIES: GROWTH IN REAL AGGREGATE AND PER CAPITA PRODUCT

(Average Annual Percentage Change)

	Aggregate Product				Per Capita Product			
	(1)	*(2)*	*(3)*	*(4)*	*(5)*	*(6)*	*(7)*	*(8)*
	1954–55	*1957–58*	*1960–61*	*Average (2) & (3)*	*1954–55*	*1957–58*	*1960–61*	*Average (6) & (7)*
A. Indonesia	5.5	2.2	...	...	3.7	—	...	...
B. China (Taiwan)	8.0	6.7	7.8	7.2	4.0	3.5	4.7	4.1
Korea (South)	4.6	7.8	2.5	5.1	1.6	4.7	—	2.3
C. Burma	5.0	3.0	4.5	3.7	3.5	2.5	3.0	2.7
Thailand	6.6	−0.7	8.3	3.8	3.5	−3.5	5.1	0.8
Japan	7.2	4.7	14.1	9.4	6.4	3.6	13.0	8.3
India	4.7	2.0	4.4	3.2	2.3	—	2.2	1.1
Philippines	6.6	4.3	5.0	4.6	3.3	1.1	1.8	1.4
Ceylon	5.0	2.4	4.6	3.5	2.4	−0.2	1.8	0.9
Federation of Malaya	...	1.8	...	...	...	−1.3	...	...

Sources: United Nations, *Yearbooks of National Accounts Statistics*, and other national official sources.
General Note: The series are at factor cost for India and Malaya.

However, the government was able to offset the excess demand pressure by a substantial drawing down of foreign reserves from 1952 until mid-1954, when additional restrictive measures were imposed.

Up to the end of 1954, inflation was still moderate. But as budget deficits and import restrictions continued and remaining stocks were exhausted, the situation worsened and in 1955, high inflation set in. As government deficits rose higher and higher, the rate of increase in money supply accelerated, with the exception of 1959 when there was a monetary reform. Increasing government deficits have been largely due to increasing security expenditures. The rate of increase in money supply and the cost of living index during the 12 months ending January, 1962, were 46 and 128[5] percent, respectively.

The economy of *China* (Taiwan) was at a low ebb when the Nationalist government of China moved its seat to Taiwan in 1949. Between Japan's surrender in 1945 and the fall of the Chinese mainland in 1949, the island's economic development was at a standstill. The already distressed situation was intensified in 1949 by the influx of Chinese from the mainland, including a great number of troops and government workers, by the reinforcement of inflationary trends due to heavy military expenditure and the resettlement of the civil agencies, and by the rising demand for goods, especially imports.

The period of rehabilitation between 1949 and 1952 has been succeeded by a period of marked economic growth under the first (1953–56) and second (1957–60) Four-Year Economic Development plans. During the eight years of implementation, a substantial increase was achieved in production; real national and per capita income increased by about 63 percent and 32 percent respectively. During the period, money supply increased by about 170 percent; increase in credit to the private sector and to official entities contributed largely to this increase. The annual rate of increase in the cost of living index during the period was 10 percent.

The objectives of the government have been to maintain a heavy military establishment on the one hand, and to improve the economic welfare of the growing population on the other. It is much to the credit of the country that both these objectives have

---

[5]International Monetary Fund, *International Financial Statistics*, October, 1952.

been attained. A rapid growth rate was achieved within a short period after rehabilitation started, and the rate has been maintained since. This was due to the determination and efforts of the government to achieve growth, the technical know-how and the spirit of the Chinese people, and foreign assistance. This growth could have been achieved with greater stability if it had not been for the high defense expenditures of the government, which comprised, on the average, about 50 percent of the total government expenditures, and about 10 percent of the gross national product, one of the highest rates in the region. However, even so, inflation has slowed down since 1961, and the increase in the cost of living index was 4 percent in 1961 and 3 percent in the 12 months ending June, 1962.

The *Korean* economy suffered from a long-suppressed inflation during the war years of 1937–45, a hyperinflation from 1945 to 1947, galloping inflation from 1950 to 1952, and a high inflation from 1953 to 1955. During 1956–60, Korea experienced a moderate inflation. The inflation during 1945–55 was largely attributed to the disintegration of the pre-existing network of production, trade, and distribution by the partition of the country into North and South Korea in 1945, a huge government deficit resulting mainly from the slow improvements in both the revenue system and its administrative machinery, coupled with the increased requirements of government expenditures to restore and maintain social order, and the Korean War during 1950–53.

During 1945–55, the average annual increase of both money supply and prices was more than 200 percent. The excess demand pressure was reduced in 1956 when the amount of budget deficit was reduced, mainly because of a slowing down in the rate of increase in defense expenditure, coupled with the accumulated effects of economic reconstruction and expanded foreign aid. During 1957–60, the Korean government adopted an annual financial stabilization program, and a further stability was achieved, chiefly through a tighter fiscal policy and a slower rate of increase in private consumption demand than in the previous years. The annual average increase in money supply was 16 percent and in prices, 8 percent in this period.

The average growth rate during the rehabilitation and recovery period, 1953–59, was relatively high. Largely because of political and economic uncertainties and the completion of the process of recovery, the rate of growth during 1960 and 1961 slowed down considerably.

III

In the moderate inflation to stable group, group C, are Burma, Thailand, Japan, India, Philippines, Ceylon, Federation of Malaya, and Vietnam (South). The growth rates in these countries,[6] with the exception of Japan, are between 3 and 5 percent. Changes in money supply in this group are, on the average, within 5 percent points of the changes in gross national product.

Thus, we can see that the relationship between inflation and growth in Burma, Thailand, India, Philippines, Ceylon, and Malaya follows a certain pattern. The common factors underlying this relationship are: relative political stability, low per capita income (below $200 with the exception of Malaya), and financially conservative governments with a long history of monetary stability. Low per capita income is one of the important factors, because it compels the government to take the sociopolitical decision of keeping the prices of mass consumption goods stable; moreover, the absence of large government contractual payments, such as social security benefits, and of large government expenditures directly creating employment opportunities in these countries makes it easy for a government to cut down its expenditures whenever the need arises.

It is quite evident that in those countries of groups A and B which have been experiencing a strong, prolonged price rise, the effective demand has by far exceed the supply of goods and services. But, in the countries of group C, where price increases have not shown a clear trend, the presence of excess demand pressure will have to be ascertained by looking at some other indicators: the presence of exchange restrictions for balance-of-payments reasons, quickly falling foreign exchange reserves, rises in real estate values, and bottlenecks in some sectors.

Among the countries in group C, Burma, Ceylon, India, and Japan maintain restrictions on imports for balance of payments reasons. The Philippines lifted restrictions only in January, 1962, when the exchange rate for the peso was allowed to fluctuate.

The foreign exchange reserves of the above countries have gone down to critical levels at one time or another, and any recovery has been only for a short period. On the other hand, Malaya and Thailand have not experienced any balance of payments crises, and their reserves have been on an increasing up trend in recent years. Thus,

---

[6]Growth data is not available for Vietnam and, hence, comparisons cannot be made with other countries of the region.

looking at the indicators, it seems reasonable to conclude that excess demand pressures have been present, at one time or another, in Burma, Ceylon, India, the Philippines, and Japan. However, if these pressures have been present, they have not been strong enough to lift the top off and push the economies onto a strong inflationary path. The pattern in these countries seems to be that whenever development efforts and/or adverse terms of trade contribute to a pressure on foreign exchange reserves, exchange restrictions are imposed or tightened and some fiscal and credit measures taken to slow down the drain on these reserves. About the time the level of reserves becomes critical and further drain is not possible, development efforts may be cut back and stronger credit measures taken to lessen the excess demand pressure and thus slow down the pressure on the price level. Should the corrective measures or other factors, such as an improvement in terms of trade, strengthen foreign reserves, as in Japan, the Philippines, and Burma, there would again be a step-up in development efforts and the cycle described above would be repeated. By pulling back from the brink before the disturbance to monetary stability becomes too serious, these countries have been able to maintain a reasonable balance between growth and monetary stability.

Japan's case has been presented as a case study in Section V below, because, being a mature industrial economy, its problems have differed from those of other countries of the region. The experience of Burma, India, and the Philippines will be studied below.

The case of *Burma* illustrates clearly how seriously the external-demand factor can interrupt planned development in an export economy. After having accumulated sizable foreign reserves during the Korean War boom, Burma launched an Eight-Year Plan in 1952. The plan aimed at an annual increase of national income at a rate of 7.4 percent and of per capita income by 6.2 percent, so that by 1959 the prewar level of living standards could be restored or even slightly exceeded. The actual achievement, at 4.6 and 3.6 percent, respectively, fell substantially below the targets. The gross domestic product barely surpassed the prewar level, and per capita output was 17 percent below that of prewar.

Two years after the launching of the plan, foreign reserves started to decline, resulting from heavy foreign expenditures under the plan, and a sharp fall in export receipts reflected a fall in the price of rice, the main export of Burma. Even after a tightening of exchange restrictions in early 1955, foreign reserves continued to decline, and they reached a critical level in 1955. The government took more drastic measures by cutting budget allocations for both current and capital expenditures, and, in general, only those projects on which work had been started or equipment purchases committed were allowed to continue. Thus, the Eight-Year Plan was virtually abandoned and was soon superseded by the first Four-Year Plan (1956–57—1959–60), which had no income target. It emphasized the objective of consolidating the projects that had been started, and the starting of new quick-yielding projects. The second Four-Year Plan was adopted in 1961 with the same emphasis as the first Four-Year Plan.

During the first Four-Year Plan, the rates of increase of GNP, money supply, and cost of living index were about 5.3, 6.4, and 2 percent, respectively. Thus, due to the less ambitious nature of the Four-Year plans, which base their investment expenditures on more realistic estimates of resources, excess demand pressures have lessened and foreign exchange reserves have been increasing, except in 1960–61, when exports declined due to poor harvests. Burma now has a comfortable reserve position and is on the verge of launching a bigger development program for the public sector than that set forth in the second Four-Year Plan.

In *India*, during the first Five-Year Plan (1951–1956), the national income increased by 18 percent, as against the target of 12 percent. During the second Five-Year Plan (1956–1961), on the other hand, the increase in national income was 20 percent as against the target of 25 percent. Over the ten years, real national income increased by 42 percent. The average rate of increase is low in comparison with most other countries under review and leads one to a discussion of the investment pattern. The trends in capital-output ratios were favorable in the First Plan period largely because of the large agricultural outturn and the utilization of considerable unutilized and underutilized industrial capacity. In the Second Plan period, not merely did the agricultural sector fail to experience the same increase in output in relation to investment, but the pattern of investment was one that made for high capital-output ratios. This was due to a concentration to a larger extent than hitherto on steel, basic capital goods, and heavy-engineering industries, whose gestation period is longer and in which the returns in relation to capital investment are likely to be lower.

The development efforts of the First and Second plans had no doubt resulted in an increase in the money supply. However, over the ten years covered by the two plans, the rate of monetary expansion was 47 percent, compared with the rate of increase in the same period in real national income of 42 percent. The principal factor behind the expansion in the money supply has been the increase in bank credit to the government sector; the significance of this factor, however, has been lessening in recent years, and the increase in credit to the private sector has emerged as a major expansionary factor.

The First Plan imposed no strain on the external account, and the favorable experience was followed by a liberalization of imports in 1956–57. The surge of import demand that resulted partly from this liberalization led to a rapid depletion of India's international reserves and the tightening of restrictions. In November, 1958, it was decided to cut back the public sector outlay by about 6 percent; India also obtained a much larger volume of external assistance than had been planned for, following the meetings of the Consortium sponsored by the IBRD in 1958, 1959, and 1960.

The lesson to be drawn from the Indian experience is that the success of government efforts to maintain monetary stability depends, to a great extent, on the availability of food through domestic production and imports. In a larger context, food availability measures what may be termed the investment potential of the economy. It would seem that in the First Plan period, when food supplies posed no serious problem, the investment potential of the economy was not fully realized; the converse was true of the Second Plan period, when food supplies fell short not only absolutely but even more so in relation to the stepped-up rate of investment.

In the outlook for the immediate period ahead that is, for the Third Plan period (1961–65), food availability appears assured for the projected investment rate. This is so not merely because some of the earlier investment in agriculture is now coming to the stage of fruition, but also because in the agricultural sector itself a change has occurred in favor of projects with short gestation periods. In the industrial sector, although the investment program continues to be oriented toward the fulfillment of the objective of a self-reliant economy, some of the earlier investment will be reaching the stage of production and thus will tend to bring about a more favorable balance between investment and output. Internally, the financing of the plan appears to pose relatively little problem, as the experience of the previous periods has shown, in the Second Plan, the tax effort exceeded the tax target, and in these first two years of the Third Plan it would seem that enough taxes have been levied to cover about two thirds of the tax target of five years. Finance for the private sector is forthcoming as well, and a further increase in private investment seems limited not so much by lack of domestic financial resources as by a shortage of foreign exchange. Recent buoyant trends in the capital market, the rising volume of life insurance, the growth of small savings, and the increase of time and savings deposits of the banking system all point toward an outlook of confidence.

For more than a decade, the *Philippine* economy has been characterized by a rapid growth in production. Rehabilitation from the extensive ravages of the war was essentially completed by 1950, and the prewar per capita income level was probably restored around 1953–54. The growth was particularly striking from 1950–54, a period of recovery. Since then, total national output has risen at an average annual rate of about 5 percent, and per capita output in excess of 2 percent.

From about 1954 onward, the country has pursued a conscious policy of accelerating economic development. As much of the development expenditures were financed by deficit financing and bank credit expansion, excess demand pressures developed and, consequently, the balance of payments weakened. To combat the payments difficulty and the dangers of a continuous excessive domestic expansion, a number of corrective measures in the fiscal and monetary management fields were adopted in late 1957 and continued well into 1958. These were organized into a so-called stabilization program in early 1959, when several new instruments of restraint, particularly a 25 percent levy on nearly all foreign exchange sales, were adopted. Accordingly, the balance of payments improved markedly in 1959 and remained favorable in 1960.

The fairly strong position of the economy in 1960, the need for achieving a more basic improvement and providing a better framework for future growth, and public pressures for relaxing controls, led the authorities to adopt a gradual exchange decontrol program in April, 1960, so as to bring about an adjustment to a more realistic level of exchange rates and permit the progressive liberalization of trade and payments. However, in 1961 there again occurred excessive domestic monetary expansion and external payments difficulties, but this may be attributed largely to the political exigencies of an election year and exchange speculation. In January, 1962, with the implementation by the new administration of the fourth phase of the decontrol program, virtually all exchange controls were terminated, and the peso was allowed to float pending the eventual establishment of a fixed exchange rate at a realistic level. This step was accompanied by monetary and fiscal measures designed to restore domestic stability. Judging from the effects thus far on the domestic monetary situation, balance of payments, and prices, the authorities seem to have achieved considerable success in stabilizing the economy. Exports have recorded a significant increase, and the balance of payments has improved sharply in the first half of 1962. Price increases to date have also been moderate. Financial developments, influenced by the complementary measures of restraint, have been characterized by relative stability of the money supply and the achievement of a large fiscal cash surplus in the first half of the year. Encouraged by these favorable developments on both the internal and external fronts, the authorities have once again started to move in the direction of an easing of financial policies so as to shift the emphasis from short-run stability to longer-run growth.

IV

As mentioned above, *Malaya* and *Thailand* have no restrictions for balance of payments reasons, and they have had a comfortable level of exchange reserves for some time. Moreover, the cost of living index for Malaya[7] shows remarkable stability. Thus, on the whole, it may be concluded that there have been no excess demand pressures in either Malaya or Thailand during most of the last decade.

Malaya's terms of trade have been the most favorable among the Asian countries (Table 6); Japan and Thailand are next to Malaya. In Malaya, with the exception of the program for the improvement of the rubber industry, planned economic development commenced only with the inauguration of the first Five-Year Plan, 1956–60. It did not contain aggregate targets and was never seriously put into operation. The second Five-Year Plan, 1961–65, is somewhat more ambitious and contains some targets; however, they have been set quite conservatively. The plan's preface stated: "The targets envisaged in the Plan have been framed not in terms of ideal ambitious goals but in terms of objective feasibility . . . in relation to the resources and capacity of the country."

The average annual income growth in Malaya during the plan period, 1956–60, was 3.6 percent and compares with the growth rates in the same period in the following other Asian countries: Japan, 9.5 percent; Burma, 5.5 percent; South Korea, 4.7 percent; Philippines, 4.4 percent; Thailand, 4.0 percent; India, 3.7 percent;

---

[7]A reliable cost of living index for Thailand is not available. The cost of living index for Bangkok shows a 5 percent annual increase during the last decade. It is conjectured that the annual increase for the whole of Thailand will be less.

and Ceylon, 2.2 percent. However, due to the high annual population growth of 3.4 percent during the same period, growth in per capita income was negligible.

It is of interest to ask why Malaya and Thailand have been able to maintain their growth rates with less inflationary pressures than other countries. But countries have had political stability for quite some time, and the small population density has also contributed to minimizing the various sociopolitical pressures for a hasty embarkation on ambitious development plans; they have enjoyed large amounts of foreign aid to defray a large part of security expenditures; public sector development outlays have hitherto been quite modest despite the ample availability of both internal and external financial resources, largely because of a number of physical and administrative bottlenecks. The increase in money supply is less pronounced in Malaya than in Thailand, and this stability has been mainly due to the Currency Board arrangement, under which Malaya has had, so far, a currency backed 100 percent by sterling.

V

The record of postwar *Japan* in achieving economic growth without unduly disturbing monetary stability has been remarkable. During the nine years 1953–61,[8] gross national product increased in real terms at an annual average rate of about 9 percent; the increase per capita was no less impressive inasmuch as the annual rate of population growth was only about 1 percent. In the same period, prices, as measured by the gross national product deflator, increased at an annual average rate of about 2.5 percent. This price increase was almost entirely in consumer prices of goods and services;[9] the wholesale price index has been remarkably stable.

The factors behind this performance of the Japanese economy can be seen in the answers to two broad questions: First, why were no upward pressures exerted on costs and prices by the exercise of market power by some factors of production, as has happened in other countries in recent years? Secondly, why did not the phenomenally rapid rate of economic growth exert a strain on resources and result in an aggregate demand pull inflation?

Considering the first question, upward pressures on prices unrelated to demand conditions would arise chiefly because of cost in-

---

[8]The years 1946–53 are excluded because they were clearly the years of postwar recovery; the Korean War was an additional abnormal factor in the last two years of this period.

[9]The increase in these prices has accelerated in recent years.

creases resulting from autonomous increases in wages. Wages have indeed increased rapidly during the period under review. Comprehensive statistics on wages are difficult to obtain in a country like Japan, with its large number of small-scale productive units, and readily available wage statistics relate to regular workers (that is, not temporary or day laborers) in enterprises employing 30 or more workers. They show that monthly wage earnings[10] per regular worker in all nonagricultural industries increased during 1953–61 at an annual average rate of somewhat over 7 percent; the increase in manufacturing industries alone was a little faster—about 8 percent. The rate of increase was over twice as much as the increase in the cost of living and also compared favorably with wage increases in other industrial countries.

Despite this rapid increase in wages, efficiency wage costs—that is wage costs per unit of output[11]—in fact declined during the period under review, as productivity of labor increased even more rapidly. Comprehensive indices of productivity, again, are difficult to obtain; however, an indication of the pace of increase in productivity in manufacturing is provided by the fact that while during 1953–61 manufacturing production increased by almost two and a half times, the employment of regular workers in the same sector about doubled; if total employment, that is, inclusive of temporary and day workers, were considered, the increase would be somewhat less. Even after making allowances for the crudity of this productivity indicator, it would seem that efficiency wages in manufacturing decreased at an annual average rate of about 2 percent during this period.

The sharp increase in Japanese labor productivity must be attributed principally to the fact that in postwar years Japanese labor has been working with increasing quantity and improving quality of capital equipment. During the decade of the fifties, gross domestic investment (public and private, fixed capital and inventory) averaged as high as 30 percent of gross national product. Gross[12] private investment in plant and equipment alone averaged over 14 percent; since 1956, it has averaged almost 19 percent.

---

[10]An index of wage rates is available, but it does not take account of substantial mid-year and end-year bonus payments to labor which are an intrinsic feature of the Japanese wage-payments system.

[11]As is well known, wage costs are only a part of total labor costs in Japan, fringe benefits also being an important component. However, no information is available regarding the relative movements of the two components.

[12]"Gross" investment rather than "net" is more relevant here, as replacement of capital rarely involves replacement by the same type of machinery.

The increasing amount of capital per worker implies not only more capital intensive methods of production in the old light-manufacturing industries, but also the development of new lines of industry—heavy and chemical industries—which require larger amounts of capital per worker. This is evident in the rapidly increasing share of these latter industries in the total output of manufacturers. Today, the relative importance of these industries in the total manufacturing sector is greater in Japan than in other advanced industrial countries—France, Germany, the United Kingdom, and the United States.

The ultimate explanation of the high levels of investment cannot, of course, be given in terms of the high capital requirements of the newly growing industries. It should come rather in terms of more fundamental factors—the plenitude of savings; the existence of the infrastructure necessary for growth and the availability of complementary factors of production like skilled labor; rapidly growing markets; and, in the past two or three years, the defensive need to prepare for the day when import restrictions are removed. The initial impetus to Japan's rapid postwar economic growth came from the process of reconstruction and recovery, heavily supported by United States aid, immediately after the war. The rapid expansion of markets in this period and during the Korean War, by engendering expectations of further expansion, created strong incentives to invest. The undertaking of investment was facilitated, of course, by the fact that Japan already possessed the necessary overhead capital and economic organization, and a skilled labor force. A particularly important factor in explaining the achievement of high levels of investment without having to force savings by raising prices is the traditionally strong propensity of the Japanese to save; while various new influences have impinged on this aspect of behavior since the end of the war, the strength of this propensity has certainly not declined.

The need to maintain international competitiveness has always provided an important incentive to invest for modernization and rationalization of industry. The relevance of this factor is not confined to the export side, inasmuch as Japan's economic growth has always been characterized by a substitution of domestic products for imports. Perhaps the most important factor behind the investment boom of 1958–61 was the need to strengthen the domestic industry so as to be able to withstand the competition of imports that was expected to arise with the implementation of the government's import liberalization program.

While these high levels of investment have kept productivity advancing at a rapid pace, a part of the explanation of the lag of wages behind productivity lies in the fact that the substantial degree of unemployment and underemployment that still exists in the Japanese economy hangs on the labor market and dampens the rise in wages. Perhaps it can also be argued that there is inevitably a lag before wages can catch up with productivity; indeed, the gap between the two seems to be narrowing, and in 1961, for the first time in recent years, the increase in wages exceeded that in productivity. This important change in the Japanese situation reflects principally the marked slackening of population growth (to a rate of less than 1 percent per annum) and the rapid growth of output in recent years. Shortages of certain types of skilled labor and of young labor have already become evident; they are likely to become more pronounced and spread to other types of labor if the present population trends continue.

In addition to the reduction in efficiency wage costs, another favorable factor on the cost side has been the reduction in the prices of imports. In particular, import prices of textile raw materials in 1961 were 27 percent lower than in 1953, of fuels, 9 percent lower, and of minerals and metals, 2 percent lower.

We can turn now to the question of why the rapid economic growth did not lead to a demand pull on prices by exerting a strain on resources. It should be noted, first of all, that such pressures did indeed arise during periods of cyclical expansion. Thus, for example, during 1956, wholesale prices increased by 9 percent. Nor was the evidence of strain confined to the price picture alone. In 1956 and the first half of 1957, bottlenecks were encountered in three sectors of fundamental importance in the industrial process: steel, electric power, and transportation facilities. Order books lengthened, especially in the machinery industry. Imports increased sharply, the competitiveness of exports suffered, and in the first half of 1957 there was a sharp deterioration in the external payments position.

An interesting feature of the Japanese experience is that the price increase during postwar boom periods has tended to be offset during recessions. As just mentioned, wholesale prices increased 9 percent in 1956. They remained stable during January–April, 1958, the final months of the boom, but declined almost continuously in the following recessionary period; the total decline by October, 1958 was 8 percent. A similar downward flexibility of prices is also being witnessed in the most recent recessionary experience. In any event, the more important thing for the present purpose is that the rise in prices during cyclical upswings was moderate relative to the expansion secured.

As discussed above, the relatively ample availability of labor resources during the fifties meant that this important source of pressure did not exist. Pronounced tightness emerged in the money market during each boom period but the increase in interest rates was not large. This is chiefly because the monetary authorities pursued a policy of active ease as long into the boom as possible; that is to say, by their own liberal lending policies they kept credit conditions easier than could have otherwise obtained. Moreover, in general, credit restraint is exercised more by restricting the availability of credit than by raising its cost.

The impact of rapid output growth on prices of raw materials and machinery was mitigated by the official policy of permitting imports of these materials to come in as freely as possible. This meant, of course, that the emergence of strains on resources was reflected more in the balance of payments position than in the domestic price picture. Thus, each of the three booms in the 1950's, 1952–53, 1956–57, and 1960–61, culminated in rather serious external payments difficulties. Except on the first occasion, these difficulties arose despite substantial increases in exports; in all three cases they were the result of sharp increases in imports of raw materials and machinery. Indeed, it is perhaps fair to say that during the fifties the authorities awaited such a deterioration in the external payments position, rather than domestic signs of a strain on resources, to take determined financial measures to check booms. On the whole, these measures succeeded rather well in slowing down the economy. In comparison with an average growth rate of 8 percent in 1952–53, the growth in 1959 was less than half as much; in comparison with an average growth rate of about 9 percent in 1955–57, the growth in 1958 was only one third as much. The year 1962, again, is likely to witness a marked deceleration in the growth rate in comparison with 1959–61. Along with the slackening of the economy, the drain on foreign exchange reserves was arrested each time.

Over the period 1951–61 as a whole, foreign exchange reserves have indeed increased. This has been supported in part by a net inflow of foreign capital, especially short-term capital. However, Japan's basic trading position has also strengthened considerably over this period, as a result of the improvement in productivity, increased diversification of industrial output, and relatively stable domestic prices.

CONCLUSIONS

There are only three countries in Asia, Indonesia, China (Taiwan), and Korea (South), which have experienced high to moderate inflation during the last decade. Heavy military expenditures have largely contributed to inflation in these countries, and this should be noted in making a comparative analysis of the experience of inflation and growth in different regions. These countries have varied experiences in growth; while the growth rates of Indonesia and Korea have been low, the growth rate of China (Taiwan) has been quite high. This is largely due to the fact that, in spite of high military expenditures, China also put great emphasis on economic development. Also, the availability of technical skills in China (Taiwan) is relatively greater.

In the moderate inflation to stable group, with the exception of Japan and Thailand, the Asian countries are newly independent countries which before independence had a long experience of monetary stability, and their monetary systems have been closely tied to important Western currencies. Since their attainment of independence, economic growth has been the main ambition of these countries. They have pursued this objective with different degrees of success. The growth rates of the countries in the group have varied according to their preparedness, conservatism in financial policies, emphasis on social versus economic development, the pattern of investment, and other factors.

However, in most cases these development efforts have resulted in the emergence of inflationary pressures of varying degrees. Nevertheless, these countries have tried to keep to a minimum disturbances to the monetary stability which they have enjoyed for so long.

TABLE 4

SELECTED ASIAN COUNTRIES: PER CAPITA PRODUCT
IN U.S. DOLLARS

Country	1950	1961
Indonesia*...........................	115†	127‡
China (Taiwan)......................	106	156
Korea (South).......................	66§	74
Burma.............................	39	55
Thailand...........................	76†	93
Japan..............................	113	501
India..............................	48	69
Philippines.........................	153	194‡
Ceylon.............................	113	120‡
Federation of Malaya................	233‖	238‡

Sources: United Nations, *Yearbooks of National Accounts Statistics*,
and other national official sources.
  *At 1955 prices and exchange rate.
  †For 1951.
  ‡For 1960.
  §For 1953.
  ‖For 1956.

TABLE 5

SELECTED ASIAN COUNTRIES: INDICATORS OF DEVELOPMENT EFFORT IN RECENT YEARS

A: Gross fixed investment as percent of gross national product.
B: Government gross fixed investment as percent of total gross fixed investment.
C: Government gross fixed investment as percent of total government purchases of goods and services.
D: Government current revenues as percent of gross national product.

(Annual Average)*

	Indonesia	China (Taiwan)	Korea (South)	Burma	Thailand	Japan	India	Philippines	Ceylon	Federation of Malaya
A.	...	13	12	19	14	24	13†	5†	13	9
B.	...	18	27	48	34	34	29	29	54	27
C.	...	12	19	40	32	42	13	21	36	13
D.	14	20	10	19	12	17	10	8	22	18

Sources: United Nations, *Yearbooks of National Accounts Statistics*, and other national official sources.
*The periods to which the average relates in different countries are as follows: *Indonesia:* 1951–59; *China (Taiwan):* 1952–59 for series A–C, and fiscal years 1952–60/61 for series D; *Korea:* 1953–60; *Burma:* fiscal years 1950–51 to 1960–61 for A–C, and 1952–53 to 1960–61 for D; *Thailand:* 1953–59 for A and B, 1953–57 for C, and 1951–60 for D; *Japan:* fiscal years 1950–51 to 1961–62; *India:* fiscal years 1955–56 to 1960–61 for A and C, 1951–52 to 1960–61 for B, and 1950–51 to 1960–61 for D; *Philippines:* 1950–60; *Ceylon:* 1950–60 (data on government revenues is on a fiscal year basis); *Malaya:* 1955–59.
†Gross fixed investment as percent of national income.
‡Generally believed to be substantially underestimated; a more correct estimate is believed to be about 10 percent.

TABLE 6

SELECTED ASIAN COUNTRIES: TERMS OF TRADE, 1950–60*

(1953 = 100)†

		1950	1951	1952	1954	1955	1956	1957	1958	1959	1960	1961
Indonesia	(1)	...	161	113	96	110	103	102	96	105	98	87
	(2)	...	116	110	92	92	94	90	93	83	92	82
	(3)	...	139	103	104	120	110	113	97	126	107	106
China	(1)	...	...	112	104	110	104	116	99	90	93	88
(Taiwan)	(2)	...	...	111	109	111	107	111	107	100	100	98
	(3)	...	...	101	95	99	97	105	92	90	93	90
Korea	(1)	...	...	...	...	...	...	100	82	90	104	103
(South)	(2)	...	...	...	...	...	...	100	92	86	83	83
	(3)	...	...	...	...	...	...	100	89	105	126	124
Burma	(1)	67	73	91	77	62	62	60	62	57	56	59
	(2)	189	130	131	93	89	82	91	98	...	...	...
	(3)	36	56	70	83	70	76	66	63	...	...	...
Thailand	(1)	113	122	102	111	109	100	99	102	108	111	109
	(2)	141	149	97	105	106	106	109	105	104	105	106
	(3)	80	81	105	106	103	94	91	97	104	105	102
Japan	(1)	86	119	106	97	91	94	97	93	92	94	92
	(2)	98	127	115	97	98	102	110	92	87	88	88
	(3)	88	94	92	100	93	92	88	101	106	107	105
India	(1)	98	143	117	102	100	101	101	100	100	109	106
	(2)	90	110	112	94	93	94	103	97	90	95	95
	(3)	109	130	104	109	108	107	98	103	111	115	112
Philippines	(1)	97	104	82	89	81	83	84	87	94	93	85
	(2)	94	106	105	96	96	97	100	102	104	106	109
	(3)	103	98	78	93	84	86	84	85	90	88	78
Ceylon	(1)	105	127	98	111	116	109	104	102	107	107	97
	(2)	84	101	108	92	86	90	95	87	86	86	88
	(3)	125	126	91	121	135	121	109	117	124	124	110
Federation of	(1)	...	...	133	96	136	126	119	109	131	137	114
Malaya	(2)	...	...	103	90	82	84	88	84	82	84	84
	(3)	...	...	129	107	166	150	135	130	160	163	136
Vietnam	(1)	...	...	...	...	99	92	97	84	85	81	69
(South)	(2)	...	...	...	...	95	90	92	92	86	89	88
	(3)	...	...	...	...	104	102	105	91	99	91	78

Sources: International Monetary Fund, *International Financial Statistics*, and other national official sources.

*(1) Unit Value of Exports. (2) Unit Value of Imports. (3) Terms of Trade = (1) Unit Value of Exports divided by (2) Unit Value of Imports.

†Except for Korea, where the base year is 1957

SELECTED ASIAN COUNTRIES: BALANCE OF PAYMENTS, 1951–61

(In Millions of U.S. Dollars)

A: Exports; B: Imports; C: Net Services
D: U.S. Government Expenditures
E: Private Capital and Donations
F: Official Loans and Grants
G: Change in Reserves and Related Items*

Country		1951	1952	1953	1954	1955	1956	1957	1958	1959	1960	1961
Indonesia	A.	1,296	920	669	774	881	843	848	647	817	881	766
	B.†	−923	−1,009	−634	−583	−554	−744	−652	−487	−582	−727	−746
	C.	−243	−168	−155	−220	−230	−264	−281	−225	−210	−216	−231
	E.	−8	−19	14	−1	2	3	3	5	1	20	−11
	F.	…	…	2	2	−10	30	49	66	139	130	87
	G.	…	…	−117	−33	+89	−126	−29	−3	+142	+96	−186
China (Taiwan)	A.	93	120	129	96	127	124	148	156	157	164	196
	B.	−143	−208	−193	−205	−185	−222	−245	−274	−264	−287	−330
	C.	−5	−11	−17	−22	−13	−8	2	−5	−15	−8	3
	E.	7	6	12	11	3	8	9	52	37	52	27
	F.	62	94	85	88	90	96	96	85	77	100	116
	G.	+12	+2	−17	−33	+28	+1	+8	+19	−7	+19	+8
Korea (South)	A.	…	…	40	25	18	25	20	17	20	33	41
	B.	…	…	−345	−252	−329	−386	−442	−377	−302	−341	−310
	C.	…	…	26	32	44	28	35	48	54	46	71
	E.	…	…	—	12	17	20	26	33	17	23	23
	F.	…	…	194	154	241	314	380	316	215	243	225
	G.	…	…	−86	−29	−9	+3	+20	+39	+5	+2	+47

(Continued on next page)

TABLE 7—Continued

Country		1951	1952	1953	1954	1955	1956	1957	1958	1959	1960	1961
Burma (c.i.f.)	A.	210	249	251	235	234	230	242	196	235	237	223
	B.	−137	−170	−203	−231	−196	−196	−327	−175	−209	−236	−207
	C.	−12	−13	−28	−42	−34	−31	−28	−32	−36	−25	−24
	E.	−13	−15	−10	−8	−1	−3	−5	−2	1	−2	−5
	F.	7	1	10	−41	−22	18	82	43	37	19	5
	G.	+37	+47	+16	−81	−19	+13	−40	+32	+25	−6	−17
Thailand (c.i.f.)	A.	367	329	323	283	335	361	390	307	357	407	473
	B.	−310	−333	−356	−329	−333	−364	−410	−386	−424	−450	−480
	C.	−5	−13	−21	−17	−19	−14	−17	1	−1	8	18
	E.	3	0	−4	−7	−6	−3	3	10	5	3	22
	F.	2	10	16	10	29	36	47	28	59	51	37
	G.	+84	−22	−41	−19	+26	+14	+8	−20	6	+45	+79
Japan	A.	…	…	1,258	1,611	2,008	2,483	2,847	2,876	3,413	3,982	4,150
	B.	…	…	−2,050	−2,040	−2,061	−2,608	−3,242	−2,500	−3,047	−3,711	−4,741
	C.	…	…	−236	−254	−252	−433	−640	−314	−357	−517	−774
	D.	…	…	802	603	510	498	449	404	381	413	389
	E.	…	…	3	115	204	31	98	73	−17	−44	37
	F.	…	…	−12	47	46	16	−63	−193	3	−47	−65
	G.	…	…	−256	+134	+354	+2	−547	+414	+405	+110	−950
India	A.	1,574	1,363	1,126	1,150	1,370	1,323	1,463	1,185	1,319	1,317	1,388
	B.	−1,852	−1,620	−1,241	−1,343	−1,566	−2,124	−2,625	−2,219	−1,969	−2,221	−2,083
	C.	85	140	136	141	98	125	132	101	120	77	−40
	E.	23	30	19	29	86	139	121	69	41	28	60
	F.	87	136	35	44	69	131	37	643	647	753	636
	G.	+146	+37	−64	−17	−101	+404	+630	+266	−90	+68	+41

Philippines	A.	428	346	398	401	401	453	431	493	529	560	500
	B.	−489	−421	−452	−479	−548	−506	−613	−559	−523	−604	−611
	C.	−95	−81	−93	−108	−125	−112	−135	−101	−106	−122	−88†
	D.	97	124	139	122	126	113	108	93	89	82	87
	E.	13	37	54	48	68	61	62	59	78	99	−7‡
	F.	8	15	17	6	30	26	64	26	67	52	6
	G.	−56	−1	−9	−26	−63	+11	−125	−9	+78	+27	−139
Ceylon (c.i.f.)	A.	375	296	314	362	398	372	350	341	372	377	358
	B.	−325	−358	−343	−291	−311	−332	−370	−360	−411	−420	−376
	C.	−15	−9	−5	−2	−6	−12	−13	−8	−3	−8	−5
	E.	−25	−17	−20	−24	−28	−22	−22	−17	−11	−8	−5
	F.	—	—	3	26	6	8	17	16	29	15	9
	G.	+18	−72	−49	+64	+60	+10	−45	−27	−42	−41	−2
Federation of Malaya	A.	...	...	...	...	...	...	...	...	...	953	853
	B.	...	...	...	...	...	...	...	...	...	−658	−689
	C.	...	...	...	...	...	...	...	...	...	−105	−95
	E.	...	...	...	...	...	...	...	...	...	−76	−64
	F.	...	...	...	...	...	...	...	...	...	14	14
	G.	...	...	...	...	...	...	...	...	...	+113	+18
Vietnam (South)	A.	...	...	...	...	59	54	89	57	62	89	66
	B.	...	...	...	...	−282	−345	−245	−182	−217	−236	−275
	C.	...	...	...	...	−52	−42	−30	−23	−14	−8	−12
	D.	...	...	...	...	119	10	3	—	—	—	—
	E.	...	...	...	...	−5	20	24	11	16	16	10
	F.	...	...	...	...	267	308	171	176	178	181	163
	G.	...	...	...	...	+94	+12	+15	+34	+25	+40	−48

Source: International Monetary Fund, *Balance of Payments Yearbook*.
*The sum of items A to F is not fully reflected in item G because of errors and omissions.
†Imports, c.i.f. for 1951–54, c. and f. for 1955 and f.o.b. for 1956–60.
‡Does not include reinvested earnings.

d. COMMENT
Michael Kaser

No observations on Professor Montias' paper would be just that did not draw attention to the novelty of his statistics and to the historical exposé which his figures permit. For economists in the eastern European field, sheer data collection is still an important preliminary to analysis, and there are many who will be grateful to Professor Montias solely for this work.

The interest to Latin America of the eastern European experience which Montias describes may be put very briefly: when eastern European governments have activated economic growth without overt inflation they have drawn upon the potentialities of an administrative execution of policies in general and of central planning in particular. When their growth has nevertheless been accompanied by a significant degree of inflation, the causes must be sought in straightforward errors of planning. This comment can thus readily be interpreted within the current Latin-American debate. First, the administrative measures applied outside the strictly economic mechanism may be seen in the framework of structural change. Secondly, given the conceptual priority in eastern European planning of the physical production-distribution plan over the financial program, and—in recent years—the aim of price stability written into the latter, monetary techniques largely account for success or failure in integrating the flows of physical assets with those of funds.

ADMINISTRATIVE POLICIES OF STRUCTURAL CHANGE

As Montias points out, the terms of trade between agricultural and industrial products turned strongly against the farmer. This was not the result of free market forces, but of the government's price policy with respect to agricultural procurements. This is, of course, contrary to trends in Latin American policies, as papers to the conference show. Escobar takes as his basic assumption that a secularly increasing trend prevails in prices of agricultural products; Tun Thin observes it as Indian experience. The eastern European government's ability to procure at prices increasingly unfavorable to the peasant is a function of its power to influence the producer by noneconomic instruments. The precollectivization period—the early fifties in eastern Europe—was that of the severest administrative rule of the cult of the personality, with Stalinist regimes everywhere installed. The by-and-large general renunciation of the coercive methods then practiced has coincided with the completion, save in Poland, of farm collectivization. The state, having political control over the collectives, can insure a supply of farm produce to the rest of the economy at prices which it itself determines and it can in large measure ignore price movements in the private sector. It is significant that it is only in Poland, the exception to collectivizations, that a real danger of inflation exists today. In the Soviet Union the same decisions on collectivization and compulsory procurement were taken almost three decades ago: the Bazarov-Bukharin-Preobrazhensky-Stalin controversy of the late twenties was in effect on whether the peasants should pay for industrialization. Erlich's recent book[1] on the debate is a timely reminder that coercion of the farmers was a tool to secure industrial growth without inflation, and if price stability was not attained in the first half of the thirties—as Holzman[2] and Montias show—the programming techniques were inadequate.

The fact that coercion of the farmers—put into a political context as "the liquidation of the kulaks as a class"—was an anti-inflationary device in Soviet-type economies does not mean that eastern European experience is irrelevant to governments unwilling or unable to exert such pressure. It serves rather to emphasize that the turning of the terms of trade against the farmer in the interests of industrialization without inflation requires the operation of some potent noneconomic influence. In Latin-American conditions they would no doubt range from the purely moral (self-abnegation after a peasant-supported revolution) to the purely economic (fostering of rural activities which divert purchasing power away from industrial products). As Dell's paper and the contribution in debate of Chamberlain and Perloff have brought out, the problem of wage-push inflation is similarly capable of administrative solution if some degree of legal constraint is admitted. It is thus relevant that the opposite has been true in eastern Europe: Montias shows that control over wages has in practice been less complete than over farm incomes.

[1] A. Erlich, *The Soviet Industrialization Debate 1924–1928*, Cambridge (Mass.) 1960.

[2] F. Holzman, "Soviet Inflationary Pressures, 1928–1958: Causes and Cures," *Quarterly Journal of Economics*, May 1960, pp. 167–88.

MONETARY INSTRUMENTS

Shortcomings in eastern European planning embrace, in a perhaps wider sense than Montias indicates, both bad planning and the bad execution of good plans, and the better execution of poor plans. Initial inexperience with new plan and control mechanisms and chronically inadequate monetary statistics may be termed the exogenous errors in planning. Montias puts most of his emphasis on the first, but "the absence of comprehensive financial and monetary data" testifies not only to concealment from the outsider but also to insufficient knowledge. One could well attribute the Soviet and Bulgarian monetary reforms of 1961 (a free exchange of currency on the French or more recent Bolivian pattern, but comprising immediate demonetization of notes) largely to their governments' desire to know the extent and distribution of money hoards. Both countries accompanied the reforms with campaigns of criminal prosecution of "speculation" leading even to capital punishment. Montias puts the avoidance of such speculation—any unplanned redistribution of incomes or assets—as a major objective of Soviet-type monetary policy. Failure to achieve this aim may be seen as an endogenous error in planning.

As just suggested, the plan itself may be "wrong"—inconsistent with its own objectives, with its own variables, or with the conditions over which it has no control—or it may be correct in all such respects but wrongly implemented. Montias devotes a substantial part of his paper to the formulae articulating the plans for production flows and transaction flows. A reading of this alone shows the dangers to consistency arising from the multitude of estimates required to determine the plan variables. Needless to say, the detail of the concordance is vastly greater in a centrally planned economy than that for macroeconomic planning and analysis, considered by Messy and Pedersen and their discussants. As a corollary to the complexity of integrating production and transaction plans, Montias draws attention to the use of a budget surplus "capable of offsetting such failures in the course of the plan-year". Buffers to absorb plan errors are written in explicitly or tacitly in other forms (enterprise and centrally held inventories are the most important), but hitherto they have been needed more to fill the gaps in the articulation of production and financial plans rather than to correct forecasts of initially consistent variables. In the entire history of Soviet-type planning, only one program has been drafted *ab initio* from a macroeconomic model: Kalecki's six-year Plan for Poland, now in operation, albeit considerably amended. The three break-downs of national income specified as in use by Montias are drawn up, but as orientational guides rather than as planning models. For annual, as for long-term, plans the key decisions have been and still are taken on physical production targets, including investment allocations and completions. As Montias points out, only eastern Germany constructs a balance for all incomes of the private sector and Varga—of Budapest University and the chief exponent of monetary theory in eastern Europe—elevates this omission to a rule. The private sector, he contends, may be ignored, since it cannot disturb state financial planning; its price movements can be offset by adjustments in turnover tax (or subsidies, which he describes as a negative turnover tax) upon state-supplied goods,[3] and one could go further and argue, with Zielinski[4] that failure to use prices as demand signals (reliance is placed on retail stock change) and consequently to adopt—by taxation—prices to the demand pattern, falsifies consumer information on cost relatives and precludes establishment of an optimal plan.

But production and redistribution in the private sector is only part of the incomplete articulation. The state sector, too, is full of gaps. However many material balances are established—and Levine[5] reports up to 1,000 as having been used in the U.S.S.R.—their aggregation into values does not cover all input and output flows. Zauberman[6] has recently described the Soviet problem in this respect and John, of the School of Economics of East Berlin,[7] points out that even production flows cannot be identified, for data are defined by administrative groupings; supply flows are from enterprise to enterprise, not product to product; delivery indivisibilities reduce unit input costs under conditions of joint supply, and so on. The relevance of these problems is evident from the correspondence

---

[3]S. Varga, "Die Rolle des Geldes während des Übergangs zum Kommunismus" (The functions of money during the transition to socialism), *Osteuropa*, No. 10, 1961, pp. 723–37.

[4]J. Zielinski, "An Attempt to Construct a Realistic Theory of Socialist Economy," *Ost-Ökonomi*, July, 1962, pp. 87–104.

[5]H. Levine, "The Centralized Planning of Supply in Soviet Industry", *Comparisons of the United States and Soviet Economies*, Washington, D.C., 1959, Part I, pp. 151–76. See also Levine, H. "Recent Developments in Soviet Planning," *Dimensions of Soviet Economic Power*, Washington, D.C., 1962, pp. 47–66.

[6]A. Zauberman, "The Present State of Soviet Planiometrics," *Soviet Studies*, July, 1962, pp. 62–74.

[7]F. John, "Grundfragen der zentralen Bilenzierung der Finanzbeziehungen im Rahmen der Perspektivplanung" (Basic problems of the central balancing of financial transactions in the framework of the long-term plan), *Wissenschaftliche Zeitschrift der Hochschule für Ökonomie*, Berlin, No. 3, 1962, pp. 197–208.

of the Soviet-type system of balances and those adaptations of SNA proposed for Africa by ECA.

The difficulties of fitting costs to physical input aggregations are present at all stages of planning: for the base-year matrix (which is established in the course of that year), for the annual plan when scope for offsetting tolerances in cost projections is relatively small, and for the five-year plan, when technical progress involves many unknowns.

The extraordinary complexity of fitting together production balances and their flow of funds counterparts has led to the now well-known eastern European experiments with input-output tables. None of the initial tables was fine enough to be used for cost planning, but the 83 x 83 Soviet table (described by Treml[8] and Serck-Hanssen[9] was inverted to verify the consistency of the 1962 annual plan and the 40 x 40 Hungarian matrix was used for the 1965 five-year plan.

In theory, this new orientation in planning should make for a better fit of production and financial plans, but Soviet planners have some way to go before even attempting such an integration. The Soviet work program in this field to 1965 contains no mention of flow of funds, of any coordination with financial plans (some study on prices apart), or, among the score of institutions affected, of the collaboration of the Research Institute of Finance. Poland—as Montias points out—has experimented with a flow of fund matrix but only Czarkowski[10] and John[11] seem to have envisaged the integration problem in detail.

But even if the integration with flow of funds projection is achieved, it will come at a time when decentralization begins to introduce occasions for divergence in fulfillment from a consistent plan. This was a problem under the five-year plans, when the central authorities decided on changes of plan priorities[12]. As they usually downgraded consumer goods targets, only Hungary escaped—by massive credit imports from the U.S.S.R.—a second round of currency confiscations in eastern Europe, and the Soviet Union evaded

[8]V. Treml, "The Soviet 1959 Inter-Indutry Study," Prepared for the Winter 1962 Pittsburgh Meeting of the Econometric Society.

[9]J. Serck-Hanssen, "Input-Output Tables in the USSR and eastern Europe," *Öst-Ökonomi*, July, 1962, pp. 65–72.

[10]J. Czarkowski, "Równowaga monetarna w naszej gospodarce narodowe" (Monetary equilibrium in our people's economy) *Wiadomości NBP*, May 1962, pp. 210–15; June, 1962, pp. 253–56.

[11]F. John, *op. cit.*

[12]M. Kaser, "The Nature of Soviet Planning," *Soviet Studies*, October, 1962, pp. 109–31.

a second refunding by a moratorium on the national debt. Central amendments to the better plans of today are still required because the technical coefficients are not "verified within the system, so that the best methods of producing given outputs cannot be chosen, but are taken from outside the system"[13] and prognosis by inquiry among technicians, an innovation in the preparation of the Seven-year Plan,[14] or among businessmen in, for example, the British So-cial-Accounting Matrix,[15] does not automatically take account of forecasts of cost relatives. Brown suggests that this might be over-come by confronting respondents with the shadow prices implied by their forecasts and making second round corrections. But at pres-ent the main source of divergence from plan lies in the devolution of decisions: the now famous proposal of Liberman, of the Kharkov Institute of Economics and Engineering[16] to restrict commands to the enterprise to a profit target—a system now being tested in Soviet plants[17]—would presumably produce input combinations and in-terenterprise money flows incapable of advance definition. This is just the problem the Soviet-type planners have so far been able to avoid: their semiprojections for the year during which the plan is drawn up could ignore financial flow divergencies from produc-tion flows; increasingly the statistical needs raised by Messy and Pedersen will be posed.

THE EASTERN EUROPEAN ATTITUDE TO INFLATION

With their governments committed to a policy of monetary sta-bility, economists and officials in eastern Europe tend to deny the possibility of inflation at home, attributing it solely to capitalism. The Bulgarian Minister of Finance, Lazarov, described the money savings accumulated before the 1952 reform—which as Montias shows almost quartered cash holdings—as "not resulting from in-flation."[18] Such double standards are general in their monetary

---

[13]J. Zielinski, *op. cit.*

[14]M. Kaser, "Changes in Planning Methods during the Preparation of the Soviet Seven-year Plan," *Soviet Studies*, April 1959, pp. 321–38.

[15]R. Stone and A. Brown, *A Computable Model of Economic Growth,* Cam-bridge (Eng.) 1962.

[16]E. Liberman, "Planirovanie proizvodstva i normativy dlitelnogo deistviya" (The planning of production norms for continuous operation), *Voprosy ekono-miki,* No. 8, 1962, pp. 104–12. See Footnote 6 for reference to an English sum-mary.

[17]"V Gosplane SSSR" (In the State Planning Commission of the USSR), *Planovoe khozyaistvo,* No. 10, 1962, p. 95.

[18]K. Lazarov, "Parichnata reforma" (The monetary reform), *Finansy i kredit* No. 7–8, 1952, pp. 10–24.

theory: Varga has pointed out that Aftalion's income theory of money is perfectly consistent with the conditions of socialism but is nevertheless repudiated by eastern European Marxists,[19] and as Seers pointed out, the Soviet-type economies still teach the quantity theory. In two countries, however, the problem of inflation has been squarely faced. Montias refers to the Hungarian discussion, but there was more acute controversy in Polish provincial journals. The debate began in March, 1957 in a short-lived Cracow periodical *Myśl Gospodaroza:* the banners of the initial tourney were more startling than the jousts themselves. Under titles of "The Struggle Against the Danger of Inflation," (Oyrźanowski[20]) "The Inflationary Policy of the State Budget (Siemiętkowski[21])," "On the Correct Policy for Money Issue" (Czarkowski[22]) and "On the Value of the Zloty" (Krźanowski[23]) the merits were argued of the quantity and income theories for money under socialism, culminating in sharp attacks on Oyrźanowski's original contentions (Sulmicki[24], Mlynarsky[25] and a rejoinder by Oyrźanowski[26]), and, perhaps more significantly, an implicit repudiation of the "double standard" in Fajans' "The Struggle against Inflation in Capitalist Countries"[27]); the editors annotated the latter as a "purely technical," that is, non-political, study. At this, however, the organ of the Finance Ministry, *Finanse,* intervened with a condemnation of *Myśl Gospodarcza* in general and of the inflation debate in particular (Fedorowicz[28], later reiterated more forcibly[29]); the debate was formally wound up

---

[19]S. Varga, *op. cit.* See also Varga, S. "Das Geld im Sozialismus" (Money under socialism) *Weltwirtschaftliches Archiv.* Vol. 78 (1957 I), pp. 223–87.

[20]B. Oyrźanowski, "Walka z Niebezpieczeństwem inflacji" (The struggle against the danger of inflation), *Myśl Gospodarcza,* No. 1, 1957, pp. 7–26.

[21]L. Siemiztkowski, "Inflacyjna polityka budzetu państwa" (The inflationary policy of the State Budget), *Myśl Gospodarcza,* No. 1, 1957, pp. 27–34.

[22]J. Czarkowski, "O prawidlowa politike emisyjna" (On the correct policy for money issue), *Myśl Gospodarcza,* No. 3, 1957, pp. 3–19.

[23]W. Krźyzanowski, "O wartości zlotego" (On the value of the zloty), *Myśl Gospodarcza,* No. 4, 1957, pp. 59–70.

[24]P. Sulmicki, "Pojecie inflacji w gospodarcze socjalistycznej" (The idea of inflation in a socialist economy), *Myśl Gospodarcza,* No. 5, 1957, pp. 127–42.

[25]F. Mlynarski, "Walka z niebezpieczeństwem inflacji" (The struggle against the danger of inflation), *Myśl Gospodarcza,* No. 5, 1957, pp. 143–54.

[26]B. Oyrźanowski, "Jeszcze raz o teorii pieniadza i inflaciji" (Once again on the theory of money and inflation), *Myśl Gospodarcza,* No. 5, 1957, pp. 155–73.

[27]W. Fajans, "Walka z inflacje w krajach kapitalistycznych" (The struggle against inflation in capitalist countries), *Myśl Gospodarcza,* No. 4, 1957, pp. 71–87.

[28]Z. Fedorowicz, "Nad pierwszm numerem 'Mysli Gospodarczej' " (On the first issue of "Economic Thought"), *Finanse,* No. 7, 1957, pp. 53–60.

[29]Z. Fedorowicz, "Diskusja o inflaciji" (The discussion on inflation), *Finanse,* No. 5, 1958, pp. 51–59.

by the two main protagonists (Sulmicki[30] and Oyrżanowski[31] and soon afterward the journal itself suffered the same fate. Save for a brief comment by Krzak and Toeplitz in 1958[32] the debate was quiescent until a successor journal appeared in Cracow in 1960— *Folia oeconomica cracoviensia.* It seems to have run to only three issues. Oryżanowski's opening shots[33] included a novel differentiation of inflation in a socialist economy (cash inflation for consumers' goods, bank-money inflation for producers' goods), but Czarkowski[34] and Mlynarski[35] little more than reiterated their 1957 views in the second and third issues. Another local periodical helped Czarkowski to keep the debate going[36]. He allied himself with Varga's theories[37] in a Poznan journal but he did not have a metropolitan platform until the National Bank published his fundamental paper of mid-1962[38]. This paper is important for its analysis of the stages of inflation . . . . "primary" when stocks have no more than fallen below their normal level, "full" when "decisions to purchase exceed the values available for the disposition of the population." For the delectation of monetarists, he affirms that "inflation, as much as deflation, is an economic evil, both unwelcome and unhealthy."

---

[30]P. Sulmicki, "Przydatnośe praktyczna formul teoretycznych" (The practical use of theoretical formulae), *Myśl Gospodarcza,* No. 10, 1957, pp. 101–11.

[31]B. Oyrżanowski, "Po raz ostatni o teorii ilosciowej" (Closing the discussion on the quantity theory), *Myśl Gospodarcza,* No. 10, 1957, pp. 113–23.

[32]M. Krzak, and J. Toeplitz, "S Varga o teorii pieniadza w socjalizmie" (S. Varga on the theory of money under socialism), *Zycie Gospodarcze,* No. 11, 1958, p. 4.

[33]B. Oyrżanowski, "Zagadnienie inflacji w socjalizmie" (Problems of inflation under socialism), *Folia oeconomica cracoviensia,* Vol. I, No. 1, 1960, pp. 73–83, and in D. Hague (ed) *International Economic Association, Conference Elsinore, 1959, Inflation,* London 1962.

[34]J. Czarkowski, "Formula dochodowa a równanie wymiany" (The income formula and the exchange equation), *Folia oeconomica cracoviensia,* Vol. I, No. 2, 1961, pp. 29–53

[35]F. Mylnarski, "Paradoksalne dzielanie ilości pieniadza" (The paradoxical operation of the quantity of money), *Folia oeconomica cracoviensia,* Vol. I, No. 3, 1961, pp. 31–67.

[36]J. Czarkowski, "Teoretyczne aspekty równowagi monetarnej" (The theoretical aspects of monetary equilibrium), *Polskie towarzystwo ekonomiczne, Oddizial w Poznaniu-Rocznik 1958–59,* Vol. VI, 1960, pp. 29–45.

[37]S. Varga, *op. cit.*

[38]J. Czarkowski, "Równowaga monetarna w naszej gospodarce narodowe", *op. cit.*

e. COMMENT

Gustav Ranis

The title of this particular session, "Comparative Analysis of the Experience of Other Countries" led me to believe, perhaps naïvely, that, to the extent possible, the experience of other parts of the world was to be viewed here as a laboratory from which at least useful insights, hopefully even a framework for analysis, with respect to growth and development in Latin America might be distilled. I was therefore somewhat surprised to find that not one of the three authors has directed himself to this problem—at least not in the papers before us. Tun Thin essentially does little beyond telling us what has been happening in various Asian countries; nor does the Sidney Dell replay of essentially familiar arguments about cost-push *vs.* demand-pull inflation in the advanced economy, with hardly a reference to the less-developed world, advance the cause; finally, Montias' analysis of the Soviet bloc's experience with inflation and development fails to attempt to elicit the distinctive features of socialist economies or to show how this analysis might or might not have been made relevant to noncentrally planned economies.

I shall spend most of my time commenting on the Montias paper, partly because his is the only paper I've had for more than a day (and thus is virtue rewarded), but mainly because his paper seems to me the only one before us which makes an attempt to conceptualize usefully the problems of inflation and development and relate them to an economy's plan and real resource magnitudes, before "jumping" either into economic history or policy prescription.

I found Mr. Montias' paper most useful in that it gives us a chance to see how people think about inflation and economic development in the bloc countries of eastern Europe. In what I would call his analytical section, he very competently utilizes a four-sector financial balance device to explore the problem of a possible disequilibrium in the system between financial and real balances and to trace the adjustment mechanism in the context of the controlled bloc economy. As he puts it, the primary (I would say the only) task of financial planning in the bloc countries (as elsewhere) is to accomplish the economy's growth objectives. And his analysis of the monetary instrumentation available to insure consumer goods price stability leads him, not unexpectedly, to government budgetary surpluses (achievable presumably by changes in the turnover tax) as the main lever. He emphasizes the importance of three major sources of disturbance to monetary equilibrium: changes in the planned investment ratio (which for some reason he calls "structural change"), changes in labor productivity, and changes in the productivity of intermediate inputs (both of which he calls "deviations from plan"). Unfortunately, in spite of a very promising framework, he fails to take the necessary steps which might have permitted him to generalize his analysis with appropriate modifications. It is true that he mentions some of the important parameters in the disequilibrium and adjustment process, but only by way of presenting a series of interesting problems and not as part of a framework which could lend itself to answering other equally interesting, problems. Too much of what he has to say, therefore, strikes one as correct but remaining on the intuitive level and missing the full chance 'for extension and transferability which it deserves.

To be quite specific, if monetary stability is to be maintained—or, to satisfy the "inflationary five percenters" here, a particular rate of increase in prices is not to be exceeded—simple resort to national income accounting concepts at Montias' level of aggregation will yield the following explicit relationship between the real wage w and three parameters: b, the fraction of income going to consumption, that is, the ambitiousness of the plan; a, "the intermediate inputs to total output ratio"; and c, the productivity of labor:

$$W = b (1 - a)c$$

As Montias points out, this relationship states that, given a monetary disequilibrium through an increase in the money wage, the aim of monetary stability can be maintained only if labor productivity *goes up* or the portion of national income consumed *declines*. The fact that the relationship between wages and prices must run through labor productivity and the investment ratio is thus nailed down precisely.

But much more than such selected conclusions could be squeezed from Montias' model: for example, the real wage is always directly proportioned to the "nonambitiousness" of the plan and, in fact, we know the precise factor of proportionality. If the plan is to be more ambitious—as Mr. Montias stipulates—and a rise in consumer goods prices is to be prevented, either the money wage must fall, or labor productivity must increase, or the intermediate input—final output ratio must fall. Both of the latter may be relatively "costless" and merely involve technological change which, incidentally, is not anywhere referred to. Similarly, if the productivity of intermediate input increases is less than expected during a plan period and this is not offset by an increase in labor productivity, or an increase in the import surplus, or a change in the money wage, a decline in consumption must occur. The final consequence will be either a decline in the real wage, as consumer goods prices increase, or rationing (a form of induced savings), or a drawing down of inventories, thus violating the intended investment ratio.

The second part (and bulk) of Mr. Montias' paper recounts the experience of several East European countries with respect to growth, disequilibrium, and the restoration of equilibrium. For me at least, this survey was both highly interesting and educational. My only further comment would be that Mr. Montias' purpose would have been better served by concentrating on one or two countries in depth and by linking the historical section more precisely (or less casually) with the preceding analytical section. This, I think, more than anything else, leads to a certain lack of cohesiveness in the presentation and fuzziness in the conclusion. For example, Mr. Montias compares the experiences of Hungary and Poland for particular periods. In the Hungary of 1959, the initial disturbance is a shortfall in the proportion of total consumer goods delivered to markets, and inventories bear the brunt of the adjustment. In the Poland of 1956, on the other hand, the initial disturbance—one which we all remember—was excessive wage disbursals, and the adjustment effected through changes in monetary circulation. In one place the Polish experience is analyzed by appealing to differential savings propensities between farmers and the urban population. The point seems to be that where there is a disequilibrium such as is caused by excessive money wage disbursals, a transfer of income from low savings urban to high savings rural groups takes place, thus minimizing the need for inventories to decline. This means that people begin to put on rucksack and buy directly from the farms. But this picture of the farmer serving as a passive shock absorber is peculiarly unconvincing. Why, for example, should he indefinitely continue to accumulate idle balances? Sooner or later he is bound to work less, refuse to sell and/or induce black market operations in industrial goods.

From the point of view of the basic purposes of this conference, it is too bad that no reference is made to the special features of the controlled socialist economies so that important differences and similarities with respect to the "mixed" economies of Latin America could be brought into focus. Just to pick some random examples, the relationship between inventory adjustments and the phenomenon of virtually full capacity, that between centralization and decentralization and sectoral imbalance, and that between revenue flexibility and the need to suppress demand via direct controls are worthy of investigation.

Sidney Dell's paper is very interesting, but the question arises as to its relevance here. Most of it is given over to the pursuit of an old feud between the six experts of the OEEC and Dell's own World Economic Survey. These are controversies of considerable importance to the mature or developed economy but it is their adaptations to the less-developed world which might have been of interest here. For example, although the author makes no attempt in this direction, two of his remarks may be relevant. He asserts that inflation is bad only if "explosive," which he defines as a rate of price rise which is nondamped. This assertion is based on a theoretical anticipations argument by Lipsey which has never been empirically tested and thus, at least to my mind, constitutes somewhat premature policy medicine. Secondly, Dell makes a good deal of the uniqueness of sectoral imbalances and bottlenecks, first of food supplies in the immediate postwar years and, later, of capital goods. Where there are no autonomous cost-push factors, what is left for conventional aggregate demand analysis to explain is not clear; surely orthodox demand inflation—and this is undoubtedly what we had after the war—does not necessarily assume complete homogeneity in the system and the absence of relative price changes. Extreme structuralists (of which there are, of course, none present) might take notice.

Perhaps both Mr. Montias and Mr. Dell did not conceive of the relevancy to underdeveloped areas as part of their charge in writing these papers. But it is more difficult to excuse Mr. Tun Thin along these same lines. The experience of the countries he is concerned with, the underdeveloped countries of Asia, are in fact, not related in any systematic fashion to our conceptual problem, much less to the Latin-American context. Tun Thin proposes three catgories of Asian countries, those with high, high to moderate, and moderate inflation, and promises to analyze the causes of the differential experience among these categories of economies. But, essentially all we get is a series of thumbnail accounts for each country in the region which read more like excerpts from central bank annual reports. No real attempt is made to explain differences in performance via differences in such exogenous factors as the initial resource base,

foreign aid, harvest conditions, or via the favorable value of parameters in various key behavioristic relationships.

Tun Thin's observation on the availability of food in India as
measuring the investment potential of the economy, however, is an
interesting one. Might it not be well to divide countries into those
with surpluses of staples and those with shortages and those where
agricultural productivity changes are possible, in terms of their
relative tolerance for accepting deficit financing in the development
effort? Tun Thin, in spite of his recognition of Japan as a special
and largely irrelevant case, treats her postwar experience at great
length. Had he turned to nineteenth-century Japan, we might have
benefited considerably more. For example, we might have become
aware of the fact that considerable deficit financing at both federal
and local levels was accompanied by only very moderate price increases. And we might have noted that during the same period agricultural productivity increased at a reasonable rate. Neglect of the
agricultural sector, which seems a not uncommon phenomenon in
contemporary Latin America, leads to a deterioration of the industrial sector's terms of trade and may have irreversible consequences
in terms of a premature upturn of the real wage—long before the
surplus agricultural labor force, as augmented by population, has
been exhausted. Such "agricultural-neglect—push inflations" may
have less to do with the structure of external demand than with the
structure of the planners' vision of what constitutes progress.

Finally, I would briefly suggest more emphasis on some other considerations which have been neglected thus far. One is the possible
role of inflation in mopping up middle-class savings in case the fiscal
mechanism is inadequate. Another is that we ought really to talk
less about deficit financing or the absence of deficit financing, but
rather about the safe limits of deficit financing. And I would suggest
that we use here the basic Cambridge equation which Ray Goldsmith advertised, taking account of the decrease in income velocity
as (1) the economy becomes increasingly monetized, (2) the use of
checks rises and the income expenditure period lengthens, and (3)
the use of money hoards increases with increases in income. Studies
of Pakistan's experience in the 1950's, for example, show that the
ability to safely deficit finance was not fully exploited.

Finally, the worst danger of inflation, whether caused by agricultural neglect or money supply changes in excess of computed safe
limits, may not, in fact, be the various disincentives and erosions so
often cited. More damaging may be the consequent damming up of

inflationary pressures behind a mass of direct controls, the continuous imposition, evasion, and modification of which often becomes a major national pastime, constituting a negative sum game from the point of view of the economy's scarce entrepreneurial and administrative resources.

7. COMPARATIVE ANALYSIS OF LATIN-AMERICAN COUNTRIES: I.

a. INVISIBLE HANDS IN INFLATION AND GROWTH[1]

Joseph Grunwald

THE STRUCTURALIST ARGUMENT

The essence of the "structuralist" debate with the "monetarists" is whether monetary expansion has been a necessary by-product of structural changes in most of Latin America. Increases in the supply of money and price increases are obviously related, and while this relation is not perfect because of velocity and other changes, no structuralist will deny that it exists. The monetarist answer to the question of why the money supply has increased revolves around the notion of financial irresponsibility, while the answer of the structuralist is that the hands of the authorities are forced by exogenous circumstances. The structuralists then proceed to show what these exogenous factors are and why and how "invisible hands"[2] have led most governments in Latin America into policies that have

---

[1]There are three major works which form the background material for this paper. The first is "Inflation and Growth," a six-volume study prepared by ECLA (1961) (mimeographed), representing essentially a structural analysis of Latin-American inflation experiences. Also the article by Dudley Seers in the *Oxford Economic Papers* of June, 1962, "A Theory of Inflation and Growth in Underdeveloped Economies Based on the Experience of Latin America," which constitutes a rigorous statement of the structuralist position.

The second is a detailed study of Chile's recent economic development by the Instituto de Economía of the University of Chile, entitled "La Economía Chilena en el Periodo 1950–1961" (preliminary draft of October, 1962 [mimeographed]), and also a previous book by the Instituto de Economía, "El Desarrollo Economico de Chile 1940–1956" (Santiago: Editorial Universitia, 1957).

The third is a set of three articles which appeared in *Latin American Issues*, a volume edited by Albert O. Hirschman for the Twentieth Century Fund, (New York, 1961): "Two Views on Inflation in Latin America," by Roberto de Oliveira Campos, "An Alternative View of the 'Monetarist-Structuralist' Controversy," by David Felix, and "The 'Structuralist' School on Price Stability and Development: The Chilean Case," by Joseph Grunwald.

[2]In this paper the term "invisible hands" is used as nearly synonymous with "exogenous factors."

made inflation inevitable. In many cases these have been policies of inaction.

The fundamental exogenous force, according to the structuralists, is the collapse of export earnings in Latin America after 1929.[3] Exports have not yet recovered in many countries of the area. The decline is measured either in terms of per capita export earnings, or purchasing power of exports,[4] or exports as a ratio of gross domestic product. (See Tables 1–13.) In at least two countries, Argentina and Chile, the decrease was also in absolute terms (Tables 2 and 3). As can be seen from the tables, the decrease can be attributed almost exclusively to the great depression of the 1930's. Since then, there has been a steady increase in exports in most of the countries, although some have again experienced significant declines in their export purchasing power in recent years.

The "Inflation and Growth" study by ECLA shows very eloquently the structural problems introduced by this development. We shall not repeat this analysis here but indicate only its broad outline. The nucleus of the argument is that in those countries where a process of import substitution has been "forced" upon them by the collapse in the capacity to import, the supply structure was not sufficiently flexible to adopt itself readily to increases and changes in the composition of demand.[5] Changes in the demand structure are based upon a set of factors among which the most important are, first, a rapidly growing population, second, the process of urbanization, which is accelerated as industrialization proceeds, third, increased per capita consumption due to rising incomes, and, finally, changes in tastes.[6] One of the important reasons for changes

---

[3] See chap. v, section A of ECLA, *op. cit.*

[4] The concept of the "purchasing power of exports" takes into consideration the terms of trade by deflating current export values by an import price index.

[5] The industrialization was imposed not only by foreign exchange shortages but also by the difficulties in obtaining the needed supplies from abroad during the war and immediate postwar period, when foreign reserves accumulated.

The ECLA study divided Latin America into those countries which maintained a gold or gold exchange standard even after the Great Depression of the 1930's, and the countries that had to abandon these standards. The more relevant aspect of this distinction, however, is that the nongold standard countries generally were also those which industrialized most rapidly and therefore developed the greatest bottlenecks and structural problems. It is obvious that they were usually the South American countries (with the major exception of Venezuela) where a sufficiently large market permitted significant import substitution. In some of these countries industrialization already had progressed substantially before the depression.

[6] Changes in tastes are usually taken as a separate function of time (See D. Seers, *op. cit.*, p. 176), but they are implicit in the urbanization process and in the consumption effects of rising incomes, if income elasticities are calculated from time series rather than from cross-section data.

in demand composition is that the increase in per capita consumption of different commodities will vary widely because of different income elasticities.

These changes will put pressure on the structure of production, and the question as to where the bottlenecks will emerge depends on the relative elasticities of supply of various sectors. The population movement from the country to the city will have a particularly strong effect on agriculture and the production in that sector will have to grow very fast even though the income elasticity for food is low.[7] Demand for intermediate goods and certain manufactured goods also will increase sharply because of high-income elasticities, urbanization, and changes in tastes.

On the supply side, the structural problems arise out of certain rigidities. Among the important ones is the land-tenure system, characterized by a highly unequal distribution of land, inefficiency on the minifundia level, and a low land utilization on the latifundia level. Land ownership and cultivation are often several steps removed. A second important factor is a low labor mobility, principally because of the lack of education and training and also because of social barriers. Thus, acute labor shortages arise side by side with an abundant supply of unskilled (and much "unemployable") labor. While, for similar reasons, there may also exist a low mobility of entrepreneurs, enterprise is enormously complicated by a low perception of investment opportunities[8] and a very rudimentary capital market (which usually implies a monopolistic market). Monopolistic conditions in many sectors of the economy, particularly in manufacturing and wholesale distribution, add to the inelasticity of supply. In addition to all this, a deficient government revenue and rigid expenditure system limits the possibilities of needed investment in the country's economic infrastructure.[9]

---

[7]For instance, if the population increase is 3 percent and the proportion of urban population increases from 50 to 51 percent of the total population, then there are about 5 percent more people to be fed through market channels (the assumption is that the nonurban population consumes on the farm). Even if the income elasticity of food is only 0.6 and per capita incomes increase by 2 percent, it means that agricultural output has to grow by about 6.2 percent to keep up with demand—a rather large order, even for countries where agriculture is dynamic. (See also David Felix, *op. cit.*, p. 87).

[8]Another way of saying this is that entrepreneurs seem to have a sharply declining marginal utility of money and a very low, or negative, or sharply declining marginal utility of risk-taking.

[9]The problem of needed investments for modernization of equipment for publicly owned utilities is a different problem, since this question revolves around government price policies for transportation and other public or semipublic enterprises.

Of course, inelasticities of supply become a problem only because of limitations in the capacity to import. If there were no balance of payments difficulties and imports could be obtained in unlimited amounts, no problems would emerge from the existence of structural factors. As it is, foreign exchange shortages have been a fact of life of recent Latin-American economic history[10] and therefore it does matter whether domestic production can or cannot expand with some facility. The question that remains is whether and to what extent the demand changes and supply rigidities are policy-induced.

The Chilean Case

In regard to agriculture, it would be absurd to talk about a bottleneck for internal consumption in certain countries such as Argentina. Even though domestic output may not meet foreign demand requirements, export of food products can be varied and may be decreased in order to augment domestic supply.[11] In many of the industrializing countries, however, neither agricultural production increased fast enough nor were there edible exports which could be curtailed while, as is always assumed in the structural argument, import possibilities were limited due to the balance of payments problem. Chile is the classic case in point here.

The Chilean case in the first half of the 1950's seems to satisfy both the structuralist and monetary explanations. In the early part of the period there was a considerable increase in industrial production (27 percent in 1951 and 12 percent in 1952),[12] while agricultural output increased almost imperceptibly. From 1940 to 1952, agricultural production increased by about 1 percent per year, which is not much more than half of the population growth during that time. Since 1952 agricultural production has risen by nearly twice the rate of population increase.[13]

On the other hand, there was a sharp increase in government expenditures without adequate financing. This was reflected in the expansion of bank credit on government accounts (44 percent in

---

[10]The present paper always views these shortages as relative to the needs as they arise from a desired growth path.

[11]At the cost of foreign exchange earnings for vital capital goods imports, of course.

[12]Instituto de Economía, *op. cit.*, Table 196.

[13]Livestock production grew at a considerably lower rate and even showed a slight decrease in the first half of the 1950's, accompanied by an increase in prices of about 50 percent. (*Ibid.*, Tables 167–70 and 174.)

1950, 59 percent in 1951, 74 percent in 1952).[14] Private credit expansion, while much less, was substantial (20 percent, 29 percent, and 39 percent for 1950, 1951, and 1952, respectively) and wages and salaries rose significantly.[15] Yet prices increased at rates considerably less than public and private credit expansion (17 percent, 22 percent, 22 percent for 1950, 1951, and 1952, respectively). Thus the increase in the money supply was accompanied by greater liquidity of the system; there was a decrease of both income and circulation velocity. Monetary restriction played an important role in putting the brakes on inflation in 1950, and a dramatic increase in imports restrained price increases in 1951 and 1952 (imports increased by over 41 percent in 1951 and an additional 8 percent in 1952).[16]

In the following years there was a decline in total supply because of a fall in the capacity to import but, at the same time, government spending rose.[17] Monetary policy for the private sector tended to be passive, permitting the financing of rising wage and material costs. When prices reached an all-time high in 1955, a recovery of exports probably contributed to prevent an even stronger inflation.

Price increases in the second half of the 1950's are more difficult to explain on economic grounds. Of course, it is always possible to say that the expansion in the supply of money[18] permitted the price increases during that period but, in the absence of any serious demand pressures, this is not a very useful statement. There were no particular bottlenecks in the manufacturing sector. Thus it would be stretching the imagination to talk about supply inelasticities in the existing Chilean manufacturing industry from about 1956 to 1962. During this period excess capacity existed side by side with a substantial rate of inflation.[19]

---

[14]*Ibid.*, Table 253.

[15]*Ibid.*, pp. 979–80.

[16]*Ibid.*, p. 980. While exports did not increase by similar amounts, there was a greater proportion of foreign exchange returned to the country by the mining companies, principally in the form of taxes and wages.

[17]*Ibid.*, pp. 902, 909, 923.

[18]Between 1956 and 1960 the money supply increased at an average annual rate of 33.3 percent, while consumer prices increased at an annual rate of 34.1 percent (*ibid.*, p. 885).

[19]A sample survey of Chile's manufacturing industry undertaken in 1958 by Chile's Development Corporation ("Corporación de Fomento") in collaboration with the Chilean Association of Manufacturers ("Sociedad de Fomento Fabril") showed that industry operated at less than 50 percent of capacity while ·consumer prices increased by about 20 percent from 1957 to 1958 and by about 30 percent from 1958 to 1959. Even after allowing for a normal rate of operation of 80 percent of capacity, production could have still been increased by one half with-

The structuralists will point out that the decline in production levels in Chile after 1955 was due to monetary restrictions introduced as part of the stabilization program in 1956.[20] It is also indicated that the curtailment of cost of living wage adjustments in the same program cut purchasing power. Yet here was no structural problem in the strict sense because, if there was insufficient purchasing power and excess capacity, from where did the price pressure come? In that period even agriculture could not have been the bottleneck because the relative prices of agricultural products (not including livestock) had declined since 1952[21] and, as already indicated, production had increased significantly faster than population. Agricultural output per capita (including livestock production) was about the same in the late 1950's as it was in the early 1940's.[22]

Two sets of factors might assist in explaining the inflation during this period. One was connected with rising costs, the other with psychological forces. There was a significant increase in labor costs. First of all, wages and salaries continued to rise, although they were kept below the previous year's consumer price increases during most of this period. More important, however, was the burden of the employers' social security contributions. Another cost factor was the low efficiency of operations because, as already noted, production was far below capacity during this period. This problem was aggravated by the fact that the internal terms of trade went against domestic industry. Because the rate of exchange was kept at a constant level for imports (1.053 escudos per dollar) from January, 1959 to the end of 1962 in spite of rising internal costs, prices of imported

---

out adding to capacity. (CORFO, "Programa Nacional de Desarrollo Económico 1961–1970" [Santiago, Chile, 1961], pp. 38 ff.).

It could be argued that elasticity of supply was low, in spite of vast excess capacity, because of the shortage of skilled labor. Much of the increase in capacity derived from the installation of new machinery during the inflation boom of the mid-fifties and specialized manpower was needed to operate this equipment. But in the case of Chile this was not a seriously limiting factor for increasing the rate of utilization of existing capital stock.

[20]This program was based upon the recommendation of a United States consulting firm which was contracted for by the Chilean government. (See "El Programa de Estabilización de la Economía Chilena y El Trabajo de la Misión Klein & Saks," Santiago, Chile, May, 1958.)

[21]With 1940 = 100, the index of "real" agricultural prices excluding livestock (nominal agricultural prices deflated by the wholesale price index) declined from 137.4 in 1952 to 90.2 in 1959. Livestock prices, which had been lagging, increased sharply until 1954 but dropped dramatically after that. Thus the total agricultural price index in "real" terms (including livestock) declined from a high of 138.6 in 1954 to 97.5 in 1959. (See Instituto de Economía, *op. cit.*, Table 174.)

[22]*Ibid.*, p. 533.

goods became cheaper relative to domestic products. As the weakest firms were forced out of business, industry became less competitive and thus any increase in costs was immediately translated into higher prices.

Psychological factors, which perhaps could fit into the structuralist classification scheme as "propagation" factors, seem to have played a much more important role in the Chilean inflation picture since the mid-fifties than economists are usually willing to ascribe to them. In spite of a relatively vigorous stabilization program and reduced purchasing power and economic activity, it just was not possible for businessmen to adjust their price expectations radically downward after 1955, a year when inflation reached a rate of 84 percent. After a nearly continuous price acceleration during the first half of the decade, businessmen continued to advance their prices in anticipation of any cost increases until they were stopped by a concerted governmental campaign of moral suasion in the late 1950's. Thus, the inflation of the second half of the 1950's was neither "monetary" nor "structural" unless one wants to stretch the concept of "structural" to include cost push and psychological aspects.

By the end of the decade there was a sharp slowing down of price increases. Consumer prices rose by about 5 percent in 1960 and by less than 10 percent in 1961. What finally put the brakes on inflation? The explanation lies principally with the balance of payments and with noneconomic factors. Monetary restraints also played a role. But most important was an impressive expansion of imports in 1960. Because of the artificially maintained rate of exchange, imports became relatively cheap. The demand for foreign goods could be satisfied in part through an increase in the country's foreign indebtedness.

On the other hand, the high labor costs made labor-saving investment more attractive. Thus, labor-saving capital goods were imported and output per man-hour increased. Improvement in efficiency was also forced upon domestic production through the competition of foreign goods.

In addition to the halting of the rise in costs, inflation was dramatically curtailed by a forceful effort to exert moral pressures. At the end of the fifties, a committee for the defense of the consumer was organized, under semipublic auspices ("Comité para la Defensa del Consumidor"), which made it morally very difficult for businessmen to raise prices because they would be publicly denounced in the press, radio, and air-borne loudspeakers. To the surprise of many economists, this undertaking seems to have had a high decree of success. Only at the end of 1961, when it became obvious that devaluation was inevitable, did price increases commence to accelerate again, principally because of higher cost anticipations by the business community.

In a summary fashion it can be said that in the decade of the fifties inflation in Chile tended to be demand-induced until about 1956, when pressures on agricultural supply were particularly strong. Since then, with agricultural production expanding and imports easing but labor costs weighing more heavily in industrial production, inflation has tended to be more cost-induced[23] (although occasionally cost increases were imaginary, so that price rises were generated by expectations rather than actual increases in costs).

The Recovery of Imports in Latin America

As has already been pointed out, the key event in generating structural problems in Latin America, according to the structuralists, is the great depression of the thirties. The collapse in export earnings after 1929 was truly dramatic in some countries, such as Chile, and the lack or slowness of recovery to predepression levels is made out to be a significant point.[24] The crucial question from the point of view of the structural discussion is not what happened to exports and their purchasing power but rather what was the course of the volume of imports which could be used to supplement domestic supply and to correct structural bottlenecks. Here there are important differences between the rates of recuperation of export earnings and of imports since the depression.

In most of the countries considered in the ECLA study, imports recovered considerably faster than export earnings, even after taking account of the terms of trade effect. Table 1 shows that for all of Latin America the rate of growth of imports was about 50 per-

---

[23]From this point of view the "structuralist school" could be related more easily to the "demand pull" classification of inflation rather than the "cost push" type although, because of its policy implications and other obvious reasons, structuralist thinking has commonly been more associated with "cost push" inflation.

[24]It hardly need be pointed out that the reliability of the data diminishes the further back one goes, and some doubt might arise about the comparability of current foreign trade statistics with 1929 data. In the ECLA study (*op. cit.*), 1929 is used as the principal bench mark year for the predepression period and the question might be raised as to how representative this year is for some countries. However, some data are available for other years for a few of the countries. At any rate, the post—1929 figures leave no doubt about the severity of the depression.

cent higher than the growth of the purchasing power of exports since the beginning of World War II. Even during World War II, the quantum of imports[25] increased faster than the purchasing power of exports in Chile, Colombia, Mexico, and Peru among the nine countries listed in Tables 2 through 10.

In the following paragraphs, the foreign trade trends since the depths of the depression will be briefly indicated for nine Latin-American countries.

Argentina. Argentina had difficulty maintaining her imports during the war years—imports dropped during both World War II and the Korean War—but the growth of imports in the immediate postwar periods more than made up for the previous declines (Table 2). While the purchasing power of Argentina's exports decreased somewhat since 1940, physical imports increased by almost as much as gross domestic product. From Table 11 it can be seen that the importance of exports in GDP declined very sharply since the mid-forties. On the other hand, the import coefficient index almost doubled.[26]

Brazil. Brazil is one of the few countries where the current volume of both exports and imports exceed the predepression levels, (Table 3), although on a per capita basis foreign trade is significantly lower. There was a sharp recovery in the immediate postwar period which lasted until the early fifties, and imports increased at more than twice the rate of GDP. Imports sagged, however, in the mid-fifties, principally because of an acceleration of import substitution and a decline in coffee prices. At the end of the decade imports were far below the peak levels reached during the Korean War, although purchases of capital goods from abroad increased substantially. Yet, over the whole period, since the beginning of World War II, import quantum grew more than twice as fast as the purchasing power of exports, exceeding even the growth rate of GDP (Tables 3 and 11).

Chile. The picture was not too dissimilar in Chile. Since 1940, imports grew at a faster rate than the purchasing power of exports, surpassing somewhat the growth of population, (Table 4). Most of this increase is accounted for by capital goods imports which rose at an average annual rate of 6.6 percent per capita during this pe-

---

[25]The "quantum of imports," which is equivalent to the terms "volume of imports" or "physical imports," is the index of import value deflated by an index of the unit value of imports.

[26]The indices of import and export coefficients are represented by the quantum indices of exports and imports respectively divided by an index of gross domestic product in constant prices.

riod, reflecting the needs of the industrialization effort. The importance of exports relative to GDP not only did not recover predepression levels but in the fifties remained below the magnitudes reached during the depression in the mid-thirties. On the other hand, the import coefficient is about the same now as it was then (Table 11).

Colombia. Colombia is the only country of the nine under consideration whose import quantum since 1940 grew at a somewhat lower rate than the purchasing power of its exports (but nearly twice as much as its physical exports). Even so, the growth of real imports about equalled the growth of GDP in this period and they would have grown much faster had there not been a sharp drop in the second half of the 1950's, partly because of a decline in the purchasing power of exports due to the fall in coffee prices, and partly because of the acceleration of import substitution (Tables 5 and 12).

Ecuador. El Salvador. As one would expect, both exports and imports recovered rapidly in Ecuador and El Salvador, which were listed in the ECLA study among the countries without significant structural problems until recently (Tables 5 and 6). While in these countries also there was a significant decline in foreign trade after 1929, by the end of the 1940's the purchasing power of exports and import quantum exceeded predepression levels. In both countries the terms of trade operated in their favor and imports increased at a considerably faster rate than GDP. Also in both countries, the export coefficient has declined since the mid-forties while the index of imports as a percentage of GDP has risen sharply (Table 12). In the second half of the last decade, problems arose in Ecuador as the terms of trade suddenly worsened. A decline in import volume resulted and the country is now facing a period of readjustment.

Mexico. In Mexico, per capita imports at the end of the 1950's were considerably above predepression levels despite sharp drops in exports. Imports in physical terms increased much faster than exports or their purchasing power in the postdepression period (Table 8). Since the depression also, imports have grown more rapidly than GDP while the export coefficient has declined steadily ever since 1929 (Table 13).

Peru. Some early information is not available for Peru but export data indicate that the effect of the depression was comparatively mild in that country. In any case it is evident that although the purchasing power of exports did not keep up with the growth in GDP in the two decades between 1940 and 1960, the import quantum increased much more than GDP. Only toward the end of the fifties was there a slowing down of import growth, primarily because of a deterioration in the terms of trade, but even then imports rose faster than the purchasing power of exports (Tables 9 and 13).

Venezuela. While in Venezuela the quantum of exports did not decline significantly after 1928, there, too, export prices collapsed as in other Latin-American countries.[27] It is interesting to note that in Venezuela, which falls into the "nonbottleneck" category of ECLA, the volume of imports remained depressed until the end of World War II.[28] After the war, imports shot up for well-known reasons, reaching nearly five times the 1928 level in 1957. Imports declined somewhat after that in the face of a continued rise of exports, reflecting the initiation of a process of import substitution. From the early forties until the end of the fifties here also imports increased more rapidly than the purchasing power of exports and exceeded by far the country's rate of growth of GDP which was the highest in Latin America during the period (Table 10).

Summary. From about 1940 to 1960 in all of the nine countries considered here (and also singled out in the ECLA study), the import quantum grew more rapidly than population, and in eight of the nine countries the import volume grew faster than the purchasing power of exports.[29] In all countries except Chile the import quantum grew at least as fast as real GDP and in most countries it grew much faster in this period. The same picture appears for Latin America as a whole. In most of the countries, as well as for all of Latin America, imports (quantum) constituted a higher ratio to GDP (in constant prices) at the end of the period than at the beginning. The reverse is true of the export volume.

In examining the 20-year period in more detail, one finds that the growth of imports in the majority of the countries under consideration was more rapid in the decade of the forties than in the fifties. This was a reflection, in part, of a reversal of the postwar trend in the terms of trade which for many countries became adverse after the Korean War. On the other hand, in the industrializing countries, while imports expanded at a faster rate than GDP in the earlier dec-

---

[27]ECLA, *op. cit.*, Statistical Appendix Table X—V.

[28]ECLA, *op. cit.*, Statistical Appendix Table X–VII. The import quantum index fell to one fourth of the 1929 level in 1935 and, after a slight recovery, declined again during the war. In the case of Venezuela, however, it might be misleading to take 1929 as a bench mark, since imports were unusually high in that country in that year.

[29]Even in Colombia, the only exception, this was true up to the mid-fifties.

ade, in the fifties GDP grew faster than imports. This in turn was in part a reflection of an acceleration of import substitution in some of these countries. Nevertheless, even in the fifties, the volume of imports grew considerably faster than the purchasing power of exports in all countries except Chile.

Is There an Import Bottleneck?

It can be seen that in the postdepression recovery period the slowly growing purchasing power of exports failed to effectively curtail a faster import expansion. The countries found other means than exports to increase needed imports. Part of the gap was filled by foreign investment, increased United States aid, earnings from services (tourist trade in Mexico, for instance) and, in a few countries, by decreasing an export surplus.

There is no doubt, however, that most of the additional imports in excess of export growth were financed by increased foreign indebtedness. Table 14, which includes seven of the nine countries considered, (Ecuador and El Salvador are excluded),[30] shows that United States private investment was more than offset by profit and interest remittances since 1950, so that United States investors received from these countries nearly $4 billion more than the new money they put into them.[31] United States aid after interest and debt repayments could not offset this outflow in most years of this period. Of course, Table 14 should be read only within the current balance of payments situation and must not be interpreted as revealing any magnitudes of the contributions of United States private or public investors to the Latin-American economies. The table does show, however, that the bulk of the "excess growth" of imports over exports could not have been financed through the inflow of foreign investments and aid, but must have been obtained through foreign loans and credits from international agencies, private banks, and also on private account.[32]

From this vantage point it is difficult to conceive of the balance

---

[30]The seven countries account for almost 90 percent of Latin America's foreign trade and gross domestic product.

[31]Venezuela received the major part of United States direct investment in Latin America during that period, over $700 million for the purchase of oil concessions in 1957 alone, which not only enabled the country to increase its imports by about 40 percent in that year but also made this the only year since 1950 in which the investment inflow exceeded the remittance outflow in the seven countries. Venezuela also accounted for almost three quarters of the profit and interest remittances in the seven-country total.

[32]Almost 60 percent of the net United States aid shown on Table 14 was in the form of interest-bearing loans rather than grants.

of payments as the principal bottleneck, as is implicit in the structural argument. Experience has shown that the countries can increase merchandise imports in spite of balance of payments difficulties. The question remains whether imports would have increased significantly had the purchasing power of exports risen faster. One can only speculate about this, but there is some doubt as to whether credit from international agencies, official loans, and grants from the United States Government would be available or would be used to the same extent had exports been growing more vigorously. Therefore it is quite possible that not much more would have been imported with greater export earnings.

Of course, a lasting export boom would unquestionably result in higher imports but, judging from past experience, the increases probably would be in response to consumer demands rather than to the needs of increased productivity and industrialization. On the other hand, when the capacity to import is more limited, a country will tend to ration its imports, orienting them more directly toward the requirements of economic growth. In the problem countries where detailed data are available, there is clear evidence that there has been a shift in the composition of imports in favor of capital and intermediate goods.[33] Thus it might very well turn out that with a more rapid growth in export earnings imports would be less geared toward eliminating the structural bottlenecks in the economy (even though the import total may be higher) than when low export earnings limit the use of foreign exchange.

In any case, Latin America managed to obtain imports over and above what export growth would have warranted. No "invisible" hands were at work because this has been purely a matter of government policy. Whether the price was too high relative to what was accomplished through these additional imports is another thing and is of no concern here. The fact of the matter is that in spite of increasing per capita imports the structural problems have persisted throughout the period, as manifested by continuing inflation (and/or economic stagnation).

STRUCTURAL PROBLEMS AND ECONOMIC GROWTH

There are three general explanations for the failure to achieve stability with growth despite the relatively rapid growth of imports since the beginning of the war. One is that imports were not high enough to permit the elimination of bottlenecks nor were they suf-

---

[33]See Tables 3 and 4. Also Table III–52 on p. 264 of ECLA, *op. cit.*

ficiently oriented toward this end. Another is that it takes time to effect structural changes and that a 20-year period is not long enough for the necessary adjustments to work themselves out. The third interpretation is that structural adjustment cannot be expected to come mainly via the balance of payments, but must be based primarily on fundamental reforms deriving from within the economy.

In respect to the first point, it already has been pointed out that unlimited imports can resolve a lot of problems, including inflation[34] and also, given enough time, structural maladjustments. This, however, is not a basis for any realistic argument because imports can never be expected to grow sufficiently fast to maintain stability and correct imbalances at the same time. After all, even United States aid is limited. It was also shown that imports generally have been oriented in the "right" direction, with the share of machinery and equipment increasing. Perhaps with more vigorous and better coordinated policies consumer goods imports could have been reduced even more in some cases, but it is unlikely that this would have produced basic changes.

It seems that the heart of the problem lies with the other two points mentioned, namely, that structural adjustments take time, and that they must come from within the economy. The foreign sector can provide the means for holding action to permit the necessary changes to be effected. This, essentially, has been the function of foreign trade in the industrializing countries of Latin America in the recent past. It is clear that the more rapidly an economy grows, the more readily and faster can the necessary structural changes be carried out. In the meantime, imbalances will persist and, therefore, it is likely that this process will be accompanied by financial instability.

It is also self-evident that, just as stability does not insure rapid economic growth, inflation in itself is not a sign of economic dy-

---

[34]Strictly speaking, it is the size of the import surplus rather than just the size of imports which is the relevant concept in relation to inflation. As was pointed out in the case of Argentina, in a country where the principal export products form a significant part of domestic supply, a curtailment of exports (relative to imports) will increase supply and thus have a dampening effect on inflation. In the mineral exporting countries, however, the import surplus has less relevance to price changes than the growth in imports. In the discussion on Chile it was indicated that the very high increases in imports of 1960 and 1961 kept the rate of inflation to below 10 percent in each year despite the much greater expansion in the money supply. Carlos Massad of the Instituto de Economía has shown in an as yet unpublished study that there is a high correlation between the rate of change of imports and the rate of inflation in Chile.

namism. It is best to separate the forces of growth and inflation, although there are obvious interconnections.[35] The countries which have shown the fastest economic growth in recent years, such as Brazil, have also had the greatest possibilities for import substitution. In some of these countries, such as Colombia, this process commenced comparatively recently. Most of them have started their rapid growth experience from very low per capita income levels and their labor movements are still weak.

Industrialization through import substitution in countries with a highly unequal distribution of income is principally geared to the middle income groups.[36] In large countries, such as Brazil for instance, the inequality of the income distribution matters less because the absolute size of the middle groups will be large, and therefore the import substitution process can proceed vigorously for a longer period of time. Since the market in these economies does not depend very much on the purchasing power of labor, even a decline in real wages will not dampen the sales potential of enterprises, but, to the contrary, will increase profit margins and therefore provide incentives to private investment.

On the other hand, in the smaller of the industrially more advanced countries of Latin America, notably Chile, the income distribution matters much more. The process of import substitution of consumer goods has just about come to an end there. For almost a decade now, the Chilean economy has grown not much more than its population, while the basic imbalances have continued to produce one of the highest inflation rates in the region. It is very unlikely that, in the absence of a significant change in the income distribution and the size of its market, this economy could sustain an acceleration in its rate of growth for an extended period of time.

The complicating factor in the case of Chile is a relatively balanced distribution of power among its major social sectors. Labor has achieved certain economic status and strength, both through a comparatively strong labor union movement and through political representation. The white collar sector, including small business and the professions, has become firmly entrenched since the advent of the "popular front" government in 1939. The larger business in-

[35]Mr. Goeffrey Maynard addresses the major part of his recent book to this particular question ("Economic Development and The Price Level" [London, MacMillan & Co., Ltd., 1962]).

[36]The lower income groups will be largely out of the market and the upper income groups will tend to orient their demand toward imports whenever possible, including making purchases during trips abroad.

terests and landholding classes still have great economic and political power.

What this adds up to is that the continuing struggle of these sectors for the economic pie adds fuel to the inflation while at the same time it dampens profit expectations and, therefore, incentives to invest. Enterprise finds its labor costs to be high, not only because of constant cost of living wage adjustments, but also because of heavy social security contributions and other nonwage payments. It is difficult in Chile for prices to run away from wages for any length of time, contrary to the experience in other countries where this factor is one of the basic elements in recent economic growth.

In Argentina there has also existed a balance of power, although of a somewhat different nature than in Chile, but government policies have played a much more important role in that economy's semistagnation than in Chile.[37]

Countries like Colombia, Peru, and Venezuela can still go a long way in carrying forward industrialization on the basis of consumer goods import substitution, which they have begun comparatively recently. Eventually, however, economic development in the "old" and "new" industrial countries of Latin America will depend upon a widening of the markets. In a normal process of industrialization, this should come naturally as a by-product of development, but in most of the Latin-American countries severe obstacles will have to be overcome before a basic improvement in the distribution of income can be achieved. This is part of the economic significance of such fundamental measures as land, tax, and educational reforms. This is also the rationale of the striving toward a common market in Latin America which would make capital goods import substitution an economic feasibility even in the smaller countries.

Thus, whether a country grows or not depends primarily on factors other than the existence of inflation. Nevertheless, inflation can have important effects on economic development through its influence on savings and investment decisions. Its effects will not be detrimental as long as price increases do not exceed the range which the (business) community continues to anticipate and does not deem severe enough to compel the government to introduce effective stabilization measures.[38] It is obvious that these limits would be much higher in Chile than, say, in the United States.

---

[37] See of ECLA, *op. cit.*, Vol IV.

[38] Of course, anti-inflation policies can have beneficial effects upon investment decisions through instilling in the business community a sense of confidence in governmental "soundness." There is evidence that investment of the largest
(Continued on next page)

CONCLUSION

The notion of balanced growth which is implicit in the structuralist argument is rather utopian if taken at face value. To obtain a structure of production sufficiently elastic to meet without friction the demand changes inherent in economic development is too big an order to fill. By the nature of "underdevelopedness" one cannot expect the developing countries to accommodate the shifts in demand through their internal production. It is natural, therefore, that the responsibility would be shifted to imports to meet these new needs and the balance of payments becomes of primary importance.

Thus we have come full circle regarding the position of the balance of payments in the structural model: the basic problem arises because of the collapse in export earnings due to the depression of the 1930's and the unreliability and long-term deterioration in the commodity markets for Latin-American exports. This has led to an industrialization effort through import substitution which in turn has created the imbalances that are the core of the structural problems. And now we return to the balance of payments in order to resolve these.

While one cannot seriously question the primary role of the balance of payments as the initiator of the structural process, its second emphasis in the model as a cure-all seems to divert attention from the heart of the matter: the resolution of the imbalances is essentially an internal problem. Assistance from the balance of payments in this effort is often very important but, as pointed out, it will always be limited, given real world conditions. At best it can help to achieve certain stability, particularly in prices, as in Chile in 1960 and 1961, which may be an important factor in the process of making structural adjustments. But since this process takes time, even this function may be lost (as in Chile) unless imports can be sustained not merely at a high level but at a fast-growing pace for an extended period.

It has been shown here that imports are not as limited by export

---

manufacturing enterprises increased in Chile in 1956 and 1957 after the introduction of a strong stabilization policy. But the absence of vitality of the Chilean economy soon reversed businessmen's expectations despite the continuance of stabilization efforts and by 1960, when price increases fell to the lowest point in about three decades, private net capital formation was close to zero. Investment of small business enterprises fell immediately after the introduction of effective anti-inflation measures, because of their dependence on credit which was restricted. (See Instituto de Economía, *op. cit.*, and "Formación de Capital en las Empresas Industriales," Santiago, Chile, 1961 [with English summary].)

earnings as has been claimed. Yet our argument states that imports cannot resolve structural imbalances, but that these adjustments are essentially a thing of internal policy. This policy might be circumscribed somewhat by external factors, such as an anticipated censure by other countries, but this cannot be too important in a sovereign country. On the other hand, social and institutional barriers impose a policy limitation only if they are assumed to be absolute. But it is just one of the fundamental tasks in correcting the imbalances to modify the institutional framework, and institutional change is a matter for internal policy decisions. It is clear that to change institutions and social structure takes time. That is why it will take time to eliminate the imbalances in order to achieve long-run growth with long-run stability.

If one goes deeper in analyzing the "invisible hands" question, it becomes apparent that even the initiation of the process which results in the structural imbalances is at least implicitly policy-based. While the balance of payments problem is the starting point, the process of import substitution must be built upon explicit or implicit policy decisions to industrialize. Tariff protection, foreign exchange and other subsidies, import quotas, etc., are just a few manifestations of such policies. Thus, the fundamental assumption underlying the structural model is the existence of economic aspirations of the community to maintain an accustomed rate of growth (or to accelerate it). The aspirations must be strong enough to be translated into government policies which are at least permissive, if they do not directly foster industrialization.

The aspirations of the community and the policies based on them are not an exogenous matter, although it may be claimed that there is very little the government can do but act upon them. In economically advanced countries where the balance of payments is important, like the United Kingdom, a severe drop in export earnings will either be compensated for by a shift of resources to nonexport industries or, as in the lesser-developed countries, result in unemployment and a decline in income. In the latter case, the retrenchment until the recuperation of exports, or until resources can be transferred to other sectors, can be endured more easily than in the developing countries, where income levels of large population groups are close to subsistence and where, because of low factor mobility, the retrenchment period is likely to last much longer.

How much the hands of the policy makers are tied in reacting to the economic aspirations of the developing countries is a matter of debate. Perhaps they can do no more than be permissive regarding the expansionary pressures, which fact alone may lead to inflation. There is no doubt that the social and political, as well as the economic, forces are very powerful, and the policymaker may feel that his range of action is therefore severely circumscribed. But to treat permissive or expansionary policies as completely exogenously determined is too easy a rationalization. It does not take a Christlike leader to be able to exact sacrifices from the population in a poor country. Recent Latin-American history is full of cases where large segments of the lower income groups have suffered stagnation or even deterioration in their real incomes without going to the barricades.[39]

There is no doubt that in the long run the generally small countries of Latin America existing in semi-isolation from one another cannot individually fulfill the aspirations for dynamic economic growth. There is nothing exogenous about the need for supranational economic integration, and policies toward this end are based upon endogenous decisions and national efforts.

This boils down to the fact that the only major "invisible hand" in the structural model is the initial export decline. But it is conceivable that structural problems may arise without any exogenous factors. Even in the absence of an export decrease, government policy, either acting upon its own initiative or upon the basis of community aspirations, may, in an effort to accelerate economic growth, embark the country on the path of industrialization through import substitution. Whether this will actually lead to imbalances or not will depend upon the size of the growth effort relative to the economy's capabilities. Under the heading of "capability" we must include not only the magnitude of factor endowments but also all the things that go into the concept of "elasticity of supply," such as various types of factor mobility, feasible rates of technological adaptation, the flexibility of agricultural production, the possibilities for the government to provide the necessary infrastructure, and, not least, the economy's capacity to import. No matter how fast exports grow, there can always be a rate of desired growth in GDP for which exports would become a bottleneck sector.[40]

---

[39]In spite of the growing power of labor, there is evidence that the lower income groups would willingly make sacrifices for future economic betterment if the government had their confidence. (For instance, the Christian Democratic labor movement in Chile included wage restraints in its policy pronouncements in connection with the 1958 presidential campaign.)

[40]If a certain growth in exports is anticipated, then the desired growth rate can be pushed up to outdistance the possibilities of getting sufficient imports to support the required industrialization process. However, if export growth is not anticipated but does occur, then the additional (windfall) imports could be oriented to achieve some degree of structural adjustment.

The balance of payments alone does not make for structural problems. The structural inflation problem is rooted in the desire to grow and industrialize faster than the present structure of the economy can accommodate.

The emphasis of this paper in placing the responsibility for structural adjustments on internal policy does not mean that the situation is hopeless. If the hitherto remarkable social tranquility in Latin America can last a decade or so longer there might be time to remove the obstacles to accelerated growth with relative stability before the social breaking point is reached. There exists already the germ of a free-trade area in Latin America. Most countries in Latin America have now passed initial legislation for land and other reforms. No one claims that inflation can be cured through agricultural reform but reform does constitute a basis upon which to build for future development with greater stability. Of course, some of this present legislation may be insincere and may represent only an ineffectual token to satisfy United States aid requirements. However, it is a significant beginning, no matter how small, and has put in motion a process which will be difficult to stop.

The oligarchies are still in existence in Latin America, but their political power has waned noticeably since the war. While they may yet win temporary victories, they are fighting a losing rear guard battle. This is the challenge for the exogenous hand of United States aid. It can be applied to prolong the rear guard action, or it can be applied to help in the acceleration of basic structural changes and to lessen the sacrifices which become necessary in this revolution.

TABLE 1

LATIN AMERICA: ANNUAL COMPOUND RATES OF GROWTH OF EXPORTS AND
IMPORTS, GROSS DOMESTIC PRODUCT, AND THE CONSUMER PRICE INDEX

1928–1960

	Export Quantum	Purchasing Power of Exports*	Import Quantum	Gross Domestic Product in 1955 Prices
1928/30–1940/42	−1.9	−5.9	−6.7	3.0[1]
1940/42–1944/46	4.7	6.8	4.9	4.25
1944/46–1949/51	0.7	5.7	11.6	5.1
1949/51–1954/56	2.8	2.3	2.3	4.55
1954/56–1958/60	5.35[2]	0.95[2]	7.6[2]	4.6[3]
1940/42–1958/60	2.9[4]	4.3[4]	6.45[4]	4.7[5]
1949/51–1958/60	3.5[6]	1.9[6]	3.8[6]	4.6[7]
1928/29–1959/60	0.7[8]	−0.2[8]	0.4[8]	4.0[9]

[1]1929/30–1940/42
[2]1954/56–1957/58
[3]1954/56–1957/59
[4]1940/42–1958/59
[5]1940/42–1957/58
[6]1949/51–1957/58
[7]1949/51–1957/59
[8]1928/29–1957/58
[9]1929– 1958/59

Source: ECLA, "Inflation and Growth," 1961, statistical appendix and respective country study chapters.

*Index of export value deflated by the index of unit value of imports.

TABLE 2

ARGENTINA: ANNUAL COMPOUND RATES OF GROWTH OF EXPORTS AND IMPORTS,
GROSS DOMESTIC PRODUCT, AND THE CONSUMER PRICE INDEX

1928–1960

	Export Quantum	Purchasing Power of Exports*	Import Quantum	Gross Domestic Product in 1955 Prices	Consumer Price Index
1928/30–1940/42......	−3.0	−2.9	−6.0	1.9[1]	2.65[1]
1940/42–1944/46......	2.2	2.7	−6.85	4.1	6.5
1944/46–1949/51......	−6.3	−3.0	16.4	4.3	20.6
1949/51–1954/56......	1.15	−4.8	−3.7	1.55	17.0
1954/56–1958/60......	4.7	5.8[2]	5.04[2]	1.7	38.0
1940/42–1958/60......	..	−0.7[3]	2.6[3]	2.9	19.8
1949/51–1958/60......	2.7	−0.9[4]	−0.5[4]	1.6	25.8
1928/29–1959/60......	−1.55	−2.0[5]	−1.2[5]	2.3[6]	13.2[6]

[1]1929/30–1940/42
[2]1954/56–1958/59
[3]1940/42–1958/59
[4]1949/51–1958/59
[5]1928/29–1958/59
[6]1929–   1959/60
Source: See Table 1.
*Index of export value deflated by the index of unit value of imports.

TABLE 3

BRAZIL: ANNUAL COMPOUND RATES OF GROWTH OF EXPORTS AND IMPORTS,
GROSS DOMESTIC PRODUCT, AND THE CONSUMER PRICE INDEX

1928–1960

	Export Quantum	Purchasing Power of Exports*	Import Quantum	Capital Goods Imports Quantum	Gross Domestic Product in 1955 Prices	Consumer Price Index
1928/30–1940/42....	2.0	−2.6	−3.95	..	3.3[1]	5.4[1]
1940/42–1944/46....	4.0	11.2	9.3	..	3.3	17.8
1944/46–1949/51....	−0.2	5.9	13.7	..	6.4	10.8
1949/51–1954/56....	−2.1	0.75	−0.9	−6.65	4.5	17.8
1954/56–1958/60....	3.1	−2.6[2]	2.7[2]	16.0[2]	5.85	23.2
1940/42–1958/60....	0.9	4.0[3]	6.3[3]	..	5.1	17.0
1949/51–1958/60....	0.2	−0.5[4]	0.4[4]	1.5[4]	5.1	20.2
1928/29–1959/60....	1.8	0.9[5]	1.5[5]	..	4.4[6]	12.4[6]

[1]1929/30–1940/42
[2]1954/56–1958/59
[3]1940/42–1958/59
[4]1949/51–1958/59
[5]1928/29–1958/59
[6]1929–   1959/60
Source: See Table 1. Capital goods imports calculated on the basis of data, ECLA, *op. cit.*,
Vol. IV, p. 47.
*Index of export value deflated by the index of unit value of imports.

TABLE 4

CHILE: ANNUAL COMPOUND RATES OF GROWTH OF EXPORTS AND IMPORTS, GROSS DOMESTIC PRODUCT, AND THE CONSUMER PRICE INDEX

1928–1960

	Export Quantum	Purchasing Power of Exports*	Import Quantum	Import Quantum Per Capita	Capital Goods Imports Quantum	Capital Goods Imports Quantum Per Capita	Gross Domestic Product in 1955 Prices	Consumer Price Index
1928/30–1940/42	0.9	−4.35	−4.6	...	...	...	1.9[1]	7.8[1]
1940/42–1944/46	−0.25	−2.8	0.1	−2.1	2.6	1.5	5.8	15.45
1944/46–1949/51	−1.45	1.5	4.7	3.0	18.2	15.6	3.2	19.8
1949/51–1954/56	1.7	4.3	−0.4	−2.6	3.3	2.3	3.6	42.0
1954/56–1958/60	3.8	−0.5	6.5	3.7	9.25[2]	6.3[2]	2.8	33.0
1940/42–1958/60	0.8	1.75	2.6	0.4	8.8[3]	6.6[3]	3.8	27.5
1949/51–1958/60	2.6	3.9	2.6	0.2	6.4[4]	3.8[4]	3.2	38.0
1928/29–1959/60	0.6	−1.5	−0.3	...	...	...	3.0[5]	19.4[5]

[1] 1929/30–1940/42
[2] 1954/56–1958/59
[3] 1940/42–1958/59
[4] 1949/51–1958/59
[5] 1929– 1959/60

Sources: See Table 1. Also, Instituto de Economía, 1962, "La Economía Chilena en el Período 1950–1961," and "Desarrollo Económico de Chile 1940–1956," Santiago, 1957; Banco Central de Chile, Boletín, August–September, 1962.

*Index of export value deflated by the index of unit value of imports.

TABLE 5

COLOMBIA: ANNUAL COMPOUND RATES OF GROWTH OF EXPORTS AND IMPORTS,
GROSS DOMESTIC PRODUCT, AND THE CONSUMER PRICE INDEX

1928–1960

	Export Quantum	Purchasing Power of Exports*	Import Quantum	Gross Domestic Product in 1955 Prices	Consumer Price Index
1928/30–1940/42	1.35	−3.3	−3.0	3.7[1]	..
1940/42–1944/46	6.7	7.8	8.1	3.5	12.7
1944/46–1949/51	−0.2	10.6	7.55	4.4	13.5
1949/51–1954/56	2.4	5.2	10.2	5.1	5.2
1954/56–1958/60	2.0	−6.9[2]	−14.05[2]	3.4	9.9
1940/42–1958/60	2.5	5.1[3]	4.3[3]	4.2	10.2
1949/51–1958/60	2.25	0.5[4]	0.4[4]	4.35	7.3
1928/30–1959/60	2.4	1.3[5]	0.6[5]	4.1[6]	..

[1]1929/30–1940/42
[2]1954/56–1958/59
[3]1940/42–1958/59
[4]1949/51–1958/59
[5]1928/29–1958/59
[6]1929– 1959/60
Source: See Table 1.
*Index of export value deflated by the index of unit value of imports.

TABLE 6

ECUADOR: ANNUAL COMPOUND RATES OF GROWTH OF EXPORTS AND IMPORTS,
GROSS DOMESTIC PRODUCT, AND THE CONSUMER PRICE INDEX

1928–1960

	Export Quantam	Purchasing Power of Exports*	Import Quantum	Gross Domestic Product in 1955 Prices	Consumer Price Index
1928/30–1940/42	0.55	−1.8	−2.1	..	..
1940/42–1944/46	5.5	11.8	8.4	4.2	13.1
1944/46–1949/51	−1.9	7.5	10.1	7.4	19.2
1949/51–1954/56	7.6	13.2	15.6	6.2	2.4
1954/56–1958/60	7.3	−0.95[1]	−3.15[1]	3.6	..
1940/42–1958/60	4.4	9.2[2]	9.6[2]	5.5	8.65
1949/51–1958/60	7.5	8.95[3]	9.9[3]	5.0	1.3
1929/30–1959/60	3.1	4.3[4]	4.4[4]	..	..

[1]1954/56–1957/58
[2]1940/42–1957/58
[3]1949/51–1957/58
[4]1928/29–1957/58
Source: See Table 1.
*Index of export value deflated by the index of unit value of imports.

TABLE 7

El Salvador: Annual Compound Rates of Growth of Exports and Imports, Gross Domestic Product, and the Consumer Price Index
1928–1960

	Export Quantum	Purchasing Power of Exports*	Import Quantum	Gross Domestic Product in 1955 Prices	Consumer Price Index
1928/30–1940/42......	−0.05	−1.9	−3.7	..	..
1940/42–1944/46......	2.7	6.5	5.45	..	13.0
1944/46–1949/51......	4.7	12.2	14.1	10.3[1]	6.5
1949/51–1954/56......	1.5	8.8	12.6	5.3	5.1
1954/56–1958/60......	15.0[2]	6.25[2]	6.7[2]	5.1[3]	0.5
1940/42–1958/60......	4.4[4]	8.9[4]	10.5[4]	6.9[8]	6.1
1949/51–1958/60......	5.2[5]	8.0[5]	10.9[5]	5.2[6]	3.0
1929/30–1959/60......	2.6[7]	3.7[7]	3.8[7]	..	..

[1]1945/46–1949/51
[2]1954/56–1957/58
[3]1954/56–1958/59
[4]1940/42–1957/58
[5]1949/51–1957/58
[6]1949/51–1958/59
[7]1928/29–1957/58
[8]1945/46–1958/59
Source: See Table 1.
*Index of export value deflated by the index of unit value of imports.

TABLE 8

Mexico: Annual Compound Rates of Growth of Exports and Imports, Gross Domestic Product, and the Consumer Price Index
1928–1960

	Export Quantum	Purchasing Power of Exports*	Import Quantum	Capital Goods Imports Quantum	Gross Domestic Product in 1955 Prices	Consumer Price Index
1928/30–1940/42....	−5.9	−5.0	−1.1	..	6.2[1]	..
1940/42–1944/46....	2.0	10.2	19.4	22.4	6.55	19.6
1944/46–1949/51....	5.7	7.4	3.4	5.1	6.5	10.0
1949/51–1954/56....	6.1	3.5	4.4	6.5	6.1	8.0
1954/56–1958/60....	1.55[2]	−4.3[2]	7.4[2]	6.1[2]	5.0	7.0
1940/42–1958/60....	4.35[3]	5.3[3]	8.0[3]	9.75[3]	6.1	10.8
1949/51–1958/60....	4.8[4]	1.2[4]	5.2[4]	6.4[4]	5.6	7.5
1929/30–1959/60....	−0.4[5]	0.4[5]	3.1[5]	..	6.1[6]	..

[1]1929/30–1940/42
[2]1954/56–1957/58
[3]1940/42–1957/58
[4]1949/51–1957/58
[5]1928/29–1957/58
[6]1929–   1959/60
Sources: See Table 1. Capital goods imports calculated on the basis of data in ECLA, *op. cit.*, Vol. V, p. 72.
*Index of export value deflated by the index of unit value of imports.

TABLE 9

PERU: ANNUAL COMPOUND RATES OF GROWTH OF EXPORTS AND IMPORTS,
GROSS DOMESTIC PRODUCT, AND THE CONSUMER PRICE INDEX

1928–1960

	Export Quantum	Purchasing Power of Exports*	Import Quantum	Gross Domestic Product in 1955 Prices	Consumer Price Index
1928/30–1940/42......	−0.2	..	..	..	1.3[1]
1940/42–1944/46......	6.8	2.0	5.6	..	12.1
1944/46–1949/51......	−5.7	5.75	9.3	4.3	18.4
1949/51–1954/56......	9.1	4.7	6.5	5.3	7.4
1954/56–1958/60......	6.2	0.7[2]	1.6[2]	2.6[2]	8.2
1940/42–1958/60......	3.7	4.0[3]	6.2[3]	4.5[7]	11.6
1949/51–1958/60......	7.8	3.95[4]	4.65[4]	4.6[4]	7.7
1929/30–1959/60......	2.1[5]	..	..	..	7.4[6]

[1]1929/30–1940/42
[2]1954/56–1958/59
[3]1940/42–1958/59
[4]1949/51–1958/59
[5]1929– 1959/60
[6]1928/29–1958/59
[7]1944/46–1958/59
Source: See Table 1.
*Index of export value deflated by the index of unit value of imports.

TABLE 10

VENEZUELA: ANNUAL COMPOUND RATES OF GROWTH OF EXPORTS AND IMPORTS,
GROSS DOMESTIC PRODUCT, AND THE CONSUMER PRICE INDEX

1928–1960

	Export Quantum	Purchasing Power of Exports*	Import Quantum	Gross Domestic Product in 1955 Prices	Consumer Price Index
1928/30–1940/42......	2.3	−4.6	−5.1	2.6[1]	..
1940/42–1944/46......	14.5	13.3	15.0	8.9	7.9
1944/46–1949/51......	9.9	19.4	21.8	7.0	6.6
1949/51–1954/56......	7.9	7.6	6.1	8.8	1.0
1954/56–1958/60......	6.9	3.6[2]	8.5[2]	7.0	1.95
1940/42–1958/60......	9.7	11.55[3]	13.0[3]	7.9	4.2
1949/51–1958/60......	7.5	6.1[4]	7.0[4]	8.0	1.4
1928/29–1959/60......	7.2	5.0[5]	5.0[5]	5.9[6]	..

[1]1929/30–1940/42
[2]1954/56–1958/59
[3]1940/42–1958/59
[4]1949/51–1958/59
[5]1928/29–1958/59
[6]1929– 1959/60
Source: See Table 1.
*Index of export value deflated by the index of unit value of imports.

TABLE 11

LATIN AMERICA, ARGENTINA, BRAZIL, AND CHILE: INDEX OF RELATION OF
EXPORTS AND IMPORTS TO GROSS DOMESTIC PRODUCT

(*Index Numbers of Three-Year Averages, 1928–1960, 1955 = 100*)*

	Latin America		Argentina		Brazil		Chile	
	Export Quantum GDP	Import Quantum GDP	Export Quantum GDP	Import Quantum GDP	Export Quantum GDP	Import Quantum GDP	Export Quantum GDP	Import Quantum GDP
1928–1930.....	248	285	390	291	24[2]	15[2]	222	322
1934–1936.....	193	92	351	169	220	114	152	124
1939–1941.....	141	93	223	140	216	97	165	143
1944–1946.....	137	81	196	58	190	103	144	102
1949–1951.....	111	106	131	114	139	144	107	100
1954–1956.....	100	100	100	100	100	110	100	100
1958–1960.....	99[1]	100[1]	129	101	90	102[3]	102[4]	127[4]

[1]1957–59
[2]1929–31
[3]1957–59
[4]1959–61
Source: ECLA, *op. cit.*, statistical appendix.
*Three-year average of quantum index as indicated divided by three-year average of GDP.

TABLE 12

COLOMBIA, ECUADOR, EL SALVADOR
INDEX OF RELATION OF EXPORTS AND IMPORTS TO GROSS DOMESTIC PRODUCT

(*Index Numbers of Three-Year Averages, 1928–1960, 1955 = 100*)*

	Colombia		Ecuador		El Salvador	
	Export Quantum GDP	Import Quantum GDP	Export Quantum GDP	Import Quantum GDP	Export Quantum GDP	Import Quantum GDP
1928–30.......	158[1]	086[1]	..	..	..	..
1934–36.......	141	075	..	..	..	..
1939–41.......	128	074	140	049	..	..
1944–46.......	138	065	148	056	134	57
1949–51.......	110	076	094	063	110	72
1954–56.......	097	096	098	094	100	100
1958–60.......	089	058[2]	116	087[3]	107[4]	95[4]

[1]1929–1931
[2]1957–1959
[3]1956–1958
[4]1957–1959
Source: ECLA, *op. cit.*, statistical appendix.
*Three-year average of quantum index as indicated divided by three-year average of GDP.

TABLE 13

MEXICO, PERU, VENEZUELA:
INDEX OF RELATION OF EXPORTS AND IMPORTS TO GROSS DOMESTIC PRODUCT
(*Index Numbers of Three-Year Averages, 1928–1960, 1955 = 100*)*

	Mexico		Peru		Venezuela	
	Export Quantum GDP	*Import Quantum GDP*	*Export Quantum GDP*	*Import Quantum GDP*	*Export Quantum GDP*	*Import Quantum GDP*
1928–30.......	445[1]	158[1]	. .	. .	78	141
1934–36.......	308	089	. .	. .	76	34
1939–41.......	126	088	108[3]	55[3]	66	63
1944–46.......	099	132	106	71	98	61
1949–51.......	096	115	91	87	105	108
1954–56.......	095	106	100	.100	100	100
1958–60.......	089[2]	108[2]	123	86	98	96

[1]1929–1931
[2]1956–1958
[3]1941–1943
Source: ECLA, *op. cit.*, statistical appendix.
*Three-year average of quantum index as indicated, divided by three-year average of GDP.

TABLE 14

SEVEN COUNTRY TOTAL: BALANCES OF PAYMENTS EFFECTS OF NET NEW U.S. DIRECT INVESTMENT AND U.S. OFFICIAL AID AND REMITTANCE

ARGENTINA, BRAZIL, CHILE, COLOMBIA, MEXICO, PERU, VENEZUELA

(U.S. $ Million, Except Per Capita Imports)

	A	B	C	D	E	F	G	H
	Net New U.S. Direct Investment	Profit and Interest Remittances on U.S. Direct Investment	Net New U.S. Direct Investment Less Remittances (A–B)	Total Net U.S. Aid	Official U.S. Debt Repayments	Interest on Debt to U.S. Govt.	Total Net U.S. Aid Less Debt Repayments and Interest (D–E–F)	Imports
								Millions $
1950........	$ 27	$399	$ –372	$ 87	$ 29	$13	$ 45	$3,991
1951........	150	495	–345	126	32	13	81	6,026
1952........	344	454	–110	97	36	13	48	5,799
1953........	132	475	–343	399	41	16	342	4,874
1954........	27	494	–467	103	64	27	12	5,515
1955........	134	635	–501	141	104	30	7	5,581
1956........	537	712	–175	182	109	30	43	5,879
1957........	1,051	784	267	247	122	30	95	6,925
1958........	215	571	–356	611	132	39	440	6,283
1959........	119	549	–430	389	156	57	176	5,885
1960........	85	632	–547	262	168	65	29	6,290
1961........	144	675	–531	740	158	71	511	6,612

Sources: U.S. Department of Commerce, AID, IMF.

b. SOME NOTES ON INFLATION
Arnold C. Harberger

The subject matter with which this conference deals falls, to my mind, into two quite separate parts. There are many things which can be said about inflation, but most of them have relatively little to do with economic growth. Likewise, of the many things which can be said about economic growth, few have much relevance for the study of inflation. I have chosen to concentrate my remarks on the problem of inflation, not because I believe it is more important than, or as important as, the problem of growth, but simply because I believe that the technical apparatus with which economists work enables us to say substantially more about inflation than about growth. There is still a great deal of mystery surrounding the problem of growth: for example, we really do not know why Brazil has been able to progress so much more rapidly than Chile, or why Mexico has been able to achieve a growth rate so much greater than Argentina's. On the other hand, our technical apparatus does permit us to explain reasonably well the differences in the rates of inflation which different countries have experienced. It also gives us a reasonably good understanding of the inflationary process, and enables us to derive a number of conclusions which are important for policy decisions. It is partly on these grounds that I have chosen to concentrate on inflation. The other part of my reason is that, regardless of what our technical apparatus permits, I feel that the remarks which I may make on the problem of inflation will be substantially more concrete and useful than the remarks which I would be able to make on the problem of economic growth.

Having decided to write mainly about inflation, there remained the problem of organizing my material. I found that there was no single thread connecting the remarks which I wanted to make, but that instead my remarks fell into three quite distinct classes. This fact determined the organization of the present paper.

In Section I, I attempt to set out a number of propositions on which I believe general agreement may be possible. These propositions are not particularly novel, but it seemed to me that it would be useful for the participants in a conference such as this to attempt to define explicitly where they agree and where they disagree.

In Section II, I make a few remarks connected with my paper,

"The Dynamics of Inflation in Chile," which was submitted as a background paper for this conference.

In Section III, I attempt to set out a simple theoretical model in terms of which we can analyze the effects of devaluation on the internal price level of a country. Most of my efforts were concentrated on this section because I have sensed in Latin America a tremendous divergence of views on this subject.

I. SOME PROPOSITIONS ON WHICH GENERAL AGREEMENT MAY BE OBTAINED

1. It is abundantly clear from the available evidence that there is no close relation between the rate of inflation and the rate of economic growth. There have been countries with low rates of inflation which have had the full gamut of experience with respect to economic growth. The same is true with respect to high rates of inflation. It seems to me that we cannot accept a position at either extreme, either one which holds that having a substantial inflation would rule out the possibility of a substantial rate of progress in real income or one which holds that some inflation is necessary in order to achieve a high rate of economic growth. Whatever connections we may establish between the rate of inflation and the rate of economic progress are likely to be rather weak, tenuous links rather than strong and fundamental relationships.

2. In this paragraph I set out what I believe to be the principal argument against inflation as the promoter of economic growth. This argument is not really an argument against inflation itself, but rather an argument against the way inflations appear to have worked in practice. It is possible to imagine an inflation which went on steadily at, say, 30 percent per year, and which was completely and accurately anticipated by everybody, and in which the separate prices of all the different commodities and services in the economy rose steadily at the same pace. This "ideal" type of inflation is not what we have observed in the real world. The inflations of the real world are, by and large not at all accurately anticipated, and in them there occurs substantial disparity in the rates of rise of the prices of different types of goods and services. The failure to anticipate accurately and, in particular, the disparity in the pace of adjustment of particular prices blur, so to speak, the vision of the people who are responsible for economic organizaiton. In a country which has a stable general price level it is possible for enterpreneurs to make a judgment that a new process will save, say, two cents in the dollar of production costs, and it is likely that within a stable

environment such a new process would in fact be adopted with alacrity. If, however, the economy is undergoing an inflation of, say, 20-30 percent per annum it will be difficult for entrepreneurs to act on this kind of improvement. They will not know whether the saving of two cents in the dollar of costs will be erased by a rise in wages or in prices of materials in the very near future. During any big inflation all absolute prices are constantly adjusted. They adjust at different rates, and in a pattern which is not at all precisely predictable. I would venture to guess that where in a stable environment entrepreneurs would be happy to make alterations in their method of production on the basis of information which appeared to suggest a saving of two cents in the dollar of costs, in an inflationary environment entrepreneurs might require information suggesting that they might save ten cents in the dollar of costs before they would be willing to undertake a substantial overhaul of their methods of production. This obviously means that fewer growth-producing innovations will take place in an inflationary setting than in a more stable environment.

3. The above should not be taken as presenting a total picture. Inflation sometimes can help to keep the economy operating at its full potential. Economists like to pretend that it is possible to maintain full employment while keeping the general price level constant. The evidence, however, does not appear to corroborate the economists' view. Moreover, a little reflection will indicate that the economic policy of a country probably should have a certain inflationary bias. Consider the economic costs to a country of having, on the one hand, a situation in which there are present inflationary pressures whose ultimate effect would be to raise the price level by 5 percent; consider, on the other hand, a situation in which there are present deflationary pressures whose ultimate effect would be to lower the price level by 5 percent. In both of these cases there would exist inequities due to the differential impact of inflation or deflation on different groups in the economy. By and large, those who would gain from inflation would lose from deflation, and I do not see any reason to consider that, on equity grounds, inflation is either better or worse than deflation. However, allowing deflationary forces to work themselves out would entail, in virtually any present-day economy, substantial unemployment of labor, and perhaps also of capital resources. This effect is present when the pressures are deflationary and absent when the pressures are inflationary. It seems to me self-evident that the social costs of allowing deflationary pressures at the rate of, say, 5 percent per annum are very much greater

than the social costs of allowing inflationary pressures at the rate of 5 percent per annum to work themselves out in the economy. So long as there is this asymmetry between the social costs of a deflation of *x* percent per annum and the social costs of inflation of *x* percent per annum, it is clear that public policy should not operate on the assumption that one is as bad as the other. Some bias toward inflation should result from any rational calculation of the costs and benefits involved. The way in which this bias toward inflation might reasonably work itself out would be through a monetary and fiscal policy which was tight in periods of boom, and sufficiently loose in periods of slack to produce some rise in the general price level, as a consequence of the effort to eliminate or reduce the slackness in the economy. Just to put an order of magnitude on the kind of inflation that might result from this sort of policy, I can easily imagine that it could produce inflation at an average rate of 1, or 2, or 3 percent per annum. So as not to err in my judgment, let me set the limit at something like 10 percent per annum. It seems to me that it would be extremely difficult to defend a policy which produced inflation at more than 10 percent per annum on the ground that this rate of inflation was necessary to eliminate slackness in the economy.

4. It is my impression that the basic force which has created the inflationary pressure in Latin-American countries has been a chronic budget deficit. But I think it is important to realize that budget deficits do not invariably produce inflation, and that there is a reasonable amount of room in which budget policy can move without having inflationary consequences.

Economic growth is the principal reason that budgetary deficits can be maintained continuously without necessarily producing inflation. In a growing economy some provision must be made for a secular increase in the money supply if stable prices are to be maintained. If economic growth is taking place at 3 percent per year in real terms, it is likely that the increase in the money supply required for price stability will be somewhat greater than 3 percent per year, for the evidence from a number of countries suggests that the income elasticity of demand for real cash balances is typically somewhat in excess of unity. Moreover, if, as may be the case in some developing economies, there is a secular tendency for the real rate of interest to fall, there will arise from this source also a tendency for secular increase in the demand for real cash balances. It is thus possible that a country with a 3 percent rate of growth of real income might be able to sustain a 4 or 5 percent rate of growth of the money supply without inducing inflation.

One can conceive of many ways of providing the increase in money supply necessary for maintaining price stability. At the base of the money supply we have what has come to be called high-powered money—currency plus the deposit liabilities of the central bank. (It is called high-powered money because it can serve as reserves on the basis of which a secondary expansion in the money supply can take place, via deposit creation in the commercial banks.)

The money supply in the hands of the public and the government may be conceived as representing the liabilities of the banking system as a whole, at least in those cases where currency consists overwhelmingly of central bank notes. Any increase in the money supply will, accordingly, have as its counterpart some increase in the assets of the banking system as a whole, and an increase in bank assets can represent either private sector obligations or public sector obligations, or both. If a 5 percent per annum increase in the money supply is desired, it could, in principle, have as its counterpart exclusively increased holdings of government obligations by the banking system. It is unlikely, however, that such an extreme position would represent wise policy for the long run, for this would mean that there would be no expansion of bank loans and investments in the private sector, in spite of the fact that the economy as a whole was growing. A situation which appears to mc more reasonably to approximate a sensible norm for the long run is that the banking systems' holdings of both private obligations and government obligations would expand at roughly similar rates. (I do not mean to imply by this that there is any profound reason for maintaining a fixity in the proportions of the two classes of assets held by the banking system; I only suggest that maintaining a fixed ratio seems to be a more plausible norm than concentrating all increases in bank assets in one sector or the other.) Let us suppose a situation in which the assets of the banking system consisted initially of half public and half private sector obligations, and in which these proportions are to be maintained throughout the process of money supply expansion. Then, assuming that the money supply is to be expanded at the rate of 5 per cent per year, half of this expansion would be accounted for by increases in bank holdings of government obligations. On this account alone, one could justify a government deficit which each year was equal to 2½ percent of the country's money supply.

Unfortunately, the amount of deficit that can be justified in these terms is substantially less for underdeveloped countries than for advanced countries. In advanced countries the money supply often amounts to a third or a half of a year's national income, so that a government deficit equal to 2½ percent of the money supply would amount to between, say, ⅞ of 1 percent and 1¼ percent of the annual national income. In underdeveloped countries, on the other hand, the money supply typically amounts to something between one fifth and one tenth of a year's national income. Here, a deficit equal to 2½ percent of the money supply would amount to between ¼ of 1 percent and ½ of 1 percent of a year's national income.

I do not mean to imply by the above that somewhat larger deficits would not in some cases be possible. Certainly, where there exists a tradition of government bonds being sold to and held by the general public, there would presumably be some possibility of having a secular expansion in this class of government obligations, and it is also possible that some governments would be able to obtain a secularly increasing volume of credit from abroad. But, having mentioned these possibilities, I shall now put them aside.

5. The fact that the money supply amounts to such a small fraction of annual national income in most underdeveloped countries operates to produce a particular proclivity to inflation. Suppose, on the one hand, an advanced country in which the money supply amounts to one half of a year's national income. Let this country experience a deficit amounting to 2 percent of a year's national income, and let this deficit be financed by the sale of bonds to the banking system. The resulting increase in the money supply might range between 4 percent and, say, 8 percent. (The 4 percent figure assumes that the government divided its sales of bonds between the central bank and the commercial banks in such a way that the government absorbed the full increase in the money supply. The 8 percent figure assumes that the government sold the bulk of its bonds to the central bank, and that there was a secondary expansion of money supply on the basis of the reserves thus created, the secondary expansion being equal in magnitude to the amount of primary increase in the money supply.)

Suppose, now, an underdeveloped country in which the money supply amounts to only one tenth of a year's national income, and suppose, once again, a government deficit equal to 2 percent of a year's national income. In this case, on the same assumptions used above, the resulting increase in the money supply would range between 20 percent and 40 percent rather than between 4 per cent and 8 percent. The same deficit (expressed in terms of national income) goes a great deal farther in generating price inflation in the underdeveloped country of the above example than in the advanced country. This is an unfortunate fact, particularly so since it is likely that underdeveloped countries in general have less refined means of controlling their budgetary situation than are available to more advanced countries. I do believe, however, that this simple reason goes far to explain why inflation has been so much more serious a problem in underedeveloped countries than in advanced countries.

6. It is highly unlikely that any country can avoid a substantial rate of inflation if its government has a perennial and large deficit of which a significant proportion is financed by the sale of bonds to the central bank. This has been the case in many Latin-American countries, and the record clearly bears out the above proposition. It is possible, for a time, to offset the inflationary pressures generated by the sale of government bonds to the central bank, through contractions in the amount of credit granted by the banking system to the private sector. But there are limits to the use of this offsetting device (if private sector credit is contracted by a certain amount each year, it will some day be cut to zero). Moreover, long before the ultimate limit is reached, the squeeze on private sector credit is likely to have other undesirable effects. It seems to me that the efforts made in many Latin-American countries to stem the tide of inflation have very often been of this type. I would conclude that programs designed to stem the rate of inflation should be assigned very low probability of success unless they include a serious attack on the problem of chronic and substantial budget deficits. Purely monetary measures will not be sufficient so long as chronic deficits of substantial size persist.

7. It is more difficult to obtain general agreement about the role of wages in the inflationary process than about the points already discussed. But it is possible that agreement can be achieved as to what wages *can* do, as distinct from the way in which they do in fact operate. In this and the next five paragraphs I shall accordingly focus on the possible ways in which wages might work in the inflationary process. First, an autonomous rise in wages *can* cause a rise in the general price level even if the money supply is held constant. If the money supply is held constant in the face of rising wages it is likely that the level of output will be reduced and the rate of unemployment increased. If the monetary authorities are sufficiently stonyhearted, and refuse to increase the money supply even in the face of substantial unemployment, it is likely that ultimately the rate of unemployment would be reduced again, either through wages being forced down or through rises in productivity, which gradually produce a situation in which the economy can attain full employment at the given wage level. But either of these processes

of adjustment is likely to be slow and painful, entailing substantial amounts of unnecessary unemployment if the autonomously-set wage is significantly above the equilibrium wage. The lesser evil is surely for the monetary authorities to add sufficiently to the money supply to permit the economy to produce at or near full employment in the face of the new, higher level of wages.

8. An autonomous rise in wages, above and beyond that justified by recent productivity increases in the economy, is fairly easy to identify in an environment in which prices have been stable for a period preceding the wage rise. We have indicated above that such a wage rise would probably cause a rise in the price level, regardless of whether it was "financed" by the monetary authorities or not. But where the process goes from here is a matter about which we can be less sure. If workers are willing to see the apparent gain in real wage implicit in the initial wage rise partly or wholly eroded by subsequent increases in prices, then there is no reason to expect a continuing inflation. The price level will adjust to the autonomous wage rise, but it will be a once-and-for-all adjustment, so to speak. On the other hand, if workers bargain for, and get, a second rise in wages to compensate them for the loss in purchasing power coming from the price rise caused by the first rise in wages, then a second round of price rises will be initiated. This process can continue indefinitely, at least in the case where the monetary authorities "finance" each successive wage rise. In short, if in the first instance an unrealistic level of real wages is set (unrealistic in the sense of precluding full employment), and if workers successfully bargain for the re-establishment of this unrealistic real wage after every successive round of price increases, then a continuing inflation can be generated, especially if the monetary authorities "finance" the successive wage rises in the effort to generate full employment. This is a real case of wage inflation.

9. In order for an autonomous wage rise to function in the way indicated in the preceding paragraph, it must be fairly general. If the autonomous rise occurs only in a limited sector of the economy, it is likely that the unemployment generated by the wage rise will be small, and it is possible that the people who become unemployed as a result of the wage rise will find employment elsewhere in the economy (through wages in the rest of the economy rising less rapidly than they otherwise would have done). Moreover, the workers in the affected areas would have to have substantial bargaining power in order to be able to enforce successive readjustment

of real wages to an unrealistic level, or the government would have to intervene to strengthen the position of the workers. My own judg- ment is that these conditions may have been met in Argentina, where the real wages of urban workers were raised to unrealistic levels during the Peron era, and where a tradition of strong union- ism remained after Peron fell. It is possible, though less probable, that these conditions were met in Chile. The possibility emerges be- cause of the responsiveness of private sector wages to the readjust- ments periodically made by the government in the *sueldo vital*. It is less probable because, by and large, unions are not particularly strong in Chile, and because in the course of Chile's great inflation of the last two decades the share of wages in the national income ac- tually fell quite perceptibly. This last piece of evidence makes it hard (though not impossible) to argue that real wages were being maintained at unrealistically high levels.

10. It should be recognized that the mere existence of periodic and substantial readjustments of wages does not in itself imply that wage rises are an autonomous force in the inflationary process. Per- haps the simplest way to demonstrate this is to talk in terms of the Chilean tradition of annual readjustments. Suppose that these ad- justments take place every year in January, and envision a process in which prices rise fairly steadily through the year while wages rise in discrete and substantial steps each January. Real wages will then be highest in January of each year, and will be progressively eroded by the steady rise of prices during the year, only to take a big jump upward when a new readjustment is declared the next Janu- ary. Now we can conceive of a "right" order of magnitude for the real wage—that real wage which would have to rule if the economy were to maintain reasonably full employment in an environment of reasonably stable prices. It is to be presumed that somewhere dur- ing the downward drift of real wages which takes place each year this "right" real wage will prevail. The question is, will this point be in January, at the beginning of the process, or in December, when real wages are lowest, or somewhere in between? If real wages are "right" in January, they are never "too high"; in this case it would be utterly wrong to attribute to wages an autonomous, causal, inflationary impact. The fuel for inflation would be coming from somewhere else, most likely from monetary expansion. If so, then the increase in money supply necessary to finance this January's wage rise will already have been issued last year. This January's wage rise, bringing wages up to their "right" level, will not require

any additional expansion of the money supply in order to maintain full employment.[1] If, on the other hand, real wages are "right" in December of each year, then they are above the "right" level during all the rest of the year. Here wages should certainly be assigned an autonomous role in the inflationary process; indeed, this is precisely the case referred to in paragraph eight, above.

11. Between the extremes discussed in the preceding paragraph, there exists a whole continuum of possibilities—real wages can be "right" at any time from February through November. If the truth is anywhere within this continuum, wages will play what I have called a transmitting role in the inflationary process. On the one hand, the wage rise of this year will be influenced by the price-level rise of last year; on the other hand, some additional expansion of the money supply will likely be necessary this year, in order to prevent the development of serious unemployment in the face of this year's wage rise, and this in turn will add fuel to this year's price inflation. It is probably idle to quibble about the point in the February-November range at which we would begin to consider that wages become an autonomous force in the inflation, for their transmitting role must be recognized to exist at any point in this range. But I think it should be accepted that in an inflation in which wages definitely did not play an autonomous role, but which was expected to continue, it would be perfectly reasonable for the January readjustment to incorporate some anticipation of the inflation expected for the coming year. That is, it would be reasonable to expect real wages to rise above the "right" level in January. In a rough way, I would argue that the dividing line should be based on the average real wage for the year. If, on the average, real wages were above the "right" level, I would argue that wages were exerting an autonomous force in the inflation. If, on the other hand, real wages averaged out to be lower than the "right" level, I would find it difficult to argue that they were playing an autonomous role. Nonetheless, even when real wages averaged less than the "right" level, they could be playing a very significant transmitting role in the inflationary process.

12. Implicit in the above analysis is the idea that wages need not be playing the same role throughout a protracted inflation. The

---

[1]Certain assumptions about the dynamic processes involved in inflation would require qualification of this statement. I do not want here to get into an involved analysis of the problem. The basic point is that if real wages are never higher than the "right" level, wages cannot be assigned an autonomous, causal role in the inflationary process.

Chilean government, in particular, has followed quite different policies in deciding on the wage readjustments to be granted at different points in time. There have been times when the wage readjustments exceeded the rate of price rise since the preceding adjustment by a substantial amount, and other times in which the readjustments fell far short of the rate of price inflation experienced in the preceding year. Efforts to establish empirically that wages always play the same role, and in the same way, are thus likely to be frustrated, and theories in which a particular role of wages is critical are unlikely to fit the facts.

13. The importance of lags between monetary expansions and the price rises they induce has been insufficiently recognized in most discussions of inflation in Latin America. I have for a long time suspected that a failure to recognize lags has been one of the reasons why the intermittent attempts at monetary stabilization in Chile have so often been short-lived. The process that I imagine runs something like this: Price inflation and monetary expansion have been going along for some time at a rate of, say, 30 per cent per year. A strong finance minister gets into power and decides on a program of monetary stabilization. He has to contend with a board of directors of the central bank in which the principal beneficiaries of easy money—industrialists, agriculturists, traders have a heavy representation. They do not respond favorably to the minister's first efforts to obtain a tight-money policy; he must wheedle, persuade, and convince them. In the process, he raises high hopes of stemming the inflation rapidly, of getting quick effects. Finally, he gets the central bank directors to go along with his policy—but only reluctantly. The printing presses are stopped, and the quantity of money ceases to expand. Now, however, the lagged effects of past monetary expansions come into play, and the price level continues to move upward, even in the face of a constant stock of money. The central bank directors and the forces they represent become increasingly restive—they cannot obtain more credit even though prices are rising. The central bank board may itself decide to abandon the tight-money policy; or perhaps political pressure from the beneficiaries of easy money may force the minister to resign or abandon his policy. In either case, the failure of the minister to "deliver" on his promise of quick results leads to an early abandonment of the program. With an adequate awareness of the probable importance of lagged effects of prior monetary expansions, the minister could at least have avoided promising something he could not deliver. Of course this would have lowered his chances of getting his program

adopted. Recognizing the importance of lags, it might be wiser for the minister to strive for a gradual tapering-off of the rate of expansion of the money supply rather than an immediate stoppage of the printing presses. This policy would operate gradually to reduce the amount of unspent inflationary force in the economy, and would not produce any abrupt reduction in the real value of the total amount of loans outstanding. From the standpoint of the borrowers from banks, this policy would be far less painful than the policy of abruptly halting the expansion of the quantity of money, and on this account alone I would accord it a far greater probability of success.

14. With respect to the effects of a devaluation on the general level of prices, it should be recognized:

1. that these effects can be very powerful for massive devaluations
2. that these effects, when very powerful, are difficult to offset by fiscal and monetary constraints
3. that these effects appear to be much more manageable for small devaluations than for large ones
4. that when certain conditions apply prior to a devaluation, there may be no effects of devaluation either to raise the internal price level of import-type goods or to raise the prices of domestic goods through substitution away from import-type goods.

Since these conclusions emerge from section III of this paper, they will be developed at further length there.

II. COMMENTS RELATING TO "THE DYNAMICS OF INFLATION IN CHILE"

15. Perhaps my main reason for distributing "The Dynamics of Inflation in Chile" as a background paper was my feeling that one should not preach what one does not practice. I wanted to preach— or, perhaps better, plead—in favor of hard empirical work, and I thought my pleas might be more sympathetically received if they were accompanied by supporting evidence that I had acted on them. I have long been impressed—and not only in Latin America—by the high proportion of total professional energy which is spent in glorified debate between opposing points of view, with only intermittent and casual appeals to evidence, and by the low proportion of total energy spent in the hard work of digging out the facts and organizing them so that they can discriminate fruitfully among alternative hypotheses or theories. I do not mean to argue against theorizing or theoretical controversy as such, nor against "casual empiricism." Anything that can lead a man voluntarily to change his mind is a

useful instrument for the advancement of science, and men can sometimes be convinced by logical argument; sometimes by a demonstration that their assumptions were implausible; sometimes by a demonstration that their model has implausible implications in ways they did not realize before; sometimes by the uncovering or presentation of a single critical fact; sometimes by a simple correlation, etc. But when an argument goes on for years running, with all contenders sticking to their guns, one can probably infer that most of the possible simple ways of convincing one another have been tried and have failed. What is required is more work—both in framing the theory in such a way that alleged effects are susceptible to measurement and alternative hypotheses susceptible to confrontation, and in assembling and processing the data to do these jobs.

16. One of the interesting outcomes of this process is that, very frequently, the simpler versions of opposing points of view are quickly left behind. This certainly was the case with the "Dynamics" paper, where the confrontation of extreme "monetarist" and extreme "antimonetarist" hypotheses resulted in the rejection of them both. Another, almost invariable outcome is that interesting relationships are discovered that were not previously imagined to exist but that require explanation. A case in point from the "Dynamics" paper is the statistical significance of the wage variable in explaining import price changes. No causal connection could be established here, and the timing of the variables precluded the possibility that the import price variable used could have been a causal force leading to changes in the wage variable used. The only plausible interpretation that I could give to these results was that the Chilean government chose to time its devaluations so that they tended to coincide with, or to follow shortly upon, upward revisions in the *sueldo vital*—on the theory that a bitter pill is easier swallowed when accompanied by a sweet one. This interpretation was borne out in the work on house rents, where once again wages appeared to have a statistical influence that could not be explained by direct causation in either direction. Here the bitter-cum-sweet pill explanation applies, because for most of the period which I examined the rent index represented controlled levels of rents; it is reasonable that the government should tend to time its upward adjustments in controlled rents so as more or less to coincide with upward adjustments in the *sueldo vital*.

17. When trying carefully to test hypotheses one also has to make up one's mind as to precisely what is being tested, and this process can have interesting consequences. This is illustrated by the work on the wages-versus-monetary hypotheses in the "Dynamics"

paper. Having been led by the data to reject extreme versions of both hypotheses, I inquired into which of the two types of variables appeared to account for more of the variation in the rate of inflation. I initially thought that this test would tell us, granted that both mechanisms have theoretical validity, which of them in some real sense was the more important. On this interpretation, and discounting as noncausal the apparent relationship between wage changes and changes in import prices and house rents, the monetary hypothesis wins hands down. When monetary variables and wage variables compete to explain the variations in the rate of inflation in Chile, wage changes end up explaining a substantially lower fraction of these variations than do money supply changes, and in many cases wage changes do not appear to have any significant explanatory power at all. But what does this really mean? In particular, is it adequate evidence on the basis of which to say that autonomous wage changes would have no important influence on the price level if unaccompanied by money-supply changes? The answer to this last question is no. The general theory in terms of which the test was framed posits that both wage changes and money-supply changes can affect the price level. The evidence clearly does not reject this theory. Indeed, one can construct examples of cases, within the general theory, in which results such as those observed for Chile are the expected results. And one can also construct cases in which the opposite results—of wage changes explaining more of the variation in the rate of inflation than money-supply changes—are the expected ones. The key distinction between these two classes of cases is the monetary policy of the country in question. "A monetary policy which was generally tight, which yielded at times but not always to wage pressures, and which strongly resisted 'overfinancing' a wage rise, would tend to produce a high partial correlation between wage changes and the rate of inflation. On the other hand, a monetary policy which was generally easy, which tended to finance wage rises even in its tighter periods and to overfinance them by varying degrees in its looser periods, would tend to produce the sort of results we have observed for Chile, of typically higher partial correlations between monetary variables and the rate of inflation than between wage changes and the rate of inflation."[2] The observed results do not call for the rejection of the general theory in terms

---

[2]Arnold C. Harberger, "The Dynamics of Inflation in Chile," *Measurement in Economics: Studies in Mathematical Economics and Econometrics in Memory of Yehuda Grunfeld*, Carl Christ *et al.* (eds). (Stanford: Stanford University Press, 1963), section IV, 7.

of which the experiment was framed, but they say a great deal about what the monetary policy of Chile would have to have been like in order for the theory to remain valid. And appeal to external evidence confirms convincingly that Chile's monetary policy during the period was indeed of the easy-money type which would produce results like those observed, within the framework of the general theory utilized in the experiment.

18. The "Dynamics" paper yielded a number of conclusions which are rather more straightforward than those discussed above. The principal additional findings were:

18a. The lags in the adjustment of the price level to changes in the money supply are significant. For both wholesale and consumer prices, and for most of their main components, we can expect that changes in the money supply between a year ago and six months ago will have a significant influence on price changes in the quarter to come. In the case of house rents, the lags are even longer. This year's change in money supply appears to have virtually no influence on this year's change in house rents, but last year's change in money supply, and the change in money supply during the year before last, both have a substantial influence on the movement of rents this year.

18b. The ultimate total effect of an extra 1 percent increase in the money supply is an extra increase of about 1 percent in all categories of prices; the ultimate total effect of an extra 1 percent increase in real income is that prices will rise by roughly 1 percent less than they otherwise would have done.

18c. If the rate of inflation has been increasing in the recent past—in particular if last year's rate of inflation was greater than that of the year before last—this fact alone will probably produce some extra inflation this year. Conversely, if the rate of inflation has been declining in the recent past, this fact alone will probably make the rate of this year lower than it otherwise would have been; that is, a greater increase in money supply can be absorbed without inflationary consequences than would have been possible if the rate of inflation had been constant in the recent past.

19. When an empirical study has been done for a period ending some time ago (the "Dynamics" paper used data from 1939 through 1958), it is certainly fair to ask how well the results explain later events. The answer in this case is "not very well," but I hasten to add that the simple hypotheses which were rejected in the course of the "Dynamics" analysis do not do very well either. For the year 1959, prices rose substantially more than predicted by the equations

in "Dynamics," and for 1960 and 1961 they rose substantially less than predicted. Three reasons occur to me which may possibly explain these discrepancies.

19a. In late 1958 and early 1959, a tight-money policy was introduced in Chile. Marginal reserve requirements of 50 percent were placed on peso demand deposits, and reserve requirements on time deposits in pesos were raised as well. There resulted a substantial slackening in the pace of expansion of peso deposits, especially so in the case of demand deposits (which are the only kinds of deposits incorporated in the official Chilean money supply series used in the "Dynamics" study). Thus, the official money supply series did not expand greatly in 1959. However, at about the same time as the tight-money policy was introduced in respect of peso deposits, new regulations were introduced which permitted the commercial banks to receive demand and time deposits in dollars, and to make loans in dollars. The ostensible motive for these new regulations was to make it possible for the banks to induce Chileans to repatriate capital which they had invested abroad, by offering the convenience of a hedge against inflation "right here at home," and by offering attractive interest rates on time deposits in dollars. There resulted an expansion of over $70 million in the amount of dollar deposits, which initially had been negligible in magnitude. More than half of this increase represented not repatriation of dollars held abroad but multiple expansion of dollar deposits by the Chilean banking system. The dollar became a sort of second currency in Chile, in which loans, transactions, and deposits were made just as in domestic currency. In a sense, the dollar was "more money than money," for while it satisfied the other motives for holding cash just as well as the peso, it provided a hedge against inflation which the peso did not provide. This is the main explanation that I can offer for the fact that prices rose faster in 1959 than the "Dynamics" equations predicted. If the full increase in dollar deposits is added to the increase in the peso money supply in 1959, the discrepancy between the actual and the predicted rate of inflation is reduced to small dimensions.

19b. In the third quarter of 1959 the tight-money policy was extended to all deposits—time and demand, dollar, and peso. Marginal reserve requirements of 75 percent became the norm for all commercial banks, though exceptions to this rule existed from the beginning and became quite important later on. As a result of this policy there was a dramatic reduction in the rate of inflation between 1959 and 1960, which was only moderately reversed by a slight increase between 1960 and 1961. For the modesty of their inflation, 1960 and 1961 were years without precedent in more than a decade. Readers of "Dynamics" will recall that I there accepted, largely on the basis of Deaver's evidence, the hypothesis that the secular rise in the velocity of circulation in Chile during its great inflation was the product of the inflation itself. People manage to get along with lower real cash balances when they expect inflation to wipe out 20 or 30 or 40 percent of their value within a year than when they are reasonably confident of price level stability. In "Dynamics" (sec. I., 5) I expressed some qualms about the crudeness of the "acceleration" variable which was used to try to isolate the effect of the above-mentioned type of adjustment of cash holdings upon the rate of inflation itself, and I also expressed doubts that the process by which cash holdings were adjusted was sufficiently regular to show up well in an analysis explaining variations in the annual or quarterly rates of inflation as against an analysis explaining variations in real cash balances themselves. Both of these considerations would operate to introduce a downward bias in the coefficient estimated for the "acceleration" variable in my analysis and to reduce its statistical significance. If such a downward bias exists, correcting for it would improve the predictions—certainly for the year 1961 in all cases, and probably for the year 1960 in the cases of the quarterly regressions.

19c. In spite of an inflation of over 30 percent in 1959, and of subsequent price rises amounting to an additional 20 percent or so in 1960–61 combined, Chile was able to keep the exchange rate stable from December 1958 to early 1962. This was accomplished largely on the basis of the very substantial grants and loans which were received from foreign governments, international agencies, and foreign banks and businesses. It is not easy to measure the effect of this exchange stability in moderating the price level increases of 1960 and 1961, but it unquestionably operated in the direction of moderating them. The difficulty of measurement stems from the fact that I was not able to introduce changes in the exchange rate as an explanatory variable for changes in the price level, owing to the existence of multiple exchange rates and a welter of other special devices for the bulk of the period with which I dealt. As to the way in which exchange rate stability can moderate the rate of price inflation, this is simply the converse of the way in which devaluation can cause increases in the general price level. It is to this latter subject that I now turn.

III. THE EFFECTS OF DEVALUATION ON THE PRICE LEVEL

20. In this section I propose to discuss the way in which devaluation can influence the level of prices in the devaluing country. My thinking on this subject has been much influenced by my experience in Chile and Argentina. In Chile there has existed for many years a powerful school of thought which held that devaluation can be expected to have very serious consequences on the level of prices. I must confess that for a long time I tended to minimize this possibility. More recently I have come to modify my earlier views quite substantially. Part of the stimulus which led me to revise my views came from the experience of Argentina in the first half of 1962. During this period the internal price level rose by some 35 percent or more, and the money supply rose by only about 15 percent. It was thus difficult to explain the observed rise in the price level on the basis of the concurrent change in the money supply. It also proved difficult to explain the observed price inflation as being significantly influenced by a lagged response of prices to prior changes in the quantity of money. Casting about for an explanation of the rapid rate of price increase in the first half of 1962, it was hard to overlook the fact that a substantial devaluation had occurred in the early part of the year. The price of the dollar had increased from a level of around 80 pesos to a level around 120 pesos. Faced by this experience, I set out to inquire whether a theoretical structure could be developed which would plausibly explain the devaluation's having had such a profound influence on the level of internal prices. There emerged from this effort a simple model in which, I believe, the main forces are captured in a reasonably orderly way. I do not claim any significant originality in respect to this model for, as will be seen, the concepts incorporated in it have been accepted parts of economic theory for many decades. I rather looked on the model as a device for ordering our thoughts on the subject and for establishing in a fairly rigorous way the conditions under which devaluation can be expected to have a strong, weak, or intermediate effect on the level of prices.

21. I assume that the country in question is "small," in the sense that it has no capacity to influence the world market prices of either its imports or its exports. This means that as a consequence of devaluation, the internal prices of imports and exports will go up in the same percentage as the exchange rate. Thus if imports account for 10 percent of the national income, a rise in the exchange rate of 50 percent would produce, from this source alone, a rise of 5 percent

in the general price level of goods consumed or invested within the country. Likewise, if exports accounted for, say, 8 percent of the national product, a devaluation of 50 percent would, from this source alone, account for a rise of some 4 percent in the price level, of goods produced within the country.

22. Let me here digress for a moment to discuss what concepts of the general price level appear to be appropriate for this sort of analysis. It seems to me that there are at least two concepts which cannot be rejected. On the one hand, one may choose to deal with the price level of goods consumed and invested within a country. This price level would cover imports plus all home-produced goods which were not exported. On the other hand, one could choose to consider a general price level of all goods produced within the country. This would include exports but would exclude imports. The important thing to note is that neither of these general price levels include both exports and imports.

23. In considering the direct impact of devaluation on the price level I have up to now neglected the possibility that import-type goods may be produced within the country and that export-type goods might be consumed or invested within the country. Suppose that import-type goods amounting to 10 percent of the national income are produced and consumed within the country, and that export-type goods amounting to 6 percent of the national income are produced and consumed at home. The prices of both of these classes of commodities will tend to be governed by movements in the exchange rate in much the same way as the prices of imports and exports themselves. If we now attempt to measure the direct impact of a devaluation of 50 percent on the price level of goods consumed and invested internally, we must recognize that goods accounting for 26 percent of total consumption and investment are directly affected by movements in the exchange rate (10 percent imports plus 10 percent import-type goods produced and consumed at home, plus 6 percent export-type goods consumed at home). And if we look at the price level of goods produced at home, we must note that 24 percent of the total will here be affected directly by the rise in the exchange rate (8 percent actual exports plus 6 percent export-type goods plus 10 percent import-type goods produced and consumed at home). We must accordingly expect that, as the direct and immediate consequence of a devaluation of 50 percent, the general price level of goods consumed and invested at home would rise by some 13 percent, while the general price level of goods produced at home would rise by some 12 percent.

24. This "impact-effect" of the devaluation tells only part of the story. As a consequence of the rise in the prices of import-type goods and export-type goods, there will emerge an inducement for the substitution of domestic goods for these other categories. I define domestic goods as those which are neither import-type nor export-type, that is, those which do not enter at all into the international trade of a country. Virtually all the services, all construction, and many other goods with heavy transport costs would fall into this category. To facilitate the exposition which follows, I shall similarly define international goods to include all those goods relevant for a particular general price index whose prices would automatically move in proportion with the exchange rate. For the price index of goods consumed and invested at home, international goods would include imports, locally produced import-type goods, and locally consumed export-type goods. For the general index of prices of goods produced at home, international goods would include exports, locally consumed export-type goods, and locally produced import-type goods.

25. If there is a substantial substitution of domestic goods for international goods, there may result a substantial induced rise in the price level of domestic goods, which may operate to augment the total increase in the general price level attributable to devaluation. Obviously, if the supply of domestic goods is completely elastic no rise in price will occur; the less elastic the supply of domestic goods, the greater will be the effect of devaluation on this class of prices.

26. We must also recognize the possibility that devaluation may have an effect on the level of output of an economy. If there are, at the time of the devaluation, significant amounts of unemployed resources within the economy, there will be significant possibilities for expansion of output. The international goods sector will have a strong inducement to employ additional resources as a consequence of the rise in the price level of international goods. And, to the extent that there is a substantial substitution in domestic demand for international goods, there will be an incentive for the expansion of domestic goods production as well.

27. If the economy is initially fully employed, there can be of course no significant expansion in aggregate output as a result of the devaluation. In this case the incentive to expand output would tend to produce an excess demand for factors of production, which in turn would lead to rises in factor prices. It is highly likely that the general price level will rise more in a situation in which wages are rising than in one in which wages are stable. By the same token, a model which demonstrates the possibility of substantial price

rises even when wages are constant is in a certain sense more "interesting" than a model in which devaluation would have an important effect on the general price level which operated via wages. I shall accordingly assume, in the model which follows, that unemployed resources are available at the prevailing wage rate, that wages are rigid in a downward direction, and that, owing to the existence of unemployment, no serious pressure for upward adjustment of wages emerges as a result of the devaluation.

28. In the model below, I shall take the demand for any class of goods to be a function of the real output of the economy and of the relative price of the class of goods. Given that the price of the principal variable factor of production—labor—has been assumed to be fixed, I shall take the supply of any class of goods to be a function of the absolute price level of that class of goods. The simplest form of the resulting equation system is as follows:

$$(1) \qquad dH^d = b_h(dp_h - dp_i) + c_h dy$$
$$(2) \qquad dH^s = e_h \, dp_h$$
$$(3) \qquad dI^s = e_i \, dp_i$$
$$(4) \qquad dy = dH^s + dI^s$$
$$(5) \qquad dH^d = dH^s.$$

The above system of equations contains the following five unknowns: dH^d, dH^s, dI^s, dy, and dp_h. The change in the price level of international goods, dp_i, is governed by the movement in the exchange rate itself, hence is not a variable to be determined by the system. In setting out the above equations in the form of differentials I implicitly assumed that quantity units of each of the two classes of goods were so chosen that their initial prices were equal to unity. This assumption permits us to consider dp_h and dp_i as percentage changes in the price levels of domestic and international goods, respectively. It also permits us to consider the quantity $(dp_h - dp_i)$ as the percentage change in the relative price of domestic goods. dH^d is, of course, the change in the quantity of domestic goods demanded, and dH^s and dI^s are the changes in the quantities supplied of domestic and international goods, respectively. The choice of units so as to make initial prices equal to unity comes in again in equation (4), where dy can be interpreted as the change in national output valued at initial prices. Equation (5) imposes equilibrium between the demand and supply of domestic goods. This is reasonable, since by assumption these goods are insulated from the international market. It will be noted that there is no corresponding assumption of equilibrium in the market for international goods. In fact, in the five equations listed, there is not even a demand function for international goods. Such a demand function surely exists, and could be written:

(6) $$dI^d = b_i(dp_i - dp_h) + c_i dy .$$

But this equation is not necessary for the determination of dH^d, dH^s, dI^s, dy and dp_h. These five variables, given dp_i, will be determined by the first five equations. Given the values of dp_i, dp_h, and dy thus determined, one can then obtain the value for dI^d, and, using it along with dI^s and dp_i, determine the effect of devaluation on the balance of trade. Since in this particular exercise we are not directly interested in the effects of devaluation on the balance of trade but rather in the effects on the general price level, we can operate with the first five equations alone, leaving (6), so to speak, in the background.

29. Also in the background are some assumptions about monetary policy. We have imposed upon a system the constraint that money wages remain constant. Given this constraint, the system will determine the way in which the level of income and the particular price levels will respond to devaluation. It is highly unlikely that there would be no alteration in the demand for cash balances if income and price levels change. In fact, we may write the function:

(7) $$dM^d = e_m dy + f_m dp_h + g_m dp_i .$$

This can be viewed as a sort of liquidity preference or demand-for-cash-balances function, indicating the change in the demand for cash holdings which would be induced by devaluation, assuming the wage level to remain constant. The assumption about monetary policy underlying the model is that the monetary authorities will accommodate this change in the demand for cash. The monetary authorities in this model operate passively; they do not themselves ignite the fire, but neither do they operate in such a way as to deprive it of oxygen.

We now proceed to the solution of the model.

Substituting equations (2) and (3) into equation (4), we obtain

(8) $$dy = e_h dp_h + e_i dp_i .$$

Substituting this expression for dy into equation (1) and equating dH^d from (1) with dH^s from (2), we obtain:

(9) $$dp_h = \frac{(-b_h + c_h e_i)}{e_h(1-c_h) - b_h} \cdot dp_i .$$

30. Let us first inquire as to the presumptive sign of dp_h. We know that b_h, which measures the effect on demand for domestic goods of a rise in the relative price of domestic goods, will be negative. Since b_h enters in both the numerator and denominator of (9)

preceded by a negative sign, it contributes a positive term to both numerator and denominator. c_h represents the marginal propensity to consume domestic goods; we accordingly expect it to be positive, but less than unity. e_i measures the response of supply of international goods to a rise in their price; it, too, has a presumptive positive sign. The term $c_h e_i$ in the numerator (9) is therefore positive. In the denominator we have e_h multiplied by quantity $(1-c_h)$; both of these have presumptive positive signs as well. We therefore can say that the "normal" result of a devaluation will be for the price level of domestic goods to rise, so long as the conditions underlying our model are met. In the limiting case, where the supply of domestic goods is infinitely elastic, e_h will be infinite, and the expression for dp_h will be zero. Another extreme case obtains when the elasticities of supply of both domestic and international goods are zero. This implies that $e_i = e_h = 0$, and under these circumstances it turns out that $dp_h = dp_i$. This sort of result might indeed occur in an economy in which there was very little short-run mobility between the sector producing international goods and the sector producing domestic goods. However, in reality the international goods sector, containing as it does import substitutes produced at home as well as export-type goods, is likely to be intermingled in the same general labor markets as many domestic goods industries. It is unlikely, therefore, that there would be no resource mobility between sectors, and it becomes interesting to inquire under what circumstances other than zero resource mobility one might obtain a high response of the domestic price level to devaluation.

31.   One way to examine this question is to ask under what circumstances the numerator and denominator of (9) would be equal. It is easy to see that this would happen whenever $c_h e_i$ was equal to $e_h(1-c_h)$. This does not strike me as a very stringent condition. To demonstrate this, let me note that:

$$(10) \qquad e_i = I^s E_i \; ; \text{ and } e_h = H^s E_h \, ,$$

where E_i and E_h are the elasticities of supply of international and domestic goods, respectively. Furthermore, let me assume that trade was initially balanced, so that we start from a position in which $I^d = I^s$, and let me also assume that the marginal propensity to consume international goods is equal to $(1-c_h)$. This last assumption is perhaps less plausible than the others because it implies a marginal propensity to hoard of zero. But it is not downright implausible, since c_h and c_i, though I have for convenience called them marginal propensities to consume, are in fact marginal propensities to consume and invest. Rather than introduce here a lengthy discussion of this, I shall proceed on the basis of the assumptions indicated and then present qualifications later. Using the general relationship between slopes and elasticities, we can write:

$$(11) \qquad c_h = \sigma_h \cdot \frac{H^d}{y} \; ; \; c_i = \sigma_i \cdot \frac{I^d}{y} ,$$

where σ_h and σ_i are the income elasticities of demand for domestic and international goods, respectively. Using the expressions from (10) and (11) we can write:

$$(12) \qquad c_h e_i = I^s E_i \sigma_h \frac{H^d}{y} \; ; \; e_h(1-c_h) = e_h c_i = H^s E_h \sigma_i \frac{I^d}{v}$$

It is evident from these expressions that in order for $c_h e_i$ to equal $e_h(1-c_h)$, all that is necessary is that $E_i \sigma_h$ be equal to $E_h \sigma_i$, assuming that we depart from a position in which H^d equals H^s and in which I^d equals I^s. The condition that $E_i \sigma_h = E_h \sigma_i$ simply states that the income elasticities of demand for domestic and international goods should be proportional to their price elasticities of supply. A high income elasticity of demand for domestic goods operates to induce a strong response of the domestic price level to devaluation. A high price elasticity of supply of international goods operates in the same direction. People are prone, in thinking of Latin America, to jump to the conclusion that international goods have a very high income elasticity of demand. In doing this they had in mind luxury consumer goods, in all likelihood. However, it should be realized that wheat and meat are international goods in the cases of both Chile and Argentina, in the first because they are imported and in the second because they are exported. These commodities are not likely to have very high income elasticities of demand. On the other hand, it should also be realized that those luxury consumer goods whose importation is, in effect, prohibited become domestic goods for purposes of this analysis. Suffice it to say that it is by no means self-evident that the income elasticity of demand for international goods is greater than that for domestic goods. As far as elasticities of supply are concerned, we have less strong grounds for presumption than in the case of income elasticities of demand. It is quite possible that the internal production of international goods would be relatively more responsive to a given percentage price rise than the internal production of domestic goods. The opposite is also possible. I conclude accordingly that, depending on the supply elasticities particularly, one can quite plausibly imagine a situation in which domestic goods prices would rise by the full, or by nearly the full, percentage of devaluation, even though wages were held constant throughout the process.

32. There are a variety of qualifications which should be made to the above line of argument. In the first place, if the marginal propensity to hoard is positive rather than zero, this will reduce the extent of rise of the domestic goods price level associated with any given devaluation. Secondly, if trade is initially unbalanced, with I^d significantly exceeding I^s, once again this will operate to moderate the degree of rise of domestic prices. Finally, even though one cannot establish strong presumptions as to the relative magnitudes of the elasticities of supply of domestic and international goods, what little one can say appears to work in the direction of moderating the responsiveness of the domestic price level to devaluation. In the first place, at least in Latin America, a larger fraction of agricultural products would appear to be in the international goods sector than one would predict on the basis of the over-all ratio of international goods to national output. Since the supply of agricultural products is notoriously inelastic in the short run, we would expect a tendency for a somewhat lower elasticity of supply of international goods than of domestic goods. Secondly, a very high elasticity of supply in any part of the international goods sector would mean that even a small devaluation would produce a large expansion of output in that part. The strenuous efforts which have been made in Latin America to promote import substitution and the development of additional exports would suggest that most possibilities in these directions have already been exhausted, at least as far as short-run effects are concerned. (I should point out here with some emphasis that this is a short-run analysis.) Third, when we consider the possibility of absorbing unemployed resources there are many parts of the domestic goods sector—particularly the services—where such absorption could take place in response to an increase in demand with little or no rise in price, so long as we maintain our assumption that wages do not rise.

33. In Table 1, I present the results of a few calculations showing how domestic prices would respond to a 50 percent devaluation under alternative assumptions as to the key parameters involved. First, however, the method by which the figures are derived should be explained. In a fashion similar to that used in (10) and (11), b_h can be expressed as $H^d B_h$, where B_h is the price elasticity of demand for home goods. Now this, plus the results from (10) and (11), can be substituted into (9) to obtain:

$$(13) \qquad \frac{dp_h}{dp_i} = \frac{-H^d B_h + \dfrac{H^d}{y}\, \sigma_h\, I^s E_i}{E_h H^s \left(\sigma_i \dfrac{I^d}{y} + c_s\right) - H^d B_h}$$

Here we used the identity $c_h + c_i + c_s = 1$, where c_s is the marginal propensity to hoard—that is, the marginal propensity to save minus the marginal propensity to invest. Now we can use equation (5), $H^d = H^s$, to simplify (13) to:

$$(14) \qquad \frac{dp_h}{dp_i} = \frac{-B_h + \dfrac{I^s}{y}\, \sigma_h E_i}{E_h \left(\sigma_i \dfrac{I^d}{y} + c_s\right) - B_h}$$

TABLE 1

RESPONSIVENESS OF DOMESTIC PRICES TO A DEVALUATION OF 50 PERCENT UNDER
ALTERNATIVE COMBINATIONS OF KEY PARAMETERS

Parameters Column	1	2	3	4	5.	6
B_h	$-.2$	$-.2$	$-.2^*$	$-.4$	$-.4$	$-.4$
σ_h	1.0	1.0	1.0	1.0	1.0	1.0
σ_i	1.0	1.0	1.0	1.0	1.0	1.0
c_s	$.05^*$	0	0	0	0	0
E_h	1.0	1.0	1.0	1.0^*	2.0	2.0
E_i	.2	.2	.2	.2	$.2^*$	.6
$\dfrac{I^s}{y}$	.20	$.20^*$	.25	.25	.25	.25
$\dfrac{I^d}{y}$	.25	.25	.25	.25	.25	.25
Results						
$\dfrac{dp_h}{dp_i}$	.48	.53	.56	.69	.50	.61
dp_h resulting from a 50% devaluation	24%	26½%	28%	34½%	25%	30½%

B_h = price elasticity of demand for domestic goods.
σ_h = income elasticity of demand for domestic goods.
σ_i = income elasticity of demand for international goods.
c_s = marginal propensity to hoard.
E_h = price elasticity of supply of home goods.
E_i = price elasticity of supply of international goods.

$\dfrac{I^s}{y}$ = percentage share of international goods production in total output.

$\dfrac{I^d}{y}$ = international goods consumption (+ investment) as a percentage of total output.

Note: In setting up Table 1, I made it a point to change only one parameter at a time, the change being marked by an asterisk between the successive values for that parameter.

34. It remains to establish that the values chosen for the different parameters are of plausible orders of magnitude. First, B_h, the price elasticity of demand for home goods, is given values of $-.2$ and $-.4$. They are rather low values because domestic goods make up a larger fraction of the national income than international goods in most countries, and the only substitution that takes place in this model is between domestic and international goods. The price elasticity of demand for international goods would be three times as high as the price elasticity of demand for domestic goods in a situation such as is assumed in the table, where domestic goods accounted for three quarters, and international goods for one quarter, of the total consumption and investment.[2] Thus these assumptions imply a price elasticity of demand for international goods of $-.6$ (when $B_h = -.2$) and -1.2 (when $B_h = -.4$). These strike me as pretty well spanning the plausible range for this elasticity. σ_h and σ_i were set at unity throughout. Since, broadly speaking, the income elasticities of all goods have a weighted average equal to unity (with a small qualification where the fraction of income saved varies as income varies), I chose to set them both at this average value. It cannot be an implausible order of magnitude. Setting C_s at .05 reflects a marginal propensity to save of .10 to .15, from which must be deducted something for the marginal propensity to invest. As can be seen from a comparison of the results in columns 1 and 2, changing C_s from .05 to zero doesn't much affect the results; nor would changing C_s from .05 to .10. In setting E_h substantially higher than E_i, I followed a course consciously biased against obtaining a large effect of devaluation on the price level of domestic goods. I was not so much aiming at "most plausible" estimates as trying to be sure that my estimates were not implausible in a certain direction. In the first four columns E_h is five times E_i, in the fifth column it

---

[2] For a derivation of these relationships see my paper, "Some Evidence on the International Price Mechanism," *Journal of Political Economy*, Vol. LXVI, December, 1957, p. 514. The relationships apply in an exact way when the price elasticities considered contain a substitution effect only. This is the case in the model being examined. The first order of income effects of a rise in domestic goods prices are to reduce the real income of people in their role as consumers of domestic goods and to raise correspondingly the real income of people in their role as producers of domestic goods. No net loss is involved. Similarly, under our assumption that the foreign currency prices of its imports and exports are unaffected by the actions of the country in question, a devaluation represents a loss to consumers of international goods which returns as a benefit to the domestic producers of international goods. Some very minor adjustments in the relationship may, however, be warranted when the country starts from a position of unbalanced trade. But these adjustments would not affect the orders of magnitude indicated.

is ten times E_i, and in the sixth column it is $3\frac{1}{3}$ times E_i. I arbitrarily maintained $\frac{I^d}{y}$ at .25 throughout the table. The change in $\frac{I^s}{y}$ from .20 to .25 can therefore be regarded as a change from unbalanced trade (an import surplus equal to 5 percent of the national income) to balanced trade. These figures appear to me to span a plausible range of values for the trade balance as a percentage of national income.

35. I find the results of Table 1 quite striking. Innocent-looking values of the parameters lead to rises in the price level of domestic goods averaging, over our examples, more than half the percentage rise in the price of foreign currency. And it should be recalled that in these examples the general price level of goods consumed and invested would be weighted 25 percent with international goods and 75 percent with domestic goods. The percentage rise in the general index associated with a 50 percent devaluation would be between 30½ percent (from column 1) and 38.4 percent (from column 4) for all the situations covered in Table 1.

36. Certainly one must conclude from this analysis that devaluations can have very substantial effects on the level of prices—not only through their "impact effect" on international goods prices, but also through their effect in raising income and in inducing the substitution of domestic for international goods. The strength of the effects obtained in Table 1 is all the more surprising when it is recalled that our model holds money wages constant throughout the process.

37. It is certainly possible that at some times and places policymakers may want to do something to limit the substantial price-level effects of devaluation which our model suggests can quite plausibly occur. We accordingly now inquire into what they might do. In the first place let us recognize that the rises in internal prices predicted by our model are not necessarily "all bad." Except in cases where the elasticity of supply of a class of goods is zero, rises in the price of either good are associated with rises in its output. However, if the economy is operating at or near full employment, the effects which in our model come out as increased product would in that model be largely reflected in increased wage rates and in still greater increases in the general price level than our model predicts. So we probably should not place too great faith in the rises in output that our model would predict, and we probably should also consider the predictions of price level change coming from our model to be particularly conservative as full employment is approached. These con-

siderations lead us back to the question of what can be done to limit the price-level effects of a devaluation.

38. Since this is basically a Keynesian model, let me frame the answer in Keynesian terms. Domestic goods prices rise because demand for them has increased; to hold down the price rise we must hold down the rise in demand. A suitable policy instrument to achieve this purpose is taxes. I shall incorporate taxes into this model in the simplest way possible—by defining the change in disposable income as $(dy - dT)$, where dT represents the change in taxes. dT is a policy variable, but not exclusively so; tax receipts can change simply because income changes, with the policymakers doing nothing. But policymakers can intervene to push tax receipts up or bring them down to the sort of magnitude that they, the policymakers, believe that taxes should have. For simplicity, I shall continue to treat dT as a policy variable in this sense.

The model (1)-(5) is now altered by making:

$$(15) \qquad dH^d = b_h(dp_h - dp_i) + c_h(dy - dT) .$$

The general solution for dp_h now becomes:

$$(16) \qquad dp_h = \frac{(-b_h + c_h e_i)\, dp_i - c_h dT}{[e_h(1 - c_h) - b_h]} .$$

Equation (16) is identical with (9), except for the addition of the term $-c_h dT$ in the numerator. It is therefore possible to ascertain, for given values of the key parameters, what effect a given change in taxes would produce.

39. I find especially interesting the case where it is desired to use taxes to offset entirely the effects of devaluation on the price level of domestic goods. In this case the solution is:

$$(17) \qquad dT = \left[\frac{-b_h}{c_h} + e_i\right] dp_i .$$

Using the same procedure as was used in deriving (16) from (9), we obtain, from (17):

$$(18) \qquad \frac{dT}{y} = \left[\frac{-B_h}{\sigma_h} + \frac{I^s}{y} E_i\right] dp_i .$$

This expresses the required change in tax receipts as a percentage of national product. There are three effects involved. $\dfrac{I^s}{y} E_i$ represents the effect of increased output of international goods upon demand for domestic goods. Since there can be no change in output of domestic goods unless their price changes (except in the limiting case of an infinite supply elasticity), the increased output of the international goods sector also represents the change in y; the second term in the bracket in (18) thus reflects the fact that the larger the change in income operating to increase demand for home goods, the larger will be the tax rise necessary to offset it. In the first term, the $-B_h$ in the numerator reflects the fact that the demand for home goods will increase more as a result of substitution away from international goods, the more price-elastic is the demand for home goods. The σ_h in the denominator reflects the fact that the higher the income elasticity of demand for home goods, the lower will be the rise in tax receipts required to achieve a given reduction in demand. σ_h does not appear in the second term because, in effect, it works both sides of the street. A high income elasticity will mean a greater rise in demand for home goods as a result of a given rise in income; but it will also mean a greater cutback in demand for home goods from a given rise in taxes. These two effects of a high σ_h nullify each other in the case of the second term of (18).

40. We may now evaluate the expression for $\dfrac{dT}{y}$ for the six sets of parameters used in Table 1. The fraction of national product that would have to be raised by increased taxes in order to maintain constant the price level and the output of domestic goods in the face of a 50 percent devaluation is as follows for columns 1–6 of Table 1, respectively:

$$12\%, \quad 12\%, \quad 12\tfrac{1}{2}\%, \quad 22\tfrac{1}{2}\%, \quad 22\tfrac{1}{2}\%, \quad 27\tfrac{1}{2}\%,$$

Obviously these are substantial magnitudes. They simply reflect the other side of the coin from our earlier results. If devaluation by itself provides a big stimulus to the demand for domestic goods, it probably will take a pretty big sedative to offset the stimulus. This is what we are finding here. I see no plausible ground for altering the parameters of column 1 to obtain a result for $\dfrac{dT}{y}$ lower than 12 percent. I would be reluctant to raise the income elasticity of demand for home goods significantly above 1.0; this parameter could not in any event get higher than 1.33 in our example, unless international goods as a group had a negative income elasticity, which is absurd. I would not feel easy, given the accumulated evidence of multitudes of demand studies, pushing B_h to a lower absolute value than .2. A figure of .25 for $\dfrac{I^s}{y}$ seems to me to be fairly close to the truth for several Latin-American countries, and I would be reluctant to change it. In fact, I would suspect it to be around .25 in the larger countries, and perhaps still greater in the smaller countries, which have greater relative dependence on international trade. We are left with the assumed value of .2 for the elasticity of supply of international goods. Even reducing this to zero, while maintaining the other parameters as in Table 1, would mean that 10 percent of the national income would have to be raised in extra taxes in order to offset the effects of a 50 percent devaluation just on the price level of home goods.

41. It appears that Latin-American countries are probably going to have to go on living with "inflationary" devaluations, for I cannot imagine any country in Latin America which would be able, let alone willing, to accompany a 50 percent devaluation with a tax increase amounting to 10 or 20 percent of the national income. Given this alternative, the prospect of domestic goods prices rising by 25 or 30 percent does not seem so bad. And trying other alternatives to fiscal policy—such as, for example, monetary or credit policy—would probably lead to similar frustrations. The impulse given by a major devaluation to the domestic goods price level is simply too strong to be countered by measures that are less than heroic.

42. What can be done about it? The model of this section was framed on an assumption which I feel has been fairly descriptive of the cases of several Latin-American countries during long periods. This assumption is that the internal price level of international goods moves with the exchange rate. The internal price level of international goods will (so long as tariff rates do not change) move with the exchange rate so long as people can freely import at that exchange rate, paying whatever tariff duties may apply to the merchandise imported. But in a circumstance where foreign exchange is seriously rationed at the going exchange rate prior to devaluation, there may be no price-level effect of devaluation at all on the prices of import-type goods. Let us suppose that the amount of foreign exchange being allocated among importers was simply the proceeds of normal exports—say, $100 million. If, at the going exchange rate, there is demand for substantially more than $100 million of foreign exchange, then the scarcity value, inside the economy, of imported goods will be greater, and probably substantially greater, than $100 million times the official exchange rate. If a devaluation occurs, and the same $100 million are now made available at a higher price, some reallocations may occur among the buyers of foreign exchange, but there is no reason to expect that the internal price level of im-

port-type goods will be any higher than it was prior to the devaluation. In the long run, the price level of import-type goods may even fall as a consequence of devaluation, as exports respond to the devaluation incentive and bring in more foreign currency to be allocated among demanders. This sort of price fall as a consequence of devaluation could, however, only emerge if the devaluation raised the price of foreign currency by less than the amount necessary to completely clear the market for the existing ($100 million) rate of export earnings.

43. The reason there are no import price level effects of devaluation in the case discussed in the preceding paragraph is that the price level effects have all occurred before the devaluation took place. To see this, let us start at a time when the internal scarcity values of imports are equal to foreign currency values times the official exchange rate. Now let demand for imports increase, or exchange proceeds fall, and let a system of licensing be introduced to distribute the available foreign exchange among demanders, with the government selling foreign exchange to the licensees at the same official rate as before. The price level of imported goods will obviously creep up in this circumstance (though not necessarily all individual product prices), and there will also be induced a substitution of domestic for the imported goods whose internal prices have risen. If this procedure of licensing of foreign exchange goes on, as demand for foreign exchange at the old official rate continues to increase while supply is stagnant, the internal price level of imported goods can get arbitrarily far "out of line" with the price level computed by applying the official exchange rate to the foreign currency prices of imports. And with each successive rise in the price level of import-type goods, there will be induced successively more local production of this class of goods, and progressively more substitution of purely domestic goods for import-type goods, with the same sort of effects on the domestic price level as are induced by the way a devaluation operates on import prices.

44. In the case discussed in paragraphs 42 and 43, devaluation still has an effect on the prices of export type goods, and on the domestic goods price level through substitution of domestic goods for export-type goods consumed at home. What can be said here is that even when a case is chosen which appears on the surface to reveal little connection between devaluation and the internal price level, some connection is likely to remain on the export side, and the connection which apparently was absent on the import side has just worked in a different way: instead of devaluation leading the price

change, here we have a price change leading to a disequilibrium, which ultimately could force such a step as devaluation to be taken.

45. If this discussion has any hopeful conclusion, it is that the effects of small devaluations on the price level are undoubtedly easier to cope with than effects of large devaluations. This is not because the derivative dp_k/dp_i has lower values for small than for large changes, but because the organs of policy can cope with a 5 percent devaluation (implying, say, a 2½ percent price rise if not offset, and an extra tax of 1 percent of national income if offset) much more easily than they can handle a 50 percent devaluation (implying, say, a 25 percent price rise if not offset and an extra tax of 10 percent of the national income if offset). Devaluations can be taken in frequent small doses rather than infrequent large ones, and there are other arguments which suggest the wisdom of this course. Just to suggest two of these arguments:

45a. In resource allocation, it is, by and large, relative prices that count. A policy which attempted to keep the relative price of foreign exchange stable in the face of an internal price inflation would undoubtedly be wiser, from the standpoint of resource allocation, than a policy which tended to keep the nominal rates of exchange constant for long periods of time, and which was periodically forced by the cumulative rise of internal prices to take the step of massive devaluation.

45b. I have often wondered what are the nightmares that plague central bankers. One good candidate for this nightmare class is the dream in which the Latin-American central banker remembers all the exchange rates that he defended almost to the last dollar of foreign-exchange reserves, only to have to yield the fort, and then to struggle manfully to build up reserves until once again it became possible to defend another, higher, equally untenable rate with valuable reserves. Etc., etc.

8. COMPARATIVE ANALYSIS OF LATIN-AMERICAN COUNTRIES: II.

a. COMPARATIVE ANALYSIS OF POLICY INSTRUMENTS IN MEXICO'S EXPERIENCE

Alfredo Navarrete

In order to reach an "optimum economic policy," the real alternatives of action in terms of the political feasibility and practical implementation of policy instruments must be sufficiently identified, analyzed, and weighed by the responsible public officials at the time of decision. Let me tell you about the experience of my country as I have observed it from inside the policymaking and executive machinery of the Mexican government for the past 20 years.

First, whether you were or were not a "structuralist" in 1934, a credit and financial policy had to be decided upon in order to carry out Mexico's first development plan of six years. The plan contained as major targets: the accelerated redistribution of land of the still-remaining feudal latifundia and the rapid industrialization of the country. Could we have established at the time either direct-income taxation or an indirect-expenditure tax system? Experience has shown that a modern tax system requires a modern administration to go with it. And this you cannot invent or produce overnight. Could we have resorted to a nonexistent capital market or could we have appealed directly for the voluntary savings of the wealthy, opposed as they were to the revolutionary program of agrarian reform?

This is to give you a clue as to why my country, in order to finance the agricultural and industrial development programs, resorted, at that time, to an ample overdraft on the government account with the central bank. This action contributed to a 14 percent average annual rate of inflation in the late thirties and early forties. The peso was twice devalued, from 2 to 3.60 pesos per dollar and from 3.60 to 4.85 pesos per dollar.

Second, whether or not you were a "monetarist" at the time, you had to realize, during the decade initiated in 1940, that the second world war meant the curtailment of imported industrial supplies and that the income expansion connected with increased exports of strategic raw materials was imposing a strain on food supplies.

The industrialization drive received a strong impulse from the substitution of imports. But this meant importing the equipment and machinery for the industry in question; importing, likewise, some basic raw materials, replacements, and parts; in sum, what I termed in my Harvard dissertation, 15 years ago,[1] a "production effect" of economic development on the balance of payments. But besides this effect, two additional effects had to be added. The machinery and equipment had to be installed, which required roads of access to the site, buildings for the new factory, and housing, market, and water facilities for the laborers. These so-called local expenditures amounted to nearly as much as, if not more than, the value of the imported machinery. Following this first injection of fresh purchasing power came the multiplier reaction, all of which resulted in the "income-effect" of economic development on the balance of payments.

And how do you get trained laborers to operate modern machines in an underdeveloped country? Well, like walking, you learn by walking. This means that you hire inefficient unskilled laborers and expect that they soon will become skilled. Unit costwise you produce dearer than do the efficient industries in the more developed countries. If you wish from the start to operate with skilled workers, you have to draw them from their relatively well-paid present employment, and this requires raising the prevailing wage rates in order to attract them, so that cost of production per unit of output is again affected upwards. We have also to bear in mind that the underdeveloped local market usually precludes lower costs derived from economies of large scale. All this was the "price-effect" of economic development on the balance of payments. Adding the three together: production, income, and price effects, I arrived at a hypothesis as to why in Mexico, short of full compensatory measures—either reduced internal consumption, or increased external savings, or a combination of both—there was . . . during the period analyzed . . . an inherent balance of payments instability in the process of internal economic development, given the lack of

---

[1] Alfredo Navarrete, "Exchange Stability, Business Cycles and Economic Development: an Inquiry into Mexico's Balance of Payments Problems, 1929–1946." (Written 1948, deposited Harvard University Archives, May, 1949.)

rapid structural changes in domestic output and voluntary savings and in export levels and their composition. Mexico devalued again to 8.65 pesos to the dollar in 1949 and to our present rate of exchange of 12.50 pesos per dollar in April of 1954.

Third, whether or not you are a monetarist or a structuralist, you had better try to be a common sense "down-to-earth" economist. Since 1954, Mexico has increased significantly its fiscal burden. Federal tax revenue at present accounts for 10 percent of national income, although considering local governments, the social security contributions of workers and business, and the surpluses of official enterprises, overall public receipts so-defined reach 16 percent of national income. The securities market has rapidly expanded and now channels and finances at least 15 to 20 percent of domestic investment. The rate of inflation has diminished to a 6 percent annual average from 1953 to 1960. But we have had four years—1959, '60, '61, and '62—with a less than 5 percent rate of increase in prices. We keep on trying to increase even further the federal revenue and to attain significant surpluses in key industries of the public sector. The volume of internal credit has doubled in the last four years. Exports of industrial goods have expanded (textiles, bulk chemicals, cement, and steel). We used to import food. Now we are self-sufficient. Economic development has been maintained at a 1½–2 percent rate of growth of real per capita income[2] and we have had exchange stability for nine years.

Since this rate of growth is below the 2½ percent annual average rate set as a target for this decade under the Alliance for Progress —agreed among the governments of the American republics under the Charter of Punta del Este—we are aiming for a higher rate of growth of aggregate output, with a meaningful betterment for the majority of the rural and urban labor force, by both raising the level of investment and structuring its composition so as to provide an adequate share in the social field (education, introduction of potable water and electric power to far-off communities, as well as roads, irrigation, and drainage). In addition to increased domestic savings, we expect to count on an adequate volume of external funds, mainly long-term, low interest credits, to help balance the financial accounts with the real output and welfare targets, con-

---

[2]For the sophisticated, these price and output rates of growth show that the price elasticity of output has been roughly one, although we have said very little as to the role of price expectations in the process of investment under inflation and as to the shifts in financial assets among wage earners, profit recipients, and the government that it entails.

sidering the not too favorable balance of payments outlook in relation to the required expanded investment program. In this connection, I wish to emphasize that the thinking of business and government people in the more advanced economies has to become oriented more toward the growth needs of backward economies, especially as regards providing them access to their markets (and I refer to the European common market, the European Free Trade Association and the great Anglo-Saxon market).

From the foregoing remarks it appears to me reasonable to conclude that the analysis of price rises associated with economic development is one problem, and that the role which inflation may play as a weapon of policy to attain or accelerate growth is a separate problem. As to the latter, it seems to me that in the absence of ready and adequate tax systems and capital market to provide the necessary financing for launching and sustaining a well-oriented investment program, inflation may serve for a time as a weapon to exact the needed higher volume of savings; but certainly its usefulness wears off and inflation eventually becomes self-defeating as it encourages consumption in the private and public sectors alike. Further, every structuralist action has a financial implication and every financial decision should consider its possible structuralist effect. Let us beware of generalizations or would-be panaceas from either source. In Mexico we have resolved the structuralist-monetarist controversy in a pragmatic way. This implies that there can be no structuralist justification for sheer monetary mismanagement and fiscal irresponsibility, but it also means that financial decisions have to be closely geared to sensible policies in the field of investment, productivity, and economic development.

b. ARGENTINA'S INFLATIONARY EXPERIENCE (1943–1962)

Javier Villanueva

I

Inflation has accompanied the economic experience of many Latin-American countries. Some of them have known it for long periods of their history, others have become familiar with it in more recent times. Argentina belongs to the latter group of countries. Its inflationary experience, which started soon after the second world war, is still a cause of major concern among the policymakers of the country.

Concern regarding inflation is reaching a climax in Argentina. Other countries of Latin-America have been showing great worry about the same problem. The intensity of this wave of concern may be due in part to the general feeling that under the mask of inflation major political issues are hidden and, in part, to the fact that the stabilization of prices is one of the elements considered of paramount importance in the policy kit offered to Latin-America in exchange for financial assistance to overcome recurrent balance of payments difficulties. It is reasonable to suppose that in previous times policy makers did not flatly ignore inflationary problems but rather chose to adopt permissive attitudes, considering inflation an undesirable side-effect of policies thought to be necessary. This type of attitude perhaps resembles that of those who accept unemployment as a regrettable outcome of a stabilization program.

II

Within the span of time from 1943 to 1962, Argentina has witnessed a cycle of changes in matters of social and economic organization.

Perhaps a fruitful angle of study would be to envisage the economic experience of Argentina in these 20-odd years as a continued process of response to the challenges put forward by a set of persistent constraints that delimitated the area within which economic decisions had to be taken.

Through the years, even under different leadership, the economic restrictions facing policy makers remained about the same. This is particularly so from 1949 on, a year in which a short-lived period of wider margins of choice abruptly ended. The straight forward elimination of the restricting conditions has either not been carried out or has been only timidly attempted. The corresponding alternative has been consistently evaluated as too costly. It is interesting to note that policy makers have instead chosen to explore several of the combinations allowed within the limits of the given unbending parameters.

III

The fundamental borderlines that set the territory within which economic choices have been taken are:

1. *Unfavorable terms of trade* that made it necessary to accelerate exports so as to at least stand still in imports.

2. *Rigid agricultural supply* which made it necessary for governments to watch relative price trends in order to maintain certain levels of incentives for the rural sector.
This was certainly a difficult task in view of the downward inflexibility of industrial prices. The situation being still complicated by the fact that, even with favorable relative prices, agricultural supply response proved to be very slow.

3. *Internal consumption,* which competes with foreign markets in regard to use of exportable goods.

4. *A developing industry* needing capital equipment and an abundant supply of imported inputs in order to maintain its activities.

Unbalanced growth, resulting from points (1) and (2) has tended to be expressed by price rises in the agricultural sector. Politically influential labor unions, pressed by food price increases, sought and obtained nominal wage increases. These increases in wages were passed on to the public in the form of industrial price increases, thus sending upward the general price level. Undoubtedly, rigidity of industrial margins and a slowly progressing productivity in the same sector are conditions for such a process to take place.

The agricultural sector did not respond to price signals with production increases, possibly because of institutional rigidities, old fashioned systems of production, the system of property ownership, and fluctuations in relative prices.

In effect, relative prices tended to fluctuate due to the reasons previously advanced. The sequence may be described as follows: (1) a rise in agricultural prices; (2) a rise in food prices; (3) a rise in money wages; and (4) a rise in industrial prices. At the end of the cycle the advances in relative prices gained by the agricultural sector are eliminated. In order for relative prices to be again set in favor of the farm sector, new increases in food prices must take place, thus again setting the merry-go-round into operation.

IV

Within the framework of the above mentioned restrictions, administrative reactions with respect to inflation have varied considerably in Argentina. During the years 1943–55, with a centrally controlled economy, the government grew more and more self-conscious about the inflationary pressures which plagued the country. However, with the exception of the period 1953–54, in which strong and successful stabilizing efforts were made, the administration adopted, in general, permissive policies.

During the years following the "Revolución Libertadora" (1955) inflation was perforce only one among the many problems that a transitory administration, such as it was, had to cope with during such a period of social and political readjustment.

It was only in the last months of 1958 the stabilization became the axis around which the program of the government in power worked. Paradoxically, the years from 1958 on coincide with the most intense inflationary pressures of the whole postwar era: in 1959 the cost of living index reached the highest average relative yearly increase since 1943.

Critics of such a program concur in pointing out that one of its major weaknesses was to rely on conditions that were absent in the economy. For example, it is cited, the program called in vain for a readily available supply of alert and flexible entrepreneurs who could respond promptly to price signals, thus facilitating the desired process of reallocation of resources.

No quarrel will be started here with these critics in connection with the fact that "stabilizers" assumed too much from national reality; however, it is our impression that in the short run the greatest burden of their program relied more on international than on national conditions. In this scheme, the mobilization of local investment was probably considered subsidiary to the mobilization of international capital.

Perhaps the basic resolution to be made was whether economic development was to be entrusted exclusively to domestic capital or whether foreign capital was to be given an important role. The first alternative was probably discarded because it would have implied institutional arrangements which were considered either undesirable or difficult to implant without drastic changes in the organization of the country. The second and more palatable alternative was chosen: development was to be attempted with a predominance, in the short run, of foreign private capital rather than foreign public capital. It is reasonable to suppose that foreign contributions were assigned two principal roles:

1. To contribute to the formation of basic capital equipment in order to leave export proceeds free to be used in the acquisition of raw material imports necessary to maintain a sustained growing import-competing industry;

2. To stimulate the economy, and to help in the process of reorientation of national resources by creating external economies.

A fundamental condition for the success of the program was that foreign capital pour in at a reasonably fast rate and in considerable amounts. The task of attracting foreign contributions was left principally to a stablization program, a free exchange mechanism, and the possibility of abundant profits.

More than a desired end in itself, stabilization seems to have been predominantly a device to overcome risk aversion on the side of foreign investors. In accordance with the program, restrictive wage and monetary policies were applied.

New attitudes with respect to negotiation with foreign oil companies, plus the settlement of a long-standing dispute between the American and Foreign Power Company and the Argentine government and a law of December, 1958, allowing unlimited repatriation of capital and profits, were all signals destined to overcome the doubts of possible foreign contributors. The case was, however, that foreign private contributions, even if noticeably larger than in previous years, did not flow in as expected. Moreover, foreign investment did not have the calculated freeing effect over foreign exchange proceeds, since in many cases they had a high import content. A well-known case is that of the automobile industry, whose expansion during the years 1959–60 meant substantial increases in imports.

Foreign investment entered Argentina under law 14.780 of 1958, and during the years 1959, '60, and '61 represented only 6.7 percent of the average gross domestic investment.[3]

More important, perhaps, in magnitude than private foreign capital entries were the amounts made available to the country for stabilization purposes in the form of short-term loans. These types of loans necessarily gave flexibility of maneuver in the immediate subsequent years.

At the end of 1958, the country received, in short-term loans, about 329 million U.S. dollars, and for 1959, 300 million.[4]

The stabilization program produced an excess supply of manufactures and a reduction in employment. The devaluation of 1959 at the same time sent prices upward, but internal absorption of exportables was not restricted in the expected degree. Even though relative prices favorable to the agricultural sector increased 12.2 percent from 1958 to 1959, agricultural production (agropecu-

---

[3]Private foreign investment followed a classical tendency of this type of contribution from the point of view of geographical location; Greater Buenos Aires and the Province of Buenos Aires absorbed 48 percent of the total amount invested by foreign private companies. The U.S. contributed independently about 40 percent and had a part in the contribution made by associations of countries, Switzerland being the second largest single investor.

[4]IMF, U.S. commercial banks, European commercial banks, the U.S. Treasury.

aria) rose only 1.8 percent. Export increases in 1959 were also small. The development of an extrabank internal credit with high interest reoriented available funds in the direction of nonessential industries. Thus, in many senses the program was not a success.

The central difficulty to overcome was that in order to attract foreign capital, a stabilization program was needed. But the conditions which the economy was facing made it difficult for stabilization policies (deflation, devaluation) to survive for long. And long-standing stability was required if foreign investors' doubts were to be overcome.

In 1962, foreseeing the imminent necessity of devaluating the peso again, and in view of the fact that the stabilization plan had to be maintained even though it had unpopular repercussions, the government sought to obtain a greater popular backing. In the attempt to obtain it, a political crisis was touched off which finally toppled the administration.

c. INFLATION AND STABILIZATION PROGRAMS: THE CHILEAN EXPERIENCE

Tom E. Davis

I. INTRODUCTION

Chile's long experience with inflation, interspersed with abortive stabilization programs in 1895–98, 1925–31, 1951–52, 1956–57, and 1960–61 has given rise to a substantial literature, too extensive and variegated to be summarized here.[1] One characteristic of this writing is the considerable divergence among authors with respect to their interpretation of the cause of the persistent Chilean inflation. The terms "monetarist" and "structuralist" evolved in Chile as labels for the two categories into which alternative explanations were classified. Widely disparate views necessarily were given a common

---

[1] See the references in the Grunwald and Felix papers in this volume and in my forthcoming article in the *Journal of Political Economy*, "Eight Decades of Inflation in Chile, 1879–1959—A Political Interpretation."

label by such a restrictive system of classification.[2] Consequently, the search for a common denominator—a proposition to which all monetarists or all structuralists would agree—had to be conducted in most elementary terms.

II. THE MONETARIST VIEW

A proposition that could well serve as a common denominator for monetarists would be: (1) that secular inflation cannot persist without secular increases in the money supply (at rates in excess of the rate of increase in the output of real goods and services) and (2) that inflation cannot be halted over a prolonged period without limiting the rate of expansion of the money supply (to correspond approximately to the rate of growth of aggregate output). This common denominator, however, does not succeed in differentiating the monetarist from the structuralist; the structuralist would not deny the validity of the proposition, but would simply argue that monetary expansion (in excess of the growth in real output) is a *proximate* and not a *fundamental* cause of inflation. The problem, according to the structuralists, is to explain *why* the money supply continually outsprints the growth of real goods and services in the system.

An answer, acceptable to many a monetarist and *fundamental* in terms of his conception of the limits of economic science, is that the central bank sets the upper limits to the growth of the money supply. With respect to the U.S. economy, the monetarist's reply virtually exhausts what can meaningfully be said on the subject, even by those not constrained by self-imposed limitations upon their field of investigation. Even a political scientist or a cultural anthropologist could not shed additional light, in all probability, for the structuralist, on the fundamental causes determining the rate at which Mr. Martin ordains that our money supply shall grow—for no less an expert than James Tobin has referred to the Federal Reserve System as an independent source of political power, a latter-day "fourth estate."

In the Latin-American context, however, if not elsewhere, the central bank is an integral part of the machinery of government and subject to the outcome of the political process. Thus, the structuralist justifiably feels "fobbed-off" when told that the failure of the latest stabilization program was due merely to the fickleness or perfidy of the head of the central bank (probably already a political suicide as a result of support given to the stabilization program).

[2]During the conference, a rather involved nomenclature evolved that permitted each participant to describe concisely his particular position.

III. THE STRUCTURALIST VIEW

Trying to find a unique common denominator for the structuralists is not easier than for the monetarists. The unifying proposition would probably be that in Latin-America supply schedules generally, and foreign exchange in particular (due to highly adverse "terms of trade"), are substantially less elastic than those in more developed countries. However, few, if any, monetarists have taken issue with this assertion; and one suspects that the majority of monetarists would agree that, coupled with a continually changing structure of demand, such inelasticity of supply schedules might account for persistent inflationary pressures, if it be further assumed that a "ratchet effect" (perhaps in the form of "administered prices") prevents declines in the prices of factors for which demand had fallen, producing politically unacceptable unemployment in the absence of monetary expansion.

While the monetarist might accept these assumptions as a valid explanation for the "creeping" inflation of the 2–3 percent per annum type, or even expand the range to 5–10 percent per annum in the Latin-American context, he understandably balks at the notion that these same factors account for inflation that in Chile has proceeded at an average rate in excess of 25 percent per annum over the past three decades. A structuralist reply is that these *fundamental* factors set in motion the pure wage-price spiral which determines whether the economy experiences an inflation of the 5, 30, 50, or 80 percent variety. But nothing is more evident than the fact that the inflation in Chile, as elsewhere in Latin America, is of the "repressed" type, with controls over the key prices in the economy, especially interest rates, exchange rates, and public utility prices, and is far from what Sir Roy Harrod has referred to as "pure wage-price spiraling." The controls have been imposed precisely for the purpose of redistributing income via the inflationary mechanism, in order to benefit the dominant political groups at the expense of the politically inert.[3] Thus, the Chilean

---

[3]Elsewhere I have contended that:

. . . greater monetary stability presumably would benefit the following groups: the export industries (since the permitted increase in the price of foreign exchange usually fails to keep up with the rise in domestic factor prices); the smaller firms in important and reasonably competitive industries, such as food processing, textiles, leather products, and wood products, which firms obtain direct access to bank credit only at a positive real interest rate; and finally the unorganized laborer and the self-employed person in small-scale industry and agriculture, who bear a disproportionate burden of the generally regressive inflation tax. The explanation for the failure of these groups to constitute a

inflation is far from neutral, not simply a tax on cash balances resulting from pure wage-price spiraling, but rather a conscious policy that constitutes a common "second-best" for:

. . . the conservatives (that) have the power to block increased direct taxation; the Radicals and the Left (that) have sufficient power to block any attempt to reduce the real wages of government employees and organized labor permanently; . . . (and) the private sector (or at least the larger firms) . . . (that have) sufficient power to insist that loans to the (larger firms in) the private sector expand *pari passus* with those to the government.[4] Stabilization programs are politically feasible only when it appears to these groups that inflation might conceivably "get out of hand"; but opposition reappears when the rate of inflation has been reduced to what historically seems to constitute "safe" levels.

IV. THE TACTICS OF STABILIZATION

If the inflations characteristic of Latin America were pure wage-price spiraling, and not repressed inflations, there might be considerable merit, or at least little latent political dynamite, in Sir Roy Harrod's and Professor Lutz's suggestion that, in attempting to implement a stabilization program, the authorities employ the "shock" (or perhaps better, Schacht) tactic of immediately curtailing, rather than gradually reducing, the rate of expansion of the money supply. Since the pure wage-price spiral would presumably have had little impact upon the distribution of income or allocation of resources in the economy, why delay the inevitable! This argument, a hallmark of orthodox monetarism, depends completely upon the diagnosis that the inflation is of the predicated type—pure wage-price spiraling. If the inflation is of the repressed

---

political force proportional to their numbers or to the fraction of total output contributed by their efforts is rather obvious. These are the foreign and the migrant, the unorganized and the unlettered, the distant (from the capital) and the remote (from urban centers). A government that would attempt to rely upon such a fragmented base for support in implementing a stabilization program and thereby alienate the "middle sectors," would immediately be threatened by the totalitarian extremes. Tom E. Davis, *op. cit.*

[4]Davis, *op. cit.* Even with the subsidies implicit in loans at negative real interest rates, the return to investment in Chilean corporations actively traded on the Santiago Stock Exchange have not exceeded the return on comparable investments in the United States. Nor, apparently, has the vast expansion of the public sector or the creation of an ambitious social security system increased the real wages of public employees. See *Economic Developments in South America* (My testimony in Subcommittee on Inter-American Economic Relationships, Joint Economic Committee, 87th Cong.) (Washington, D.C.: U.S. Government Printing Office, 1962), pp. 7–9 and Appendix A.

type, the more drastic the restriction in the rate at which the money supply expands (and the shorter the period in which inflation is halted), the more painful will be the adjustments to be made by the dominant political groups that previously benefited from the repressed inflation. Consequently, it should come as no surprise that the shock treatment has led to acute political unrest where attempted in non-Schachtian political systems and is strongly resisted by Latin-American governments of a "democratic" character.

Monetarists would undoubtedly settle for a gradual approach to stabilization if such a tactic increased the prospects for eventual success. The short-lived Chilean stabilization programs of 1951–52, 1956–57, and 1960–61 certainly provide little encouragement on this score. This same disillusioning experience, however, virtually compels Chilean politicians to hope that the monetarists are incorrect in their assertion that inflation and economic growth are incompatible, and to grasp at the more hopeful structuralist notion that if governments in Latin America concentrate their attentions upon structural problems, especially land, tax, and educational reforms, the resulting higher rate of economic growth may militate against the inflationary pressures that have proven so intractable politically in the context of virtually stagnant economies.

d. SOME OBSERVATIONS ON THE BRAZILIAN INFLATION

Werner Baer and Isaac Kerstenetzky

Observing the data available concerning the Brazilian inflation in the dozen years up to 1961, and the changes in the structure of the economy, it becomes obvious that the experience of this country will require economists to do some new thinking about economic relationships during an inflationary process.

The basic facts are that Brazil has had a high rate of inflation since the early 1950's (averaging 25 to 30 percent), the rate rising in the later period, but, at the same time, the average real growth rate was between 6 and 7 percent, being higher in the later than in the earlier years. In 1961, the rate of growth actually reached 7.7 percent.[1]

During the postwar period fixed capital formation as a proportion of GNP did not vary much, averaging 15 percent at the beginning of the 1950's and also in the early 1960's. This implies a high and even rising output-capital ratio, which is an interesting phenomenon because in the latter 1950's and early 1960's the proportion of infrastructure capital formation was rising, and one associates this type of investment with a falling output-capital ratio. No rigorous study of this phenomenon is yet available.

Although foreign capital contributed to the growth of real income through increasing balance of payments indebtedness and direct investment, there can be no doubt that a substantial share of this growth was due to domestic savings. Foreign financing was never above 20 percent of total investment and was usually substantially below this proportion. Domestic capital formation was characterized by a rising share of the government sector, the proportions being 59 percent for private and 41 percent for government investment in 1950, while in 1960 the proportions were 55 and 45 percent, respectively. Since private capital formation as a proportion of GNP is smaller than private savings as a proportion of GNP, it would seem that government capital formation was partially financed by private savings. This was achieved, especially in the latter part of the period examined, by a process of forced savings.

How much evidence is there of such a forced savings process, a process in which inflation redistributes claims on real resources from the consuming sector to the investment sector, and/or from one part of the investment sector to another part of it? On the surface, it would seem that no such event occurred, because the remuneration of labor as a proportion of total income increased from 41 percent to 47 percent in the period from the late forties to the early sixties. But these shares represent income before taxes. The largest proportion of Brazilian tax revenue, more than 60 percent, comes from indirect taxes. Although there does not exist at present a study of tax incidence, it can be stated with confidence that the principal burden of indirect taxes falls on the lower income groups. Taking this into account and observing that indirect taxes as a share of income increased from 11 percent to 19 percent in the years from the late 1940's to the early 1960's, that is, by a larger

---

[1]The source of the data used in these comments is the Fundação Getulio Vargas' National Accounts Data, which are published every March in the *Revista Brasileira de Economia*.

amount than increases in labor's share of pretax income, one could claim that evidence does point to an actual diminishing of labor's share in the national income during the long inflationary period, especially during the latter fifties and early sixties. Although the share of interest payments and rents remained almost constant during the postwar period, at 1 and 4 percent respectively, profits increased from an average of 8 percent to an average of 11 percent in the middle fifties, falling again to 9 percent in the late fifties.

Unfortunately, a distribution of income according to various types of income groups is not available for agriculture. National income data for agriculture are only presented on a net output basis, making distributional estimates impossible. The share of agricultural income of national income, in current prices, has remained roughly 27 percent throughout the postwar period. This was due partly to the government support program of coffee and to the fact that agricultural production has lagged behind the growth of industrial production, and especially of the growth of the urban population, which resulted in the turning of the internal terms of trade in favor of agriculture. The latter was not as damaging to capital formation as it could appear. Due to an archaic agricultural distribution system, the agricultural producers have benefited little from the more favorable terms of trade. It is the middlemen who have profited the most and it is quite plausible that their windfalls have been invested in industry rather than in the agricultural sector.

For inflation to perform its role of forced savings, there must be some lag between wages and prices and/or between the prices of different types of goods. Some indication of this is given by the legal minimum wage which is readjusted at different time intervals. In the greater part of the fifties there was a definite lag in the adjustment of minimum wages to price changes. This is clear from the accompanying table. The much more frequent readjustments in the last few years, and the fact that adjustments have been faster than price changes, are taken to mean that inflation has lost its forced savings aspect. This is doubtful. First of all, no one knows precisely the impact on the wage structure of minimum wage revisions. Secondly, it can be shown that in the last few years, for certain areas where a sample of wages has been attempted, the gap between the minimum wage and wages above this minimum has been diminishing. Between 1946 and 1957 the real minimum wage increased by 166 percent, while the real median wage in manufacturing increased by only 21 percent. Finally, it can be shown that during the postwar period price increases have not coincided so much with minimum wage changes as with changes in the salaries of government employees.

We would like to pause briefly at this stage in order to venture a hypothesis. A forced savings type of inflation can only occur in a society where some income groups, especially the wage-earning sector, are not strong enough to maintain constantly a certain share of the national income. This does not necessarily mean that per capita incomes in real terms will have to fall, but rather that a greater proportion of the increment of the national product will go into the capital formation sector, via private or governmental investment, than into consumption. The greater the proportion of the economy not yet part of the monetary economy, the greater will be the weakness of the wage-earning sector in maintaining its share during an inflationary bout and, also, the greater will be the flow of new migrants from the nonmonetary sector to the urban sector. It takes a certain length of time for a newcomer to the money economy to become sophisticated enough to protect himself thoroughly against inflation. This might explain the relative success of forced savings through inflation in Brazil. A large part of its population is still illiterate and living in the nonmonetary sector but every year new migrants come to the cities. The disappearance of the cultural lag is slow enough for many of these new groups to fall behind during the inflationary process.

It has been claimed that one basic distortion resulting from the Brazilian inflation has been the increasing participation of the government sector in the economy. We very much question this argument. A good claim can be made for the view that increased government participation, especially in the infrastructure sector, was an inevitable trend in the economy bound on accelerating its development. Furthermore, it can be argued that for a government bent on increasing its participation in the investment sector but faced with an antiquated and weak fiscal system which it will take a long time to modernize, inflationary finance is the fastest way of achieving its aims. Distortions might indeed have existed in the government sector, but as a result of wrong types of government investment decisions rather than the participation per se of the government sector.

To sum up, we are convinced that the forced-saving mechanism played a definite part during the inflationary period of the last dozen years. In the earlier period, it was the private sector that mainly benefited from lags inherent in this process, while toward the later fifties and early sixties it was mainly the government that financed its increased investment expenditures through inflationary methods.

A comment is also called for concerning the degree to which the inflation was responsible for any general investment distortions.[2] The evidence available suggests no obvious drastic distortions. First of all, in Brazil, there has been no relation between the rate of inflation, or changes thereof, and the investment proportion, which has been fairly constant. Secondly, a recent study of changes in the structure of capital formation between the late forties and late fifties shows that relative increases have occurred in the manufacturing and transport sectors rather than in construction and similar inflation-hedge sectors. There is also no general evidence of any out-of-proportion rise in apartment-building and other housing construction in the fifties or early sixties. Thirdly, except for coffee, there has been no increase in the proportion of inventories, as is evidenced both by national accounts data and by data of the balance sheets of the principal industrial corporations. And the rate of change of inventory accumulation has absolutely no relation to the changes in the rate of inflation. Finally, if, with all its weaknesses, one takes the output-capital ratio as an index of the country's investment efficiency, one finds that this ratio has risen from the early fifties to the late fifties and early sixties, despite the fact that in the latter period the infrastructure content of investment was higher. Again, with all its deficiencies, this would indicate an increased productivity of investment in the midst of an increased rate of inflation.

Our aim was not necessarily to defend the Brazilian inflation, but rather to show that the concomitant high rate of economic growth and other unconventional phenomena give the economist a lot to think about and place certain easy generalizations about inflation in question. In an arbitrary fashion one can divide the Brazilian inflation into three parts. First, there is the completely unnecessary part which is due to wasteful spending on the part of government (overstaffed bureaucracies, etc.). Secondly, there is the part played by certain structural bottlenecks, such as the lag in agricultural production and the antiquated agricultural distribution system which helps to push prices up. And thirdly, there is the forced savings part (due in part to a backward fiscal policy

---

[2]Baer, W., "Brazil: Inflation and Economic Efficiency," *Economic Development and Cultural Change*, July 1963, pp. 395-406.

mechanism), in which the private investment sector and, especially, the government sector appropriate, through inflationary policies, a large portion of the increment in the national product for investment purposes.

TABLE 1

Rio de Janeiro, GB—Real Minimum Wage, 1940–62

Years	Minimum Wage Cr. $	Cost of Living 1940 = 100	Real Minimum Wage (1940 Prices)	Index Real Minimum Wage	Annual Change
1940	240	100	240	100	
1941	"	111	216	90	− 10.0
1942	"	123	195	81	− 9.7
1943	380	136	279	116	43.1
1944	"	153	248	103	− 11.1
1945	"	179	212	88	− 14.5
1946	"	208	183	76	− 13.7
1947	"	254	150	63	− 18.0
1948	"	263	144	60	− 4.0
1949	"	274	139	58	− 4.1
1950	"	299	127	53	− 8.6
1951	"	335	113	47	− 11.0
1952 (January)	1,200	356*	337	140	198.2
1953	"	450	267	111	− 20.8
1954 (July)	2,400	550*	436	182	63.3
1955	"	679	353	147	− 19.0
1956 (August)	3,800	834*	456	190	29.2
1957	"	954	398	166	− 12.7
1958	"	1,094	347	145	− 12.8
1959 (January)	6,000	1,234*	486	203	40.1
1960 (October)	9,600	2,106*	456	190	− 6.2
1961 (October)	13,440	2,912*	462	193	1.3
1962†	"	3,816	352	147	− 23.8

Source: Instituto Brasileiro de Economia (Fundação Getulio Vargas).
*Monthly index
†January–November average

9. COMPARATIVE ANALYSIS OF POLICY INSTRUMENTS

a. MONETARISTS, STRUCTURALISTS, AND IMPORT-SUBSTITUTING INDUSTRIALIZATION: A CRITICAL APPRAISAL

David Felix

The monetarist-structuralist debate is more than the Latin-American version of the international dispute concerning the efficacy of monetary controls in stabilizing the price level. It also involves a deep disagreement over the ability of the price mechanism to bring about a socially acceptable rate of growth and distribution of income in the Latin-American context. Finally, the temperature of the polemics tends to be heated by mutual accusations of political bias to a higher degree than is characteristic of professional debates elsewhere. The interweaving of these three issues accounts for some of the murkiness of the monetarist-structuralist debate. This paper deals, however, with only the first two issues.

The practical focus of the debate has been whether the package of policies—credit constraints, devaluation, the elimination of exchange and price controls, and related measures—invoked in a number of Latin-American countries in recent years to halt inflation would succeed, and, if so, whether success would be at the expense of economic growth. These programs have generally been undertaken under the aegis of the International Monetary Fund, in that the IMF has insisted, as a condition for granting stand-by credits, on the setting of limits to the rate of credit expansion, unification of the exchange rate, and complementary measures.[1]

---

[1]For tactical reasons, the specific terms of the agreements are not publicized, so that it is not possible, except on the basis of "inside knowledge," to know the precise range of commitments nor the degree of flexibility permitted in carrying out the commitments. It is clear, however, that as the going got more sticky, the authorities tended to push credit expansion beyond agreed-upon limits and to fudge on other commitments, and that the IMF was often forced to accede, albeit reluctantly.

It is evident that the IMF's ability to impose terms has depended in good part on the willingness of U.S. governmental lending agencies, with their more ample resources, to make the granting of credits contingent on an IMF agreement being reached. Such collaboration was the rule during the Eisenhower administration, but under Kennedy's Alliance for Progress the two suppliers of credit have tended at times to part company, and as a result the IMF's leverage has been weakened.

It is by now evident that the stabilization programs have been largely unsuccessful, particularly in the larger Latin-American countries. In Argentina, after a period of exchange rate stability between May, 1959 and March, 1962 and of near price stability between January, 1960 and March, 1961 (there was an 8 percent rise in the cost of living in this period), the dam broke, and by 1962 accelerating inflation and exchange depreciation were again underway. A similar, if as yet less dramatic, denouement also occurred in 1962 for the Chilean stabilization program.[2] In neither country, moreover, was there a sustained rise in the growth rate during the stabilization period. Uruguay is at this writing still maintaining its exchange rate, but without the price stability and export expansion needed for long-run support. Peru, with moderate inflation and a stable exchange rate anchored in expanding exports, is apparently the one important victory in the array of partial or total defeats.

Events seem, then, to have given the debating cup to the structuralists. But was this because the stabilization programs miscalculated political limits, or because they were economically misconceived? Would the Argentine and Chilean programs have succeeded if the authorities could have held on a bit longer or turned the screws a bit tighter? It is the contention of this paper that the basic fault lay elsewhere, that the programs were simply not reallocating resources in the *directions* needed to create viable growing economies. This seems to have been due to excessive confidence in the efficacy of the price mechanism and to a failure to take account of the adverse effect of the import-substituting pattern of industrialization followed by Argentina and Chile on the structure of consumer demand and on the capacity to import.

[2]The Chilean effort has had two phases. The first stabilization plan (the so-called Klein-Saks program, after the Washington consulting firm which drew up the plan and advised the Chilean government) was instituted in late 1955, and was patently running down by 1958. A second effort followed in December, 1958 under a new presidential regime. The Argentine program was begun in January, 1959.

The first defect has been a central part of the structuralist critique, but the second has not.[3] This paper is, thus, also a partial critique of standard structuralism. It is, however, structuralist in spirit, and its policy suggestions share the greater catholicity in the choice of policy instruments which is characteristic of this school of thought.

THE IMF STABILIZATION PROGRAMS AND THEIR RATIONALE

Two features of the IMF-sponsored stabilization programs should be emphasized at the outset. The first is that credit tightening was only one of a composite set of measures designed to achieve exchange and price stability and to stimulate the rate of growth. The second is that the programs were premised on the explicit awareness that supply rigidities were retarding the growth rate. These rigidities were, however, considered in large part the consequence rather than the cause of inflation. That is, they could in effect be classified into two types: "distortions," engendered by price expectations built up during the long inflation, and supply inelasticities which were the result of "distortions" in the structure of relative prices due to controls.

The first type refers to inflated business inventories, luxury construction, and similar manifestations alleged to be associated with inflationary expectations. In fact, it is not at all easy to sort out behavior due to inflationary expectations from that related to more enduring socioeconomic determinants. Inventorying in poorly integrated economies relying heavily on long distance imports is bound to take a larger share of investment than in advanced economies.[4] Babylonian excesses have been more conspicuous in

---

[3] *Inflation and Growth,* the valuable five-volume mimeographed study prepared by the Economic Commission for Latin America for the Rio Conference on Inflation and Growth, in particular the sections on the Argentine economy (Vol. IV) and the Chilean economy (Vol. V).

[4] A. S. Shaalan finds that in 1953–59 underdeveloped countries put twice as large a percentage of their gross investment in inventories (exclusive of agricultural surpluses) than did advanced countries. In addition, he finds an *inverse* correlation in his sample group of underdeveloped countries between the average rate of inflation and the percentage of inventory accumulation in gross domestic investment. He does, however, find a positive correlation for some Latin-American countries, including Chile, between rises in the rate of inflation and increases in the inventory percentage of gross investment. ("The Impact of Inflation on the Composition of Private Domestic Investment," *International Monetary Fund, Staff Papers,* Vol. IX (July, 1962), pp. 243–63.)

The latter relationship for Chile is supported by a recent analysis of the asset structure of a sample of large Chilean firms, which also indicates that inventories rose more when the rate of inflation rose. See Instituto de Economía. Universidad de Chile, *Formación de Capital en Las Empresas Industriales* (Santiago, 1961), p. 124, Table III.

Caracas, where there was until recently virtually no inflation and easy importation of more mobile forms of conspicuous consumption, than in the residential and commercial construction in and about Santiago or Buenos Aires, where neither condition has prevailed. It is not clear how much the stabilization programs hoped to alter such behavior, although attacks on luxury housing, of course, made good public relations material for the programs.[5]

The second type of "distortion" referred primarily to overvalued exchange rates, underpriced public services, and underpriced agricultural prices. That is, an inadequate capacity to import, power and transport bottlenecks, and a poor growth rate of agricultural output were explicitly recognized, just as in structuralist analysis, to be key points of strangulation. The "over- and under- pricing" viewpoint, however, assumed that there was an attainable set of equilibrium prices which would remove these bottlenecks.

In reality, it was much less a matter of removing price controls, despite some loose usage, than of trying to change the relative position of controlled prices. This was obvious for public utility and transport rates. But the same also was true of the exchange rate. For while the full goal of the programs was the establishment of a single stable rate in place of multiple rates, to be held by orthodox pegging operations, in actuality it was only the form rather than the substance of exchange control which changed. After the initial devaluation and formal unification of the rate there was less stress on quantitative import controls. But the shifting of goods between a permitted and a prohibited list of imports in order to protect industry and to meet foreign exchange pressures was one of the important tools of foreign exchange policy. In place of a formal structure of multiple rates, import deposits and other temporary surcharges and direct controls on invisible transfers were also varied in a discriminatory manner to achieve the same two objectives. In Argentina, in addition, export taxes were selectively reduced on occasion to encourage exporting, although reduction was limited by the importance of these taxes in the federal budget.[6] Only when these methods failed, and exchange

---

[5]Construction fell drastically during the Klein-Saks period in Chile, generating high rates of unemployment among construction workers. The drop, however, was due in good part to cutbacks in public works and the general slowdown of economic activity. There was a similar decline in construction during the first year of the Argentine stabilization program, which seems also to have been due in large part to similar causes. In the second Chilean effort, construction rose at the outset from the extremely depressed 1958 level as a result, in part, of a more active public works program.

[6]They were the third most important source of tax revenue. Compare Bank of London and South America, *Quarterly Review*, January, 1961, pp. 116–22.

reserves plus the availability of new stabilization credits were patently inadequate, was the exchange rate allowed to fall once more. Severe and unexpected declines in international prices for the major exports did complicate the effort of the Klein-Saks program of Chile to attain an "equilibrium" exchange rate. Copper prices fell from an average of $0.44 per lb. in 1955 to a low of $0.247 in 1958. But no such declines disturbed the other two efforts. During the second Chilean effort, begun at the end of 1958, copper prices rose moderately, the average for the three subsequent years being slightly below $0.30 with little annual variation.[7] Moreover, annual export volume of the foreign owned mining sector in 1959–61 averaged 10 percent higher than in 1955–58. Similarly, Argentine export prices and terms of trade were moderately higher during 1959–62 than in the previous three years.

Apart, therefore, from special difficulties for the Klein-Saks effort from falling copper prices, the common problem for all three stabilization attempts was to limit the general rise of domestic prices in the private sector while bringing about a relative rise of agricultural prices, as well as of controlled prices, sufficient to remove the critical bottlenecks in supply.[8]

The first part of this problem was met primarily by efforts to

---

[7] London price for electrolytic copper. See Banco Central de Chile, *Boletín Mensual*, April, 1962.

[8] The stress put by protagonists on the favorable effects which the removal of domestic price controls in the private sector would have on the structure of relative prices is difficult to fathom. In the first place, such controls as were applied were weakly enforced. At most they had a short-run delaying effect, which in shortage economies subject to severe speculative flurries is probably justifiable.

Secondly, they did not alter the direction of movement of relative prices which excess demand conditions suggested would take place. In Chile, for example, agricultural prices rose 1.32 times more than industrial prices during the prestabilization period 1940–55. During the subsequent six years of progressive decontrol, it was industrial prices which, interestingly enough, rose the more rapidly. (See ECLA, *op. cit.*, Vol. V, p. 57; and for the more recent period the components of the wholesale price index in Banco Central de Chile, *Boletín Mensual*, April, 1962.) In Argentina also, except for the short period in the late 1940's when a strong effort was made to hold agricultural prices, they rose in 1949–59 almost 1.5 times more than industrial prices, with the relationship reversing direction in 1960 and 1961. (See ECLA, *op. cit.*, Vol. IV, pp. 44, 53.)

Thirdly, after formal decontrol the governments continued to use informal pressures to restrain price increases. In Chile, for example, the government decreed decontrol but threatened to restore controls unless industrialists held the line on prices. To check retail price increases, consumer committees were organized to publicize establishments guilty of raising prices. Probably these methods were about as effective as the previous price controls in restraining price increases.

restrict the expansion of credit to the private sector and of money wages. In Chile, during the Klein-Saks period the rise in money wages was held down by utilizing the already existing pattern of legislated annual wage adjustments, but restricting the increases to a fraction of the previous year's rise in the cost of living. This policy, however, ran into increasing opposition, so that the fraction was back to unity in 1958. The subsequent Chilean stabilization effort also began with a fractional adjustment in 1959, with the fraction forced upward in subsequent years by labor unrest and political pressures. In Argentina the principal device used seems to have been a tougher policy toward unions on the part of the government. However, this, too, ran into increasingly heavy sledding.[9]

The second part of the problem would, it was hoped, be solved by an elastic response of the private sector to more profitable opportunities to export and to increase agricultural production, to be supplemented by a greater inflow of private foreign investment which more stable prices and exchange rates would hopefully induce. The transportation and energy bottlenecks would, it was recognized, take more time to resolve, since they required heavy investments by the public sector. While these could be met in part by long-term loans from the IBRD and other foreign sources, the noninflationary financing of such investments would also require a substantial current account surplus in the public sector through cutbacks in current expenditures and increases in tax revenues, as well as higher rates for public services.[10] Thus fiscal reform and a cutback of current budgetary expenditures were key elements in the stabilization programs. However, to bridge the

[9]According to an informed observer, while labor relations in Argentina had shown "remarkable stability" in the "face of a substantial reduction in real wages in 1959 and 1960," there were significant signs by the end of 1960 of "a more militant attitude of trade unions indicating that the working classes are not prepared to accept any further reductions in their standard of living." (Bank of London and South America, *Quarterly Review*, January, 1961, p. 113.)

[10]A relatively quick response was achieved in Argentina in removing the heavy drain on foreign exchange from petroleum imports. The state petroleum agency was authorized to open up oil reserves to foreign firms, who were guaranteed remunerative prices for all their output and liberal profit transfer rights. Domestic oil production rose rapidly as a result, so that Argentina by 1961 was largely self-sufficient in crude petroleum. However, the longer-run gain in foreign exchange savings from the reduced outlay on the import of petroleum products is being partly offset by the substantial profit transfers which the foreign contracts entail. In point of fact, many of the contracts were made in 1958 before the formal initiation of the stabilization effort, but they were clearly consistent with the economic philosophy motivating the stabilization program.

interval required to achieve such reforms and to promote the expansion of the private sector, short-term credits were obtained from the IMF, various U.S. and European governmental agencies, and foreign banks. These were to meet budget deficits in a noninflationary manner as well as to amplify imports and sustain capital formation during the critical adjustment period.[11]

Tactics differed on how rapidly to attempt the relative price changes and the retrenchment of governmental current expenditure. The Klein-Saks program took the most gradual approach, perhaps as much because of governmental foot-dragging as from the original intent of the program advisors. The second Chilean effort tried to make many of the adjustments more speedily; the exchange rate adjustment in 1959 was particularly abrupt. The Argentine effort was the most abrupt of all, setting off a spiral of prices and wages in 1959 during which wholesale prices rose 145 percent and real wages fell by about 25 percent.[12] The last two efforts, however, were each followed by about three years of exchange rate stability and a shorter period of near price stability, while the Klein-Saks effort, bedeviled by falling copper prices, never achieved even this brief triumph. Nevertheless, since all three efforts ultimately failed, the most evident lesson to be drawn seems to be that differences in timing were probably unimportant in explaining the ultimate failure of the efforts.

REASONS FOR THE FAILURE OF THE STABILIZATION PROGRAMS

Why did the programs fail? It is quite arbitrary to single out any one of the propagating factors, to use ECLA's terminology, as responsible. The collapse of exchange rate stability in all three cases did set off a more rapid price rise. But in each program the exchange rate came to be held up by drawing on foreign credits and exchange reserves long after rising prices had already wiped out the initial cost-price gap created by devaluation.[13] The rise in

---

[11]They are the main reason why the Chilean balance of payments deficit on current accounts, which was negligible during the early 1950's, rose to 27 percent of gross capital formation during the Klein-Saks period (1956–58) and to 22 percent in 1959–60. See UN, *Yearbook of National Accounts Statistics, 1961,* section on Chilean accounts.

[12]ECLA, *op. cit.,* Vol. IV, p. 41; Vol. III, p. 126.

[13]The exchange picture is currently most critical for Argentina. Despite a number of earlier debt renegotiation agreements, the short-term external debt obligations (five years or less maturity) of the central bank and government were reported in Fall. 1962 as follows:

domestic prices, in turn, can be attributed alternatively to wage pressures or to budget deficits which forced an expansion of the money supply and thus permitted the upward adjustment of wages and prices. But, since wages had substantially lagged behind prices during the earlier phase of the stabilization efforts, it seems uncharitable to blame the workers for resisting further cuts in real wages. Similarly, rising prices and the disappointingly low rate of growth of output and employment undoubtedly made it more difficult to cut back public employment or to resist raising badly lagging public salaries. Hence one of the key elements in the failure to create a current account surplus was the inability to slow markedly the increase of current expenditure. In particular, initial gains in public transport and utilities tended to be lost through rising operating costs.

The failure significantly to increase tax revenues can be less easily dismissed in this manner. A larger tax bite would not have generated widespread destitution among the Argentine or Chilean higher income classes, particularly during a period when their relative and absolute position had significantly, if temporarily, improved. However, given the slow longer-run growth of income in the private sector, resistance to increased taxation was understandably sharpened. Moreover, the substantial increase in taxes needed for stabilization would probably have led initially to a further curtailing of private construction, reduced employment in some of the more sumptuary domestic industries, and an increase in the relative importance of the public sector which would run counter to the economic philosophy of the managers of the stabil-

---

1962	$ 277,200,000
1963	384,500,000
1964	459,700,000
1965	318,500,000
1966	246,500,000
Total	$1,686,400,000 (U.S. dollars)

In addition the external debt of the private sector, chiefly short-term, was reported as $283,700,000, while the long-term external debt (maturity of over five years) was reported as $751,600,000. (Bank of London and South America, *Quarterly Review*, October, 1962, p. 216.) This is even more serious in the light of the fall of central bank gold and foreign exchange reserves from a high of $705 million in the first quarter of 1961 to $215 million in the third quarter of 1962, and average annual exports in recent years of $1,000,000,000. Moreover, profit transfers from the foreign petroleum contracts and the increased inflow of private direct investment in 1958–61 are now generating an additional service demand for foreign exchange.

ization program.[14]   Hence, despite the commitment of the programs to budget balancing (apart from foreign loans for capital expenditures), there was a general dragging of feet on tax questions.

How does one break through this circle? Leaving the tax question to one side for the moment, the most promising entry is via the slow growth achieved during the stabilization efforts. Actually, growth declined markedly from the prestabilization rates only during the Klein-Saks period, and even in this case the decline had already set in during the preceding quinquennium. In the second Chilean effort, the growth rate in 1959–61 was about equal to that of the Klein-Saks period, while in Argentina output and employment fell absolutely in 1959, recovered in 1960–61, with the average over the three years only slightly below the sluggish rates prevailing in the preceding decade. What this meant, however, was that in none of these cases did the economy respond to the apparent opportunities opened up by the wage lag, devaluation, and foreign credits, either with increased exports or with a sustained rise in domestic output.[15]

The General Structuralist Explanation

The failure of the programs to overcome the sluggishness of the postwar Argentine and Chilean economies strengthens the view that the major rigidities are deeper-rooted than had been assumed by the monetarists, and were causes rather than results of inflation. Of these, two are singled out by the structuralists as, in effect, primordial: the slow growth of agricultural output and the limping capacity to import. The first is attributed primarily to institu-

---

[14]This was particularly the case in Argentina, where *smithianismus* had gotten a new lease on life as a reaction to the Peron era. In Chile, however, there has been a marked shift in emphasis to public investment since 1960. This seems to have been due partly to the disappointingly slow growth of the private sector, but it was also impelled by reconstruction needs resulting from the earthquake of May, 1960. The change of heart, however, has not yet affected tax policy.

[15]The moderate increase in exports in the foreign-owned mining sector in Chile during the second stabilization effort had relatively little to do with the stabilization programs. The firms of this sector are not required to return their foreign exchange receipts to the central bank or government except as needed for local outlays on labor and materials or to pay taxes. Local nontax outlays have averaged less than 30 percent of sales in the postwar period, so that devaluation can only have a modest effect on production costs of these firms. Moreover, as taxes, which since 1955 have been levied on profits, take up a larger percentage of sales receipts, the modest gains from lowered production costs as a result of devaluation are partly offset by increased tax payments.

tional defects in agriculture, the second to unfavorable trends in world primary products markets.[16] The consequences of these two rigidities on output and inflation can be rather summarily treated, since their analysis is by now a familiar feature of economic development literature in Latin America and elsewhere.[17]

Briefly, in a closed economy, with money wages and industrial prices rigid downward, prices will rise if the growth of her capita income times the income elasticity of demand for food exceeds the rate of growth of food production per capita. Since the income elasticity of demand for food in poor countries is likely to be quite high—on the order of 0.5–0.6—a slow rate of growth of food production per capita (in Chile the rate has been negative over the past 25 years) limits the noninflationary increase in aggregate output per capita to perhaps twice the rate of growth of food output per capita. There is, moreover, a redistributive effect if the noninflationary limit set by the food supply is exceeded, since food outlays take up a larger share of working-class than of upper-class budgets. Thus money wages are likely to react to rising food prices, generating a wage-price spiral. In other words, excess demand inflation in the agricultural sector becomes cost inflation for the rest of the economy.

Opening the model to bring in the capacity to import makes it more realistic, since underdeveloped economies depend on imports for some of their consumer goods including food, much of their industrial materials and fuels, and most of their capital goods. With the income elasticity of demand for imports greater than unity, cost pressures are felt via import shortages and rising import prices when the capacity to import grows less rapidly than domestic output. These shortages and rising prices, however, also provide opportunities for import substituting industries to develop, although this development will be associated with a rising price level.

The model now becomes more complex and can take off in various directions, depending on the relative growth of food output and the capacity to import, the nature of the labor market

[16]However, in the case of Argentina, whose exports are predominantly agricultural, the inadequate capacity to import in the 1950's has been related to agricultural supply rigidities as well as to the unfavorable trend in world agricultural prices. See ECLA, *op. cit.*, Vol. IV, pp. 10–21.

[17]The food-price relationship is explored in considerable detail in Geoffrey Maynard, *Economic Development and the Price Level* (London; Macmillan & Co., 1962). See in particular Chapter III. The other is part of the well-known Prebisch thesis. Both are elaborated upon in ECLA, *Inflation and Growth*.

and wage pressures, the rate of growth of productivity in industry, etc. For example, if we separate the industrial enterprise sector from the household sector, it will be noted that the redistribution effect of substituting domestic production for consumer imports works against the higher income households in whose budgets such consumables take up a larger share than in working-class budgets. The extent to which this is compensated for by profits received as owners of industrial enterprise depends on wage and productivity trends in the industrial sector and on the dividend policy of corporate enterprises. For example, in Argentina and Chile real wages in corporate industry prior to the stabilization efforts seem to have risen at least as fast as man-hour productivity,[18] although workers in smaller enterprises and in services fared much worse. Profits of the Chilean corporate sector tended downward in the 1950's, and firms resorted to progressively higher profit retention to finance inventory and fixed capital formation.[19] The fact that household savings turned negative in Chile during the 1940–55 inflation may, therefore, be due at least in part to the redistribution effect of import-substituting industrialization, rather than to the supposed depressing effect of inflation as such on the propensity of households to save.

Thus, whereas in the closed model there is a strong presumption that the share of wages will fall and the aggregate savings rate will rise as a result of inflation, in the open model there is no firm basis for such a presumption. In point of fact, the wage share was quite stable in Chile during the 1940–55 inflation, tending downward only during the subsequent stabilization period.[20] In Argentina there was a remarkably large rise in the wage share during the late 1940's, the share subsequently sagging somewhat and then falling rapidly in 1959 to the early postwar level. In both countries the savings rate declined in the 1950's.

Industrial growth, however, may still proceed fairly rapidly despite unaccommodating wage movements, as long as there is a large margin of consumer imports to be compressed and foreign exchange to be diverted to import-substituting industries at subsidized rates. Thus inflation and exchange discrimination in favor

---

[18]For Argentina, see ECLA, op. cit., Vol. III, p. 130, graph 2. The short period fluctuations in the relationship have been quite substantial, so that it is possible to claim an up- or down- trend, depending on the choice of dates for measuring the trend.

[19]Instituto de Economia, op. cit., pp. 110–11, 166–69.

[20]The reference is to the Klein-Saks period. I have not seen any income shares data for the more recent period.

of industry may for a time raise the growth rate of the economy beyond what would occur from a policy of monetary constraints designed to keep the rate of growth from upsetting price and exchange rate stability. But as consumer imports contract toward an incompressible minimum, the ability to divert foreign exchange to the industrial sector falls correspondingly, although such diversions to new industries may still occur at the expense of the older ones. And since inflation is unable progressively to depress the wage share, industrial capital formation and economic growth decline. This is the stage which Argentina and Chile had reached by the 1950's, according to structuralist analysis, and since the two primordial rigidities have continued to prevail during the stabilization periods, the rate of growth has remained low.

The structuralist model is, in fact, more richly embellished with sociopolitical propositions than the above skeletal statement. Other constraints are also recognized as coming into play during the inflationary spiral; for example chronic infrastructure bottlenecks due to lagging transport and energy prices and cuts in public investment in order to restrain mounting budget deficits. Such constraints are judged, however, to be largely derivatives of the two basic rigidities. That is, the apparently greater confusion and contretemps in Argentine and Chilean policy than in the policies of some other Latin-American countries is related to two essentially sociological observations. One is the plausible proposition that growth with a lagging capacity to import puts more severe pressure for rapid adjustment not only on the economic structure but also in the administrative and policy-making machinery. The second, rather paradoxical, proposition is that the more industrialized and technologically advanced Latin-American economies with their correspondingly greater urbanization adjust less easily to economic shocks than do the less-developed countries. Thus the greater success of the recent stabilization effort in Peru is attributed in large part to a comparatively favorable capacity to import, which in turn put less pressure on the economy to industrialize.[21]

---

[21]ECLA, *op. cit.*, Vol. III, pp. xiv–xv. The assumption that Peru's favorable capacity to import in recent years has been due more to exogenous factors than to astute monetary and exchange rate policies is by no means implausible. In the foreign-owned mineral industries—most notably in copper—and the partially foreign-owned fishing industry, investments to expand capacity were under way some years before the stabilization effort in 1959. They came to completion fortuitously when the stabilization effort was under way.

Import-Substituting Industrialization and Structural Rigidities

Has the sluggishness of agricultural supply and of the capacity to import been, in fact, grounded in institutional or exogenous forces? In the case of Chilean agriculture, the evidence that this is so appears convincing enough. That is, neither the trend in relative prices, nor agricultural taxation, nor the evidence on agricultural profits suggest a situation which should have depressed a reasonably responsive, technologically alert agricultural sector.[22] Argentine evidence is not as clear cut. Government price fixing, which depressed relative agricultural prices by 25 percent in 1946–49, undoubtedly damaged agricultural output. However, the sluggish supply response to the rise of about 50 percent in relative prices during the subsequent 13 years plausibly suggest institutional deficiencies.[23]

The capacity to import presents, however, a more complex picture. Granted that world excess capacity in minerals, coupled with import restrictions by a number of leading industrial powers, have held down earnings from Chile's mineral exports. Granted that a somewhat similar situation has prevailed for Argentina's agricultural exports.[24] Granted also that in the circumstances a lavish resort to devaluation or to greater concessions to foreign mineral investors might be only a beggar-my-neighbor policy which would evoke mutually damaging responses from other depressed primary exporters. What remains to be explained is why Argentina and Chile, with their sizeable industrial sectors, have been unable to become significant industrial exporters both prior to and during the stabilization efforts. This calls for closer analysis of the import-substituting industrialization pattern. But since what follows is not based on research in depth, careful economic analyses of Latin-American industries being still rather sparse, the discussion will perforce be in rather general terms. To the extent

---

[22]Supplementing the data referred to in the ECLA *Inflation and Growth* study is a recent calculation of Chilean agricultural production over the longer run which indicates that the average annual increase in 1921–40 was 1.9 percent, or only slightly in excess of the rate of population growth. In the period 1941–57, the annual increase fell to 1.7 percent, while the population growth rate rose to over 2 percent per annum. See Tom E. Davis, "The Growth of Output, Employment, Capital Stock and Real Wages in Basic Sectors of the Chilean Economy," in *Hearings before the Sub-Committee on Inter-American Relationships, Joint Economic Committee,* 87th Cong., 2nd sess. (Washington, D.C.; Government Printing Office, 1962), p. 104, Table 1.

[23]Compare ECLA, *op. cit.,* Vol. IV, pp. 11, 17–22.

[24]In actuality, the slow growth of agricultural output and relatively favorable home prices have also depressed the volume of Argentine exports in the postwar period.

that it is valid, however, the analysis may fit other industrializing economies of Latin America—Brazil, for example—as well as Argentina and Chile.

In form the import-substituting pattern recapitulates the conventional pattern of capitalist industrialization. That is, the initial industries are generally consumer goods or building materials producers with a relatively simple technology and a low capital requirement per worker and per unit of output. They are then followed by consumer goods industries requiring a more sophisticated technology and larger capital outlay, shading subsequently into industries producing relatively complex consumer durables, steel, engineering, and chemical products.

The patterns diverge, however, in two important respects. The first is that, in contrast to European, North American, or even Japanese industrialization, Latin-American countries have lacked an extensive structure of handicraft industries from which to draw skilled labor and entrepreneurial talent. The development of such a structure was inhibited by the highly stratified two-class society which characterized most Latin-American countries prior to World War I, in particular by the absence of a middle class of farmers and merchants to provide an extensive market for such industries. Argentina, it should be noted parenthetically, is a partial exception, since much of its population was of recent European, albeit of largely poor peasant origin. The industrialization efforts, therefore, have been forced to draw on a particularly inexperienced stock of human inputs. To a varying degree, deficiencies in entrepreneurship and capital accumulation have been compensated for by foreign firms which have established branches and subsidiaries, in good part to avoid a threatened loss of the local market due to import restrictions, and by government-financed industries when capital outlays have been too large to interest private investors. But at the same time the highly protected monopolistic market environment which has been created to induce private investment lessens pressure on industrial firms to increase productive efficiency. To this must be added the notorious lag of Latin-American education in developing trade and technical schools to augment the supply of industrial and scientific skills. The consequence has been that even with modern plants and low wages, domestic industries tend to have considerably higher unit costs than foreign equivalents.[25]

---

[25]For a detailed appraisal of the factors involved in one important industry, see ECLA, *Labor Productivity of the Cotton Textile Industry in Five Latin American Countries* (New York, 1951).

The second major difference is that widening of the industrial spectrum has taken place more rapidly than had been characteristic of the conventional pattern of capitalist industrialization. The pace has been more rapid the more sluggish the capacity to import, for then the saving of foreign exchange by encouraging import replacing industries became high policy. This has also tended to give the industrialization pattern a bias toward producing middle class products, such as consumer durables, since it is the less essential imports which have been restricted most severely. But even when efforts are made to check this bias, policy still tends to favor the allocation of foreign exchange and tax concessions to establish new industries which would save foreign exchange, as against the modernization and expansion of existing industries.

Two significant consequences have followed from this precocious widening of the industrial spectrum. Firstly, it has meant a rapid movement toward the production of technologically sophisticated products in which complex economy of scale factors are especially critical determinants of production costs, even though the domestic market has often been inadequate to exploit such economies. These scale economies relate not merely to the size of individual plants, but also to the size of the intricate complex of feeder firms. Thus, whereas in advanced economies with larger domestic markets supplemented by exports, the market size and level of organizational competence permit complex flow production within and between plants, the smaller markets and lower organizational competence in Latin-America has meant batch production, lags in supply, larger inventories, and other cost elevating deficiencies. Secondly, output curves have tended to be kinked, rising rapidly when exports are being replaced, but flattening out when further growth of demand has been grounded in the growth of domestic income. Profits have also followed this kinked pattern. Thus industries have moved rapidly from high profit and growth to precocious "maturity," at which point they fall back to monopolistic quiescence with lower profit rates, a reduced level of investment, and aging plant and equipment.

The inability of even the more industrialized Latin-American countries to develop export markets follows from the general pattern described. The initial cost disadvantage stemming from the lack of skills and deficient organization could, taken by itself, be overcome in time, particularly in industries of lesser technological sophistication with relatively low capital-output ratios. Precisely because the initial skill differential vis-à-vis older foreign competitors is great, the learning curve in Latin-American countries is likely to slope more steeply, despite the absence of internal competitive pressures. This, plus a slower growth of real wages relative to foreign competitors, plus devaluation, might bring down costs in such industries to a profitable exporting level. However, even this possibility could well be thwarted by the effect on wages of relatively rising food prices. For the relevant wage relationship is real wages in terms of industrial product, and the latter would rise more rapidly than real wages as such when the industrial terms of trade are worsening.

But even if these adverse terms of trade do not completely thwart the narrowing of the cost gap, the added effect of the relative aging of the capital stock in industries with export potential may well do so. For one of the convincing generalizations emerging from contemporary analysis of productivity is that its growth is positively correlated with the growth of capacity because this results in a stock of plant and equipment which is more *au courant* with the latest technological developments in the industry. This is due not merely to a more rapid addition of capacity, but also to a more rapid rate of replacement. The combined effect of an inadequate growth of food production and of the import-substitution pattern followed in Latin-America may, therefore, create a continual state of dynamic cost disadvantage.

The argument can be developed more formally. Whether or not an import-substituting industry reaches exporting efficiency depends on the interplay of at least four sets of forces: (1) the effect on the industry's productivity of the growth of other industries; (2) the effect on its productivity of its own growth in output; (3) the growth in productivity of competitors abroad; (4) wage and exchange rates trends.

The first set of forces, the external economy-diseconomy problem, may for our purposes be disposed of quickly. If the establishment of new industries always lowers unit costs in existing industries, then the rapid widening of the industrial spectrum would be broadly justifiable, and the case against continuing import-substituting industrialization much the weaker. But, clearly, industries also compete for scarce resources. Indeed, deepening shortages of foreign exchange (imports) and public services have, as already indicated, been a major cause of the slackening of industrial growth in recent years in Argentina and Chile. Between specific subclusters of industries, complementary relations in production may perhaps outweigh the competitive ones,[26] but this would still

---

[26] The *pôles de croissance* theory of François Perroux is built on this notion

(Continued on next page)

mean that the choice of industries to encourage can critically affect a country's ability to become an industrial exporter.

The other sets of forces are combined in Diagram 1, which, after a necessary if tedious explication of its components, will be used to

DIAGRAM 1

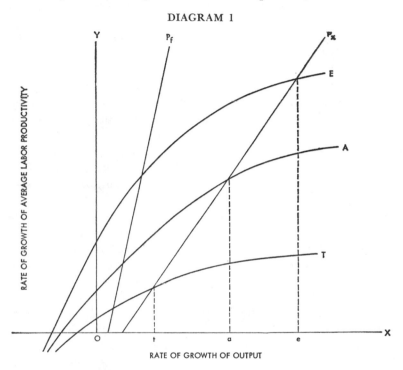

RATE OF GROWTH OF OUTPUT

illustrate how the interplay of these sets of forces can render import substituting industries incapable of exporting.[27]

The T (textiles?), A (automotive?) and E (electronic?) industries are selected to represent industries in different portions of the industrial gamut created by import substitution. They broadly represent an ordering in terms of increasing technical sophistication

of complementary clusters. "Note sur la notion de pôle de croissance," *Economie Appliquée*, January–June, 1955, pp. 309–20.

On the other hand, the view attributed to Nurkse (perhaps wrongly) that complementarity in demand insures that the external effects between industries are positive, is analytically incorrect. See Marcus Fleming, "External Economies and the Doctrine of Balanced Growth," *Economic Journal*, June, 1955, pp. 241–56.

[27] This is a revised version of a diagram in the original draft of this paper presented at the Rio conference. I am grateful to the Quantitative Seminar of the London School of Economics for useful criticisms which caused me to reconstruct the diagram. Far from the revised version being the responsibility of the seminar, however, its members would probably resent such an implication.

and probably, also, in terms of recency of establishment, although the last is incidental to the argument. The ordering is assumed capable of being extended to other industries, so that we may imagine an array of curves filling the space around those actually depicted. The *Pf*-line represents the annual rates of increase in labor productivity in the equivalent exporting foreign industries. For our purposes this is simply exogenous information. The line slants to the right because the evidence suggests that in recent years the productivity increases have been higher the more technically sophisticated the industry.[28]

The *Px*-line is the export-efficiency line. Starting from current levels of output, let us provisionally take both the exchange rate and the differences between domestic and foreign wages and between other factor prices also as given. Let us fix the time interval at the end of which the industrial sector is to become capable of exporting. There will then be a point on each industry curve representing the rate of increase in its output and productivity necessary to allow it to export. The *Px*-line connects such points. As drawn, no industry is initially capable of exporting—approximately the current situation in Latin-America.

The curves are derived by combining four functional relations between industry output and productivity. A fifth is incorporated in the *Px*-line.

The first relation we call the Salter effect.[29] New technology is incorporated in any industry mainly through gross investment in currently most advanced equipment. Since plant and equipment is durable, each industry, soon after its founding, comes to consist of layers of plant and equipment of different vintages, the older the vintage the less efficient the equipment. Consequently, the faster the growth of output, the younger will be the age structure of the industry's plant and equipment and the larger the growth of average productivity of its capital and labor. Higher rates of growth of output will hasten both the expansion of capacity and the obsolescence rate for old equipment. The relationship between growth of output and productivity is curvilinear, approximately as in Diagram 1, rather than linear, for reasons which should be apparent to the reader.

---

[28]For a bit of evidence on this, see UN, *World Economic Survey, 1961,* Tables 2-13.

[29]After W. E. G. Salter, who first made important use of a major fact about capital structures which had been ignored by capital theory. See his *Productivity and Technical Change* (Cambridge: Cambridge University Press, 1960).

The curves array themselves approximately as indicated in the diagram because of a second relationship, the economy of scale effect. It is generally accepted that Latin-American industries suffer in varying degrees from inadequate scale of output. The productivity effect of this is depicted in rather oversimplified form by Diagram 2, where current rates of output are taken as given. The diagram assumes that the more sophisticated Latin-American industries suffer most from inadequate scale of operations. This is

DIAGRAM 2

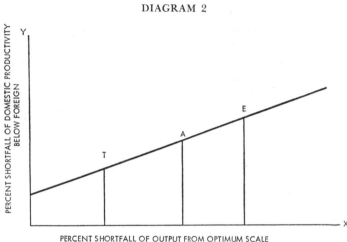

PERCENT SHORTFALL OF OUTPUT FROM OPTIMUM SCALE

more likely to be true if by scale we refer not to individual plants alone but, as already mentioned earlier, to industrial complexes. It should then follow that the industries which are further from optimum operations will have the higher rate of increase in productivity for a given increase in the output rate, because the economy of scale effect will be reinforcing the Salter effect the more strongly.[30]

The third relationship, the learning effect, simply shifts the industry curves upward. This effect says that with a given plant,

---

[30]For a perfect ordering, it is necessary for the downward sloping section of all long-run industry cost curves to have approximately the same slope. This is unlikely to be the case, although how far off the mark such an assumption is cannot be assessed directly, since we have limited information on the shape of such curves. It can, however, be assessed indirectly by testing our model's prediction that, for example, the industries in Argentina or Chile with the highest increases in productivity per given increase in output also have the greatest shortfall in productivity levels relative to foreign competitors. This prediction depends on the legitimacy of arraying the industry curves as in Diagram 1, and the array is derived from the economy-of-scale ordering in Diagram 2.

equipment, labor force, and rate of output, productivity will rise over time because production experience will increase labor skills and the coordination of operations. The effect is likely to be greater for the more technologically sophisticated industries, and the curves in Diagram 1 are drawn this way.[31]

The fourth is between the degree of utilization of plant and equipment and productivity. The extension of the curves to the left-hand quadrant of Diagram 1 indicates that productivity increases as output falls below the full capacity level.

Finally, industrial efficiency may be enhanced for technological borrowers, such as Latin-American countries, if they can lower unit costs by adapting imported technology to their lower wages and higher capital costs. The consequence of effectively substituting labor for capital is to increase total productivity, but to lower labor productivity. Such substitution would therefore lessen the increase in output per head and the corresponding rate of increase in output required to attain export efficiency. The Px-line and the industry curves may thus be expressed in terms of labor productivity, as in Diagram 1.[32] The more sophisticated, however, the imported technology, the less the ability of Latin-American countries, with their limited engineering and managerial cadres, effectively to make such adaptations. Empirically, this should show up for each country in smaller differences between the capital-labor ratios at home and abroad per given plant, the more sophisticated the industry. That is, the capital-labor ratio for T-type industries should be lower than in foreign equivalents by a greater percentage than for A- and E-type industries, a hypothesis which I believe is broadly valid, and should at any rate be testable.[33] The Px-line, therefore, slants further to the right than the Pf-line, because it is given an added tilt by the declining ability to substitute labor for capital as we move from the less to the more sophisticated sections of the industrial spectrum.

----

[31]This is also an oversimplification. The learning-by-repetition influence on the efficiency of a given plant, equipment, and labor force should peter out in time. Correcting for this should, however, strengthen rather than weaken the main conclusions derived from Diagram 1.

[32]The Salter, economy of scale, and learning effects presumably influence total productivity, that is, both capital and labor efficiency, proportionately. Hence, the resulting curves should be the same whether expressed in labor or total productivity.

[33]Alternatively, a possible definition of that sexy but imprecise concept, technological sophistication, could be concocted in terms of ratios between capital-labor ratios at home and abroad. This, however, might be giving too many hostages to stochasticism.

We may now, at long last, manipulate Diagram 1 to indicate a number of conclusions concerning import-substituting industrialization:

1. Despite higher rates of increase in output per head, the more sophisticated industries will require greater sustained rates of increase in output to reach export efficiency than the T-type industries; $Oe>Oa>Ot$. Under the import-substituting pattern of industrialization, interindustry differences in the levels and rates of growth of labor productivity are misleading indicators of comparative industrial efficiency.

2. The shorter the time interval in which it is desired, say for balance-of-payments reasons, to become an industrial exporter, the greater will be the rate of increase in industrial output. That is, if the time period is cut from x to $x/2$, the Px-line shifts to the right.

3. Widening the difference between foreign and domestic industrial wages can reduce the needed rates of output growth, that is, it can shift the Px-line to the left. The effectiveness of such a policy is, however, limited by three considerations. The first arises from the linkage between industrial wages and food prices. If food prices are chronically rising by more than industrial prices, as has been the case in Argentina and Chile, the fall in wage costs per unit of industrial product may be much smaller than the widening of differences between domestic and foreign real wages. The second is that if industrial wage costs are reduced by a sufficient cut in wages, consumer demand would shift from T-type consumables to sophisticated A- and E-type consumer goods. The implication of this for the failure of the Argentine and Chilean stabilization programs is discussed in the following section. The third is that if it is necessary to depress industrial output and employment in order to force down real wages, productivity falls. That is, we move into the left-hand quadrant of Diagram 1. Although the Px-line may have been moved to the left by the fall in wages, the output and productivity gap which has to be bridged in order to reach export efficiency can remain as wide as ever.

4. Devaluation as a means of promoting industrial exporting is also subject to at least two constraints germane to the model. The first is that if the redistributive effect of devaluation is toward greater income inequality, the shift in consumer demand will be toward A- and E-type goods. This point is elaborated below. Secondly, the ability of devaluation to shift the Px-line leftward is limited by the degree to which higher price of imports feeds back on industrial costs. The degree appears to be substantial, because

the import-substituting pattern relies heavily on Professor Hirschman's strategy of establishing industries and letting the backward linkages come along later. Hence, the industrial sector develops with a heavy dependence on imported materials, fuels, and parts.[34]

5. The extension of import substituting to capital goods establishes new industries which are likely to be in the A- and E-range of the industrial spectrum. Whether the Px-line shifts to the right or left depends on whether the higher price of such goods to industrial users is offset by more ready availability and, hence, lower inventory costs. There is no a priori reason for assuming that the extension will improve the prospects for industrial exporting. It depends on which industries are established and what their economy of scale shortfall might be.

6. Economy of scale deficiencies are obviously less of a problem the larger the domestic market. Hence the industry curve array should be narrower for Argentina than for Chile, and somewhat narrower for Brazil than for Argentina.

The general presumption is that economies which have pushed import-substituting industrialization in the context of stagnating agriculture to the extent to which Argentina and Chile have, tend to box themselves in. As industrial growth slows down when imports become less compressible, the industrial sector, for reasons suggested by the above analysis, is unable to revive its momentum by exporting. Clearly the analysis needs to be tested more carefully against the facts than I have been able to do. The model, however, provides us not only with a plausible set of reasons for the incontrovertible fact that neither Argentina nor Chile (nor Brazil) has been able to become an industrial exporter, but also, I believe, with a useful agenda for empirical research on this problem.

Import-Substituting Industrialization and the Failure of the Stabilization Programs

The analysis also helps explain why, despite the fall in real wages, devaluation, and foreign credits, the IMF stabilization pro-

---

[34]This has been brought out in a number of recent ECLA studies of the growing "rigidity" of imports in the more industrialized Latin-American countries.

Due to the monopolistic character of Latin-American industry increases in costs are also passed along rapidly, and even anticipated. Wage demands may then set off a wage-price spiral which can wipe out in short order the gain from devaluation. This is clearly a serious problem for economic policy. The points made under 4, however, concern not the speed of adjustment of money incomes but whether devaluation can shift resources so as to facilitate industrial exporting.

grams failed to promote a breakthrough to industrial exporting. Basically it was because the programs worked against the realloca-tion of resources needed for such a breakthrough. There appear to be three major reasons for this.

The first is that the reduction of real wages and the wage share tended to divert investment in the industrial sector excessively and indiscriminately to consumer and capital goods industries in the A- and E-portions of the industrial gamut. This resulted partly from the fact that the less-sophisticated consumer goods industries at the T-end of the gamut are generally industries whose demand depends more heavily on wage income.[35] The resulting stagnation of T-industry demand was further accentuated by sharp changes in relative prices for manufactures consumed by the nonwage house-holds whose real income position had improved. Recall that import-substituting industrialization and the restrictions of sumptu-ary imports when the capacity to import is tight tend to raise drastically the prices of goods which are more important in the budgets of nonwage than wage households. The most glaring exam-ples in Argentina and Chile in the 1950's were, of course, auto-mobiles, which because of import restrictions sold for five to six times their price in the United States or Europe. But price dispari-ties of a significant, if less spectacular, degree existed for most con-sumer durables, even when domestic production or assembly was the main source of supply. Some of the greater supply of foreign exchange made possible by stabilization credits was used to increase imports of consumer durables and luxury goods. A much larger share was used to import equipment and supplies for new durable consumer goods industries and to enlarge the output of existing ones. The particularly high income elasticity of demand for such goods among nonwage households combined with the fall in their relative prices to divert a major share of the increased nonwage income to industries producing these products. In turn, this stimu-lated the demand of domestic supplies to these industries and en-couraged their expansion. Parenthetically, the falling wage share may also help to explain why, contrary to the expectations of the

---

[35]However, since they are also industries with lower capital-labor ratios, they should reap the greater cost benefits from lower wages. Offsetting this is the fact that they tend to be less dependent on imported inputs and thus benefit less from a greater availability of foreign exchange. The argument in the text is, therefore, essentially an empirical judgment that the cost advantages which might have accrued to the T-industries from the stabilization programs were not enough to offset the disadvantages stemming from the shifts in consumer demand.

program, the removal of price controls was followed by a fall in relative agricultural prices.[36]

Secondly, most of the augmented inflow of foreign manufacturing investment during the stabilization periods[37] also went into A- and E-type industries. This was due not only to the increased demand for such products from the income distribution changes described above; it was also related to the special characteristics of such investment in Latin-America. This investment tends to be limited-risk investment designed to obtain or keep a foothold in the local market when direct exporting is blocked by import restrictions, hence is made despite the fact that local costs of production are often substantially higher.[38] It is limited-risk investment because, to the maximum degree commensurate with local regulations, foreign manufacturing firms seek to rely on imported parts and other inputs, and to finance operations from local borrowing and retained profits. The gains to the parent firms tend to come from the sale of goods and services to their Latin-American subsidiaries as much as from the profits of these subsidiaries. Thus, despite the fact that profit rates of U.S. branches and subsidiaries in Latin-America declined progressively in the 1950's,[39] and from 1951 on have averaged much less than the profit rate after taxes earned in U.S. manufacturing, the annual inflow of such investment rose until 1958. The flow of such investment tends, therefore, to be heavily influenced by the prospective availability of foreign exchange for importing and, to a lesser extent, for the transfer of profits. But it reacts only slowly to changes in the rate of profit earned by branches and subsidiaries.[40] The greater availability of foreign exchange during the earlier phases of the stabilization effort attracted, therefore, an increased volume of manufacturing investment which went into the partial domestic production of sophisticated products. The most notorious example was, of course, the Argentine automotive industry. Between December, 1958 and November, 1961, Argentine

---

[36]See footnote 9. The greater impact of devaluation on industrial costs was probably the other main factor.

[37]The inflow, however, was negligible in Chile during the Klein-Saks period.

[38]For a more detailed discussion of this characteristic, see *United States Business and Labor in Latin America*, prepared at the request of the Subcommittee on American Republic Affairs, Committee on Foreign Relations, U.S. Senate, 86th Cong. (Washington, D.C.: Government Printing Office, 1960), Chapters I–III.

[39]*Ibid.*, p. 12, Table 9.

[40]In contrast to investment in extractive industries for export. *Ibid.*, pp. 13–15, Charts 1–3.

authorities approved automotive investment plans submitted by foreign firms to the amount of $97 million (U.S.). This resulted, by 1961, in the establishment of 22 automotive firms, wholly or partly foreign-owned, in a country with an estimated market potential for motor vehicles in the half-decade ahead of at the most 200 to 300 thousand units per annum. In 1961 alone, the industry imported $153 million in parts, supplies, and equipment, or about 16 percent of that year's imports, in order to produce 136,000 units.[41] An additional volume of imports, impossible to quantify without an input-output table, was consumed by the steel industry and domestic-parts manufacturers in order to fill orders for the automotive industry. While there were no such spectacular examples in Chile, an accumulation of small-scale partial production of sophisticated consumer goods, including automotive assembly, took place, to which foreign investors contributed.[42]

The third reason is that the policy of tighter credit diverted private finance to A- and E-type firms. When credit is tight, the activities of firms with higher rates of profits are usually less affected, since they are better able to finance internally through retained earnings and also have superior credit ratings. This seems to have been true in both Argentina and Chile.[43] Moreover, since credit was tightened primarily by imposing global limits on bank lending to the private sector, a nonbank lending market emerged in each country with extremely high interest rates, in which the more profitable operations could obtain marginal funds but which was too costly for less profitable firms.[44] It is difficult to assess the quanti-

---

[41]Bank of London and South America, *Quarterly Review*, July, 1962, pp. 124–30.

[42]There was a particularly heavy concentration of such new industries in the northernmost province of Tarapacá. In order to offset the decline of the nitrate industry, ports in this province were given free importing privileges. It became highly profitable, therefore, to locate industrial activity in these ports, even though the market (the central provinces) was located 1300 miles to the south.

[43]For Argentina, see Bank of London and South America, *Quarterly Report*, July, 1962, p. 148. For Chile, some rather indirect evidence is indicated in Instituto de Economía, *Formación de Capital*. The latter shows that while domestic loans financed a decreasing percentage of gross capital formation for the sample of corporations studied, the firms with the most rapid growth of real assets had both the highest rate of retained profits and received a higher rate of loans as a percentage of profits. In addition, see some general remarks in ECLA, *op. cit.*, Vol. III, pp. 86–103.

[44]Interest rates in the nonbank credit markets in Chile during the Klein Saks period and in Argentina during the recent stabilization period ranged to well over 40 percent per annum. For Argentina, see Bank of London and South America, *Quarterly Review*, January, 1962, pp. 25–26. The most important single use of the high interest credit in Argentina was to finance motorcar sales.

tative importance of these diversions, although their direction seems clear enough. During the earlier phases of the stabilization programs, when budget deficits were largely met by foreign credits, the squeeze on the private sector as a whole does not seem to have been very severe. But, as the net inflow of foreign credits fell off, a larger portion of government budgets had to be financed by central bank borowing. To keep within the credit limits agreed upon with the IMF, loans to the private sector were restricted more severely, chiefly by raising marginal reserve ratios of the commercial banks. The effect was felt most acutely, evidently, by less profitable firms. In Argentina, in particular, this led to a serious credit crisis in June, 1962, during which the central bank had to undertake the emergency rediscounting of industrial paper to enable firms to meet wages and other current commitments.[45]

TABLE 1

	Argentina 1952 = 100		Chile 1953 = 100	
	Manufacturing Production	Manufacturing Employment	Manufacturing Production	Manufacturing Employment
1957.......	..	..	103.7	95.7
1958......	123.7	95.7	106.9	91.8
1959.......	107.4	91.6	122.1	93.4
1960.......	109.5	84.2	119.3	96.9
1961.......	120.1	81.6	127.5	102.6

Sources: Argentina: Dirección Nacional de Estadística y Censos, *Boletín Mensual de Estadística*, January, 1961; March, 1962. Chile: Banco Central de Chile, *Boletín Mensual*, April, 1962.

In sum, the effect of the IMF stabilization policies on the industrial sector was mainly to shift an excessive proportion of resources to A- and E-type industries. The cul-de-sac into which the industrial sector had worked itself prior to the stabilization efforts was made a bit roomier, but no breakthrough to exporting occurred because the stabilization policies, rather than directing resources to industries with export potential, continued the pattern of precocious widening of the industrial spectrum. Even the apparent gain in labor and productivity for the industrial sector as a whole was partly illusion. (see Table 1) For, while tighter credit proba-

---

[45]Earlier in the same year, the Minister of Economy had appealed to the automotive industry to obtain foreign funds for retail financing in order to relieve pressure on the local credit market. (Bank of London and South America, *Fortnightly Review*, March 24, 1962, p. 233.)

Inflation and Growth in Latin America

bly did force an increase in efficiency, part of the apparent gain in productivity seems to have been merely due to a shift in output toward industries with higher capital/labor ratios made possible by greater capital imports.[46]

TABLE 2

	Argentina					1952 = 100					
	Vehicles and Nonelectrical Machinery		Electrical Products and Machinery		Rubber Products		Food and Drink		Textiles		Leather	
	O*	P†	O	P	O	P	O	P	O	P	O	P
1958.......	99	102	128	109	123	103	133	121	102	122	90	101
1959.......	80	97	123	115	119	105	114	115	81	117	70	98
1960.......	103	111	136	116	144	114	110	123	85	116	66	107
1961.......	109	123	122	105	199	140	115	131	90	122	73	110

	Chile						1953 = 100							
	Metal Products Other Than Machinery		Electrical Products		Chemicals		Rubber Products		Food Products		Textiles		Leather	
	O	P	O	P	O	P	O	P	O	P	O	P	O	P
1957........	118	108	111	101	112	101	93	89	103	106	93	106	103	104
1958........	124	112	104	118	122	109	99	106	99	102	93	112	103	110
1959........	149	132	106	131	121	106	134	140	107	110	107	127	103	122
1960........	155	130	112	134	126	109	147	139	111	93	95	121	90	91
1961........	195	149	115	139	134	114	161	150	114	84	103	122	102	123

*O = Output
†P = Labor productivity (Man-hour output in Argentina; per worker output in Chile).
Source: See footnote 41.

The need for drastic measures to slow inflation and stimulate growth in Argentina and Chile has been obvious beyond question. One cannot but conclude, however, that the IMF-type programs were based on a misappraisal of where some of the leading difficulties lay, as well as on an erroneous normative perspective. The contention that under quite restrictive assumptions a free market economy will allocate resources with optimum efficiency simply does not support the corollary that the performance of a half-free economy will necessarily be improved merely by making it 60 percent free. Yet it is this sort of reasoning, buttressed by an un-

---

[46]Two-digit industry classes are too gross to be very illuminating about output and productivity trends. Moreover, it is not clear how well the data gatherers make allowance for new products in these classes. (The small rise in output of the Argentine vehicle and nonelectric machinery class does not seem to conform with the information on automotive expansion.) For what they are worth, the sectoral data in Table 2 are offered.

critical faith in the benefits of private foreign investment, rather than detailed analysis of the structure of the Argentine and Chilean economies, which seems to have guided much of the stabilization programs.

POLICY IMPLICATIONS

If the analysis of this paper is broadly correct, Argentina and Chile have reached another major impasse in their frustrating climb to self-sustaining growth, similar to that of the 1930's. Then, the decline and stagnation of their primary export markets made clear that the economic growth of Argentina and Chile could no longer be supported primarily by a handful of primary exports for which substantial Ricardian rents provided by nature offset the technological backwardness of the economy. The impasse, temporarily overcome by import-substituting industrialization, has now reappeared in a new guise. Import-substituting industrialization has also proved inadequate to elevate the economy to growth-sustaining efficiency. Continued agricultural backwardness, inadequate investment in public overhead capital, and precocious widening of the industrial spectrum have combined with a fall in the external terms of trade to bring Argentina and Chile to their present impasse. How is this to be overcome?

Firstly, the preceding analysis underlines—if such emphasis is still needed—the necessity to accelerate agricultural development by agricultural reforms and related measures and to augment substantially public investment in education, transport, and power. The attempt to outflank technological backwardness by import-substituting industrialization without such ancillary measures has failed. Nevertheless, the attempt has given Argentina and Chile a substantial heritage of industrial skills and experience which should now be utilized to supplement their primary exports. Indeed, the viability of their economies requires this, for the growth of their traditional exports is hardly likely alone to support their import needs, even under optimistic projections of world primary market trends. In brief, they must also turn to industrial exporting. But the existing demand structure as well as ingrained industrial habits stand in the way of a simple market solution to the problem of restructuring their industrial sector. What are required, therefore, are more direct and drastic measures, conceived in the spirit of Mrs. Robinson's dictum that the "task is not merely to study the coefficients but to change them." More specifically, the following lines of policy are suggested:

1. Taxation should be used to alter the structure of consumer demand. It is not sufficient to raise taxes in order to finance more public investment. The tax incidence must also fall much more heavily than is now the case on consumer durables and other sumptuary items of consumption, whether imported or domestically produced, with the object of curtailing new investment in such products. This requires some combination of heavy indirect taxes on A- and E-type consumables and augmented and progressive taxation of *personal* income.

2. A larger share of industrial investment must be directed to T-type industries with good export potential. This implies cost and market studies to identify such industries and input-output studies to estimate the direct and indirect demand for foreign exchange of alernative industrial investments. Given such information, exchange and capital issues controls, tax concessions, and public funds will probably have to be used to help proportion industrial investment so as to maximize net foreign exchange availability and to direct entrepreneurial perspectives outward rather than toward the domestic market. Since the required scope and rigor of such measures would vary inversely with the buoyancy of traditional exports, the authorities should link these measures to medium-term projections of traditional exports. Similarly, government outlays on power, transport, manpower training, and industrial research should be channelled to facilitate the industrial exporting effort.

3. Foreign manufacturing investment must also be screened with the same criterion in mind. The authorities must not be seduced by the appearance of direct-exchange saving, or by the fact that such investments may not compete with existing industries, into overlooking possible indirect defects of such investments in augmenting the demand for foreign exchange and stimulating low priority complementary investment.

4. Foreign technical assistance should be sought to assist in modernizing promising T-industries.

5. Vigorous efforts should be made to get the United States and Europe to open their markets to T-exports from Latin-America.

In short, the emphasis, particularly while the exchange crisis resulting from stagnating markets for primary exports lasts, must be on export-promoting industrialization. The focus, however, should be on raising promising industries to long-run exporting efficiency, not on indiscriminately subsidizing industrial exports.

Let me finally anticipate three lines of criticism.

The first is that world demand for T-industry products has

generally risen less rapidly than for A- and E-industry products. While this is not necessarily the case for all items, it is broadly true for the general class of less-sophisticated industrial products. Yet it is also true that world demand for such products has expanded more rapidly in recent years than for primary products. Moreover, in more advanced industrial economies the rapid rise of A- and E-industries has been pulling up real wages and labor costs in T-industries, so that imports have been progressively supplementing and even replacing domestic production of many T-type items. Coupled with this is the growing middle-class taste in these countries for exotics, which also favors the demand for technologically less-sophisticated industrial imports. To hasten our gradual process in the advanced countries of substituting imports for domestic output of T-products undoubtedly requires further liberalizing of the import restrictions against T-imports.[47] What is disturbing is that, while the industrially more advanced Latin-American countries are pressing hard for the removal of import restrictions against primary products, they have shown little interest in measures which would promote industrial exports to hard-currency markets.[48]

The second objection is that the Argentine and Chilean governments have been singularly inept in administering controls. This is, however, a *tu quoque* argument, for neither has the private sector been notably efficient. More importantly, the objection tends to confuse the essential issue. As indicated in the preceding dis-

[47]The Alliance for Progress could well devote some of its efforts to promoting such liberalization and to encouraging the industrial export potential of the relatively industrialized countries of Latin-America. The benefit to their balance of payments and to their industrial confidence might lessen the danger of the Alliance becoming little more than a supplier of stabilization credits to demoralized economies. Such funds could be used to better mutual advantage even if partly spent in the United States to ease the transfer of resources out of industries adversely effected by the liberalization of entry to Latin-American industrial exports.

[48]The Latin American Free Trade Association is not an exception to this statement, since at present it is largely an effort to extend import-substituting industrialization in A- and E-type goods to the entire region. This is not necessarily a criticism, although it is clear that the limited amount of intraregional trade, the timidity of the Montevideo Treaty, and the difficulties of compensating the less developed members of the LAFTA for the burden of diverting their imports of A- and E- goods to higher-priced Brazilian, Argentine, or Chilean production makes it likely that expansion of intraregional trade in industrial products will be slow. It does not provide, therefore, a sufficiently persuasive argument for foregoing the effort to develop hard-currency industrial exports. The LAFTA consultation machinery, on the other hand, could be used to coordinate plans for developing T-type exports, so as to avoid needlessly competitive efforts.

cussion, a strong measure of discriminatory controls in Argentina and Chile is unavoidable. The quest, for example, for an equilibrium exchange rate proved to be chimerical. Exchange controls took on different guises in the stabilization periods, but have shared the major weakness of earlier efforts; namely, they attempted to check immediate symptoms without central guidance on allocation priorities from a general development program. It would be far the wiser course to recognize the inevitability of discriminatory controls and to concentrate more fruitfully on relating them to a coherent development strategy, of which the promotion of industrial exports should surely be a major component.

A third objection is that the stricture against excessive A- and E-type investment overlooks that the feedback on industrial skills and managerial experience is greater from such industries than from T-industries. There is some merit to this criticism, although one should not overlook the favorable feedback on cost and quality control and marketing skills which would derive from exporting T-products. The basic problem is to determine the point at which the educational gain from establishing A- and E-industries is being purchased at too great a cost in short-run resource misallocation. If we use the growth rate as a rough guide, it seems reasonably evident from the critical plight of the Argentine and Chilean economies in the past decade that they have gone beyond the point, and need now to find more economic ways of picking up industrial skills and experience.

Growth economics is not able, of course, to indicate any single right path to maximizing the long-run growth rate, although it can indicate some of the necessary conditions for mounting each path successfully. There is, for example, the path formalized by the turnpike theorem and illustrated, perhaps, by the Soviet Union. That path would indeed call for an intensification of A- and E-investment in capital goods, heavy outlays on education and technical training, compression of real wages and consumption whenever necessary to offset bottlenecks and misallocations in the capital goods sector, and other hard, painful measures. It is possible that by taking this dangerous, long, and tortuous detour the turnpike to rapid economic growth can be reached. I doubt that Latin-Americans, who are notoriously wild drivers, are capable of managing the difficult detour. But even if they are tempted, they should at least realize that the Russian people did not make it over the detour to the turnpike in Zils and Moskvitches or outfitted with household durables. If one prefers a less distant payoff in such goods, then one had better choose an easier, if perhaps ultimately slower, road to travel. But even on this road it is possible to break down from the weight of excess baggage, or to tip over from a badly unbalanced load.

b. FINANCIAL POLICY AS AN ANTI-INFLATIONARY INSTRUMENT

Javier Márquez

Definitions

We shall adopt the traditional definition of inflation as a persistent balance of payments deficit or increase in prices, or both, simultaneously or succcessively, deriving from a relative increase in demand. "Development" will be construed as long-term growth in real income as a result of increased production.

These definitions should be given their proper shading. The type of development to which this paper refers, and which will be qualified in certain instances as "accelerated" or "good," is development at a faster pace than that permitted by spontaneous market forces (although allowing for individual years or periods of downward fluctuation) and one that brings out a leveling of income greater than is customary in Latin-America, or in any event does not accentuate the existing uneven distribution of income. The "social content" requirement for development means preventing not only a general price increase, but also sectorial price increases if the latter affect unfavorably the lower income groups. This does not detract from the fact that sectorial price movements are unquestionably desirable if they serve as a guide to investment. Furthermore, over-all price increases not in excess of those occurring in the countries with which a given Latin-American country conducts most of its trade will not be considered inflation for purposes of this study, unless they affect income distribution or the balance of payments.[1]

---

[1] It is mainly for this reason that we are not particularly interested in price increases—even persistent ones—of the order of 2 percent or 3 percent per year, but are referring to inflation "Latin-American style." Inflation exists, Tinbergen says, when prices increase more than is considered desirable; and he feels that slow upward movements are as acceptable as no movement at all (J. Tinbergen,

(Continued on next page)

A development that can fulfill all these requisites is admittedly very difficult to achieve with stability (but even more so without it). Some economists are skeptical of the capacity of Latin-American countries to attain this desideratum. However, much of the controversy regarding the problem of stability and stabilization explicitly or implicitly revolves around such development, although one has at times the feeling that mutual accusations are based on two different definitions of development: the one indicated here, and the other where the type of development sought is that produced by spontaneous market forces.

Controls

The thesis that there can be no development (particularly of the type indicated) with stability, that development brings inflation with it, has fallen into a great deal of discredit, and reference has even been made to the "false dilemma" of stability and development. As a matter of fact, in the long run the choice does not lie between "good" development with inflation or without inflation, but between "good" development without inflation or stability without development, whether good or bad. However, if we seek economic development at a greater rate than that produced by market forces and with a well-defined social orientation in line with the preferences of the authorities, by definition we cannot expect it to result, together with stability, from the action of market forces alone. Within the free enterprise system that we would like to preserve to the fullest extent possible, these forces are very useful, one might even say indispensable, but they are not enough. Perhaps the proper approach would be to attempt to turn them to the purpose at hand but be prepared to counteract them when they produce undesirable results.

To achieve the combination of objectives outlined, we need different kinds of controls, although there will be differences of opinion as to which type is preferable. The acceptance of controls presupposes acceptance of loss of liberty, and there will also be different attitudes in response to the type and degree of liberty that is lost. Income may be legitimately exchanged for freedom, or freedom for income.[2]

Economic Policy: Principles and Design, North-Holland Publishing Company, Amsterdam, 1956). Furthermore, the acceptance of price increases is necessary if a timid or excessively conservative economic policy is to be avoided as it should, for it would not favor development.

[2]Here we are defining control very broadly as any official measure that com-

No one in his right mind can argue that there is one single instrument (or control) capable of achieving accelerated development with a given social content and unaccompanied by inflation. But on occasion it is asserted that the single-control approach has indeed been attempted. Perhaps this is owing to the fact that sensible persons have concerned themselves with only a part of the task, with only some of the instruments. This does not mean that they are unaware of the others or believe them unimportant. Another contributing factor may have been that the specialized fields of certain agencies have prevented them from entering into those of others,[3] thus giving the impression that they exaggerate the importance of the instrument in which they specialize. This leads to a mutual assumption of a bias that actually does not exist. It is also possible that those specializing in a given aspect of economic policy have great power of conviction or possess particular strength, and that the country's authorities regard everything they say as *the* policy instruments (techniques), and pay little or no attention to what others have to say.

Quantitative and Selective Control of Expenditures. Just as controls are necessary to step up the rate of investment or channel it in a given direction, or both, within a climate of stability, so also are they needed to block attempts to expand the absolute volume of investment beyond the level that the capacity of the economy would dictate. After all, no country can develop at an unlimited pace. To attempt to exceed the economy's absorption capacity of investments, however well oriented these may be, constitutes a certain threat of inflation.[4] It is not easy to escape the impression that

---

pels or induces individuals to behave differently than they otherwise would. These controls will vary in terms of severity and scope, but we feel that the problem is one of degree, of the type of technique that leads to action or inaction, rather than one of principle. A specific end is sought, and it may be attained in different ways, some more expeditious than others, depending on circumstances, place, or governmental preference. Obviously, it would be very desirable, if not indispensable, for controls to be applied with a view toward favoring a development plan which, in turn, should lay down the guidelines for such controls.

[3] A certain claim to monopoly seems to be made on occasion in some fields, and it is difficult for different specialized agencies to conduct joint projects, as would be advisable, when the problems for study involve policy matters where one or several of the prospective contributors doubt that their points of view can be made to prevail or are afraid that they will be authoritatively and publicly discussed by somebody else. All this leads to confusion in the minds of those called on to determine policy.

[4] A great deal of insistence has been placed, particularly in ECLA, on the thesis that the limits on Latin-America's development capacity are set by her (limited and fluctuating) capacity to export—in other words, by the availability

(Continued on next page)

Latin-American development plans and economic thought have placed too much emphasis on specific areas of investment, and on the necessary volume of such investment, that the authorities, rightly enough, desire to encourage. It also seems that not enough consideration has been given to the concomitant need to reduce, or prevent, the "other" investments that may be of an induced nature (principle of acceleration), and which, if made, will detract real factors from the more desirable ones, will compete with them and create the inflationary pressures that we want to avoid. In other words, not enough attention has been paid to the consequences of permitting "indifferent" or prejudicial investments to be added to the desirable ones.

The foregoing obviously argues in favor of selective controls. The attitude with regard to such controls forms the dividing line between those who consider full employment the primary objective of economic policy (supposing that spontaneous investment is the greatest and best obtainable) and those who believe economic development to be the basic objective (supposing that spontaneous investment does not imply maximum volume or optimum orientation).

The argument of a more general character in favor of selective controls is that economic development cannot be balanced—that if such a development were possible, the world would have no underdeveloped countries. This argument might be qualified in many ways, in the sense that economic development cannot, and need not, be unbalanced to a very great degree, but the thesis still stands: An underdeveloped country cannot do everything at the same time. Attempts in that direction will lead to slow development, for if resources are limited and "semi-specific," many things will be badly done, on an insufficient scale, etc. If this were not true, an extraordinarily rapid rate of development would be entirely feasible. The maximum rate will vary from one country to another, but the possibilities are not infinite.

At the same time, the type of development attainable will also

---

of foreign exchange. True enough. But this limitation does not alter the fact that the availability of other factors can also exert a restrictive influence. Those who put the accent on foreign exchange are aware of this circumstance, but fail to give sufficient emphasis to those other factors that curb the rate of development—perhaps because the foreign exchange problem is the easiest to solve. Savings are also a limiting factor, but, like foreign exchange, do not suffice for accelerated development in the absence of complementary factors. The outside limit on development will undoubtedly be a shifting one, and economic and other policies (for example education) should seek to move that limit upward.

vary, because each country possesses the combination of factors necessary for a certain volume of *a given type* of investment, and no other. It is also obvious that the rate of development is not independent of the orientation of investments, or of the productivity of the ones that are feasible. The reference is to absolute as well as to relative productivity, for the volume of production varies in accordance with the nature of the investments and the degree of ability displayed in their management.

Certain investments are more productive, efficient, or socially desirable than others; hence, to the greatest extent possible, it will be necessary to seek the combination of productivity, efficacy, and social desirability that most closely approaches the optimum. Further, a policy of accelerated development that is socially oriented and accompanied by stability must make use of instruments that, ideally, will quantitatively restrict investment ex ante to the maximum that the economy will be able to absorb ex post, and will, moreover, channel that maximum in the best directions as determined by the combination of factors available and the social goals sought. (A telling argument in favor of *good planning.*)

Very few countries in Latin-America have made adequate efforts for quantitative or selective control. Some nations, for example, have favored indiscriminate importation of foreign capital, to the exclusion of all other considerations, as though foreign capital were the only factor needed for investment, as though investment could reach any limit provided foreign exchange were available, and as though foreign capital investment did not require national inputs that take away factors from other investments, or lead to new ones that the economy might not be able to absorb without inflationary pressures.[5] These and other countries have established quantitative credit controls without regard to the volume of investments or other expenditures which could be made without credit, and have controlled selectively bank credit, as if these prevented expenditures on consumption and investment which it would be advisable to discourage. In other countries, finally, selectivity has been imposed in favor of certain expenditures (investment or consumption) without quantitative control of the total, just as though an expediture effected with banking and nonbank resources and in

---

[5]See comment on foreign exchange, footnote 4. The capacity to save, the spirit of enterprise, the availability of skilled labor, income distribution, etc., are all additional limiting factors. The battle must be joined against them all as a part of the development-with-stability endeavor.

excess of the maximum absorption capacity of the economy were not harmful.

Instruments for quantitative and selective control of investment and consumption—an indispensable adjunct to accelerated development without inflation—may be of a monetary-banking nature only to the extent that investment and consumption depend on bank credit. However, we know that most expenditures are made out of current income rather than out of credit.

However, the influence of selective credit control can be great in some sectors, such as durable consumer goods expenditures. Apart from a certain effect on total expenditure on these goods, the influence in this case will be of short duration (lasting somewhat longer than the time consumers need to accumulate the resources required for the purchase of durable goods). One area in which selective credit control can have great and long-lasting effects is construction, for there it is difficult to replace institutional credit to any appreciable extent or over very long periods. To the extent that these and other expenditures are inflationary factors that the authorities wish to discourage, the policy of selective credit restriction can do the job *if the controls are efficient,* that is, if evasion is prevented. Many of us are skeptical regarding the latter possibility.

Generally speaking, monetary policy by itself will not be a good "selective-restrictive" instrument for controlling consumer or investment spending in Latin-America, because that policy affects only a part of such expenditure, is of short duration, or can easily be eluded. On the other hand, it can be a good expansive, and "selective-expansive." By making the necessary available to consumers and investors, monetary policy can be very useful in the sense of permitting the type of spending which it is desired to encourage.

In the case of investment the most obvious of the effective "selective-restrictive" control instruments would be a system of licensing. Under it, anyone desiring to make an investment must obtain from the authorities an appropriate permit. Licenses of this type are granted only in the measure that investments are deemed desirable (in terms of the country's estimated capacity to absorb them) and are channeled to the activities best suited to the type of development sought. This system is already in use to a certain extent in Latin-America.[6] However, it would appear to be better to

---

[6]Several countries use an import licensing system, superimposed on the customs tariff. In some nations in the area prior permits are also required for the establishment of new business enterprises.

seek whatever limitations are deemed necessary through fiscal devices: that is, increasing or reducing the profitability of investments through selective taxation, thereby encouraging those deemed desirable and discouraging the others.

The imposition of direct taxes of a general nature would probably not achieve the desired results, for they would tend to discourage total investment. The proper fiscal approach would involve selective taxes on investment and consumption, with the emphasis placed more on restriction than on stimulus. Monetary policy should subsist within a development-with-stability program, but it will be more important as a means toward selective expansion and quantitative restriction than in any other respect, for however selective monetary policy tries to be, "excessive" expansion will in all likelihood favor evasion and lead to excessive demand, thus reducing the efficacy of the selective fiscal restriction. But in the final analysis, the less restrictive monetary policy is, the more restrictive fiscal policy will have to be. The more restrictive monetary policy is, the more selective fiscal policy must be.

In Latin-America, the fiscal system has been used selectively—and successfully—to limit expenditure on luxury and semiluxury consumer goods, particularly through import duties and special taxes on luxury items in general. However, with the possible exception in some instances of residential construction, selective fiscal controls have not been applied to discourage some investment spending,[7] or, at any rate, not as widely and progressively as would be both feasible and desirable. The resistance to fiscal devices will always be less than that to administrative decisions which, with or without reason, are ordinarily suspected of being arbitrary.

Joint monetary and fiscal policy admittedly cannot solve the entire problem of rapid development with a social content and stability. Development of this nature is very complex, and wage policy, for example, is as important an element as any.[8] If action is not taken with respect to wage rates, the monetary authorities may find their hands tied. The same may be said of foreign trade policy (as distinct from fiscal policy), policy on public education, etc. But,

---

[7] The much-used restriction on credit to commerce has no limited stocks, but simply has transferred them to producers, or has placed on the latter's shoulders (acting as bank intermediaries) the burden of financing wholesalers and retailers.

[8] "In many countries wage rates are not considered a feasible instrument of economic policy in that government intervention in wage negotiations is not considered desirable; it may be questioned whether this attitude is wise in the long run. With an increasing desire to consider full employment and a constant price level as important targets of economic policy, the need for these instruments will have to be recognized." J. Tinbergen, op. cit., p. 139.

with the possible exception of wages, these points are not subject to as much debate as the relative importances of the fiscal and monetary policies or, as we prefer to call them, financial policy.

Considered independently, monetary policy has the great virtue of ease of application and rapid results. Its importance may therefore be greater for stabilization.

The Role of Monetary Policy

Two arguments have been adduced against the use of monetary policy for stabilization purposes in the presence of inflation. One of these holds that monetary policy should not be employed because its effects are too harsh. When credit is reduced, or is not permitted to increase in response to price rises, a deflationary situation is created that is inimical to accelerated development, to social or political stability, etc., and is, generally speaking, worse than inflation itself. The cure is worse than the disease. The other stand (most frequently encountered among nonprofessional economists), is that monetary policy should not be used because it is ineffective; that is, relative monetary contraction does not influence demand and hence does not curb the price rise or balance of payments deficit.

Some are inclined to take intermediate stands, of which two are worthy of mention. One group believes that monetary policy should be used only when there is "demand inflation," not when there is "cost inflation."[9] Another maintains that monetary policy should be employed when investment is the expenditure to be restricted, whereas fiscal policy is the one best suited to the purpose of limiting consumption.[10]

In demand inflation, monetary policy suppresses cause and effect, but it is futile against cost inflation because it does not attack the root of the problem, which consists of all the institutional and other obstacles that hinder development and are—the argument goes—beyond the reach of such policy. Effective action in this case would be to change the system of land tenure, the distribution of income, the fiscal system, the propensity to import, the orientation of investments, etc. According to the other school of thought,

---

[9] This thesis frequently coincides with, or forms a part of, the argument that restrictive monetary policy is too harsh.

[10] The thesis that very progressive direct taxes serve to restrict luxury consumption (together with private investment), and indirect ones hold the other forms of consumption in check is, perhaps, a variant of the theory under discussion.

monetary policy is useless as a means of limiting consumption, for it depends only in small measure on credit, or at any rate on credit susceptible of monetary policy control; on the other hand, credit restriction does serve to contract investment.[11]

Certain sectors of opinion, then, feel that monetary policy should not be used at all (with some claiming excessive severity and others claiming inefficacy); while some are in favor of its use only to combat certain kinds of inflation.

Then there is another group (to which the writer belongs) according to which stabilization always requires the use of monetary policy measures. No member of the group would exclude other policies or measures from the company of the monetary ones. The latter do not replace, but rather are superimposed on, policies for accelerated development having a social content.

The idea that monetary policy cannot do the whole job by itself has perhaps not been sufficiently stressed because it was felt to be quite obvious. (Here, however, let me observe, with Talleyrand, that "things that go without saying go still better when they are said.")

This position is eclectic or opportunistic insofar as the relative importance of monetary or other policy measures as stabilization tools is concerned, for such importance is deemed to be contingent on the particular circumstances of each case, time, and place. It is a pity that there are no strict formulas for application, but such is the case. The thesis is based on the contention that stabilization calls for a relative reduction in certain demand (for consumer goods or investment, or both) that has increased because of inflation, and for the maintenance or expansion of certain investments designed to sustain or increase development and satisfy demand; and in this endeavor monetary measures can contribute *to some extent*.

By and large, those who are most opposed to the use of monetary policy as a stabilization instrument, or who would limit its use to certain kinds of inflation, seem to mix, or confuse, two things that it would be better to keep separate: the development process with stability, and the way out of inflation—in other words, how to ward off inflation, and how to be rid of it when it is already present. At any rate, for emergence from inflation they appear anxious to apply measures that could have been used to better advantage to ward it off.

---

[11]One of the advocates of this thesis (Harrod) acknowledges that if inflation is severe fiscal and monetary policy should be used to limit consumption. (See Sir Roy Harrod, *Policy Against Inflation*, London, Macmillan, 1958.)

In some instances, the policies recommended to put an end to inflation are essentially measures for development with stability, since they seek to eliminate institutional and economic obstacles that stand in the way of such development. There appears to be some acceptance of continuing inflation as a lesser evil, as long as the underdeveloped status persists. Prescriptions for recovering from inflation recommended by this group are almost always of a long-term nature, as is development itself. However, in the long run, good development, within a private enterprise system, is incompatible with inflation.

Moreover, even if the element of compatibility were present, these prescriptions (with due recognition of their good points as an adequate guide to development, to the choice of investments, and to appropriate means of financing them) do not take the bull by the horns, for the anti-inflationary effects they produce are not speedy enough to satisfy the authorities. When the latter embark on a stabilization program, they do not do so with a view toward having their efforts produce effects at a much later date; they are not asking how to achieve development with stability but how to get rid of inflation *fast*. Governments are aware of the fact that it takes several generations to attain a high income per capita and one that is better distributed: What they are interested in is stabilization at short term. They undoubtedly know that an effort is involved, but nevertheless persist in their desire. It is necessary to *superimpose* the stabilization plan on the development plan, obviously not to substitute the former for the latter. The thesis under discussion offers no way to skirt the short-term problem: the need to contract demand or change its orientation or both, for inflation will have increased it (over-all or in certain sectors) to a point beyond that which the economy's productive and importing capacity would permit.

Any economic line of reasoning, any policy recommendation, can stumble (and many, indeed, are doing so) against the argument that existing situations do not permit its adoption, that it is politically or socially impracticable. Fully aware of the difficulty of imposing a stabilization plan "come what may," when faced with *de facto* situations the economist does not have a great deal to say. Or, perhaps he might observe only that inflation will not be overcome and, because of that fact, development, if there is any, will proceed at an ever-slower rate or in a socially perverse direction (the less perverse, the less development), and that tensions of all types will continue. If the rate is slow or the orientation different from that desired by the majority, the time will come when *something*—more or less violent—will happen to put an end to inflation by reducing effective demand for certain things). By the time this happens, however, the general situation of the economy will have become worse and, therefore, the penalties and sacrifices involved will be greater.[12] (Somebody told me once that the trouble with inflation is that it has to be stopped.) Continuation of inflation is not the way to achieve accelerated development having the social content that we consider desirable. Structural distortions will not be corrected and may even become more acute if inflation persists. Sad but true, resistance and hardship will unquestionably arise. But the way to fight an actual inflation is not to contend that, since there will be hardships, and since inflation is due to certain specific causes, it should not be combated *with the weapons available*, that we should content ourselves with doing things that will not put an end to it.[13]

It is difficult to see how a country can emerge from inflation without sacrifice. Stabilization without tears could occur in the case of a slow inflation, but we believe it is not possible when emergence from inflation is sought at short term, and when short-term emergence is indeed desired and, furthermore, necessary in order to achieve good development, as well as beneficial effects (such as political stability), on other fronts.

Efficacy of Credit Restrictions. Credit expansion directly and indirectly permits an increase in effective demand, in expenditures, which must be held in check if inflation is to be curbed. To the extent that spending is reduced as a consequence of credit restrictions, or at any rate does not increase, inflationary pressures are lessened. Is this actually the case?

Latin-America's experience has been that, while the velocity of money has never gotten out of bounds, it nonetheless has "some" elasticity. In the presence of a stable money supply (defined in the traditional manner), velocity increases under inflationary pressures.

---

[12] The invisible hand will fall, but there is no assurance that it will have a lighter touch than the visible one

[13] The preceding passages are a commentary on the "general impression" derived from reading the major document on the subject: Dr. Prebisch's work, "The False Dilemma Between Economic Development and Monetary Stability" ("El Falso Dilema entre Desarrollo Económico y Estabilidad Monetaria", *Boletín Económico de América Latina*, Vol. VI, No. 1, March, 1961, pp. 1–26). From this study, one can extract concrete statements that contradict the general impression, but they do not fit in very well with he basic thesis: the discussion of appropriate ways and means of emerging from cost inflation within a short time.

Up to a certain point businesses manage to get along with less cash. However, the real unemployment that has arisen on occasion (for example, in building) with stabilization plans that include as a main feature relative credit restriction proves that the elasticity of the velocity of money has well-defined limits, and disproves the point that credit restriction does not curb demand.

But every economy reacts in a different manner and degree to a given economic policy measure; furthermore, the increase in the velocity of money cannot be forecast (except within a very broad range), *nor is it the same in all sectors.* The last-mentioned circumstance may support the position of those who maintain that restrictive monetary policy has no influence on demand (perfect elasticity of velocity) and of those who claim that it has too much (constant velocity, or direct correlation between the money supply and velocity). As a matter of fact, both arguments may well be true at the same time: restrictive monetary policy may be too harsh for certain sectors of the economy, while exerting little, if any, effect on others. For maximum efficacy of a restrictive monetary policy (within the sort of development policy that we seek to encourage), credit restrictions should adversely affect the activities to be discouraged, because they stand in the way of desirable ones, and either exert no effect on, or provide stimulus for, the latter.

What really happens? Here again, generalization is impossible. In different countries and at different times some activities will call on institutional credit more than others and will be in a better or worse position to get by without it if it should be restricted. But it is quite possible that quantitative credit restriction will produce the most unfavorable effects in the very areas the authorities would like to see least affected. In other words, such restrictions may produce results that are contrary to the ones intended.[14]

This is due to the fact that, in Latin America, activities that contribute little to, or jeopardize, the type of development we seek can easily give rise to problems by becoming the object of strong demand. Faced with a limitation of total credit, financial intermediaries are prone to impose the greatest restriction on the financing provided for the "least luxurious" portion of expenditure.

Thus, restrictive monetary policy does limit total spending, since

---

[14]According to some, banks do not restrict credit to their rich friends. This may be true; but the economic effect of such a situation does not necessarily have to be perverse, and even the social implications may not be negative. One would have to know what type of rich friends are involved.

velocity is not perfectly elastic, but cutting credit enough to compress total demand within the desired limits (and keeping velocity in mind) can be very hard on the more desirable activities, and perhaps all the harder on these activities the greater the relative contraction imposed in order to counteract the increase in velocity. The obvious conclusion to be drawn from the foregoing is that restriction should not be sought through monetary policy alone but through a coordinated monetary and fiscal—that is, financial—policy.

A Stabilization Period

As indicated earlier, when governments really want to stabilize, they want to do so within the shortest term possible; they want to be rid of their problems in a hurry. But the stabilization endeavor will differ, depending on the length of time inflation has been in effect.

The basis for this distinction lies in the distortions that inflation induces in the structure of demand and, consequently, in that of supply. How much damage has been done, and of what type? Inflation that has existed for only a short while may have disturbed demand, but cannot have had time as yet to alter the supply structure to a corresponding degree. On the other hand, inflation that has lasted for quite a long time will have changed supply as well as demand. For, within a free enterprise system, inflation over a period of time will create a supply of consumer and capital goods, plus a series of services, tailored to inflation-induced demand: that is, demand that has been molded by the less equitable distribution of income, by changes in consumer preferences, by alterations in investment possibilities, habits, expectations, and similar factors—all deriving from inflation. Stabilization policy should seek to influence that demand structure within a short period. If it is successful in doing so, it will also affect the spontaneous supply structure.

Now then, the change in the spending pattern may, on the one side, encounter inelasticity in the supply of goods and services earmarked for promotion, and, on the other, unemployment will most certainly arise in the activities that formerly supplied the inflation-induced demand.

These problems must of necessity be faced when carrying out a stabilization plan; hence, the program should include policies designed to change the demand structure in the case of a short-term inflation, and to change the structure of both demand and supply when inflation has lasted a goodly number of years. A policy that produces such consequences is bound to encounter bitter and stubborn resistance on the part of all those who consider themselves the injured parties—and these will be many.

The psychological impact of a stabilization plan can influence expectation and bring other positive results. Specifically, expenditure habits can be changed to a certain extent, through propaganda, and demand expectations can influence the direction taken by private investments.[15] However, this may not be enough, in which case some additional mechanism will have to be resorted to. One that comes to mind would be to deliberately exert an upward influence on prices of "undesirable" goods and services, perhaps through the fiscal system, although this might mean a rise in the general price index. Such an increase, however, we would not regard as a cause for concern. In any event, the stabilized price level following on a severe and prolonged inflation will always be higher than that prevailing at the time the stabilization plan is put into operation.

The authorities will also have the problem of finding means of shifting to new activities the factors released by the loss of public favor in certain lines. In other words, adequate instruments must be found that will lend *mobility* to such factors. One of the means of attaining this end is public works programs scheduled over the shortest time possible—and preferably without requiring the physical displacement of individuals—that will absorb the factors released. Another method would involve the search for, and encouragement of, alternative uses of equipment left idle as a result of diminished demand in certain areas.

The desirability of shifting factors toward other areas of employment, and thus combating the relative inelasticity of supply of those goods that the authorities desire to make the object of new demand (apart from the function of temporarily offsetting the depressive effects of general or sectorial unemployment) is perhaps the decisive element leading to the thesis that, in the event of prolonged inflation, it would be desirable for stabilization not to be instantaneously imposed, *if this can be avoided*. It would be preferable to constitute a process the duration of which will depend, among other things, on the authorities' ability to tap savings

---

[15]Joseph Grunwald ("The 'Structuralist' School of Price Stabilization and Economic Development," *Latin American Issues*, A. O. Hirschman (editor), The Twentieth Century Fund, New York, 1961, pp. 95–123) reports that public relations campaigns of this type met with success in Chile.

(including foreign exchange) needed for new investments, to induce private enterprise to carry out such investments, and, above all, to provide factor mobility.

Obviously, the lesser the degree of factor mobility and the smaller the amount of available savings, the greater the hardships that stabilization will bring. The availability of foreign exchange will permit an extension of the stabilization period and, consequently, render it less severe. As a matter of fact, the gradual approach presupposes the existence of foreign exchange. By definition, as long as the stabilization process is running its course, stability does not exist; and, in the absence of stability, the pressure on the balance of payments will persist in some degree. The existence of a dynamic entrepreneurial class that readily adapts to new circumstances by channeling its savings to activities best fitted for development-plus-stability in like measure obviates the necessity for the authorities to undertake such activities and to strain the tax-levying machinery.

However, no matter how strong the desire that private enterprise take the lead, it is foolhardy to expect a country to emerge from the type of inflation we have in mind without provoking violent disturbances, if all or most of the task is left up to the private sector. In Latin-American countries private enterprise is not sufficient, nor will it adapt with the necessary speed to new circumstances of this nature. A "wait-and-see" attitude is unavoidable. With relative frequency Latin-America has observed how readily private investment will contract in the face of events a good deal less spectacular than stabilization programs. Entrepreneurs will not be willing to take risks without having checked out the persistence and virtues of a stability with which they are unfamiliar, have forgotten, or in which they do not believe. Moreover, certain of the development tasks that come in the wake of a lengthy inflation are not the type customarily associated with private enterprise.

For these and other reasons it would appear inevitable that in the early stages of a stabilization program the state will assume more managerial functions than in normal times. Its task will consist of filling the investment gaps left by inflation, initiating other new investment programs, and, by absorbing them, lending mobility to the factors displaced by the shift in demand. It would therefore be very desirable for the state to have a plan for investments (some appropriately its own on a permanent basis and others taken over temporarily in substitution for private enterprise) that would contribute to the continuation, reorientation, or initiation of development, and would absorb the factors displaced by stabilization.

Rather than being the marginal last-resort investor, under the circumstances outlined the state would become the main investor.

The problem of organizing and carrying out a program to increase such varying types of investment as will be required is obviously not an easy one; nor is it a simple matter to obtain noninflationary financial resources for the purpose. Managerial efforts put forth by the government to promote factor mobility may find the latter to be relatively specific and may encounter other obstacles. Therefore, however effective the government's performance in the fiscal, administrative, or managerial fields, a certain degree of unemployment will have to be allowed for in the activities affected by a thoroughgoing stabilization program. In addition, the plan may of necessity incorporate the disappearance (or creation of idle capacity in each case) of certain activities faced with a contraction of demand within a system of stability.

To effectively discourage inflationary expectations is an indispensable requisite for stabilization, but it is important that this be accomplished without detriment to *development* expectations. The business community must be convinced that the authorities, in the interest of encouraging private enterprise, are determined to curb inflation and possess the necessary means to do so without braking the country's development. If development expectations are lacking, private initiative will not be dynamic, but will simply settle down and wait.

Administrative, fiscal, and managerial ability, accompanied by political strength, must be present if a country is to emerge rapidly from a prolonged and severe inflation with a minimum of hardship. Will these ideal circumstances be present?

It has been said[16] that the emphasis placed in Latin-America on the use of monetary instruments for stabilization purposes may be owing to the fact that the region is, in general, suffering from a dearth of administrative ability, and that monetary tools are the easiest to manage and, moreover, capable of producing more rapid results.

The very fact that prolonged and severe inflation has occurred would appear to be sufficient proof of a lack of administrative or fiscal ability, and would point to inadequate political power (in terms of enforcement of decisions), or perhaps the two together. It has been asserted that inflation is the instrument of weak governments.[17] There is much truth in this contention.

---

[16]Grunwald, *op. cit.*, p. 122.

[17]W. Arthur Lewis, *Theory of Economic Growth* (London, George Allen & Unwin Ltd., 1955).

The institution of a stabilization plan carries with it the tacit assumption of the existence of political strength, for from the very beginning political strength is a minimum requirement *if the desire to stabilize is actually sincere* and not just a matter of lip service. (On the other hand, it is possible that a government may believe itself endowed with sufficient political power when such is not the case.) Technical ability is also presumed to be present.

The existence of fiscal and administrative ability, however, cannot be taken for granted. It cannot be improvised, and inflation proves that it did not exist before. While it is acquired, so as to enable the application of other measures on a certain scale (independent of the intensity with which these others may be employed from the beginning),[18] monetary policy, along with wage policy— where the emphasis is more on authority than on administrative capacity—may constitute the only feasible and effective anti-inflationary weapon of any importance. Moreover, its utilization may be necessary in order to achieve stability. In other words, inflation is not the most propitious climate for acquiring fiscal and administrative ability. It is true that, in this case, the stabilization process will not be accompanied by accelerated development, and what development does occur will not have any very great social content, but it will be the biggest and best obtainable.

Monetary policy unquestionably constitutes the instrument, or group of instruments, that lend themselves to easiest management. Technical ability is ordinarily available, and the practical application of monetary policy (as in the case of wage policy) is a matter of political authority. To limit credit to the banks or the government, or to devalue the currency, does not call for a great deal of administrative ability.

It may be that a combination of coordinated programs for the imposition of relative restrictions on bank credit, together with successive currency devaluation, is an *easy way* to achieve stability. Devaluation may be one of the few practicable instruments for counteracting a wage level that is presumed to be irreversible (falling back on political power to curb further wage increases). This would obviously mean that the price level during stability will be higher than that in effect at the time the program is initiated. Such an effect, for that matter, would be inevitable, for the price level at the time a stabilization program gets under way will always be the result of income from an earlier period rather than the current one. The inflationary potential must be exhausted.

---

[18]If political power exists, there will always be a certain ability to levy and collect additional indirect taxes.

But one should entertain no illusions regarding the consequences of such a program which will be harsh indeed; for private sector depression, which cannot be entirely avoided even in the presence of administrative, fiscal, and managerial capacity on the part of the government, will be proportionately worse in the measure that such capacity is lacking. In other words, the fewer the elements that are made to accompany the monetary (and wage) policy, the harsher the stabilization will be, and to that extent one may have to "forget" about simultaneous development. Attention will have to be centered on stabilization as such, on public works that can be executed with whatever fiscal resources happen to be available, or with foreign exchange obtained from outside sources in the absence of domestic reserves. At the same time, properly oriented development plans must be prepared and held in readiness for application as the administrative, fiscal, and entrepreneurial (managerial) capacities are acquired.

c. COMMENT
Sir Roy Harrod

Mr. Felix raised the question as to how far we should apply the maxim *tout comprendre c'est tout pardonner* to the recent performance of Latin-American countries. We should certainly seek to be fair, but not incline to undue leniency, in our appraisals. But what makes me tend somewhat to the side of "pardonner" is that we are in a field of discourse, namely the relation of growth to inflation, about which little is known, so that the validity of any advice that may be tendered is often very problematic. Greater blame could be assigned for deviations if prescriptions were more reliable.

I therefore assume the mantle of humility as regards anything that I may venture to say. I am humble in another sense also, in that, although you have been good enough to ask me to this conference, I have to confess myself a person who knows little about Latin-American affairs as such.

1. It strikes me that the most important evil here is the spiraling between wages, prices, and wages. Both Felix and Márquez in their papers touched on the inelasticity of food production as of key importance in this connection. Mr. Kaldor also made a statement on

which it would be hard to improve, showing the mutual relations involved. To judge from this testimony, it seems to be the case that food production in this region is inelastic to price increases.

Having regard to this awkward fact, the minds of some of those present seem to have moved toward the reform of land tenure. This may be right, but, although an ignoramus, I should suppose it to be political dynamite. Should not economists try, if possible, to steer clear of that? Could not the matter be approached by a different route? Could one not start with a stated policy of increasing food production? Marketing boards might be a useful device. They might offer guaranteed prices over a term of years for certain quantities of output on a rising scale. Although I say it with great hesitation and reluctance, it might even be expedient to insert escalator clauses. Vicious although these can be in certain circumstances, they might be justified if they actually got an increase of production, if that would be really important in checking the inflationary spiral. Differential pricing might also be useful, as instanced by its effectiveness when employed by the British Milk Marketing Board before the war. Although it was accused of taking milk from the mouths of children and turning it into processed objects, it did get an increase in milk production. If and when a definitive policy, using whatever means were appropriate, was seen to be frustrated by the attitudes of landlords, then the question of land reform would come up naturally.

2. A sharp distinction should be drawn between inflation due to excess demand and that due to wage-price spiraling. It appears to have been assumed in the discussions that excess demand has been widely prevalent, taking the form, notably, of unbalanced government expenditures. Here again Mr. Kaldor has given an analysis that cannot be surpassed. If there is a margin of expenditure that ought to be covered, if demand inflation is to be avoided, then, if this is done by taxation, the burden on the general public can be limited to the precise sum required. But if the margin is not so covered and leads to price and profit inflation, then, over and above what the general public has to pay, in this case through higher prices, profit makers can take a rake-off of unlimited size, which they can then proceed to deploy on luxurious consumption. Thus the burden on the general public is far greater if the necessary funds for the governmental expenditures are found by inflation than if they are found by taxation.

When adopting disinflationary measures, we should be very careful to assure ourselves, if possible, that there really is a demand inflation proceeding, which is something entirely different from the wage-price spiraling that has been referred to. This may be difficult to discover, especially in view of the unreliable character of many Latin-American national income statistics. I could not help being struck by the figures provided by Mr. Baer to the effect that profit has not been increasing disproportionately to national income in recent years in Brazil. It is for you to judge how much we can rely upon this figure. You may think it a very weak reed. But there it is, and perhaps we should not ignore it completely. What it points to prima facie is that there has not been demand inflation in Brazil, but only spiraling inflation. As counterevidence, we ought to require something specific, like the existence of mounting backlogs, other than those due to specific bottlenecks.

I can only conclude this by stressing that the greatest crime to which the free world is prone is to reduce demand below the growth potential of the economy in order to combat wage-price spiraling.

3. I was much impressed by what Felix had to say about industrial protection. The basic assumption in discussions about developing countries is that the government should be responsible for *doing* something to foster growth. Its easiest course, if there is a certain amount of entrepreneurship available, is to proceed by the imposition of import restrictions. If export markets are inhospitable and import requirements for materials, capital goods, etc. grow year by year, the temptation will be to go through the whole spectrum of possible import-competing industries, thus extending protection over a wide range. But this, in and by itself, may well be something that hampers growth to the extent that the protected industries are not efficient, and the real cost of their products to the consuming public will be higher than it was when these were imported.

Surely the principle of comparative costs suggests that, instead of continually widening the spectrum of protected import-competing industries, we should narrow the range with a view to the protected industries' in due course becoming export industries also. This came home to me very much when I was the "observer" at a conference of 15 Asian countries in Karachi a short time ago. There one was faced with the fact that they could not rely on the export of primary products alone, since the world demand for them was not sufficiently elastic, while they would be confronted with a steep rise in import requirements. It was absolutely necessary for them to think in terms of exporting such manufactured goods as they might become proficient in producing. The thing would be, instead of protecting all possible import-competing industries, to select a more limited number, with the view that, according to comparative costs, they should eventually grow from "infancy" into export industries. Of course, getting an export industry going is a hard task, but it will be more conducive to growth than the other plan. Arising also out of my Asian experience was the idea that it would be desirable to get some agreement among the countries about the lines on which each would specialize. I am doubtful that a free trade area alone will achieve the desirable specialization, in this age of much planning and government interference, without specific agreements between governments about what they will encourage in their own countries.

4. I do not think that subsidies are necessarily to be frowned on, if the main problem is to put an end to wage-price spiraling. I was not completely convinced by the case of Ceylon cited by Mr. Dorrance, presumably as a warning, since there might have been much more wage-price spiraling there if the subsidies had not been given. Illustrative of the principle of subsidies as an anticost-inflationary measure was the classic case of Britain's food subsidies during World War II. These subsidies were definitely demand inflationary, but they were also cost deflationary, and I am sure that their net effect was that we had less price inflation than we should otherwise have had. Of course any policy of that sort would have to be combined with a drastic attempt to grapple with the wage problem. Is it really impossible to get some kind of wage restraint in these countries?

5. I am very much worried by the question of devaluation. Undervaluation of a currency is the surest way of inflaming a tendency to wage-price spiraling. On the face of it, one would suppose that in some Latin-American countries devaluation has been an integral part of the spiraling. One gets a round of wage increases, price increases, devaluation, price increases, wage increases, price increases, another devaluation, etc. In certain cases, if there was a really resolute attempt to break into this spiraling, it might be expedient to keep the currency a little overvalued in the foreign exchanges, so as to get a respite during which other parts of an antispiraling policy could be put into effect. Drastic measures might be needed to prevent black market developments. Someone has referred, from this platform, to capital punishment in Bulgaria for currency offenses. A historic instance of currency reform was that of Queen Elizabeth I of England, which was a landmark of world significance in the history of coinage. Governments had previously been the

victim of Gresham's Law, by which, when one wanted from time to time to refurbish the coinage, one had progressively to debase new issues, lest they be driven out of circulation by the old coins. Queen Elizabeth refused to tolerate this, and ordered that all the coins then in circulation should be collected and withdrawn from circulation on the occasion of her new issue, so as to evade Gresham's Law—a heroic administrative achievement in those days. Various regulations had to be issued, and anyone contravening them was to be "hung, drawn and quartered!"

That is the spirit one might need, if one was really to break into this vicious spiraling, which does so much harm to growth prospects.

d. COMMENT
Jorge Mendez

It is evident that the structuralists as well as the monetarists are narrowing their differences. The efforts to achieve development by orthodox methods have failed in underdeveloped countries. The more orthodox international institutions have had to think about such failures, and it seems that they have come to the conclusion that, in addition to monetary and exchange policy, there are some old structural problems to be overcome; otherwise stability would only be achieved at the cost of development, and it would be weak and transitory. This was shown by the experience of Argentina and Chile.

The basic policy instrument to achieve development without inflation should be a development program. A development program consists basically of a set of targets which must be balanced among themselves.

A key problem is that of the balance of payments. The process of development requires additional imports which cannot be paid for by traditional exports. The consequence is to submit the country to successive devaluations or to limit the rate of development. Until now, the solution to this dilemma in Latin-America has been to adopt ambitious plans of import substitution. I agree with Professor Felix that in order to avoid distortions of an excessive import substitution we should try to expand those traditional industrial goods which could be exported. I realize that it is not easy to make practical decisions on these matters.

In reality, there is no true choice for planners between import-substitution industries and the expansion of traditional industries. In existing institutional arrangements, there is a very limited possibility for exporting traditional industrial goods. The choice is thus limited, for the time being, to import substitution.

Nothwithstanding greater comparative advantages, or smaller disadvantages, in traditional industries as compared with industries with greater capital intensity, it is very difficult for the former to compete with the latter in world markets. Abundant and cheap factors that enter into the production of traditional goods do not compensate for both the high cost of scarce factors and the low productivity of the technical process. In textiles, the traditional Latin-American industry, the productivity of the spindle man in the United States is four times as high as in Latin-American countries, where, however, important progress has been made of late. In other lines, the difference is still greater.

Successive devaluations have not been a real stimulus toward diversification of exports. The causes for the lack of competition must be found elsewhere.

e. COMMENT
Osvaldo Sunkel

I fully accept Mr. Marquez' definition of development—that it can be faster than the rate of growth produced by spontaneous market forces, and that development should take place with a progressive redistribution of income. The logic of development requires substantial direct public action, adequate for both short- and long-run objectives. Monetary instruments cannot be used as such but should be adjusted to the special conditions of Latin-America.

Considering the recent experience of stabilization programs in a number of countries, I cannot understand how anyone could recommend with enthusiasm the bitter medicine of stabilization. The recent experiences show that classic stabilization policies are doomed to failure. These policies can only succeed if the economy can be held in a semi-paralyzed state. But this state obviously cannot be maintained for a long time. The Latin-American experience of the last decade is very instructive in this respect.

In the 1950's, a number of Latin-American countries were confronted with a fundamental dilemma of economic policy. Until 1952–54, exceptionally favorable conditions which existed in the world market for primary products produced an abundance of foreign exchange, which permitted the imports required by the process of industrialization. Many countries wasted their foreign exchange on nonessential imports as if the foreign exchange bonanza would last forever. But, since the middle of the decade of the 1950's, conditions in the international market for primary products have severely deteriorated, thus adversely affecting the rate of development.

In the face of such a situation, the majority of the less developed countries of the region, predominantly agricultural, with substantial subsistence sectors, a weak industrial development, and a small degree of urbanization—and thus with weak political representation of the large salaried masses—were in a position to use traditional policies to adjust to unfavorable external conditions.

In the group of relatively more advanced countries, the policy dilemma created by a foreign trade crisis presents a more complicated situation, resulting in more difficult decisions to be taken. The short-run problem created by the crisis in the foreign sector in the middle of the last decade increased the long-run domestic rigidities and disequilibria, which were slightly attenuated during the postwar decade thanks to the exceptional bonanza of the world markets.

In the face of the impossibilities of limiting imports and government expenditures in a substantial manner in a relatively short period, such countries run into strong balance of payments and budgetary deficits, thus adding fuel to the existing inflationary process. The readjustments of the exchange rates, of tax rates, and of prices were followed by massive readjustments of wages and salaries, giving rise to the inflationary spiral.

On account of the danger of hyperinflations and the difficulty of getting foreign aid to honor foreign debts unless inflation was stopped, several countries followed stabilization programs. Such programs consisted basically of such measures as curtailing monetary expansion, postponement or elimination of wage readjustments, attempts to eliminate the budget deficit by reducing expenditures and raising tax and public-utility rates, readjustment of the exchange rate by a substantial devaluation, and the partial liberalization of price and import controls. It was expected that such measures would produce price stability and a decline of real wages, and that all this, combined with a certain freedom to import, would stimulate competition, raising efficiency and diminishing costs of private firms. As a consequence, there would be a substantial inflow of private foreign capital and a strong expansion of exports, which would put the whole development process on a more healthy basis.

Such hopes were completely disappointed. In fact, neither stabilization nor development were achieved. It is true that the rate of price increases was reduced, but only at the expense of low income groups, and through an extremely liberal policy of imports of foodstuffs and industrial consumer goods. Both measures hurt domestic manufacturing industries whose level of activity declined, causing unemployment.

On the other hand, investment was the more flexible element of public expenditures, and its contraction caused a violent decline in the building industry. As is well known, this is an activity which employs an important proportion of the labor force, and, at the same time, has a strategic importance on the level of activity of the private sector. As a result of the general decline of the level of effective demand, greater competition of imported manufactured goods, and the difficulty of channeling industrial products into foreign markets, and insufficient agricultural output, the level of private investment also declined. Domestic private savings were oriented toward speculative activities, or were wasted on imports of luxury goods or trips abroad. Given this general picture of stagnation and lack of stimulus, foreign private capital did not show any interest, except when exceptional opportunities were offered in export industries.

The budgetary and balance of payments deficits, whose elimination constituted one of the main purposes of the stabilization programs, in reality increased. The budgetary deficit increased the contraction of economic activity curtailed in part the tax base, while, at the same time, the level of public expenditures was not reduced; the balance of payment deficit due to an excess of freedom to import and to the persistence of unfavorable conditions in world markets for basic products. Consequently, these countries accumulated, in the last three years, huge short-run foreign debts, without such debts having made any contribution to the increase of the productive capacity of the country.

In the face of the pressures from the business sector and of unemployment, governments were forced, after a period of strictly pursuing a stabilization policy, to expand public investments and to slacken credit restrictions. With such a new increase of effective demand and of economic activity, structural inflationary pressures appeared once more, as a consequence of inelastic supply of food-stuffs and due to the rigidity of certain basic services. Above all, the balance of payments crisis became more acute, due both to the increase of imports caused by the recovery of the level of activity and domestic incomes, and to the difficulty of controlling the excess of imports as a consequence of the abandonment of the system of import controls, which was part of the stabilization policy itself.

Thus, these countries found themselves in the midst of a situation similar to that of five or six years before, but with much greater foreign debts, and having lost the opportunity of correcting some of their structural problems. In addition, as a direct consequence of stabilization policy, income distribution became more unequal, unemployment and underemployment went up, the replacement and increase of social overhead capital was neglected, and deficiencies of housing, medical care, and education became more acute. Nothing, or almost nothing, was done to raise income and to improve the supply elasticity of the agricultural sector, or to introduce the necessary changes in the tax system.

Historically, in the region, several ways out have been suggested. These were not, however, solutions to an apparent incompatibility. In the past, and even today in many countries, unions are still weak, and inflationary pressures have been kept at moderate levels by breaking the resistance mechanisms of wage earners. But this cannot be accepted anymore. Inflation as a method to avoid a solution to the underlying contradictions of the economic structure has caused, after some time, negative effects and has finally led to stagnation. Stabilization, as an objective in itself, and in the form that was tried to achieve it during the last years, was also a sad failure. Short-run massive foreign indebtedness as an alternative or complement to previous policies does not provide a solution to the basic problems that causes instability and, at the same time, hinders future development.

The difficulty stems from the fact that structural deficiencies have long-run roots and solutions. Consequently, the achievement of stability in Latin America during a period of transition, until structural reforms begin to yield results, must be based on the simultaneous use of several instruments. Among these we must emphasize a distribution policy of agricultural output; a fiscal and monetary policy oriented toward the achievement of the objectives of development plans; the use of taxation in the foreign sector and international negotiations as a means of attenuating fluctuations in the markets of basic products; the reorientation of public and private investment according to the objectives of development plans; an efficient control of imports that would make possible a foreign trade policy consistent with the development objectives; an aggressive policy of exports; an adequate mechanism of international cooperation that would assure foreign aid whenever needed and that would not be conditioned by the adoption of internal and external policies or instruments inconsistent with development policy.

Finally, this whole set of measures must be simultaneously combined with other measures that would start a land reform and changes in the fiscal and educational systems, and with measures that would attack the great concentrations of power, wealth, and income that are the main obstacles to a dynamic and balanced economy in Latin America. Let it not be said that it cannot be done because these are long-run measures—this kind of attitude is a guarantee that they will never be started. It is true that the *effects* will appear in the long run, but policy *measures* simply are adopted or not. Besides, these measures do not represent just the economic conditions necessary to achieve a development process but are also the basis for getting a strong and permanent popular support without which it will not be possible to pursue a policy of balanced economic growth.

In conclusion, complaints, resistance, violent criticisms, and complete failures met by stabilization programs in Latin America are basically due to the fact that they were presented as alternatives and substitutes for a legitimate and realistic policy of economic and social development.

PANEL SESSIONS

Part III

10. PANEL: CHANGES IN ECONOMIC STRUCTURE

Guido di Tella

Structural problems show up particularly in two interrelated problems, first the balance of payments deficit and second the problem of inflation. The interpretation put upon the causes of these two problems influences economic policy recommendations.

In the case of the balance of payments deficit, the most obvious diagnosis is that of an overvalued exchange rate, the solution being a policy of devaluation. This recommendation is generally accompanied by the suggestion that inflation be restricted through reduction of the budget deficit and printing of new money.

This approach to the problem assumes the existence of a rate of exchange that corresponds to the equilibrium in the exchange market. It assumes also that devaluation is not an important cause of inflation, which to our mind presents several difficulties.

First, we might have to face elasticities of supply or demand of exchange that would make a devaluation inconvenient or, as in the more normal case, would call for a substantial devaluation in order to influence effectively the balance of payments.

Still less satisfactory than this argument, the importance of which has sometimes been exaggerated, is the possibility that devaluation might represent one of the most important inflationary stimuli and lead to a rise of domestic prices that would make necessary new devaluations, thus causing a devaluation-prices-wages spiral that might reach very dangerous proportions.

In this context Harberger's contribution to this conference is extremely interesting because it shows that even in the more favorable case of fixed wages, a spiral of this kind might occur which would turn out to be still more dangerous in the more normal case of a possibility of wage increases.

Such successive devaluations might increase in size, leading to explosive, divergent solutions. But, even assuming devaluations of diminishing size and a procession of convergent adjustments, the final solution might require a long period of time.

What is important here is the conclusion that a policy of devaluation does not necessarily lead to balance of payments equilibrium, and that even in the case where it does, too large a devaluation might be required, thus making equilibrium attainable only after at long process of successive devaluations which would certainly cause a very dangerous cost inflation.

Thus the solution of simultaneous exchange devaluation and putting a stop to inflation combines contradictory measures because of a wrong diagnosis of reality. A correct diagnosis requires probing into the fundamental causes, of which the foreign bottleneck and the tendency toward price increases are mere symptoms.

For this reason we have directed this panel discussion toward analysis of appropriate policies for the primary sector, particularly the agricultural sector, the secondary sector, and the sector of social overhead, especially the public sector, which constitute the areas where the battle against inflation must and can be conducted.

Before the panel gets into these three areas I would like to submit some general reflections.

Regarding the primary sector of exports it is necessary to distinguish between those countries which consume what they export and those which do not.

This is, of course, a matter of degree. To some extent, at least potentially, every country consumes its own export products. This problem arises more often in countries that export foodstuffs of which they are immediate consumers than in countries that export industrial raw materials, in which case the domestic demand will only be felt at the final stages of the process of development, that is, when the country has already developed its industrial sector.

In the case of exports of foodstuffs there exists the possibility that improvement in the standard of living, particularly at the early stages, will produce smaller supplies of exportable products. This would be the case of a "backward bending" supply curve.

Such has in fact been the Argentine case. In the Brazilian case, apparently because the export product (coffee) represents a small proportion of the minimum diet, there was no tendency toward leveling off or retraction of exports.

It is well to bear in mind the dangers of generalizing from the experience of countries that are exporters of raw materials which they do not consume to derive conclusions which in practice are inapplicable to countries that export foodstuffs which they normally also consume.

Regarding the government sector, it is worthwhile to examine briefly the problem of the budget deficit.

The deficit of the government sector has notoriously been one of the common problems of the Latin-American countries. This deficit has two main causes—one dangerous from the point of view of development, and the other of a completely different nature but neutral from this point of view.

The budgetary deficit, in the first place, might be due to a policy of directly or indirectly subsidizing the private sector. Such subsidies can be provided explicitly or through government enterprises, especially in the field of public utilities, such as transportation, energy, etc., that are getting for their services a price that is lower than their costs, which obviously implies a transfer from the government sector to the private sector. Such a policy is neutral from the point of view of development. The important question here is the rationality of such subsidies. A case can be made for them when they are aimed at low income groups.

The other cause of budget deficits, dangerous from the point of view of development, stems from inefficiency in the government sector, both in public administration proper and in government enterprises. In this case the question is not whether or not to cover the costs but whether or not the latter are in themselves too high. We can even think of cases where there is no deficit because the cost of the services is being totally covered, but where the level of these costs is abnormally high, due to the previously mentioned inefficiency. There are also cases of deficits arising from a policy of transfer of incomes from one sector to another, although services are being efficiently operated. This constitutes a situation somewhat less undesirable than the previous one. There are in Latin America cases of deficits mainly caused by inefficiency. In such cases, balancing the budget might hide inefficiency without eliminating it.

In addition, we must bear in mind that both the existence of inefficiency in the government sector and the need or motivation for subsidizing certain types of consumption represent structural problems of countries in the process of development.

Some of the oversimplified recommendations regarding the elimination of the budgetary deficit simply fail to consider fundamental problems.

Concerning the development of the industrial sector, it is very important to analyze where it is in conflict with the theory of comparative advantages. It is generally assumed that this theory assigns to countries such as those of Latin America the role of primary producers. In this context it seems that a policy of industrial development would strongly contradict the theory of comparative advantages. Even structuralist economists have admitted that industrial development is undertaken in conditions of comparative disadvantage but that it produces changes in the industrial structure that could not otherwise have been induced.

This apparent contradiction between a country's industrialization policy and the initial comparative disadvantages arising from its application can only be eliminated if we introduce into the traditional theory of comparative advantages the concept of *social* costs and prices in place of *private* costs and prices.

The type of development that leads to structural changes thus assumes a very strong and important external economy. Such an external economy, if computed in industrial costs, by reducing them, would lead to the conclusion that the country has a comparative advantage in industrial activities.

This seems to be a more positive approach than the well-known argument that attributes to the theory of comparative advantages universal validity but which maintains that in the real world, because the great nations do not follow the free trade rules of the game, the small nations are not able to follow them either.

Such an argument, even where valid, has a taste of "second best."

These reflections do not lead to the conclusion that all the Latin-American countries have a comparative advantage in all industrial activities. It is very important to bear in mind that the problem of high industrial costs constitutes an important problem, especially for the development of nontraditional exports.

Behind such high industrial costs all kinds of inefficiency of the economic structure are probably hidden—be they of the labor, entrepreneurial, or government sectors.

Great care must be taken in the use of rates of exchange for the purpose of international comparisons of any type of product, including industrial products. The rate of exchange would be relevant only in the case where there are no overcharges of any kind and especially where we have a situation of balance of payments equilibrium at such a rate.

It seems apparent that the price mechanism alone cannot work as a sufficient inducement to fundamental change in the economies of Latin-American countries. The balance of payments problem, and the problem of inflation, are only the consequence of profound existing maladjustment. Rather than attempting to attack the ultimate manifestations of the problems, it will be better to focus on eliminating their causes, which stem from the structure of the economy itself.

Hollis Chenery

I shall start with a brief outline of the main structural changes that take place in an economy as it develops, in order to have an idea of the order of magnitude of some of the changes involved.

Despite the fact that we are discussing structural changes, I think it is quite difficult to give a definition of what we mean by structure or structural change. In general, economists define "economic structure" as the set of institutional, technological, and psychological factors which condition economic behavior. To distinguish a predicted change in a variable from a change in the structure depends on the model which you have of the economy. Assume that the income elasticity of demand for food is .6 and the elasticity of demand for automobiles is 1.8, and we see that as a response to an increase in per capita income, automobile consumption increases more rapidly than food consumption. I would not call this a change in the economic structure, although a lot of people in talking about structural change would describe it as that. We need to have in mind the changes in composition of demand, of output, of trade, of factor use, whether they are predicted by the model we are using or whether they involve some changes in the parameters of their model. I would define structural change as a change in any of these parameters, to distinguish it from a change brought about by varying income or price levels.

As Mr. di Tella has said, the notion of adapting the economic structure is not an issue among people prescribing for inflation and growth. Everyone recognizes that there are structural changes. The issue is whether they will come about more or less automatically in response to the working of the market, or whether the government needs to intervene to correct the automatic forces. I think that the main difference between the less developed and the more developed countries in this respect is in the magnitude of the changes which take place as per capita income increases. If we take, say, the objective of countries in Latin America, which is to have a growth of GNP of something like 6 percent, you need a growth in industry of 10–12 percent, in agriculture of 3–4 percent, and in the various service sectors something in between. The analysis of exports which we have had, stemming from the ECLA studies, has distinguished between the cases of countries in which exports do not keep up with income and those which do. Industry has to compensate for the lack of growth of exports to provide balance between supply and demand, sector by sector.

When most people use the term balanced growth, it is not in the sense of a country producing everything for itself, but in the sense of production satisfying the demands of the economy as income increases. This can be done either through trade or through domestic production, so that the term balanced growth is, I think, neutral with regard to the path that the production structure takes. It is just a requirement of economic equilibrium which recognizes consumers' preferences as to what they choose to buy.

The main structural problems arise, I think, in the ability of the market to transmit the right signals to producers, and in their adequacy in bringing about the very large changes which would be required, particularly in the cases where exports do not expand as rapidly as GNP. This case is not unique for Latin America, and I would not agree with the distinction that was made earlier between Southeast Asia and Latin America in a structural sense. I think the Asian countries have very similar problems in adjusting their structure to the growth of income. Much of what we will say about Latin America would be equally applicable to Asia. They may have taken different policies, but the structural problems were very similar.

The analytical question is to identify for the policy maker the areas in which the market may not work properly, so that he can be prepared to take such steps as are necessary to compensate for the deficiencies of the market. I think this is an approach which should have a wide range of acceptance, both among monetarists and structuralists. If, in fact, the market does adequately lead to adjustment in the structure, which has been the case in a number of countries, then the argument for more direct kinds of interference is rather weak. The selection of the kinds of structural policy that are needed varies considerably from country to country; in some cases one industry will respond properly and in other countries there will be a different industry, so there is no uniform structuralist policy prescription. Rather it depends on the entrepreneurial talents in the country, the mixture of public and private ownership, and a whole range of other things.

Against this background, I will now outline some of the main kinds of structural change which may cause difficulty and which, I think, will provide a focus for further discussion.

One kind of change which everybody has pointed out is the response of agriculture, which is more a question of access to land and of information on demand rather than anything innate about agricultural producers. In many countries, agricultural producers are extremely responsive to price change. Even very primitive, illiterate agricultural producers have sometimes surprised planners by their reaction to price changes. It is not that all agriculture is unresponsive to the market; often the market doesn't give the right information.

We have the fact that agricultural performance in Latin America has not been adequate. What we need to do is determine why it has not been adequate and what the proper policies are.

A second main area which everybody has pointed to is the export sector. Here again, I don't think we can just assume that exporters don't respond to prices or that devaluation never has the proper response, or that all demand elasticities for Latin-American products are inelastic. We need to look at what information the market has been conveying to exporters, whether governments have allowed the prices to reflect the real price of foreign exchange. Here we come to the question of accounting prices. In many cases, by keeping overvalued exchange rates and not letting the market transmit the right information to exporters, countries have prevented the adapation which might very well take place through the market. This mechanism has brought about increases of exports in countries like Japan, Israel, and other countries where structural changes have been achieved through the play of market forces. Again, we cannot jump from an observation of the inadequate performance of a sector to the conclusion that there is something innate about that sector that does not respond. We need to look at the institutional setting within that sector and to see whether governmental policies may interfere with the proper response.

The third area I will touch on is that of the interdependence among the various branches of industry, and between industry and overhead facilities. It is well known that economies of scale prevent the market mechanism from working properly. You don't get the right investment decision on marginal principles where there are economies of scale. This is particularly true in steel, metal-working, electric power, and heavy chemicals, which in the countries starting into this phase of industrialization have to be created more or less at the same time.

In this case, it is well known on theoretical grounds that the market does not give all the information needed for the right investment decision. All economists will admit that some sort of intervention is needed. They will disagree, however, on the form the intervention might take. It may be the French type of planning, in which the information is given to the producers. It may be necessary to follow the Indian model and have the government actually invest in steel and other industries in order to bring about these changes. Here we have to recognize it is not just that the economy is not like the theoretical model; the theoretical model itself tells us that there should be some sort of governmental intervention on a sector basis.

In conclusion, I would just indicate some of the policies that are relevant to all sectors. One would be a policy to make factors more mobile, so that sectors that are expanding rapidly will not be starved of skilled labor and entrepreneurship while the traditional sectors have a surplus. Another structural policy is the improvement of information other than prices, so that investment can be based on market forecasts and not just prices which happen to result from the current working of the market. Another structural policy would be to remove obstacles to entry, both in agriculture and industry. Finally, there are policies affecting the working of the public sector itself, which, as many people have pointed out, is one of the least responsive in many of the countries we are talking about.

Robert T. Brown

I would like to sharpen one point in Hollis Chenery's introduction. I don't think that the only point at issue is whether or not the structural changes which have to occur in any country which is growing will take place automatically in response to price stimuli, but we must also look at the timing of the structural changes. It is true that countries such as England were able to make the structural changes within a free market environment, but it took a good part of a century in order to do it.

One of our problems now is that Latin-American countries are not prepared to wait out that kind of a time period for the structural changes.

Earlier Japan was mentioned as a country which achieved a successful structural change while depending primarily on the free market. But even in the case of Japan, the way in which the government conscientiously uses its taxation policy in agriculture to bring about important structural reforms, the kind of reforms which would be necessary here in South America, is certainly relevant. This may be just a little off the point, but as a structuralist I would like to say that the point at issue in structural changes is especially their relationship to planning.

At no time have any of the structuralists advocated centralized dictatorial planning for South America in order to bring about structural changes, primarily because they are matters of law. Tax reforms and agricultural reforms are matters of law, and at least of the ABC countries it is certainly true that in both Brazil and Chile this kind of reform would be carried out only through law. We hope that even Argentina, which is temporarily away from it, will get back to a democratic frame.

Anibal Pinto

I shall try to clear up some points with reference to changes in agriculture. Let us see what can be expected from agriculture under a development process. As you all well know, one would like to see the supply of agricultural goods increased in order to satisfy the increasing demand of both the nonagricultural and the rural sector. It is also expected that the agricultural sector, which is a great reservoir of labor, can free labor for the sectors which will expand more rapidly than agriculture in the future.

I would like to call your attention to the fact that there are some situations in Latin America where agriculture could play its expected role in the development process. For example, Argentina and Uruguay are, or were, countries with great agricultural surpluses which could direct part of the food formerly exported to the rising numbers of their populations active in the industrial and urban sectors. I wish to call attention to the difference between these countries and those which are not in such a fortunate position.

In the case of most of the South American countries, agriculture has not grown fast enough both to sustain the increasing consumption of the urban populations and at the same time to make its contribution to the balance of payments position. The latter has increased in importance as a consequence of the requirements of industrialization programs, causing increased importation of machinery and raw materials. Thus, there is an urgent need for increasing exports. It is obvious that the problem is even more serious for countries depending on the importation of foodstuffs in addition to industrial products. So the increase of agricultural output, given natural resources, is of strategic importance for their future development.

What can be done about this problem? As is well known, the expansion of the agricultural sector depends on technical progress and its dissemination. We have already said that a basic function of agriculture is to supply labor. Latin America faces a unique situation in this respect, since, in many countries, there has already occurred an excessive transfer of population from the rural to the urban sector. Thus, certain types of dissemination of technical progress in the agricultural sector would cause a relative urban overpopulation. There are two ways to increase agricultural production. One would be to increase labor productivity by using more machinery. This would burden the balance of payments and would release labor not needed in urban areas. The second method would be to increase the use of fertilizer, use better seeds, etc., thus increasing the yield of the land without aggravating the labor absorption problem.

The other key problem is in the receptivity to technical progress of the Latin-American agricultural sector. One should differentiate between the behavior of the export-oriented and the subsistence sectors. The former is usually dynamic, while the latter lags behind and only in some cases, is barely keeping up with population growth. Besides the emphasis on the lack of structural changes in the agricultural sector due to the tenancy system, we must take into consideration other elements to explain why such a structure shows a certain flexibility when it is working for the external market, while it is rigid when it has to produce for domestic consumers. The problem is one of effective demand, related to the distribution of income. Since the latter is very unequal, additional income goes more to the upper and middle classes, rather than to the masses of low-income wage earners. This, however, is hidden by the averages. Thus, with a small agricultural market for the masses, there is little stimulus to innovate in the domestic-oriented agricultural sector. Consequently, we must avoid the error of thinking only in terms of obstacles from the supply side.

Robert T. Brown

I am going to refer to the sectors of transportation, power, and communications, not to the entire sector of services. I would like to point out a few of the characteristics of these sectors, then mention a few points on how they have contributed to the inflationary pressures in Latin America, and finally to discuss some of the repercussions of inflation on these sectors. In most of the Latin-American countries the existing state of transportation, power, and communications is poorly suited to the demands of new industries, especially when these new industries are located outside the traditional producing centers or the traditional centers of concentrated population. But different countries show quite markedly different patterns of transportation in Latin America at the present time. For example, we have some countries, Argentina being perhaps the best example, where the present transportation network was well developed and quite appropriate for the period when the entire economy was oriented toward exports. They have good transportation networks to bring food produce especially to the ports for exportation. Other countries, such as Venezuela and Brazil, have vast areas which are yet to be opened up, where there is no transportation and where it will be necessary to make really massive investments if the development of these regions is to be possible. Then there are still other countries, such as Chile, where you do have the major elements of a national transportation system, but these countries face very difficult adjustments to motor vehicle transport, which has placed great comparative pressure on the traditional media such as railways and coastal shipping. In this sense, the problems of Chile cannot really differ basically from those in, say, England. It is also worth pointing out that in nearly every Latin-American country the government is already heavily committed in the transportation sector. In Chile it owns nearly 100 percent of the railways, the major coastal shipping company, the ports, and the most important airlines. It is also engaged in the building and maintenance of highways. As these public transportation companies have been run as public services, and because at times it appears that the operating loss is taken as a measure of the public service being rendered, their financial deficits represent an impressive burden on the national budget.

The situation with respect to electric power and communications is quite similar. The capacity in these sectors is completely inadequate even in the traditional urban centers, where new investments have lagged far behind the growth of population. In new areas the problem is serious and power plus communications links among the different regions are practically nonexistent. To a greater extent in power and communications than is true in transport, you have considerable private ownership, especially foreign ownership. This has led to frequent attacks of the respective governments on foreign-owned companies, because they have not invested sufficiently to keep up with the growing demand. You have countercomplaints from these foreign companies of low rates which do not permit renewed investment. A short time ago *Time* magazine published a glowing account of the International Telephone and Telegraph Company's Telstar satellite and the great breakthrough it represented, and the following week *Time* printed a letter from a Santiago resident saying something like "Now that T and T's brainy engineers have achieved a brilliant breakthrough, perhaps they can solve a small, much lesser problem and get me a telephone, as I have been on the waiting list for 5 years."

Now, with respect to the pressure that this inadequate investment puts on inflation, it is quite clear that the level of prices could, and probably would, be lower if there were adequate capacity in power and transportation. What happens is that as the demand for finished products increases, the effects on prices will depend on the shape of the supply curve. To the extent that the increase in production of transporation can only be secured at increasing cost, a price increase is necessary to call forth the increased output of the finished goods. In the extreme case where no transportation facilities exist, as in Chile for example, you can have rising potato prices in Santiago simultaneously with potatoes rotting in the extreme south because of lack of transportation facilities. This inadequate investment causes inflationary pressures in these countries. New investments to overcome inadequate capacities would also be inflationary, if, as is common, they are financed by an increased budget deficit.

Finally, the heavy operating losses of state enterprises which I mentioned are also inflationary in that they add to the over-all governmental budgetary deficit. There are a number of reasons for the deficits of the operating companies. One is that governments have tried to subsidize public services in order to reduce the wage-price spiral.

In the second place, the unions in this sector are traditionally strong and have been successful in mantaing average wages above those of the private sector. And, in countries where you have a delicate political coalition in the government, strikes on the railways—in Chile the railways are the biggest single employer—or in ports are political dynamite.

Thirdly, productivity in the public utility sector is notoriously low and even falling in the case of the state railways of Chile, as the state transporting companies are used to absorb the faithful party members who are represented in the coalition government.

And, finally, in the case of Chile, you also have growing deficits because of the competition of highway transportation.

It is really quite difficult to think of ways in which inflation has been able to speed up expansion of capacity. First of all, in facilities which are still in private hands investments have been reduced because of inflation. This is not only a problem of inadequate rates, as I mentioned before, but also one of the general environment which rapid inflation creates and uncertainty concerned with remittances, exchange rate policy, tax policy, etc. The latter are extremely important, especially in investments with long life.

Hollis Chenery

Most countries are reaching the ceiling on import substitutions at present income levels. This does not mean that they are not able to produce anything else, but that the cost of producing the remaining imports is so high that it is not advantageous to undertake production when the cost is going to be twice or more the import price. Again, export policies should be a central element in any such prescription, and we have examples of a number of countries which have managed to break into the international market. One trouble is that in this case it requires quite a different attitude of both government and industrial producers, that the traditional policy of inducing producers to undertake production by protection be completely abandoned. Protection and the high cost production which has resulted from it are really handicapped when it comes to exports, because quality, costs, delivery times, and all kinds of marketing arrangements are neglected so long as one is producing for a protected market.

Thus the very policy which was successful in inducing industrialization up to a certain point now works against the next stage of industrial development, which is production for an export market. It seems to me that things can be learned from some of the latecomers in parts of the world outside Latin America, such as India, Pakistan, Israel, or Middle Eastern countries which are now exporting some kinds of industrial commodities. The import substitution ceiling has been hit by so many countries that the problem is not peculiar to Latin America.

The other main problem in terms of the range of structural policies would be the extent to which planning seems to be required to supplement the ordinary incentives that governments provide for industrialization. If one looks at Latin America as a whole and tries to figure out, as ECLA once started to do, what the location of industry would be if you had achieved an integrated market as compared to the present pattern of industry, one would see that some very large changes and movements of resources would be necessary in order to achieve integration. The very magnitude of these movements impedes integration, because some producers will be hurt. It is probably not as serious as the problem which faces the European countries, which were all industrialized when they started to integrate. Many industries in Latin America are just getting started. But every year integration is postponed there are more industries that are going to be hurt. I think the automobile industry is a clear case. But, if you have anything like an integrated Latin-American market, most of the efforts which do not now even make sense in the national context would make even less sense in a regional Latin-American context.

11. PANEL: INVESTMENT POLICY

John H. Adler

I would like to suggest a systematic expósition of the effects of
inflation on the level and composition of investment in Latin America—or for that matter, in any underdeveloped country. The simplest way of doing this is to enumerate a few characteristics of investment which I believe are prevalent in underdeveloped countries
even in the absence of inflation, and then to speculate about the effects which inflation has on these characteristics. I am using the
term speculate advisedly, because, as Mr. Chenery and Mr. Goldsmith have already pointed out, we are discussing a subject in
which data are disagreeably scarce, while hypotheses abound. I am
confining my remarks to domestically financed investment, although
I think that much of what I have to say also applies to foreign-
financed investment.

We can all agree on some basic propositions regarding investment in Latin America. The first is that a high level of investment
is desirable and that it is a necessary but by no means sufficient condition for a high rate of economic growth. This, I suggest, is true
whether it is argued that the level of savings (supplemented by resources obtained from abroad) or the difficulty of making investment decisions is the decisive factor limiting investment. It is still
true—perhaps even more true than before—if we take account of the
growing recognition that what has been called investment in human
capital, through increased current rather than capital expenditures
on education, research, technical training, health, and so on, is also
a major factor contributing to economic growth.

Second, I believe that all or at least most of us would agree to the
proposition that the composition of investment is unsatisfactory.
The major characteristics seem to be a larger proportion, perhaps
an excessively larger proportion, of investment going into such
things as inventories, high-cost housing, and not enough into economic and social overhead facilities, agriculture, manufacturing industries, and low-cost housing. There is not likely to be agreement
on the specific reasons for this bad pattern, and it may even be ludic-
rous to try to find any general reason which would be applicable to
all countries. But what I want to stress is that this tendency toward
a less than optimum composition of investment exists in Latin-

445

American countries with or without inflation, and—to take account of earlier observations of Professor Haberler—irrespective of the degree of government in the economy.

Third, although the level of investment is only a very partial explanation of the rate of economic growth and it may well be, as Professor Kaldor pointed out, that the rate of capital formation is also the result of growth and not just one of its causes, its importance from the point of view of policy makers is that it is operational. Policy measures can be devised to increase the level of investment and improve its composition. It may well be that Everett Hagen is correct in his assertion that some sort of psychological dissatisfaction is at the root of all development endeavors.[1] But I am sure that it is easier to increase investment and improve its composition than to produce a set of dissatisfied grandparents to increase the supply of entrepreneurship.

Given the "structural" problems adversely affecting the size and composition of investment. I shall now examine whether inflation helps to solve these problems or makes them worse. In order to answer this question, I suggest that it is necessary to distinguish between the type of inflation which prevails and the conditions surrounding the inflationary process. It is necessary to stipulate whether administered prices are adjusted immediately or after a long time lag; whether exchange rates are permitted to fluctuate or are fixed and adjusted periodically; whether interest rates are institutionally sticky and whether investment funds at those rates, from public or private sources, are available or not.

I could go on, but I think I have made my point: it is very difficult to find a combination of these policy and institutional factors which would lead to the conclusion that an inflation of any significant size would increase the level of investment, except perhaps for a short period, or improve its composition.

The conclusion is reinforced if we take into account the adverse effects of inflation on the balance of payments. This I think is true irrespective of the existence or absence of exchange controls and irrespective of whether we have fixed or fluctuating rates. If export earnings decline, or the price of foreign exchange increases, or domestic prices rise relative to the cost of imports, we either get an adverse change in the composition of investment by sector, or we may get the wrong choice of technology—too much imported equipment and not enough domestic labor.

---

[1]Everett Hagen, *On the Theory of Social Change, How Economic Growth Begins* (Homewood, Illinois: Richard D. Irwin, Inc., 1962).

There is presumably one exception to this generally negative conclusion. If, during an inflation which is expected to continue, loan funds are available, and if the level of capital formation is determined by the "Hirschman mechanism," that is, it is limited by the willingness and ability to make investment decisions and not by available savings, then inflation may raise the level of investment. But it also would adversely affect its composition.

At this point I should like to add that my conclusions are not symmetrical in the sense that a deflation would stimulate investment or improve its composition. Deflation of any kind I could think of would obviously make the problem of capital formation worse. But I suggest deflation is not the problem we must worry about in Latin America.

The last observation I want to make is that the most important factor determining the efficacy of investment is the growth process itself. I remember a remark by Professor Kafka, some years ago, to that effect in relation to the Brazilian economy. But this is true for other economies as well. In a fast-growing economy, mistakes and distortions in the investment pattern, whether aggravated by inflation or not, tend to be automatically cured, absorbed, so to speak, in the dynamic movement of growth itself.

Isaac Kerstenetzky

As the more general aspects of the influence of inflation on the level and composition of capital formation have already been discussed by Dr. Adler, I am going to make just a few remarks concerning some aspects of the Brazilian experience in this respect.

The period 1947–61 has been characterized by a fairly high average rate of growth (6 percent).

There is no clear evidence that the rate of inflation had any substantial influence either on the rate or on the composition of capital formation behind the rate of growth.

The structural change of the economy during the period is indicated particularly by the increase of the share of the industrial sector in the domestic product at constant prices, from one fourth to one third, with a relative increase of more than 250 percent.

As for capital formation behind such growth, there is only evidence in relation to the aggregate level.

During the period 1947–60, gross fixed capital formation represented, on the average, 14 percent of the gross domestic product, which indicates a relatively low capital-output ratio of 2,4:1 for the period as a whole.

As for the sectorial composition of capital formation according to its apparent destination, notwithstanding the rise of prices the share of building declined between 1949 and 1958, from 57.8 to 49 percent, increasing the proportion of equipment from 42.2 to 51.0 percent of the total.

During this period there was substantial import substitution—the import content of equipment declined from 53 to 33 percent.

In the development process, the foreign sector played an important role. During the first part of the period, the growth of the economy was greatly conditioned by the rise of the capacity to import as a consequence of the improvement of the terms of trade. With the worsening of the latter, the deficit of the balance of payments increased. The rate of growth could be sustained, and even increased at the end of the period, through indebtedness and a substantial inflow of foreign capital.

Some important distortions must be pointed out. There seemed to be an insufficient increase in the supply of foodstuffs, in relation to the high rate of growth of population of more than 3 percent per year, due mainly to an imperfect distribution system.

The greater share of the government in the economy was accompanied by certain negative aspects. Expenditures for the transportation system and for education, for instance, were characterized by a disregard of cost-benefit considerations. Expenditures of the central government on coffee accumulation represented from 2 to 3 percent of the gross domestic product in recent years, with no increase in the capacity of production of the country and with an important absorption of the storage capacity in some regions. Thus, the main distortions observed during the last 15 years were less a consequence of inflation than of a lack of an adequate system of government planning.

Jorge Franco

In considering the effect of stabilization programs on investment, I would like to state that I am definitely against inflationary methods as a means of development in Latin America. I strongly believe that inflation is highly disadvantageous and in consequent I do not consider that there is a choice between having or not having stabilization programs, but rather that they are an absolute need. Thus the problem is to choose the best possible stabilization program in accordance with the peculiar circumstances of the country in question and the diagnosis made.

In order, however, to make a good diagnosis, it is essential that a clear distinction be made between monetary demand and aggregate effective demand. Speaking in general terms, the problem in Latin America is not one of excessive aggregate effective demand; on the contrary, there is a clear insufficency of effective demand, since real purchasing power is low, markets are very small, etc. On the other hand, however, monetary demand is in general very high, causing constant rise in prices, since supply factors tend to be rather inelastic.

This being the case, it does not seem reasonable to curtail investments in Latin-American countries, as would be done in more developed countries, in order to reduce aggregate demand. The problem cannot be handled in that way because it would penalize the economic potential of Latin-American countries, this being contrary to one of their most evident and obvious aims, that of achieving the highest rate of economic development possible..

It is, however, necessary to curtail monetary demand, since inflation inevitably also causes a subutilization of available resources. Thus, stabilization programs should be aimed at reducing or even stopping inflation, without at the same time lowering aggregate effective demand, and in consequence the rate of growth. There lies the great difficulty.

Probably the best way to achieve this twofold aim is to attack the problem in a roundabout manner, monetary measures being the logical complement of this policy. There are two basic fields in which action would seem particularly effective. In the first place, measures should be taken to break up the wage-price-devaluation spiral. There are many possibilities; among them I believe that those directed at encouraging the production of wage-goods, particularly foodstuffs, would be especially useful, since they should have the effect of increasing or, at least, maintaining real wages.[2] If this is achieved, there are at least some better chances of breaking the spiral than would otherwise be the case.

A second effective way of dealing with the problem would be for the economic authorities in the Latin-American countries to care-

---

[2]Even subsidies might be used to lower the retail prices of wage goods.

fully revise their policies, adopting strong measures to encourage production for export and avoiding the creation of import substitution industries in which Latin-American countries have no comparative advantages vis-à-vis the more developed countries. This latter point is rather important because, in general, Latin-Americans do not seem to recognize that there are some industries in which their countries do not possess comparative advantages. Obviously there are such industries; for example, the manufacture of jet planes.

Once these measures aimed at resolving structural problems are taken, monetary policy can regain some of its lost autonomy and become more fully effective. It can then act, under the framework of general stabilization programs, with much better chances of success, that is, assuming a fuller use of available resources and a higher rate of overall economic growth.

I believe that stabilization programs should be undertaken within a framework of freedom, since, to my thinking, this is the only way in which they can be really successful. Latin America suffers from undue and immoderate state intervention, which is justified by its advocates in any situation. If the economic conditions are stable these advocates maintain that the state should intervene in order to raise the level of public investment, achieve a better income distribution, etc.; if the situation is unstable and inflationary, they argue that the state must control the situation. Always they argue for more state control. This is a wrong view, for the simple reason that it does not take into account the obvious but not usually recognized fact that state intervention should be aimed at promoting freedom rather than curbing it. It should thus take the form of indirect measures rather than direct controls.

Stabilization programs through indirect measures, such as those mentioned, under a framework of freedom, will promote stable development without penalizing productive investment and help Latin-American countries get nearer to their more immediate objective, which is that of attaining self-sustaining growth.

Krieger Vasena

For the first time in this century, Argentina had, during the first decade of the postwar period, an acute inflationary process. The investment rate had been around 20 percent, but when the GNP ceased growing from 1949 on, it was insufficient to finance investments. Stagnation of per capita income prevented net capital formation.

Let us look at the composition of investment during the first years after the war, the period of acute inflation. We shall see how inflationary policy not only has not boosted real resources but actually led to their inadequate utilization. When per capita income of a country increases, there will be reduction in the investment and transport sectors. The contrary occurred in the postwar period in the Argentine case. The net product per capita stagnated, but there was a dangerous intensification of investments in the unproductive sectors. According to ECLA's studies during the 1944-55 period, only 25 percent of the investment went into productive sectors, and 75 percent went into the other sectors. We should add the transportation sector, in which we not only had no increase of capital but a reduction of 1.3 percent between 1945 and 1955. In agriculture, investments were not made to the extent which was called for by technological advancements, as in other countries. And in the period considered industry was the only sector which increased its proportion of total investment. But most investments were not adequate for the development of the country. For the particular period in question, capital formation was oriented toward the production of consumer rather than capital goods.

Between 1946 and 1955, the production of consumer goods increased 127 percent, strongly dependent on imports of parts and raw materials. But capital goods increased only 45 percent. There is no doubt that the production of consumer goods means satisfying needs, but its excessive demand in a period of creeping inflation and stagnation of the GNP compressed the production of capital goods, as well as the possibilities of new industries using local raw materials, especially for export. We must add to this the unfavorable effect on the balance of trade, as it meant a greater demand for import of raw materials for those industries. Other sectors of activities, such as mining and electricity, during the first phase of the postwar period, showed a notable reduction. In other words, the necessary resources were not oriented toward the bottlenecks of the economy. Let us see where most of the investments went during the period considered. 75 percent of the increase in capital went into the sectors not producing goods. This increase of 75 percent breaks down as follows: 35 percent for the state sector, 34 percent for public buildings and housing, and, for other sectors, 6 percent. After the end of the war, the country went through a period of nationalization of important sectors, such as the railroads and telephones.

When these basic sectors were concentrated under the state, it was essential to maintain and increase their capacity for operation. But if we analyze separately the amounts annually earmarked for electricity, highways, railroads, oil, and so on, we observe that there is a very low proportion of investments in relation to the importance that they had achieved within the over-all structure of public investments. After the war, public expenditures involved a very high percentage of the gross national product (from 20 percent prior to the war to 30 percent). And the state absorbed one third of the increase of labor in the country which, in turn produced serious anomalies in connection with the increase of public current expenditures. The current expenditures of the state, that is to say wages and subsidies, increased, and the proportion of capital expenditures was insufficient. These figures lead to important conclusions: on the one hand, the public sector for a long period absorbed a considerable portion of the resources of the country, part of which could have been utilized by the private and public sector to increase capital formation. As Argentina began to feel the consequences of an acute inflation by 1951, subsidies were used on a large scale, especially in connection with foodstuffs, such as bread and meat, in which Argentina had been at one time the first world supplier. Apart from lacking an investment program in this period, the state also distributed inadequately the available savings and this is one of the most important causes of the structural problems which created obstacles to economic growth in Argentina during the first part of the postwar period.

Let us see how investment behaved from 1959 on, when stabilization plans were instituted. The main instrument was monetary policy. At the same time, a great deal of emphasis was laid on the necessity for development, but a specific plan establishing priorities and objectives was not drawn up. As inflation continued, due principally to massive salary increases without any relation to productivity, internal resources were oriented to unproductive sectors. The very important flow of funds coming from abroad, in the greater part short and medium term, helped, but of course they also increased the foreign debt of the country.

Considering investments in this period, the favorable aspects lay mainly in the fields of oil, electricity, and industrial re-equipment. In the oil sector, where there was a great deal of private investment, production increased substantially, but still there are no definite conclusions regarding the real economy in foreign exchange which has been obtained. In electricity, the loans from agencies such as the

Eximbank and the World Bank helped new investments considerably and there was a substantial improvement for the first time in the postwar period in this sector. In the industrial sector there was a change in the composition of imports, in other words, a considerable increase in import of parts, equipment, and machinery. But, at the same time, financing was done with foreign credits, especially on short terms. The IMF reports on Argentina stimulated a massive flow of hot money, also attracted by a high rate of interest. This industrial re-equipment, lacking an over-all plan, led to certain new distortions, like the striking automobile expansion (more than 20 new entities started to build and assemble cars).

Relatively few improvements were achieved in railroads, highways, and agriculture. The stabilization program correctly brought out the fact that the country might once again, as in the past, have a capital market in which it might be possible to finance not only the private sector but also the public sector. May I point out something which has been discussed, but not sufficiently, in this conference, and yet is fundamental for development.

Anyone who has been secretary of the treasury or has held high posts in this field knows how hard it is to manage a budget with investments in the public sector if you do not have among your resources, besides taxes, the placement of loan papers which would make it possible to provide adequate financing for the requirements of the public sector. It is a *sine qua non* to have a capital market, that is to say, we must have a supply of loanable funds which the state can shovel into public investments. Something of this started with the stabilization program; and the country has, as in the past, once again placed bills internally and loans abroad. But as the inflationary pressure continued, due particularly to the lack of relation between wage increases and productivity and inefficiency in the administration of public entities (railroads, telephones, oil), this possibility disappeared very soon. And, furthermore, it should be stressed that an important factor to be borne in mind in future stabilization plans is that global restriction of credit through the banking system, if you do not at the same time adopt fiscal measures and draw a development program, creates a parallel financial market at very high interest to be used by the less important sectors.

In summary, Argentine experiences as regards investments, not only in the immediate postwar period, in which there was an acute inflation, but also in the last four years, indicate without doubt that to get real monetary stabilization and a persistent growth rate it is necessary, within an over-all program, to draw a plan for investments, not only for public sectors, but also for the private sector.

Albert Hirschman

I must warn you that I am going to be a bit roundabout insofar as investment policy, the topic of our panel, is concerned. In effect, I shall behave here like a structuralist, for a structuralist seems at first sight an oddly roundabout fellow, someone who, faced with the task of containing inflation, refuses to use the "obvious" tools of monetary restraint and tells you to concentrate instead on illiteracy, the distribution of income, geological surveys, etc.

I shall stop right here and get my word in on this debate with the promise that I will lead you back eventually to investment policy. As a result of my current study of policymaking processes in Latin America, I can perhaps contribute something to an understanding of why monetarists and structuralists seem to be engaged in what the French call a "dialogue of the deaf."

Let me put it quite briefly and schematically: at any one time every society goes through certain clusters of difficulties which are considered as "problems" if there is some feeling that something can and should be done about them (difficulties that almost everybody agrees cannot be remedied at all are not felt as problems). Now, it is almost always possible to forge a fairly convincing causal link between one problem and another, of this sort: problem A causes problem B, hence if, and *only* if, problem A is taken care of, will problem B disappear or be alleviated. Why do structuralists feel the need to engage in this kind of linking while monetarists have no use for it and even consider it slightly absurd? For a very simple reason: monetarists come largely from societies in which each major problem is taken up or is expected to be brought to the attention of the policy makers *independently*, under its own steam. These are societies where interest groups, that is, groups of problem victims, are manifold, active, vociferous, and constantly regrouping. As a result, each problem, be it medical care for the aged, agricultural distress, or inflation, gets access to the policy makers and is treated pretty much in isolation from the others: there is little need, in general, for one problem to ride the coattails, so to speak, of another.

But then we have other societies—and I talk about Latin America now—where some problems have long lacked direct access to the policy makers: the problem victims—the submerged classes, as they are often called—have not been able, or have not been allowed, to organize themselves into effective pressure groups; the problem victims have no direct channel to the policy makers. But suppose there is one problem, such as inflation, that does arouse the policy makers. It may then be possible for intellectuals, deeply concerned over the other, neglected problems, to secure *indirect* access for them by connecting them causally to the privileged problem of inflation, which does get a hearing. Looked at in this fashion, the structuralist position is really an attempt to get some external economies out of the problem of inflation, to utilize it for the purpose of bringing some new pressure and of rallying some new forces for the purpose of solving the other, perhaps more fundamental but less "loud", problems which the society faces.

Hence, the difference between monetarists and structuralists is neither, as Mr. Dorrance proposed, between optimists and pessimists, nor as Mr Seers believes, between superficial and deep thinkers, but between two ways of problem-solving—one typical of societies where each problem is tackled and nibbled at independently, and the other where there is a great difference in the access different problems have to the policy maker and where there is, therefore, a tendency to link problems together.

I would add that, from this point of view, the structuralist position strikes me as a transitional one: it fills the void between the state in which the neglected problems are completely voiceless and the state in which they are able to assert themselves on their own, without the need to get smuggled in, so to speak, with the help of inflation. Mr. Sunkel said at one time here that some causes of inflation are more profound than others. I would amend this by saying that a *given* set of circumstances in a *given* situation is picked by us as a cause, and as a more or less profound cause, depending on whether we can do something about it or not. The maldistribution of land *became* a cause of inflation in Latin America only after the possibility arose of doing something about it. And, because the desire of compassionate intellectuals and economists to see something done outran the ability of the peasants to organize themselves, the result was structuralist theorizing rather than peasant action, violent or otherwise.

Structuralism, as I have already mentioned, is an attempt to utilize inflation, as long as it exists, anyway, for something worthwhile. This is a topic that has not been given nearly enough attention. As long as it seems to be a fact that inflation is with us in much of Latin America during eight years out of ten, we ought to reflect not only on how to fight it most effectively, but also on how to make the best of it while we are stuck with it. This brings me a bit closer to the topic of our panel. What are the possible uses a policy maker can get out of inflation from the point of view of investment policy?

Usually it is said that inflation distorts the investment pattern. We have already seen that the empirical evidence on this point is by no means conclusive. Let me now point to one way in which moderate inflation may contribute, *or could be made to contribute,* to a more efficient pattern of investments than might prevail in the absense of inflation. One of the reasons for the low efficiency of public investment is frequently the appropriation of funds in response to a variety of local political pressures without any coordination, let alone prior study of individual projects. Now, it may be easier to resist such pressures when the finance minister does not have to argue about the project per se, but can merely point to the developing inflation and say: you can see easily for yourself that we cannot afford this project just now. This is a very similar tactic to the one the French ministers of finance used to follow when they hid away in some hard-to-identify accounts any cash they happened to have on hand. Note that one of the principal advantages of having a development plan lies in providing policy makers with a similar tactical weapon against pressures for haphazard expenditures. A plan joined with a mild inflation may be a very powerful defensive combination against appetites on the loose.

Inflation also provides the much needed incontrovertible proof that taxes must be raised to finance investments. The forces favoring higher and more progressive taxes may well have to marshal the evidence of inflation to win their battle. We are apt to forget that big spurts in taxation have become possible in the advanced industrial countries only under the impact of major emergency and crisis, generally in wartime. The calamity of inflation may be the equivalent of war in countries fortunately deprived of this particular stimulant toward forceful taxation.

Another way of looking at the possible uses of inflation is to look at the changes in relative prices that always come with inflation and to examine whether these changes are development-promoting or not. I have a strong suspicion that the long coexistence of inflation and growth in Brazil is due to the fact, perhaps not entirely based on sheer good luck, that the relative price changes that resulted, for example, from the lag of some exchange rates behind the internal price level were just what the doctor would have ordered at that particular stage of Brazil's industrialization. Thus, the setting aside of foreign exchange at low cost for machinery and equipment throughout the fifties enormously facilitated Brazil's industrial boom; moreover, the abolition of that privilege in 1961 appears to have also come just at the right time to give a strong fillip to some machinery industries for which the economy was ready by then. Similarly, certain inflation-induced distortions of consumption patterns—for example, the shift from cash to durable consumer goods—may lead just to additional pressures on the balance of payments in a country whose industry hasn't gotten beyond the textile-cement-beer complex, but may be quite useful in one that is starting domestic production of automobiles, refrigerators, and washing machines.

The effects of inflation on the distribution of income and on reinvestment policies of business firms should also be looked at in this fashion.

Once inflation exerts this kind of investment and growth-promoting effect, you get, of course, a feedback in the form of public acquiescence in the inflation and a widespread resistance to forceful measures designed to stop it. It is for this reason that the prolonged coexistence of inflation and growth is not a matter of pure luck. Once inflation has proven itself as an ally of growth in these ways, it, in turn, picks up a variety of allies. This sequence suggests that before tackling an inflationary process that has gone on for a considerable period of time, we ought to have a good analysis to ascertain whether the inflation profiteers are to be found in the parasitic or the dynamic sectors of the economy. The stabilization effort that is called for may have to be very different, depending on whether we have a Brazil- or an Argentina-type inflation to deal with.

Roberto Campos

I would like to speak about the relationship between inflation and the mobilization of foreign resources. Any comments will be both very brief, for lack of preparation, and very narrow. I shall address myself to the relationship between the problems of inflation and the ability or inability of a country to capture foreign resources to supplement its domestic effort in development or stabilization programs. The initial distinction, which is obvious when considering this matter, is between the effects of inflation on the mobilization of foreign private investments and on the mobilization of

loans and credits, both public and private. In regard to private
investment, one perhaps ought to confine oneself to the question of
direct investment, because, at least in Latin-American experience,
portfolio "private investments" have practically disappeared as a
consequence of debt default in the disorganization of bond markets
and, last but not least, the very presence of inflation and serious balance of payments difficulties. One would say that, prima facie, other
things being equal, the effect of an inflationary situation would be
to discourage foreign direct investments. The first reason for this
is that inflation increases the exchange risks, by rendering mercenary
periodic exchange-rate devaluations.

It is true that this exchange risk may be temporarily offset by
windfall profits to the foreign investors when for short periods there
is exchange overvaluation.

In the experience of quite a few Latin-American countries, devaluations have lagged well behind internal inflation. For brief
periods, then, foreign investors may derive a windfall benefit, since
internal profits and prices reflect the inflation while the exchange
rate for remittances may remain overvalued. This, however, is likely
to be of short duration; moreover, overvaluation is likely to be accompanied by exchange controls which inhibit profit remittances.
The second reason that inflation discourages foreign investments is
that it adds to uncertainty, particularly in the case of slowly ma-
turing investment with a long gestation period, and particularly in
the case of investors from countries that are used to a long tradition
of stability and have not developed the peculiar gymnastics and
mental flexibility of those who are used to doing business in an
environment of inflation. (Some of our Brazilian investors and exchange operators are really ambulating IBM machines.)

To sum up, then, to the extent that inflation creates actual balance of payments disequilibria or the expectation of such imbalances, it is likely to have a discouraging effect on private investments. But, here, still another distinction is called for between direct investment in price-flexible and in price-inflexible sectors. In
situations of repressed inflation, when attempts are made to combat
inflation by the freezing of "critical" prices, creating very serious
rigidity in certain sectors, the effects of inflation are likely to be
partcularly discouraging. This is the problem faced, for instance, by
investors in public utilities, which, not only for political, but for
technical reasons, are a price-inflexible sector. The problem, of
course, is even more serious for foreign than for domestic investors,
since in addition to the problem of internal profitability, the latter
have the problem of transfer. In price-flexible sectors, the constraints

are less serious; the investors may continue to invest for quite a while in the expectation that, through periodical devaluation or through the adoption of flexible exchange rates, controls on profit remittances can be relaxed and the profitability of the investment preserved. Therefore the distinction between price-flexible sectors and price-inflexible sectors appears important in this context.

This whole picture would seem, on balance, to postulate clearly a negative relationship between inflation and the inflow of direct investments. Yet there are cases, such as that of Brazil, in which even a sharp and prolonged inflation has coexisted with a very substantial amount of direct foreign investment. This has been made possible by a number of counteracting measures or influences, such as, for instance, the size of the expanding market, the optimistic price expectations in the inflationary boom, the portective effect of exchange protectionism and exchange controls, which elicit foreign investments designed to maintain a foothold in the domestic market. Exchange controls thus have a somewhat ambivalent effect. To the extent that they impede or retard profit remittances, the impact on foreign investment is negative. To the extent, however, that they create an additional instrument for protection of the home market (and if his home market is substantial to start with) the effect may be quite positive. It is true, again, that this effect is differentiated, because it exerts itself much more on expansion of existing investments than on the influx of new investment. Finally, there are special measures that can be taken to encourage certain sectors of investment even under conditions of inflation. Brazil has had substantial success in this regard by such measures as exchange rate preferential treatment for certain sectors, reservation of markets, and fiscal incentives. The major cases of deliberate and successful promotion of foreign direct investments, even under conditions of inflation, have been the automobile industry, the shipbuilding industry, and, I may also add, the heavy mechanical industry—all of which have benefited from a very notable inflow of foreign direct investment in the last few years, despite rather gloomy forecasts that the inflationary climate would frighten away investors. To sum up this part of the discussion: inflation is likely to have a discouraging effect on foreign direct investment mainly because of its expected adverse effects on the balance of payments. These effects, however, can be, in individual cases, counteracted by other incentive measures, particularly in situations where inflation is associated with the growth of an internal market, as has been the case in Brazil.

Last year, Brazil experienced a substantial decline of foreign investment. This, however, was perhaps not mainly due to inflation or to the sharpening of inflation (although this may have been a contributing factor) but rather to the effect of a special legislation on profit remittances, which established quantitative limits for yearly remittances and excluded reinvested profits from the capital basis for computation of future remittances. It is not clear how long this discouraging effect will last, but it certainly exists. The picture, therefore, which initially had looked very simple, is becoming a little bit complex as we proceed along.

The next topic I wish to discuss is the effect of inflation on public loans and private loan financing. In relation to public loans, it seems clear that inflation renders more difficult the securing of financing from international agencies, as well as from the United States government, European suppliers, and so on. There are several reasons for this. The first is the technical linkage which exists, or is supposed to exist, between inflation and balance of payments disequilibria, affecting future ability to pay. A by-product of this is the discouraging effect of inflation on export behavior. Second, in addition to this linkage, there is also a psychological barrier in the developed countries, always prone to forget their past inflationary experiences, which leads them to regard inflation as somewhat more repulsive, even when accompanied by growth, than a situation of monetary stability accompanied by stagnation. According to the conventional mores of credit institutions, it is somehow more sinful to be inflated, even though dynamic, than to be stable, even though stagnant. Thirdly, there is an implied acceptance of some sort of deterministic link between inflation and social and political instability.

Be that as it may, it is clear that inflation does render it substantially more difficult to obtain financial assistance from foreign sources. Having been at this game for a while, I can claim, perhaps, to be an expert on international public loan financing. With regard to private financing, we may again distinguish between united loan financing and suppliers' credits. United private loan financing has practically disappeared from our scene, just as portfolio "loans" were a casualty of the last depression. What remains are suppliers' credits. It is indeed surprising that, even in the face of substantial balance of payments disequilibria and inflationary expectations, it is still possible to mobilize very substantial amounts of suppliers' credits. Of course, the supplier in this particular case does not act as an investor, but rather as an exporter. But whatever his motivation may be—it is not really assistance or aid but mainly export promotion—it has been possible, fortunately, even in the face of major difficulties in recruiting public loans, to continue to obtain suppliers' credits. In fact, we have here some sort of vicious circle. The international financial agencies, in particular, adopt a restrictive attitude in loan financing because of expected balance of payments difficulties or inflationary situations. This puts the developing countries in the hands of private equipment exporters, who offer suppliers' credits without bothering to investigate whether there is a stabilization plan or whether long-run projections of the ability to pay are satisfatcory. Of course the inadequate financial terms of the suppliers' credits contribute to aggravate the problem at the second turn.

I might, finally, mention some types of financing that have occurred in the past which I might describe as *involuntary financing*. Consciously or unconsciously, the developing countries may have been making the best of the situation, following perhaps Professor Hirschman's advice, in a different sense, by attempting to maintain imports even in the face of lack of financing. This has been done through the formation of commercial arrears, an experience which has been only too frequent, both in Argentina and Brazil. This leads to involuntary financing by foreign governments, who find themselves compelled to absorb exporters' claims and extend compensatory financing.

I would like to propose a general conclusion: weighing all the pros and cons, the effects of inflation on recruitment of public funds are generally unfavorable. With regard to private funds or credits, the possibilities are limited to suppliers' credits and also to involuntary financing through the formation of arrears. It makes, of course, a lot of difference in this whole context, whether or not the balance of payments disequilibria resulting from inflation, among other factors—it is of course clear that inflation is only a part of the problem, since balance of payments disequilibria can exist in the absence of inflation—are part of a pluriyear plan. In fact, if you have stabilization programs for gradual disinflation and if you plan the balance of payments gap, the whole exercise seems suddenly to become very respectable. If there were no other reason for planning, this selfish and narrow-minded reason would be an inducement to lead the developing countries in this direction. The mere forecasting of a balance of payments deficit as part of a multiyear plan gives an aura of respectability to large deficits which unplanned deficits would never have.

12. PANEL: INTERNATIONAL POLICIES

Gottfried Haberler

Whenever I speak on integration, I cannot forego the pleasure of quoting Alfred Marshall. Marshall once said that it is very difficult for the economist to be a patriot and to be regarded as one. When we speak on integration in Europe, it is very hard to be a good European and to be regarded as one. By the way, this is not an allusion to my European origin, because I have always found that the best Europeans you will find are in the United States. I could vary this statement by saying that it is very hard for an economist to be a sincere friend of underdeveloped countries and to be regarded as one. Now, let me come to the topic of economic integration. This is, of course, an extremely popular subject and Mr. Chenery observed that he would put it at the head of a list of agendas for Latin-American economic policy. What he meant, if I understood him rightly, was that regional integration is the best method to get out of autarchic protectionism. Maybe I should not say protectionism, since the modern "child" is "import substitution policy."

I will first say a few words about the European common market. Briefly speaking and from the propaganda standpoint, the common market has been a tremendous success. There is no doubt about that, and they have really developed the most efficient propaganda machine which has been seen for hundreds of years in that area. You have to go back 130 years, to the Anti-Corn Law League against Great Britain, in the first half of the eighteenth century, to find a ruthless demagogic propaganda machine as efficient as that of the common market. One difference, of course, is that the Anti-Corn Law League fought for free trade, but this is not unqualifiedly so for the common market. Tariffs have been radically reduced. On the other hand, the propaganda has exaggerated the actual economic impact. There can be no doubt that they are trying to give the impression that the recovery of Europe and the rapid growth of the Six is due to the common market. To my mind this is simply not so.

Let me come to the implication of the common market for the outside world, that is, in our case, for Latin America. I shall not

462

say anything about the direct damage done to outsiders and to Latin-Americans through trade diversion. The great disservice of the exaggerated claims of success of the common market is that they have led Latin-Americans to try to do the same. There is a certain imitation in the Latin-American free trade area, a demonstration effect if you like. I always feel that a demonstration effect is much more important in the field of policy than in the field of private business and consumption. I doubt that this type of integration will do much good. I am afraid that the conditions in Latin America for integration, the political as well as objective economic and geographic conditions, are much less favorable than in Europe. To begin with, the geography of these countries is much less integrated than in Europe and trade among them is, I think, 10 percent or less. And the transport situation is not very good. As has been pointed out to me, Brazil and Peru, though neighbors, cannot trade across the land, and even shipping is rather expensive. I was told by an Argentine friend that freight charges between Buenos Aires and Rio are frequently as high or higher than those between Buenos Aires and New York. This is a little amazing, but I was told that this is so because trade there is regarded as coastal trade and is reserved to the respective governments' shipping companies, which operate extremely inefficiently, and so this situation arises. This is one of those structural defects, in this case a man-made structural defect. I am afraid there are quite a few of these, and I would wish our structuralist friends would pay a little more attention to these man-made structural defects than to geography and other things, including the terms of trade, about which it is not so easy to do anything. There are quite a few man-made structural handicaps which could possibly be removed. This is the first reason why Latin-American integration cannot be as effective as European.

The second reason is concerned with different degrees of inflation. These countries have different degrees of inflationary pressures, and it is very hard to see how countries which pursue such different monetary policies, say Mexico on the one end and Brazil and Chile on the other, can really integrate. The third reason relates to the much higher degree of government intervention in the economic process. That again makes integration much more difficult. Fourthly, the whole setup of the Treaty of Montevideo is very different from that of the Treaty of Rome. The terms of the Treaty of Rome provide for broad tariff categories, while according to the Treaty of Montevideo there is no across-the-board cutting of tariffs.

Using the terms "trade creation" and "trade diversion" gets on the nerves of some people, but I still think that this is an absolutely fundamental distinction. Trade diversion is simply the protectionist effect of integration; you buy less from the outside and more from each other, that is, you get exactly the same effect as with a national tariff, and therefore every free trader is, of course, against trade diversion. Professor Viner, who has developed this distinction, and Professor Meade, who has followed him, were quite consistent in judging such a scheme to see whether trade creation or trade diversion is more important. Now, I do not want to take an extreme free trade point of view here. I think there is no free trade in the world. Surely one must allow for exceptions, and the most important exception from the free trade rules would be something like the infant industry argument, or nowadays we would call it import substitutions. A certain amount of trade diversion can be justified. The question is, how much? Mr. Chenery said that even an economist who does not like the comparative costs doctrine would not go so far as to say that it is profitable to produce something at home which you can import at half the price from abroad. Hence, if trade diversion takes on a form where these countries buy from each other at double the price for which they could buy somewhere else, that kind of trade diversion is a little too much. I would agree, on the other hand, that a certain division of labor is a good thing, and you could argue that regional import substitution is less objectionable than national import substitutions. I would not deny that, but here one has to consider that, national substitution may be so absurdly expensive that it is not done, while regionally it may be irrational, but not absurdly irrational and expensive. Thus, it is not 100 percent correct to say that regional import substitution is better than national import substitution. I think that the infant industry arguments have been greatly overdone, and a policy which comes much nearer to free trade would be much better.

Let me just mention one example. There is one Latin-American country which cannot pursue protection and, I might mention, cannot pursue inflation, namely Puerto Rico. Puerto Rico is in the U.S. customs area and has dollar currency, so the Puerto Ricans cannot have an inflation, at least no more so than the United States, which is very little by Latin-American standards. They cannot protect themselves against the competition of American industry and yet Puerto Rico has done better than any other Latin-American country. Puerto Ricans pursue development policies all right, but those two weapons which we are told are essential for development, inflation and protection, they cannot use.

But now let me ask this question: "Suppose a certain amount of trade diversion is all right, who is going to specialize in what?" I think the simplest method would be for each of the Latin-American countries to adopt a fairly uniform ad valorem import tariff over a wide range of commodities. Then, inside this framework, free enterprise, the forces of demand and supply, would automatically select the industries which would specialize here and there. That, it seems to me, would be the ideal solution.

Nicholas Kaldor

I have been asked to talk to you on the problem of the terms of trade, which is a perennial problem of all underdeveloped countries who get the bulk of their export revenues from one or a few primary products. An immense amount of discussion, thinking, and literature has emerged about this problem of the terms of trade, a lot of which goes back to periods preceding the second world war. I have recently been asked by Dr. Prebisch to preparte a paper for the Economic Commission of Latin America on what I think, as an individual economist, are the most promising methods for stabilizing the terms of trade of underdeveloped countries. I shall try to give brief summary of my views.

This paper begins by stating the position with regard to the terms of trade. The terms of trade have been deteriorating continuously since 1954. If you take the overall terms of trade of all the underdeveloped countries of the world, the deterioration has been about 12 percent. The postwar terms of trade have been much better, not only compared with the prewar terms of trade, but also with the terms of trade of the decade which preceded the great depression. The outlook for the future, according to all the experts, is very bad. Now, again, I want to issue a warning in this field of the terms of trade, where experts very often went wrong. When they prophesied falling prices, prices rose, and when they prophesied rising prices, prices fell. This could very well happen again. However, if you look at the picture as do some international organizations, such as FAO, which examines this systematically, it does look as if somethink like a great structural overproduction of primary commodities is in the making.

This is partly due to rapid technological progress, giving higher acreage yields for a number of primary commodities. Partly, it is due also to a sort of long cycle by which, in periods of high prices, there is a large amount of planting followed by a long gestation period. The high prices up to the early part of the 1950's led to large plantings which are only just now beginning to come into production. For all of these commodities the markets are narrowing and increasing in competition with synthetic materials, or are facing changes in the pattern of demand of industrial production, which makes less use of either minerals or products of tropical agriculture. There is the fact that the elasticity of demand from high income areas is very low, and thus consumption is restricted by revenue duties or by import restrictions, as in the case of the Communist countries. And there is the final threat, a very serious threat indeed, of the European common market, which adopted about 18 African and Caribbean countries as special wards and gives them privileged and preferential terms. That will very much stimulate the production in these countries and therefore narrow the market considerably for Latin America and for other unfortunate underdeveloped countries not entitled to wear the badge of Overseas Associated Members of the European common market.

What can we do about this?. Up until the war, the main efforts were concentrated on stabilizing the prices of individual commodities by means of international commodity agreements. In the 17 years that followed, few agreements have been concluded, despite innumerable international conferences, negotiations, study groups, intergovernmental consultations, and what not. Of the few that have been concluded, there are not more than two or three which for any prolonged period helped the underdeveloped countries in making their prices higher than they would have been otherwise. One agreement, the wheat agreement, was successful in keeping prices lower during the period of its effective operation than would have been the case otherwise. So, gradually governments became more disenchanted with individual commodity agreements and recently there have been proposals for an attack in a different form, the so-called compensatory finance schemes, which are not trying to stabilize commodity prices individually or in a group, but merely offer financial compensation to countries whose export receipts decline. I don't believe that this is an effective alternative. I greatly welcome all these schemes—they are very nice and very fine—but they are, after all, a new and more automatic form of financial aid from the rich to the poor countries. I don't think that the countries which are willing to provide the financing for these schemes will be ready to provide it quite so automatically as envisaged, I am not sure that they should. In no case can these schemes be regarded as an effective alternative to stabilizing the terms of trade.

The best way to stabilize prices is by individual commodity agreements. These agreements should be export quotas or export restriction agreements of the type which was attempted for a number of commodities before the war. Since the war, there have been only two agreements of this type: the International Sugar Agreement of 1953 and the International Coffee Agreement, which was negotiated in the summer of 1962. I think these are the most promising methods for tackling the problem in the future. Underdeveloped countries sell in highly competitive markets; they buy in monopolistic markets. They sell in markets where they are the price takers and buy in markets where the sellers are the price makers, and that makes a tremendous difference. They suffer under a structural handicap. I feel that it contributes to the welfare of humanity, and it is not a negative but possibly a positive contribution, if this great structural handicap is lessened or eliminated by commodity agreements. The question is: can it be done?

I think the opposition of importing countries can be overcome, as the negotiations which led up to the 1962 Coffee Agreement have shown. Importing countries are naturally very disapproving of restrictive types of commodity agreements. But if the producing and exporting countries show that they can really come together and do something, the importing countries, who may be opposed, will change their tune rather than let the exporting countries do it on their own. That is what happened in the case of sugar, and in the case of coffee. There are three main reasons, in my opinion, why these agreements have not been more permanent and more sucessful. First, it is very difficult to get everybody in, because the more countries that come in, the greater the temptation of the remaining exporters to stay out. Second, while you can regulate exports by means of quotas, if you do not succeed in regulating domestic production as well, you put an increasing strain on the agreement, which would mean that sooner or later it would break down.

The third reason, and this seems, to my mind, the most important defect of export quota agreements as long-term measures for stabilizing commodities prices, is that such agreements tend to freeze the pattern of trade and the pattern of trade cannot be frozen for more than an ordinary period. The pattern of all commodity trade is constantly changing, sometimes very dramatically. There was a time when all the sugar in the world came from Brazil. Later it came from Cuba and the Caribbean. All the coffee at times came mostly from Brazil, but in the last eight years the African countries have increased their share of world exports from practically nothing to 20 percent of the whole coffee trade. So the pattern of trade is constantly changing as new low-cost areas compete with the existing areas. A commodity agreement is naturally based on the quotas of the previously attained shares of the world market. This can be done for a time, but beyond that time it breaks down. There comes a time when, for a low cost producer, it is better to take the risk of falling prices and get an increase in the share of trade than to stick to the agreement.

If agreements are to be successful, they must provide for three things: full participation, effective regulation of production, and a steady and gradual change in the distribution quotas in favor of the low cost producers. If it freezes the pattern of trade, no agreement will survive for very long.

If the objection to my scheme is simply that the countries are not ready for it, I am sure I am just as much aware of that as everybody else, but still you have to begin somewhere. The most important suggestion is that production regulations should be by means of a variable export levy. Each participant country should be obliged to have an export levy, and this levy should be raised whenever domestic stocks exceed a certain amount and are increasing, and should be lowered whenever they are beyond a certain minimum and are decreasing. You can always get domestic production down in the export quotas. But so long as it is not down, you go on raising the export levy, which means that you lower the price received by the actual producers. Although supply may be inelastic in a short period or for some time, I believe that price regulation is an effective way of restricting production if it is carried far enough.

Once you get each country's production limited to the requirements of all world trade by means of these export levies, you can use the export levy as an automatic instrument for an ordinary adjustment in the distribution of the quotas. You will find that there are some countries which require a very high levy to keep their production down to the quota. Those are evidently the low-cost producers. Other countries, the high cost producers, need only a moderate levy to keep their production down. Such agreements should contain a provision whereby after a lapse of some years, say after three years, there would be a revision in the basic quotas by some modest amount, not more than 5 percent for each country, from those whose export levies as a proportion of their FOB prices are relatively low and to those whose export levies are relatively high. That, of course, will lead to an adjustment in the export levies themselves. Those whose quotas are increased will have to reduce the export levy to be able to fulfill their quotas. Those whose quotas are cut have to raise their export levy in order to reduce their production. Thus, all the time there will be a tendency, maybe a slow one, to get a situation where the export levies of all these countries tend to a uniformity as a percentage of their export prices.

I am not suggesting that this method can be applied to everything. I do not think it can be applied to temperate-zone foodstuffs, to commodities where exports are marginal to domestic consumption. I am mainly thinking of commodities like coffee or cocoa in Ghana, or sugar in Cuba, where the great bulk of domestic production is exported. I do not think that this in itself would be sufficient to solve the problems of trade in underdeveloped countries. The problems that Professor Haberler was talking about, of preventing discrimination in securing access to the big markets of western Europe, I think are equally involved. But I think there is no doubt that the memories of the 1930's are fading, though they were a tremendous lesson, and it could happen again. Despite the brave words, all the international trade charters, all the new ideas and principles since the second world war, very little has been done to prevent the recurrence of this.

Enrique Lerdau

Repeatedly at this conference some very interesting and pertinent remarks have been made on the relevance of the foreign sector to the problem under discussion, namely, growth with a minimum of inflation. I would like to try to recapitulate the subjects which in my opinion have emerged as central under this heading, by looking at the foreign sector from two points of view: exports considered as a foreign exchange bottleneck and regional integration as a development tool. I do not propose to take sides in the controversy on whether the deterioration of the terms of trade and the inability to expand exports form the core of the structuralist position or just one of several centerpieces. I gained the impression that both agreed that the foreign sector did indeed pose a special problem, especially as Grunwald's finding that an import quantum rising faster than the capacity to import was accompanied by a rise in indebtedness casts doubt on the permanence of this process.

But, what is the nature of the problem? Let me first of all repeat here what I have recently expressed in writing:[3] I think that the discussion of the declining terms of trade of primary producers has consistently stressed only one side—albeit an important one—namely, demand phenomena, and ignored the enormous impact of postwar supply developments. This can be shown statistically: in the 40 years before the second world war, world industrial production rose substantially faster than that of primary products, but since the war the opposite has occurred. Given reasonably low price elasticities of demand, this can be taken as a major determinant of the declining terms of trade.

Part of the problem arises in the stimulus to primary production which protectionist policies have brought about in the industrial countries. Western Europe's emerging self-sufficiency in sugar and meat, as well as the better-known cereal and cotton surpluses of the United States, have done their share in bringing about the overall glut. Of great importance also is the development of Africa, where cotton, coffee, and banana,[4] to mention only three important instances, have been the targets of active development policies.

This raises a problem to which I wish to refer at least in passing. What ought to be the policies of international lending institutions when faced with requests for capital to expand the production of commodities already in oversupply on the world market? Since most individual borrowers are likely to add only marginally to total supply, if the resource endowment is favorable, the arguments in favor of complying with individual requests may be extremely plausible. And yet an extension of the same approach to large numbers of underdeveloped countries producing the same product might seriously hurt the development efforts of many, since the ensuing price effect might reduce export receipts of the traditional exporters. The law of comparative advantages, for obvious reasons, can only be a very partial guide under such circumstances. It will serve if all that has to be weighted is the question of where the gap between the first and the second (etc.) best export commodity is widest, but it will not do if relevant criteria also include the time it would take traditional exporters to switch to other lines, their access to world markets, the impact of the transition on their development programs,

---

[3]See my "Stabilization and the Terms of Trade," *Kyklos* 2, and "Some Notes on the Terms of Trade and Economic Development," *Quarterly Journal of Economics,* August, 1962.

[4]It may sound hard to believe, but the development plan of the Ivory Coast, to cite one instance, envisages a 94 percent increase in banana production in ten years. Demand projections for the industrial countries, made by the FAO as well as by the OAS, coincide in predicting an annual growth rate of around 2 percent.

and a host of other considerations which practical men will have to take into account and which economists have only recently begun to include explicity in their models.

It is true that the expansion of traditional export commodities has not, in the past, been the main activity of the larger international financial agencies, but in particular cases the problem is very real. In the meantime, it is hard to see how the agencies could always avoid policies which make sense in a national setting but are inconsistent when viewed as a whole. The fault lies not with them but with the world and with us: on the one hand, it is too easy in too many places to grow too many things for which demand is too sticky, and on the other hand, the ability of the profession to integrate these harsh facts fully into its analytical framework has so far been less than totally satisfactory.

Obviously we cannot leave the matter here. What are the remedies? Export receipt stabilization schemes have a lot to commend them. Inasmuch as they facilitate national planning by making exchange availabilities more foreseeable, I do not think that Professor Kaldor's dismissal out of hand of such schemes is justified. But I am sure that we all agree with him that such schemes touch the surface, not the heart of the matter.

Reference was made to the need to increase exports. I suggest that for many countries there is a perfectly logical avenue in the increasing processing of their traditional exports. I also submit that the objection raised at this conference by Professor Goldsmith— that this was tried in Australia without success—is not valid. General equilibrium theory would lead you to expect such lack of success in countries in which the marginal productivity of labor is as high in the primary export industries as in manufacturing. Now Australia and New Zealand were probably the only countries in the world where this premise held, but it seems quite the opposite in most of Latin America.

In some countries, processing of traditional raw materials is obviously an insufficient answer. But in the smaller and poorer countries, it is to be expected that this is where "guided comparative advantage" policies would lead them. It is doubly regrettable, therefore, that industrial countries impede the importation of such semiprocessed raw materials by tariffs that are a multiple of those on unprocessed goods. Take an extreme example: the EEC's common external tariff on cocoa will be around 5 percent, but that on chocolate—depending on sugar content—may be as high as 80 percent.

One last word about "guided development." I should like to register my dissent from Professor Haberler's dichotomy between planning industrialization—bad—and letting the price mechanism do the job—good. The true choice in Latin America is a different one, namely, that of trying to foster those industries which, according to our present imperfect knowledge, seem to have the best chance of becoming dynamic forces in the economy, or, alternatively, to foster industries through subsidies and tariffs on a haphazard, corrupt, and inconsistent basis. The latter has been the system in many countries. Planning does not *necessarily* imply a greater degree of intervention, only a more systematic one, and, if it is intelligent planning, administered with integrity and responsiveness to the public's needs and desires, a more useful one, too.

It is of little use in this connection to appeal to historical experience in Latin America. True reliance on the price mechanism has not been seen often in recent decades, and where it has occurred it has not always been associated with the most rapid or the most stable development. The opposite position will gain just as little comfort from simple references to history: intervention per se has been no guarantee for growth, either. The reason for this deadlock on a question apparently both simple and fundamental is quite clear: it is the wrong question. Much more pertinent would be the extent to which a particular country is ready for *any* government action designed either to promote growth or to avoid inflation. The pre-eminence of particular vested interests in the legislative process, in the administration of justice and of the public business, the independence and objectivity of the civil service, in short, the maturity of the body politic, these are the touchstones on which the development effort will depend. The kind, not the degree, of intervention is the issue. Professor Silvert's statement on methodology, and Mr. Davis's paper, each in its different way, illustrate what I have in mind.

Now a few words about integration. The theoretical arguments for regional integration are based on a belief in the existence of very strong internal economies of scale. Without these a free trade area makes little sense. I would like to suggest that this also implies either of two conditions: (1) that external economies of the usual kind—labor skills, public utilities, etc., are not too important, or (2) that the member countries start out with roughly comparable infrastructures. If neither condition obtains, it will be almost impossible to avoid a concentration of industries that are already the most advanced—say the ABC countries and Mexico. Might premise

(2) be one reason for the relatively greater advances made in Central America's integration than—until now—under LAFTA? If so, perhaps further thinking is needed along several lines, one of which refers to the importance of differences in size of country and in degree of development. The size problem will have additional bearing once important trade flows develop: at that time differential rates of inflation will make the choice of a regional payments and exchange system of great importance, even under conditions of full multilateral convertibility.[5]

Krieger Vasena

I wish to raise a concrete subject in relation to zonal joint action which I think should receive attentive consideration at the present time. If you look at the trends of world trade you will see that Latin America, which previous to the war participated in about 10 percent of world trade, has come down in the last years to scarcely 6 percent. This constitutes a position quite contrary to that sometimes claimed by some governments, especially in Europe, when they compare the statistics in 1945, just after the war, with 1958 or 1962, in which naturally there is a relative increase in the exports of the Latin-American countries. But, as is explained in detail by a group of experts in a recent study sponsored by ECLA, (see report in the *Economic Bulletin,* October, 1962) the Latin-American countries as a whole have suffered severely from their participation in world trade during the last 20 or 25 years. Various and different causes will be found for the deterioration of their trade position. One of them has already been mentioned by Professor Kaldor in relation to the adverse terms of trade against Latin America during the period starting with the decade of the fifties.

In the price structure of Latin-American exports, undoubtedly the preferential treatment in favor of other areas, as in the case of tropical goods, the increase of protectionism and discrimination in favor of the agricultural sectors of more developed countries in Europe, and the continuation of subsidizing exports, as in the case of the U.S., are factors which have seriously affected the trade of

---

[5]Needless to say, in the meantime among the financial aspects of integration, those pertaining to *producing such increases* in trade flows (export credits, tax credits or rebates, etc.) are much more important than the settlement of potential bilateral trade imbalances that might emerge among members once the trade exists.

Latin America. If you look at the trade distribution of Latin America, you will see that exports to Europe (the common market and the free trade area) have substantially declined during the postwar period in relation to the figures for 1935–38, while trade of Latin-American countries (with the exception of the temperate country producers) with the United States has been increasing in relation to the period prior to the war. And in the last years, especially the last two years, some new areas are appearing as clients for Latin-American exports.

The continuous balance of payments crisis and even the political crisis, so difficult to understand outside, have a direct relation to the failure of Latin America in the world trade of primary products, at the same time that little or nothing has been done to favor new products. The first restrictions after the war were supposed to have been imposed by the difficult monetary conditions confronted by the European countries. But when at the end of 1958 most of the European countries arrived at monetary convertibility, not only did these restrictive measures and protectionism not disappear, but new schemes appeared instead, particularly in the common market countries. With the Rome Treaty and, more specifically, the common agriculture policy approved in January, 1962, there is no doubt that the present situation can even worsen.

As we know, until 1961 the import of primary products by the common market countries was subject to quotas and other direct controls. Now these direct import controls have been replaced by new schemes which, in my opinion, are much more dangerous than those existent before. I call to your attention the system of levies, part of a very refined and complicated system launched by the six countries, with the name of a common agricultural policy. The import levy is to cover the difference between the internal fixed price and the lowest price offered by the most efficient exporter of any country in the world. And more is to be added. These levies, collected by the countries in a special fund of the common market, will be used to maintain subsidies on agricultural products in Europe. On the other hand, these funds can also be used to subsidize exports to third countries. All these ingenious achievements of the last years naturally have affected Latin-American possibilities of increasing their traditional exports. And if that is the prospect for the traditional trade, for the primary products in which Latin America is on a competitive basis, what are our possibilities for new markets for manufactured goods which we indispensably and urgently need to export in the future?

If the GATT structure and spirit seems incapable of impeding this excessive protectionism and the appearance of new forms of it, what can be expected from cooperation to safeguard our new products?

I think that coordination of the commercial policies of the countries of Latin America is essential and that we should act as quickly as possible in considering our different problems together. I am sure that we shall be better understood if we present a coordinated and well-prepared position than if we go on as at present with bilateral negotiations.

David Pollock

I should like to ask the panel two questions, mainly concerned with whether certain international trade and aid policy approaches, now under active consideration or already in existence, give an incorrect or at least a misplaced emphasis to resolving the problems of many developing countries, especially the Latin-American area. One refers to the sharply increased attention that has been given in recent years, concentrating upon the problem of short-term export instability. The second solicits the panel's views on whether there would be some value in establishing automatic or partially automatic access to international short- and long-term financial assistance, possibly through formula-based techniques, rather than relying solely upon the principle of managed assistance, such as is the case at present.

I would like to place these two questions in a rather general and brief statistical framework, to indicate what I have in mind. First, if you look at the postwar years, divide them into three fairly equal time periods, and measure the trend of Latin-American export earnings at current values, you find some rather unusual developments. First, from 1946 to 1951, the trend of Latin-American export earnings was sharply upward. From 1952 to 1956, the trend was still upward but at a much slower rate of growth. From 1957 to 1962, it flattened off and turned down. If you then measure the amplitude of the annual swings in export earnings around these three different medium-term trend lines, you will find the following: from 1946 to 1951 an amplitude from peak to trough of export earnings equal to 16 percent per year; in the second period, from 1952 to 1956, swings of only 6 percent; in the third period, from 1957 to 1962, swings of only 3 percent per year. It is my feeling that the characteristics of the third period, namely, a stagnant trend around which oscillations are relatively moderate, is the picture that will persist throughout most of the decade of the sixties. Therefore, stabilizing around a declining or even a flat trend strikes me as of rather limited utility and I feel it should be given a limited priority. But there is a corollary to this, namely, that to maintain the import capacity of Latin America during the rest of the sixties, some international approach should be of high priority, pushing the import capacity back up in the only apparent way which can be institutionalized, namely, through long-term financial flows.

This leads me to my question on the automaticity of aid. There have been many criticisms of the new automatic compensatory financing mechanisms dealing precisely with this feature. But I wonder whether that is not really an advantage which we have not been able to obtain during the postwar period. The principle of managed assistance means that the preconditions are attached to international financial assistance. But it seems to me that one of the necessary elements in a valid international aid policy is continuity of international financial assistance as well as the volume of it. To have aid proceed in a lumpy pattern, which has been so characteristic of the postwar period, is still a problem which has not been resolved. I am not saying that the short-term and long-term financial assistance agencies that impose preconditions should be superseded by an automatic mechanism. I would like to ask the panel what their views are on supplementing aid by an automatic mechanism that would provide continuity. To summarize, I would welcome the panel's views as to whether, first, short-term export stabilization emphasis has the relevance today and during the rest of the sixties that it had in the first ten postwar years, but not in the last five years, and secondly, whether a supplemental international credit mechanism explicitly designed to guarantee access to short- and long-term financial assistance should receive high priority or, at least, some priority, unlike the situation presently existing.

Michael Kaser

A number of speakers, in fact all of the speakers at the panel today, have raised questions posed by the creation of the European common market. Those raised by Professor Felix, Mr. Sunkel, and the present chairman have also referred to the possibility of eastern

Europe as a likely market for Latin American products. There are four choices facing Latin America: first, the promotion of the traditional exports; second, the promotion of exports of a higher degree of processing within the zone, or the creation of new lines of exports, notably in manufactures; third, import substitution; and, fourth, a switch of domestic demand into noninternationally traded goods.

The first three are concerned with zonal integration. This is self-evident in the case of export promotion, but in the case of import subsitution we have had Professor Haberler mention that this could be more cost-minimizing if the Latin-American free trade area led to economies of scale within the region. The specialization aims of the Central American common market are surely an example in point. In the long run, markets might eventually be found in other regions for products which started as import substitutes in Latin America. What we have seen are problems which need to be solved on an intergovernmental level.

Professor Haberler mentioned the need for the Latin-American free trade area, particularly as a negotiating body vis-à-vis the EEC. In fact, he could have added, also vis-à-vis the CMEA, the Council for Mutual Economic Aid in Moscow. The Moscow body is just becoming as centralized a decision maker as the EEC is likely to be when the full provisions of the treaty come into operation.

Another focus for intergovernmental discussion on this prospect is the United Nations Programming and Projection Center, created by the General Assembly last year, with its subcenters, one of which cooperates with ECLA, providing a forum for discussions at governmental levels of costs, output, and eventual trade possibilities in a world-wide matrix.

Dudley Seers

I would like the panel's view on a proposal for amending the procedures of the IMF in the light of what has been said about the rather gloomy prospects for Latin-American exports. I want, for the purpose of this proposal, to put myself in the position of a member of the IMF staff and ask myself how the situation in the region would look to me. Now, I think, if I were a member of the IMF's staff, I would be a little bit worried at the emotion which the IMF rouses in the region, at the degree of hostility which must be evident to it, and not merely at the hostility, but also at the nature of some of its support, which comes rather highly correlated with organs and political parties which also oppose tax reforms and other social reforms in the region. I would be inclined to worry lest the end result of this might be that the IMF would find itself associated with military dictatorships of one kind or another, and that as a result there might be secessions from the IMF, and that the United States and other industrial powers might be inclined to give it less support. I am not making any prediction, I am just pointing to what must be an obvious risk in the present situation from the point of view of the IMF.

I shall try to see if I can put my finger on the reason why this situation has developed. If we go back to the Bretton Woods agreement, we find that it was conducted in a very different atmosphere from that of the international economic problems of today. It was conducted by a group of economists from industrial countries, trying to find out how to prevent the spread of international recessions, like that of the 1930's, which was very strong in peoples' minds. There are two aspects of this agreement I would like to draw attention to. One is that the object was to make drastic restrictive financial policies unnecessary in the world. And the second was that the people taking part were the industrial countries' representatives, thinking of the problems of the industrial countries.

Now, subject to correction from the IMF's representatives, I would guess that the main customers today are not the industrial countries but the underdeveloped countries, who are not facing the same sort of problems as were envisaged when the Bretton Woods Charter was discussed and drawn up.

Moreover, the extent to which the IMF accepts the stabilization terms put to it determines whether other organizations which are primarily concerned with development do or do not give financial aid to the country concerned.

And now, how can one think in terms of adjusting the IMF procedures, or, to put it another way, why have not the IMF procedures been adjusted to this new type of situation? My own preference—I seem to have lost my character as a member of the IMF—would be for some automatic procedure, such as has been discussed by the panel, because it seems to me, for a large number of reasons, impossible and improper for people to tell governments how they ought to conduct their own affairs.

Werner Baer

I have a brief remark to make about Professor Haberler's reference to the Puerto Rican case. My principal objection to using the Puerto Rican example is that it is such a special case. First of all, Puerto Rico is in the same tariff and currency area as the United States. Secondly, the Puerto Rican government is not burdened with the usual types of governmental duties. For example, it does not have any defense burden. No taxes have to be paid to the United States government, which offers various services. Thus, it is in a position to attract capital due to its special tax incentive program. There is no political risk involved in investing in Puerto Rico. The amount of capital which flowed in due to the special incentive programs, due to the political and economic stability, and due to the island's special relations with the United States was way out of proportion to that which has flowed into in any other Latin-American country.

Let me close by saying that this does not mean that Latin-American countries have nothing to learn from the Puerto Rican experience. I believe that the type of planning that Puerto Rico has undergone would be certainly worth-while studying. I believe that if you look at the situation in Brazil, for example, the SUDENE programs, due to the political and economic stability, and due to to attract capital are similar to Puerto Rico's. Thus, the Puerto Rican experience might be worth-while studying for SUDENE planners and planners in areas with similar conditions.

Gottfried Haberler

I should like to address my remarks to the very stimulating paper by Professor Kaldor. I think we almost agree that the primary producing countries have a considerable degree of monopoly power when acting jointly, and very little monopoly power when acting individually. Some effort on their part to exploit this power in a reasonable way would not be entirely bad. The Kaldor plan requires a tremendous amount of cooperation among many producing countries, which will be difficult to achieve. In addition to its adequate enforcement, it also requires the cooperation of the consuming countries as well. I think that this poses a great practical difficulty for its implementation. I would like to note that this plan does operate through restrictions of output and of exports via taxes.

I do not think the plan gives adequate recognition to the appearance of new suppliers or to changes in relative costs.

The African coffee producers would never have obtained their present position in the field if they had been allowed to expand at the rate of only 5 percent on their original very low export rates. The Kaldor plan does not have a mechanism which keeps the world price moving in relation to costs. You may start out at a certain level, let us say the 1954-55 level in all commodities. Some commodities may experience a doubling of real costs, others may have real costs cut in half. There should be a mechanism for the adaptation of the world market price to changes in overall costs.

I prefer an alternative plan which I believe meets the objections which I have noted. We must know, first of all, that 80 to 90 percent of the exports from most primary products go to the United States and to the European common market, at least if we include the United Kingdom. My plan is for the United States and the countries of Europe to agree to collect duties on given primary products and to remit them to the producing country. I was happy to note that Professor Gudin made a similar suggestion. His was for a loan; mine is for a simple remission of these duties. Here we only need an agreement essentially between two organisms, the common market and the United States. They are obviously capable of reaching an agreement. And, moreover, in some cases, where they themselves produce the primary product, these duties will have the added advantage of providing a certain amount of protection for the internal producers and therefore may become more politically acceptable, as in the case of nonferrous metals in the United States. I would suggest that the tariff would have a mean value of 25 percent when the price net of tax is above the average value of the last three years. The percentage of the tariff could also be reduced according to a certain formula. When the price fell below the average of the last three years, the percentage of tariff could be increased, according to that formula. Whatever the trend of prices then, the tariff would always tend back toward the 25 percent level.

There are a few minor additions to the plan. I would suggest that any country caught subsidizing its exports would not be entitled to receive the rebate, whereas any country taxing its exports would receive the rebate, because the tax could not be regarded as an attemp to capture the rebate otherwise due to other components. I think possibly also a discriminatory arrangement may be included in the plan whereby imports from more developed countries would not receive the rebate. Where the governments have difficulties in maintaining fiscal discipline, it might be appropriate, instead of paying the rebate all in one lump sum, to pay it out over a period of three years, so that the rebate received by the country in any year would be the average due over the past three years and would tend, therefore to, fluctuate considerably less than in the case where rebates were all remitted in the year in which they were collected.

13. PANEL:
FISCAL AND FINANCIAL POLICIES

Alexandre Kafka

There is only one point which I would like to stress: the policy instruments and institutions which we are going to discuss should, I think, be examined from three points of view. The first is in regard to their use for preventing, in a context of desirable growth, unnecessary price instability. I think that we can dispense with further discussions of the controversy between monetarists and structuralists. Everyone will decide what he considers a necessary price increase. The second aspect from which we should discuss the use of these policy instruments, is concerned with the way they can be applied to stop inflation after it's on the way. And the third refers to how we can adapt them if we have to live permanently with a positive rate of price change. I think the last may be unsympathetic to many people. But, especially for those who are convinced that rising prices in a process of growth are unavoidable, it is absolutely necessary that we discuss what adaptations should be made to policy instruments and institutions in the financial and fiscal fields. Our habitual instruments and institutions can take 2 or 3 percent of annual price increases, but those of you who believe that higher rates of price increases may be necessary will have to show in what way they have to be adapted to correspond to such a change in the financial environment.

Friedrich Lutz

I am speaking here as a general economist without any special knowledge of South American conditions though with personal knowledge of inflations, as I have lived through one of the worst inflations in economic history—the post-World War I inflation in Germany.

The main task assigned to me on this panel is to discuss the use of monetary policy as a means of stopping inflation. But first I want to make clear where I stand with respect to the inflationary issue. I can summarize my position in a few statements.

Like everybody else I do not believe that structural problems can be solved by stabilizing the value of money. Other methods of economic policy are required for this purpose.

I can see that structural difficulties may cause inflationary pressure, but I cannot see how they can explain an inflation of 60 percent per year.

An illness may be a cause of fever, but the fever is not a cure for the illness. In the same way inflation, though it may be caused by structural difficulties, is no cure for them. On the contrary, I believe inflation makes these difficulties worse and adds new ones by its distorting effects on resource allocation, which come into the open once stabilization is achieved. The most important reasons for this belief are:

1. The fact that the real rate of interest is negative and that a sufficiently accurate cost accounting becomes well-nigh impossible, making a rational investment policy difficult, if not impossible, both for the private and the public sector.

2. Relative price changes which are necessary to overcome bottlenecks are rather ineffective instruments for resource allocation in an inflationary environment, where every enterprise is, or at least seems, profitable, where nobody is threatened by losses but, at worst, only by smaller profits than are made by others, and where the degree of uncertainty is so great that for this reason alone a shifting of resources does not seem worth-while.

3. Inflation prevents foreign capital from coming into the country and causes domestic capital to leave the country.

4. Inflation makes the balance of payments bottleneck worse.

5. Inflation, for obvious reasons, reduces productivity.

Against these harmful effects of inflation one might set the beneficial effects of so-called forced savings. These result from a change in income distribution in favor of entrepreneurial income, a large part of which will be invested. I think that there is no justification at all for squeezing investments out of the economy at the expense of the poor. Frankly, I am quite shocked by the equanimity and even glee with which these forced savings are contemplated by many economists.

Now to my main task: what can monetary policy do to stop inflation? I think it is generally agreed that the inflation in Brazil is of the demand pull type, since wages and salaries lag behind the price level. The immediate cause of this type of inflation is overexpansion of the credit supply either to the private sector or to the government. If it is the latter, the obvious method to deal with it is to balance the budget. Fiscal policy, however, is a topic that will be taken care of by other members of this panel and I shall say no more about it.

However, it is worth pointing out that even if a large budget deficit is the main cause of inflation it is not impossible to stabilize the value of money chiefly by monetary policy. The outstanding example of such a stabilization is the Italian one in September, 1947, after a period of inflation comparable to the one in Brazil. The stabilization succeeded in spite of the fact that the budget deficit was still growing—it was higher in the fiscal year 1947–48 than in 1946–47. The way in which the inflation was halted can be described very briefly: The introduction of reserve requirements for the banks forced them to stop credit expansion. For lack of credit, business was unable to continue inventory accumulation; it even had to throw inventories onto the market. The result was a sharp general price decline in the weeks following the credit restrictions. The fall in the price level restored the public's confidence in the lira, and the income velocity, which had been rapidly rising before the stabilization, returned to normal. This increase in the demand for money to hold enabled the government to continue to finance the budget deficit predominantly by recourse to the banking system, without any inflationary effect on the price level, although the money supply increased in the year after the stabilization even more than in the year before. In subsequent years, the deficit was reduced and Italy started on the path of development, where it achieved—with stable money—one of the highest growth rates in the world.

The Italian experience shows that inflation can be stopped by monetary policy even though the budget deficit is growing and is mainly financed by the banking system. But in order for such an experiment to be successful, two conditions must be fulfilled: firstly, the authorities must be willing to administer a shock to the economy and, secondly, they must be able, during the breathing space which the decline in the velocity of circulation of money grants them, to reduce the budget deficit to an amount that can be financed in a noninflationary way.

It goes without saying that if inflation results from excessive credit expansion to the private sector, a restrictive monetary policy is the proper method to deal with it.

One more question must be faced in this connection: Is it possible to stop inflation gradually, or must it be done suddenly with shock therapy? All the rapid inflations I know of have come to an end suddenly. I do not deny that it is possible to draft a model in which inflation is brought to an end gradually. But I can't help being skeptical about the practical success of a gradual stabilization program. For one thing, so many unforeseen things are likely to happen during the period envisaged for bringing the inflation to an end, so many pressures are likely to develop which create new inflationary impulses, that for this reason alone I feel that a program of slow stabilization has little chance of being carried out successfully. But, more important, experience as well as theoretical reasoning lead me to believe that a change in the public's expectations about the future movement of prices is a prerequisite of stabilization. And this change can only be brought about by administering a shock to the economy. I think that in an economy which is inherently vigorous and dynamic—and I believe this to be true of the economy of Brazil—the harmful effects of such a shock are short lived and are far outweighed by the benefits that derive from stable money later on.

Now I should like to take up one more topic which can be said to be one of monetary policy only if the latter term is interpreted in a very broad sense. Suppose inflation continues and one has to live with it, is it advisable for the government to support and even further the development of protective devices which always tend to spring up in an inflationary environment? Should new debt instruments be created which contain a purchasing power clause to protect the lender? Should wage contracts, social security claims, and the like be equipped with an escalator clause? Should monetary authorities see to it that the interest rate itself is enough for the real rate to be positive?

It seems at first glance reasonable to move in this direction. But, on second thought, it will become evident that the shorter the time lag between the increase in the price level and the adjustments of wages, rents, social security payments, etc., the greater must be the degree of inflation that is necessary to turn the same amount of resources over to the public sector or to entrepreneurs. The use of such protective devices is therefore bound to accelerate inflation.

Nicholas Kaldor

I wouldn't claim that fiscal reform would necessarily bring Latin-American inflations to an end; however, I don't think they can be brought to an end without it. Nor would I claim that monetary stability is the most important reason for fiscal reform. I think the most important reason for fiscal reform is to achieve a better and more rational use of resources of the countries of Latin America. Latin-American countries, far more than other countries of the free world, have a tremendous dead burden to carry in the form of maintaining the "idle rich." I think there is plenty of evidence that the proportion of the gross national product taken up by the consumption of property owners in a typical Latin-American country is two or three times as high as it is in a country like the United States or the United Kingdom. That means that the added burden of maintaining the "idle rich" is comparatively greater to the poor Latin-American countries than the whole burden of military expenditures is to the United States.

This is becoming increasingly recognized. Recently I attended a conference on fiscal reform in Latin America which was remarkable for the degree of unanimity among the participants. It was agreed that the overwhelming need of Latin-American countries is for greater public revenue. This is needed to make it possible to enlarge the scope of useful public expenditures, which are recurrent but nevertheless vital for accelerated development, for education and health, and for the maintenance of communications systems like roads, for more public investments, and certainly to achieve a better balance between revenue and expenditure.

The conference also agreed that the most important cause of the insufficiency of revenues in Latin America is the inability of Latin-American governments to tax effectively the benefits derived from property ownership, either in the form of income, in the form of capital gains, or in the form of any other benefits which the ownership of disposable wealth confers. It is not that the masses of the people are taxed too lowly in relation to other countries. It is simply that the taxation is regressive, in the sense that the vast bulk of taxes fall on the mass of the people, and the rich people—whether their wealth is derived from land or from industry or commerce—escape taxes almost entirely.

Finally, the most important reform to put an end to this situation consists in two things: first, to have a radical reform, or a comprehensive reform, in personal income taxation or in progressive personal taxation generally, and secondly, to have a radical reform in the taxation of land. A lot of the property owned is in land, and if the ownership of land could be effectively taxed an important incentive for improving the situation in agriculture would be created.

As regards personal taxation, it was agreed that the most important reform is to introduce a comprehensive income tax of the type existing in the United States, England, or in the Scandinavian countries. This would replace a series of separate taxes on various schedules, as is the custom in Latin America. It was therefore recognized that more direct tax rates, not necessarily high tax rates, were needed. But that requires a good administration. It also requires some essential legal reforms; you cannot, under the present conditions in Latin America, have a progressive income tax on income derived from capital or property so long as you stick to the prevailing system, under which the ownership of any individual—his wealth —is a top secret. This is the legacy and largely the consequence of the prevailing system of what we call in Anglo-Saxon countries "bearer shares" and, on the French pattern, "Anonymous Societies" (Sociétés Anonymes). This is a wonderful French invention to make wealth completely anonymous, and it was copied in all Latin-American countries. In Mexico even real property hides behind holding companies, which makes it impossible to know who owns what, in either urban or agricultural real estate. Now, the institutional arrangements, in some form or other, which are necessary to force individuals to disclose their wealth to the revenue authorities, if not to the public at large are an essential precondition.

Henry Bloch

A number of theoretical models have been evolved which may serve as a basis of discussion for new solutions to fiscal problems. Several of these models, in more or less perfect form have, however, already been tested by a number of governments and it is useful to evaluate this technical and administrative feasibility in the light of the practical tests to which such models have been exposed.

Never before has there been in this hemisphere such active exchange of information on how taxes are applied under different conditions in different parts of the world. While it has frequently been said during this and earlier conferences that the experience of India is particularly relevant, I would also like to draw attention to the reconstruction of European tax systems after the holocaust of war and postwar inflations. I am drawing the attention of the Latin-American tax reformers particularly to the experience of England in preventing inflation through a variety of means which included a graduated purchase tax, to the experience of France in the application of a value-added tax, and to the purchase tax of Holland. The practical studies of the German treasury on the possible introduction of a value-added tax are also of interest. The experiment in the use of value-added tax by the European Coal and Steel Community may be of value in considering future techniques of taxation for the LAFTA. So would the broader studies of the Common Market Tax Commission. I might add here that the administration of investment allowances, write-offs, and depreciation in the rapidly growing economies of France, Italy, and Holland, deserve close study by Latin-American tax administrators.

European models may be more significant for Latin America than Asian models, especially where the tax system has a Latin origin and went through the transition from schedular to unitary taxes and from complex to simple taxes. As different types of taxes are applicable, it may be useful to consider that the present stage of economic development in the majority of Latin-American countries cannot be compared with India. While in some respects India may have a better civil-service system, it does not possess the highly developed and broadly based industrial class which can be found today in Mexico, Brazil, Argentina, Colombia, and some other Latin-American countries. In an inflationary period, the greatest danger in a massive application of the income tax is that it becomes very rapidly a wage tax. While a wage tax may be an important and powerful anti-inflationary instrument, it also has the disadvantage of discriminating against workers and employees. Furthermore, it does not strike with full force as far as the inflationary gains of the self-employed are concerned. In the United States, the self-employed and the employee are on a pay-as-you-go basis, but this practice has nowhere been fully extended to companies. The U.S. 1963 tax proposals provide for the placing of all corporations that pay over $100,000 in income tax upon completely pay-as-you-go —like individuals—gradually over the next few years. These corporations are already partially on a pay-as-you-go basis. Thus, the U.S. Internal Revenue Service provides an extremely desirable model for those countries which are in the throes of inflation and where the deferment of tax payment would provide an unjustified and undesirable special privilege.

The conditions for effective administration are first of all to be found in the possibility of "institution building." Even if there is no conscious effort to change the structure during an inflationary period, there is an automatic and fundamental alteration of the pattern of tax burdens as the income distribution is being distorted. It is at this point that the government must learn about taxpayer experience and that it must be concerned indeed with the requirements for introducing structural changes. The purpose of building fiscal institutions is to create a machinery for implementation of policy decisions which can function both rapidly and effectively. Relying on automatic flexibility of tax devices is impossible in countries where the number of taxpaying units is relatively small as far as direct taxes are concerned, and where indirect taxes strike at a large number of very different items often administered by a variety of authorities. Nevertheless, the administrative flexibility of indirect taxes is normally much greater than that of direct taxes.

As taxable capacity in an inflationary period becomes a "moving target" in countries where inflation is rampant, and as the role of "tax reserves" of private companies and shareholders is very small, the adjustment of direct revenue objectives involves a considerable time lag. With few exceptions, base and rate structures are quickly altered in character by changes in money value and the changing value of assets. The time lag problem is even more significant in the case of organizing and adjusting property taxes.

Some taxes require more, and some less, institutional infrastructure. For instance, taxes on agriculture which are intimately linked with the agrarian structure—unless they are export taxes—require, normally, a very difficult institutional framework. The infrastructure includes the legislative framework. Frequently a reform of agrarian property and commercial legislation is needed to provide the base for a decent tax system.

An excessive reliance on statutory reform, as against administrative reform, is a real danger. In other words, there is normally a decreasing desire to innovate as one proceeds from the idea man to the legislative draftsman to the author of administrative instructions, to the man who transmits instructions. Especially in the tax field, there is frequently quite a hiatus between fiscal thought in central banks, planning boards, and at ministerial levels, on the one hand, and in tax administrations on the other hand. This is partly remedied where there are occasional shifts of bright young men from one service to another. As technical services become more significant in tax administration, the service should become more flexible. Staff and line services may coexist as two distinct careers but the research man in the new tax research division should be given a chance to obtain some administrative experience. The direction of the specialized career concept and the rigid civil-service legislation have not been a universal blessing. In those administrations where habit and acquired rights have led to erosion of initiative, very senior officials often act as mere agents to transmit instructions, whereas major changes are being initiated through the technical services. The technical services have sometimes a brainier but dangerously inexperienced personnel as far as administrative practice is concerned. This is indeed the dichotomy which confronts the policy maker in attempting implementation of decisions involving innovation and change.

In addition to the necessity for proper administrative inspection, there is also a need to organize statistical services in such a manner that they can be used as an instrument of administrative control. Knowledge of yields of taxes levied upon specific categories of taxpayers in various parts of the country will frequently lead to the discovery of geographic differentials in the efficiency of administrative personnel and in the coverage of various strata of taxpayers. While mechanization renders the processing of mass data more effective and provides the tools for a broadly gauged information and collection machinery, it also provides the tools of measurement to the analyst.

The existence of communication channels within the administration, and from the policy makers to the administrators, remains a necessity for proper understanding of the taxing process. Mere gadgetry, ignoring these complex management problems, cannot succeed.

The administrator who is directly in contact with the taxpayer is the best judge of possibilities whenever the question of speed is involved. A crash program is practically doomed if it does not receive the support of the lower levels of the administration. The building of the capacity of the lower administration levels to react speedily does require time. Yet, at top levels, outsiders, personnel who know fiscal affairs but did not rise from within the administration, can often intervene with surprising rapidity if given responsible posts in tax administration. Such outsiders are not burdened with loyalties to existing routines. Postwar experiences have proved this point in many countries.

In certain Latin-American countries, the administrative infrastructure which is the backbone of European tax administrations is indeed nonexistent. Administrative reform will, therefore, have to come from above and not from below in the administration. A reform from above has to rely much more on techniques of measurement, on knowledge of quantitative aspects, on knowledge of the impact of the tax instrument, than a reform which relies on a large number of well-trained middle and lower level civil servants who are quick to report and understand negative aspects of taxes on the taxpaying units. Such a possibility exists in European countries. Yet some European countries, especially France, also provide the model for an effective administrative elite which was created at a time when there was no infrastructure of solid employees, and which continued to play an important role.

One of the questions asked during the discussion was whether a fiscal crash program is possible in Brazil and other countries where taxation seems to be neglected. It is wrong to link the idea of a fiscal crash program with the notion of increase in taxation.

Actual figures indicate that the countries which suffer from inflation do not necessarily have a relatively low tax burden. The root of the evil is frequently in the expenditure volume and in the distorted pattern of the tax structure. The expenditure volume cannot be reduced as fast as the tax volume can be increased, and a distorted tax pattern is more difficult to remedy than a low level of taxation.

The accompanying data are obtained thanks to Dr. Giertz of the U.N.F.&F. branch. Their reading may be of interest to some students of the problem of tax administration.

Part of the difficulty of tax administration in countries like Brazil or Argentina is that they already have a very high level of taxation. Such a level, if combined with a bad tax structure, may have rather destructive impacts on specific enterprises in an inflationary period. Rearranging the tax structure should therefore be based not only on a study of aggregates, but also on careful microeconomic analysis. This is particularly significant when direct taxes are involved.

As it is necessary to watch out for negative effects of taxation on production, any strengthening of the income-tax mechanism must take into account the necessity for judicious use of depreciation, write-offs, and similar devices. All this is highly technical and not understood by the ordinary tax administrator. Furthermore, it is necessary to make special arrangements for the large income-tax payers whose problems are more complex than those of the masses of small income-tax payers. The possibilities of evasion by large payers are also more likely. Consequently, a small elite group of specially trained officials should deal with the large companies in the underdeveloped countries.

FEDERAL, STATE AND LOCAL TAXES IN PERCENT OF NATIONAL INCOME FOR SELECTED COUNTRIES*

		Estimated National Income	Tax Receipts	Tax Receipts in Percent of National Income
		In Millions of National Currency		
Argentina	1938.......	8,857	1,010	11.4
	1950.......	51,900	11,784	21.5
	1959.......	492,300	60,898	12.4
	1960.......	626,000	119,121	19.0
Brazil	1938.......	33,111†	6,870	20.8
	1950.......	212,600	40,561	19.3
	1959.......	1,403,900	331,003	23.7
Mexico	1938.......	5,323	438	8.8
	1950.......	37,500	3,333	9.0
	1959.......	109,000	10,715	9.9
Austria	1937.......	5,653	1,202	21.1
	1950.......	41,800	8,662	20.6
	1959.......	107,500	29,912	28.0
Belgium	1938.......	65,200	11,143‡	17.1
	1950.......	275,500	58,098	21.1
	1959.......	424,200	94,338	22.4
Sweden	1938.......	11,970	1,104‡	9.2
	1950.......	26,758	8,323	30.9
	1959.......	53,006	19,677	37.1
U.S.	1938.......	67,395	8,889	13.3
	1950.......	241,000	51,000	21.2
	1959.......	396,500	99,636	25.1

*Social security charges, surplus of government enterprises and other non-fiscal revenues are excluded.
†Estimate for 1940.
‡Local taxes excluded.
Source: Computed from official statistics:

Estimated national income
    United Nations Statistical Yearbook, 1948, 1952, and 1961.
Tax revenues
    Argentina: Boletin Mensual de Estadistica, September, 1961.
        Annuario Estadistico de la Republica Argentina, 1957.
        Annuario Estadistico de la Republica Argentina, 1951.
    Brasil: Annuario Estadistico do Brasil, 1951 and 1961.
    Mexico: Annuario Estadistico, 1951–52.
        Annuario Estadistico, 1953.
        Informe Anual, 1960—Banco de Mexico.
    Austria: Statistisches Handbuch für die Republic Österreich, 1962.
        Wirtschaftsstatistischen Handbuch, 1959.
    Belgium: L'Economie Belge, 1953.
        L'Economie Belge, 1961.
        United Nations Statistical Yearbook, 1948.
    Sweden: Riksräkenskapsverket Årsbok, 1958—Stockholm.
        Statistisk Årsbok for Sverige, 1961—Stockholm.
        United Nations Statistical Yearbook, 1948.
    U.S.: Statistical Abstract of the United States, 1952.
        Statistical Abstract of the United States, 1961.

Furthermore, a sectorial approach is often necessary, as financial institutions, agricultural and industrial sectors, commercial enterprises, and the mining sector require different treatment as far as the base of taxation is concerned.

In Latin America the cultural tradition in business circles and even in the academic world is frequently what the British call "oral tradition." Consequently, Latin America should be a natural territory for the use of intensive hearings and similar possibilities of testimony by witnesses. The royal commission approach in the U.K. and the somewhat different congressional hearings in the U.S. should provide useful models. If taxpayers are given an opportunity to present their views on the feasibility of new taxes, on their experience with certain types of taxes, they can make a major contribution. Yet the hearings must be managed and staffs must be developed to organize the mechanism and handle the documentation. This device should appeal to Latin-American governments especially, as it is also an exercise in democratic procedure. The professional accountants and the attorneys can become most important elements in this process of tax reform based on the understanding of realities.

Robert Sammons

I speak from the conviction that the price system is still the most useful and best allocator of economic resources that we have yet devised. Even if you do not accept this opinion, one thing we do have to remember is that prices have their effect on supply and demand; and that any attempt to maintain any kind of price for considerable length of time at a level which does not equate supply and demand is bound to cause distortions in the economy and to produce misallocations of economic resources.

The position of the monetarists is that the role of monetary policy in the economy extends far beyond its power to control inflation. Most, if not all, monetarists that I know hold that monetary policy can also have a positive effect in encouraging production and growth. I believe that monetary policy is not only a defensive weapon but can be used in an aggressive manner to encourage growth with general price stability. But I was assigned the specific task of discussing exchange policy within the broader framework of fiscal and financial policy.

Exchange policy, particularly exchange-rate policy, has frequently been brought into this discussion. Sir Roy Harrod and others have expressed the view that exchange devaluation is to be avoided, because of the effects on the wage-price spiral of the resulting increase in prices of imported goods in terms of local currency. This seems to me to be quite consistent, as I understand it, with the general structuralist position, according to which foreign trade, particularly the foreign trade of underdeveloped countries, is controlled mainly by income elasticities of demand. In this view, price, including the price of foreign currency, has a relatively minor influence on foreign trade. This view was also implicit in an earlier comment to the effect that there could be fundamental long-term disequilibrium in the balance of payments which would not be appropriately cured by exchange rate changes.

Obviously I disagree, as will be clear from my remarks. Those who oppose exchange rate changes as a mechanism of adjustment should be very careful in their selection of arguments. If not, they will find themselves taking a position which, when carried to its logical extreme, would mean no exchange rate would ever be changed at any time or under any circumstances. All we have to do is try to imagine the Brazilian cruzeiro still at 18 to the dollar to realize that this is not a serious possibility; and I'm not sure that even Sir Roy Harrod believes that the pound could still be valued at $4.86.

Some of the views expressed here reflect, perhaps, a misunderstanding of what I conceive to be the principal role of an exchange rate under modern monetary conditions. It seems to me the exchange rate is a price and should be permitted—perhaps with some official interference—to serve the function of a price. It is a very special kind of price; there are very strong arguments for holding it steady as long as possible. But, like any other price, if it is held for a long period of time at a level which does not equate supply and demand, it is bound to create problems.

There are three alternatives open to underdeveloped countries which are growing and are threatened with inflation.

One is to hold an exchange rate as long as possible and then, when finally forced to make a devaluation, make it a big one. This course of action raises a host of problems. For speculators, it provides a relatively riskless avenue for capital flight and a large profit when the adjustment is finally made and the capital is brought home. Also, I think that what Sir Roy so greatly fears, the effect on the domestic wage-price spiral, is much more to be feared when devaluations are large. But it seems to me that the greatest disadvantage of this policy is that it is bound to leave the currency overvalued most of the time. An overvalued currency is completely inimical to production and growth. It tends to subsidize imports against domestic production; it tends to penalize import-competing domestic industries.

Incidentally, I worked up a few figures recently just for the main industrial countries in the last few years. It was interesting that, when ranked in the order of the rate of economic growth for the last four or five years (admittedly a fairly short period) and ranked also in the order of degree of undervaluation of the currency as measured by the increase in foreign exchange reserve (because I think an increase in foreign exchange reserves, everything else being equal, is evidence of undervaluation), there was a fairly close correlation in the rank order; the countries with the highest growth seem to have had the most undervaluation.

A second alternative is the so-called "adjustable peg system" where, either *de facto* or *de jure,* the exchange rate is changed in small amounts rather frequently, but has official support in the meantime. This system has many of the disadvantages of both the fixed rate and the flexible rate systems and none of the advantages of either. The Latin-American countries, particularly, have sought a compromise in the way of a fixed rate for merchandise trade transactions, and a free market rate for capital transactions. I think that this is better than an overvalued unitary rate. I certainly do not like to see capital flight subsidized by overvaluation. But this system has its own problems. When you are dealing with money you have to remember at all times that there are great psychological influences. When there are two prices for a currency, or even three or four or five prices, it seems to me that this always creates uncertainty about what its real value is. People who get fewer units of foreign exchange for their money think they are being cheated—and they probably are. Even relatively small differences between the official rate and the free rate cause distortions, and lead to many schemes for evading controls—for instance, trying to get the free market rate for exports, which everybody feels he is entitled to, anyhow.

As an economist, one must admit that multiple exchange rates have much the same economic effects as differential import surcharges, preferential tariffs, but somehow as a central banker I feel that tampering with the currency, so to speak, is somewhat different from setting different rates of taxation on different commodities.

This brings us down to flexible rates, as the term is generally understood, either with no official intervention in the market whatever, or with a minimum degree of official intervention designed, as the Canadians had it in the 1950's, to minimize daily and other strictly short-term fluctuations in the exchange rate. The case for and against flexible rates has been made extensively in the literature. I admit that the system cannot be used by a reserve currency and probably would not be beneficial to an industrialized country with a broad spectrum of exports and imports, whose currency is widely used in international trade. But for underdeveloped countries greatly subject to outside influences, and particularly if it seems to be impossible to avoid at least some degree of inflation, a flexible rate system has much to commend itself.

In summary, I would like to make the following points. First, I believe that overvalued currency is a great impediment to economic growth, to full employment, and to export diversification. For this reason, I regret that underdeveloped countries, in particular, seem to have such fears about the direct impact of currency devaluation on the internal price level and the cost of living. At the least, I think, these fears have been greatly exaggerated. I admit that account must be taken of what might be called the psychological impact. Many people seem to hold the view that whatever changes are made in the exchange rate, the internal prices should follow. I think, however, that this problem can be dealt with by an appropriate monetary policy, coupled with "structural" changes designed to weaken monopolistic elements in the economy. In the last analysis, if you want a free economy, you cannot continue with an exchange rate which does not equilibrate the demand and supply of foreign exchange in the market.

Celso Furtado

I would like to say a few words about the issues on economic policy that are being dealt with by the Brazilian government and which, of course, have been the object of discussions by all the participants of preceding sessions.

I would like to say just a few words as a member of the Brazilian government rather than just as an economist. Nevertheless, a number of my fellow economists have pressed me to avail myself of this opportunity to say something, not specifically on such technical problems as are in fact implicit in our government's economic policies and planning, but on those difficulties of a practical nature which confront us in Brazil and are indeed of interest to all.

When the government of Brazil decided to take some measures with a view toward drawing up a plan for the country's economic and social development, there were two objectives defined which precisely involve the two essential subject matters of this conference. The issue at stake was that of achieving simultaneously these two objectives: first, to maintain the high rate of growth in the Brazilian economy, and second, to eliminate progressively those tensions leading to the inflationary process.

How are we to face up to this only too apparently simple problem of growth with a diminishing rate of inflation? We are all familiar, here in Brazil, with the potentialities and possibilities of our national economy. We know, for instance, that in the last 15 years the country's economy has been growing; we furthermore know that this rate of growth for the past 5 years has become even faster; and we know, finally, that the rate of growth has been sustained, in spite of great difficulties related to the country's participation in international trade.

However, to the extent that development took place in the last few years, mainly based on internal production of equipment, the inflationary pressures increased. We know, therefore, that the problem of inflation was directly connected with the way in which the economy was managing to transform its savings into investments. It was therefore essential to consider the problem of investment directly, to draw up a policy aiming essentially at correcting the insufficiencies in the process of financing investment. We knew that investments had indeed been made, in other words, that a given rate of capital formation had been achieved. But the way in which this investment had been financed was in reality the essential factor that created inflationary pressures.

This being the case right from the start, it was possible to divert the attention of the congress and of the government from the problem of excess demand to the problem of insufficiencies of ways and means to finance the process itself. However, it would be difficult in an underdeveloped economy to tackle this problem without any further considerations.

The Brazilian inflation in the last 15 years must be understood as a complex process within which two perfectly differentiated phases came in succession. The conventional idea about inflation as a mechanism guided toward obtaining forced saving and tending to lose its effectiveness within a relatively short time period, ought to be set aside in the case of the Brazilian historic experience. In the course of a first stage, characterized by a substantial improvement in terms of trade, inflation acted mainly as a mechanism for the redistribution of income against the export sector (traditional agriculture) and in favor of the industrial sector. The exchange policy led to a transfer of the increase in income created by the improvement in the terms of trade for industry, due to relatively low prices for imported equipment. With the decline in relative prices of equipment, the marginal efficiency of capital invested in manufacturing rose. Therefore, the mechanism of redistribution acted upon the increase in income generated by the improvement in the terms of trade. The type of inflation which started in the second half of the 1950's, and is still prevailing, constitutes a new wave with characteristics completely different from the first one. Its primary cause lies in a deep disequilibrium of the public sector, which was called forth to take up concrete responsibilities in the process of capital formation, without regard to the fact that the fiscal apparatus had not undergone the necessary adaptation.

The responsibility of the government in that inflationary process was connected primarily with insufficient financing of public expenditures, and we have always discussed this in the light of the need for a basic reform of the tax system, essential to eliminate this type of inflation. However, this inability to adequately finance public expenditures has been one of the major difficulties in a country such as Brazil.

To understand the difficulties which we are facing now in order to restore the equilibrium in the public sector, it is necessary to bear in mind certain characteristics of the develoment process in this country. From every side there arise pressures upon the government to improve health and educational services, create overhead basic services, and complement private enterprise insofar as private investment is concerned.

This situation leads the congress and the government to plan each year an expenditure which is above and beyond its means. Although expenditures are cut by the so-called "plan of retrenchment" through the executive branch, every year federal expenditures still become transformed into an inflationary force.

In short, we annually start the year with a planned public expenditure which corresponds to 18 percent of the gross national product, and we end the year with a public expenditure amounting effectively to 13 or 14 percent of the GNP. This disparity between actual and planned expenditures causes a tremedous inflationary pressure. And one of the fundamental purposes of the Three-Year Plan was that of planning a public expenditure which might be sufficiently large to avoid unemployment created by the government itself, and at the same time so small as to avoid inflationary pressures caused by the public sector itself. This is the essence of the program: to reduce progressively inflationary pressures. We estimate that, given the present institutional framework, it would be far from easy to reduce inflationary pressures to more than one half in the first year, if we intend to keep up the rate of growth of the GNP obtained in recent years. This will allow us to have a fiscal reform and then be able to reduce the inflationary pressure in the second year and up to the third year. This is a highly complex problem; it is unfortunate that it would take up too much time and this prevents me from telling you more about it.

Nicholas Kaldor

I'd like to congratulate Professor Lutz for his admirably presented, and I would say moderate, statement coming from such a distinguished representative of the monetary school. I don't know why in this particular conference I always find myself complimenting people with whom I'm normally in strong disagreement. And I don't want to withdraw my remarks about Professor Harberger in the light of later events either. I just want to say that the Italian example was frequently mentioned, but what was not mentioned is that Dr. Einaudi in 1947 had the classical situation in which monetary measures were the effective remedy, and it is wrong to suggest that all inflations, or most inflations, are just like that.

In 1947, in Italy, real incomes were rapidly rising as the result of the recovery from the war, but inflation was merely felt by inflationary price expectations leading to excessive inventory accumulation and stock holding. These inventories were financed by private credit. By restricting credit, the private sector could be forced to release stocks, immediately moderating prices, and even causing a slight fall in prices, which wiped out the inflationary expectations. That was a classic case of bringing inflation suddenly to a halt, followed by a period of remarkably rapid economic growth combined with complete monetary stability. But there are other examples. I would remind Professor Lutz that another of his colleagues made a monetary stabilization many years earlier, and I am referring to Dr. Salazar, who is also a professor of political economy like Professor Einaudi. Dr. Salazar's monetary stabilization was followed by 30 years of hard currency, stable prices, and a completely stagnating economy. I would like to ask Professor Lutz if he was ever in a position, in a sort of imaginary world, an imaginary Brazil, where there was a presidential election in which he had to choose between electing President Kubitschek or Dr. Salazar—where would he put his vote? I will not allow him to abstain; abstention is ruled out. Of course, I agree with him that when inflation comes to an end, it will come to an end suddenly and not gradually. There will be a point, looking back into history, at which we can say: this is the point where stabilization took place. But that does not mean that in an inflationary situation such as Brazil's, it is possible to bring inflation to a dead stop overnight, or to believe that if Professor Lutz were made dictator of Brazil tonight that tomorrow morning he could stop the inflation. This is impossible, and I think that, as Minister Furtado said in this context, Brazil suffers from inflationary pressures mainly due, or exclusively due, to insufficient fiscal revenue in relation to government expenditure. The remedy to that is fiscal reform. But fiscal reform can only take effect gradually.

Sir Roy Harrod

I am not opposed to a shock treatment. It might be a very good thing. What I object to is a slow and continuing policy of bringing demand down below the growth potential of the economy as a way of correcting the wage-price spiral. This is wrong. If you would have a shock treatment with the psychological effects described by Dr. Lutz, that might have an effect on the wage-price spiral. I am sorry that Dr. Kaldor threw some cold water on this idea in relation to the Brazilian situation. He defined the Italian situation, and he claims that the sudden ending of this rather rapid inflation by shock treatment has not been confined to this particular case. For instance, I am thinking of the French case 20 years earlier.

Dr. Kaldor also said that you have to attend to features, such as accumulation of inventories, under periods of inflationary influence. But don't these conditions apply in Brazil? I'm afraid I know nothing about inventories in Brazil but what I have heard is that inflation has been leading to inventory accumulation. I submit that we also have a strong growth potential in the Brazilian economy, so it seems to me that the two conditions are the same as with Einaudi in Italy.

Werner Baer

All I can say about the Brazilian inventory situation is for Professor Harrod to look at the background paper I wrote for this conference, in which I found the surprising fact that there doesn't seem to be any direct correlation between the rates of inflation and inventory accumulation in Brazil.[6] In that paper I also gave evidence that there is no obvious direct connection between the rate of inflation and a misallocation of investment resources.

I'd like to address myself briefly to the remark made by Professor Lutz about the forced savings school. What hit home, as far as I was concerned, was Professor Lutz's remark that forced saving is a bad thing, especially because you are producing growth at the expense of the poor, who are usually losing out in an inflation where forced savings occur. I would like to point out two things: first, it is quite elementary to all of us economists that in a growing economy, and one which is starting to industrialize, a large proportion of the increment in the national product has to be reinvested. This is what happened in the nineteenth century in Britain; this is what the Russians have been doing, too, where the increment of national output for several decades went back into investment goods. And I suggest that this might be happening in Brazil. The forced savings process did not result in a lowering of the population's living standard. It simply resulted in a redistribution of the increment in the national output in favor of investments. It seems to me from the data I gave a few days ago that that increment was appropriated mainly by the government. What I was trying to emphasize in my talks was that if you have a country which has a weak fiscal system, unable to redistribute the increment in the national output to the investment sector, you may have to resort for some time to forced saving through inflation. Thus, I think that putting it in black and white terms—which Professor Lutz did—might be slightly unfair.

---

[6]Baer, Werner, "Brazil: Inflation and Economic Efficiency," *Economic Development and Cultural Change*, July 1963.

Arnold Harberger

I would like at the beginning to emphasize what I consider to be of great importance in tax planning in Latin America. As a country is moved toward developing national plans, one must realize that tax planning is an essential component of a total plan. Tax planning in Latin America must not only cope with the problem of providing the government with an increasing revenue over the long run but, in addition, must cope with the very difficult short-run fiscal problem which emerged because of the ups and downs in the world market, and indeed also because of the pressures which sometimes arise calling for increases in government wages and salaries in a very short period of time. Without having the mechanisms to increase revenue on short notice, governments are bound to fall into difficulty. I would like to emphasize three points.

One is the great importance of the development in Latin-American countries of a progressive system of indirect taxation. During the period when most luxury goods were imported there was indeed in Latin America, through import duties, an effectively progressive system of taxation. But with the development of substantial import substitutions, particularly in the luxury consumer-goods field, it has worked out that a great many luxury consumers goods get off scot-free. The Santiago Conference, previously mentioned, was in virtual agreement about the importance of this move, particularly because it is something which can be done rather quickly and which does not entail the enormous reforms of administrative structure which are necessary to improve the yield of the personal income tax.

The second point, particularly favorable for Latin America, concerns investment incentives. The countries of Latin America have had a very distinct propensity for attempting to give incentives to one or another activity by means of tax exemptions. These exemptions have operated to stimulate particular activities, but in the course of time in many countries, they have become so widely generalized that one sees no particular pattern of preference emerging that might come from an effort at planned development of only particular sectors of the economy. What one sees is rather a large number of exemptions whose ultimate effect is to reduce the revenue of the government without augmenting the total flow of private or public savings. I think that we must be continually aware, when dealing with the question of investment incentives, that investments and savings happen in the end to be the same. And if a tax incentive does not have an effect on total savings, its only method of working will be through altering the pattern of investment without changing its total amount.

Thirdly, I would like to turn to the question of assessment. I proposed at the Santiago Conference the mechanisms of self-assessment which would work for both urban and rural properties. The general principle would be that each property owner would be required to declare the value of his property, that his declaration would be placed on public record and the only enforcement would be that any individual or company bidding 20 percent more than this declared value could obtain the property that the owner would be required to sell. This strong version of the self-assessment technique ran into some heavy sledding at the conference. A number of people did not like the idea of a forced sale. Professor Kaldor suggested an amendment whereby the owner of the property on which a bid had been made could refuse to sell, but he would be required to revalue the property up to the amount which was bid. And, moreover, the frustrated bidder would be entitled to a reward perhaps equaling the implemental tax coming to the government from the upward readjustment of the assessment in the implemental tax for the first year or the first year-and-a-half. This modified version of the self-assessment scheme received great support at the conference. A few people felt, however, that self-assesssment was a device which should be adopted as a short-run measure during a period in which normal assessment would be improved. Others at the conference felt that the self-assessment device was an appropriate one for consideration, even as a long-term measure.

Alexandre Kafka

I would like to point out that the Italian model of Professor Lutz has in some ways been represented in some of the stabilization programs in Latin America. This is the aspect of the differential credit restrictions, that is, while in many of these programs credit to the private sector was cut down quite severely, credit to the public sector continued to grow due to the inability of the public sector to cut down its deficit. Of course, being subject to a top limit of credit expansion agreed very often with the IMF, and so the private sector was the residual sector, so to speak. This type of severe contraction of credit to the private sector has had some well-known effects all over the world, but I think that it is especially unfavorable in Latin America. This is due to the great concentration of banking and fi-

nancial institutions in Latin America, plus the very close relations
of these institutions with the also heavily concentrated industrial
sectors. The private industrialists who suffer more are usually the
beginning entrepreneurs. The net effect of this credit restriction is,
then, an increase in the concentration of industry, which, I think, is
one of the key propagating factors in this inflationary process.

The second point is closely related to this. You won't find that
a severe credit restriction in the private sector will cause prices to
fall, even though stocks are sold. I've been told that in Chile there
were very few cases where prices fell. Of course, in general the result of this is a tendency to favor fiscal policy because of the bad
effect of monetary policy.

Federico J. Herschel

I should like to refer to the role of expenditures and revenues,
which aim at the fundamental objective of fostering development
and also of obtaining reasonable stability.

In the first place, it seems fundamental that we should have an
over-all development plan which includes the public sector as well
as the private sector. This is important, not only for an orderly policy of public expenditures, but also to orient fiscal policy in order
to influence private activity. In most underdeveloped countries
there is a considerable need for infrastructure, and investment expenditures have to increase so as to build or augment them. The
question is: how can we make this possible? This can be done by
either reducing other public expenditures or by increasing their
overall level. With regard to the first problem we must consider to
what extent it is feasible to reduce nonessential expenditures in the
public sector in order to orient the activity of the state toward productive activities. As such we have to consider not only physical
capital but everything that contributes to increase the potential capacity of the economy as well. Thus, technical education is an example of productive activity. In this connection we can refer to
bureaucracy and the unproductive expenditures which are so frequent in many government agencies of Latin American countries.
Needless to say, every possible effort has to be made to eliminate
them.

In the second place, we must mention transfer payments—and in
this connection bear in mind the social aspect—especially income redistribution policy. It seems to me that one of the best ways to

achieve this end, at least on a short-term basis, is through fiscal policy. Regarding redistribution through fiscal policy, we can discuss whether in certain instances the best thing to do is to apply transfer payments, which probably in some cases have increased at a very fast rate, and whether in many instances a larger social benefit could be attained through current government expenditure.

As regards investment, we have to consider two problems: in the first place, there is the obvious problem of eliminating nonproductive investments, (for example, the construction of luxurious buildings to house government agencies). Then we have to contemplate a much more complex problem, the possibility of changing the existing structure of public investment in order to attain investments which are more in agreement with the needs of development programs. In the short run there will be rigidities that will prevent the immediate implementation of such structural changes. These rigidities may consist of limited administrative capacity, especially in connection with the execution of public-works programs. Furthermore, there is another rigidity caused by the existing structure of the public-works program as such, since, many works having already been started, it would be convenient to finish them, as their marginal benefit is usually very high.

In the public sector as a whole, we meet with another parameter to be taken into account. In the case of the inefficiency of the public administration we have a parameter which is less of a parameter than others, because it is certainly a factor that can be changed, although as a rule not within a very short time. It is necessary that this problem be considered within the whole framework of economic change, which is one of the conditions of economic development, that is, it fundamentally depends on a change in mentality and behavior of the population as a whole, within which we have to consider government employees. But, to a certain extent, this inefficiency is also an economic factor which can be more radiply modified. In this connection, we have to refer to the low salaries earned by public employees, especially by the high level public officials and technicians. Here we can mention the case of many technicians—many of them within the public sector—who left positions in their own underdeveloped countries in order to work in developed countries as an example of technical assistance given by underdeveloped to the developed country, which, of course, is very costly for the first group of countries. The important thing is that this problem must be considered for what it really represents, and the solution lies in improving the efficiency of government policies by all means available (including higher salaries). This may seem rather obvious, but frequently the solution sought is to transfer activities from government to the private sector. Basic bottlenecks are certainly not overcome in this way, and, what is more, sometimes new ones are created.

Next, we have to consider the revenue aspect. Since a re-allocation of expenditures is not sufficient to increase productive investment, we have to increase the level of expenditures. This not only raises the problem of the transfer of real resources, but also the problem of finance. Of course it is not possible to set up concrete rules or make out prescriptions, since the situation differs with each country, but one can outline the factors which tend to limit the possibility of increasing tax revenues, which are the most important sources of revenue.

In the first place, we must refer to fiscal capacity and ask ourselves if there really is a limit to it in Latin-American countries. Theoretically, I do not think that we can say there is a limit to fiscal capacity, but nevertheless, in the particular case of Latin America, it is true that it is difficult—although certainly not impossible—to increase fiscal capacity. Are there economic considerations which explain this difficulty? This does not seem to be the case, as in many Latin-American countries the over-all tax burden (that is, relation of tax revenue to national income) is low, not only in comparison with developed countries, but frequently also with regard to countries of similar or even lower per capita income. Therefore, we must look for other reasons—outside economics—which explain this difficulty.

First, of course, there also is the problem of efficiency and honesty among government officials, which can make the application of even the best tax difficult. But there are other, more important, reasons than this one. And here we have to refer to the political situation or, in other words, the pressures which certain groups can use to make an effective tax reform difficult. At this point, I should like to give an example of a case in which I had some personal experience. At the end of 1958 I was in charge of the preliminary studies made for the tax reform to be undertaken in the province of Buenos Aires. The essential parts of this reform consisted of an increase in the yield of the property tax (by increasing tax rates and an adjustment of valuation) which, due to inflation, had deteriorated considerably. Furthermore, the rates of a type of turnover tax (tax on lucrative activities) were increased, particularly those corresponding to the sale of luxury or unessential articles and services. What was the reaction following the enactment of the corresponding tax laws? In the most serious Argentine newspapers enormous advertisements appeared, together with editorials. In these advertisements one could see how the cows were emigrating from Buenos Aires Province, as they were forced to leave a province with such a high tax burden. Of course, at the same time it was argued that foreign capital was either leaving the province or was prevented from coming in. In my opinion, there was not much truth in these arguments, but the fact remains that this campaign was sufficiently strong to prevent the tax reform from being made effective in its original form, and in consequence many changes had to be made which greatly diminished the effectiveness of the measures recommended.

In this connection, another problem to be mentioned is the high degree of tax evasion. Even at the risk of stressing a quite obvious point, it is necessary to emphasize it time and again and to insist on the need for stronger action against tax evaders—including imprisonment. The enactment of frequent tax amnesties or other types of concessions to tax evaders is decidedly an undesirable practice. Last but not least, we must mention the existing tax structure, since any change takes time. Of course, even the ideal tax system suited for each particular country depends on its degree of development, but I believe that, on the whole, the existing tax systems in Latin America are still quite far away from this ideal level. There are only a few countries—like Argentina and Colombia—where a global income tax exists, although in the case of Argentina dividend income is not included. In most countries there are only schedular taxes. In many countries consumption taxes make up a considerable part of the total tax revenues and in many cases within consumption taxes, those levied on luxury or unessential items are low.

Regarding other revenues, we have to mention the fact that the capital market is unimportant in most countries, and its significance is even more reduced due to inflationary pressures. Finally, in some Latin-American countries—as in Chile and Argentina—the deficits existing in public enterprises significantly contribute to the over-all government deficit.

If we want to make a realistic appraisal, we have to mention inflation, and here precisely is the point where the goal of inflation and development touch each other. The problem is certainly most acute in those countries where a considerable deficit already exists. The problem to discuss or solve is whether or not to eliminate the deficit. I think that insofar as it is possible to increase tax returns or other government revenues, it is convenient to do so, but great care must be taken that the reduction of government expenditures does not imply the postponment—sometimes of long duration—of those government expenditures which are investments (in a wider sense) fundamental to development or when it involves substituting open unemployment for the existing disguised unemployment. The elimination of rigidities or bottlenecks is not only a fundamental means to achieve economic development but, at the same time, a way to reduce basic inflationary pressures. On the other hand, the reduction of excess demand, which gives more impetus to inflation, must be contemplated within a global framework. This means that expenditures of low social priority must be decreased, but this type of expenditure must be diminished whatever its origin, that is, within the private as well as the public sector. In other words, it can be quite dangerous to reduce government expenditures—for instance, through the not too sophisticated instrument of not paying government employees—if at the same time demand and supply of television sets or other luxury items is encouraged, thereby creating an "affluent society" before its time. Therefore, the solution must consist of a global appraisal of all expenditures, and for that purpose all available instruments should be used (fiscal, monetary, or even direct controls). We must take good care, nevertheless, when putting these instruments to use, not to commit what Sir Roy Harrod called a capital crime, that is, to reduce demand below the potential rate of growth of the economy. This seems even more important in underdeveloped countries.

14. PANEL: INCOME DISTRIBUTION

Lloyd Reynolds

I hope I will not be violating my instructions if I say one or two things in general about income distribution before discussing recent developments in the United States. In thinking about what one can say about income distribution in a few minutes' time, it occurred to me to raise the following question: What measures of policy are likely to be effective in reducing the inequality of personal incomes, and among these measures, which will contribute also to the promotion of economic growth? If one could find measures which would both promote growth and reduce inequality, I imagine most of us would be inclined to favor them. This way of putting the question implies that income distribution in the Latin-American countries is less equal than would be desirable. I've studied welfare economies and I realize perfectly well that as an economist I'm not entitled to say anything about what constitutes a proper distribution of income, but I'm going to do it anyway. I'm going to speak of a shift toward greater equality of income as an *improvement,* and a shift toward greater inequality as a *worsening* of income distribution. This is a value judgment, if you wish.

I'm talking about distribution of personal income among individuals and households. This is only one way of viewing income distribution, but I think it is an interesting and important way. I'm talking also about the distribution of income *before* taxes, and about methods of reducing pretax inequality.

I will pass over quickly some negative reactions toward measures which I think are not very effective. I don't think, for example, that it is feasible to capture profit income by pushing up the general level of money wages. At least, I'd like to be shown a case in which this has been done successfully. This does not seem very practical because employers have such an easy escape through price increases. I don't think, either, that one gets very far by trying to reduce wage-salary differences for different occupational levels by commanding them to be smaller. This was tried in the U.S.S.R. during the 1920's, but it led to serious supply bottlenecks in the upper occupations and to other difficulties, including evasion of the legal wage rates.

Thus, policy on this point was reversed and differentials were widened again during the 1930's. The approach to this problem by legal regulation is not likely to be effective because it is so easy for either a private employer or a state employer to pay people more than the prescribed rate in one manner or another.

Let us go on to more positive suggestions. In the rural sector, reorganization of agriculture is obviously the key problem. I know that land reform is a very treacherous term. Everyone has his own version of what true land reform should be, but I think most versions involve giving the actual cultivator of the land greater responsibility for management of production and a larger share in the fruits of production. The point of this is partly that it provides an institutional setting in which financial incentives, agricultural education, farm credits, and other supporting services can be put to work effectively in raising productivity. This is obviously desirable. Many would say that it is essential to a successful over-all development program.

The effect on income distribution is somewhat uncertain. The incomes of the old landowners will probably shrink in relative importance. Even nice land reforms, such as the two Japanese reforms, seem to end up with the old landowners being done out of most of their property. Japanese landlords were paid off, as you know, in government bonds, the value of which was then eroded by inflation, so that their real income shrank very substantially. But the new landowners, the new small proprietors, will not all be equally efficient, their land will not be equally good, and so on. So there will continue to be substantial variation in agricultural incomes under any conceivable tenure system. But this is the kind of inequality which rests on a productivity basis and which has the economic function of calling forth productive effort. So one can conclude that the new pattern of income will be superior to the old. Whether it will be more equal in a pure statistical sense, I don't know; but in a functional sense it will be a superior pattern of income.

The second thing on which I wanted to say a few words is the desirability of heavy investment in educational and training facilities. The most sensible way to bring down the relative earnings of people in the higher occupations is not to pass a law but simply to train many more people for these occupations. This means heavy investment in secondary education and higher education to train technical, professional, and administrative staff, not to mention the great array of lower white-collar occupations which are so important in a modern economy. It means also attention to industrial training programs for skilled manual workers. These things not only have a healthy effect on the distribution of income but also contribute directly to economic growth by breaking or even anticipating serious manpower bottlenecks. All this is quite obvious, but unfortunately governments don't always do the obvious. I suspect that most governments, and not only in the less developed countries, are underinvesting in development of human productive capacity and are overinvesting (relatively) in accumulation of physical capital. These are things which, as I said in the beginning, contribute both to an improved distribution of income and also to economic growth.

I'd like now to turn the question and ask whether the process of economic growth itself may be expected to improve the distribution of income. If you somehow get a vigorous process of economic development underway, what will this do to income distribution? We should recognize that in the short run it is possible, and even probable, that rapid economic growth will worsen the distribution of income. The reasons were suggested a long time ago by the classical economists and have been re-emphasized more recently by Professor Arthur Lewis and others. Industrial profits increase as a percentage of national income, and these profits go mainly to a small minority. Supply bottlenecks in the higher occupations cause a relative rise in their earnings, while the real wage of the common laborer may rise little or not at all. I realize also that the "short run" may last quite a long while—20 years, 30 years, 40 years. But if a nation has the endurance and the leadership to live through this period, I believe that these disequalizing tendencies which mark the early stages of industrialism will eventually be reversed. From that point onward, greater equality and continued growth march hand in hand. Most of the Western industrial nations passed this point 30 or 40 years ago; and if time permitted I believe I could show that the reduced dispersion of pretax incomes which one observes in these countries was intimately related to the growth process. I believe that the U.S.S.R. also passed this point sometime during the 1950's, and that from here on we shall see a reduction of the real income differentials which were so prominent in the early stages of Soviet industrialization.

Rather than engage in abstract argument on this point, it may be pertinent to say something about the recent experience of the United States. Some of the things that have happened there can be taken as possibly being typical of a growing economy in the later stages of its growth. We have reasonably good statistics of personal income distribution in the United States for selected years, and they suggest that the distribution of pretax incomes today is considerably more equal than it was a generation ago. The shift occurred mainly during the 1940's, that is, between 1939 and 1949. There doesn't seem to have been much tendency in either direction since 1950.

Why was the 1949 distribution of income somewhat more equal than the 1939 distribution? There were several contributing factors. First, the much higher level of employment in 1949 was obviously a significant factor. More people were able to work a full year and thus reach a higher income level. Second, there was a marked shrinkage of wage differences among occupations over this period, a narrowing of the gap between unskilled labor, skilled craftsmen, and white-collar employees. This was due partly to the very high demand for labor in the 1940's, which somehow caused the lowest wage rates to rise faster than higher wage rates, and thus telescoped the income distribution. It was due also to the continued increase in the number of people who get more years of schooling. The proportion of the children entering primary school who eventually graduate from high school has been rising quite steadily, and the percentage of people graduating from college is also rising. This is one reason why the earnings of white-collar people have been declining relative to those of manual workers.

Another thing that contributed was a reduction of the gap between agricultural incomes and other incomes. This gap is still substantial, but it was considerably narrower by the late 1940's than it had been during the 1930's. This was due mainly to higher urban employment and income, to increased demand for agricultural products, reinforced by government price support policies. There has also been a dramatic shrinkage in the relative size of the agricultural sector. Agriculture is now down to less than 5 percent of GNP and only 7 to 8 percent of employment. This by itself will reduce the measures of income dispersion. If you have a sector with subnormal incomes, which is also a shrinking sector, this reduces overall inequality.

There has also been reduced dispersion of property ownership, particularly of stocks, bonds, and other types of income-yielding property. Professor Kuznets has calculated that during the 1920's the top 5 percent of income recipients got more than 80 percent of the dividend payments and more than 55 percent of all property income. By the late forties they were getting only 70 percent of the dividends and about 40 percent of total property income.[7] Since

---

[7]Simon Kuznets, *Share of Upper-Income Groups in Income and Savings* (New York: National Bureau of Economic Research, 1953).

1950, unfortunately, this tendency seems to have gone into reverse. More recent studies show that during the fifties there was some increase in concentration of stock and bond ownership.

Then there is the influence of the progressive income tax, which was a much more substantial factor in the 1940's than in earlier times. But this is in Dr. Pechman's domain.

For all these reasons, then, you had an equalizing tendency in the United States during the 1940's. Since 1950 there seems to have been little change. So it may be that marked changes in income distribution occur in sharp bursts, and that it takes some catalytic agent such as a war or a great depression to set them off. But the main direction of change is reasonably clear. If we had right now income distributions for 1980 and 1990, I would be surprised if they were not more equal than the distribution for 1963; and I think this will be true for the other mature industrial nations. How comforting this is to the countries in the early stages of development, I don't know. It may amount to saying, "When you get rich enough your problems will be easier—including the problem of income distribution!"

Joseph A. Pechman

My assignment on this panel was to discuss the relation between taxation and the distribution of income. I shall begin with a summary of the situation in one highly developed country—the United States—but my major purpose will be to apply the lessons of that experience to underdeveloped countries.

The stiuation in the United States is, in brief, the following:

1. Direct taxes on individual and corporate incomes constitute the backbone of the federal revenue system. We have had a corporate income tax for 54 years and an individual income tax for 50 years. For the past quarter of a century, the rates have been high by almost any standard. At the present time, the individual income tax rates range from 20 percent in the lowest taxable income bracket to 91 percent at the top. The corporate rates are 30 percent of the first $25,000 of profits and 52 percent on the excess over $25,000.

2. We have also had an estate tax for 47 years and a gift tax for 31 years. The estate tax is levied at progressive rates which reach a maximum of 77 percent; the gift tax rates are set at three quarters of the estate tax rates, or to a maximum of 57¾ percent.

3. The U.S. income taxes are probably the largest in the world in relation to GNP or in relation to total tax revenues. Federal in-

come taxes amount to more than 13 percent of GNP and about 85 percent of federal revenues (including social insurance contributions).

4. Although we are still striving to improve compliance, the degree of voluntary compliance is at a very high level. I would guess that we collect about 95 percent of what should be collected under the law.

5. Despite this heavy reliance on income taxes which are not evaded in a wholesale manner, the facts seem to suggest that this tax system has not greatly altered the distribution of income in the United States. Some redistribution seems to have occurred during the thirties and early forties, but this so-called "income revolution" stopped during World War II. Department of Commerce estimates indicate that there has been virtually no change in the relative distribution of personal income exclusive of capital gains since the end of World War II. There are no official estimates of the distribution of income *including* capital gains, but it is fairly certain that the inclusion of capital gains would reveal a trend toward greater inequality in recent years. Moreover, the major share of the redistribution that occured during the thirties and early forties is accounted for by the change in the distribution of income before tax, which reflected the drastic reduction of property incomes during the Great Depression. The effect of the tax system, though not insignificant, is dwarfed by the change in the distribution of income before tax.

6. As far as the distribution of wealth is concerned, a recent study by Lampman has shown that there was a substantial movement toward equality between 1929 and 1949, but about half of this had been reversed by 1956. The movement toward greater inequality in the distribution of wealth since 1949 is consistent with the proposition that the distribution of income *including* capital gains has become more unequal in recent years. It is a pretty fair guess that the present distribution of wealth is only slightly more equal than it was during most of the 1920's.

What accounts for the relatively small impact of the U.S. tax system on the distribution of income and wealth?

In the first place, even at the rates of income tax imposed in the United States, it is arithmetically difficult to budge the distribution of income. To take an extreme example, suppose that an income tax falls entirely on the top 20 percent of income recipients and that it amounts to 10 percent of total personal income. (This is about the current percentage collected in the United States, and it is doubtful that any other country—developed or underdeveloped—approaches it.) Suppose also that the top 20 percent accounts for 60 percent of total income, while the bottom 20 percent accounts for 3 percent, that is, the per capita income of the top quintile is 20 times as high as the bottom quintile. The distribution of income before and after tax in this example are shown in the following table:

Quintile	Income Before Tax	Income Tax	Income After Tax	
			Amount	Distribu- tion
Bottom 20 percent.............	3	0	3	3.3%
2nd 20 percent................	7	0	7	7.8
3rd 20 percent................	10	0	10	11.1
4th 20 percent................	20	0	20	22.2
Top 20 percent...............	60	10	50	55.6
Totals....................	100	10	90	100.0%
Ratio of top to bottom quintile....	20	..	16.7	..

It will be noted that, despite the concentration of this heavy income tax entirely in the top class, the percentage of income of the top quintile declines from 60 percent to only 55.6 percent, while the ratio of per capita income between the top and bottom quintiles declines from 20 to 1 to 16.7 to 1. By contrast, the disparity between the top and bottom quintiles would be reduced to 10 to 1 if incomes in the bottom quintile were doubled (I do not want to suggest that doubling of per capita incomes in the lowest strata is easy to achieve in a short period of time, but I do think that this goal can be approached over a longer period through land reform, improvements in education, stimulation of mobility, and other methods of increasing the productivity of the poor.)

The second factor accounting for the relative weakness of the redistributive effect of income taxation is that we do not tax total income in the United States or elsewhere. In particular, I know of no country that has been able to tax capital gains and profits, particularly profits of unincorporated enterprises, at rates approaching those that apply to other incomes. This enormous gap in our personal income tax system is probably the major reason why the cumulative effect of high progressive income taxation seems to be small. It is also true that estate and gift taxation is generally ineffective, and this reinforces the weakness of the redistributive effect of the personal income tax.

Although I believe that the redistributive effect of income taxation can at best be moderate, I do not want to be interpreted as suggesting that underdeveloped countries should de-emphasize the income tax in their tax systems. On the contrary, income taxation is the only practical method of achieving progression, and it is hardly likely that a nation will accept the tax burdens required to achieve higher rates of economic growth unless there is some progression in the tax system. But I would urge the adoption of a progressive income tax on pragmatic grounds as well. Development requires the allocation of increasing shares of the national income to capital formation, both public and private. Since voluntary saving is usually inadequate, the bulk of investment funds must be provided by the government. A progressive income tax automatically provides some of the financing as incomes increase. Where development is associated with rising prices, the income tax serves the dual role of moderating inflationary pressures and of increasing the rate of national saving.

I should like to illustrate this point with another simple example. Suppose a nation collects 10 percent of its personal income in taxes. If it has a regressive tax system, it will be required to increase rates or expand the base periodically to maintain taxes at 10 percent. Of course, it will fall behind during the years in which tax rates remain unchanged. Suppose, on the other hand, that half of total taxes is collected by an income tax averaging 5 percent of income with a marginal rate of, say, 10 percent (that is, the income tax has an elasticity of 2), and that the remaining taxes have an average elasticity of 0.8. Then, if income doubles from 100 to 200, taxes will increase as follows:

Income	100	200
Income tax......................	5	15
Other taxes....................	5	9
Total taxes		
Amount.....................	10	24
Percent of income.............	10%	12%

I know of no more practical way of increasing the rate of personal saving by 20 percent as national income doubles than through such automatic action of the personal income tax.

It should be emphasized that highly graduated rates are not necessary to achieve a satisfactory degree of progression. Experience shows that the imposition of unrealistically high rates creates pressures for the exclusion of particular incomes from the tax base as well as tax evasion. The proliferation of special benefits to particular groups creates resentment and dissatisfaction and leads to further erosion of the tax base, thus offsetting much, if not all, of the progression achieved through the high rates. It would be simpler and more effective to enact a broad-based income tax from the beginning, and to keep rate graduation to within modest limits.

I suppose that the reaction to this suggestion will be to regard it as setting up an impractical goal. The underdeveloped countries, it will be argued, do not have the expertise or the taxpayer morale to levy and administer an effective income tax. Nor is there any evidence that they can avoid erosion of the tax base any more than the developed countries. I can only repeat here what Sir Roy Harrod said the other day in another connection: achievement of a good income tax will yield handsome dividends, and underdeveloped countries should "give it a good try." On the few occasions I have had to discuss these problems with officials in this hemisphere, I have been persuaded that there is more ability to administer income taxes than Latin Americans will admit to themselves. The achievement of an effective income tax is well worth the effort.

Aldo Ferrer

Since the liberalization of the exchange system in Argentina and the establishment of a "free and fluctuating" type of exchange rate in January of 1959, the peso has suffered successive and pronounced devaluations. In 1958 the effective exchange rate of the peso was 28 for one U.S. dollar. In 1959 the rate was around 75, becoming stable at around 82 for one dollar until April of 1962. Since that time, a new devaluation has taken place, reaching a maximum of 153 pesos to the dollar in December of that year.

The sharp depreciation of the peso plays a key role in the economic development of the country. I shall attempt to describe the relationship between this devaluation, the redistribution of income, and the process of industrial disorganization.

The Exchange Rate and the Price Structure. It is not possible to understand the forces acting on the value of the peso without recalling the Argentine export structure. On the other hand, what happened to the peso since the beginning of the nineteenth century, when the Pampa area started to become an important supplier of agricultural products destined for the world market, makes it possible to see present problems in their proper historical perspective.

Around 95 percent of Argentine exports are made up of agricultural products, basically meat, wool, leather, livestock by-products, cereals, and oils. These exports come almost entirely from the Pampa area. Of the total value of agricultural production in the Pampa area, exports presently make up 30 percent; in the past the proportion was much higher, reaching 70 percent in 1929.

Traditionally, the price in pesos received by exporters had been conditioned by the price in foreign exchange for the exported products and the exchange rate. The price in foreign currency depended and still depends on conditions in the world market. With few exceptions, Argentina has never influenced the international prices of its exported products. Traditionally the internal price of agricultural products has been conditioned by export prices (in pesos). In this way, the type of exchange rate has always had decisive influence on the internal prices of farm products. Because the prices of other production sectors (industry and services) do not move automatically in the same magnitude and direction as the prices of agricultural products, a devaluation of the peso must change the relative prices of farm products. *Modification of relative prices* implies transfer of income to the agricultural sector. In 1959, for example, as a consequence of devaluation, agricultural prices increased by 137.2 percent, while those of industry went up 100.1 percent and those of the services 80.9 percent. Deflating these increases by the implicit deflator of the gross domestic product, one can see that the real prices of farm produce increased by 37.2 percent, while those of industry were kept constant, and those of the services fell off 10 per cent. This modification of price relations provoked the transference of 2.500 billion pesos (*as of* 1950) from the rest of the economy to the agricultural sector, which would be approximately 500 million dollars today.

The devaluation of the peso makes for a division of interests between the separate socioeconomic sectors of the country, for while one sector (agriculture) benefits from it, the others (industry plus services) are hurt. This situation differs from that of other countries, such as England, for, given a diversified structure of exports, the devaluation affects the community as a whole, without the appearance of such marked difference of interests between the distinctive sectors of the community. It is natural, as a consequence, that in Argentina the export sector has always been interested in depreciation of the peso and it is useful to analyze, in this respect, past history from the beginning of the nineteenth century until 1930.

Redistribution of Income. The modification of the price structure produced by devaluation not only generates intersectorial transfers of income, it also changes the distribution of income between wages, interest, and profits. This occurs in the following ways:

1. Participation of labor in net income is not equal in all sectors of economic activity. In the agricultural sector, remuneration of labor represents about 25 percent of the net income generated in the sector and profits, interest, and rents the remaining 75 percent. In industry and services, on the other hand, the remuneration of labor represents about 55 percent of the net income generated in these sectors and the remaining factor shares, 45 percent. Thus, if a modification in price structure is brought about and the sectors of highest labor participation in income (industry and services) transfer income to other sectors with less labor participation (agriculture), there will necessarily result a diminution of the share of labor in the national income. This has occurred in Argentina due to transfers of income from industry and services to the agricultural sector, resulting from the alteration of the price structure produced by devaluation.

2. According to a recent investigation of the agricultural sector, agricultural capital and enterprise tend to absorb at an early stage the transfer of income received from the rest of the national economy. Between 1958 and 1960, for example, the participation of labor in the net income of the agricultural sector dropped from 29 percent to 21 percent.

Data gathered between 1958 and 1960 seem to show that because of factors 1 and 2, the devaluation of the peso has strongly affected the participation of labor in the income of the economy as a whole. While in 1958 this participation represented 53.1 percent of the net internal income, since 1959 it has fallen to below 46 percent. The fall of labor participation in net internal income has been so intense since 1958 that it has dropped to the low level observed during the five year period before the second world war, when industry and services had an importance relatively inferior to that of the present in the whole of the national economy.

The Devaluation-Wage-Price Spiral. Devaluation of the peso has immediate repercussions on the general price level, due, first, to the simultaneous increase of the prices of commercialized agricultural output and the prices, in pesos, of exports, and second, due to a cost increase of industries which utilize imported inputs.

The internal price increase of agricultural output and industries which utilize imported inputs causes a fall of the real wage due to the increase of prices of consumer goods (of agricultural and industrial origin) bought by the workers. As a consequence of devaluation, the real wage fell 20 percent between 1958 and 1959.

The fall of the real wage produced a quick reaction on the part of the workers, who demanded an increase in wages to compensate for the fall of their income. It must be remembered that in Argentina the high level of organization of the workers' movement permits them to demand a readjustment of wage levels from a strong bargaining position.

On the other hand, the shrinkage of the real income of the working class causes an even greater fall in the demand for less essential industrial consumer goods because a growing proportion of real income is absorbed by expenditure for food and shelter. Given the high level of concentration of the major part of the country's industrial production in a reduced number of enterprises, the adjustment of the latter to the lower demand level is brought about by a reduction of the quantity produced and not by a fall of prices. The increase of real income in the agricultural sector does not compensate for the demand shrinkage of urban masses due to the expenditure composition in the agricultural sectors. Given the large participation of high-income sectors (especially of big landowners) in the income of the agricultural sector, expenditure is deviated from industrial consumer durable and nondurable goods to luxury consumption and investments (for example, costly homes) and to hoarding of foreign exchange.

In this way, the monetary devaluation, wage decreases, shrinkage of effective demand, and the growing idle capacity of industry, should produce a wave of secondary effects on the price level. They produce, furthermore, a growing pressure on the value of the peso and a new devaluation, which will give rise to an inflationary spiral —more precisely, a devaluation-wage-price spiral.

A proper appreciation of the role which devaluation plays as the key element in the modification of price structures and the activating of the inflationary process permits one to understand how the price level continues to increase rapidly in Argentina, in spite of the shrinkage of effective demand and the fall of real wages. It also permits an evaluation of the real significance of the recent stabilization policy.

It is understood that devaluation, raising the general price level, and putting into action secondary inflationary mechanisms which operate on the side of wages and industrial prices, should necessarily increase the level of costs and, in consequence, the financial needs of the private sector (especially in industry) and the total expenditures of the public sector.

Public expenditures have increased because of the impossibility of dismissing large groups of employees, increases in remunerations brought about by the rise of the cost of living, and the impossibility of achieving in the short run the self-financing of public utilities. Concurrent with these pressures which tend to raise the expenditure level of the public sector, public revenue has remained constant, due mainly to the shrinkage of economic activity. The logical consequence of these processes is the continued increase of the budget deficit.

The great demand for means of payment by the private sector, the growing budget deficit, and the increase in wages, operate in the present as the "propagating mechanisms" of inflationary pressures, which have their origin in the continued devaluation of the peso. Upon trying to eliminate these mechanisms of propagation through the shrinkage of credit to the private sector, the suspension of discounting government bonds in the Central Bank, and the dampening of the workers' demands, a serious financial penury has been produced in the private sector. Government payments were stopped, and a great decline of real wages occurred, with subsequent growth of social tensions. These factors have produced, in turn, a sharp shrinkage of the effective demand and a growing underutilization of installed capacity, which has let loose a spiral of real deflation, while the price level has continued to rise.

The inflationary impulse which has its origin in the devaluation of the peso is much stronger than that produced by the autonomous expansion of public expenditure, the credit to the private sector, and the huge wage increases. Between 1946 and 1949, in the midst of an expansionary policy of public expenditure, of cheap money and general wage increases, the cost of living went up 98 percent. Between 1958 and August, 1962, with a policy of credit restriction to the private sector, of reduction of the budget deficit and dampening of workers' demands, the increase in the cost of living has been about 323 percent.

An important variation, introduced together with the liberalization of the exchange rate system in January of 1959, has been the obtention of foreign credits to enable the Central Bank to enter into the exchange market to protect the value of the peso.

Together with these agreements, a sharp devaluation of the peso has taken place, and with the consequent operation of the propagation mechanisms described before, import demand tended to grow more strongly than the effective capacity to import. This resulted in the exhaustion of reserves formed on the base of external credit.

The conclusion of this experience has been a new devaluation, the acceleration of inflation, and the increase of foreign debt. Generally, the Argentine experience seems to reveal the weakness of stability schemes and liberalization of the exchange rate system when they are realized concurrently with a strong devaluation.

Sergio Molina

The subject of income distribution in developing countries has not received all the attention it should on the part of Latin-American economists. Perhaps the reason for this phenomenon has been a preoccupation with conditions which promote a more rapid growth. Some of our economists had expected that growth would automatically bring about a better distribution of income.

I personally believe, given the present circumstances of Latin America, that redistribution is indispensable, not only from the social, but also from the economic point of view. Redistribution cannot be felt as a by-product of development. It must reinforce development, step by step, because structural conditions do not permit automatic redistribution in a reasonably short period of time.

Income has its origin in the ownership of the means of production and/or in the work of individuals. A more or less equitable distribution of income, generated by property such as profits, interest, and rents, will depend, in large measure, upon the larger or smaller concentration of ownership which creates them. For the purpose of later statistical analysis, property has been divided into:

1. real estate (urban & rural)
2. real assets of firms
3. financial assets (banks, insurance companies, etc.).

In another way, the distribution of wages will depend upon the range of opportunities which the society offers to its members.

In turn, the factor which conditions these opportunities in a more deterministic way is education. Thus, it is possible to say that the concentration of rent as wages will be greater when the population has less access to the higher levels of education.

There are, of course, other elements, such as the differences in natural aptitudes and the sociopolitical structure, that is to say, the greater or lesser imperfection of democracy.

It is necessary to add, finally, that those who obtain a larger proportion of income are those who are able to arrive to the highest educational levels. On the other hand, those who maintain an important share of the ownership control, or at least have easy access to, the financial system.

The analysis of income distribution can be made through the national income accounts, from which we can obtain some information about share of wages versus the share which corresponds to profits, interest, and rents.

The type of information generally available places a high banking or industrial executive among the salaried workers and next to peasants with salaries at subsistence levels. Likewise, among the entrepreneurs appear the big proprietors together with the artisan who lives under worse conditions than any employee. I make these observations with only one objective, to point out how important it is to give due priority to these questions. Otherwise, we will continue to talk about generalities on the basis of misleading estimates. In all events, available data shows with sufficient clarity that in Latin-American countries a small proportion of the population earns a high percentage of total income.

In accordance with the investigations of ECLA, while in more developed Western economies one frequently finds that 10 percent of the higher income bracket receives nearly 30 percent of the national income, the proportion for Latin America, based on partial data, comes to more than 50 percent.

Although these earlier facts show clearly the existence of a bad distribution of income, I now wish to put forth some additional information on ownership structure which, in my opinion, conditions bad distribution.

To support this argument, I will take the case of Chile, even though I am certain that Chile is far from being the worst case in Latin America, and in fact I might go so far as to say that, in comparison, it seems to be one of the more favorable cases.

If one considers the distribution of land ownership, for example, one arrives at the following conclusion: 85 percent of landlords own 12 percent of the land and 3 percent own 62 percent. It can be supposed, as a consequence, that this concentration of land ownership also creates a concentration of income.

As for urban ownership, a sample taken in a residential district in Santiago indicates a smaller concentration than in the rural sector, but here, too, it is surprising to find that 25 percent of the real estate owners own 60 percent of the total value, and that 10 percent have 37 percent of the total value.

In the case of corporations, a sample of the largest firms shows an enormous concentration. In fact, if one compares cumulatively the number of stockholders with the accumulated value of the stocks they own, one arrives at the following figures:

50% of the stockholders hold 1.4% of the total value
95% "   "   "   "   " 31.0% "   "   "   "
 1% "   "   "   "   " 46.0% "   "   "   "

If one takes the case of banks and insurance companies, the concentration found in corporations is repeated, but with slightly less intensity. From past data one arrives at the conclusion that 50 percent of the stockholders own 2 percent of the total value, 95 percent of the stockholders own 39 percent of the total value, and, finally, 1 percent of the stockholders have 35 percent of the total value.

The figures shown represent an incomplete sampling, but they serve the purpose of illustrating some of the structural factors which condition the distribution of income.

I am not among those who feel that the solution to a poor distribution of income is to take from the rich and give to the poor. I say that this is not enough, because making a redistribution of income effective requires a change in the quantity and quality of production, and this is not done from one day to the next. Neither is it possible to think that changes in income will be produced without inflation. A transfer of income to less-favored sectors will induce a change in the demand structure which may be in favor of goods of inelastic supply. This produces transitory inflationary pressures.

Lastly, I wish to point out one of the determining aspects of bad income distribution originating in the "monopoly of knowledge."

In countries where illiteracy sometimes exceeds 50 percent of the population, opportunity to obtain well-paying positions are extremely limited.

I wish to return to the case of Chile, which stands out from the rest of Latin America because it has a more or less efficient educational system. The illiteracy rate comes to about 20 percent, however. A high proportion of students abandon primary school in the first two years. This causes what educators call "illiteracy through disuse," or rather, loss of acquired knowledge through lack of usage.

Less than 30 percent of the pupils who enter primary school pass to the secondary level and approximately 9 percent finish secondary school.

Finally, less than 1 percent of the students who entered primary school graduate from the university.

This shows a great concentration of knowledge and, as a consequence, a tremendous dissimilitude of opportunities, which is translated into a sharpening of bad income distribution.

In face of the magnitude of structural problems posed, the traditional redistributive policies appear to be insufficient and are being replaced by more direct measures.

A typical example of this tendency has been the impulse given to agrarian reforms, which tends to break the present structures of land ownership.

Also, a tax system is being drawn up with emphasis on a tax on wealth and with much higher progressive taxes on personal income and inheritances.

To make the distribution of income originating in corporations more equitable, reforms of the rules which control corporations and which regulate relations between capital and worker are increasing.

Finally, no one denies the urgent need in our industries to carry out a thorough reform of the educational system, which would enlarge the opportunities of our growing population and make use of human talent which today is not utilized.

In a word, reforms in structure which permit improvement of income distribution and reduce gross injustices are shown each time to be more evident and necessary. It is our duty to furnish the technical means to carry them out, and it is the duty of the politicians to create the national conditions in which they can be applied.

Charles F. Schwartz

My discussion of "Income Distribution" will cover three aspects of the subject: (1) effects of inflation on the income distribution; (2) achievement of a more equal income distribution in Latin America; and (3) statistics on income distribution, with particular reference to the emphasis that should be given to them in the region's over-all statistical program.

1. *Effects of inflation on income distribution.* The effect of a strong or continuing inflation on the broad distribution of income

as between profit-receiving and wage-earning groups is likely to be small. Or, perhaps more precisely, the available evidence does not permit us to say that any significant change will occur one way or another. (After a period of lag, increases in money wages tend to become as large as increases in prices.)

However, many individual wage-and-salary earners, pension recipients, and others are affected adversely by inflation. Moreover, within the profits category itself, there is likely to be a shift from entrepreneurs engaging in "productive" activity (combining factors of production to add real value to commodities in the productive process) to those engaged in speculation—those who hold commodities, without transforming them or adding to their value, purely for purpose of speculative monetary gain. Inflation thus creates a class of "profiteers," and this is certainly a very unfavorable qualitative aspect of inflation.

But this matter of the effect of inflation on the income distribution should not be left with observations such as these on the "direct" effects alone. In consideration of what may be termed the "indirect" effects, I shall start with the proposition that inflation hampers the rate of economic growth. This was the subject of the comprehensive paper which Graeme Dorrance presented to this Conference, and I refer you to it for analysis and documentation of this proposition. Quite briefly, however, these are the main ways in which inflation affects development: community saving is reduced, and a significant part is channeled to foreign instead of domestic investment; inflow of capital from abroad is discouraged; a substantial part of the reduced flow of resources for domestic investment is directed to uses not of the highest social priority; accumulations of inventories and other short-term investments are encouraged, as well as housing for the wealthy; savings are diverted from capital markets; real rates of return become obscured and rational choice on the part of entrepreneurs is inhibited; and balance of payments pressures arise, and may lead to controls and restrictions which create distortions and protect uneconomic production.

Whereas inflation may be said to hamper the rate of economic growth, growth itself leads to a more equal distribution of income. From the scanty evidence available, as well as from direct observation, we know that the income distribution in Latin-American and underdeveloped countries generally is highly skewed. Labor is plentiful; capital is scarce. The marginal product of labor is relatively low; the marginal product of capital is relatively high. Economic development and growth lead to an increase in the ratio of capital to labor and to a shift in the ratio of their marginal products. In the process of development, since development leads to a greater complexity of production, there is an increased demand for higher-skilled, better-educated, higher-wage types of labor. Now, these types of labor are all of the middle class, and they tend to substitute for unskilled manual labor in the development process as the quality of the work force improves through such means as education and training and the enlargement of opportunities. In short, by these considerations the process of economic development and growth leads to a rise in the share of wages in total income and to the emergence and development of a middle-income class.

Therefore, since inflation hampers economic growth, and economic growth leads to a more equal distribution of income, it may be said that the effect of a strong, continuing inflation is to retard the equalization of incomes and the development of a middle-income class in society. This kind of "indirect" effect of inflation on the income distribution does not, of course, show up directly in the statistics on income distribution. However, it is of fundamental importance for a number of Latin-American countries, and should not be overlooked.

2. *Achievement of a more equal income distribution.* It follows more or less from what I have said to this point that I believe that the main hope for the achievement of a more equal distribution of income lies in the encouragement of a higher degree of economic growth—combined with, and facilitated by, an improvement in the allocation of resources.

At the outset, let me say that I believe strongly that financial policy has an important role to play in the encouragement of economic growth. Achievement and maintenance of a reasonable degree of financial stability should be a direct, purposeful element of economic policy in Latin-American countries. All too often in the economic analyses for Latin-American countries, it is evident that the fiscal and monetary aspect either is neglected altogether or is brought in only very partially and indirectly.

The policies necessary to bring about financial stability will, in themselves, contribute to a more equal distribution of income. Perhaps the major example of this is fiscal reform. This should include the substantial reduction or elimination of fiscal deficits, which, as Professor Kaldor stressed earlier in this Conference, arise in large part from subsidies that benefit recipients of profits rather than the large mass of individuals. Further, if governments are to fulfill their developmental obligations, fiscal reform should also achieve, as a general proposition, a very substantial increase in tax levies, including really effective progressive income taxes, property taxes, and expenditure taxes. (These expenditure taxes should be centered on consumption of goods purchased by high-income groups, and would have results for economic development similar to the expenditure taxes proposed by Kaldor and others.) Moreover, the fulfillment of their developmental aspirations will also require most Latin-American countries both to increase the volume of expenditures by the central governments and to shift the composition of these expenditures toward a greater emphasis on investment, including social investment such as education and health.

I have already touched upon the fact that financial policies may be expected to contribute toward a more equal distribution of income (through achievement and maintenance of a reasonable degree of financial stability and through fiscal reforms). Nonfinancial policies directed toward economic growth and development also may be expected to contribute toward a more equal distribution of income. Important examples are sound, well-designed programs of land reform and improvements in agricultural techniques (seed, fertilizers, farming methods, etc.) Better farming techniques not only would raise incomes of the small individual farmers, but also would increase the supply of food in urban areas and thus, in that respect, contribute to the real incomes of urban wage earners.

3. *Statistics on income distribution.* As I have mentioned earlier, we know in a general way that the income distribution of Latin-American and other underdeveloped countries is highly skewed.

It seems highly doubtful to me that the availability of time series on the distribution of income by size classes—covering an extended period in the past—would be very useful in the establishment of economic policy targets for the period ahead. That is, I doubt that in general such policy targets would be changed—or should be changed—by the availability of historical estimates of the size distribution of income. I say this because I feel that the broad purpose of economic policy in Latin-American countries should be the acceleration of economic growth and development.

For this general reason alone, I would be inclined to give a rather low priority to estimates of the size-distribution of income in the statistical program of Latin-American countries. Moreover, it would be extremely difficult and costly to develop such estimates. In the highly developed countries, this work has been just about the most difficult and complex in the entire field of national income accounting, and it always has waited upon the successful development of other parts of the field. In particular, it is necessary to have reliable aggregates before attempting to make breakdowns of the aggregates into size-of-income classes. In the highly developed countries, income tax returns and field-survey information (household surveys) have constituted the principal kinds of raw data for developing these breakdowns. In many Latin-American countries, reliable aggregates are lacking, the available tax-return data would be of very limited value for this purpose, and household-survey information would be exceedingly difficult to collect—much more so than in highly developed countries, where there has been developed over a long period of time a tradition of reporting information to the government and other institutions. (There is not time to develop the point, but the problem of handling the agricultural sector in size-distribution estimates in Latin America would prove extraordinarily difficult.)

In the earlier session on "Statistical Requirements," I emphasized the need for setting up a schedule or system of priorities in carrying out any statistical program for Latin America. My own suggestion was that a high priority should be given to such statistical series as receipts and expenditures of the central government, exports and imports and the balance of payments generally, industrial production, wages and salaries, cost of living, agricultural production and income, and population and its characteristics. Further, I recommended that some of these series—notably trade statistics, government finance statistics, industrial production, and consumer prices—should not only be strengthened but should be made available on a current monthly or quarterly basis as promptly as possible. It was no oversight that I did not include size-distribution estimates in my list of priority statistical series. I fully recognize the importance and necessity of making income size-distribution estimates from time to time for individual Latin-American countries as the particular purpose at hand may indicate, but I do not think it would be advisable to allocate any large amount of resources to the development of such estimates as an integral part of any overall statistical program.

APPENDIX A

c. COMMENT FOR SECTION 4, "STATISTICAL PROBLEMS"

Charles F. Schwartz

The paper by Roger Messy and Hans Pedersen is a useful one. They have given us a comprehensive and detailed report; and any one who studies it will acquire greater knowledge about the quantity and quality of statistical information in Latin America, especially with regard to the national income accounts. At the same time, a fundamental question of interpretation is raised by this paper. Is the kind of statistical program proposed by the authors really a suitable one for Latin America at the present time? I would answer this question in the negative.

In the early part of their paper, Mr. Messy and Mr. Pedersen stress the value of national accounts tables for economic analysis and planning. For Latin-American countries, they would like to have national accounts tables available on a fairly detailed basis for at least a decade in the past, and they would like to have these tables kept up to date currently. Also, they would want the national accounts estimates to be reliable, for they point out, quite correctly, that "figures with too large a margin of error may lead to erroneous and harmful policy conclusions."

The authors next spell out the national accounts series which they consider to be necessary for economic analysis and planning. Among these series are gross domestic product by industrial origin and by sectors, at current and constant prices; gross national product by expenditure categories, at current and constant prices; gross fixed capital formation according to various types of breakdowns, at current and constant prices; direct estimates of private consumption, broken down by expenditure categories, at current and constant prices; national income by type of income, at current prices; breakdowns of government income and expenditures by economic and functional categories; a statement of international transactions;

530

a complete system of national accounts; and an input-output table for some recent year.

Mr. Messy and Mr. Pedersen believe that it would be "quite insufficient" to limit the statistical programs to the national accounts only. So they next go on to list the so-called "specialized statistics" which should be developed in the Latin-American countries. Such statistics, as defined by the authors, cover population and the labor force; agriculture, forestry, and fishing; mining, manufacturing, construction, and energy; transportation; private services; money, finance, and prices; and external trade.

Having drawn their outline of a statistical program for Latin America, the authors next evaluate the adequacy of the existing situation. They find that the statistics are generally deficient, and they cite the widely held opinion in professional circles that "a great effort has to be undertaken" to improve the quality of the statistical instruments. The authors cite numerous gaps which "seriously limit any quantitative economic research" in Latin America, and they refer to the "lack" of resources which prevents statistics in the region from being adequate to the needs of policy-makers.

Now, what does all this add up to? It is the belief of Mr. Messy and Mr. Pedersen that they have set forth a "minimum" program— one which they say "refers to the essential priorities and is not an exhaustive list of statistical activities." But this judgment is surely open to question. What in fact the authors are proposing is more like a "maximum" program, calling for a dramatic leap forward. It would entail an exceptionally large expansion in the quantity of statistics, as well as a very marked improvement in their quality. The center piece of the authors' proposed program would be a well-developed, relatively reliable, up-to-date system of national accounts, and this would be coupled with a buttressing of statistics in a whole array of "specialized" activities. Since, as the authors themselves emphasize, the basic statistical data presently available are sparse and weak, numerous comprehensive censuses and other systems of data collection would be required to fill the existing gaps; and the difficulty of carrying out such a gigantic task would be compounded by the widely recognized inadequacy in the supply of trained professional personnel.

But one does not have to speak of a "gigantic task" in terms of the national accounts and "specialized statistics" taken together. The task of simply strengthening the national accounts work in Latin America—to the point of assuring reasonable standards of quality in the estimates and getting the estimates out much faster—would appear to be both time-consuming and costly. At this stage, any full-fledged, heavy concentration upon the national accounts could readily absorb all the additional resources that are likely to become available for statistical work.

I would say, therefore, that the statistical program proposed by Messy and Pedersen definitely raises the question of priorities. Taking into account the rudimentary state of the basic data, the needs of analysis and policy, and the desirability of allocating the available statistical resources to their potentially most efficient uses, I would think that numerous other series of statistics should be accorded priority ahead of any elaborate effort on the national accounts in their entirety. Those series which come to mind in this connection are receipts and expenditures of the central government, exports and imports and the balance of payments generally, industrial production, wages and salaries, cost of living, agricultural production and income, and population and its characteristics. Some of these series—notably trade statistics, government finance statistics, industrial production, and consumer prices—should not only be strengthened but made available on a current monthly or quarterly basis as promptly as possible.

For the most part, the statistical series I have just singled out are covered in the "specialized statistics" category in the Messy-Pedersen paper. However, their category has a number of other series in it as well.

Next, I should like to mention some of the ideas that came to mind in picking out the types of statistics which I think should be given particular emphasis in Latin-American countries.

1. Almost all the series in my list are important for current economic and financial analysis.

2. The strengthening of these series would improve the statistical system generally and would provide a very good basis for subsequent development of the national income accounts themselves. Surely, one cannot visualize an adequate system of national accounts in Latin America without satisfactory, timely data on transactions of the central government, exports and imports, industrial production, wages and salaries, consumer prices, agricultural income and output, and population (including labor force).

3. International trade statistics are vitally important for economic analysis and policy-making in Latin-American countries. Until these statistics have been improved and put on a current monthly basis, why should the scarce statistical resources in these

countries be allocated to tasks which by any reasonable standard are less urgent?

4. I would make the same generalization about financial statistics, including the monetary as well as fiscal accounts. These, too, are key statistics and should be improved and updated before any serious thought is given to filling out many of the uninteresting items in the national income accounts.

5. The expanded work which I recommend on international trade statistics and financial statistics would appear to be entirely feasible. It would be based mainly on administrative statistics collected for other purposes, so that the "payoff" in these areas would be substantial and quick.

6. It would be just about impossible to obtain current monthly measures pertaining to aggregate production, aggregate income, and average prices of all goods and services. But it would be feasible, although not easy, to develop current monthly measures of industrial production, wages and salaries, and consumer prices. In putting these items on my list of priority statistics, I have no doubt whatsoever of their usefulness and value. They would certainly be most helpful for analysis of inflation and growth.

7. I have put population and agricultural production and income on my list because these statistics would seem to be particularly "basic." In some sense, a country cannot be said to have much of a statistical system if it does not have at least fairly good information on the number of its people and on their principal characteristics, including status in the labor force. But more to the point, we need adequate figures on population because it is only increases in per capita income or production that properly can be called growth or development. As to the agricultural sector, that, of course, is predominant in most Latin-American countries, and statisticians must tackle the difficult problems in that sector if they want to get very far toward any comprehensive economic measurements. Specifically, there is no point in planning a detailed, elaborate set of national accounts until you have achieved satisfactory statistical coverage of the agricultural sector. Admittedly, this is very difficult, in major part because of the thorny problem of handling the "subsistence" part of the total.

8. My view of the statistical situation in Latin-American countries was influenced in still another way. You can get a very good idea of the statistical situation in these countries, compared with that in other countries, simply by looking at the tabulations on the

individual country pages included in International Financial Statistics, the monthly statistical bulletin published by the International Monetary Fund. You will find, for instance, that the latest data available for Latin-American countries on exports and imports are generally several months behind those for the countries of Western Europe and North America. Information on government finance in Latin-American countries is either lacking altogether or is incomplete and out of date. Figures on cost of living and wholesale prices, apart from their recognized weaknesses, are not very current for the countries of Latin America. Estimates of industrial production, wages and salaries, and industrial employment—again by reference to the country pages of *I.F.S.*—are available for very few countries in this region. Also, less than half of the Latin-American countries yet have estimates of their total population for any time in 1962. So, I ask again: With this kind of situation prevailing with respect to statistical series so important for economic and financial analysis, why should a primary emphasis at this time be put on the derivation of elaborate aggregative statistics? Some idea of the status of these aggregative statistics can also be gotten from *I.F.S.*, which shows that several Latin-American countries do not have national income estimates at all, and that for nearly all the other countries of the region the latest available estimates pertain to the year 1959 or 1960. No Latin-American country has yet prepared a quarterly series for the national income accounts.

If I may, I should like to close on a semipersonal note. My objection to a heavy concentration on national accounts work in Latin America does not reflect a professional bias. I spent a long period of time in the U.S. Department of Commerce helping to produce the highly developed, detailed system of national income accounts which have been available for the United States for a good many years now. I do not have to be told, or convinced, of the great utility of national economic accounting. I recognize the value of national accounts work for Latin America (especially for developmental analysis and planning), but simply believe that at this stage it would not be very rational to try to put a large-scale effort into it.

INDEX

INDEX*

A

Accelerated economic development with stability, prerequisites, 8
Adler, J. H., *445*
Agriculture, 14
  agricultural policies, 32
  Latin America, 439
  reforms, 28
  statistics, 119, 122, 135
Ahn, C. S., 41n.
Aitken, H., 161n.
Alliance for Progress, 25, 95, 175, 354, 399
Ames, E., 228n.
Argentina, 12, 43, 60, 65, 253, 298, 311, 316, 318, *355*, 371, *450*, 492, *517*
Assets; *see* Business fixed assets
Ausch, S., 237n.
Austria, 492

B

Baer, W., *364*, 368n., *479, 501*
Balance of payments, 13, 28, 29, 59, 306, 425
Balanced growth, 306
Balogh, T., 98n.
Banking, 37
  bank credit, 39
Baykov, A., 216n.
Bazarov, 277
Beckerman, W., 207
Belgium, 192, 213, 492
Berthet, P., 118
Bhatia, 39n.
Bloch, H., *487*
Bochkova, V., 240n.
Bolivia, 43, 60, 253
Bottleneck sectors, 14, 109, 292
Brazil, 11, 43, 45, 54, 60, 109, 110, 253, 298, 311, 316, 318, 319, *364*, *447*, 479, 492, *496*, 501
Brown, A., 281n.
Brown, R. T., *438*, 440
Browne, M. H., 197n.

Bruton, H. J., 37n.
Budget, national 115
Budget deficit, 21, 23, 46, 110, 322, 425, 432, 433, 484
Bukharin, 277
Bulgaria, 226
Burma, 252, 259, 270, 271, 272, 274
Business fixed assets, 55ff.

C

Campbell, C. D., 41n.
Campos, R., 290, *457*
Canada, 192
Capital, foreign, 32, 49ff., *457*ff.
Capital formation, 29
  statistics, 116, 123
Ceylon, 46, 47, 50, 251, 252, 255, 270, 271, 272, 275
Chamberlain, N., *176*, 277
Chenery, H., *435, 443*, 462
Chile, 12, 22, 54, 60, 105, 156, 253, 293ff., 298, 306, 312, 316, 318, 319, 330ff., *360, 371*, 523ff.
China (Taiwan), 10, 252, 254, 255, 256, 270, 271, 272, 273
Christ, C., 332
Classical doctrine, relevance to Latin America, 94
Coffee Agreement, International, 467
Colm, G., 166
Colombia, 11, 12, 253, 299, 300, 313, 316
Commodity Markets, 95
Common Market, 16
  European, 355, 462ff.
  Latin-American, 462ff.
Comparative costs, principles of, 420
Construction, statistics, 137
Consumption, 32, 117
  mass consumption, 33
  personal, 29, 30, 32
  reduction of, 33
  statistics, 123
Controls, government, 58
Cost of living, 28, 76, 87
Costa Rica, 253
Credit control, 13

---

*Entries in the Index in italics indicate papers or contributions to the discussions.

This book has been set on the Linotype in 10 on 12 and 9 on 10 Baskerville Light. Part numbers and part titles are in 24 pt. Radiant Medium. The size of the type page is 25 by 44 picas.

ECONOMIC GROWTH CENTER
BOOK PUBLICATIONS

*Werner Baer, *Industrialization and Economic Development in Brazil* (1965).

Werner Baer and Isaac Kerstenetzky, eds., *Inflation and Growth in Latin America* (1964).

*Bela A. Balassa, *Trade Prospects for Developing Countries* (1964).

Carlos F. Días Alejandro, *Essays on the Economic History of the Argentine Republic* (1970).

*John C. H. Fei and Gustav Ranis, *Development of Labor Surplus Economy: Theory and Policy* (1964).

*Gerald K. Helleiner, *Peasant Agriculture, Government, and Economic Growth in Nigeria* (1966).

*Lawrence R. Klein and Kazushi Ohkawa, eds., *Economic Growth: The Japanese Experience Since the Meiji Era* (1968).

*A. Lamfalussy, *The United Kingdom and the Six* (1963).

*Markos J. Mamalakis and Clark W. Reynolds, *Essays on the Chilean Economy* (1965).

*Donald C. Mead, *Growth and Structural Change in the Egyptian Economy* (1967).

*Richard Moorsteen and Raymond P. Powell, *The Soviet Capital Stock* (1966).

*Frederic L. Pryor, *Public Expenditures in Communist and Capitalist Nations* (1968).

Clark W. Reynolds, *The Mexican Economy: Twentieth-Century Structure and Growth* (1970)

*Lloyd G. Reynolds and Peter Gregory, *Wages, Productivity, and Industrialization in Puerto Rico* (1965).

*Donald R. Snodgrass, *Ceylon: An Export Economy in Transition* (1966).

*Available from Richard D. Irwin, Inc., 1818 Ridge Rd., Homewood, Ill. 60430.